The Empress Eugénie

1826–1920

By the same Author

THE TRIAL OF MARSHAL NEY

THE EMPRESS EUGÉNIE

The Empress Eugénie

1826-1920

BY

HAROLD KURTZ

Illustrated

Houghton Mifflin Company Boston
The Riverside Press Cambridge
1964

Copyright © 1964 by Harold Kurtz

Printed in Great Britain

FOR
MR. AND MRS. G. A. LYWARD
With permission

CONTENTS

ILLUSTRATIONS

ACKNOWLEDGEMENTS

THE AUTHOR has to acknowledge gracious permission from Her Majesty The Queen, to make use of material from the Royal Archives at Windsor Castle.

Next, the author wishes to express his deep gratitude to His Royal Highness the Duke of Windsor, K.G., who spoke to him of his encounters with the Empress and gave permission to quote from letters written long ago after visits to Farnborough Hill.

The author wishes to put on record his special sense of obligation to the Hon. Mrs. H. R. A. Adeane, and to Lt. Col. Sir Michael Adeane, G.C.V.O., K.C.M.G., P.C., Her Majesty The Queen's Private Secretary. He was given most generous assistance by Mr. R. C. Mackworth-Young, Librarian at Windsor Castle, Miss Price-Hill, Miss Olwen Hedley, and Miss Scott-Elliot.

The Duchess of Alba allowed the author unhindered access to the Empress's private papers. In going through them at the Palacio de Liria in Madrid, the author was given every help and support by the Duchess of Alba's learned librarian, Don Ramón Paz. While in Spain, the author was most courteously helped by a large number of people: by Señor Roland, then Chief of Protocol at the Ministry of Foreign Affairs; the Duchess de Santo Mauro; the Marqués de Villalobar; the late Count de Albiz, descendant of Red Comyn; Count de Bailén; Mgr. Cheli, of the Papal Nunciature; Señorita Alcon, of the *Patrimonio Nacional* at the Royal Palace, Madrid; the officials of the Historical Section of the Ministry of War at Madrid and Segovia. For the details of the earthquake in Granada on May 5th, 1826, the author is obliged to Father Antonio Due, S.J., of the Cartuja Observatory at Granada, the Instituto Geografico y Cadastral at Madrid, and Mr. J. Piegza, of the Kew Observatory. During his work in Spain, the author received every encouragement from H.M. Ambassador, Sir George Labouchere, K.C.M.G.—help that was not discontinued when reluctantly he had to leave Spain and rely for research on correspondence.

The Marqués de Santa Cruz, Spanish Ambassador in London, and Sir Charles Petrie, Bart., provided valuable introductions and suggestions for research in Spain.

In Paris, the author was helped by M. Fleury, Prince Napoleon's Secretary; by Father P. Teisseire, O.S.B.; by Comtesse de Viel Castel; by Comtesse Jean de Pange; by Comte de Rilly who with extreme kindess copied out an entire manuscript dealing with the family antecedents of Napoleon III and provided other information besides; by Comte Antoine de La Bédoyère; by

H.R.H. Princess Eugénie, Princess of Greece, one of the Empress's god-daughters; by Vicomte Hubert Jurien de la Gravière; by Dr. Parturier, editor of the masterly final edition of Mérimée's correspondence; by M. Max Terrier, of the Museum at Compiègne, M. Pierre Schommer, of that at Malmaison; by M. Paul Léon, *membre de l'Institut*; by the Director-General of the Archives de France; by the Administrator of the Archives of the Préfecture de Police, Paris; by the Service Historique de l'Armée at Vincennes; and very much not least by Miss Nancy Mitford.

In Germany, Wolfgang, Prince of Hesse, searched among the archives at Friedrichshof for letters from the Empress to the Empress Frederick. H.R.H. the Margrave of Baden and his archivist, Dr. Krebs, very kindly supplied copies of some of the correspondence of the eleventh Duchess of Hamilton and diplomatic documents from the Minister of Baden in Paris, Baron Schweizer.

The author is obliged to Herr Dr. Blaas of the Haus-Hof- und Staatsar-chiv of Vienna for sending him copies of unpublished correspondence exchanged between Paris and Vienna during the Second Empire.

In England, a large number of people have been haunted and harried in the quest for authentic information. The list must be headed by Miss Vesey, at ninety-five the oldest survivor of those who knew the Empress really well. The author was given several opportunities for admiring Miss Vesey's miraculous memory, her eagerness in recalling the days at the Empress's side, and her generosity in lending him letters and other documentation. The author has also been very fortunate in meeting Dr. Wilfrid Attenborough, the Empress's doctor at Farnborough who, like Miss Vesey, communicated his memories of the Empress and her circle, speaking of it all as if it had happened last month. The author is greatly obliged to Mrs. Wroughton for lending him Lady Lintorn Simmons' unpublished diary which throws much new light on important events at Chislehurst and Farnborough; to Earl Haig for giving permission to search among his father's, the Field Marshal's, papers for references to the Empress; to the late Miss Violet Vivian, to Lady Alexandra Trevor-Roper, and Lady Victoria Scott; to the Marquess of Salisbury, K.G.; to the Marquess of Anglesey; to the Earl of Avon, K.G.; to the Earl of Clarendon; to Lord Kinross; to Sir Anthony Rumbold, Bart.; to Sir Ivone Kirkpatrick. He is most grateful to Captain R. E. Huddleston, R.N., of Sawston Hall, Cambridge, where the Empress stayed when Countess de Teba; to Mr. A. J. P. Taylor; to Dr. G. P. Gooch, O.M.; to Dr. Theodore Zeldin; to Mr. Roger Fulford; to Mr. E. E. Y. Hales; to Mr. Ivor Guest; to Mr. Harold Acton; to Mr. George D. Painter, the definitive biographer of Proust; to Mr. Ernest Weal, Secretary of the London branch of *Souvenir Napoléonien*; to Mrs. Nathaniel Lloyd; to Miss Claire Blount; to the Hon. Mrs. Balfour, of New-tondon, Scotland; to Mr. T. A. B. Corley, author of the latest and most original biography of Napoleon III, *Democratic Despot*, without whose vigilant co-operation several essential sources of information would have been missed; to Mr. Noel Blakiston who permitted a pre-publication glimpse of his important work on Odo Russell in the Rome of Pio Nono. The author remembers with abiding gratitude his several conversations with Sir Harold Nicolson at Sissinghurst—in the gardens in the summer, in the book-lined cottage in the autumn and winter—conversations that went from the Empress to Lloyd George (" did he know where Alsace-Lorraine was? ", Sir Harold wondered), to the Kaiser and Clemenceau and Mr. Arthur Balfour and Lord Carnock and M. Maurice Paléologue.

The author is under the greatest obligation to Mr. W. C. Dalgoutte of the Foreign Office Library, to the Librarian of the Admiralty, the Director of the Wallace Collection, to the Librarian and staff of the London Library, to the Rev. Dom Silvester Houédard, O.S.B., formerly Napoleonic Librarian at St. Michael's Abbey, Farnborough, to the Prior and community of that monastery,[1] to Lt. Col. G. A. Shepperd, Librarian of the Royal Military Academy, Sandhurst, to Lt. Col. C. B. Appleby of the Sandhurst Museum, and to the Librarian and staff of the Kent County Library, Maidstone.

The author has again had the expert assistance, both as to form and contents, of Mr. Christopher Sykes, who read the book in typescript and proof and gave his time and knowledge as unsparingly to the Empress as he did to Marshal Ney.

The Empress lived for ninety-four years and two months. At a conservative estimate, three lies were told about her for each day of this long life, two *per diem* by her enemies and one by her friends. To piece together a more truthful picture was therefore a lengthy process, entailing a number of protracted research operations and urgent sorties towards the true sources. The author wishes to express his sincere appreciation of the exemplary patience and support he was accorded by his publishers, Mr. Hamish Hamilton and Mr. Roger Machell.

The book was written at Finchden Manor, Mr. G. A. Lyward's house in Kent where, under his authority and care, some forty ' disturbed ' boys and young men are living in the security provided by the abundant potentialities of a real community life. In the specific spirit and setting of Finchden Manor, writing about dead people and distant events acquired an enlivening justification through sharing life and purpose with wide-awake young people trying to come to terms with their future, with each other and themselves.

---

[1] The Abbey Church is in urgent need of repairs, and the Prior has launched an appeal for funds. It is greatly to be wished that the physical survival of the Empress's final resting place will be ensured by the generosity of her admirers in England, France, Spain and elsewhere. (1964)

I. THE EARLY YEARS
1826-1853

CHAPTER 1

A FEW MONTHS before her ninety-fifth birthday, the Empress Eugénie
travelled from England to Spain by way of Cap Martin. She reached
Gibraltar on April 22nd, 1920, and there an old friend, Colonel Willoughby,
Verner, was waiting to escort her and the small group of people travelling
with her across the bay into Spain. He had been on calling terms with her
for twenty-five years, but it was only during the First World War that he
had come to know her well. He had been a frequent visitor at Farnborough
Hill, the Empress's house in Hampshire, a wing of which had been turned
into a hospital for officers, and had often talked over with her the problems
and anxieties of the Great War. He found that she would discuss matters—
'some of them of the highest importance'—with a first-class knowledge
of the facts, with incisiveness and brilliance. Here, the Colonel realised,
was not someone who had shut herself away for fifty years among the
melancholy relics of the past. 'What a grotesque travesty of her life!' he
wrote. 'Nothing could have been less melancholy than her manner and
conversation at all times.' He was impressed by the unflinching courage
with which she faced the crises and setbacks of the war, he praised her
spirit, he admired, above all, her 'cheerful countenance'. Nearly ninety
in 1914, her attitude towards the war was prescient, compassionate
and alert. She became, in those final years after 1914, a figure of our own
time.

Now as they were motoring from Algeciras to Jerez through the shimmering countryside on a perfect day of spring, the Colonel found her filled
with joy and animation at being back in the country of her birth. Someone warned her to put on dark glasses, but she replied that the sun of
Andalusia had never done her eyes any harm. 'I smell the old scent of the
blossoms,' she said, 'the sun is my friend.' Later, standing on the terrace
of Colonel Verner's house in Jerez above the trimmed hedges and the flowerbeds, she talked delightedly of the *romero*, the wild rosemary of Spain
which had grown in such profusion outside her father's house at Teba,
and of her joy at feeling again the beauty and the sunshine and the wildness of Spain. In the afternoon, an English officer who had been in Zululand with her son called on her, and the bitterest grief of her life pierced
her once more and brought back the tears. Next morning, her nephew, the
Duke of Alba, came to take her to Madrid in his motor-car. It was another
radiant day of Southern spring and, says Col. Verner, 'no young girl could
have shown more vivacity or more charm than the Empress as she bade us

farewell. It was a delightful incident that will endure in one's memory for all time.' It was the last time he saw her.

She died at Madrid in the following July. Had she gone to Spain because she wanted to die there? To anyone as economical and fatalistic as the Empress the thought of making arrangements to meet death was scarcely likely to occur, but, not unnaturally at ninety-four, there had been presentments. When before she left Farnborough for France Lord Stamfordham, King George V's private secretary, came to wish her a happy journey, she took with her own hands von Angeli's fine portrait of the Prince Imperial from the wall and gave it to Stamfordham who had been her son's comrade in the Zulu War. It was a gesture of admission that she might not see him again. But when after a short stay in Paris she arrived at her house on Cap Martin, she gave her gardener detailed instructions for a number of changes to be carried out in time for her visit the following year. When the doctor from Rocquebrune came to see her and, unlike Dr. Attenborough at Farnborough, endeavoured to dissuade her from going on to Spain she replied : 'But doctor, I really am not immortal. I absolutely must die one day, and I want to see Spain once more.' 'Before I die,' she told the Duke of Alba, whom she had summoned to Cap Martin, 'I want to see Spain again. Besides, I am losing my sight, just as my mother did. I do not mind solitude, I am used to that, but life without reading, without books, without newspapers—that would be intolerable.' 'I feel,' she told her young companion Miss Vesey at Cap Martin, 'like a lamp of which the light is growing very dim and will soon flicker out.' And to the Duke of Alba she said : 'It is quite likely that in the country where I first saw the light, I shall also see it last.'

She had accustomed herself to the thought of dying, but she travelled to Spain because there she had first known life; from the moment she stepped ashore on to the soil of Spain, delightedly blowing kisses to the ground, her old vigour and gaiety were restored to her. The old lady who returned to her native land was a great European figure, belonging as much to England as to France and yet not wholly identified with either. With her passion for ideas, with her large and precise understanding of the problems of the age and with her implacable loyalty to her own standards and ideals of conduct, she had remained wholly unaffected by the chauvinism and hysterical nationalism of the period and achieved a distinction and eminence that were unique. Yet, in undertaking the journey at her great age, she yielded not merely to the natural desire to seek the South and the sun after the hard war-years in England, to find again the warmth and the ease and the waywardness of Spain. She went out in a mysterious impulse to link her end to her beginnings. Even as a Toledo blade, Othello's 'sword of Spain', can be bent into a full circle until its tip touches the hilt, so the Empress bent the long line of her life towards its origins. The steel of the Toledo blade which the Castilian craftsmen temper by plunging it, still hissing from the fires of the forge, into the ice-cold waters of the Tagus, carries within it the living tension between the extremes of heat and cold: 'a sword

4

of Spain, the icebrook's temper'. It expresses some of the elemental tensions of the Empress's life and destiny. On her last journey she travelled towards the sources of her life, to the country where nearly a century earlier she was born on a day when the earth shook and trembled in convulsions—on the day which was the fifth anniversary of the death of Napoleon I.

The date was May 5th, 1826. She was born at Granada, second daughter of the Count and Countess of Teba. Her father, Don Cipriano, was a younger son of the noble house of Montijo, among whose ancestors figured the famous knightly clan of the Guzmans, St. Dominic, the founder of the Dominican Order, the Count-Duke of Olivarez, Prime Minister to Philip IV, Cardinal Portocarrero who had negotiated the French succession to the Spanish throne with Louis XIV: a roll-call of Peninsular history that reached back to the days of the Moors and added up to an impressive record of great positions in State, Army and Church. But if the father was a man of ancient lineage, he was, in the age dominated by the rise and fall of the first Napoleon, also a man of modern convictions. His courage as a soldier was equal to his political courage as a liberal Progressive, as a Bonapartist, who believed that with Napoleon the principles of the Revolution, tamed but not denied by the Emperor, had lost their most powerful defender.

The Empress's mother was of Scottish descent, belonging, paternally, to the Kirkpatricks of Closeburn. William Kirkpatrick, one of eighteen brothers and sisters, had arrived at Malaga in 1788 and entered, prosaically but successfully, the wine and fruit trade. Twelve years later, he was commissioned American Consul. He married Mlle de Grévigné, daughter of immigrant traders from Liége, who had given him his first employment in the wine-trade. His daughter Manuela, the Empress's mother, was born at Malaga in 1794. Her family background was thus one of solid middle-class affluence, Scottish efficiency enlivened by a generous and cosmopolitan hospitality. Not alone among American Consuls during the Napoleonic period, when the British were blockading the coast-line of the Continent, William sided with the Emperor rather than embattled Britain, and his daughter Manuela received some of her education in Paris in the heyday of the First Empire. In Paris, she stayed with her aunt's family; her mother's sister had married Count Mathieu de Lesseps. It is possible that she was in Paris in 1805, the year of Ulm and Austerlitz, when her cousin Ferdinand, the Canal builder, was born. She was certainly in the French capital in 1813, and in that year saw something of a young Spanish nobleman serving in the Emperor's army who was the brother and heir of the rich Count de Montijo and was a frequent caller in Count Mathieu's house. He did not, in 1813, use his Spanish title, Count of Teba, but called himself Colonel Portocarrero. The pale beauty of his face beneath the auburn shock of hair was made the more striking by the patch he wore over his left eye. His tall, supple and erect appearance enhanced his well-bred bearing, and he was the sort

5

of man who is not easily forgotten. Nor was he by Doña Manuela. She saw him again in 1817. Napoleon was in St. Helena, France and Spain were ruled by the restored Bourbons, but in Malaga the house of the American Consul remained open to all who were unreconciled to the return of that oppressively uncontemporary dynasty. Doña Manuela, the Consul's youngest unmarried daughter, was now twenty-three, and had become a beautiful, ambitious and vivacious young woman combining, wrote an American visitor, George Ticknor, 'Andalusian grace, English genuineness and French facility'. A certain tendency to domineer was also noted by some, while the Marquise de Lage de Volude, who hoped that the Count of Teba would marry her own daughter, wrote that Doña Manuela was 'worth millions and as beautiful as the day'. Teba, still wearing the black patch over his eye, came to the Kirkpatrick house at Malaga in the course of 1817. Lonely, unhappy and dissatisfied like most of his generation in the age of the Holy Alliance, he had started out from his house at Teba on a tour of Andalusia on foot and horseback, making the Kirkpatricks part of his vague and aimless itinerary. Who proposed, Doña Manuela or he? It is difficult to know. We next find him in earnest conversation with William Kirkpatrick, to whom he was pointing out that as a grandee of Spain he had to have the King's approval for marrying—a Kirkpatrick. William produced documents from Lyon King of Arms in Edinburgh, tracing his descent back into the farthest mists of Scottish history, as well as to more recent patents and matriculations of nobility. Teba submitted these proofs to His Catholic Majesty, King Ferdinand VII, who said: 'By all means let the noble Teba marry the daughter of Fingal.'

After the marriage celebration held at Malaga on December 15th, 1817, the young couple went to live in Granada. The new Countess quickly resumed the kind of life in which her social, intellectual and musical accomplishments had the greatest opportunity to shine. Her Parisian education and her years in Malaga had turned her into a witty conversationalist in several languages. She had a very pretty singing voice and a good ear for music. From the start, she strove to attract to her house politicians and diplomats, men closest to the fountains of power, for to her, as to Mme de Staël, 'to talk politics was to live'. With considerable consistency she argued in her salon through the years that Europe was waiting to be saved by 'a tyrant of genius'. She had seen the First Empire at the height of its authoritarian might and doubtless she hoped that the tyrant of genius would pass through her house on the road to supreme power. Her husband, by contrast, had witnessed Napoleon's abdication and fall. Under the impact of those stark events he had become committed to the Napoleon of the Hundred Days whose rule had been cut short by the 'King-making victory' of Waterloo. Don Cipriano's professed admiration for Napoleon— a transformed Napoleon whose existence the statesmen of the European Alliance were compelled to deny—became the most formative influence on the adolescence of his second daughter. From early childhood, Eugénie idolised her father. Her love for Spain, her life-long devotion to the Bona-

6

partist formula of freedom and authority, both derived from her dangerously possessive feeling for him.

The way in which Don Cipriano became so closely identified with Napoleon is, for his daughter's sake, worth a glance. Under the somewhat Quixotic Spanish caste system he was, though a grandee of the first class, quite penniless. He therefore joined the Royal College of Artillery at Segovia as a gentleman cadet at the age of fifteen. Four years later the battery in which he was serving as a Sub-lieutenant was put aboard a Spanish ship of the line and he sailed away in the combined Franco-Spanish fleet to meet the English off Cape Trafalgar on October 21st, 1805. He received his baptism of fire from British naval gunners, and emerged from the experience with his left shoulder and arm maimed for life. He remained in the service and took part in further Franco-Spanish actions against the British, including the siege of Gibraltar.

Spain at this time was ruled by the trinity immortalised by Goya—the Royal favourite Manuel Godoy, Prince of the Peace, the weak and foolish Bourbon King Charles IV and his hideous wife who was Godoy's mistress. The King's son and heir, Ferdinand Prince of the Asturias, had already been caught plotting for the overthrow of the ' earthly trinity ', but in the spring of 1808 Teba's brother Don Eugenio, Count of Montijo, put himself at the head of an open rebellion which demanded the King's abdication in favour of Ferdinand. The King yielded, the Prince of the Peace was nearly lynched, Ferdinand was proclaimed King, and Count de Montijo was the hero of the hour.

At this point, however, Napoleon, committing what was without doubt the gravest blunder as well as the basest act of treachery in his career, intervened, luring the Royal family, including Godoy and Ferdinand, to Bayonne, and thence to imprisonment beyond the Pyrenees. It is relevant to add that even as the Emperor was engaged upon his disastrous negotiations with the Spanish Royal family, a messenger, René de Villeneuve, arrived at Bayonne from Paris to announce that Hortense, Queen of Holland, had given birth to a son on April 20th, 1808. The future Napoleon III was born on the very day that Napoleon I informed the Spanish Bourbons they had ceased to reign. All along the frontier French guns saluted the birth of the Emperor's nephew, and on the following days French columns were crossing the mountain passes into Spain and the Peninsular War.

After their conquest of the peninsula, the French formed the ' Royal Corps of Spanish Artillery ' under their orders.[1] Teba, in joining it, became Colonel Portocarrero. He served in it up to the Vittoria campaign, was badly wounded in the leg in an action against the English, and lost his right eye in an accident when he was temporarily in charge of the artillery arsenal at Seville. ' Isn't it fortunate,' he remarked with the dry wit that Eugénie was to inherit, ' that God has created us with two legs, two arms

[1] The British Army under Wellington had been withdrawn from Spain into Portugal in 1809, and the Spanish were temporarily on their own.

7

and two eyes? Thus, I still have one of each left.' Towards the end of the Peninsular war, he served on the staff of General Dedon, King Joseph Bonaparte's Colonel-General of Artillery. He left Spain for France in 1813. In March of the following year he fought in the campaign of France against the Allies, and in the defence of Paris he commanded the pupils of the *Ecole Polytechnique* who manned the guns on the heights of Montmartre. 'The last cannon shots,' wrote a friend of the Empress many years later, 'which delayed our shame by a day, were fired by Colonel Portocarrero.' In the same month his brother Montijo, emerging from the hiding place to which French rule had driven him, was put in charge of the Royal Administration of Granada in the name of the returned Ferdinand VII. In Paris, where Ferdinand's cousins, the French Bourbons, were being restored to the throne, Colonel Portocarrero resigned from the army. On 31st August, Montijo, appointed *capitán-general* of His Catholic Majesty, King Ferdinand VII, publicly reproached his subordinates for their mildness towards the French party, the *afrancesados*. On 17th October, on the other hand, His Most Christian Majesty, King Louis XVIII of France and Navarre, conferred on Colonel Portocarrero the dignity of a 'Knight of the Royal Order of the *légion d'honneur*'. The two brothers had stood in what the Spanish call the War of Independence on opposite sides, but in the mild and agreeable atmosphere of 1814 it did not seem that the conflict need pursue them into the golden age of peace. For the time being Don Cipriano decided to remain in Paris.

When Napoleon escaped from Elba in March 1815 to begin his second reign, Don Cipriano became a chamberlain in the household of Joseph Bonaparte, since as a much-wounded and one-eyed veteran he could hardly go on active service. He lived through the Hundred Days in Paris and watched the great experiment of the liberal Empire. After Waterloo, he remained as close to the fallen Emperor as Joseph Bonaparte did himself and so witnessed the second abdication, the proclamation of Napoleon II as Emperor, the farewells at Malmaison late in June. Unlike ex-King Joseph, however, he decided against an escape to the United States and was still in Paris when Louis XVIII, restored a second time to the throne of St. Louis, became *Louis deux fois neuf* to his unenthusiastic subjects.

But, in 1815, a cold and angry storm was raging through France and Europe, and the mild spring breezes of 1814 became a distant memory. The French military authorities, with unblushing meanness, declared Portocarrero, since he was a Spaniard, a prisoner of war, but before he could be sent to a fortress he had joined his old comrades in their encampments south of the Loire to which they had been withdrawn in accordance with the armistice arrangements. There he was hidden among the veterans of the wars of the Revolution and the Empire who formed a solid front against any attempts on the part of the Royal authorities to arrest wanted or proscribed Bonapartists. Finally, he left the protection of the 'brigands of the Loire', as the French army was called by the vindictive Ultras of the French Restoration, and made his way back to Spain where he was

8

soon in trouble with the no less vindictive Ultras of the Spanish Restoration. He had left Spain as an *afrancesado*, but he returned as a Bonapartist. For Bonapartism was the fruit not of the conquests of the Empire, but of the reforms of the Hundred Days. It was a protest, not against Waterloo, but against the punitive treaties of 1815. It offered the principle of nationality evolved in freedom and based on the sovereignty of the people as an alternative to the international absolutism of the Holy Alliance with its persecutions of patriots and its belief in the divine right of Kings. The Bourbon rule in Spain, France and Naples; the oppressive Metternich system in Germany and the vast dominions of the Habsburgs; and the regressive incompetence of the Pope's temporal rule in central Italy all helped to confirm the Bonapartist opposition in their hopes and aspirations. Even as Don Cipriano, escaping from the French authorities, made his way back into Spain, ex-Queen Hortense with her little boy Louis Napoleon took the road of exile into Switzerland. Napoleon's sister-in-law had been peremptorily ordered out of Paris by a Prussian general, and it took her son all but forty years to return in freedom to the city of his birth, become Napoleon III and marry the daughter of the Spanish ex-Colonel who, like Queen Hortense, was driven from France by the provisions of the imposed treaties of peace.

Teba was not a politically-minded man, but such were the circumstances he found on his return to the Spain of Ferdinand VII that his allegiance to Napoleon almost automatically turned into a strong sympathy for the party of the *liberales*. The word was now entering the European vocabulary as a fighting term, and the treble constellation of nationalism, liberalism and Bonapartism stood visible for long in the skies above Spain, Greece, Italy, Poland and elsewhere during the long night of the Holy Alliance. Don Cipriano joined the *liberales* because the reactionary and clerical camarilla ruling Spain from the Royal Palace in Madrid persecuted the opposition with an arbitrary and panic-stricken cruelty that Spain had not known since the days of the counter-reformation. In later years the Empress, talking of this period in her father's life, would speak of the time when he was 'the prisoner of the Inquisition'. Teba communicated to his daughter much of the doctrine which he acquired in the Spain of the Bourbon counter-revolution, making it impossible for her ever to regard unfettered political Catholicism with undivided favour.

Immediately on his return to Spain in 1815, Teba was put under police supervision. Montijo, still the King's supreme representative in the South, seems to have done what he could to make his brother's life tolerable, and so Cipriano settled in Andalusia. As we have seen, he was still able to visit his friends, the Kirkpatricks, in Malaga, to obtain Manuela's hand in marriage and take his bride to Granada. There they were overtaken by the revolution of 1820.

As in the days of Napoleon, Don Cipriano and his brother supported opposing parties in the new conflict. The *liberales*, basing their rule on the famous Cadiz Constitution of 1812, remained in power until 1823, but

9

Montijo, faithful to Ferdinand VII, laid down his office as *capitán-general* as soon as his King became dependent on the constitutional party. Don Cipriano, already well-known for his liberal convictions, came out in open and active support of the new authorities at Granada. Monarchical Europe, meanwhile, perturbed by the martyrdom of the King of Spain, assembled in Congress at Verona and decided on armed intervention to free Ferdinand from his constitutional jailers. The Ultras of France, led for a time by Chateaubriand, sent a strong army into Spain under the command of the Duke of Angoulême, Louis XVIII's nephew. Only England stood aside from this demonstration by the Holy Alliance. The Foreign Secretary, Canning, decided to give official recognition to the independence of Spain's former colonies in South America, Mexico included. If France was to hold Spain, he declared, it must be 'Spain without the Indies'.

However, French armed intervention with its strong international backing could have only one result. Ferdinand VII was restored to absolute power. Immediately on his liberation, he embarked on a ghastly programme of suppression and revenge, and even Count Montijo did not return to office under the new conditions. Don Cipriano, having supported the *liberales* at Granada, was thrown into prison and then banished to Santiago de Compostella in the North. Some eighteen months later he was permitted to serve his term of imprisonment at Granada and, as he was a grandee, allowed to live with his wife in a small house at 12, Calle de Gracia. He could not travel, visitors were restricted and he remained under the closest surveillance. The police found it more difficult to keep Doña Manuela under control. She easily overcame their petty chicanery and managed, even under these conditions, to establish the semblance of a *salon*. Among her friends who braved police disapproval was José de la Pena, a liberal writer and man of law who was to serve in various governments of the future, and a young attaché from the French Embassy, Louis de Viel Castel, whose father had been the Empress Josephine's chamberlain at Malmaison after the divorce.

Cipriano's and Manuela's first daughter Paca, the future Duchess of Alba, was born on 29th January 1825. For the confinement, Doña Manuela had gone to her father's house at Malaga where the rich old man lavished all the medical care then available on his favourite daughter. She returned with the baby to her prison-home. For all her ambitious worldliness she never, in those days, hesitated to share her husband's wretchedly limited existence in a provincial backwater.

When the spring of 1826 brought tremors and earthquakes to Granada, Doña Manuela was pregnant once more. In the morning of May 5th, sub-terranean rumbling presaging disaster drove her into the garden where, since the earthquakes of the previous month, a tent had been erected. In this tent she gave birth to her second daughter. There had been no time to reach the comforts of Malaga or even to arrange for ordinary medical help to arrive in time, since the tremors had brought on the mother's pains unexpectedly and the birth was premature by some weeks. It evidently gave Doña Manuela no consolation that it had occurred on the anniversary of her hero Napoleon's death. Her feelings for her second daughter were long overshadowed by recollections of terror and pain.

The child was christened on the following day and was named Eugenia after her Montijo uncle in Madrid. This had been Don Cipriano's express wish, and so the name which the Empress was to make so famous celebrated the friendship of two brothers, sons of an ancient house who would not let the bitter feuds of the times break the bond between them. The imprisoned liberal gave his daughter the name of the head of his family who was also the friend of the Royal jailer. It was a gesture of conciliation.

CHAPTER 2

DON CIPRIANO'S detention lasted until 1830 and it nearly cost him his Montijo inheritance. Don Eugenio had, after the death of his wife, taken to living with a lady whom in later years the Empress coldly described as *une fille des rues*. She had been the mistress of his cousin, the Count de Parcent, and Montijo, lonely and ageing, had been prevailed upon to marry her. But not long afterwards he suffered a paralytic stroke which left him unable to move or speak; and then word reached Don Cipriano at Granada that his brother's new wife was expecting an heir.

The terms of his imprisonment did not permit Cipriano or his wife to travel to Madrid and exercise their right, as next of kin, to attend the birth. They knew that the child could not be Don Eugenio's, but as the day of the confinement approached Doña Manuela, insisting on her status as a grandee of Spain, succeeded in being admitted into the King's presence when the Court was at Valencia. Ferdinand, apparently much impressed by the beautiful and determined Countess of Teba, gave the desired permission, 'although,' as the Empress assured her Alba nieces in later years, 'he detested my father'. Doña Manuela hurried to Madrid where she surprised the household in the midst of elaborate arrangements to introduce an orphan child as the legitimate Montijo heir. The lady from the streets, when she heard of Doña Manuela's unexpected arrival, put herself shriekingly to bed and attempted to stage a dramatic *accouchement*, but found her visitor not so easily hoodwinked. The intrigue, set on foot by Parcent who no doubt disliked the prospect of the Montijo riches going to a notorious liberal, collapsed ignominiously, but it is pleasant to report that Doña Manuela adopted the orphan boy cast for the principal part of the comedy, giving him a home, a name and, later, a career. He was mentioned in Don Cipriano's will and became a military engineer; 'a good soldier,' the Empress remarked once, 'but no eagle'.

Don Cipriano was freed from detention by a new development in the labyrinth of Spanish politics. After three barren marriages, Ferdinand VII had at last been given an heir to the throne by his fourth consort, Marie Christine of Bourbon-Naples. The long-expected heir, however, was a girl, Isabella; hitherto the King's brother Carlos, obedient tool of the absolutist and clerical parties, had been the heir-apparent. To gain support for the succession of Isabella, the King had now to form an alliance with the liberals he had hitherto persecuted, and so he decreed the forming of a 'progressive' government based, with modifications, on the Constitution

12

of 1812. Consequently, the prisons emptied, the Universities reopened, the tribunals of the Inquisition were closed down, and Don Cipriano was a free man.

He was forty-four when he emerged from his detention. His good looks, the pale face under the auburn-red hair, were as striking as ever, but his friend Miraflorés was dismayed to see how rarely he smiled; other visitors to Doña Manuela's salon found him withdrawn and silent. With the paralysed Montijo still retaining a hold on life at Madrid, the Teba family found themselves relatively poor. But their acquaintances were surprised to observe that Don Cipriano had come to regard a Spartan simplicity of life as a matter of personal pride. When Paca and Eugénie were taken to visit affluent relatives, they did not travel in carriages, but rode on horseback or mules. Their naïve gasps of astonishment at the opulence of other people's houses became a byword.

Eugénie greatly resembled her father in looks. She had inherited his auburn hair, fair complexion and blue eyes. Paca with her dark hair, brown eyes and natural femininity took after Doña Manuela. With Eugénie Don Cipriano liked to go on long rides across the countryside and spend nights by a fire under the stars. She was no more than six or seven when she became a familiar and fascinated visitor among the gipsies round Granada with their music and their dances and their ancient superstitions. Eugénie grew up wildly and in freedom. At an early age she caused much anxiety and anger by her marked aversion from children's parties or similar social occasions. They bored her, she showed it, she was reprimanded, there were tears. That she was self-willed and determined was quite obvious.

Though her grasp of political affairs was precocious, there was never the slightest danger of her becoming a blue-stocking. Her insight and understanding were awakened not by books but by the fascination she felt for her father. For all his eccentricities, Don Cipriano belonged to a class never famous for its earnest pursuit of book-learning. But he was equally free from prejudice against the learned; he treated men of letters with courtesy and respect, and one of them, repaying the compliment, described him as 'the soldier-philosopher who so nobly bore the disgrace of having loved France and freedom too much'. 'Philosopher' was not inappropriate.

Eugénie's upbringing was cosmopolitan. With her parents she spoke mostly French, always wrote to them in that language and was twelve when she first began to read Spanish. In the pleasant house on Granada's Calle del Sordo, to which the Teba family moved after their father's liberation, she heard her mother's visitors speak Spanish, English, French. The latter language in particular was, for some months in 1830, represented there by a young Parisian who spoke it with consummate art, wit and distinction: Prosper Mérimée.

Don Cipriano had met him, on one of his first travels as a free man, on the stage-coach from Madrid. When the pleasant-looking stranger revealed conversationally that he was a liberal, a writer and a Frenchman, the enchanted Don Cipriano took him along and introduced him to Doña

13

Manuela. He could have rendered his wife and Eugénie no greater or more enduring service: Mérimée became their friend for life. To both Doña Manuela and the future Empress this wise and disillusioned student of the human heart brought the solace of his compassion, his intelligence, his honesty, his humanity. In 1830, when he was twenty-seven, he had already published a number of short books, some with a Spanish theme, and all of them distinguished by a subtle irony of style. His fame as a writer was assured, his notoriety as a highly amusable man about town was as yet confined to Paris; the bitter secrets of his heart were still hidden from the world. Stendhal said of him that like himself he was 'an example of non-charlatanism among writers', and his friend Augustin Filon wrote that what saved Mérimée from being ruined by the devouring dissipations of Paris was 'his innate sense of measure'. For this victory the world has reason to be grateful.

In him Doña Manuela welcomed something of a lion into her house. She understood him from the beginning while he became fascinated by the family's lively and sociable style of living and by his hostess's widely-ranging sympathies and interests which closely followed his own. 'Do you remember,' he wrote to her gratefully many years later, 'the beautiful stories you told me about the Alhambra and the Generalife Gardens, in 1830, in the Calle del Sordo? " And to Stendhal he wrote from a different journey in 1836: 'When I return I shall take you to meet an excellent Spanish lady whom you will like for her wit and her naturalness. She is a wonderful friend, but there has never been anything carnal between us. She is the Countess of Montijo, formerly Countess of Teba, of whom I have often told you. I am greatly and gravely in love in a different direction. . . .' His friendship with Doña Manuela survives in the 400 or so letters which he wrote to her from the beginning to the final one of September 1870 in which, a fortnight before his death, he made his excuses for not attending on the Empress that Sunday when she was besieged in the Tuileries by the Paris mob. These letters mirror forty years of European history.

He returned from Spain to Paris in December and found that ' the special spectacle given for our benefit', namely the July Revolution and the advent of Louis Philippe, had resulted in his being given official duties in the new government. The Mérimée family had always been protégés of the ducal family of Broglie whose present head, Duc Victor, was one of the country's new leaders. Mérimée became *Chef de Cabinet* to the Minister of the Marine, from where he slowly gravitated to the Inspectorate General of Ancient Monuments. In this post he was to render his country special services, in partnership with his friend Viollet-le-Duc. Another of the new men, Adolphe Thiers, signed the document appointing him to this post on May 27th, 1834. It carried a salary of 8,000 francs per annum.

The year 1834 also brought great changes in the life of his new friends, the Tebas. Don Eugenio de Montijo died in July. Not long before his death, his two nieces were brought along to see him and Eugénie gazed on a helpless figure in a large armchair. His brother's death made Don Cipriano

14

Count of Montijo and gave him a whole new string of titles. The family moved into the splendid Montijo mansion on the corner of the Plazuela del Angel in the centre of Madrid, close to the Puerta del Sol; Mérimée, during the numerous outbursts of unrest and popular risings which punctuated the reign of Isabella II, always deplored that the Montijo *Palacio* should occupy 'the strongest military position in Madrid'. On the day known in Spanish history as 'the massacre of the Friars', little Eugénie watched in horror while two monks were stabbed and tortured to death in the wide square below. The Plazuela del Angel certainly held a strategic position, being on the line of march whenever the people of Madrid surged from the poor quarters towards the Puerto del Sol, the Plaza Mayor or the Royal Palace beyond. The sinister rumbling and shouting of a mob bent on violence and bloodshed was a sound familiar to Eugénie from her early youth.

The new Count of Montijo did not find it necessary to let prosperity and the possession of a great name affect his conviction that simplicity and economy provided the healthiest basis for his daughters' upbringing. He looked on their wearing silk stockings as an irresponsible luxury, he wanted them to use the same dresses summer and winter, he still disliked their driving out in carriages. Doña Manuela, on the other hand, became increasingly concerned with providing a more conventional education for Paca and Eugénie. The Montijos had inherited the country property of Carabanchel near Madrid, and there Eugénie would go as often as she dared to escape from the tyranny of social life and be with her horses and animals and country pursuits. These she shared with her little friend Abelino, another orphan-boy adopted by her parents and, like Count Parcent's unsuccessful changeling, treated as one of the family. Abelino and she became inseparable, but the day came a year or so later when in the full maturity of her ten years she would write from Paris: 'I can no longer enjoy myself with Abelino, but shall always preserve the friendship which I once had for him.' But a few weeks later she sent another message for him: 'I cannot forget him, my heart is constant.'

The parents chose Paris for the education of the two girls for a variety of reasons—the unsettled state of the country during the Carlist War; an outbreak of cholera early in 1835; the love they both felt for the French capital, over which a liberal King was now reigning. Moreover, their marriage, so close and happy in the days of persecution, was, under the more difficult strains of prosperity, showing signs of a rift. Manuela and Cipriano agreed, in truth, on very little. In the civil war, for example, she favoured the Carlists, or *apostolicos*, with their absolutism and traditionalism, while Don Cipriano naturally remained a partisan of the liberal idea. Doña Manuela was confirmed in her outlook by a new habitué at the Plazuela del Angel, George Villiers, since July 1833 English Minister and, after 1838, fourth Earl of Clarendon. This personable young diplomat, clever, empirical and frivolous, had very quickly formed the opinion that 'the Spanish people hates what is called liberal government, liberal institutions, liberal men, because by experience it knows that worse usage comes from that than from a single despot. . . . Give trial by jury, liberty of the press, or any other *desideranda* of rational beings to such a community as this, and you only descend into a lower pit of hell.' Villiers could not, of course, express such views openly in Doña Manuela's drawing-room, but she gave him his opportunities for a safer and more convenient intimacy elsewhere. The fact that their friendship was soon noticed by Madrilene society no doubt made a sojourn abroad seem still more desirable.

The family arrived in Paris in the spring of 1835. By Doña Manuela's wish, Paca and Eugénie were sent to the Convent of the Sacré Coeur in the Rue de Varenne, then much in vogue among the fashionable and the rich of Louis Philippe's Paris. Doña Manuela, herself, went visiting in the South, but her husband remained in Paris to renew old friendships in a city which he had last known during the Hundred Days. The two girls wrote their parents letters, apologising for calling them *vous* for the first time—'my mistress has told me,' wrote Paca, 'that to call you *toi* would not be respectful'. Similarly Eugénie wrote to her mother at Toulouse, that although she called her *vous* she still loved her. Apart from this, the girls' letters written from their smart convent school were unremarkable.

Don Cipriano returned to Spain in November 1835, unaccompanied by his wife, and did not come back to Paris until the spring of 1837. They had gone their different ways in France almost as if the cradle of the Napoleonic Empire had further accentuated their differences. For even in their Bonapartism, which they both regarded as an essential element of their political thinking, husband and wife did not see eye to eye. Ex-Colonel Portocarrero, the former chamberlain of Joseph Bonaparte, had convinced himself of the viability of the liberal Empire with its balance between representative institutions and executive authority while Doña Manuela, who had known the Empire in its noonday of power and splendour, believed in Caesarism unadulterated and supreme. No letters from his wife reached him during his absence.

Unlike their mother, Paca and Eugénie wrote to Don Cipriano regularly, and Eugénie's letters show that she took the separation hardly: 'Write to me at once if you are ill,' she implored him in her first letter and in every following one she impatiently counted the weeks until the reunion which he had to delay time and again. When he sent a miniature of his portrait by Vicente Lopez she wrote that 'every time I look at it I think of the face I have not kissed for so long'. In January 1837 she commented sadly that this had been the first Christmas they had spent apart and went on: 'You know, my dear Papa, it is quite impossible to live in Paris, they are trying to kill the King all the time, the other day there was an explosion in the street, and we were told that some people had set fire to the gas. What was so funny was that soldiers came running along with their arms thinking it was a Revolution. . . . I am longing to kiss you, Papa, and when I see the other side of the Pyrenees, my heart will not have enough room for its joy. . . .'

The two girls left their convent school in July 1836 and were given an English *institutrice*, Miss Cole. Following Don Cipriano's preference, they now attended the *Gymnase Normale, Civile et Orthosomatique* which Colonel Amoros, late of the Pestalozzi Institute of Madrid and the Napoleonic army, had opened in Paris for the physical training of children of both sexes. The institution was the last word in progressive education, a great contrast to the traditionalism of Sacré Coeur. Meanwhile in Spain, Don Cipriano had entered on an active political life and become Senator for Badajoz. This made visits to Paris still more difficult, but it also made it easier for Mme de Montijo to explain her husband's absence: 'The Queen,' wrote Paca to Madrid, 'did not want to let you come to fetch us.' Eugénie continued to write like an impatient woman in love: 'What is the arm that keeps us apart? It is the war. Time hurries forward and we remain behind, and we have less time to kiss each other. . . .' When finally he reappeared in Paris, he stayed apart from his family at an address in the Rue d'Angoulême, but took the girls to the theatre, the circus or boating on the lake. It was a short stay, his career and the Carlist War recalling him to Madrid after two months. 'The evening you left us,' Eugénie wrote early in April 1837, 'the Duke of Alba took us to his house and I looked at the clock all the time. When it struck seven I knew that this was the hour of your departure. . . .'

Later in the same month, Mme de Montijo took the two girls to a board-ing school at Clifton near Bristol. Again they did not remain long. In her old age the Empress always discouraged questions about this early English episode, and it seems clear that she was not happy among the girls of this establishment. She once confessed that she was much teased on account of her red hair, the other girls inelegantly calling her 'Carrots', so that she was driven to comb it with leaden combs in the belief, happily mistaken, that this would dull its glory. 'We hope to be your interpreters when you come here,' she wrote to her father from Clifton, 'but there are no public amusements here, everybody always stays at home and you don't see nice people in the streets.' Paca, also from Clifton, told her father without enthusiasm that they were staying at school all day, learning English. The Empress remembered an Indian girl at the school who so fired her imagina-tion with marvellous tales of the splendours of the East that Eugénie and her friend decided to find an India-bound ship in Bristol harbour and escape from their dismal life in the English *pension*. However, their absence was discovered before they reached Bristol.

They were back in Paris in July 1837, and with them came Miss Flowers, their new English governess, who remained in the service of the Montijo family until the 1880s. Eugénie had not done well, academically speaking, at either school; the reports had been bad and she apologised to her father for causing him sorrow in this respect, promising to do better for his sake 'next year'. The Pestalozzian Colonel Amoros, on the other hand, reported most favourably about her work at the gymnasium. He praised her strong liking for physical exercise, called her character 'good, generous, active and

firm ', her temperament ' sanguine and nervous '. Mérimée taught her how
to handle, and fire, a pistol. ' You have told us,' she wrote to her father on
one occasion, ' to read Napoleon [sic] and learn his history, it has made me
cry. . . .' And Paca wrote: ' Isn't it true, Papa, that the Spaniards are
generous in loving Napoleon after all the bad things he has done to them?
We are not like the English who have sent him to St. Helena with an
atrocious jailer like Sir Hudson Lowe whom everybody detests, even the
English. We know a gentleman called Monsieur Beyle who is very kind
and very good to us. In Napoleon's time he was employed at Court and
carried out all kinds of jobs for him, and now he is able to tell us everything
that went on in the days of the Empire.'

Mérimée had introduced Stendhal—he remained Monsieur Beyle to both
sisters all their lives—some time in 1836, and when Mme de Montijo
brought the girls back from England, the two writers were regular visitors
at their house. For Eugénie, Stendhal's memories of the Empire, of Napoleon
himself, were the ideal, the deeply exciting continuation of her father's
tale while M. Beyle greatly enjoyed his audience of two small girls who
listened to him with bated breath and could never hear enough. To them
he dedicated the Waterloo chapter in La Chartreuse de Parme, for them he
endeavoured to speak of epic grandeur and misery as simply, as clearly and
as truthfully as he could. A friend of Mérimée's wrote later that Eugénie
and Paca saw Stendhal ' at his best, knew perhaps the real Stendhal without any affectation and distortion since, in order to be understood, to be
worthy of his little friends, he wanted to be pure and deigned to be
simple '. These Thursday evenings when M. Beyle called and the two girls
were allowed to stay up were perhaps Mme de Montijo's most fruitful
single contribution to Eugénie's education. With her wide and cultured
intelligence Doña Manuela understood the value of these sessions when
lived history was offered to young minds by a writer of genius.

Monsieur Beyle's reminiscences found a complement in Mérimée's
watching as a tutor of sorts over Eugénie's and Paca's French compositions,
handwriting and spelling. Then he would take them out to have a look at
the new Arc de Triomphe, where Napoleon's victories were engraved on
stone of gleaming white, or hand them over to Miss Flowers and English
lessons.

Late in February 1839, word reached Doña Manuela that her husband
was gravely ill. She hurried at once to Madrid, making arrangements for
the two girls and Miss Flowers to follow in the following month. They left
Paris on March 20th. ' I cannot tell you,' wrote Mérimée to the mother,
' how their departure grieves me. At their age women change completely
in a few months, and it seems to me that I shall lose them. When one
becomes separated from a friend like yourself one knows that one will find
again the woman one has left, but in the place of our two little friends I
fear I shall see two prim and stiff young ladies who will have forgotten me.
I see in the papers that Lord Clarendon is leaving Madrid which is a loss to
you. Sorrows never come singly. . . .' On March 25th he received a letter

THE COUNT OF MONTIJO

THE COUNTESS OF MONTIJO

PACA, DUCHESS OF ALBA

from Doña Manuela telling him that Cipriano had died on March 15th, a week before the two children had reached Madrid.

'You know how much I loved the Count, and how much I love you,' he wrote in his letter of condolence. 'You have been put to a cruel test, but despite the pain which that heart-rending scene must have caused you, it is better that you were present. You have the consolation of having soothed his last moments. . . . When you are able to write to me, please reassure me about your health which must have been violently upset by the shock. Lord Clarendon, passing through Paris, expressed some anxiety about the Count's testamentary arrangements in so far as they concern you. I hope to hear that you will be satisfied in this respect. . . .'

It was the end of Eugénie's childhood. She had loved her father with all the ardour of her nature. He had given her life, freedom, a sense of values, a spirit of adventure. Now she stood before his grave, as in the future she was to find herself again looking on the graves of those she had loved with a disturbing and unrequitable passion. She was thirteen.

CHAPTER 3

AFTER HER husband's death, Doña Manuela was a dutiful, but far from affectionate mother to Eugénie. Her own preference, which she took little pains to conceal, belonged to Paca, and before long Eugénie began to feel rejected and even wronged. The situation was not without its dangers to one who, for all her precocious intelligence, was still so young in years. Already, her life had given her little outward stability, and only her father had infused an element of continuity into the constant changes of school and domicile. Now that they were all, as it were, re-naturalising themselves in their native Spain, Eugénie's old aversion from the obligations and restrictions of social life further aggravated her mother's impatience. 'We have no friends here,' Eugénie wrote to Stendhal in December 1840, 'for the young girls of Madrid are so stupid that they speak only of their clothes, unless they talk scandal about each other. You must be very happy because they are bringing back Napoleon's mortal remains. I know I am, and wish I could be in Paris for the ceremony.'

Her mother's underlying hostility, coupled with her own overwhelming grief at the final separation from a father of whom in the last years she had seen all too little, bitterly discouraged Eugénie and filled her with a sense of inadequacy. Would she ever fit into the world of ordinary men and women? Remembering Don Cipriano's intoxicating tales of Napoleon and his loyalty to a cause that seemed to have vanished from the world, she was assailed by the fear that hers was a destiny which, in the contemporary world, could never be fulfilled. She kept such sombre thoughts to herself until a tragic experience suddenly brought her lonely struggles to light. Her outward reputation, not surprisingly in view of these tensions, was that she was over-excitable, too high-spirited and sometimes alarming company. By the time she was seventeen, she had grown to unique and breath-taking beauty. Her proud and erect bearing, the blue eyes set in an oval face of milky whiteness, the Titian-red hair cascading down to perfect shoulders, had driven more than one young man from among Doña Manuela's habitués into passionate declarations of love and devotion. For Eugénie, though rarely unprotestingly, played at her mother's receptions and *tertullias* the part that Doña Manuela expected of her, and met the world unflinchingly. Yet when among the young men who thronged round her she chose one with whom to share the happiness of love, her hopes were crushed in a way that was to mark her emotional life for ever.

20

Among the familiar visitors at Doña Manuela's receptions at Madrid and Carabanchel was the Duke of Alba and Berwick, a shy and somewhat taciturn young man of twenty of whom they had already seen something in Paris. He lived in one of the great Madrilene houses, the Palacio de Liria, where behind a restrained Louis XVI façade there were rooms hung with paintings by Titian, Velasquez, Murillo, Zurburan and Goya and magnificent tapestries given to an earlier Duke by Louis XV. The owner of all this splendour was a childhood friend of the two Montijo girls, and Doña Manuela, who did little without a purpose, saw to it that the friendship continued. Soon he was as often at the strategic mansion in the Plazuela del Angel as she took her daughters to the Palacio de Liria or to Alba's famous hunts at Aranjuez. Alone among all the Osunas and Ayerbes and Ardales who, according to Mérimée, were 'smitten' with Eugénie's exotic beauty, it was only the silent Duke whom she seemed to notice. When she had fallen passionately in love with him, she made no secret of her feelings. Was he in love with her, was he in love with Paca? Nobody knew then, nobody knows now. But Eugénie told him that for him she would go begging in the street, for him she would consent to her own dishonour. In the ensuing drama, Alba's part was one of polite passiveness.

For what happened (of this we can be certain) was that Doña Manuela stepped in with ruthless briskness and saw to it that Alba declared his intentions for Paca. She had intended all along to marry her elder daughter off to this great nobleman. When she became aware of the depth of Eugénie's feeling, she chose to announce his engagement to Paca in a manner that ignored Eugénie's rights, humiliated her pride and ridiculed her feelings. Eugénie poured out her despair in a letter to Alba:

16th May 1843.

My very dear cousin,

You will find it odd [she began, writing in French, calling him *tu*] that I should be writing to you like this but all things must come to an end in this world and so to me the end is approaching and I want to explain to you what is in my heart. It is more than I can bear. I have a strong character, it is true, I do not want any excuses for my conduct, but also when people are good to me I would do everything they want of me. But if I am treated like an animal, if I am beaten in public—this is more than I can stand. Many people think that nobody in the world could be happier than I am, but they are wrong. I am unhappy because I make myself unhappy, I should have been born a century earlier, because my most cherished ideas are ridiculous nowadays, and I fear ridicule more than death; I love and I hate in excess and I don't know which is better, my love or my hate; passions mingle in me, some terrible, all of them strong: I fight against them, but I lose the battle and in the end my life will finish, miserably lost in a welter of passions, virtues and follies.

You will say that I am romantic and stupid, but you who are good will forgive a poor girl who has lost all those she loves and is treated with indifference even by her mother, by her sister and, dare I say it, by the man she loves the most—that man you know. Don't say I am mad, I beg of you, but have pity for me: you don't know what it means to love and be despised. But God will give me courage to end my life quietly in some cloister and nobody will know that I ever existed.

There are people who were born for happiness: you are one of them. May God grant that it will always be so. My sister is good: she loves you, your union will not be postponed long, and then nothing will be missing from your happiness. If you have children, love them also: remember that they are all your children and never wound their good feeling by showing more affection for one than for another. Follow my advice and be happy—this is the wish for you of

Your sister,
Eugénie.

Do not talk me out of it: it would be useless. I shall finish my life far from the world and its affections: with God's help nothing is impossible and my mind is made up, for my heart is broken.

Not for her the solace of the cloister, the escape behind convent walls! She was meant to live in the world, even though it required yet another defeat in love before she was able to accept the fact that happiness was to be no part of her life. Her lines to Alba are so revealing because they show us not only her pride and her deep self-doubts, but also her horrified awareness of the intensity of her own feelings. Was it not this aspect of her character that so alarmed her friends and suitors? Did she not, whenever she committed herself to any person, idea or cause, invariably betray an inner passion that compared with sudden flashes of lightning on a summer sky? As the years went by, she was to learn that while many were attracted to her beauty, only few could bear her more than natural intensity for long.

More extraordinarily still, when she lost Alba she transferred the love she had felt for him to her sister Paca. Until her son, the Prince Imperial, was born, she bore no deeper, no more passionate love for any human being than she did for the dark and quiet Paca. All her life, she cherished the name of Alba beyond all others in her world, watching over the welfare of Paca's children and grandchildren in the years to come. One may record in gratitude that Paca's grandson, the late Duke of Alba, transformed some of the stately rooms in the Palacio de Liria into a worthy and moving memorial to the Empress. She had known the house as a young girl in love, she returned to it in extreme old age to die. Her heart was truly constant.

After the Alba wedding, held early in 1844, Eugénie spent five uninterrupted years in Spain. She showed, at first, a certain defiant recklessness of conduct and threw herself into sporting amusements—riding bare-backed horses through the streets of Madrid, appearing at bull-fights in spectacular costumes, swimming, fencing and even, an enemy reported, smoking cigarettes. But her quieter occupations continued also: drawing and painting lessons, English with Miss Flowers (at no time in her life did she manage the aspirates). More surprisingly, she suddenly studied the works of Fourier, the last of the pre-industrial Socialists, as they were being published during the 1840s. These volumes left a lasting impression on Eugénie's roving and inquisitive mind. Her conversation became tinged with comments on Fourier's concepts of the problems of property and class, and Doña Manuela did not take kindly to her daughter turning her *soirées* into debating societies of a progressive tendency.

And Bonapartism? Both Doña Manuela and Eugénie had in 1843 made the acquaintance of an authentic Bonaparte Prince who had turned up in Madrid and quickly become a regular caller at the Montijo mansion. This was Prince Napoleon, son of Napoleon's youngest brother Jerome, ex-King of Westphalia, and known informally as Plon-Plon. Was he the 'tyrant of genius' for whom, according to Doña Manuela, Europe was waiting? After a few conversations with him she firmly decided that he was not. She found him witty, handsome and endowed with the fascination of the Bonapartes, but he was not, she said, *the* Bonaparte. He was, of course, banished from France like the rest of the family, but his sister, Princess Mathilde, married to an immensely rich and equally unpleasant Russian and therefore able to live in Paris, was already endeavouring to persuade Louis Philippe to let her brother return. Prince Plon-Plon, travelling for pleasure, made an extended stay in Madrid. He was soon paying court to Eugénie, but she made it abundantly clear that she had no wish to be part of his present programme. 'Tell me,' wrote Mérimée to Doña Manuela from Paris, 'what sort of man is the Bonaparte who has come to play Don Juan in your house?' In later years, the Empress was to learn that hell knows no fury like a Don Juan scorned.

Now that Paca was married, Mérimée, with all the zeal and conviction of the confirmed bachelor, in almost every letter expressed his hope that 'Eugénie will let herself be influenced by her sister's example'. 'What I fear for Eugénie,' he wrote again, 'are penniless lieutenants in the Hussars with fine moustaches and brilliant uniforms. I hope to see her settling down, before she has begun the first chapter of a romance of that sort. . . .' When no engagement was announced, he wrote with some sarcasm of 'the caprices of the señorita', and commiserated with the mother over 'the innumerable *calabazas* of mademoiselle, your daughter'. It hardly occurred to him that even a beautiful young woman of good family might wish to live her life in independence, without paying much attention to smitten noblemen or cavalry officers.

How delicately and tactfully Eugénie dealt with unwelcome suitors may be seen from the experience of an Englishman who was Doña Manuela's guest for several weeks in 1846. Ferdinand Huddleston, of Sawston Hall,

Cambridge, and St. James's Street, London, was a landowner and a Roman Catholic. He was an obliging and kindly man, was soon regarded as a friend with whom Miss Flowers could talk English and whom even Madame Gordon, a somewhat adventurous person staying in the house, found wholly acceptable. When he left, he amiably offered to take on various commissions for the ladies in Paris and London, but great was Eugénie's surprise when not long after his departure she received a letter from him containing a proposal of marriage. She took a little time over replying, and then told him of how surprised she had been by his letter, perhaps she had not quite understood what he was saying? 'It was enough for me to hear,' she went on, 'that my mother had invited you to Carabanchel to find it all very agreeable.' The next sentence was written in English: 'As a *friend* I shall always be happy to see you. You tell me,' she went on in French, 'that I am undecided, and you would wait for me to make up my mind. But I feel too much friendship for you to raise hopes which I could never fulfil. At the risk of losing your friendship I prefer to act loyally towards you. I hope nevertheless to see you here again, if not at present, then later on. You know that you will always find in me a friend.'

Madame Gordon—one fears one must call her a *demi-mondaine*—also wrote to Huddleston on the subject. He had trusted her with his secret, perhaps he had been rash enough to try and enlist her support, at all events she had talked with Eugénie frankly. 'She has told me,' the lady wrote brutally, 'that she would rather be hanged than marry an Englishman. She did not bind me to secrecy when she told me this. You are frankly in love—eh bien! frankly I tell you that you have not one single chance of success, and you had better realise that I am right and that my advice is good. If you want to burn yourself, that is your affair, there are forms of suffering which are not without their charm and yours is no doubt of that kind. Adieu, monsieur, I wish you luck and joy, and I hope that chance, which has brought us together here, will defeat distance and re-unite us.' Sadly, Mr. Huddleston returned to Cambridgeshire.

What was so crude and blunt a person as Madame Gordon doing in Madame de Montijo's house? The lady was an *artiste*. Some years previously, Doña Manuela and Eugénie had visited a watering place in the Pyrénées and heard Mme Gordon sing at a musical *soirée*. The singer was presented and revealed in conversation that she had played a conspicuous part in Louis Napoleon's attempted coup at Strasbourg in 1836. When Eugénie heard that the Napoleonic claimant was, after a second unsuccessful attempt made four years later at Boulogne (this time without Mme Gordon's assistance), serving a life sentence at Ham, she at once expressed an urgent desire to visit him. Mme Gordon gave her to understand that visits could be arranged, that she herself was about to travel North for the purpose. . . . Mme de Montijo seemed inclined to grant her daughter's wish and even to go herself and meet the great Napoleon's imprisoned nephew, but a few days later news (it is not clear of what sort) reached her which made an immediate departure for Madrid imperative. The voyage was abandoned, but Mme Gordon was invited to come to Spain after her visit to Ham and give mother and daughter further news. Eugénie was never to know that this same woman, who stirred her imagination with stories of the Napoleonic conspirator in his misty fortress above the Somme, had at the same time dealt so downrightly with poor Mr. Huddleston's feelings.

Eleanora Gordon belonged heart and soul to the Bonapartist advance-guard. 'The cause that I defend openly and aloud,' she said in 1839, 'is to me so noble, great and holy that it is my religion, a religion of which I shall always be a faithful and devout disciple.' Her enthusiasm still blazed brightly when she came to Carabanchel with tales of 'her Prince', as she invariably referred to the prisoner of Ham. Put on trial for her share in the Strasbourg affair she had been asked, in open court, whether she was in love with Louis Napoleon. 'Politically—yes,' she replied and then added: 'Frankly, he produces on me the effect of a woman.' To Eugénie she brought a revelation of the fortunes, past and future, of the Napoleonic idea. The encounter with Prince Plon-Plon had not revealed that men still fought and suffered for the cause into which her father and M. Beyle had initiated her.

Through her intimate friendship with Narvaez, one of the alternating strong men of Spain[1] and head of its government since 1843, Doña Manuela was at long last given a position of acknowledged power. In October 1847, Queen Isabella made her *camarera mayor*, the highest position in her household and, as such, a political appointment. Eugénie became one of the Queen's maids of honour and so had her first taste of ante-chamber politics and palace intrigues. Once again, her apprenticeship was to be brief, for Doña Manuela was soon driven from her powerful position by an intrigue launched by Miraflorés, an old friend of Don Cipriano and, for that reason, a declared enemy of his widow. Among the objections whispered against Doña Manuela behind the scenes was her traditional friendship with succeeding British ambassadors who, it was truthfully pleaded, since Clarendon's time belonged to her circle practically *ex officio*.

But Doña Manuela did not let her brief term of power, or her fall from it, interfere with her hospitality, and throughout 1847 and 1848 the influential, the famous and the amusing flocked to her house as numerously as ever. Late in 1847 an English member of Parliament, Monckton Milnes, who in the words of his biographer had 'tunnelled his way successfully into the hieratic structure of Madrid society', surfaced in the Montijo Palacio on several occasions, danced on 'thick, dirty carpets', saw Queen Isabella and admired Eugénie's 'real Spanish beauty'. Bulwer, British Ambassador at the time, at once suspected Eugénie of having, siren-like, 'beguiled' the visiting politician.

But only Paca held her love and Eugénie was seen at the Palacio de Liria almost as if she belonged there. She still went on the hunts organised by

[1] The others being O'Donnell, Espartéro and, finally, Prim.

the Duke of Alba, to the *apartados* which he held on the eve of the chase at Aranjuez, and she found such moments of danger more to her taste than the less dramatic entertainments arranged by her mother. 'My mother,' said the Empress in later years, 'wanted to make everybody happy, but in her own way, not in theirs. . . .' Mother and daughter differed in most things. Eugénie loved the wide horizons and the wildness of the Spanish country-side, while Doña Manuela preferred the parks and the gardens and the flowerbeds around her houses in Madrid and the country. Being, as Fourier's disciple, known as *la jeune phalanstérienne*, Eugénie proved herself to be a vivacious debater, fond of long arguments on serious subjects with novel opinions strongly held and expressed, whereas to the mother conversation (and correspondence) meant subtly probing for information and gossip about people in power, fishing for indiscretions, confidences exchanged behind a fan in the interval between two valses. To Mme de Montijo social life, including matchmaking, was politics under another name: she loved power as Eugénie loved principles and ideas. Music provided another source of mutual irritation. Doña Manuela with her attractive singing voice appreciated and understood music and often put on very creditable performances of Italian opera in the little theatre at Carabanchel which gave her *tertullias* a special attraction of their own. Eugénie, although so responsive to the rhythms of Spanish music and gipsy dances, had no ear for music or sense of melody whatever. In later years, she was barely able to distinguish God Save the Queen from the anthem of the Second Empire. Her one contribution to her mother's musical entertainments, a walking-on part in Bellini's Norma, ended in her being laughed off the stage.

It cost mother and daughter constant efforts to keep relations on a reasonable footing. They both made this effort. For all the undertones of bitterness which were never absent from Eugénie's relations with Doña Manuela, she felt even then some admiration for her mother's indefatigable energy and courage. 'Listen!' said the Empress later on with great emphasis, 'you know Lesseps, my mother's first cousin? He has exactly the same temperament. Both have achieved the impossible.'

Again unlike her mother, Eugénie was no great correspondent and seems at this period to have written with any regularity only to Cécile Delessert, the daughter of King Louis Philippe's Prefect of Police and once her companion and great friend at Colonel Amoros' progressive gymnasium in Paris. Doña Manuela, on the contrary, kept up correspondence with a good many people, including Ferdinand Huddleston at Sawston to whom she sent slightly sarcastic messages for Lord Clarendon, now President of the Board of Trade. Mérimée often deplored Eugénie's aversion from ink, and we may deplore it with him, for as a result we have no word from her concerning a second disaster of the emotions she had to undergo before fate and Louis Napoleon took a hand.

The young marqués who moved her vulnerable heart and engaged her passions was Pepe Alcañisez, a stylish and accomplished man of wit, pleasure, ambition and wealth: in later years he graduated as a king-maker in the restoration of Alfonso XII. It is, once more, difficult to establish with certainty precisely what happened in that summer of 1848: but, whatever the details, the episode brought Eugénie final despair. The version believed by the Empress's closest friends and relatives is that Alcañisez gave her every reason to think that he was in love with her and that she, believing him to be truthful, in turn fell in love with him. He wrote her letters filled with ardent declarations, he sought her company wherever he could. Then she made the discovery that he had merely used her as a means of gaining access to the Duchess of Alba with whom he was really in love, that he hoped that Eugénie's easy access to her sister's house would promote his amorous designs. The story as told by one of the Empress's nieces to Ethel Smyth 'in a rare and fortunate moment of ex-pansion' at Farnborough Hill, goes on that Eugénie, annihilated by the discovery, took poison and for hours hovered between life and death, refus-ing the antidote. Pepe was brought to her sick-bed, bent over her and whispered, 'Eugénie, where are my letters?' In what Dame Ethel then calls 'a blaze of contempt', Eugénie swallowed the antidote. 'You are like the spear of Achilles,' she is said to have told him, 'you heal the wounds you made.' Soon afterwards, Mme de Montijo took Eugénie to Paris for a long visit.

CHAPTER 4

THE ALCAÑISEZ episode was Eugénie's farewell to love and happiness as the terms are understood by ordinary mortals. After the enterprising and clever marqués no other man roused and engaged her emotions as a woman. On the eve of her encounters with Louis Napoleon she had, at twenty-three, reached a stage where despair and thoughts of death loomed large in her mind, prompting her to emotional withdrawal from the heartless world of sensual, frivolous men. At the same time, however, her lively feeling for the political conflicts of the day, her identification with progressive movements, her instinctive anticipation that dramatic events and revolutions were to come, especially in her beloved Spain—all these pointed, dimly and uncertainly, to a world of struggles and hopes beyond the afflictions of the merely personal. Even so, it was to take her nearly four years of restless travelling and her meetings with Louis Napoleon before she could turn away from the shadows of her private world and take the first bold step towards her historic destiny.

In choosing Paris as the place most likely to rescue Eugénie from the shock of Alcañisez's treachery and the malice of Madrilene comments, Doña Manuela had been only partly influenced by the circumstance that in December 1848 Louis Napoleon—who had escaped from Ham not long after Mme Gordon's stay at Carabanchel—had been elected President of the Second French Republic. She simply hoped that the change and the diversity of Paris would help Eugénie to forget. However, before they left Madrid, Doña Manuela had received a letter from Mérimée: 'People do not know what to make of the new President [he wrote]. He surprises all who come near him by that air of *self-conscience* [this in English] which one associates with legitimate Monarchs. He is the only person here whom his election has not taken by surprise. Otherwise, he is said to be obstinate and resolute. The clamour of the first days has been followed by a curious silence, and people are beginning to wonder what he will do, although nobody is prepared to risk prophecies.'

Swiftly resuming her many contacts in all spheres and quarters of political Paris, Doña Manuela soon picked up a good deal of gossip about the Prince-President and the 'Elysée set' that surrounded him. Thus she heard that he was living with an English lady of indeterminate status, Miss Howard, a former actress who had amassed a considerable fortune, principally while resting, and was rumoured to have financed his recent election campaign. Poor Madame Gordon, after years of poverty in receipt

28

of a pension from the Prince, had died in hospital on March 11th, 1849, a few days before the two Montijo ladies reached Paris. Within a month of their arrival, Doña Manuela succeeded in obtaining an invitation for herself and Eugénie to one of the Prince-President's not infrequent *soirées* at the Elysée. It has been often said, and the error has given rise to much unintelligent comment, that Eugénie first met her future husband in the house of Princess Mathilde, Louis Napoleon's cousin and former fiancée. From a letter written by Doña Manuela soon after the event we find that the first meeting took place at the Elysée on the evening of April 12th, 1849. Mérimée had already taken the two ladies along to Princess Mathilde, but it was Bacciochi, the President's social secretary and *maître de plaisir*, who obtained for them the invitation to a Presidential reception.

'An enormous number of people were there,' Doña Manuela wrote to Paca. 'His looks are absolutely insignificant, but he carries himself well and is clearly in his rightful place. He talked with me for a long time, unusual for him because normally he never chats with people at all. As the Elysée is so small, it is very probable that he will soon move elsewhere.' Eugénie, when presented by Bacciochi, told the Prince-President: 'We have often, Monseigneur, spoken of you to a lady who was passionately devoted to your interests.'

'And what,' he asked, 'was her name?'

'Madame Gordon.'

It was an unwelcome allusion and Louis Napoleon addressed no further remarks to his young guest that night.

A few weeks later, Bacciochi delivered an invitation to both ladies to dine with the President at Saint-Cloud. They put on their most gorgeous evening dresses, but at the château carriages were waiting to take them to a little house on the road to Villeneuve where they found only Bacciochi with the President and dinner laid for four. Afterwards, Louis Napoleon offered Eugénie his arm and proposed a stroll through the darkening park; Doña Manuela and Bacciochi hovered uncertainly on the side. 'Monseigneur, my mother is here,' said Eugénie, reproachfully pointing out that he ought to escort the older lady. Silently he did so and Eugénie followed at Bacciochi's side on what became a somewhat formal promenade. No further Presidential invitations were received, and in June the two ladies left for Spa.

Thus Eugénie's first encounter had been with the sensualist, the man of pleasure and not of destiny, yet when she and Doña Manuela returned to Paris two years later she showed how, for all that, he had impressed her with other, less obvious, qualities. The political climate of Paris had, by the early autumn of 1851, changed out of all recognition. The Prince-President's term of office was scheduled to come to an end in May 1852 and the Assembly, preponderantly conservative in feeling, was to be dissolved at the same time. Various bills had been presented to enable Louis Napoleon to seek legal re-election for a second term, but they had all been defeated in the Assembly. Few people believed that it would be possible to 'dismiss him into private life'. During the summer, he had been touring the provinces and Eugénie read reports of his speeches in the newspapers. 'Should the day of danger arrive,' ran a quotation from one of these, 'I shall not act like the governments which preceded me and say to you: "March, I shall follow," but I shall say: "I march, follow me."' Eugénie recognised the note of daring. Before they returned to Spain in November she wrote a letter to Bacciochi in which she said that all she possessed in the world would be at the President's disposal should developments make such assistance necessary. Louis Napoleon, since his return from the provinces, had shut himself up at Saint-Cloud, receiving only his most intimate advisers, reshuffling the Cabinet, showing the world that he was bent, not on evacuation, but on consolidation. By the time he was ready to strike, Eugénie was back in Madrid and she did not hear until much later that Bacciochi had not shown him her letter until after the coup d'état of December 2nd, 1851.

Doña Manuela heard all about the great event from an English friend, Lady Clifford-Constable, who had been in Paris throughout the three momentous days from which Louis Napoleon emerged as, at first, President for ten years. This lady, wife of a landed proprietor of Yorkshire, had been present at the reception which the Prince-President gave on the evening of Monday, December 1st—the famous occasion that was to the coup d'état what the Duchess of Richmond's ball at Brussels was to the campaign of Waterloo. Louis Napoleon discussed the details of the imminent operation with his confederates—his half-brother Morny, General St. Arnaud, Fleury, Maupas and Persigny—in a discreet room down the passage to the accompaniment of sounds of revelry from the ball-room where his guests were dancing. Lady Clifford-Constable had noticed nothing. 'The coup d'état,' she wrote to Doña Manuela, 'has interested us very much. We found it possible to take walks on the boulevards on all the days except the Thursday, and even on that day it was possible to go out as usual on the Champs Elysées. On Monday evening we were at the Elysée, and on Tuesday M. Drouyn de Lhuys[1] gave a reception, as did Princess Mathilde. But the whole thing happened like a thunderbolt. I hear from Paris that many balls and fêtes are being given at the Elysée and by the Ministers, but that not many private soirées are being held. . . . I hope that you and Eugénie are well?'

The foundations of the Second Bonapartist Empire were laid and so was one of its most widely-believed legends: that Louis Napoleon's coup d'état was carried out on behalf of the Party of Order, that he 'employed a group of officers and men of order whose previous feats of arms had been victories won over Berber tribesmen and over the workmen of Paris and Lyons'. And a witty writer on the Second Empire has told us that throughout 1851 Louis Napoleon 'posed as the saviour of a society that was only too willing to be saved', since it had been artificially alarmed by

[1] Foreign Minister in the new Presidential Cabinet and an old acquaintance of the Montijos from his days at the Madrid Embassy.

'lurid publications about the Red Peril'. The significance of Louis Napoleon's position in 1851 was, on the contrary, that by then he could no longer be identified with the Party of Order whose military leaders were his rivals Changarnier and Cavaignac (the latter responsible for the massacres of June 1848 when Paris workmen were shot down in the streets). Its political managers were men like Thiers, Berryer, the aged Molé and others all of whom were, by the spring of 1851, bitterly cursing the day when they had given their patronage to this seemingly harmless, dull and docile Bonaparte Prince. 'The hour had been reached,' wrote a contemporary observer of these events, 'when the country was repelled by abstractions, however lofty or generous. Order was already a word without prestige, and what was wanted was a precise and clear formula, however daring. The President was the only man capable of personifying this.' Louis Napoleon was not concerned with the negative aim of saving society, as Orleanist party politicians understood the term, but with the positive policy of giving French society a new and meaningful unity and purpose. Nor, it must be added, would Eugénie have been greatly roused by a cardboard saviour of alarmed property owners and nervous investors. She wrote her letter to Bacciochi because she felt, not fear, but hope.

One man in Paris understood the realities behind the coup d'état. This was Eugénie's admired friend, Donoso Cortés, Marqués de Valdegamas, Spanish Minister in Paris since the autumn of 1850. Largely forgotten today, he was without any doubt one of the most profound and illuminating political thinkers of his time. A Catholic Conservative with an acute social conscience—not rich himself, he gave the greater part of his ambassadorial salary to the needy—he had, from the first, established relations of great cordiality with the Prince-President who was, before and after the coup d'état, more accessible to him than to any other foreign diplomat. This gives his dispatches to Madrid a special and authentic interest. Donoso Cortés was convinced that the salvation of France, her inner security and European influence, could not come from the Party of Order, from Orleanist or other party politicians. 'These men,' he wrote, 'are only interested in being Ministers, in quarrelling over the loot of office, and in nothing else.' 'In France,' the Prince told Cortés a few months before the coup d'état, 'the leaders of the old parties are quite mad—they don't understand their own interests and they do not see the way to their own salvation.' 'Parliament here is dead,' Cortés wrote to Madrid on December 1st, 1851, 'its leaders paralysed with fear. The President is master of the situation. He will carry out his coup d'état whenever he wishes and will appoint the day himself. Let me add that it will be very soon.' The prophecy was fulfilled on the very next day. 'The President,' he wrote on December 4th, 'has dared to make the boldest coup d'état known to history, and the shrewdness with which he carried it out surpasses anything hitherto experienced in the field of such operations.' Soon he was able to say to the President: 'If you solve the problems of France before it is too late, you will solve the problems of Europe. France

31

and Europe are one and the same.' In the midst of his assignment of watching Louis Napoleon's conquest of power, he was at work on one of his philosophical essays in which with alarming foresight he prophesied the rule by 'plebeians of satanic power', by 'criminals risen from the fermenting dregs of the masses' in the Europe of the not too distant future. To him, as we shall see, we owe the truth about Eugénie's marriage to Louis Napoleon, for only he came to know the inner circumstances leading to that improbable event.

By the time she and Doña Manuela were back in Paris in the summer of 1852, Eugénie's confidence and vitality were gaining the upper hand. The intervening years had taken her to many countries, places and resorts. There had been two quick excursions to England, brief meetings with political Englishmen like Lords Palmerston and Malmesbury, a ball, but no presentation, at Buckingham Palace, and a hurried stay of a few days at Sawston Hall where the faithful Mr. Huddleston, still unmarried, was still, it would appear, asking Eugénie to become the *châtelaine* of his beautiful old house with its memories of Mary Tudor and Charles II's Father Huddleston. His next-door neighbours, the Adeanes of Babraham, caught a glimpse of a beautiful foreign lady riding across the fields at Huddleston's side and said, perhaps regretfully, that 'of course, we don't know Huddleston; he is a Roman Catholic'. But Eugénie would not commit herself to any man. Mérimée, still the celibate advocate of marriage, knew that a delightful young Spaniard called Joseito Xifre was, even as the two ladies were travelling along 'the grand routes', nursing hopes of Eugénie's accepting him in marriage on her return. He told Doña Manuela that Xifre found Eugénie 'most amiable, reasonable and not in the least giddy-headed, as her enemies are always calling her. He is as much in love with her as all the white and all the blue Hussars put together, but he also has much more courage'. Xifre was the son of Doña Manuela's oldest friend, and it seems likely that she passed Mérimée's hopeful messages on to Eugénie: but there was no response. Doña Manuela understood that, during these travels abroad, she must subordinate her own concerns and interests, even her match-making talents, to her great objective of helping her daughter over the crisis caused by Alcañisez for which, in contrast to that surrounding Paca's marriage with Alba, she bore no responsibility of any sort. When these years of travel and movement so surprisingly ended with Eugénie's marriage to the Emperor of the French, Doña Manuela, who had no influence whatever on this event, could at least reflect with pride that she had watched over her daughter's well-being during the most vulnerable years of her life. She may have regarded it as a belated act of reparation, but, whatever her motives, it must be acknowledged that she ushered Eugénie into the next and most famous phase of her life with a persistent and instinctive assurance that commands respect.

The differences separating mother and daughter were too deep ever to be completely bridged. There was, in Doña Manuela, a streak of vulgarity that compelled her to speak, and write, of her daughter's beauty in a manner that puts one in mind of the merchant praising his most precious wares. 'Paris,' she wrote to Paca,

'talks of nothing but [Eugénie's] beauty. We went to the opera the other evening for the first performance of Meyerbeer's *Prophet*. All eyes were turned towards our box and everybody wanted to know who the pretty lady was. Next day, they talked more about her than the opera, and she has become the fashion of the day. I have ordered her a charming dress from Palmyre. . . .'

Eugénie was little interested in the effect her looks and beauty had and would on more than one occasion show her irritation when her mother harped on the subject. Yet Doña Manuela's master-stroke was that she punctuated these healing travels with prolonged interludes in Spain. Eugénie saw her native country with new eyes. 'I saw the Alcazar last night,' she wrote to Paca from Seville, 'it was superb. We saw the gardens by moonlight—what magic! I seemed to feel the shade of King Pedro pass at the side of Maria Padilla and all was so beautiful that I began to feel afraid. How sad that the Moors were driven from the country! Does it not look as if the Christians came merely to destroy?' She wrote delightedly of dancing to the sound of castanets, of *ballos de palillos*, of watching the gipsies dance and sing and prophesy. Of bull-fights she confessed herself an *aficienda en extremo* and wrote that she had met and talked to the fabulous Andalusian *torero* José Redondo, universally worshipped as El Chiclanero. 'I am preaching,' she told Paca with that note of seriousness that became increasingly typical of her correspondence, 'the restoration of our Spanish customs. If others supported me, we could do it. You should become a better Spaniard,' she finally told her sister, probably not very hopefully. The intoxication with the country of her birth was complete and great was her faith in what she called its 'exceptional character in the midst of all this European civilisation'. The final proof, perhaps, of her gradual transition to adult life came when she wrote to her adored Paca:

'I shall always think back longingly to the time we spent in Paris with each other. But we must forget the past. What is certain is that it all really is past.'

Paca's family was growing. Her eldest son, subsequently 9th Duke of Berwick and 16th Duke of Alba, had been born in December 1849 and her elder daughter in July 1851. 'Your star,' Eugénie had written shortly before the latter event, 'continues to shine brilliantly: such happiness without shadow frightens me.' Another time she wrote: 'You were born under a happy star which will never grow dim, or so I hope . . . there is too much happiness in your life to risk losing it.' Throughout their travels the thoughts of both strayed always towards Paca in her huge Palacio at

Madrid. 'You, my beauty, are a real treasure for your poor mother,' wrote Doña Manuela from the Rhineland and added: 'I am like a miser who always fears to lose his treasure. Adieu, my very dear, child of my predilection. . . .'

Before going on to Paris in the summer of 1852, the two Montijo ladies made a stay at Eaux Bonnes in the Pyrenees, then famous as a health-resort. Among the sporting events arranged to entertain the visitors was a rock-climbing competition in which some Spaniards from Aragon participated and lost. Eugénie took the national defeat personally. 'If you do not feel strong enough to win,' she told the unlucky team, 'you should not compete against the French.' Then she looked at them more closely, saw that fine men though they were they looked weak and pale, and word-lessly handed them some money. They told her that they were earning only 25 *sous* a day, that they had to support their families in Spain, and that they were trying to supplement their earnings by doing casual jobs in France. 'It is a scandal,' Eugénie wrote indignantly, 'that in an under-populated country like Spain, bad government should make emigration necessary. It is, I assure you, a sorry sight to see good-looking and robust men degraded by too much work and too little subsistence. . . .' The indignation came from the heart, but her reaction showed more than a passing whim of charity. The impulse behind it was political.

CHAPTER 5

PARIS WAS empty when in September 1852 Mme de Montijo and Eugénie returned from the Pyrenees to their apartment at 12, Place Vendôme. The Prince-President had left the capital for a tour of the South which, after visits to opposition strongholds like Lyons, Toulouse, Marseilles, was planned to finish with an important speech at Bordeaux in October. Society was absent from Paris, and, as the Austrian Ambassador, Count Hübner, wrote in his private journal, there was no one to see except Princess Lieven and foreign ladies passing through. The two Spanish ladies, not on the invitation list of the representative of the Habsburgs, dined occasionally at the Spanish Embassy where to Eugénie's delight Alba's younger brother Henry, Count of Galba, was serving as an attaché under Donoso Cortés.

Late in September, the faithful Huddleston appeared in Paris where he kept a bachelor establishment on the Boulevard des Capucines. The Prince-President's tour meanwhile had turned into a triumphant progress. His reception everywhere was enthusiastic—'I am telling you,' wrote on October 8th, 1852, Mme de Montijo's friend Castelbajac, 'that what I have just seen with my own eyes and heard with my own ears is something which I have never seen and never heard in our cities of the South at any of our political epochs: unless you witnessed it yourself, it is impossible to form an idea of the frantic enthusiasm of the population for the visits of the Prince-President.' Bulletins du voyage reached Paris from Louis Napoleon's principal stopping places and these the Austrian Ambassador sent to Vienna 'because they are, so to speak, the steps of the throne on which this instrument of Providence will soon place himself'. Hübner, in his dispatch of September 29th, called the progress of the 'Imperialist movement' in the South 'great, vehement and irresistible', and described its spreading to the Paris area as imminent. Yet before he reached Bordeaux on October 10th, Louis Napoleon had not himself uttered the word Empire, nor given the slightest indication of his intentions. On that Sunday, however, he finally announced the imminence of the decisive step in what was perhaps the greatest speech of his career: 'Like my uncle, the Emperor Napoleon,' he said at a civic banquet,

'I have many conquests to make. I would like to conquer and conciliate the dissident parties and direct back into the great river of the people those straggling streams that in their separation are likely to lose them-

35

selves without advantage to anyone. I would like to conquer for religion and morality that part of our people, still so numerous, which in the midst of a Christian land knows hardly anything of the teaching of Christ, which in the heart of the most fertile country in the world can scarcely command the bare necessities of life.'

Here at Bordeaux he admitted for the first time in public that the overwhelming majority of the French people desired the restoration of the Napoleonic Empire—'but,' he added in what became the most famous passage of the speech, 'there is one fear to which I ought to reply. There are the doubters who say, "the Empire means war". I tell you the Empire means peace. It means peace because France desires it: and when France is satisfied, the world has repose.'

The President's return to Paris was announced for Saturday, October 16th: Eugénie went to watch the procession from Huddleston's rooms. 'Solemn entry into the Tuileries by Louis Napoleon,' noted Hübner in his diary. 'He was pale and looked tired. One saw much cavalry and, for the first time since the coup d'état, the National Guard. The public on the whole was indifferent.' 'The public excitement,' wrote, on the other hand, a member of the British Embassy staff, Horace Rumbold, of the same occasion, 'was at its highest pitch—the President distinguishing himself by boldly riding along, on a magnificent chestnut, several horses' length in front of his brilliant staff and escort.' Hübner, illegitimate son of Prince Metternich, naturally viewed the proceedings with a more jaundiced eye than his English colleague. Rumbold had come to watch the entry with his friend William Grey, who in turn was a friend of Ferdinand Huddleston's, and they were all watching it from the latter's rooms: 'It would be extremely interesting to know,' noted Rumbold, 'with what feelings the sight was watched by a lovely girl, who, with her mother, was standing at one of the windows of this bachelor apartment. The occupier of the rooms was Huddleston of Sawston, a Roman Catholic squire of good estate and very ancient lineage, hopelessly in love with his guest, who was no other than Mlle de Montijo[1]—a few months later to become Empress of the French.'

Louis Napoleon, amid the considerable work of preparing his transformation from President into Emperor, yet found time to express to Eugénie his appreciation of the letter she had sent him on the eve of the coup d'état. She and her mother were asked to a number of receptions at the Élysée and Saint-Cloud, and while she now refrained from reminding him of Mme Gordon, he on his side took good care not to offend her with further suggestions of intimate dîners à quatre or less. On November 13th the President held a great hunt in the forest of Fontainebleau to which Eugénie was invited. She was in her element. She mounted a fine thoroughbred from the Prince's stables and, for the first time since the hunts of

[1] In Paris, Eugénie was generally referred to as Mlle de Montijo, although her correct title at this time was Countess of Teba.

Aranjuez, gave herself to the excitement of the chase. For the first time Louis Napoleon could watch her expert horsemanship, her intrepid skill, her supple strength: he hardly recognised his demure guest of the Elysée dinners. She was first in at the kill, and when the Prince and the rest of the party had galloped up while the final *Hallali* sounded from the horns they paid tribute to her skill and dash. The next day was the eve of Eugénie's name-day and Louis Napoleon offered her the horse on which she had triumphed. He presented her with a bouquet of flowers and, from then onwards, it was known that he was in love with her.

That he should, 'at his age and with his experience' (as Count Hübner put it), be capable of being 'so naïvely and so seriously in love', came as a great surprise to all who knew him, or thought they did. The Foreign Minister, Drouyn de Lhuys, felt it advisable to ask him point-blank whether he intended marrying the Countess of Teba. The Prince-President (as, in November, he still was) replied that at present he had no intention of marrying anybody. As Drouyn de Lhuys knew, a recent project of marrying Louis Napoleon to Princess Carola Vasa, daughter of the legitimate house of Sweden, had, after a promising start, ended in a somewhat abrupt refusal—the abruptness having been due, so Louis Napoleon had every reason to suppose (and Hübner later confirmed), to the veto by the Austrian Court, who paid the displaced Vasa family a small pension. Louis Napoleon had been snubbed by Legitimacy, it had been implied that as a Bonaparte he did not measure up to the exacting standards of eligibility stipulated by the Habsburgs, and Drouyn de Lhuys suspected that in his present mood of happiness the Prince-President might well feel inclined to snap his fingers at Legitimacy and marry for love—which is exactly what happened two months later.

On November 20th Fleury, one of the officers responsible for the success of the coup d'état and now styled Master of the Horse, addressed on Elysée note-paper a formal letter to Mme de Montijo apprising her of the gift of a thoroughbred for 'Mademoiselle your daughter'. On Sunday November 21st, the first day of the plebiscite in which the people of France were asked to ratify or oppose the proclamation of the Empire, the Prince-President gave a ball at Saint-Cloud to which Eugénie and her mother were invited. Eugénie wrote a hasty little note to Galba at the Spanish Embassy telling him that they would take him to Saint-Cloud in their carriage. 'You have no idea,' she told him, 'what they are saying about me since I have accepted that devil of a horse.' Eugénie cast Henry Galba, to whom she signed her letters reminiscently as 'your sister who loves you', for the role of chaperon of her public appearances, and the young diplomat played the part with distinction and grace. At the ball that Sunday Hübner noticed 'the young and beautiful Mlle de Montijo, much singled out by the President'. For the first time, Eugénie figured in the private diary of the Austrian Ambassador. Count Hübner, comparing the scene at Saint-Cloud to the aristocratic world of Vienna into which he had been so nearly born, did not much care for what he saw that night

37

and agreed with Charles de Flahaut that it was all 'far too democratic'. France had voted that same Sunday. Nearly eight million people had welcomed the restoration of the Napoleonic Empire while some 250,000 had registered their opposition. Louis Napoleon, superstitiously believing, as Donoso Cortés said, that some dates were charmed and others unlucky, chose December 2nd as the day of the Empire's official proclamation, the day being the anniversary of his own coup d'état, of the battle of Auster-litz, of the coronation of Napoleon I. Singularly enough, it was also the anniversary of the accession of Czar Nicholas of Russia and of the Emperor Francis Joseph of Austria. Eugénie and her mother attended the solemn *Te Deum* sung that day at Notre-Dame amid scenes of great and spon-taneous enthusiasm.

England recognised the new Empire without delay. The British Ambassador, Lord Cowley, presented his credentials to the Emperor Napoleon III on Monday, December 6th. His Austrian, Russian and Prussian colleagues had not yet received instructions from their govern-ments in this respect, and Hübner was extremely apprehensive as to the effect this deplorable delay on the part of the guardians of Legitimacy would have on the mind of the Emperor of the French. In the letter handed by Cowley to the Emperor, Queen Victoria addressed Napoleon III as *Monsieur mon frère*, despite the misgivings which his choice of the numeral had inspired in her Ministers. Rumbold, standing behind Lord Cowley on this solemn occasion, was secretly much amused when the Emperor in his reply expressed his gratification at England being 'the first power to recognise me'. Two days earlier, the Minister of the Two Sicilies had succeeded, by sheer importunity according to Rumbold, in being the first with recognition. To Napoleon III, the Bourbons of Naples were not a power.

As the three great Continental Courts, and the smaller German States in their wake, were still withholding recognition, the diplomatic Corps was somewhat scantily represented when, on December 17th, the first Imperial house-party of the reign gathered at Compiègne. It was a modest precursor of much future splendour. When Eugénie and Doña Manuela arrived, they found, in addition to the accustomed entourage, the rep-resentatives of the powers who had recognised the Empire, among them Lord and Lady Cowley, the Belgian Minister Baron Beyens and his Spanish wife—and Donoso Cortés. The Government was present in full—Drouyn de Lhuys, Persigny, Achille Fould, Morny, Maupas; the new Imperial family was represented by old ex-King Jerome, his son Prince Plon-Plon, his daughter Mathilde. Among personal guests was Doña Manuela's old friend, the Maréchal de Castellane and his daughter, the Marquise de Contades. The gathering, planned for four days, lasted eleven.

Most people assumed then, most people assume now, that what hap-pened in the course of that historic house-party was that the Emperor, all set to enjoy a love affair, was cleverly trapped into marriage by Mme and Mlle de Montijo. Hübner, for example, in a report to Vienna described the events of those eleven days as 'efforts the object of which was the fall of the young Spaniard [and] the result of which was to raise her to the throne', and then refers to Eugénie's 'game played with extreme skill and crowned with complete success'. Cowley wrote of Eugénie that 'she has played her game so well that he can get her in no other way but marriage'.

The British and Austrian ambassadors were strangely unanimous—not surprisingly, since they drew their information from the same sources and compared notes afterwards. These sources were the Emperor's closer entourage, the Elysée set, which felt its privileged position at the summit of the Empire undermined by a development which threatened to go beyond a mere change of mistress. They all hoped that Eugénie's presence among them meant nothing more serious than that the Emperor felt a need for distraction. But who could tell? Thus Cowley would listen to the after-dinner talk of the Colonels of the household—Fleury, Edgar Ney, Toulongeon—and heard them lay odds on the day 'on which the fortress would surrender'. He heard the ladies of the gathering contribute their comments—the Marquise de Contades, for example, who had her own private reasons for wishing that the pleasantly bohemian ways which had been the mark of the days at the Elysée would continue. Since Louis Napoleon's election in 1848, she had been the mistress of the dashing and soldierly Fleury, then a bachelor and, as we saw, closely linked to the Prince-President's fortunes. Her own marriage to the inadequate M. de Contades had ended in separation long ago, and the public tantrums of the unhappy woman who could not obtain a divorce had been one of the lesser scandals in the salons at the time of Louis Philippe. As the daughter of the Maréchal de Castellane, Sophie de Contades was an old friend of Doña Manuela and Eugénie and so the côterie, taking alarm when the fortress showed no sign of surrendering, sent her forward to make an appeal to Eugénie. Why resist? was the burden of her intervention. 'Remorse,' she warned the younger woman, 'is better than regret.' (Hübner described the whole scene in a dispatch to Vienna.) Would Eugénie not prefer the passing remorse from a moral lapse to the abiding regret at having lost altogether? The conversation finished, according to Hübner, with Eugénie replying that she had no intention of being left with either remorse or regret. Other tales relayed by one or the other of the two ambassadors included the story from some invisible informant that, thinking they were alone, the Emperor had one evening addressed the most urgent proposals to his guest only to be told: 'Yes, when I am Empress, yes.' These and similar anecdotes, under the seal of diplomatic secrecy, were passed on to Vienna and London. In Paris, too, they soon found currency.

It was surprising that Hübner should have accepted these tales so unquestioningly, since they hardly agreed with his own assessment of Eugénie's character with which he prefaced his diplomatic scandal-sheet about the goings-on at Compiègne. 'She is,' he wrote, 'passionately in love with what is new, wonderful, unforeseen, always on the look-out for movement, whether in the physical or the intellectual sense, inclined to innovations in politics, a member of the progressive party in Spain. An advanced liberal and constitutionalist by taste, she has a great love of contrariness; superficially instructed, as one is when like her one has received one's education from the nuns of Sacré Coeur; capricious, eccentric, but with a force of will and a physical courage which one meets rarely, even among women of the people. An ardent imagination, an inflammable heart, a heart which has already had romantic experiences, though of a distinctly innocent kind. . . .'

Finding so much to respect and admire in her, it is strange indeed that Hübner should merely have wondered whether the events at Compiègne were due more to art than to cynicism, or more to cynicism than to art. Cowley, for his part, confined his observations to the safe statement that 'the great one of all has been captured by an adventuress'. It filled him with some distaste that affairs of this sort should become matters of the highest political concern : but he, the nephew of the first Duke of Wellington representing his Queen at the Court of the nephew of the first Napoleon, grimly did his duty according to his lights.

The house-party at Compiègne consisted of 101 guests and 98 persons of the household, and there were 183 attendants and domestics. In this not very intimate setting, the Emperor showed his preference for the Countess of Teba in the most open manner imaginable. He was always at her side; she had only to admire a clover leaf glittering with dew to make him send Bacciochi to Paris to bring back a clover of emeralds glittering with diamonds. He would ride at her side, they would return together late; after dinner one evening he placed a crown of violets on her head. In the evening of December 22nd, the actors from Eugénie's favourite Parisian theatre performed a play, and she watched it from the Imperial box, as did Princess Mathilde, some of the Ministers, and Lord Cowley. On hunting days (*chasse à courre* on December 20th, *chasse à tir* on the 21st, *curée aux flambeaux* on the day before Christmas) Eugénie showed all her habitual intoxication with freedom and movement; at the same time she made it clear, as Fleury wrote, that at the slightest sign of disrespect she was ready to return to Spain.

Did the Emperor at Compiègne ever give Eugénie cause to regret her presence there as his guest? It seems unlikely in the extreme. Louis Napoleon must not be wholly identified with the moral level of the Elysée set. He did not live as they did and was not the man they thought him to be. He was the son of Queen Hortense. In the past, he had been self-indulgent rather than dissolute; in the days of his exile, especially in London, he had proposed marriage and been refused more often than he had pursued illicit love affairs and been accepted. Hitherto, he had always been perfectly open about his affairs of the heart, and if he was not strict or strait-laced, neither was he coarse or hypocritical. In his own way, he had been faithful to Miss Howard, but he had never allowed personal commitments of this sort to divert him from following his star in which he believed as deeply and as fervently as Eugénie believed in Paca's star. He did not see his destiny mirrored in the prosaic Miss Howard, devoted though she was; but in Eugénie he found a fierce and fiery faith in the Napoleonic idea which bore the mark of his own intensity of conviction, his hopes, his fatalism.

Someone had once cut Eugénie short in the middle of a heated political discussion with the homely remark: 'Women exist to mend stockings.' 'I knew very well,' wrote Eugénie, 'that I was not destined for that, I felt that there was a different *métier* in me.' Napoleon III understood and accepted that the woman with whom he was 'so naïvely and so seriously' in love, was not cast for any of the roles convention had assigned to her sex. He would have been an exceptionally obtuse man if he had not grasped the contrast between her and the people who surrounded him; he would have been an abysmally stupid man if he had persisted in pursuing a line designed to lower this proud Spanish grandee to the status of an established mistress; and he would have been a very poor politician indeed if he had allowed the lady and her mother to manoeuvre him into a position in which he would lose all freedom of action and be compelled to act as they wished. He was none of these things, but for the moment he was above all else a man in love.

Only Donoso Cortés knew that love was not the whole explanation of the Emperor's puzzling and, given the present public setting, provocative conduct. As at the time of the coup d'état, the Spanish diplomat was again more deeply taken into the Emperor's confidence than anyone else. The trust was well-placed, for Donoso Cortés in no way belonged to the smart, hardened and indelicate society that from long habits of cynicism bred by affluence viewed most personal relationships from the materialistic level on which it lived. Paying not a moment's attention to this tainted chorus, he reported home the realities of the event. In quoting his dispatch here we anticipate slightly, for he did not write it until after the engagement had been officially announced. We shall presently see why the Emperor, even after his own mind had been made up, was compelled to defer the announcement. Since Cortés knew the truth while they were all still at Compiègne, it is appropriate to give his account to his Foreign Minister here:

'Last November [he wrote] the Emperor was at Fontainebleau. Walking with the Countess of Teba through the park one day it occurred to him to ask her what the time was. The Countess looked at her watch and was annoyed to see that it had stopped at 6.15 that morning. The Emperor made a few jocular remarks reproaching the Countess for her carelessness and forgetfulness, and then pulled out his own watch. To his great amazement he found that his watch had also stopped, at

41

the same hour and the same minute as that of the Countess. He was startled, he went pale, his mind suddenly seemed far away. His superstitious sense had been aroused: and it was then that the marriage first occurred to him as a serious possibility.

While he was brooding on it and inclining to accept the notion, without, however, reaching a definite decision yet, another extraordinary event was reported to him. Many years ago a scientist presented a then unknown shrub to the *jardin des plantes* at Paris. At first it seemed barren, but in the year when General Bonaparte married Josephine, it suddenly produced a bloom, only to revert to its previous state of barrenness and death soon afterwards. Yet in this present year the mysterious plant has flowered once again. The Emperor, being told, there and then decided to marry the Countess of Teba.

I would ask your Excellency not to regard all this as improbable or untrue. Why should it surprise us that someone should be superstitious, if that same man, taken all in all, appears to be himself a kind of miracle? By nature, the Emperor is anything but a simple man—his is the most complex, the most many-sided, the most enigmatic nature I have come across in my whole life. Let me ask a question: where in the world would one find a man who, like the Emperor, unites in himself so many contradictory qualities, such as his mystical exaltation and his talent for the practical? The man who relapsed into a startled silence because two watches had stopped at the same minute, the man who was struck with amazement because some shrub had blossomed again, is the same man who prepared the coup d'état of December 2nd—not only planned it, but carried it to success. He is the same man who holds the ear of the masses whenever he chooses. He is the same man who is capable of uttering words that never fail to reach their targets, words that score true like the arrows of the savages. . . .'

The exceptional interest of this document is not limited to the facts narrated in it, but lies in the circumstance that, with his profound insight into the Emperor's character, Donoso Cortés was able to put these facts into their proper historical and psychological context. 'The Emperor alone knows,' he wrote to Madrid, 'that he represents two things at one and the same time: at home the authority to contain the revolutionary tendencies of the French and, abroad, The Revolution *vis-à-vis* the European Monarchies. His whole force and power rest on the fact that he has understood, fully and thoroughly, the unique nature of his position.' The Ambassador pointed out to his Minister that three motives had combined in deciding the Emperor to marry Eugénie: his love for her, his wish to defy the European Monarchies after their offensive reluctance to accept the restored Bonaparte dynasty on equal terms, and finally 'the mysterious and irresistible inner illumination', whose magic power he had so vividly experienced in incidents which to most other human beings would be merely quaint. Donoso Cortés urged his Minister not to dismiss these from his mind when 'forming a clear and trustworthy impression of this man who holds a leading position in Europe and is the absolute ruler of a neighbouring country'.

From this account, one fact emerges clear beyond any doubt: since the day at Fontainebleau, when his face had grown pale under the shock of a sudden recognition, the Emperor's mind, where Eugénie was concerned, was wholly free from all thoughts of dalliance and seduction. He may have arranged that dinner at Saint-Cloud with nothing but pleasure in mind. But at Compiègne, the problem was not whether the two Spanish ladies, the two adventuresses, would succeed with their intrigue; the question was would the Emperor, so soon after the proclamation of the Empire, be able to carry out his resolve to unite his destiny with Eugénie's in the face of the strong opposition he knew he had to expect at home and abroad? If anyone gambled for high stakes it was the Emperor himself. Eugénie, her own sense of the uncanny and the supernatural equally aroused, could do little else but trust him and wait.

As for Doña Manuela, she had been, since Fontainebleau, very much relegated to the background. The Emperor, for appearance's sake, naturally invited her to all functions attended by Eugénie, but he found it advisable from the beginning to keep her in her place and avoid all impression that this *maîtresse femme* had been pulling the strings. It has been alleged that she employed Mérimée as a go-between, especially later on when the inevitable delays of the official announcement rendered the situation difficult. Nothing could be further from the truth. Mérimée was then deeply affected by the recent death of his mother and saw hardly anyone. His entire share in the marriage was limited to drawing up a list of Eugénie's many Spanish titles and dignities for the marriage contract. Otherwise, the Emperor consulted Doña Manuela only once, and that after the gathering at Compiègne had broken up. This was on the famous occasion when he showed her an anonymous letter which alleged that Eugénie was really Lord Clarendon's daughter. 'Sire,' replied the mother coldly, 'it cannot be true, the dates do not correspond.'

Did Eugénie return the love of this man who was her senior by eighteen years? 'He is a man,' she wrote to Paca, 'with an irresistible will-power, but he is not stubborn. He is capable of great sacrifices and small gestures: he will leave the fire on a winter's night to pluck a flower in the woods and so satisfy the fancy of the women he loves—next morning, he will risk the crown rather than not share it with me.' 'He has,' she wrote again, 'a noble and devoted heart.' 'To me,' she confessed, 'life has been a desert, for I was alone.' She had been haunted by the fear that always she would be condemned to love more than be loved, and here was this man who drew her heart towards him because he loved her. Did he re-awaken memories of former disasters and defeats? Like the Emperor, she saw the finger of Providence trace her course before her, and the old fires of her imagination blazed forth again when the new Napoleon, the nephew of the great Emperor of her earliest memories, spoke to her of destiny and a crown and of love. They were both ready for a union that stood under an implacable law.

Enmeshed in their strange and ghostly preoccupations, neither was greatly touched by the gossip and other manifestations of the world around them. The gossip hardened, in the course of time, into history, even the friendliest among subsequent chroniclers judging with Cowley, Hübner and others that at Compiègne Eugénie had walked off with the greatest prize of all, that it had all been a triumph of 'contrivance and art'. The truth was that, when the party at Compiègne broke up on December 28th, Eugénie knew that no official announcement could yet be made. She returned to Paris in a state of excitable tension. The Emperor for his part prepared himself to find a way that would allow him to obey the voices of his heart and yet enable him to strengthen the future of the Empire and of his own mission in France and the world.

BEFORE THE invitations to Compiègne had been sent out, the Emperor's advisers had involved him in a new attempt to lend the Empire an aura of Legitimacy by a dynastic marriage. The French Ambassador in London, Walewski,[1] who had valuably contributed towards obtaining Queen Victoria's prompt recognition of the Empire, hoped to crown his work of reviving the *entente* with England by arranging a marriage between Napoleon III and Princess Adelaide of Hohenlohe-Langenburg, the Queen's niece through the Duchess of Kent's first marriage. Drouyn de Lhuys had eagerly taken up the suggestion and the Emperor, to whom it was pointed out that the match might lead to even closer relations with England, allowed the project to go ahead. On December 13th, 1852, four days before Compiègne, Walewski presented himself at the Foreign Office and asked for Princess Adelaide's hand in marriage for the Emperor Napoleon. There had been earlier talks of the proposal and the Foreign Office was not surprised. The Queen was informed. Not overjoyed at being given responsibility in the matter, Queen Victoria discussed it with Prince Albert and the Foreign Secretary on December 28th. She expressed the fear that the Princess 'should be dazzled if she heard of the offer'. The Foreign Secretary told her that Walewski was about to go to Langenburg 'to make an offer to the father', and the Queen spoke of 'the sad fate of all the wives of the rulers of France since 1789'. The Foreign Secretary thought that the Queen 'did not positively object to the marriage'. Princess Adelaide was staying quietly at Windsor and the Queen found her looking 'so pretty, so young, distinguished and ladylike'. Walewski left London for Langenburg, but travelled by way of Paris which he reached on December 31st.

One of the first people he saw on arrival was Lord Cowley. The British Ambassador immediately told him that the Emperor was probably going to marry Eugénie. Walewski, aghast at this threat to his project, thereupon initiated Cowley into the Hohenlohe secret and was urged to go to the Emperor and do what he could to stop what Cowley termed 'the demonstrations going on between the Emperor and Mlle de Montijo'. Walewski saw the Emperor in his study at the Tuileries. To the Ambassador's horror, Napoleon, radiant with happiness, shook him by both hands and said: '*Mon cher, je suis pris.*' Walewski, knowing who had taken

---

[1] The son of Napoleon I and his Polish mistress Walewska. He was thus an illegitimate cousin of Napoleon III.

him, reminded the Emperor of 'the other affair', and Napoleon became thoughtful. At length he promised to wait until Princess Adelaide's answer was received. This, fortunately, arrived on the following day and was polite, but negative: the Princess declined 'on account of her youth, and not feeling equal to such a position'. It is not clear whether the marriage had been turned down by Princess Adelaide or by Queen Victoria.

Napoleon told Eugénie immediately of the Hohenlohe refusal. She replied that he must think only of the interests of the throne and expressed both her sense of elevation and her humility in the face of the prospect before her. The Emperor reminded her, gravely and with absolute sincerity, that the position he offered her was not only one of greatness and brilliance, but also of hardship and danger. He spoke of the hostility of the old families of France, of the ill-will shown by the Great Powers, of the impermanence of popular favour. He spoke of plots and conspiracies against him, especially in the army, of the certainty that more than one attempt would be made to assassinate him at her side. 'So you see,' he concluded, 'that you need have no scruples about sharing my fate, its bad chances are probably equal to its good ones.' Eugénie, to whom these words confirmed everything she had ever felt about Napoleon, reported the conversation to her mother word for word. Doña Manuela, on the same day, wrote it all to the Marquesa of Santa Cruz who, in turn, communicated the conversation to two people—by letter to Lord Clarendon in London, by word of mouth to a Belgian diplomat in Madrid. Through the latter King Leopold of the Belgians came to hear of it and he told his niece, Queen Victoria. Clarendon told it to Henry Greville, who summed up the general impression when he said that the Emperor's words were calculated 'to engage and attach any woman of high spirit and generosity'. It was a first turning point. Napoleon and Eugénie were after this regarded with a new respect in influential places.

Next, the Emperor had to prepare the way for the official announcement. Walewski having been the first to be told, Napoleon summoned Drouyn de Lhuys to his study to inform him. The Minister implored him to change his mind before it was too late; he told the Emperor that the crowned heads of Europe would never accept the marriage, that it would be fatal to the future of the Empire, that if the Emperor persisted he would have to resign from office. The Emperor told him to think it over. St. Arnaud protested in the name of the army. Would a marriage at this point not mean peace? For the army, in contrast to opinion in the country, was gaily convinced that the Empire meant war. 'The army,' wrote Lord Westmeath to Lord Clarendon on January 5th, 1853, 'would invade the moon, if transported there, for service and promotion. The idea of a descent on England has taken root.' Another friend of Lord Clarendon reported to him the following conversation between a Frenchman just returned from the United States and a Colonel on the staff: 'You had better,' said the Colonel, 'enter the Army, we are about to have a war. 'A war with whom?' asked the astonished civilian. 'With England.'

'How?' 'By invasion.' 'But my dear friend,' remonstrated the civilian, 'what is all this about? You have no quarrel with England.' 'You astonish me,' exclaimed the Colonel. 'Have you forgotten Waterloo? We shall be at war in six months from now.' Not for nothing had Napoleon spoken to Eugénie of plots and conspiracies in the army. His sources of information were quite as good as Lord Clarendon's.

Against the opposition to the marriage bearing down on him from all sides the Emperor maintained an imperturbable calm: he was certain of the course he had set by his stars. The only support he found in his own circle came from Achille Fould, financier and Minister of State, one of the Empire's most capable and constructive men, and from his half-brother Auguste de Morny.[1] This elegant and accomplished man of affairs, at home equally in diplomacy, high finance and the ballet, but endowed with exceptional gifts of intelligence and judgment, had liked Eugénie from the first, and encouraged the Emperor to persist with the marriage.

Meanwhile, the question of his recognition as the Emperor Napoleon III, in which England had given a lead as long ago as December 6th, was still hanging fire four weeks later. A month after the proclamation of the Empire, the ambassadors of Russia, Austria and Prussia as well as a whole shoal of lesser German diplomats were still in the ludicrous position of remaining accredited to the defunct Republic, since their new credentials, made out to the Emperor of the French, remained unpresented. This was due to the Russian letter of credence containing the slight of replacing the traditional phrase of *Monsieur mon frère* with *notre très cher ami Napoléon, Empereur des Français*. The Emperor refused to receive a document couched in terms which no other European sovereign had ever been asked to accept. To this the other envoys of the Concert of Europe replied that in that case they would not present their letters of credence, although these were correctly made out. A major diplomatic rupture seemed imminent as late as the morning of January 5th and Hübner began to think in terms of war. On that day, however Napoleon decided to yield and avoid, perhaps only postpone, a rupture with Russia; Hübner says that Morny, always a friend of Russia and of the stock exchange, had prevailed over the Emperor. At all events, the Russian Ambassador was enabled to present his credentials, as made out by Czar Nicholas, in the afternoon of January 5th and, if the word of the Russian attaché Meyendorf who was present is to be trusted, the occasion gave the Emperor the opportunity for one of his most felicitous remarks. 'I am,' he said, 'very sensible of the Czar's kindness, for we put up with our brothers, but we choose our friends.'

The other ambassadors followed suit, much relieved by the termination of this embarrassing interval which had permitted the Emperor to make sarcastic comments about great powers waiting for 'orders from Russia'. Hübner presented the Emperor Francis Joseph's letter on January 11th

[1] He was the son of Queen Hortense and Charles de Flahaut. He did not meet Louis Napoleon until 1848.

47

and was received by Napoleon III in the presence of Drouyn de Lhuys, of the Duke of Bassano as Great Chamberlain and the Duke of Cambacérès as Master of Ceremonies, Baron Feuillet de Conches acting as the Imperial introducer of Ambassadors. The new Court was taking shape.

In Princess Lieven's salon someone whispered into Hübner's ears on January 7th that Mlle de Montijo would in all probability become Empress. Elsewhere people no longer whispered, but spoke loudly, derisively, indignantly. Even at this stage hostility to the match was extremely vocal. Pamphlets, often printed in Belgium and Germany to evade the police, began to appear in the bookshops and in the streets, anonymous letters were received at the Tuileries and elsewhere with information that Eugénie and Paca were the daughters of the present Queen Mother of Spain, of a different Montijo, of all manner of people except Don Cipriano. Not since Philippe Egalité, Duke of Orleans, and the two brothers of Louis XVI circulated their libels and calumnies about Marie Antoinette on the eve of the great Revolution had Paris known so scandalous a campaign directed against a lady who was unable to reply.

The Emperor was still engaged in winning over the leaders of the country to his marriage by individual persuasion when an incident at the Court Ball of January 12th compelled him to precipitate matters. The Ministers, the diplomatic Corps, leaders of politics and finance attended the ball at which the Emperor caused some astonishment by appearing in court breeches and silk stockings, garments that had not graced Court functions at the Tuileries since the Restoration. Doña Manuela was escorted to the Hall of the Marshals, the inner sanctum of the privileged on such occasions, by Baron James de Rothschild, Eugénie following at the side of the Baron's son. All eyes were on these four as they moved towards the *banquettes* along the wall on which some ladies were seated. There the two Rothschilds bowed to their charges and withdrew. At this moment Mme Drouyn de Lhuys was seen to rise, whisper into Eugénie's ear and sit down again. Eugénie said something to her mother and the two ladies stood in obvious embarrassment. The Emperor hurried over and escorted both to the dais where the Imperial Family were sitting.

The Foreign Minister's wife had told Eugénie that the *banquettes* were reserved for the wives of Cabinet Ministers. But when the Emperor, bowing over her chair, asked Eugénie what had happened, she begged him in a heated whisper to wait until later when they could talk under less public conditions. Mme Drouyn de Lhuys meanwhile, as declared an enemy of the marriage as her husband, found it difficult to remain calm under the malicious smiles of her companion ladies who, like herself, saw that she had not humbled, but raised Eugénie. The hilarity among the diplomatic Corps was, says Hübner, as great as the confusion of 'the severe lady guardian of the rules of etiquette', but when he wrote an account in his diary after the ball, he added that what they had witnessed that night had been nothing less than the Emperor's official declaration of intent.

Lord Cowley, also present, wrote to the Foreign Office that throughout the ball the Emperor had 'seemed woefully out of sorts'. It was not surprising, since it was not until late in the evening that he was able to talk to Eugénie about the incident. Eugénie's distress was acute and genuine. All the latent hostility, venom and disrespect of which she had been aware since the hunt at Fontainebleau had finally come out into the open before the gaze of official France. Her face, as always at moments of great stress, was as pale as alabaster, and she was roused to a high-pitch of excitability. She spoke of leaving Paris at once, of going on her travels once more, of not returning until she could be certain of not being publicly insulted. 'Tomorrow,' said the Emperor, 'nobody will dare insult you.'

From then on Napoleon endeavoured to combine his campaign of winning over the opponents with safeguarding the interests of Eugénie's position. It was all a question of careful timing, especially as his plans for the wedding were ambitious in the extreme: not only did he plan, for the religious ceremony, the greatest splendour and pomp at Notre-Dame, he even hoped, though not for long, that the Pope would come from Rome to preside over it in person.

On January 15th Achille Fould, Minister of the Imperial Household, presented himself at the Place Vendôme and delivered to Doña Manuela the Emperor's formal request for her daughter's hand:

> Palace of the Tuileries, 15th Jan. 1853.
> Madame la Comtesse,
>   I have loved Mademoiselle your daughter and wished to marry her for some time. I have therefore come today to ask you for her hand, for nobody is more capable of contributing to my happiness or more worthy of wearing a crown. If you give your consent I would ask you not to mention the project until we have made our arrangements.
>   Please receive, Madame la Comtesse, the assurance of my feelings of sincere friendship.
>   Napoleon.

On Saturday January 22nd, the Emperor summoned members of the Senate, of the Council of State and deputies of the Assembly to the Tuileries at noon in order to announce his imminent marriage in a speech which caused a sensation. For he chose the occasion to reply to the provocations which he had suffered at the hands of Legitimacy from the time when the Concert of Europe had first suspected his design of restoring the Napoleonic throne. His tone and demeanour were serious and grave, his accent still slightly German.

His very first words reminded his audience that the union he was about to contract was not 'in accordance with the political traditions of old'. That, he stressed, was its advantage. France, the cradle of Revolutions, must not seek its place among the ancient Monarchies by the pretence of a royal alliance which substituted for the true interests of the nation merely those of a family, but rather by a 'frank and upright policy'.

Besides, had the foreign princesses who had occupied the throne of France in the last seventy years not seen their reigns cut short by war and revolution? The people of France, said the Imperial bridegroom, had every right to feel superstitious in respect of foreign princesses as Queens of France. 'Only one woman seems to have brought good luck in her train: and that woman, the kind and gentle wife of General Bonaparte, was not of royal blood.' It was not the last reference to Josephine that day.

He continued:

'When, in the face of ancient Europe, a man is borne upward by the force of a new principle to the lofty height of the old dynasties, it is not by attributing antiquity to his escutcheon and by forcing himself into the family of Kings that he makes himself acceptable. Rather, it is by remembering always his origin, by remaining true to his own character, and by frankly taking up before Europe the position of a *parvenu*: a glorious title when one succeeds to it by the free suffrage of a great nation.'

And what of the lady worthy of the exalted *parvenu*? Since he had been 'obliged to depart from precedent', his marriage had become his own private affair.

'She whom I have chosen is of lofty birth. French by education and by memory of her father's blood shed in the cause of Empire, she has the advantage, as a Spaniard, of having no family in France to whom honours and dignities must be given. Endowed with every quality of mind, she will be an ornament to the throne, and in the hour of danger one of its bravest defenders. A devout Catholic, she will unite her prayers to Heaven for the welfare of France with mine. Gracious and good, she will, I do not doubt, revive the virtues of her predecessor, the Empress Josephine.'

He concluded this oration of defiance and hope with these words:

'So, gentlemen, I am here to say to France: I have preferred a woman whom I love and respect to an alliance with an unknown lady who would have brought advantages not unmixed with sacrifices. In putting independence, heart and happiness above dynastic prejudice or calculating ambition, I shall not be less strong for being more free. Soon I shall go to Notre-Dame to present the Empress to the people and the Army. Their confidence in me will assure their sympathy for her whom I have chosen: you, gentlemen, who have come to know her, will be convinced that on this occasion also I have been inspired by Providence.'

The virtues of Josephine! The phrase stuck in a good many minds. If the undoubted virtue of Eugénie had already caused ribald comment such as we have noticed, how much more would the smart wits of a

THE 15TH DUKE OF ALBA

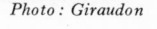

NAPOLEON III

Photo : Giraudon

hundred drawing-rooms and officers' messes exercise their gifts on the virtues of Josephine! Yet to the Emperor his grandmother's name was so closely linked with the whole miracle of his marriage that he was determined it must flower again in the minds of Frenchmen as that mysterious plant had done in the *jardin des plantes*. For the rest he spoke boldly and with an assured and stubborn dignity. Here was indeed the son of the universal suffrage who told the Monarchs of Europe that he was proud to be a parvenu since he had succeeded—'*lorsqu'on parvient*', it was a subtle play on words—by the will of the sovereign people. He put his marriage into the whole context of Revolution versus Legitimacy, but did not allow it to be quite the one or the other: instead he made it a Napoleonic event which he explained over the heads of its representatives to the people of France, the masses whose living standards he had committed himself to better.

How did his invisible audience, the inarticulate masses of France, judge the speech and the marriage? Copies of the speech were sent in vast numbers for distribution in the departments. Reactions, although mixed, showed on the whole that the peasants and workers welcomed the marriage because the bride was not royal. 'The speech,' wrote Hübner in his diary on the same day, 'most remarkable in certain aspects, had the purpose of reconciling the masses to the marriage, hence the predominantly democratic note. I don't know whether the Emperor succeeded in this. . . .' It was, indeed, difficult to know, but the Emperor felt confident. 'His speech,' wrote Eugénie to Paca, 'has had a magic effect, because he addressed it to the people and the heart, two things which in France one never invokes in vain.'

Donoso Cortés, for his part, thought that the speech was remarkable for two reasons: first, 'the Emperor's skill in exploiting the feelings of the ordinary people—the mysterious skill which is his to an extent unparalleled in the whole range of history', and, second, that 'with a daring without example he has thrown the gauntlet of defiance at the feet of the European Monarchies'. 'The marriage,' Cortés explained to his Minister,

'is by no means popular in all parts of France. The Ministers, the Senate and almost everybody else were opposed to it, and the calumnies to which the Countess of Teba has been exposed are without number. The Emperor was the only man who remained firm and unshaken, finding it hardly worth his while to pay any attention to the clamour often raised by people who otherwise cower tame and docile at his feet. The reason behind these manifestations is that the commercial men, the Ministers, the Senators and others who are against the marriage, are members of the middle class. The Emperor has no intention whatever of merely pleasing the middle class, he is far more determined to please the large masses, that surging sea whose waves obey his command and would rise up to drown the middle classes should he desire it. Louis Philippe's government would have been unable to resist that clamorous opposition whereas it moves the Emperor not at all, unless it gives him cause for amusement. Such is the great revolution that has taken place before our eyes: yesterday the middle class was everything, today it is nothing. The *bourgeois* Monarchy has been replaced by a powerful Republic ruled by a crowned dictator. . . . [All this] has never before been more clearly expressed than it was in the speech which the Emperor made by way of commentary on the imminent solemnifying of his marriage. . . .'

He concluded by saying that if by so unconventional a marriage the Emperor had formed a powerful link between the dynasty and the masses he had, by flinging the word *parvenu* into the faces of the European Monarchs, made war inevitable. Like Constantine he had exclaimed 'in this sign shall I conquer'.

If the speech, and the marriage, held some appeal to the egalitarian masses of France, articulate opinion at home and abroad was almost universally condemnatory. 'In very bad taste,' said Queen Victoria of the speech. 'It pleased nobody in the true meaning of the word,' wrote O'Reilly, a private informant of Lord Clarendon from Paris. It had, he said, brought pain to the Emperor's friends and solace to his enemies. The Republicans in particular had taken fresh hope, and the Emperor's cousin Plon-Plon was now backing that party quite openly, as his friendship with its principal spokesman, Emile de Girardin, showed.

Yet if speech and marriage were being loudly condemned, another reaction was beginning slowly to insinuate itself into people's minds and even into the dispatches of the diplomats. This was the astonished realisation that the Emperor had dared to set the world at defiance to marry for love and had succeeded. However much they misjudged the reasons for the marriage, however loudly they derided the man 'who had married to satisfy a whim', 'who transformed his flame into an Empress', the phenomenal boldness of the event won from them a reluctant respect which was not unmixed with fear. Hübner first, Cowley after him wrote home to point out that a man who had succeeded in this despite almost unanimous opposition was a force to be reckoned with, for what might he not attempt next? 'A man,' wrote Hübner in his dispatch of January 16th, 'who at the age of forty-five decided to marry for love, at the risk of losing backing in his country and abroad, such a man, especially if he is Emperor, is made to inspire apprehension. . . .'

II. THE REIGN
1853-1870

CHAPTER 1

ON THE day after the Emperor's speech Eugénie and her mother moved into the Elysée Palace which became their official residence until the wedding ceremony, now timed to take place on Sunday, January 30th, 1853. The Pope had declined the honour of being present, giving his 'great age and infirmities' as his not very convincing excuse; His Holiness was to be spared for another twenty-five years. The Emperor advanced the date of the wedding by a month; Eugénie told Paca that he had done so 'for reasons of state' without saying what these were.

The Emperor called daily and a large number of people left their cards or signed the visitors' book downstairs, but, in accordance with the customs of Spain, Eugénie did not return calls or accept invitations, and did not appear at the Tuileries for the ball on January 22nd. The Paris correspondent of *The Times* called at the Elysée and told his readers that she was 'wearing the incipient honours of her approaching rank quite as if she had the consciousness that they were not superior to her merits.'

'The moment is sad,' wrote Eugénie to Paca on the day she arrived at her new residence, 'it means bidding goodbye to my family, to my country, in order to dedicate myself exclusively to the man who loves me to the point of raising me to the throne. I love him, and this is a great guarantee for our happiness, he has a noble and devoted heart: you have to see him in his private life to understand how much one must esteem him. . . .

'Goodbye. Today for the first time people have cried *vive l'impératrice*. May God grant that it will never be otherwise, but adversity will find me firmer and braver than prosperity. . . .'

'Two things,' Paca was told in another letter, 'will, I hope, protect me —the faith I have in God and my immense desire to help the distressed classes who are deprived of everything, even work. If the finger of Providence has marked out for me so lofty a place, it means that I must serve as a mediator between those who suffer and him who can find the remedy: I have accepted grandeur as a divine mission and I thank God for allowing me to find the Emperor. . . .' And when she wrote to Paca about the extraordinary man she was going to marry, praised his irresistible will-power and the goodness of his heart, she added some words of what perhaps was to her the most magnetic quality of all: 'He does not count the cost, he always stakes his future on one card and that is why he always wins.'

On the evening of January 29th, the Duke of Cambacérès presented himself at the Elysée to escort the bride to the Tuileries where the civil marriage ceremony was to be performed that evening. Apart from the Imperial Master of Ceremonies, Eugénie was accompanied by her mother and Donoso Cortés.

The ceremony was attended by the diplomatic Corps, Hübner and Lord Cowley representing their countries, Count Hatzfeld Prussia and M. Rogier Belgium, their ladies sitting together with the wives of some of the Ministers (excluding Mme Drouyn de Lhuys) on stools facing the two thrones. This part of the ceremony ended with the guests filing with their ladies past the thrones. Hübner found the Emperor 'gay and frisky, offering the spectacle of the supreme degree of human happiness', but the bride 'pale and fatigued'. The Imperial couple retired and presently the company assembled again in the *salle des spectacles* to listen to a Cantata specially composed by old maestro Auber. Eugénie's return to the Elysée at midnight was no less ceremonious than her drive to the Tuileries four hours earlier, and she spent the night before the wedding ceremony with her mother.

The civil ceremony had also been watched by a few newspaper correspondents and the man from *The Times*, while conceding that Eugénie's 'demeanour throughout was of one accustomed to a high station', nevertheless noticed that she appeared 'agitated', that just before signing the register 'she trembled for a moment' before she took the pen. Next morning, two hours before setting out for Notre-Dame, she hurriedly wrote a brief note to Paca in which she said that 'yesterday's ceremony was superb, but I just missed being ill before we entered the room where we signed. I cannot tell you, dear sister,' she went on writing amidst the rush and bustle of the wedding morning, 'how for three quarters of an hour I suffered, sitting on the throne with everybody facing up towards me: I was as pale as the jasmine on my head.' When, after the signature, she was for the first time addressed as Your Majesty it seemed to her they were acting in a comedy. 'When I shall play my part as Empress,' she went on, 'I don't know that I shall play it from nature.' She ended:

'Goodbye, dear sister, my last memory as a girl is for you. I am going to dress and go. I love you.
Eugénie.'

Sunday, January 30th, 1853, was a fine, clear, frosty day. Paris was festooned with banners and pennants and gilded paper, a city of colour and triumphal arches, with brightly gleaming Napoleonic eagles in every street and square, with the golden Napoleonic bees glittering on green velvet hangings in the new Rue de Rivoli, and the letters N and E decorating the houses along the processional route. For days people from the provinces had been streaming into the capital—peasants on donkey carts, *communes* in little groups complete with band and banners, uncounted thousands making use of the novelty of railway travel. The troops in their bright new uniforms lined the streets, the breast-plates and helmets of the cuirassiers sparkled in the winter sunshine, the mounted guards in plumes and feathers trotted up and down the streets, and bands everywhere crashed out the marches of the First Empire. The day was the first great Royal jubilation in France since the coronation in Rheims Cathedral of Charles X in 1825,[1] but the enthusiasm was far from unanimous. Many of the public lining the street thought the whole business was much too Royal; others thought it not Royal enough.

The grim and grimy old Cathedral of Paris had been spectacularly transformed for the ceremony; the interior was overladen with colour and blazonry, with velvet and ermine, with gold, silver and precious stones, with the arms of France and Spain, with the escutcheons of the Bonapartes and the Montijos, with the shields of the cities and provinces of France. 'Splendid,' said Lady Augusta Bruce who was there as Lord Cowley's guest and wrote to Queen Victoria's mother about it, 'flags and hangings of all colours were combined and harmonised with the splendid costumes of the clergy, the uniforms, civil and military, and the magnificent dresses of the ladies.' 'Loud colours, a profusion of flowers and candles, many flags, little taste,' wrote, on the other hand, Count Hübner.

The Imperial couple arrived at the Cathedral at one o'clock. As they entered the church the orchestra of 500 accommodated behind the High Altar struck up the march from Meyerbeer's *Prophet*: 'very fine,' wrote Lady Augusta, 'stupefying,' noted Hübner. Lady Augusta craned her neck to catch sight of the bride: 'a more lovely *coup d'oeil*,' she wrote to the Duchess of Kent, 'could not be conceived. Her beautifully chiselled features and marble complexion, her nobly *set-on head*, her exquisitely proportioned figure and graceful carriage were most striking. The effect was something more than that of a lovely picture, it was aerial, ideal. On her classically shaped head she wore a diamond crown or diadem, round her waist a row of magnificent diamonds to correspond, and the same as trimming round the "basques" of her gown. Then a sort of cloud or mist of transparent lace enveloped her. . . . I suppose that a sort of national prejudice made me attribute the grace and dignity of the scene, for what there was of either came from her, to the blood of the Kirkpatricks ! ! !' Hübner, recovering from the shock of Meyerbeer, noticed that as the Imperial couple was moving down the aisle, the vast gathering filling the church remained cold and undemonstrative, much in contrast to the enthusiasm shown in the same place during the Thanksgiving Service for the coup d'état. 'Doña Eugénie,' he added, 'pale, but beautiful poor child ! has made a good beginning in her part as Empress.'

At the transept the bride and bridegroom were greeted by the Papal

[1] The return of the ashes of Napoleon I in 1840 was, of course, not a moment of 'jubilation'.

Legate and the Cardinals of France. The ceremony was performed by the Archbishop of Paris and lasted for an hour. After benediction and the presentation of the Holy Water, the Archbishop intoned the *Te Deum* to the responses of the choir and then conducted the Emperor and Empress to the West door of the Cathedral. In the wintry sunlight outside, they were greeted by the sound of drums and trumpets, of pealing bells and artillery salvos, and as the great bell of Notre-Dame droned out its majestic note, they returned to the Tuileries.

Reports on the street scene after the nuptial ceremony vary. Those by Cowley and Hübner speak of public coldness and indifference, but neither diplomat was an eye-witness of the procession, since Cowley was confined to his Embassy by illness, and Hübner sat waiting in Notre-Dame. 'No acclamations or insults,' says Hübner after hearing the reports next day, and Cowley was of the opinion that the Emperor 'could not have liked his reception by the people'. O'Reilly wrote to Lord Clarendon that 'there was—for the Emperor—no enthusiasm expressed last Sunday. The novelty and the sex interesting them, the Empress was cheered everywhere by the people'. 'There was avid curiosity everywhere,' wrote the masked noble-man who acted as an observer for the London Rothschilds and signed him-self as C. de B., 'for Parisians did not want to miss anything. The white plumes above the heads of the eight bays drawing the coach had immense success, and a wit shouted: "It's just like a young girl's funeral proces-sion!"' Lady Augusta Bruce, for her part, found that the multitudes thronging the streets 'appeared to be animated by curiosity chiefly, and that *sober* curiosity which now characterises the people of Paris. . . .'

Emperor and Empress presently vanished from sight into the Palace, but reappeared on the central balcony as the people below serenaded them before dispersing. The big double doors to the balcony were shut, and through the windows of the great palace the lights of a thousand candles were shining into the gathering night as Napoleon and Eugénie drove off to the rural house at Villeneuve l'Etang which the Emperor had bought because it adjoined Saint-Cloud. On the way they passed a little house where on a spring night in 1849 dinner had been laid for four and Louis Napoleon had stood waiting impatiently for the Countess of Teba.

'We have married the Emperor and he has retired to Saint-Cloud,' wrote Cowley to the Foreign Office on January 31st. Hübner also heaved a sigh of relief. 'I am tired out physically, morally and emotionally,' he wrote to Büol on the same day, 'for we have all been gambling for high stakes.' Hübner had been quite shocked by the 'puns, witticisms, jokes pleasant and evil', which he heard everywhere before and after the wedding and thought they represented 'the vengeance of the vanquished who realised a little late that in an access of fear they had given themselves a master'.

While in the evening of January 30th, 1853, Napoleon III and Eugénie bade farewell to their Court to retire towards Saint-Cloud, there stood among the chamberlains an erect old gentleman of seventy-six fulfilling the ceremonial duties to which the Emperor had called him. He was René de

Villeneuve, who had announced Louis Napoleon's birth to Napoleon I at Bayonne in 1808.[1] He had been made a Count of the Empire in that year and had soon afterwards left the service of the King of Holland to become Queen Hortense's principal attendant at Paris, St. Leu and Malmaison. He had spent the whole interval between the two Empires at his lovely château of Chenonceaux on the Loire, but Napoleon III had not forgotten his ' oldest friend ', as in his kindly way he called his mother's chamberlain. M. de Villeneuve died as a senator of the Second Empire and commander of the *légion d'honneur* in 1863.

[1] See page 7.

CHAPTER 2

NAPOLEON AND Eugénie stayed at Villeneuve l'Etang for only one week and were back in Paris on February 7th for a 'monster ball' given by the Senate at the Luxembourg Palace. It had been a brief honeymoon. On a fine and frosty morning a citizen had seen the Imperial newly-weds drive in an open carriage along the road to Versailles and found the sight a little formal, the Emperor and his 'pretty' consort sitting 'farther apart than seemed to me proper'. Others more aware of the problems of the new reign deplored the absence of all security arrangements on these excursions to Versailles and Trianon, but both the Emperor and Empress insisted from the first that these should be always kept to the minimum. 'If we thought of assassination all the time,' said the Empress to Mérimée, who often remonstrated with her on this question, 'we would not be able to sleep at night. The best way is not to think of it and trust in Providence.' They drove over to the deserted Palace of Louis XIV on several mornings, and through the bare and wintry park to Marie Antoinette's Trianon.

On returning to Paris, Eugénie showed, with a few rapid and well-judged strokes, how seriously she took her new *métier*. A wedding present from the City administration of Paris, 600,000 francs for the purchase of a diamond *parure*, was returned to the City Fathers with the suggestion to use it for the founding of a training college for impecunious girls. A present of 250,000 francs from the Emperor was similarly handed to public phil-anthropy, 100,000 francs to maternity societies, the rest for additional beds in hospitals for incurables. Less publicly, she persuaded Drouyn de Lhuys, still bent on resignation over the marriage, to desist. 'I told the Emperor myself,' she said to the Minister ,'exactly as you did that he must think only of the interests of the throne. It is not for me to judge whether he was right or wrong in deciding that his interests and his feelings might be allowed to coincide.' The Minister withdrew his resignation and the Emperor continued to have the co-operation of an able and experienced politician who, though rich, was honest. Such actions reaped their awards. 'The description of the young Empress's character is an interesting one,' wrote Queen Victoria to King Leopold of the Belgians who had praised Eugénie, 'and also agrees with what I have heard from those who know her well. It may be in her power to do much good—and I hope she may. Her character is made to captivate a man, I should say—particularly a man like the Emperor.'

The Emperor associated Eugénie and the marriage with an amnesty he

THE EMPRESS IN HER ROBES OF STATE

THE EMPRESS AND HER LADIES-IN-WAITING

granted to 3,000 people in detention since the coup d'état. This was about half the number of those still deprived of their freedom for political reasons. Both Emperor and Empress soon realised that the effect of such measures was disappointing, that to disarm and conciliate the intransigent Republicans was a task for the government and its policies rather than for the Sovereign and his prerogative of mercy. The Republicans were the Empire's most serious enemy, as the Republic had, since 1793, become the political ideal of a steadily growing number of intellectuals and publicists. The three years of the Second Republic had further swelled their number. As recently as 1851 Frenchmen had heard it announced from the tribune in the Palais Bourbon that 'The Republic is the form of government that divides us least.' At that time debates in the Chamber were still reported and published, a practice which the Second Empire greatly attenuated during its first eight years. Under the reigns preceding and following the short-lived Second Republic, Republicans were less a properly organised opposition than a resistance movement, because, since 1789, no French Government had succeeded in taming its enemies into a purely parliamentary opposition. In consequence France had become a country of secret societies, and conspiratorial organisations like 'the Consuls of the People' or 'Cordon Sanitaire' were keeping the Republican faith and mystique alive in a clandestine way. Republican intellectuals on the surface of national life, such as Plon-Plon's friend Emile de Girardin and indeed that princely Radical himself, were in many cases sufficiently strong, intelligent and even wealthy personages to remind the public of the presence in their midst of guardians of the Republican alternative to the Imperial government. They, rather than the Orleanists gathered round Thiers and the Duke of Broglie, or the 'pure' Legitimists with their dream of absolute monarchy, represented the Empire's most acute political problem within France. The Empress soon began to feel the weight of this menace.

That gracious measures of amnesty made small impression on the Republicans may be gleaned from an entry which a particularly fanatical member of their party made in his secret journal on February 22nd, 1853. He was a rising young lawyer, and his name was Emile Ollivier:

'Yesterday I saw Napoleon and his Montijo. They say power beautifies! I had been expecting to see a miracle before which one must stand disarmed: and I saw a woman pretty like so many others. There is something flat and dull in her physiognomy. No clarity. You do not sense the reflection of some inner light. Perhaps she is an intelligent woman, as everybody says. To look at she is not the superior woman who if necessary could save an Empire poised on the brink of an abyss. . . .'

The future held some surprises for Ollivier causing him to modify his views on the effect of power on beauty, of beauty on intelligence, but as he did not meet the Empress face to face until 1865 we may take his austere reaction to the Empress as a typical expression of Republican determination not to surrender to any aspect of the Imperial regime. It was, in 1853, a perfectly logical attitude for a convinced Republican to take.

However, as the novice Empress entered upon her profession, Republican hostility was a general rather than a specific problem, a menace in the air and not yet the direct challenge to her courage and intelligence that it became in the reign's second decade. The enmity of the Orleanists and Legitimists, on the other hand, although politically less serious, brought nevertheless thorny and harmful problems of its own into Court life and the social sphere. Its centres were the salons on both banks of the Seine, the pleasant villas at Passy and Neuilly, and the Académie Française. Names like Broglie, Decazes, Pozzo di Borgo, La Rochejaquellein and Pasquier were found among the leaders of these groups who were united only in their rejection of and abstention from the Imperial regime. The political failure of the Restoration and the scandals in high places during the reign of Louis Philippe had robbed the older nobility of much of its prestige and coherence as a class, but its power in the field of social life and opinion was far from being extinct, especially as these circles had their connections and sympathisers in the society of London, Vienna and St. Petersburg.

The Emperor endeavoured quietly to undermine the enmity of the nobility by putting certain members of it under personal obligations, such as when he made Mérimée's friend Count Léon de Laborde director of archives. In these conciliatory activities he had Eugénie's whole-hearted support. She did not allow the politics of malevolent abstention to spoil old friendships and among others she visited the Orleanist Delesserts at Passy as often as she could, although her girlhood friend Cécile was now married to the ultra-royalist Marquis de Nardaillac *en deuxième noces* and was about to depart with him for Austria and Frohsdorf to visit the Count de Chambord. The Empress intended to set a personal example in conciliation, and this intention was strongly reflected in the composition of her household.

At its head stood the Princess d'Essling, a General's daughter, who had married into the wealthy family founded by Marshal Masséna. Next to her, as principal Lady of Honour, came the bearer of another well-known first Empire title, the Duchess of Bassano. Her husband, the Emperor's Great Chamberlain, was the son of Maret, first Duke of Bassano, Napoleon's faithful Secretary of State. They were both completely won over by the Empress and no other name was to become more enduringly associated with her service than that of the second Duke of Bassano who remained faithfully at her side, in prosperity and adversity alike. The Duchess, tall and full-figured in contrast to the porcelain slightness of the Princess d'Essling, was an amiable and goodhearted lady who until her premature death lived with her husband in exemplary happiness.

Under the orders of these two highly competent ladies there were six ladies of honour who went into waiting in weekly rotation. They included the Countess of Montebello, granddaughter of one of Marie Antoinette's ladies who had been a fellow victim of the Revolution; the Baronne de Pierres, née Thorne, American by birth, her father having been one of the earliest transatlantic millionaires to prefer dying in Paris; the Marquesa de Las Marismas,[1] of the immensely rich Franco-Spanish Aguado family, who were old friends of the Montijos since the days when Alexander Aguado, *afrancesado* like Eugénie's father, had first followed the armies of the first Napoleon. If to these names we add those of the Marquise de Latour-Maubourg, the exquisitely beautiful granddaughter of Marshal Mortier, of Baroness Malaret, granddaughter of Prince Rostopchin, who was responsible for the burning of Moscow in 1812, of the Countess de la Poëze, daughter of the Marquis de Rochelambert, and of the Countess of Lezay-Marnesia, we have put a name to each of the ladies whom Winterhalter assembled around the Empress in that misleading painting which has for so many people represented the Court of the Empress Eugénie.[2]

The picture should perhaps be understood merely as a somewhat leafy Court Circular in white, pink and Bavarian blue. It gives us a catalogue of the Empress's entourage early in the reign without telling us anything memorable about the ladies or the Empress herself. Winterhalter was, as is well-known, the court painter *par excellence* of his time, and had already applied his amiable brush to the principal personages at the Court of Louis Philippe. He had painted the Queen of England and the Queen of Spain with the same reliable absence of comment, and given the Sovereigns at Munich, Karlsruhe, Brussels and Vienna the same attributes of refined *Gemütlichkeit* which no doubt flattered their mediocre sense of beauty, their modest aspirations to immortality in crimson and gold. He avoided character and individuality on his canvases as successfully as he steered clear of vulgarity and over-emphasis, and by the time he was painting the Empress and her ladies he was at the height of his renown. It might be thought that in making her Court pictorially indistinguishable from that at Laeken or Buckingham Palace the artist was conferring a kind of European accolade on Eugénie's status in the monarchical world. This, in a sense, was true. Queen Victoria felt reassured when she heard that Winterhalter was busy at the Tuileries, and the Empress, acting on the Queen's recommendation, commissioned a number of portraits, for the Tuileries and the Palacio de Liria, from this industrious and ubiquitous German craftsman.

But the importance of the Imperial Court lay not in its conformity with, but in its deviation from the accepted contemporary norm. For that reason the much-reproduced Winterhalter idyll, however interesting as a declaration of monarchical solidarity, is of small enduring value as a source of information about the Second Empire. The picture hides the fact that

[1] She herself was Scottish by descent, having been born a Macdonnell before marrying the Aguado heir.
[2] Jean Cocteau wrote that these portraits of the Empress's ladies were ' so much less reassuring than those of the first Napoleon's Grenadiers '.

this was an upstart Court. For even as the Emperor in his speech of January 22nd had described himself as a parvenu, so neither he nor Eugénie intended to disguise or dissimulate their origins. The Emperor had announced that he was seeking acceptance into the 'family of Kings' not by a fraudulent antiquity, but by a frank avowal of his democratic mandate. The Court was not exempt from this programme. The only admitted precedent was the Court of Napoleon I, where old forms had been given a new meaning and tradition for a new dynastic concept. The new Imperial Court, therefore, combined correct ceremonial with a wider accessibility, the observance of etiquette and protocol with a lowering of those barriers of exclusiveness and inbreeding which rendered the Court of the Habsburgs so remote and fossilised and those of the many German cloud-cuckoo dynasties so ludicrous and unreal.

That by the middle of the nineteenth century a departure from accepted practices was urgently needed can be seen from a glance at one rule that was being applied to the vexing question of admissibility by the traditional Courts of central Europe. For the guidance of chamberlains and similar officials mankind, so far as it could be invited to Court, was divided into three categories: (1) All-highest Ladies and Gentlemen; (2) Highest Ladies and Gentlemen; (3) Other people. Both Louis Napoleon and Eugénie had themselves been 'other people' for too long to relish such divisions. They wished to remain close to the world they knew. Their Court reflected awareness of the fact, from which other Continental Sovereigns were carefully sheltered, that society was changing. There were people living in 1853 who remembered the Court of Louis XV—old Mme de Saint-Aulaire, for example, who died in the following year aged ninety-nine, or the Duke of Bassano who as a boy had been instructed by Louis XV's fencing master, Isabey who had painted Marie Antoinette and her ladies at Trianon. Equally, men and women were born during the Second Empire who lived to see the Second World War. Poised between the charms of a dying world and the enigma of the society of the future, the Court of Napoleon III and Eugénie was closed to neither.

To some extent, the Emperor and Empress allowed themselves to be influenced by the Court of St. James's, and the Empress in particular almost always followed the advice offered by Queen Victoria or Lady Ely, who was the loyal friend of both. But in this as in everything else England was a phenomenon apart; the real progress which the Court of the Tuileries achieved may be measured by the contrast between its liveliness and verve and the stagnant atavisms of Vienna, St. Petersburg and Potsdam. The gas-lit Empire, the Empire of the crinoline—the Empire dancing to the strains of Offenbach and Waldteufel and the Empire held for a second in the glitter of grandiose fireworks cascading down from the night sky above the river—all these things existed and played their part. They were the grand gestures of the regime addressed now to the truant nobility of France, now to the visiting Sovereigns of England, Austria, Spain. But this festive elegance, this opulence and ostentation need not blind us to the fact that it was above all other things a means of persuasion, an attempt to make a new, a different, an upstart Court accepted in a world that was dozing on a volcano.

The Court divided its activities between four of the ancient Palaces of France—the Tuileries and Saint-Cloud for the great functions of State, Fontainebleau and Compiègne for the entertaining of specially invited guests. At the Tuileries, the Empress gave her audiences, from there she carried out her manifold charitable and social work. There also she attended the receptions fixed for certain dates—New Year's Day, the Opening of the Legislative Session, Napoleon Day on August 15th and so on. At the Tuileries and Saint-Cloud, she presided over the balls, grand and intimate, masked or merely *en grande tenue*, during Carnival, the concerts during Lent, the banquets, dinners and soirées throughout the year.

The regular sojourns at Fontainebleau and Compiègne demanded a more specialised skill in entertaining invited guests: the country house manner replacing the formal and more generalised posture required at the Palace. The Court visited Fontainebleau in the spring and again during the autumnal weeks immediately preceding Compiègne. Riding, excursions, sport made up the programme there, while the celebrated parties at Compiègne were of a much more ambitious nature. There the Empress would be surrounded for some weeks by the representatives of the political, diplomatic, industrial and financial world, composers, writers, scientists and artists, distinguished foreigners, ornaments of society. A large number of widely varying guests had to be made welcome and put at their ease. Count Hübner might travel down together with Alfred de Vigny, Flaubert be found at the side of a Prussian Field Marshal, Mérimée in the company of a Roman Monsignor and the Princess de Metternich in that of Louis Pasteur. The Empress had to school herself to find the particular note required for these complex and diffuse assemblies, which provided a meeting ground for people sometimes barely on nodding terms.

It was a considerable task. At the beginning, she was criticised for trying too hard, for showing a nervous desire to involve everybody in constant activity. She had much to learn, her apprenticeship in the intimate as well as the most public aspects of her duties was arduous and taxing, but she applied herself to it unsparingly. On balance, her triumphs were more numerous than her failures although, on balance, the failures were more frequently reported than her successes. The reign found its chronicler in Horace de Viel-Castel, the brother of the young diplomat whom Doña Manuela knew in the lonely years before Eugénie's birth. He hoped to be the Saint-Simon of the Second Empire, but was little more than its most assiduous and ill-humoured gossip columnist. His diaries which were not published until the 1880s prove the infinite capacity of the Orleanist upper crust for nursing its frustrations to the point of total sterility.

From 1854 onwards, Biarritz was added to the residences of the Court. The Villa Eugénie which the Emperor built for her outside a deserted and remote fishing village on the Atlantic became the Osborne of the reign.

The Court spent some weeks of high summer there each year and the Empress was able to relax from her duties within sight of Spain. Like the Tuileries and Saint-Cloud, the Villa Eugénie, as she knew it, was destroyed by fire after the fall of the Empire, but Biarritz itself is perhaps the most famous surviving example of the Midas touch which the Second Empire showed in so many of its enterprises: Napoleon and Eugénie found a forgotten place, 'the naked shingles of the world', at the extreme limit of their kingdom and left a flourishing resort.

Such, then, was the setting to which the young Empress, exchanging her freedom for a crown, had to adapt herself. 'Don't think, my sister,' she wrote to Paca not long after the return from Villeneuve l'Etang, 'that my courage is failing me, I assure you that the blood of the Guzmans does not play false.' To this she added in ironical parenthesis: 'I see that this phrase is becoming fashionable in the newspapers of Madrid.'

CHAPTER 3

EUGÉNIE WAS a swift learner. Between February and the end of spring of 1853, the great bodies of State vied with each other in the brilliance of their entertainments in honour of the newly-wed Sovereigns. The young Empress, despite her continuing aversion from glamour for glamour's sake, went to all of them. Mérimée thought that to make one's *début* in the duties of marriage and Empire at one and the same time must be a great strain. 'The days when I could say "I wish" are over,' the Empress wrote to Paca. 'I have forgotten,' she confessed, 'what *dolce far niente* means and the days pass without my finding time for reading or writing. Useless to make projects! I live from one day to the next.'

In the midst of the never-ending round of balls and receptions Eugénie found time for a task requiring much firmness and tact, that of persuading her mother to return to Spain. Doña Manuela had a European reputation for being an *intrigante* and the Emperor had publicly stressed that his bride was unencumbered by family. Realist as she was, she understood how matters stood and, when asked whether she would continue to remain in France, had replied: 'No, I have two incurable defects—I am a foreigner and a mother-in-law.' The Emperor had no intention of making her an Empress Mother, but it was Eugénie who had to convince her mother of the desirability of an early departure. 'Mama thinks of leaving in March,' she told Paca. 'Despite our unhappy relationship and the incompatability of our characters, it grieves me to think that she will be lonely and sad. Our house in Madrid is full of memories of me—but from a distance faults may disappear and only the good be remembered.'

Doña Manuela, again in contrast to her younger daughter, had always been extravagant and vague about money, apt to run up debts and to get herself into difficulties. The Emperor therefore found it convenient to make a generous financial settlement on her before she left for Spain in the last week of March. Undeterred by the ambiguities of her new situation, Doña Manuela soon filled her house at Madrid once more with diplomats and politicians, with the victims of yesterday's shift of power, with the partisans of tomorrow's dictatorship. Carabanchel also was reopened for the splendid *tertullias* set among the trees and hills of the Castilian countryside. Mérimée heard a story that Doña Manuela once encountered the Duke of Montpensier, for since his marriage that son of Louis Philippe had become a leading figure at Queen Isabella's court. He fatuously enquired how the Countess of Teba was. 'She has recently moved to a new address,' Doña Manuela assured him, 'and now lives in the apartments once occupied by Your Royal Highness's mother.'

The Empress had become accustomed to her new address. Hübner glanced at her critically during a reception of the diplomatic Corps. 'Simple in dress, strong in beauty,' he noted, adding that the Emperor seemed 'drunk with love and happiness'. His instructions from Vienna stressed the desirability of entering into closer relations with the Imperial government. 'What is the road that Napoleon III intends to follow?' he wondered uneasily. 'Where is his lode-star? Nobody knows. En attendant, they are trying to tie him up with England. Lord Cowley subordinates everything to that task. The Emperor of Russia likewise exchanges intimate letters with the new democratic sovereign. Büol's letter, therefore, defining Austria's desire to establish more intimate relations with the French Cabinet came in very good time. I read certain passages from it to Donoso Cortés, who is well liked at Court, and he found an opportunity of mentioning it to the Empress.'

In taking the Spanish Ambassador into his confidence, Hübner had chosen a harbinger of the new Austrian orientation to whom the Empress would listen with respect. With him she talked long and earnestly in Spanish and all her life would recollect in gratitude these early encounters with so profound, ardent and charitable an intelligence. The memory was especially poignant because she lost him at the time when she needed him most. Donoso Cortés died, lonely and illuminate, in May 1853 at the age of forty-four. At the funeral, the coffin was followed, not merely by the representatives of the Emperor, Empress and official France, but by those of both branches of the House of Bourbon, by the ambassadors from Roman Catholic, Greek Orthodox and Protestant countries—a sincere and spontaneous demonstration of respect given by a Europe torn by strife and fear. Eugénie felt the loss deeply and wrote to Paca that Spain, 'where the number of outstanding men is diminishing daily', had lost a statesman of stature. Others, including Lord Acton, agreed with this judgment, but Donoso Cortés survives in his written work. Eugénie's library, wherever she was, was never without these volumes, and until late in life she drew inspiration from the harsh and powerful meditations on mundane realities, on the relationship between the rulers and the ruled, which these books contain. His diplomatic work has been largely forgotten, but the literary output of this singular mystic of the nineteenth century forms, in the evolution of the Spanish mind, a link between the great writers of Spain's Golden Age and modern thinkers like Unamuno and Ortega y Gasset, both of whom have paid eloquent tribute to his achievement. The Empress never forgot the impact which he left on her receptive mind at a time when she was finding her way in the world of politics and affairs of state.

Late in April, the Empress had a fall and after a hot bath violent pains came on which the doctors were unable to alleviate during seventeen hours. On April 27th she suffered a miscarriage and remained confined to bed for a month. It was a discouraging beginning of her married life and her gradual recovery was a time of black despondency and depression. The accident brought a first intimation that, as a woman, she had to face special dangers from her physical nature, that with her instinctive awareness of being meant not for the ordinary *métier* of women but for a destiny above the conventional she had to learn the hard and harsh lesson that nature, her carnal side, was an enemy, not a source of pleasure and happiness. Her emotional precociousness had burnt itself out when the objects of her early passions—her father, Alba, Alcañisez—had been taken from her by death, by circumstances, by the ordinary meanness of human nature. After her final defeat, her instincts put up a protective barrier against all further possibility of injury and disillusionment in the field of love. The Empress, whose radiance and beauty were European bywords, had become a frigid woman. She held, all her adult life, sexual love in small esteem, regarding it not as wicked, but as unimportant and cheap. 'You mean,' she would say in tones of incredulity, 'that men are interested in nothing but that . . .?' when her ladies were chatting about the infidelities of men. And when in her last years someone told her of the break-up of a marriage in which she had been particularly interested and added, by way of excuse: 'After all, men are worth very little,' the old Empress summed up the attitude of a life-time and replied:

'Since we are alone I will tell you: they are worth nothing.'

Her greatest trials in this respect were still to come for, cruelly enough, she was married to a man who was, as an intimate friend expressed it, 'tortured by the flesh'. For the present, the incident of the miscarriage threw her back to the worst moments of discouragement and disgust with life which had given Doña Manuela so many anxious moments not many years before. Now the Empress wrote to Paca that much as she was looking forward to having children she wished for her son 'a crown that was less resplendent and more assured'.

Her sick-room reading conjured up a parade of ghosts and made her linger on thoughts of death—the little Dauphin in the Temple during the Revolution, Charles I at Whitehall, Mary Queen of Scots, Marie Antoinette. When Paca asked what had caused the accident she replied: 'What is the point of looking for reasons? I shall say with the Moors, " *esteba escrito* ", it is written.'

Queen Victoria, soon to accept Napoleon III as an ally, sent a sisterly letter of sympathy and concern for the ailing Empress. To Cowley, who delivered it and offered his own wishes for the patient, the Emperor replied curtly: 'The mistake can be put right.' Clarendon, to whom Cowley reported this uxorious remark, replied that 'an affair of this sort is not always *facile à réparer* as His Majesty seems to think'. The Foreign Secretary was genuinely anxious about Eugénie's health and wrote a long and affectionate letter to Doña Manuela expressing the hope that 'this unfortunate affair will have no adverse consequences for the

Empress's health. . . . The habit of having miscarriages is easily formed'.[1]

The Empress returned to her duties at the end of May. On July 5th, 1853, she and the Emperor attended the gala reopening of the *Opéra Comique*. Half way through the performance there was a sudden commotion in the theatre, and both Hübner and Cowley saw the police arrest some fifteen men armed with daggers who, it was learnt afterwards, had mingled with the audience in order to assassinate the Emperor after the performance. Cowley wrote to the Foreign Office that ' the Empress showed a great deal of courage and says that she is not in the least afraid of going about in public '. He added that the affair had been very serious and that it showed ' the danger threatening from the socialist tendencies of the lower orders '.

The Empress became her husband's most assiduous and promising disciple in the field of foreign affairs. He initiated her into the complexities of the European situation that was dominated, almost from the first day of the Empire, by Russia's obvious designs on Turkey. He showed her official reports and dispatches, he associated her with certain diplomatic conversations and occasions, he discussed in his acute and subtle way the aspects of a given situation with her. He even schooled her in what to say to certain people into whose opinions he wished to probe. He taught her the necessity for discretion, he lectured her on the unwisdom of coming out impulsively with remarks that she might regret having made in the heat of the moment. The latter frailty, caused in equal part by her innate honesty and her lack of self-control, he was particularly concerned to cure and a little incident, told by René de Villeneuve, who witnessed it, shows us the gentle way in which he drew her attention to her failings :

They were discussing some topic of no great importance, but, following on some remark from her husband, the Empress allowed herself to make an angry comment. There was a moment's uneasy silence. Calmly, the Emperor walked over to her, took her by the hand and led her to a large mirror. ' Why,' she exclaimed at length, ' do you make me look into this glass? '

' Take a good look,' said the Emperor.

' I see nothing but a glass,' she replied, her anger not notably decreasing.

' Perhaps so,' he rejoined, ' but it reflects.'

It was her turn to fall silent. Presently she led her husband back to the looking-glass.

' What do you see? '

[1] Several letters from Clarendon to Doña Manuela survive among the Empress's papers at the Palacio de Liria, all tender and affectionate in style. It seems possible that they gave some incompetent reader the notion that Clarendon was Eugénie's father. The Foreign Secretary's concern for the Empress's health, especially at this time when England was about to form an anti-Russian alliance with France, had political roots—even if he finished the above letter to Doña Manuela with : ' Will you be coming to Paris this summer to see your daughter? And then to London? Ojala ! Adieu, dear friend. Yours as always and for ever.' The same letter shows that Clarendon felt great respect for Doña Manuela's political ability and influence in Spain.

'Only a glass,' he said, playing up to her.

'*Oui,*' she said in what she hoped would be a crushing last word, '*oui, mais elle est polie*. . . .' Future moments of discord were to end less pleasantly.

Count Hübner soon became aware of the progress the Empress was making under her husband's expert guidance and tuition. 'This is no longer the young married woman, the improvising Sovereign whose diffidence always added to her natural attractiveness,' wrote the Austrian Ambassador in his private diary in July, 'this is the mistress of the house who makes her presence felt. . . .' 'She needed,' he wrote again, 'a throne to become serious and lovable.' 'My veneration of you, Madame,' he told her as he walked at her side across the lawn at Villeneuve l'Etang during an Imperial garden party, 'increases daily.' 'But that of your Court,' she replied drily, 'decreases at the same rate.' The Empress had, especially on men older than herself, often the effect that Galatea had on Pygmalion, and Hübner, a widower and close on fifty, was more than willing to shape the mind of this radiant novice in the school of diplomacy. The Empress, for her part, often singled him out at her Monday receptions and other occasions. During the Italian crisis of 1858/59 it was said that whenever the Empress and the Austrian Ambassador were seen in friendly conversation, the funds rose next day. At this time, when Europe was drifting, to use Clarendon's term, into the Crimean War, the Empress and Hübner exchanged many remarks—and reflections—on the new alignments within the Concert of Europe.

Hübner's position at the Court of Napoleon III was never easy. He represented one of the great Conservative powers, 'Europe's House of Lords'. Austria was also a leading guarantor of the sanctity of the treaties of 1815 to which the very existence of a new Bonapartist Empire was a defiance and a challenge. At the personal level he represented a ruling class that felt towards the upstart Emperor, his Court and government, an invincible aversion and contempt, part snobbery, part fear of the revolutionary and 'popular' origins of the Bonapartist régime. The masters, if they may be called that, of Austrian policy, and especially Count Büol, head of the Imperial Chancellery, foolishly expressed this narrow attitude in a number of prim and petty pin-pricks. Büol, for example, was responsible for circulating an order that no Austrian subject, including citizens of the Italian provinces, must wear the decoration of the *légion d'honneur* since it bore the image of Napoleon. Again, Büol boasted to foreign diplomats that he had prevented the marriage between Princess Vasa and Louis Napoleon. When, at a later date, the Austrian Emperor travelled North to meet the Czar, a meeting at which the French Emperor expressed some surprise, Büol told Hübner: 'The Emperor, our august master, is going to Weimar in order to meet his equal whom he has known for four centuries. Mark the distance between the old Monarchies and the *parvenu!*'

It must be said that Hübner was tireless in his endeavour to teach his

71

superiors the value of a more flexible and tolerant approach. When the Russian danger, especially the menace from that quarter against Turkey's European provinces which were Austria's neighbours, became increasingly acute, the Austrian government made some tentative approaches to France, as has already been noted.[1] To Hübner's way of thinking these did not go far enough. As the new and patently extremely cordial understanding between France and England grew in warmth, he energetically insisted that only Austria's unreserved accession to the anti-Russian alliance would prevent her from sinking into the isolation and impotence of a second-rate power. In Vienna, therefore, Hübner acquired the reputation of being embarrassingly pro-French, while in Paris he was suspected of being a Legitimist and reactionary. He made an honest effort to achieve a balance of sorts between the old Austria and the new France. Far more than most official Austrians he understood the potentialities of the new Bonapartist Empire while privately he always showed a marked preference for the society of the ancien régime, for the great families of the Faubourg Saint-Germain, and was heard to make nostalgic remarks on the *douceur de vivre* which for him had gone for ever in 1848, the year of revolutions. The Empress discussed the complexities of the situation with him in an open and friendly manner. 'You are too ill-natured in small matters,' she told him after one of Büol's outbursts, 'and we don't understand each other on the great issues. One catches flies with honey, not with gall.' And she added: 'I like the Austrian alliance; there is only one alliance we like more—that with England.'

France and Britain declared war on Russia on March 27th, 1854. It was a singular fact that England had in 1854 a mainly pacific government confronted by a bellicose public opinion and press, whereas in France, where the choice between peace and war was ultimately the Emperor's alone, the people showed no enthusiasm for war. The contrasting popular attitude towards war in England and France closely affected the Sovereigns. Queen Victoria, leaving Windsor Castle for the State opening of Parliament on January 31st, noted that 'from time to time there were hisses and groans, but it was evident that the people who emitted them had been placed there. We left Buckingham at ¼ past 4 and at the gates these selfsame nasty people greeted us with similar music. . . . The speech from the throne was the *least* nervous part of the affair. I shall not easily forget this day.' And on February 13th she wrote: 'My heart is not in this unsatisfactory war.'

In Paris, the Empress saw the troops depart for embarkation to the East. 'You cannot imagine,' she wrote to Paca on February 22nd, 'the effect produced by the thought of these robust men, so full of life and hope, never seeing their country and families again. Believe me, when I think of the war with this in my mind, I feel horror and regard each soldier as if he were my own son. Yet bearing in mind the stage things have reached I regard the war as a good thing.' When later that day she had to bid farewell to the officers of the Guards she said with tears in her

[1] See page 68.

72

THE ORSINI ASSASSINATION ATTEMPT

eyes that she hoped they would all return safe and sound. 'Surely *not all?* ' murmured a young Lieutenant who hoped to return at least a Captain.

On the same February 22nd, Queen Victoria noted uneasily in her journal that the enthusiasm of the crowds in the streets was reaching delirious proportions, and on February 28th the Queen rose at 6.30 in the morning to see 'the last battalion of the Scots Fusiliers march past Buckingham Palace on the way to embarkation'. A huge crowd had assembled outside the Palace, and when the Queen and Prince Albert appeared on the balcony, cheers rose from the crowds to greet them. 'The morning was fine and calm,' the Queen entered in her journal, 'the sun rising red over the time-honoured towers of Westminster which was heightened by the gradual, steady, but slow approach of the Band (which does not go) almost drowned by the tremendous cheering of the dense crowd following. The soldiers gave three hearty cheers which went straight to my heart. Carriages with ladies, sorrowing wives, mothers and sisters were there, and some women in the crowd were crying. The men were quite sober, in excellent order and none absent. Formerly they would have been all drunk! May God protect these fine men, may they be preserved and victorious! I shall never forget the touching, beautiful sight I witnessed this morning. . . .'

Thus in England war against Russia had reconciled throne and people. Lord Aberdeen's unenthusiastic government prepared themselves for a war which, it has been aptly said, was to 'alter the psychological climate of England, perhaps for ever'. The warlike demonstrations in London struck Hübner as evidence that England was becoming 'more and more revolutionary', while the American Hawthorne found that the war 'has given England a vast impulse towards democracy'. In England the Crimean War certainly speeded up the weakening of aristocratic government which had begun with the Great Reform Bill, whereas in France, as a parallel development, it helped to consolidate the Emperor's power and prestige. The public war loan was soon over-subscribed, and Mérimée saw the people of Paris forming long queues outside the banks where they could contribute from their savings. He also noticed great activity in the French ports, and sailors told him that their warships would be armed with weapons which could kill 'a thousand cubic metres of Russians with each volley'. This, he told Doña Manuela, was probably less of an exaggeration than at first appeared 'owing to the philanthropic development taken by the art of war in the last forty years'.

The English alliance led to a number of friendly demonstrations in Paris. The Duke of Cambridge, Commander-in-Chief of the British Army, and Lord Raglan, who was to command the expeditionary force, were much in evidence at parades and public reviews. In July, Napoleon watched 10,000 French soldiers being embarked on English ships at Calais for the Baltic, an event, said the stupefied Hübner, 'without parallel in the history of the two countries'. The Empress gave several English soirées in her apartments in the spring of 1854, and when in the evening of Easter Sunday Hübner saw her surrounded by the Duke of Cambridge, Lord Raglan, the second Duke of Wellington and the Duke and Duchess of Hamilton, he was much consoled when the Emperor came up to him and spoke of the day when, so he hoped, 100,000 Frenchmen would be taken across Germany by railway to join the Austrian army in Turkey. For her part, the Empress also did what she could to underline the Emperor's desire of seeing Austria join the alliance against Russia soon.

Yet soon after the Anglo-French declaration of war on Russia, Hübner learnt to his consternation that Austria was holding back because Prussia was not inclined to commit herself. Hübner saw the spectre of Austrian isolation loom larger than ever, and when in April he received an invitation to attend the wedding of the Emperor Francis Joseph with Princess Elisabeth of Wittelsbach at Vienna, he went resolved to put the case for Austria joining the alliance in the strongest possible language.

The Princess, whom Hübner saw being married to the twenty-four-year-old Emperor Francis Joseph at the Church of St. Augustin on April 24th, 1854, was a very shy, a very beautiful girl of not yet seventeen. Her wedding day marked the beginning of a destiny of sorrows. As Elisabeth's pale and nervous beauty matured and ripened with the years so did her protest against the fate which had placed her at the summit of an unquiet Empire. She soon sought escape and solitude in Madeira, Corfu or Ireland—islands on which she isolated herself before the eyes of an astonished Europe. Fleeing from her uncongenial duties, prosaic husband and his fatiguing Empire, she became an absentee Empress during most of the years to come.

Soon after the ceremony Hübner saw the young Emperor[1] and explained that if Austria remained neutral, the French Emperor would revert to his revolutionary connections, that, moreover, he would regard neutrality as the equivalent of hostility. Francis Joseph listened courteously. Hübner returned to Paris not wholly dissatisfied: at least Austria had mobilised two army corps on the Russian frontier and further precautionary measures had been decided upon by the government.

But now the war overtook the hesitant movements of Austrian diplomacy. While Büol and his Emperor allowed the summer and autumn to pass in evasions and delays, the Allies fought the battles of the Alma, Balaclava and Inkerman. The Light Brigade galloped to its destruction. In a war in which public opinion was playing a novel and major part, diplomacy, and especially Austrian diplomacy, cut a poor figure against long casualty lists, war reports from special correspondents and the concern over the ravages of cholera.

Nevertheless, when at long last Austria signed a treaty of alliance with France and England on December 2nd, 1854, the news was received with enthusiasm. Napoleon III was informed as he rose from table that evening and he ran over to the Empress to embrace her in a public access

[1] Francis Joseph ruled his dominions as an absolute Monarch, having, after his own coup d'état of December 1851—three weeks after that of Louis Napoleon—suspended the Constitution conceded to the Revolution of 1848.

of relief and gratitude. But it was soon clear that the alliance existed on paper only. It was followed by no action from the Austrian army that was of any assistance to the Western allies as they besieged Sebastopol in that wet and freezing winter. By her political accession to the Anglo-French alliance Austria estranged herself from Russia while through her military inactivity she lost the respect of France and England. When the Russian Ambassador left Vienna after the rupture he said that the young Austrian Emperor had offended the Czar so deeply that Austria would not enjoy an hour's peace so long as Francis Joseph remained on the throne. Like Francis Joseph, Eugénie lived long enough to see the prophecy come true.

Austria's indecisiveness provided a younger and more vigorous state, the kingdom of Sardinia, with the opportunity to graduate from the Italian to the European level. Under the guidance of his principal Minister, Count Camillo di Cavour, King Victor Emmanuel II joined the Anglo-French alliance in January 1855, and a new expeditionary force of 15,000 men sailed from Genoa to the Crimea in the following April. England, with whom Cavour had been negotiating for some considerable time, had made the enterprise possible. When Palmerston was in Paris in November 1854, he had discussed the plan with the Emperor who welcomed it and mentioned it to the Empress. She immediately suggested that a similar arrangement should be made with Spain: 'Spanish soldiers,' she said, 'are sober and brave, and would fight well by the side of ours.'

The Emperor took up the idea and Palmerston gave his approval. The Empress was asked to find out through her brother-in-law, the Duke of Alba, how the Spanish authorities would react to the suggestion, but Alba replied that the Spanish government disliked the project. It might, the Spanish Ministers pleaded, lead to outside interference in their affairs. 'Interference!' wrote back the Empress on December 18th, 'you should be more afraid of total oblivion.' 'The Emperor does not wish to intervene in the affairs of other countries,' she told Alba another time. 'He thinks that a fool knows more about his own affairs than a wise man about those of others. You need a man like him. They say that nobody is a hero to his valet or his wife: well, I admire my husband more and more, and I wish you could have someone as capable as he is—if it were possible to find another like him.'

She was a grateful disciple. To Paca she wrote almost apologetically how serious everything was becoming around her; she was becoming quite serious herself, she went on, telling her sister to be thankful that she did not write to her about the Eastern Question. This was in answer to a letter Paca had written from Seville: 'Nothing,' wrote the homesick Eugénie, 'that you tell me about Seville came as a surprise. There is poetry in those winding streets, in those walks, those old houses: and there you still find feelings of chivalry unknown otherwise to our high and civilised society which thinks itself so superior. In that part of the world ordinary people still have imagination, elevation of feeling. One vainly looks for such things in privileged society, so degenerate nowadays, especially in Spain.'

75

Take a man from the countryside and you can still turn him into a proper man, but soon this will become impossible with the grandees of Spain, so small have they become. . . . My hopes belong to the generation of the future.'

As the year approached its end and news from the East grew worse, the alliance grew in popularity. If French soldiers were carried to the Baltic theatre in English vessels, English cavalry were transported overland across France to Marseilles to the cries of 'Vive les Anglais' from the people of France. On October 29th, the band of the French élite regiment of the *Guides* played in their handsome dark green and gold uniforms on the terrace at Windsor. 'They had supper,' the Queen's journal tells us, 'in the Castle and drank my health with great enthusiasm.' 'These are no meaningless cries,' M. de La Verdière, the officer in charge, assured Queen Victoria, 'they come from the heart. Our men would let themselves be killed for Your Majesty as much as for the Emperor.' Much moved, the Queen talked to these elegant young musicians about the battle of Alma. 'How times change!' she noted later. 'Who would have dreamt only twenty years ago of sixty French soldiers playing on the Terrace at Windsor and drinking my health in the Steward's room! What would George III say, did he know this, he who, walking on the same terrace, used to ask the Eton boys, "I hope you hate the French."' In her free moments, the Queen was reading Philippe de Ségur's history of Napoleon I's Russian campaign of 1812.

Relations between the Sovereigns of England and France, which were soon to receive popular as well as political sanction in the famous State visits later in 1855, were, although increasingly friendly, subject to much misgiving, doubt and reserve. Prince Albert held several long talks with the French Emperor at the camp of St. Omer in September 1854. Before going, the Prince had discussed the visit and the alliance with Queen Victoria and the Prime Minister, Lord Aberdeen. He said that, once the war was over, the tide, 'that had been flowing very strongly in favour of France might flow the other way when our people saw that the Emperor continued to be a despotic ruler and necessarily an enemy of Constitutional Government'. Developing this thesis, the Prince urged that friendship with a man who later might be 'execrated' by the country was not without its dangers to the Queen who after the end of hostilities could not easily drop an ally although, in the eyes of Englishmen, he was nothing but a tyrant. Her husband's speculations made the Queen thoughtful. 'In an alliance,' she wrote in her journal, 'based in fact upon no solid footing, upon no similarity of feelings, customs, religion etc., but merely the outcome of necessity, owing to the blunders and faithlessness of the Emperor Nicholas—this is what we must guard against, in consideration of *our own* position.' On his return from St. Omer, the Prince wrote a long, conscientious and sober account of the problems involved, slightly patronising in its tone and cautiously affirmative of the Anglo-French alliance which was, he considered, 'the Emperor's best chance'.

76

At the same time, however, the Queen, the Prince and the Aberdeen government[1] did not underrate the value of the French alliance to British interests. With every show of reluctance the Queen was beginning to accustom herself to the idea of a visit to England from the French sovereigns. But as the first discussions were being held at Windsor, news arrived that the Emperor was planning to go to the Crimea and direct the assault on the Fortress of Sebastopol in person. The project shocked and dismayed the Queen and her advisers. Would it not be fatal to the alliance, the Queen argued, if the British army were to become 'contemptible and weak in the eyes of the French army' and do all the inglorious work while the French troops, led by the Emperor, were making a brilliant campaign, to return covered with laurels? 'This,' she stressed, 'we *never* could bear.' Lord Clarendon was dispatched to Paris on April 4th but, although obtaining satisfactory promises from the Emperor 'to give the honour of the British flag his first consideration', could not persuade him to abandon the plan.

In Paris, the effect of the news was equally staggering. Mérimée heard it on February 17th and at once wrote to Doña Manuela in the greatest alarm. The voyage made no sense, he said, for if Sebastopol could be taken, the Emperor's presence was not necessary, and if it could not, his presence would only do harm. 'But worst of all, people are saying that he listens only to one *person* and that that *person* whose courage you know well enough is advising him to go, and wants to go with him. She is assuming a terrible responsibility before the eyes of the world. Could you not write to her and remind her of that responsibility? Rightly or wrongly, everybody is attributing the project to her and I know on *excellent authority* that only she could stop him. . . .' A fortnight later Mérimée dined at the Tuileries while the Emperor was away and opened his heart to the Empress on the subject. The plan was being attacked with almost national unanimity. He found to his astonishment that the Empress was equally opposed to it. Who had started the rumour that she was in favour? 'I had no need of her denials,' he told Doña Manuela, 'to realise that she had nothing to do with the idea. We begin to get to know the stubbornness of your son-in-law.'

The Emperor's reasons for wanting to go were numerous: his disappointment at how badly French and British headquarters were co-operating; his hope that unified command would increase the two armies' striking power; his interest, as a gunner, in a plan to capture Sebastopol by means of floating batteries[2]—and finally the embarrassing circumstance that his cousin Plon-Plon had, early in January, returned from the war covered with no glory. The Prince explained that he had fallen ill with cholera. While the Emperor found this a valid reason for a temporary withdrawal from operations he thought it inadequate grounds for returning all the

[1] Lord Aberdeen himself had never been enthusiastic about war against Russia and regarded an alliance with Austria as a prime necessity.

[2] See Mr. T. A. B. Corley's *Democratic Despot* (Barrie and Rockliff, 1961) for an admirable exposition of this scheme.

77

way to Paris. Pun-loving Parisians turned Plon-Plon into *craint-plomb*. The Emperor felt that his cousin's ill-advised return constituted a slight on the Napoleonic dynasty for which only an act of courage on his own part could atone.

The Empress did her best to dissuade him. She had, wrote a courtier, Baron d'Ambès, 'set her face against it', and she stressed her fears that his absence might encourage political mischief-makers. Her efforts failed. She made it clear that, should he go, she was determined to accompany him, for she always regarded her presence at his side as an added protection against attempts on his life. No amount of lurid warnings from Mérimée against 'the narrow streets of Constantinople' could weaken her determination. 'I must contradict,' she wrote to Paca on March 22nd, 'two items of news you have read—I am not pregnant and I shall depart for Constantinople towards the middle of April.' It was not until May 8th that she was able to tell her sister that the voyage to the Crimea had been abandoned.

In England, meanwhile, public indignation with the conduct of the war had swept Lord Aberdeen and his coalition government out of power, and early in 1855 Lord Palmerston formed his first Cabinet, much to the Queen's and Prince Albert's grief and the horror of conservative Europe. The Queen and the Prince had consulted with a number of alternative candidates, but none felt confident of success under the prevailing conditions. When at length the crisis was resolved, by which time she had personally interviewed all the country's political leaders of importance, Queen Victoria entered in her diary: 'Everyone seems to have confidence in me excepting my poor wretched self who am so often miserable and desponding.'

Palmerston became the man of the hour. He was, wrote Sidney Herbert, the only public man in England who had a name: 'Many criticise, many disapprove, but all, more or less, like him and look upon him as the only man.' Lord Clarendon remained at the Foreign Office. On March 2nd, it was learnt that Czar Nicholas had suddenly died. Although his successor was reputed to be more pacific and amenable, Clarendon did not expect any rapid changes and dedicated himself to the preparations for the reception of England's principal ally.

'The Emperor's reception here,' wrote Queen Victoria to Lord Clarendon, 'ought to be a boon to him and not a boon to us.' The Court of St. James's remained very much on the defensive as the date of the visit drew nearer. Lord Cowley, to whom the Queen conveyed a special wish that he should be in the Emperor's entourage, wrote despondently to Clarendon: 'Heaven send we may have fine weather. How we are all to be sick in uniform and the ladies in smart toilettes I cannot comprehend.' The Foreign Secretary expressed the general gloom felt on the eve of the visit when he said that 'nothing could look worse both from a military and diplomatic point of view than the state of affairs at the moment'.

Like the thick fog that enveloped the Imperial flotilla and its escort ships in the Channel, and at Dover reduced visibility to a hundred yards, the gloom and tension lifted from the moment when the Emperor and Empress set foot on the soil of England. From Monday, April 16th when the Empress, her hand resting on Prince Albert's outstretched arm, followed by the Emperor in general's uniform, stepped ashore to be greeted by a salute from the guns and an address of welcome by the Mayor of Dover, Mr. Worsfold, to Saturday, April 21st, when they embarked from the same pier and Mr. Worsfold received a golden snuff-box from the departing Emperor, the visit was an immense success. For the Emperor it was more than a political triumph, more than a further recognition by his powerful neighbour of the Empire: it was a return to a country which, as an outcast in the Europe of the Holy Alliance, he had come to love and admire with a sincerity and affection that only ended on his death-bed. The people of England, aware of their growing influence and political importance, gave him a full-throated and clamorous reception that was in itself an exciting commentary on the Emperor's hold over the popular mind.[1]

The Empress whose acquaintance with England, and especially London, had been more cursory and less happy than her husband's, was said by one observer 'to be equally condescending in her acknowledgements'. Unlike the Emperor, Eugénie always felt uncomfortable among crowds and had therefore to exercise some self-discipline to master her nervousness and appear to be at ease. While the Emperor possessed the gift of at once rousing, and reacting to, the enthusiasm of the multitudes with an immediacy which the crowds, whether French or English instinctively recognised and applauded, the Empress, feeling lost and, in some mysterious way, even a little frightened among the masses, always appeared 'self-possessed' to friendly observers, but 'disdainful' to those who were hostile. On the present occasion, therefore, the Emperor was judged to be 'visibly moved', 'strongly affected by the cheering', while the Empress impressed the crowds more with her elegance, her poise, her seemingly gentle and wistful beauty. The 'popular' success was the Emperor's; the Empress came into her own in the interiors of Windsor Castle and Buckingham Palace. She may not have established herself deeply with the multitudes, but she won, on this as on future English occasions, the abiding friendship of a number of individual people. Above all, the State Visit saw the beginning of the life-long friendship between her and Queen Victoria. She conquered also the heart of the Queen's eldest daughter, who was to be the tragic Empress of a Germany still hidden in the future and who throughout the present visit showed an almost embarrassing *Schwaermerei* for the exotic visitor from across the Channel. The Prince of Wales, for his part, was to show *his* affection for

---

[1] The impact of Napoleon III on the people, as opposed to the individual classes, of England is a theme for which there is no space in the present study. Future events were to show that the British 'people' remained as faithful to the Emperor as he did to them. Despite Prince Albert's misgivings, the tide never flowed the other way.

the Emperor and Empress when in the following August his parents took him with them on the return visit to Paris. When, just before embarking at Dover at the end of the visit,[1] the Empress spoke to Lady Ely of the events of these six crowded days, she dwelt not on the splendid banquets in the Royal Palaces or the Guildhall of London, nor on the considerable political and military agreements which the Emperor and his staff had negotiated, nor even on the ceremony of her husband being made a Knight of the Garter: what filled her with special gratitude, so she humbly told Lady Ely who reported it to the Queen, was 'that the Queen and the Prince allowed the children to associate with us'.

[1] An account of the two State Visits has recently been published, based on Queen Victoria's *Journal*, with an introduction by Mr. Raymond Mortimer. The reader is referred to this attractive publication for the details of the two State Visits (*Queen Victoria: Leaves from a Journal*, André Deutsch, 1961).

CHAPTER 4

WITHIN A week of their return to Paris, the very real danger facing them was brought home to Napoleon and Eugénie in a dramatic episode. Shortly before six in the evening of April 28th, the Empress drove out towards the recently completed Bois de Boulogne, the Emperor and Edgar Ney following on horse-back some minutes later. At the Rond Point des Champs Elysées a well-dressed young man approached the Emperor as if to present a petition, then suddenly fired on him from close range, and missed. Ney immediately rode between the Emperor and the assailant, and after a brief scuffle the police overwhelmed the culprit, an Italian called Pianori. The Emperor and Ney resumed their interrupted ride to the Bois where the Empress was waiting in her carriage. They told her what had happened, and on their return to the Tuileries the Emperor and Empress were loudly acclaimed by the people in the streets who spontaneously formed a procession around and behind the carriage as a protective escort to the Palace. The Empress, pale and shaken, just had time to send her mother a reassuring telegram and then went to the State rooms to receive congratulations on the Emperor's narrow escape. 'The Empress sobbed convulsively,' reported Hübner who had hurried to the Tuileries, 'but the Emperor was absolutely calm and gave us the details of the crime. "Attempts of this nature," he said in conclusion, "will never succeed; to strike home you need a dagger."'

Mérimée also went to the Tuileries as soon as he heard the news. 'The Empress,' he told Doña Manuela, 'was much affected and very pale. She pressed my hand and I read a thousand things in her eyes. No discouragement.' Mérimée then resumed his favourite lecture on deficient security arrangements: 'What is the point,' he lamented, speaking of the famous *Cent-Gards*, 'of having the hundred finest soldiers in the world and giving them bullet-proof cuirasses, if one uses them only to announce the approach of the Emperor and so point him out to assassins? The man who shot at him yesterday stood on the pavement a few yards away. When he had fired his two shots, the Emperor began to smile and to salute as if he had been given a salvo of honour. . . . The assassin is an Italian. His hat and double-barrelled pistol come from London. He is generally thought to be an envoy from Mazzini and the secret societies. The Duke of Mortemart who commands a division in central France tells me that the Socialists are still fully organised and ready for anything. But they have no longer any weapons or ammunition. . . .'

Queen Victoria also thought the assassin was connected with Mazzini. 'The Emperor shot at, but not hurt, in his own Capital!' she wrote in her journal on April 28th; a few days later she added that the assassin was 'a shoemaker who had resided here, but had left before the Emperor came. We all think he must be a tool of Mazzini's'. The Queen was at no time enthusiastic about the presence of Mazzini and other 'patriotic' exiles in England, and sometimes expressed the personal wish that these individuals might commit some felony 'which would render their deportation possible.'

Paca, who happened to be dining at the Plazuela del Angel when Eugénie's telegram arrived, wrote a few days later to her sister expressing her affectionate concern. 'Thank God the danger is over,' replied the Empress. 'That sort of thing is quickly forgotten, or at least one tries not to think of it, for to live in anxiety is not to live at all. God has protected the Emperor so well this time that I hope He will continue to do so in future. This hope redoubles my courage. Shared danger makes one less afraid.'

Pianori's pistol shots succeeded where Queen Victoria's and Prince Albert's persuasions had failed; they killed the Emperor's Crimean project. The attempt on his life was an early intimation of another threat to the Empire, the Italian problem. At his trial, Pianori gave as his motive resentment at the French occupation of Rome, 'which', he maintained, 'has ruined my country'. He denied having any accomplices, but after being sentenced to death he addressed a plea for mercy to the Emperor. The French Cabinet Ministers were horrified to find that both Emperor and Empress wished to pardon the criminal. In the ensuing discussion Napoleon, normally so calm and impassive, appeared to be 'unusually agitated', put off signing the order for Pianori's execution and spoke several times of the Empress's special wish to spare the young man. In the end he yielded sorrowfully to the collective representations of his Ministers who told him that the wretched Pianori had a record of political murders in Rome and Bologna. It seems hardly possible to doubt that the Emperor's reluctance came from his close acquaintance with the secret societies, with their ghastly mystique of blood and revenge. Napoleon knew that Pianori's execution must have its sequel, that blood must atone for blood. Pianori was executed a fortnight after his attempted crime. Before then the Emperor had forbidden the presentation of any addresses of congratulation on his fortunate escape.

Walewski had kept Queen Victoria informed on the Pianori affair, including both Sovereigns' strange desire to pardon the culprit. It was his last function as French Ambassador at the Court of St. James's. The unsatisfactory developments at Vienna had induced the Emperor to accept the resignation of his Foreign Minister, Drouyn de Lhuys, who like Lord John Russell had become too closely associated with the Austrian attempt to appease Russia rather than fight in the war. Walewski became the new Foreign Minister and Persigny was sent to London as Ambassador. At his farewell audience, Walewski's beautiful Florentine wife 'spoke,' says the Queen's journal, 'with tears in her eyes of going—she is such a charming person. She will be an immense loss'. The Queen was to modify the latter sentiment radically at a none too distant date.

During May the Empress was involved in a new round of official duties: the Universal Exhibition in Paris was opened on May 15th, there was a State Visit from the King and Queen of Portugal, soon after which the Lord Mayor of London with numerous members of the corporation paid an official visit to the French capital, delighting Parisians with a rich display of traditional City ceremonial. In June the Empress, feeling ill and exhausted, was examined by the doctors and was found to be pregnant. She went to Eaux Bonnes in the Pyrenees to recuperate from the strain of the recent months. 'The doctors told the Emperor,' she wrote to Paca later in June, 'that the examination took place just in time. If we had waited any longer, I would never have been able to have children.' She was in fact undergoing a thorough and painful treatment at the little watering place—'decidedly,' she told Paca, 'I pass my life being ill. Who would have thought it when I was sixteen? *Los malos ratos*, the evil hours through which I have lived in my time have ruined my health.'

In the Crimea, meanwhile, General Pélissier had succeeded Canrobert as French Commander-in-Chief in May. This short, stocky, vulgar and brutal leader infused an air of professionalism into the Crimean War. He began by dispatching a naval force to Kertsh which destroyed vast enemy stores of corn and provisions amounting to four months' rations for 100,000 men. This was followed by a successful capture of the outer line of the Sebastopol fortifications early in June, the first victory of the year, but a fortnight later the people of Paris and London heard that their armies had suffered a considerable set-back in an attack on Fort Malakoff undertaken, after very inadequate preparation, on Waterloo day, June 18th. Raglan died ten days later. The Emperor, whom Pélissier had informed of the defeat in the most laconic terms, was greatly tempted to dismiss his rude new Commander-in-Chief but was dissuaded from doing so by General MacMahon who was passing through Paris on the way to the Crimea.

To Napoleon III the moment was critical. The collapse of the Vienna Conference, which had brought neither an acceptable peace nor Austrian reinforcements to the war effort, made the country feel afraid of a long war. The news of the defeat at the Malakoff, printed in the press as laconically as Pélissier had sent it, increased the alarm further, as that great seismograph of the tremors of public reaction, the Paris Stock Exchange, swiftly registered. 'The prolongation of the war,' we read in a confidential report to the Imperial government from Bordeaux, 'begins to cause a certain weariness to appear among a section of the population. It must be stressed that it is neither the agricultural nor the labouring classes who seem to show this, but rather the business and leisured classes who are troubled by the war in their transactions and speculations. They hope fervently for a return of peace as a vital necessity for their prosperity.'

'The promise,' reported the Belgian Minister to Brussels, 'that a great blow is about to be struck, has not been fulfilled. It is to be feared that the confidence of the country in a definite triumph may be a little weakened by the delays and ever re-appearing difficulties of the siege of Sebastopol that is unparalleled in military annals.' The Empress, sharing the general apprehensions in her Pyrenean retreat, suffered recurrent black moods, but, her letters to Paca apart, suffered them in silence. Even to Paca she wrote that she did not wish to communicate her depression 'and so,' ended one letter, 'I leave you. Adieu, I love you with all my heart'. Paca was in Paris for the exhibition, and so was Doña Manuela.

At the Tuileries, the Emperor acted. Realising that the set-back of June 18th would give tonic encouragement to his enemïes of the interior, particularly to the Russian party of the *salons*, he summoned a special session of the Legislative Assembly, asked for a further 140,000 men and the issue of another war loan which was soon five times over-subscribed. At the same time he pursued the preparations, diplomatic and otherwise, for Queen Victoria's return visit which was finally arranged to take place in the second half of August. Already the exhibition was filling Paris with large numbers of foreign visitors among whom only the elderly could remember Paris ever having been as gay and welcoming before, namely after the conclusion of peace in 1814. Behind this bright camouflage, the Emperor led the country through the crisis of confidence that followed the defeat of June 18th and reassured his English ally at the same time.

The Empress returned to Saint-Cloud in August, soon after which Queen Victoria was officially informed of her 'condition' by Mme de Persigny, the new French Ambassadress. The Queen was at Osborne, resting before her Parisian exertions. 'They are all greatly alarmed,' she noted in the journal, 'lest the Empress should fatigue herself next week, but they can rely on my not allowing this. It is a great blessing for her, poor thing, as it will make *all* the difference in her happiness and position.'

The Queen and Prince Albert left the Isle of Wight for Boulogne early on August 18th aboard their new yacht *Victoria and Albert*, accompanied by the Prince of Wales and the Princess Royal, Lady Ely, Lord Clarendon and a numerous suite. After ten days of great splendour imaginatively stage-managed under the Empress's closest supervision the English Sovereigns embarked for home on August 27th. There had been, in the midst of official engagements at the Tuileries, the Opéra, the Hôtel de Ville, the Palace of Versailles, several opportunities for intimate talks between the visitors and their hosts, especially at Saint-Cloud. Queen Victoria was able to give the Empress sound advice in respect to her confinement. The vexing question of the Queen's relations with the Orleans family in England was also discussed in complete openness and honesty on both sides and thereafter ceased to trouble what the Queen called 'the closest alliance which has almost ever existed between two great independent nations. May this ever, with God's blessing, continue!' The visit confirmed the Queen in her view 'of the altered feeling of the country' towards England and she responded to her reception in Paris with sincere enthusiasm. Prince Albert, throughout these festive days of his only visit to the French capital, was polite but cool. The Queen was convinced that the Emperor 'appreciated Albert thoroughly', but the appreciation seems to have been one-sided.

The Queen and her family returned to Osborne on August 28th. According to Greville, who frequently chatted with Lord Clarendon, the Prince of Wales had towards the end of the visit tried to persuade the Empress to get permission for his sister and himself to prolong their stay in Paris. The Empress replied that she was afraid that the Queen and Prince Albert could not do without them. 'Not do without us!' exclaimed the boy. 'There are six more of us at home, and they don't want us.' Once they were back in what Prince Albert's biographer calls 'the calm sweet home after the stir and splendour of the last ten days', the Princess Royal could show the others the fine bracelet the Empress had given her as a present. The Queen, discussing the details of the 'stir and splendour' with the Prince, found him 'naturally much calmer, and particularly much less taken by people, much less under *personal* influence, than I am'. But in her journal, she continued to reminisce and ponder, and after a few days of rest at Osborne she wrote: 'I shall ever retain an affectionate feeling for France'.

CHAPTER 5

THE PROGRAMME of engagements and functions which claimed the Empress's time and energies between the end of Queen Victoria's visit and the birth of the Prince Imperial in March 1856, was an exceptionally heavy one under which a weaker or less dedicated woman might easily have broken down. There were two further State visits, one by the Duke of Brabant and his Habsburg bride, the other by France's and England's new ally, King Victor Emmanuel II of Piedmont. The Universal Exhibition required the Empress's presence on certain special days to award prizes or escort distinguished visitors. The war, the victories in September, the peace preliminaries followed by the assembling in Paris of the delegates for the Congress of Paris early in 1856, the return of the soldiers before then, all brought their special obligations to the Empress whose health, under the strains of pregnancy, was neither normal nor stable.

She had Paca with her until the end of the year. The Albas now had a fine house in the Champs Elysées, purchased by the Empress from the Lauriston family, and Eugénie was relieved to feel that her sister and brother-in-law had a second home so near her own. Alba, apart from being the first of the grandees of Spain, occupied a position of importance in the municipal administration of Madrid and knew a great deal about the shifts of power going this way or that round the Madrid parish pump.

The Empress had asked him to lend her the correspondence between Philip II and his Duke of Alba from the archives at the Palacio de Liria, and, in her rare leisure hours, she studied history at its source. It became the habit of a life-time. Spain in her greatness, Spain in her present sealed-off provincialism were the subjects the Empress would discuss with her brother-in-law. Paca, on the other hand, did not concern herself with questions of politics and State. She was perfectly content with her status as a private person in France, and when a Court official wanted to assign her a prominent place in one of the processions during Queen Victoria's visit, she replied, 'I would much rather go on making bandages for the wounded in the Crimea. I am the Duchess of Alba and that is quite enough.'

Austria's odd position as a platonic ally led to a number of brisk exchanges between the Empress and Hübner given, and taken, in the old amicable spirit. After a dinner at Saint-Cloud on October 21st, the Empress spoke to him of Austria's predicament: 'You have not reconciled Russia, you have not resumed your ascendancy in Germany and you cannot count on the gratitude of France and England.' The Emperor talked to the Ambassador a little later in the evening, the conversation turned to the King of Naples who had had to apologise to the French government for some small incident. 'What can you do with a government,' said the Emperor, 'which finds the Jesuits too liberal?' Hübner realised that they did not care for Platonic friendships at the Tuileries. He was much struck that evening with the many Spanish names and faces among the guests— great names, small people, it seemed to him, and, strangely echoing a remark made by the Empress, wrote down: 'There is nothing so small as a grandee of Spain.'

The King of Sardinia's visit in November coincided with a crisis in Anglo-French relations over the conclusion of peace. Sebastopol had fallen on September 10th, when the French under Pélissier had stormed the key fortress of the Malakoff. Unfortunately, the simultaneous British attack on the Rédan under Raglan's successor—described by Lord Clarendon as 'that worthy old gentlewoman Simpson'—had failed under conditions which an English officer called 'the greatest disgrace that has ever fallen on the British soldier'. The British attack had started well and when the outworks were being attacked, a young lieutenant called Lintorn Simmonds came close enough to the enemy to tear off a Russian standard the black ribbon commemorating Nicholas I's death: but the bravery of the officers failed to carry the men with them and the assault had to be called off. Nevertheless, the Russians marched out of Sebastopol, having withstood a siege of seven months' duration. Pélissier's dispatch paid handsome tribute to British valour, but while Paris and France celebrated the great victory, London remained mainly quiet and the British mood sombre. Thereafter the policy of the two countries diverged for a time into opposite directions: Napoleon reflected that with the capture of Sebastopol France's immediate war aim, to keep Turkey and the Mediterranean outside Russian influence, might well receive sanction in a treaty of peace, while England hoped for a more decisive and enduring weakening of Russian power. England, where public opinion was as bellicose as ever, was now geared for war and ready to deliver a major blow against Russian might, whereas France, both morally and materially, was past the peak of her war effort and expressed a strong desire for an early peace.

The French position was put impressively into words by the Emperor when he made a speech on November 15th. The occasion was the closing of the Universal Exhibition, and the audience included the Duke of Cambridge in his Field Marshal's uniform:

'At the sight of so many marvels spread out before your eyes,' he said, 'the first impression is a desire for peace. Only peace can develop these remarkable productions of the human intelligence. You must then all wish with me that peace may be swift and lasting. . . . All of you, who think of the progress of agriculture, industry, and commerce of one nation contributing to the welfare of all the others . . . I would ask to tell your fellow-citizens, that France entertains no hatred against any nation and that her sympathies extend to all who, like her, desire the triumph of right and justice. . . . At our present stage of civilisation the success of armies, however brilliant it may be, is only momentary. In reality it is only public opinion which invariably wins the final victory.'

The speech was greeted enthusiastically, particularly so, we are assured, by the 3,000 English present.

It was known in London that the Emperor was being put under considerable pressure by the pro-Russian elements in the French capital with whom Morny remained closely associated. The Emperor's enemies in England saw their opportunity and murmured the awful words 'separate peace'. But, although England regretted the peace moves as being premature, the Queen and the government acknowledged that the Emperor upheld the English alliance against considerable opposition, and even Prince Albert admitted that only the Emperor 'as a Napoleon' could have made the alliance endure, whereas, said the Prince, 'a Bourbon would have been accused of sacrificing the interests of his country'. The Duke of Cambridge was present at this conversation and, the Queen's Journal tells us, they 'all agreed that the way in which Louis Philippe had lived, as a *Family* and not as a *Court*, had not been sufficient for the French feelings, and that the present Court with all its show, etc., pleased and satisfied their pride much more.'

Before long, England, France and Austria reached agreement on the terms which were to be submitted to the Czar in an ultimatum. England had meanwhile concluded anti-Russian defence agreements with the Scandinavian powers, and even in Madrid the Empress's idea of Spanish participation was discussed once more between the British Minister and General Espartéro, the dictator of the moment. While the question of war or peace was hanging fire, the chancelleries of Europe, at the beginning of the winter of 1855/56, began to perceive the ominous outlines of a vast European conflagration. On January 16th, 1856, the Czar announced his acceptance of the Allied terms.

The new concord with Austria improved Hübner's position at the Tuileries. When on December 16th, 1855, he sat next to the Empress during a dinner, he reminded her that when the Vienna negotiations of the previous spring had broken down and Drouyn de Lhuys returned in disgrace, she had said to him: 'Austria cheats.' The Empress at once turned to the Emperor and said: 'Louis, M. de Hübner remembers what I told him in April,' and the Emperor replied that this was an excellent opportunity for an *amende honorable*. This the Empress gave gracefully and the diplomat realised that the Emperor was in earnest with his desire to make peace.

The Empress next spoke of the Concordat which the Emperor of Austria had recently concluded with the Vatican and which signified the final disavowal of the ecclesiastical policy of Joseph II. 'What reasons,' enquired the Empress, 'could have induced your Emperor to make this medieval treaty?' Hübner said afterwards that he felt no wish to enter into a theological dispute with his beautiful neighbour, but in truth Eugénie's pointed question was unanswerable, even though she had told him that it was 'Eugénie and not the Empress' who was asking it. It enabled him to discuss the point with a mere liberal. Did the Ambassador feel, as the Empress certainly did, that the excessive clericalism of the Concordat was, in fact, indefensible? Hübner found the Empress 'looking very beautiful despite her sufferings' and 'very cheerful'.

The Empress remained at her duties until a week before the confinement, and the Emperor continued to discuss with her all the moves and negotiations behind the scenes that went on between London, Paris, Vienna and St. Petersburg in preparation for the imminent Peace Congress of Paris. Thus she learnt late in January that Austria was disinclined to incorporate certain special points, insisted on by England, into the peace preliminaries. 'Among the Allies,' she said to Hübner on January 26th, 'Austria is the power who has done least and wants to gain most—why do you oppose those special points?' Hübner's replies did not satisfy her, she became increasingly animated and finally asked the Emperor to come to her rescue. When in her ardour she insisted on taking a strong, an English, line with Russia, Hübner said, 'If your ideas were to be followed, Madame, we would have universal war.' The Empress fell abruptly silent, nor did the Emperor add a comment. Later in the evening she told Hübner, half jokingly, half seriously, that he had 'compromised' her with the Emperor, that she would be lectured by him later on.

The various peace delegations reached Paris in the course of February and each was fêted at the Tuileries with an official dinner. Russia sent Count Orloff, a fabulous grand seigneur, together with Baron Brunnow. Clarendon, with Cowley at his side, represented England, and Hübner received his own Chief, the choleric Count Büol, in Paris on February 16th. The Turks dispatched Mehmed Djemil and the Grand Vizier, Ali Pasha. Thanks to the Emperor Napoleon's special efforts, the Kingdom of Sardinia was admitted to all sessions of the Conference, Cavour and Villamarina representing King Victor Emmanuel. The admission of Prussia was subject to a difference of opinion. The English government had no wish to see the 'Russian Prefect at Berlin' participating in the deliberations as an equal, but Hübner had instructions to induce the French Emperor to dissuade England from her opposition. In the end, Prussia, rather late during the Congress, was admitted to some of the sessions, while at others the delegation, which included Bismarck, was kept in the ante-rooms. Queen Victoria approved of the Emperor's action of the question of the admission of Sardinia. 'It must ever be our object and our interest,' she told Lord Clarendon, 'to see Sardinia independent and strong as a Liberal constitutional country, opposing a barrier alike to unenlightened and absolute as well as revolutionary principles. . . .' As for Prussia, the Queen at first shared her government's reluctance to admit Frederick William's representatives to the Congress, but when Napoleon gave Austria's wishes his support, she acquiesced.

'I shall soon be obliged,' wrote the Empress to Paca on February 14th, 'to make a fuss of the plenipotentiaries of the Congress, and I rather fear that these dinners and concerts will not do me much good in my present state, especially as it will all be over in a month's time. It is extremely annoying to live in public and never have the right to be ill when unfortunately one is subject to the same maladies as everybody else.' Lords Clarendon and Cowley dined at the Tuileries on February 17th, and the Foreign Secretary told the Queen in a letter that 'the Empress was looking in great health and beauty last night. She was in the highest spirits, and full of affectionate enquiry for your Majesty.' When the Austrian delegates went to the Palace, the Empress sat between Count Büol and Hübner, the latter finding her 'animated as always'. The first session of the Congress of Paris took place on February 27th, and Hübner saw the Empress for the last time before her confinement at a reception on March 9th.

The Empress's labour began on Friday, March 14. She was in indescribable agony throughout Friday and Saturday and at times had to be kept standing erect supported by attendants to recover her breath after the spasms. On Saturday she called for Dr. Darralde, who told the Emperor bluntly that instruments would have to be used and that he could not guarantee that both mother and child would survive the birth. Whom should he save in an emergency? The mother, replied the Emperor without a moment's thought. All his famous impassive calm dissolved under the prolonged waiting in uncertainty, despite the fact that members of his family, including cousins Plon-Plon and Mathilde, and numerous officials of Court and State were waiting in the ante-room with him. Through the open door of the bedchamber the sobs and groans and cries of the Empress fighting for her and her child's life could be heard for fifteen hours.

A healthy and exceptionally strong boy was born on Palm Sunday morning, March 16th, 1856, at three o'clock. On being told, the Emperor jumped up and embraced several people standing near him in an access of joy such as he was never to show again. He finally remembered his Imperial dignity and said, only a shade more formally, that he was sorry he could not embrace everybody and thanked all those present for their patience and good will. Then he stepped softly to Eugénie's bed. 'Is it a girl?' asked her small exhausted voice from behind the curtains. The Emperor drew the curtains aside and said: 'No' to this despondent enquiry. The mother showed joyful animation—'A boy?' The Emperor, absorbed by the picture of his wife worn out after the agony, absently shook his head to discourage her from exciting herself, but then reassured her and told her that she must rest. Some say that before she fell asleep she had a last impression of Prince Napoleon giving her an evil look of hatred from his monocled eye. Plon-Plon was no longer the heir to the throne.

Outside in Paris and in every town throughout the country guns fired salutes and Palm Sunday was given over to rejoicing. From the Tuileries came the expected gestures of largesse and mercy, a hundred thousand francs to the poor, ten thousand each to the mutual benefit societies of artists, men of letters, science, and the theatre. Political prisoners were amnestied, Generals Randon, Canrobert and Bosquet became Marshals of France. The Pope telegraphed his benediction and for the first time in history the electric wire was deemed appropriate to convey it. The crowned heads of Europe sent their congratulations by the same means. The token forces left in the Crimea fired their guns, including the English and Sardinians: the Russian guns, silent since the armistice, responded with peaceful salvoes. The birth of the heir to the Empire meant peace. In the evening the boulevards of Paris formed one long line of light from the Madeleine to the Place de la Bastille, and *The Times* correspondent noticed illuminations in the poorer quarters and back streets 'where, I believe, no lights were ever hung out before'. Théophile Gautier composed verses in the child's honour, and the City of Paris presented a cradle made in the shape of a Norman boat supported by an Imperial eagle—in allusion to the city's early history and present pride. On the same day it became known that the Pope and the Queen of Sweden were to be among the infant's godparents.

Queen Victoria, like the other Sovereigns, had heard the news by telegraph within an hour of the birth. She noted 'Excellent news of the dear Empress, but distressing ones of her confinement which must have been an awful one.'

In Paris on March 18th, the assembled diplomats filed past the Prince Imperial's nautical cradle. The red ribbon of the *légion d'honneur* had been placed above the bed clothes. Hübner briefly noticed the child's beautiful blue eyes.

The Congress concluded its work on April 30th, and peace with Russia was signed. The limited aims of the Western alliance, namely, to keep the Russians out of the Black Sea and Turkey, were achieved. Navigation on the Danube became open to all nations and was placed under international control, and Russia was forced to cede Bessarabia. Turkey for the first time in her history was acknowledged as a legitimately European power.

As for the two marginal powers, Prussia and Sardinia, Bismarck's country had been confined merely to a passive ratification of the decisions arrived at, while Cavour succeeded, after the Peace of Paris had been signed, in having a special session called of which the only memorable result was that Lord Clarendon castigated the government of the Pope as 'the most detestable government in the world'. From one or two remarks made to him by Clarendon in private Cavour hoped that England's sympathy with the case of Italy might produce more tangible results. Victor Emmanuel had during his visits to Paris and London always spoken of the need 'to exterminate Austria', and to Queen Victoria he had said in December 1855 that the war in the East should develop into a war to the finish—'*une guerre à outrance*'. Queen Victoria had replied that

England had no wish for a war of this sort. England had her own grievances with the Peace—'premature and not favourable to us', wrote Queen
Victoria in her journal—and English statesmen began to feel that Continental alliances and wars were not a principal British interest.

To the Emperor Napoleon the Peace of Paris represented a solid achievement both in form and substance. The first major European Congress since
the days of the Holy Alliance had taken place under his undoubted
leadership and arbitration in Paris. Throughout his life, Napoleon had
been determined to restore French self-respect from the humiliation which
the peace of 1815 had inflicted on the French nation. The new alignment
of Europe was turned against the country that had rigidly remained the
upholder of the spirit of 1815: Czarist Russia had invited her fate.
Napoleon III was not inspired by any feelings of undue elation, revenge
or vindictiveness: the Peace of Paris punished nobody, but merely forced
Russia back behind her frontiers and faced her with a European coalition
should she propose to emerge once more to threaten her neighbours. This
system remained in force so long as Napoleon III was Emperor of the
French. It was a system that did not involve military occupation of enemy
country, excessive demands for reparations, or bland assumptions of
righteousness on the part of the victor. It was a peace in which neither
the hangman nor the firing squad were called upon in support of policy.
The Emperor's words at the closing of the Universal Exhibition in November, that France felt no hatred towards anyone, had not been meaningless
or false.

No less significant at this important moment in the history of Europe
was the Emperor's sincerity in presenting the peace, like the war, as the
result of Anglo-French understanding. When on Sunday, March 30th, the
delegates went to the Tuileries to present the signed treaty 'concluded
under his auspices' to the Emperor, and to the Empress the eagle's quill
with which it had been signed, the Emperor, so Lord Clarendon wrote to
Queen Victoria, 'turned towards Lord Cowley and myself and said that
peace had been rendered possible by the spirit of conciliation we had
exhibited'. The Foreign Secretary went on: 'as a result it was clearly
understood by the Congress that in the opinion of the Emperor the question
of peace and war had rested with England. The Emperor's remark produced
a great effect. It was uncalled for, but generous.'

The new Napoleonic style in dynastic matters informed the speech
which the Emperor made to the assembled Senate and deputies on March
18th. In the baptismal register the Emperor had written *Son of France*
behind the Prince Imperial's names—'a revival,' as he explained to the
assembly, 'of the usages of the *ancien régime*. It is not, for that reason, a
meaningless or antiquated term. For truly, gentlemen, when an heir is
born to perpetuate a national institution, that child is the whole country's
son: and this name will remind him of his duties. . . .'

The Empress had to withdraw from public life for a long time; it was
not until May that she was able to walk unsupported. The doctors told

her that she could never without the certainty of death give birth to another child. Nature's revenge was complete, yet her vitality proved stronger than the death-wish of her long adolescence. Dr. Fergusson, one of Queen Victoria's most trusted medical advisers, saw the Empress in May 1856, and reported the result to the Queen. 'The poor Empress is not ill in health,' we read in the Queen's Journal under May 10th, 'but has not yet recovered from the results of her severe confinement, which incapacitates her from standing or walking, and this may possibly last for a good time longer. It is most sad and I fear she will get into low spirits if she cannot go about with the Emperor. . . .'

CHAPTER 6

THE COUNTESS OF CASTIGLIONE was not yet nineteen when she arrived in Paris from Turin in January 1856, but her physical beauty had reached an early perfection that made her age irrelevant. She was entirely without the spontaneity of youth and her appearances in public were always calculated to suggest an aura of remoteness and mystery. She soon became the 'social sensation' of the 1856 season, as the Maréchal de Castellane noted in his diary, adding that he did not like her. This was a common reaction, especially in diaries: all who saw her gasped in amazement at the beauty of her form, but soon found that she was a woman without charm, wit or conversation. Fleury wrote that she seemed scarcely human. Yet she tantalised all by conveying the impression that she was attainable to no one outside the immediate Imperial circle. Thus she would appear, sensationally dressed, at a reception or soirée, moving silently through the throng on the arm of some distinguished diplomat or eminent courtier; those who could not see her well, climbed on chairs to catch a glimpse of the pagan divinity. When finally the Emperor made his entrance and she was presented, she would suddenly be wreathed in smiles and talk with great animation and abandon. 'She is very beautiful,' the Emperor remarked after first meeting her in the house of Princess Mathilde early in January, 'but she has no brains.'

Even as the Empress prepared herself for, and then slowly recovered from, the birth of the Prince Imperial, the ambitious Italian Countess dedicated herself to the campaign of (to quote her marching orders from Cavour) seducing the Emperor. Cavour was Mme de Castiglione's cousin and he had, as he put it, 'endeavoured to stimulate the patriotism of the very beautiful Castiglione' with that seduction in mind. Shortly before she left for Paris, King Victor Emmanuel had come to visit her unescorted and spoken to her of 'his misfortunes, his anxieties, the war'. On the evening before her departure she became the King's mistress. This sequence of events suggests Cavour's guiding hand. The idea that a shared mistress would represent a special link between the King of Sardinia and the Emperor of the French appealed to Cavour who hoped that it would be a simple matter for accomplices to become allies.

This coarse and cynical intrigue provided the Emperor with the first of that succession of *maîtresses-en-titre* in which his and Eugénie's marital dilemma came to be reflected before the eyes of the world. Some time during 1856, Mme de Castiglione succeeded in the principal objective of her mission, and Mérimée wrote sadly to Doña Manuela that the chamberlains at the Tuileries were treating the lady *en princesse*. The Emperor once told a friend that, where women were concerned, he did not believe in 'attack —I defend myself and sometimes I yield'. Mme de Castiglione had attacked successfully, but, although Napoleon III shared some of Louis XV's carnal weaknesses, she was no Mme de Pompadour. She ceaselessly directed his attention to Victor Emmanuel's 'anxieties and misfortunes' and, equipped with two of 'the King's code-books' by Cavour, assiduously reported on her work to Turin from where she received further instructions and encouragements in the same way. She had formed a personal conviction that she held the fate of Italy in the palm of her hand, but this self-deception of a trivial and narcissistic mind need not be taken seriously. Her political influence on the Emperor and his Italian policy remained at the level of her intellectual gifts which were those of an exceptionally extravagant butterfly. She maintained her position as the Emperor's mistress until the autumn of 1857, but her Italian patriotism was not, to the Emperor, her greatest attraction.

The Empress did not encounter the new addition to her Court until later in the year. The situation naturally brought with it a number of painful and even humiliating implications, but in the face of these provocations Eugénie acted as an Empress and not as a woman: she was free from sexual jealousy. Furthermore, the Empress was, until 1860 when the Italian Question got out of the Emperor's control, no enemy of the ideal of Italian freedom and unity: Mme de Castiglione was, therefore, no rival in this respect either. She favoured, as we saw, the constitutional form of Monarchy, she was not, as her remarks on the 'medieval' Concordat with Austria had shown, impressed by the political side of Papal rule. When she heard that Queen Isabella took the Austrian side in the Italian Question, she at once wrote to her former Sovereign in the hope of correcting that 'incomprehensible' tendency. The Empress was Austrian only North of the Alps— an attitude that was not to exercise any influence on events until the second decade of the reign.

Mme de Castiglione's appearance in Paris was ill-timed also for another reason: the Emperor's health. Dr. Fergusson had examined him and passed the result on to Clarendon. 'Great alterations of character may take place,' the Foreign Secretary wrote to Cowley on the doctor's diagnosis, 'apathy, irritation, caprice, infirmity of purpose are on the cards as the result of an exhausted nervous system and diseased organs which ensue from such exhaustion. The political results of this may be fearful and we may soon have to make allowances for physical infirmity.' Much of this forecast was to be proved correct. Meanwhile, Dr. Fergusson advised the Emperor 'to follow a regime to set himself right'. 'Notre Dame de Cavour' had arrived at an unpropitious moment in the life of a self-indulgent man.

The Empress was making a slow and painful recovery and returned to her duties only gradually. In May her presence was required for the official visit paid by the Archduke Maximilian of Austria, younger brother of the

Emperor Francis Joseph. He arrived on May 17th, and left for Brussels on May 28th. The Empress received the visitor once or twice in private, attended an unavoidable minimum of the official functions arranged for him, but as luncheon on most days was taken in private, she saw Maximilian frequently. She was curious to make the acquaintance of a prince who was reputed to be more liberal, open-minded and intelligent than other Princes of the House of Habsburg. Recently in her search for a ruler who might succeed Queen Isabella on the Spanish throne after the inevitable revolution she had favoured Maximilian's candidacy.

The Archduke, by training a sailor, had paid a visit to Spain some years earlier, and as he had stood before the royal tombs at Granada, had held in his hands the royal insignia of Ferdinand the Catholic, grandfather of the Habsburg Emperor Charles V. 'Proudly, longingly and yet sadly,' Maximilian had written then, 'I grasped the golden circlet and the mighty sword—what a seductive dream for the descendant of the Spanish Habsburgs to wield that sword in order to regain that crown. . . .' Spain and the Indies!

The visiting sailor prince was a figure of mystery also in another respect —was he or was he not the son of Napoleon II, the young eagle who had been held captive by Metternich at Schönbrunn? Many people believed that he was. His mother, the Archduchess Sophie, had shown her friendship for the romantic prisoner in the early days of her marriage to a cretinous Archduke, and it was generally said that Maximilian was her favourite son. But whatever Napoleonic secrets were wafting round this Prince, his first reactions towards the French Court were haughty, critical and caustic. 'There can be,' he wrote, 'no question of a good or bad tone here, for this Court is absolutely lacking in tone.' Naturally, he took great pains to hide these opinions from his hosts, but in his letters to Vienna he wrote as the traditionalist steeped to the finger-tips in Habsburg pride of lineage. At the state ball held at Saint-Cloud on May 22nd, 1856, he found the company 'inconceivably mixed', was distressed to see that the Empress's ladies shook hands with their mistress and showed 'a hearty friendliness', while the Emperor's suite consisted mostly of 'amateurs who are not very sure of their parts'. Someone pointed Mme de Castiglione out to him. The Italian Countess reminded him, with her 'free and independent bearing', of some dancer at the time of the Regent Orleans, but he also wrote to Francis Joseph that 'this person may prove dangerous to the domestic happiness of the Emperor and Empress'.

Like many other visitors past and future, the Archduke soon revised his first impressions. The daily luncheons in private showed him another aspect. 'The Emperor,' he wrote after one of these occasions, 'can be very attractive in his frankness and amiability. He speaks well and with animation, and the impression is heightened by a certain flash of the eyes. Great candour prevails in which I join with due moderation. The Empress also thaws rather more at these *déjeuners*. . . .' She thawed sufficiently to tell a little story that came to her mind which was that once, as she was riding through the park at Saint-Cloud, she had noticed a handsome young sailor, one of the crew of the Imperial Yacht, and so impressed was she that she turned and, followed by her groom, rode back to have another look. All her life, the Empress took a great and wholly innocent pleasure in good looks, whether in man or woman. When on another occasion she was driving with the Emperor down the long alley at Saint-Cloud and again spotted some personable youth, she asked her husband to make the carriage turn back, which he indignantly refused. He was surprised to see the youth in the livery of a groom a few days later, and when Eugénie told him that she had given him the post, became seriously annoyed: 'Ugénie, you are impossible.' During the luncheon at Saint-Cloud, the Archduke noticed that the Emperor, as he listened to her gay recital, 'pulled a long sour face and fidgeted and haw-hawed in his seat'. Reporting the incident, the Archduke wrote completely without censoriousness, and seems to have been genuinely amused by the way she described her innocuous adventure. 'The Empress's gaiety and naïve vivacity,' he commented, 'do not always seem to please her Imperial husband.'

When he finally summed up his impressions after reaching Brussels, he told his brother that the Emperor was 'one of those men who do not produce a favourable impression at first sight, but know how to attract on closer acquaintance by their calm, easy-going, and open nature. . . . I had occasion to appreciate the sound principles that seemed to inspire him. . . The Empress . . . invited me most cordially to come back soon, and was altogether extraordinarily friendly. . . . Her amiability remained unaltered up to the last moment.'

Paris as a city, for all the grandiose improvements, struck him as merely cosmopolitan where Vienna was 'more truly Imperial', Versailles was nowhere near as 'dignified as our Schönbrunn', and Hübner, although 'a man of great intelligence', took too rosy a view of everything French: 'it is my endeavour to check the expansiveness of this sentiment,' the amateur diplomat assured his Imperial brother. Finally he confessed that despite the friendliness of Their Majesties he had felt but small regret at leaving Paris—'I may say,' he added ungratefully, 'that I blessed the day upon which it was granted me to turn my back upon the centre of civilisation.'

The Archduke's visit had coincided with that of Prince Oscar of Sweden and Norway, grandson of Marshal Bernadotte, 'a tall, lean young man with a black beard,' Maximilian had written to Vienna, 'very pleasant and friendly, but not calculated to arouse my jealousy to any great extent. He has nothing of the soldier or sailor about him'. As Maximilian collected his thoughts 'at the well-ordered Court' of the King of the Belgians ('it is very much to be wondered,' he told Francis Joseph, 'whether the dynasty here will survive Leopold I'), Prince Oscar stayed on at Saint-Cloud. The Empress formed a liking for this slightly awkward Nordic Prince.

Her enfeebled health prevented her from accompanying Napoleon on his tour of the areas in central and southern France which had been hit by disastrous floods in the early summer. 'The Peace had no sooner offered us a calmer and happier future,' she wrote to Paca on June 6th, 'when the floods came to blow on all our hopes, so you must forgive me for being sad. . . .' The Emperor visited the affected areas and especially the towns where hostility towards the Empire and himself was most marked, and supervised arrangements for relief. At Lyons where the dyke near the Tête d'Or fort had burst and damage had been particularly heavy, the Emperor rode through the town a few days after the catastrophe. An enormous crowd pressed round him and his small escort, shouting 'Vive l'Empereur! Vive l'Impératrice! Vive le Prince Impérial!' and also: 'Vive le père du peuple! Vive notre sauveur!' The tour turned into a triumph. 'Whatever you may have heard of the success of the Emperor's voyage,' wrote Mérimée to Doña Manuela on June 14th, 'will be less than the truth. They have received him like a God. At Lyons, a worker with an enormous beard, which advertised the man's Socialism for miles, took the Emperor by the arm and said: "Monsieur, I don't like you, but I admire you.' With his usual impassiveness, the Emperor gave the man a few gold pieces. As the metal had an agreeable colour the uncouth Republican decided to keep the coins.'

Mérimée wrote this letter on the day of the Prince Imperial's baptism. 'The Empress,' he told Doña Manuela, 'was in great beauty and wore a diadem of diamonds worth no doubt two or three kingdoms. The Emperor also looked very impressive, and when after the ceremony he held up the child in his arms to present him to the multitudes, the enthusiasm was genuine and great. Those who know about such things find the boy enormous for his age while I, who know nothing, noticed that Mme Bruat, who was carrying him, clearly found this hard going. Everything went off very well, but, typical of our heroic nation, some details were muddled. The Archbishop was beginning to preach a sermon in Latin, when the music and the cannon outside cut him short. . . .'

June 14th was the earliest date on which the Empress was able to attend, and as towards six in the evening she drove with the Emperor in the great carriage of State down the Rue de Rivoli to the Cathedral, they were greeted with enthusiasm. No hostile note was heard. 'I do not know,' wrote Cowley with unusual warmth, 'that I ever witnessed a finer sight than the baptismal ceremonies, though the arrangements in Notre-Dame partook more of a National than ecclesiastical character. . . . The Empress was much overcome.'

The Pope had dispatched Cardinal Patrizzi to represent him as the infant's godfather at the christening; once again His Holiness had declined to travel to Paris in person. The Cardinal drove to Notre-Dame in a cortège of his own, but the people, whose piety had not as yet been offended by what came to be known as the Roman question, cheered him and his princely escort as heartily as they cheered the Marshals of France riding alongside the Imperial carriage. 'The Legate,' wrote Cowley, 'is taking a high line, they treat him exactly as a sovereign. . . .' 'I love talking to these Roman Cardinals,' confessed Hübner, 'there is something so agreeable, easy-going, paternal about them. It is clear that if one does not make their life too difficult in this world, they will endeavour to make yours as acceptable as possible in the next. . . .'

After the ceremony there was a great banquet at the Hôtel de Ville. The Empress sat between the Papal Legate and Prince Oscar of Sweden, the Emperor had his Beauharnais cousin, the Grandduchess of Baden, on his right and his Bonaparte cousin Princess Mathilde on his left. 'I never saw the Emperor in higher spirits,' Lord Cowley reported home. 'He told me that the excitements of the last fortnight had done him an infinity of good and that he never felt better in his life.' As at the Empress's side he was returning to the Tuileries at the end of the great day, he told her: 'The baptism has done more for us than a coronation.'

Five days later, Cardinal Patrizzi presented the Empress with the Papal gift of the Golden Rose. This was a magnificent rose-bush fashioned in pure gold, rising from an ornamental vase that stood thirty inches high on a base of lapis-lazuli and silver gilt with twenty-three roses of various sizes skilfully fashioned with petals and leaves and thorns. In keeping with an ancient tradition the Pope, blessing the gift, had anointed it with balsam and sprinkled it with musk—all, like the rose itself, mystical symbols the origins of which went back to Christianity's earliest times. The Papal Legate also handed the Empress a golden spray of flowers for the Pope's godson, the Prince Imperial. The presentation of these gifts took place in the chapel at Saint-Cloud, and the Empress expressed her delighted gratitude.

Prince Oscar of Sweden left Paris for London soon after the baptism and wrote to the Empress from London to thank her for the great kindness she had shown him during his stay at Saint-Cloud. The letter was written in terms of transparent sincerity. He expressed his conviction that the Emperor and the little Prince Imperial represented between them 'the surest guarantee, the one of the present tranquillity, the other of the future happiness of Europe'. As Prince and King, Oscar was to remain a faithful friend of the Bonapartes. His devotion to the Empress was heightened by the assistance she accorded him in his matrimonial projects. These ended in his marrying not, as the Empress and Queen Victoria had hoped, Princess Mary of Cambridge, the future Duchess of Teck and mother of Queen Mary, but Princess Sophie of Hesse-Nassau. Prince Oscar wrote from Coblenz saying that he wanted the Empress to be among the first to know and added that he hoped she would continue to show him the same 'maternal friendship' as during his long stay in Saint-Cloud. It was, for a man only three years younger, an extraordinary phrase to use, but it tells us much about the nature of Eugénie's friendships. Once she had given it, it remained, on her side, indestructible. He on his side remained in friendly contact with her until he died as King Oscar II of Sweden, but no longer of Norway, in 1907, and was succeeded by the Empress's godson, the late King Gustav V.

In accordance with Dr. Fergusson's instructions, the Emperor planned to go to Plombières at the beginning of July for a cure, after which the Empress hoped to go to Biarritz, 'if,' as she told Paca, 'the Emperor will let me take the baby'. She explained the programme for the summer to Lord Cowley. 'She mentioned,' the latter reported home, 'Dr. Fergusson's visit, and I said I trusted H.M. followed the advice he had given, to which she replied that he did so most scrupulously. But she is evidently very, very anxious about him, and I can see the Ministers are so likewise. After Plombières he is to go to Biarritz, after which the Empress hopes to get him to Fontainebleau and Compiègne, and to keep him as long as possible from Paris. She said that people mistook him—that because he had a calm exterior, they thought he had no feeling—whereas it was impossible to exaggerate the misery which the war had caused him, to which she attributed much of his illness.'

The reasons for the Empress's wish to keep him away from Paris are not hard to guess. Late in June the Emperor gave an evening fête among the lakes and ponds of Villeneuve l'Etang at which Mme de Castiglione appeared in a dress of transparent muslin with her rich dark hair falling over her shoulders from underneath an enormous hat adorned with marabou feathers. In the Empress's presence and that of Grand Duchess Stéphanie of Baden, the Emperor made no efforts to disguise his admiration. In the course of the evening he rowed the Countess about on the illuminated lake 'and then disappeared,' reported Lord Cowley, 'with her in certain dark walks during the whole of the evening. The poor Empress, I am told, was in a sad state and began to dance, then, not being sufficiently strong, she fell heavily. . . .' Yet nobody heard a word of complaint from the Empress. 'She behaves admirably,' reported Cowley, 'for she keeps her council to herself.' Even Paca was given no direct indication of her feelings. 'My little boy,' the Empress told her sister in June, 'is well, God be praised. That is the only encouraging thing I am able to see as I look around me at present . . .' and she went on to talk to her sister of the problems facing France that summer—the poor harvest, the floods, the debts accumulated in the years of war and cholera. 'All public calamities,' she added, 'affect me more than they do other people.'

To the Empress's relief, her programme of taking the Emperor and the little Prince to Biarritz was carried out later in the summer. The Imperial party arrived at the Villa Eugénie on August 21st and remained until the end of September. With them travelled Doctor Barthez, recently engaged as the Prince Imperial's medical attendant. He was a most amiable and level-headed observer who greatly enjoyed the agreeable informality which the Court liked to observe during these holidays on the Atlantic.

'The Emperor,' the doctor wrote home at the beginning of September, 'is greatly attached to his wife: he watches her at times with an expres-

100

sion which cannot be misunderstood. It has been said—it is said daily—
that he is not faithful to her. I have no means of affirming or denying
the fact. I can see in the Emperor's face some of the signs of sensual
need, but all the same, I am not mistaken in asserting that he has a real
affection for her, one of those affections of the heart. . . .'

Of the Empress he wrote:

'In the evening she is glowing with youth and beauty. She has no
need to select the women she invites in order to outshine them. Since
we have been in Biarritz there has almost always been a ball twice a
week. I do not think I have ever seen such a number of pretty women
together. But I cannot compare them with the Empress. She shines in
the midst of these ladies like the fairest flower in the garden. . . .'

And at the end of the six weeks he wrote: 'The Emperor loves the
Empress, contemplates her with a caressing gaze full of tenderness, is
weak where she is concerned, and yet rules her. . . .'

He found both parents doting on the little Prince and both 'perfectly
ignorant of what is fitting for a young child . . . the Emperor is always
nervous, the Empress never afraid—she looks forward and wants to
accustom the child to all sorts of things. . . .' Doctor Barthez was happy
to say that the last word was always with the child's English nurse, Miss
Shaw, 'who understands her business admirably'. 'My little boy,' the
Empress wrote to Paca, 'is very pretty, his eyes especially are superb, blue
like the sky and with long black eye-lashes. Already, he has a most intelligent smile. . . .' The six weeks on the Atlantic shore restored the Imperial
couple to health and happiness, and they returned to Paris early in October
to face the autumn season, the parties at Compiègne—and Mme de
Castiglione.

The Italian beauty and her husband had been invited to Compiègne
with other foreign diplomats: Hübner travelled down in the company of
Alfred de Vigny. The Cowleys were there, the Nuncio, the hereditary
Grand Duke of Tuscany, members of the government, the Marshals, old
James de Rothschild and, in the week set aside for the arts, Auber, Meyerbeer and Verdi, Vernet and Isabey. The Castigliones were submerged, as
it were, in a brilliant throng, and as the unfortunate husband was always
present and they were both officially sponsored by the Piedmontese lega-
tion, appearances were observed to a perfectly adequate degree.

Yet Mme de Castiglione was temperamentally incapable of leaving well
alone: at the little theatre in the Palace one evening—the Comédie Française were performing and the curtain had just gone up—she rose suddenly
from her seat and left the auditorium complaining loudly that she felt
unwell. The Emperor and Empress were in the Royal box, the Emperor
became fidgety, fingered his moustache in agitation and seemed increasingly distracted. During the first interval he left the box and did not

return, leaving the Empress to face the five hundred or so spectators as best she might.

Hübner talked with the Empress a few days later after dinner and found her in a melancholy mood. She spoke of Marie Antoinette and said that she would prefer assassination in the streets to the guillotine. 'Since my last confinement,' she added, 'my imagination has been badly shaken.' Yet she did not allow her dark moods to affect her role as hostess. 'We are all enjoying ourselves here,' wrote Sophie de Contades to her father, the maréchal de Castellane, 'the Emperor and Empress seem very gay and the little Prince magnificent. The Empress is in excellent form and followed the hunt yesterday.' 'They are both so natural and unaffected,' wrote Lord Cowley to London, 'and there is so little etiquette that this life is not disagreeable for a short time.' The diplomats departed on the last day of October, and the next group of guests arrived; the Castigliones stayed on. But then the Countess came to grief: during an excursion among the rocks at Pierrefonds she fell and sprained her wrist. Despite her pitiful cries, nobody came to her assistance, nobody offered to escort her back to the Palace, until the tactful Fleury organised an ambulance. Next day the angry beauty appeared with her arm in a sling and left for Paris soon afterwards.

Early in January 1857 Cowley reported home that the Emperor went to see Mme de Castiglione 'every evening between 11 and 12—how long he stays I cannot tell you'. The Castigliones had moved to an expensive house at No. 28, Avenue Montaigne, but the Count was often absent in Italy to restore his shattered finances. At the famous ball which Walewski gave at the newly-opened Quai d'Orsay on February 17th, she appeared as *Queen of Hearts* with chains formed by jewelled hearts wound round an almost defiantly décolleté costume in shimmering gold. 'The heart is a little low tonight,' remarked the Empress drily after glancing at these oddly placed ornaments. It was the only comment in public she was ever heard to make about this bizarre instrument of Italian propaganda.

The beginning of the end came for Mme de Castiglione one night in April 1857. The Emperor, emerging in the small hours from 28, Avenue Montaigne, had no sooner climbed into his private coupé when three men ran from the shadows and grabbed hold of the horses. The coachman fought them off with his whip and drove back to the Tuileries at speed: next day the police arrested three Italians one of whom, Tibaldi, confessed to being in Mazzini's pay. The Press remained silent for several days, but the salons soon knew all about the incident. The police had proof, in the shape of intercepted letters, that Mazzini was responsible for the attempt though not for its bungling execution. The three Italians were to be put on trial, but the Emperor was horrified to realise that his mistress's lack of discretion had enabled the conspirators to waylay him outside her house. Would her name figure in the proceedings? As the trial approached, it was pointed out to Mme de Castiglione that her presence in Paris was undesirable.

She went to spend some weeks in London and was invited to a ball at Buckingham Palace; King Leopold of the Belgians and the Duke and Duchess of Montpensier were among the other guests. 'A sensation was caused,' wrote Queen Victoria in her journal, 'by the appearance of the beautiful Countess Castiglione (the Emperor Napoleon's great admiration)—really a perfect beauty, tall, with a wonderful figure, shoulders, arms, a lovely face and features, and a sweet smile—very distinguée looking.' She was also invited to stay at Holland House where G. F. Watts began a portrait of her which remained unfinished as she soon grew bored with giving sittings. Appearances had been kept up sufficiently in Paris to make the Countess an acceptable visitor during the London season: Lady Holland, for example, who had often seen her in Paris, refused to believe the tale that she was the Emperor's mistress, saying that she would not have her in her house 'if I believed a word of it'.

On August 6th the Emperor and Empress paid a private visit to Osborne where they stayed until August 10th. The Emperor, Prince Albert, Palmerston, Clarendon and Walewski held long discussion about the 'Eastern Question', in the course of which, much to all participants' surprised relief, a full harmony of views was established, despite British suspicions concerning Franco-Russian relations and 'intrigues'. In her conversations with the Queen, the Empress showed herself to be no friend of the recent pro-Russian trend in French politics once more directed by the able and skilful Morny, now Ambassador at St. Petersburg. 'She is full of spirit and good sense,' noted the Queen, 'so kind and amiable, very accomplished and well informed.' There being no elaborate programme of entertainments on this informal occasion, the Queen held long talks with the Empress and felt a deepening respect for Eugénie's mind: 'Very well informed and read,' she wrote of her guest, 'much more serious than people give her credit for—understanding all the questions of the day. I am sure the Emperor would do well to follow *her* advice. Albert is excessively fond of her and I think few, if any, Princes have pleased him as much.'

'It is as well that we can not stay longer,' the Emperor said to Queen Victoria on their last day at Osborne, 'or we would finish up by totally forgetting France.' The Empress returned to Saint-Cloud in the knowledge that, for her at any rate, the friendship with the Queen was unimpaired. Clarendon, moreover, had said in her hearing that it had been 'a great blessing' to have the visit at this particular juncture. Tibaldi's attempt on the Emperor's life, his trial which began later in August, were not mentioned during the visit, although the instigator, Mazzini, was living in England. During the same month of August he was granted asylum for the second time on his return from yet another unsuccessful enterprise to stir up republican risings in the Massa-Carrara region. 'The execution of the attempt on Napoleon,' Mazzini had written after Tibaldi's failure, 'is a vital thing for Italy: almost everything is bound up with it.' Both Emperor and Empress were aware of this constant, if hidden, danger, but tactfully did not refer to Mazzini's presence in England while they were the Queen's personal guests.

Soon after their return, Tibaldi's trial showed London to be a centre of the hatching of lethal plots, but this aspect was dealt with as quietly as possible, there was no outcry against England, and Tibaldi was sentenced to transportation for life. The location of the attempt caused some embarrassment, but the defendants were instructed merely to refer to 'No. 28' without giving the rest of the address. Naturally the smart world knew the full address and made the appropriate comments. The Emperor, complaining that Mme de Castiglione 'has the need to be talked about', decided on rupture. It was done with kindliness and grace: in October 1857 the Countess was once more invited to Compiègne, but before the year was out she was back in Turin where she took up residence in a villa in the hills outside that only *seemed* inaccessible.

'Hardly had I entered life,' she wrote pathetically, 'when my role was over.' She was not yet twenty-one, and perhaps she felt that more than playing a role was over. Although we cannot share her own inflated opinion of her mission we may pity her for the illusion of grandeur and destiny to which she clung long after the memory of her brief sway in Imperial Paris had vanished. The short season of Napoleonic favour was the only period of her life in which she was happy and, so she thought, successful. Others had contributed to the deception, and later on life was to exact a heavy price for the brief moment when she had lived so daringly beyond her emotional, intellectual—and financial resources.

CHAPTER 7

'How did you know that I cough?' wrote the Empress to Paca on January 2nd, 1858. 'I have not mentioned it to you or Mama in order not to alarm you, and really it is nothing. The doctors want to condemn me to silence, but at these receptions I have to talk to everybody. What would commerce say, what would the women and the young ladies say, if I shut myself away without giving balls? And if you give them you must go to them. Pale or pink—what does it matter? The winter season must be gay, that is what matters. I am like a soldier on the day of battle: I cannot be ill, and the world is my battlefield. Do not worry, God gives us health when we have duties to fulfil. . . .'

She did not know how true her image of the battlefield turned out to be. Twelve days later the Italian question exploded literally in her face. She and the Emperor were due at a gala at the Opéra in the Rue Lepelletier on January 14th, and as the Imperial procession with its escort of lancers swung into the private carriage way, three bombs were hurled at it from across the road by Italian conspirators who were acting under the leadership of Felice Orsini, Mazzini's disciple and apostate friend. The first explosion, extinguishing all the lights, turned what had been a boisterous street scene into a tragedy of unnerving horror as the darkness was rent by the sound of crashing glass, falling horses and the cries of the dying and the wounded. Two further explosions shook the street seconds later. The Imperial carriage came to an abrupt halt after the first explosion, and the Empress saw its two doors being wrenched open on either side of her. She thought of death by dagger of which the Emperor had spoken so often and was surprised that she did not feel more fear: then she realised that the intruders were not assassins but police agents. She descended into the street, followed by the Emperor. 'Don't bother about us,' she said calmly, 'such things are our profession. Look after the wounded,' and with the Emperor walked into the foyer. The Emperor for a moment seemed to wish to turn back and talk to the wounded, but the Empress firmly piloted him inside: '*Pas si bête!*' she managed to whisper.

Inside, Fleury, Bacciochi and Duke Ernest of Saxe-Coburg, Prince Albert's brother, rushed up to meet them. It was found that the Emperor's nose had been slightly grazed and that the lid of the Empress's left eye was bleeding. Her white dress, in the few moments she had stood in the street, had been bespattered with blood. Enormous relief was felt when it was realised that the Sovereigns had escaped serious injury. All accounts,

105

including that given by Prince Albert's brother to Queen Victoria the following day, agree that throughout the drama the Empress never once lost control of herself while the Emperor at first was badly shaken. 'The Empress wonderfully composed and courageous,' the Queen noted after her talk with Ernest on January 15th, 'even more so than the Emperor. They remained through the whole performance.' Hübner heard from another eye-witness that the Emperor 'seemed completely demoralised whereas the Empress was admirable in her intrepid calm'. As they entered their box, the audience rose and greeted them with an ovation. In the interval they showed themselves on the balcony outside and the crowds in the street below gave them a rousing cheer. After the performance, the people of Paris escorted the Imperial carriage back to the Tuileries, and there officials and courtiers were awaiting in the public rooms to express their congratulations. They had already congratulated each other that their world had not gone down amid the bombs of the assassins.

Next day it was found that the dead counted ten, and the wounded some 140. The police had been able to arrest the culprits all of whom, including Orsini, showed a most elementary lack of foresight and nerve. Bombs were then a novelty in politics, and the police found that those used by Orsini and his crew had been manufactured in Birmingham. The assassins, moreover, had all recently arrived from England with passports made out in English names. 'Working people,' wrote Mérimée to Doña Manuela, 'are saying that if the English won't hand over the scoundrels who are behind all these assassination attempts, it will be necessary to go and fetch them.' France in the 1850s had become a peace-loving country, more in love with comfort than with glory, but war with England was still widely regarded as an enthralling possibility. Morny, now back from Russia and recently appointed President of the Chamber of Deputies, saw to it that this easily inflamed anti-British emotion was kept at boiling point, since it fitted in well with his determined backing of a Franco-Russian alliance. When on January 16th Senators and Deputies went to the Tuileries to offer their congratulations on the miraculous escape, Morny fulminated against the nest of vipers across the Channel where refuge was given to murderers and enemies of order. For weeks afterwards the columns of the *Moniteur* were filled with letters from the Colonels of various regiments written mostly on a vehement *Gott strafe England* note. These outpourings were gleefully reproduced by London papers. 'If your Majesty,' wrote one of the Colonels, 'should want soldiers to get at these wild beasts [the refugees] even in the recesses of their den, we humbly beseech you to choose the 82nd regiment as the vanguard of that army.'

The Emperor and Empress, not for a moment sharing this collective hysteria, did what they could to counteract it. When Granier de Cassagnac, that eloquent spokesman of Bonapartism in the Chamber and the Press, showed the Empress a virulent article which, in the most humiliating terms, demanded reparation, she begged him not to publish it: 'England,' she told him, 'will soon regain her sense of justice.' In common with other crowned heads, Queen Victoria had telegraphed her felicitations, and the French Sovereigns wrote friendly and affectionate letters in reply. 'The hand of Providence,' wrote the Empress, 'made itself clearly felt, for the Emperor and I were the only people in our carriage to escape injury. . . .' 'In the first flush of excitement,' wrote the Emperor, 'the French are determined to find accomplices everywhere. I find it hard to resist the demands for extreme measures which I am asked to take, but this event will not make me deviate from my habitual calm.'

The Empress insisted on a minimum of fuss. When Doña Manuela wrote from Madrid blaming the whole attempt on the revolutionary tendencies of the French, the Empress wrote back reminding her mother that the only people to blame were foreigners, namely Italians. 'I have,' she wrote, 'experienced both: the bombs of the assassins and the enthusiasm of the people here afterwards. Far from blaming the French, my dear mother, you should praise them because from them came our first consolation after the attempt.' When she heard that Doña Manuela had organised a *Te Deum* and asked the whole of Madrid to it, she became extremely indignant at this public display of what should be merely family feeling: 'There is something that repels me,' she wrote to Paca, 'in inviting multitudes of people in order to shed tears in front of them and ask for their pity. Had I been alone in my room in the evening of the 14th, I might have cried, but the public were present and nobody can say that they saw a single tear in my eyes. . . .'

But they were not allowed to pass the incident over without fuss. Not only was it used by the politicians to demonstrate to the world that England harboured dangerous criminals and must be taught a lesson, but the French Ministers who had been so dramatically reminded that their power and prosperity depended on the survival of a single person insisted on all necessary safeguards being taken to guarantee the future of the régime in the event of another attempt being more successful. They prevailed on the Emperor to issue legislation designed to deal the political enemy a mortal blow. The Emperor himself, moreover, drew from Orsini's attempt the conviction that the Italian question must be solved in the interests of his own survival. These issues were all tackled in the course of February, partly by administrative action and partly by secret diplomacy. Orsini's bombs caused therefore one of the great turning points in the history of the Second Empire, even as the Royalist conspiracy of Cadoudal and his friends had forced the First Empire into paths from which there was no turning back. What the execution of the Duke of Enghien in March 1804 was to Napoleon I, the Orsini affair was to his nephew and successor, for it led to the Law of Public Security of February 1858.

Before dealing with that piece of repressive legislation, however, we may glance at the changes which the situation created by Orsini's outrage brought for the Empress. It was announced early in February that in the event of the Emperor's death, the Empress would become Regent on the Prince Imperial's behalf. She would govern with the assistance of a Regency

Council consisting of the Archbishop of Paris, the Minister of State, the Presidents of the Senate, Chamber of Deputies and Council of State, of Marshal Pélissier (now Duke of Malakoff), Persigny, and members of the Imperial family. The announcement was greeted with great acclaim, especially by the army, whose spokesmen (still writing in the *Moniteur*) wrote enthusiastically of closing the ranks round a young and beautiful Empress. Some recalled the example of the Empress Maria Theresa appealing to Hungarian nobles with her infant son on her arm, while others spoke of a new Blanche of Castile. Only the salons did not share the enthusiasm: 'Blanche—yes,' they said of Eugénie *chez* Pozzo di Borgo, 'of Castile, yes: Blanche of Castile—no.' It scarcely mattered. Hübner, for all his predilection for the past, wrote that 'these salons keep going on memories rather than hopes, they live by epigrams, but, politically, they don't count.' He himself fully approved of the Empress's new dignity: 'The establishment of the Regency,' he wrote to Vienna, 'has the advantage of removing all uncertainty immediately after the Emperor's death. The Empress, by virtue of the courage she showed at the Opéra, has greatly gained in popularity, and her nomination as Regent has been well received.' In his diary, the Ambassador noted: 'People here are so exalted at the picture of a beautiful woman with her baby in her arms saving France with the help of an heroic army that the Emperor, apparently about to be removed by some exploding bomb at any moment, has practically become a negligible factor.' He saw the Sovereigns a few days later at a ball which the Empress had insisted should be held and found that 'the Emperor seemed distracted and almost depressed. The Empress, on the contrary, innocently enjoys her heroic triumph. She has recovered her spirits and looks content'.

The second measure of legislation caused by Orsini's attempt affected the whole structure and inner bias of the Empire. This was the Law of Public Security, popularly christened The Law of the Suspects. It has been said that this law was passed less as a consequence of Orsini's attempt than as a response to the elections of June 1857 in which five 'irreconcilable' Republican opponents of the Empire had been elected as Deputies of the new Chamber. The Emperor had, in fact, been under considerable pressure from his Ministers all along to pass a law against the political enemy of the interior, but had so far resisted. It was true that the Emperor had less arbitrary power than the Prince-President had held immediately after the coup d'état, but by inflicting the Law of the Suspects on the country, the Empire reverted, not to the reforms of the Hundred Days and the reign of Napoleon II, but to the First Empire in its most autocratic days.

The new law enabled the government to punish and silence all those holding inconvenient opinions, all grumblers, all *frondeurs*, all with oppositional tendencies and convictions. The Minister of the Interior, and through him every Prefect in the provinces, could remove from public life all 'who manoeuvre inside the country and abroad to disturb the public peace', and they could fine, intern or deport all those who 'excited hatred or distrust of the Emperor's government '. One paragraph mentioned those who had been sentenced 'in May or June 1848, in June 1849 or December 1851' and had since shown signs of a relapse: it applied retrospectively as well. Other offences listed included plotting to incite civil war, illegal employment of armed force, destruction and pillage of public property, and the manufacture of forged passports. People found guilty of any of these offences were now to be deprived of all legal security and safeguards and there stood no protecting force between them and an arbitrary administration of justice. Before the bill became law the liberal Billaut resigned from the Ministry of the Interior and was replaced by General Espinasse who had made a European name for himself by the manner in which he had closed down the Assembly of the Roman Republic in 1849.

Among the five irreconcilables elected in 1857 was Emile Ollivier whose comment on 'the Emperor and his Montijo' has been quoted on an earlier page. To his honour the young lawyer, who was also a skilful and effective speaker, rose in the Chamber of Deputies and in a maiden speech attacked the bill. 'Since when is it customary to deprive one's enemy of justice?' he asked. He castigated the lawlessness of the new measure—'if you violate the rights of a single person, you violate the rights of all,' and he accused the government of wishing to proceed 'against those who do not conspire, whom you cannot charge with a single offence, but whose attitude and tone of voice you do not like—those who criticise, who console discouraged friends with a few manly words, who have voted wrongly or are disliked by the police . . .' He ended with these words:

'You have ruled for nine years. You are at peace with the Monarchs of Europe. You have a strong and war-like army, an able police force, an enormous budget. Strategic roads cross the capital and you have erected formidable citadels. There is no freedom. The greatest freedom of all, that of the Press, consists merely in the right of saying things which do not displease the Minister of the Interior. And now you ask us for a Law of Public Safety! Where will you stop?'

Morny allowed him to finish. When the vote was taken twenty-four deputies came out against the law. Only one voice was raised against it in the Senate, but it was that of General MacMahon.

Thus the bill passed into law and no one then alive in France escaped its nemesis. Not all the Emperor's genuine liberalism and progressiveness, not all the Empress's dedicated intelligence and charity, could redeem the terrible effect which this law, passed under the impact of an outrage committed by a few uprooted desperados, left on the body and conscience of France. Having imposed the law in his name, the Emperor at once endeavoured to soften it, to water it down, to explain it away, to limit it to the most dangerous suspects only. Its immediate consequence was the arrest and deportation of no more than 400 persons; of its application in the future the reign's most able conservative critic, Pierre de la Gorce, has written that 'although it remained as a threat, it was hardly ever used'. And yet it was the Second Empire's most fateful internal measure. One typical example of it being applied may be quoted here although it did not occur until some years afterwards. The Prefect of Nantes one day in 1862 arrested a respected lawyer on a charge of disaffection. After a month in prison without trial, he was sentenced to deportation and had already reached Marseilles when he was pardoned and released following a public protest organised by the citizens of Nantes, but not before his son had exclaimed: 'I will avenge you.' The son's name was Georges Clemenceau. The law remained in force until 1869. It may have been sparingly used, but the Emperor was never able to undo its demoralising effect and it truly became his shirt of Nessus. It affected, one need hardly add, the Empress and the Prince Imperial as intimately and inexorably as it did the work and character of the officials and soldiers who had proposed it. The Emperor might plead that the measure was forced on him by the Ministers, a way of reasoning that might well explain why Hübner found him looking so sad and depressed. For the first time since the coup d'état the Party of Order had forced their will on the Emperor.

The trial of Orsini and his consorts—Rudio, Pieri, Gomez—opened on February 25th and took two days. The task of defending the tyrannicide was given to Jules Favre, another of the five irreconcilable Republicans and, like Ollivier, an impressive and ingenious orator. The prosecution achieved an initial effect by producing the blind and maimed in the court-room as irrefutable evidence of Orsini's terrible handiwork, but this paled into insignificance when on the second day Favre read a letter which his client had written to the Emperor. Most members of the public present in the court-room had lived these many years in immunity from most forms of freedom of speech and so could hardly believe their ears when counsel read the lapidary sentences which the prisoner in the dock had addressed to the Emperor of the French. 'Remember, Sire,' Orsini exhorted his intended victim, 'that as long as Italy is not independent, the peace of Europe and of Your Majesty is but an idle dream.' 'Is that quite clear?' Hübner added ironically when quoting this threat in his diary. Like the rest of France and Europe, he had read it in the *Moniteur*, where the trial was reported with a fullness of detail that no debate in the Chamber of Deputies could hope to rival. What was the explanation of the amazing latitude accorded to the defence and the press? The initiated knew that Pietri, Chief of the Paris Police, visited Orsini in his cell and reported to the Emperor and Empress what the prisoner had said. These visits continued even after the lower Court had sentenced Orsini, Rudio and Pieri to death, and Gomez to transportation in perpetuity. The Court of Appeal then reviewed the sentences and during this interval of two weeks it became known that both the Emperor and Empress were hoping to exercise their prerogative of mercy and pardon the culprits.

This, on the face of it, was a repetition of what had happened when Pianori had been sentenced to death after his attempt in April 1855. Then, as will be recalled, the Emperor appeared 'strangely agitated' and wanted to pardon his assailant. The Orsini case had already produced far wider international repercussions, had affected relations with England over the refugee question and had, since the reading of the defendant's letter in open court, brought the Italian question into the foreground. The Emperor knew that this desire to show clemency was viewed with suspicion abroad. Nevertheless he sounded foreign diplomats on their reaction to a pardon, and thus gave Lord Cowley the impression that he was 'regularly bitten with this miscreant'.

The Empress for her part realised that Orsini martyred by the régime he had come to destroy constituted a far greater danger to the safety of the Emperor and her son than Orsini pardoned and forgotten. She therefore moved heaven and earth to help the Emperor in his dilemma. The thought of violent death had always an unsettling effect on her, and although the Court had expressly found the defendants not guilty on the additional charge of attempting to cause the Empress's death, she was haunted by the thought of being responsible for the execution of the three Italian fanatics. In addition, her personal compassion had been roused when she received the wives of Orsini and Rudio who with their children had travelled to Paris to plead before her for their husbands' lives. Orsini's daughter remembered all her life 'the kindness which the gracious lady showed us poor orphans at the time of our father's impending death'. These appeals to her sense of charity explain her vehemence, her excitability, her tears, but they must not make us forget that throughout she was pleading a course which the Emperor wanted to pursue in 1858 as in 1855.

The Court of Appeal confirmed the sentences on March 11th and the final word now rested with the Emperor. He held a Council of State on March 12th in which he informed the Ministers that he and the Empress wished to exercise their prerogative of mercy. The Ministers attempted to dissuade him, but he seemed firm and after a protracted discussion they offered their collective resignation. Mgr. Morlot, Archbishop of Paris, suggested as a compromise that Rudio, the only defendant to have asked for mercy, should be pardoned but the other two guillotined. When the Emperor continued to resist, Fould finally implored him to remember 'that French blood had been shed in the Rue Lepelletier'. This appeal seemed to swing the Emperor round, and he yielded. Rudio was pardoned, and in the early hours of March 13th, Orsini mounted the fifteen steps to the guillotine. 'Viva l'Italia! Viva la Francia!' he called out in ringing tones that could be heard by spectators on the farthest fringes of the crowd.

A further blow was in store for the Empress in this crucial affair, and it came from England. Yielding to public pressure, the Emperor, through Cowley and other channels, started negotiations with Palmerston's government to obtain a stricter treatment of the political refugees harboured by England. Mazzini, Ledru-Rollin and Victor Hugo were specifically mentioned in these communications, but the laws of England enabled the Government (who listened not unsympathetically to the Emperor's representations) merely to arrest a certain Dr. Bernard, a French left-wing refugee living in London since 1851, who had materially assisted Orsini, and to issue warrants for the arrest of some British subjects known to have conspired with him. 'We hope,' wrote Queen Victoria in her journal, 'to do something to soothe the excitement and irritation in France, for certainly were similar assassins to be tolerated in France and come over to attempt to do something against us here, the whole British nation would demand instant reparation.' On this principle, Lord Palmerston in February submitted his Conspiracy Bill the purpose of which was to give the authorities the power of convicting, and, in the case of aliens, deporting, those found guilty of the new felony of conspiracy to murder. This was passed by a good majority, but when a few days later Milner-Gibson, an intimate friend of Mazzini, moved an amendment the wording of which expressed a strong criticism of the government's conduct since January 14th, this was also carried by a majority, though a less strong one. Palmerston made a furious speech and shocked the House by shaking his fist at his opponents. He resigned on the same day, and a short-lived Tory government under Lord Derby took over. On April 19th Dr. Bernard was tried on the charge of having been instrumental in causing the death of a French police sergeant. The judge directed the jury to find the defendant guilty, but, to everybody's astonishment, the jury acquitted him.

The Empress felt that this was hardly to be borne, and on April 18th she decided to address a letter to Lord Cowley. She was writing (so she told him) not in order to interfere in matters outside her province, but for the sake of her own peace of mind.

'You know,' she went on, 'better than anyone how great is my personal affection for England (I leave politics on one side), I admire the English powers of reasoning, the proverbial common sense which allows your people to be free in every way, for they can weigh things dispassionately, and thus justice can be done.'

And then she told the British Ambassador how she viewed Bernard's acquittal:

'Here we have two men, the one a murderer (as in your innermost heart you must know him to be) accused by the Public Prosecutor, and the other the Emperor, accused by Bernard's Advocate of being morally responsible for the crime. The former was acquitted; what can I say, I the wife of the latter? . . . You must not think that I desire the death of any man. I pleaded for Orsini in the face of public opinion, so hateful do I find bloodshed: what I regret is that moral sanction should have been given to such an act. . . . I leave to others the language of diplomacy, I can only pour out my feelings, not to the English Ambassador, but to a valued friend who will excuse the warmth of my letter. . . .'

In her grief, the Empress was consoled to learn that her feelings were shared by many English friends. Lady Combermere wrote to a close friend of the Empress on April 23rd:

'I went in the evening to the Duchess of Northumberland and to Lady Derby. There I heard much distress expressed at Mr. James's [Bernard's defence counsel] unwarrantable impertinence. The great world, as well as the small, is indignant at the result of the trial and the circumstances attending it, which are a disgrace to the English character. The acclamations proceeded from the Refugees and their friends, and outside the court from the lowest rabble. Public opinion in the respectable classes has but one cry of indignation and regret. The Army, such as it is, is, in England, as you know, essentially conservative and great admirers of the Emperor and of the wisdom with which he directs European affairs.'

When later in April Lord Cowley spent a few days in England, he found that the Queen shared the general indignation at what she called 'the most unfortunate acquittal of Bernard'. She used strong language saying that it had all been due entirely 'to the cowardice of the Jury and the shameful behaviour of the public on the occasion'. Cowley told her how deeply the Empress had felt it, while Lady Cowley told the Queen that throughout the Orsini affair the Empress's conduct had been 'admirable and devoted'.

Earlier in 1858, the Empress had been in touch with the Queen in a more pleasant context. On January 25th, the marriage between the Princess Royal and Crown Prince Frederick of Prussia had been celebrated, the Queen calling the occasion 'the second most eventful day in my life'. The Empress had sent Mme de La Bédoyère over with presents for her friend Vicky who had worshipped her so greatly during the State Visits. The presents, which included a splendid dress of *points d'Alençon* for the bride, were accompanied by personal letters of felicitation from the Empress. Lord Cowley gave a reception in Paris on the day, and despite strong advice to the contrary, the Emperor and Empress attended. The new Crown Princess of Prussia left London for Potsdam early in February, and in January 1859 their eldest son, the future Kaiser Wilhelm II, was born.

CHAPTER 8

IN APRIL 1858, the Emperor appointed Marshal Pélissier, Duke of Malakoff, to the London Embassy in succession to Persigny—'a great compliment to us,' noted Queen Victoria in her journal. The Marshal was the Empire's most renowned soldier, and in sending him to London the Emperor effectively counteracted the impression left by the Colonels who had rattled their sabres so resoundingly in the columns of the *Moniteur*. Mérimée who visited his friend Panizzi in London during April saw the new Ambassador pay a visit to the British Museum and wrote to Doña Manuela that three hundred street urchins had been running behind his carriage shouting hurrah. He also told her—Doña Manuela was in Paris at the time—that everybody he had seen had apologised to him for Bernard's acquittal. As Mérimée's visiting list included the Palmerstons in Piccadilly, the Hollands in Kensington, a good many Members of Parliament and the recently widowed Lady Ely, this information carried authentic weight, and soothed the Empress's anger at the Bernard verdict.

An interesting opportunity for one of the Empress's friendly disagreements with Hübner was provided by the question of the Danubian principalities of Moldavia and Wallachia, which nominally belonged to Turkey, but had since the Crimean War shown a marked desire for union and independence. Austria insisted on these provinces remaining as separate entities under Turkish suzerainty, while Napoleon, applying the principle of nationality, favoured their union and independence. 'We want a Europe based on treaties,' wrote Hübner, 'and they a Europe based on nationality, which would mean the end of Austria, *finis Austriae*.' The problem was being thrashed out in ambassadorial conferences held at the Quai d'Orsay between the envoys of England, Austria, Prussia, Russia and Piedmont under the chairmanship of the French Foreign Minister. 'The principalities,' said the Empress to Hübner, 'want union, as you can see.' 'No, Madame, I can only see wild intrigues going on in that region.' 'Not at all,' she replied, 'it is the national wish, they want union.' Austria continued to oppose union, but some years later could not prevent the two principalities being united in the 'one and indivisible' kingdom of Rumania under Prince Charles of Hohenzollern-Sigmaringen—one of the major achievements of the Second Empire.

Despite her predilection for England and Austria the Empress was far from uncritical of the limitations and occasional perversities shown by the governments of these powers. She always hoped that Austria would show a greater readiness to come to terms with the inevitable and not cling to the out-moded concept of keeping down the nationalities of Europe by force, as she did in the occupied provinces of Lombardy and Venetia. There, as the Empress knew only too well, the 'national wish' had been expressed with the utmost clarity these last few years, since the Peace of Paris and earlier. When the young Emperor of Austria and his beautiful consort had paid official visits to Venice and Milan early in 1857, they had everywhere encountered the most humiliating demonstrations of hostility from the nobility and middle classes. In Venice, they walked across St. Mark's Square to the Cathedral through a huge crowd which observed a glacial silence; at a reception in the Doge's Palace thirty out of an invited 130 members of the nobility put in an appearance; at a gala performance in the Teatro Fenice the boxes of the aristocracy remained empty. Silence surrounded their brief and embarrassed appearances in Vicenza, Brescia, Verona, and the authorities had to fill La Scala at Milan with officials and even domestic servants in order to avoid a repetition of the Venetian débâcle.

In 1858, Archduke Maximilian, the Empress's visitor of 1856, was appointed governor of Lombardy and Venetia in succession to old Field Marshal Radetzki. The young Prince, preceded by his reputation as a liberal ambitiously bent on improvement and reform, soon found that he was a mere figure-head, that his various suggestions were ignored and frustrated by the reactionary bureaucrats of Vienna. He experienced, as he wrote to the Archduchess Sophie, 'private friendliness and public repudiation [which] shows how powerless I am, but it also shows how irresponsibly the government trifles with the good-will of the masses'. Like Eugénie, he complained bitterly about Büol 'who gets more and more inept'. Needless to say the country's extreme anti-Austrian feelings and Maximilian's helpless isolation were well-known at the Tuileries, even before the Emperor gave his Italian policy priority over all else soon after the Orsini outrage. Yet the Italian Question became the first major operation of the reign in which the Emperor did not take the Empress as fully into his confidence as he had done on earlier occasions. For better or worse, he preferred in this problem to act as his own conscience, to enter new commitments and responsibilities without consulting his English allies, his Ministers or his wife.

Instead, he engaged in a number of clandestine meetings and negotiations with emissaries from Turin, the most crucial of which was his famous encounter with Cavour at Plombières in July 1858. On that occasion three points were agreed upon: that the might of France would support Piedmont in a war against Austria; that Piedmont would cede Savoy and Nice to France; and that the Emperor's cousin Plon-Plon would marry Princess Clotilde, Victor Emmanuel's youngest daughter. All that remained to be done thereafter was to find a cause for war which was 'non-revolutionary', could be justified before public opinion in France and Europe and would not make Piedmont appear as the aggressor. The expulsion of the Austrians from Northern Italy was to be followed by the founding of an Italian Confederation in which a Northern, Central and Southern State were to be united under the Presidency of the Pope. 'I must treat the Pope carefully,' were the Emperor's final words to Cavour, 'in order not to arouse the Catholics in France against me.'

The Empress, like the rest of France, remained ignorant of this pact until November. The programme for the summer of 1858 included a prolonged tour of Brittany by the Emperor and herself the opening event of which was to be a meeting at Cherbourg with Queen Victoria and Prince Albert. It may well be that the Emperor, knowing Eugénie's transparent honesty and impulsiveness, excluded her from his confidence for tactical reasons. He knew her gift for dissembling to be small, her sense of discretion far from strong: in confidential conversations with her august friend, the Queen of England, Eugénie might well say more than suited the Emperor at this critical stage of his great scheme.

Another lady was admitted to the secret, however. Mme Walewska, the Foreign Minister's beautiful Florentine wife, had succeeded Mme de Castiglione in the Emperor's favour. Attractive, ambitious and clever, she was very much *une femme politique*, and some people thought that the Emperor allowed her husband to remain in office mainly for the benefit of Madame his wife. Walewski, at no time one of the giants of diplomacy, certainly knew nothing about his master's Italian policy, but his wife was in a different case. The Emperor's new liaison did not escape comment for long and when in May 1858 Hübner spent an evening at Étioles, the Walewskis' country house that had once belonged to Mme de Pompadour, he heard it whispered that Étioles had become a place of worship again—*Étioles est rendu au culte*. Fortunately Mme Walewska was less ostentatious or dramatic than Mme de Castiglione, although she may have prided herself too much on hailing from the city of Machiavelli. At all events the new liaison was infinitely more dangerous for the Empress than any other during the reign. Mme Walewska, as a political woman, was the Empress's enemy. Even as Ambassadress in London, she had expressed her opposition to Eugénie's marriage, as Queen Victoria had noted once or twice. As the Emperor's new *maîtresse-en-titre* she not only monopolised his confidence while he pursued his intricate Italian schemes but began to whisper certain insinuations about the Empress's attitude into the ears of foreign diplomats such as Cowley. The latter, and some of his colleagues, naturally believed her, both as the wife of the Foreign Minister and the Emperor's mistress, to be well-informed, and she cleverly exploited her advantages to the full. She was justifiably taken more seriously than *Notre-Dame de Cavour* had been. Among other things, she implanted in Cowley's mind the notion that if the Empress disagreed with her husband in matters of policy, she did so for reasons of marital resentment. Cowley, not a subtle psychologist at the best of times, had reported to Clarendon in this sense when, in the summer of 1857, there had been an open disagreement between Emperor and Empress over a Spanish problem. The Emperor had favoured armed

116

intervention in the latest uprising in Madrid, but the Empress had opposed it. She had not thought that Spain—which, as she said, had 'thanks to a thousand stupidities lost her European position as a power of even the second rank'—was worth the risk of a major Anglo-French discord. Walewski, on the other hand, was, like the Emperor, an interventionist. Although in the end the Emperor decided to let Spain work out her own salvation, Cowley, faced with the novel experience of Emperor and Empress expressing diametrically opposite views, jumped to the obvious, to the far too obvious, conclusion that the Empress attacked her husband's Spanish policy for domestic and marital reasons (the Spanish incident had occurred at the height of the Castiglione liaison). This was what Mme Walewska wanted him to think. It was a plausible explanation, avidly accepted— and spread—by diplomats and men of State who had little time for the more complex aspects of Eugénie's psychology.

It took the Empress many years of persistent application and hard work to inspire some of these men, including Cowley, with a greater respect for the objectivity and intelligence of her political mind. At the beginning of her reign she was handicapped by being a woman and by being a beautiful woman. She also handicapped herself, in those early years in her *métier*, by her impulsive and often ill-timed honesty, even though she was learning to confine her verbal exuberance more and more to the circle of her closer friends, including her ladies-in-waiting. Mme Walewska belonged to this intimate circle, for it was the Empress's deliberate policy to show the world that the Emperor's mistress was also her personal friend—a further act of renunciation which she felt she owed to her position as Empress. By setting an example she hoped to silence gossip and lessen the ordinary consequences of scandal. Yet Mme Walewska was thus enabled to tell those she wanted to impress and influence what the Empress 'really' thought of various major issues. Being regarded, rightly, as 'a usually well-informed source', her tales were, more often than not, believed. However, unlike the recent Spanish crisis, the Italian question did not furnish her with any opportunities of spreading gossip about the Empress crossing the Emperor's path with her opposing views, for when that fateful problem at length became the great European crisis of 1859, the Empress supported her husband in his difficulties without reluctance and reserve. Mme Walewska's greatest opportunities did not arrive until after 1860.

Fontainebleau, Brittany, Biarritz, Compiègne made up the Empress's programme for 1858. The British Royal visit to Cherbourg took place from August 4th-6th and was less successful than former encounters. The Queen came filled with alarm at French naval armaments. A few days before leaving for Cherbourg she had talked to Lord Derby 'of our Navy and the formidable fact of our being for the first time in our history *inferior* to the French, the consequent immense danger to this country which would soon lapse into a second-rate power. . . .' What she saw at Cherbourg did not reassure her. 'Steam is the chief cause of it,' she wrote gloomily. She also had heard rumours about the Emperor's cult of Mme Walewska and, although she had always shown a great liking for her when she had been ambassadress in London, the Queen now refrained rather pointedly from kissing Mme Walewska when she was presented with the other ladies. Consequently neither she nor her husband attended the dinner which the Emperor and Empress gave to their visitors on board the battleship *La Bretagne*. The Emperor offered a toast in honour of the friendship between the two Sovereigns and the desire of the two nations to live in peace and friendship. When it came to Prince Albert's turn to reply, the Queen felt that this was 'the dreadful moment for my dear husband, which was terrible to me, and which I should never wish to go through again. He did it very well, though he hesitated once. I sat shaking, with my eyes *cloués sur la table*.' The Prince Consort's mistrust of the Emperor had grown considerably in the last two years, and he was at this time a great champion of an Anglo-Austrian alliance.

On August 7th Queen Victoria and her party returned to Osborne, from where they left for Prussia on the 12th. The Emperor and Empress began their tour of Brittany. Hopefully, the salons of Paris had prophesied disaster for this visit to France's most Royalist province, where the fierce battles between the *Chouans* of the Royal and Catholic Army and the soldiers of the Revolution and Empire were still a living memory. Some thought it might be as calamitous as the visits to Venice and Milan by the Austrian Sovereigns. Instead, the tour was a triumphant success: 'The Emperor,' wrote Hübner, 'is being received with enthusiasm in the country of the Cadoudals and La Rochejaqueleins. Who would have thought it possible?' The Bourbons, as Mérimée reminded Doña Manuela in a letter, had never bothered to 'pay a single visit to the Bretons who have shed their blood for them'. This remarkable circumstance may have given the Breton cheers an added fervour, but that maritime province was also highly delighted with the pronounced naval touch which the Emperor bestowed on the whole occasion. Aboard *La Bretagne*, which was escorted by a splendid squadron of warships, the Sovereigns sailed along the coast and went ashore to be welcomed vociferously in the various townships, flourishing once more thanks to the Emperor's ship-building programme.

Among the spectators at Brest was a Mlle Bouvet, daughter and granddaughter of sailors. At the ball given at the Corn Exchange she watched the entrance of the Sovereigns to the strains of *Partant pour la Syrie*:

'From that moment,' she wrote, 'everything seemed to vanish from my sight—the banquet, the people, the lights, and I remained unconscious as in a trance, in which the Empress alone appeared to me as a lovely apparition. With a graceful and stately movement, she gave a kind of circular salute, taking in the vast assembly with one look of her bright, sweet blue eyes. She was graceful and stately in her deportment, and her walk was light and supple: but what enhanced her unequalled charms above all else was the evident harmony between her physical appearance and her moral personality.'

118

The Empress, for her part, noticed the young girl among the throng, enquired who she was and as at the Emperor's side she made a final tour of the ball-room before leaving, stood and addressed a few words to Mlle Bouvet. 'Trembling with emotion and pleasure, my only replies were *Oui, Madame* and *Non, Madame*, spoken with great shyness.'

At St. Malo a few days later, the Empress again saw the timid and stammering young girl, and again spoke to her with great affability: when Mlle Bouvet stood among the crowd next morning watching the Sovereigns' departure, the Empress raised her hand to her lips in a silent salute. 'Little did I suspect,' writes Mlle Bouvet, 'that these few things sealed my destiny.' Six years later the Empress heard that the young woman and her mother had been left penniless by the father's death and, remembering these moments among the crowded visit to Brittany, made Mlle Bouvet a member of her household. To this happy story we owe books of delightful memoirs about the Empress and her reign, for from Mlle Bouvet the Empress received gratifying proof of the renowned Breton sense of loyalty and devotion to the throne.

In faraway Venice Prosper Mérimée received letters from Brittany and Paris describing the victorious tour. 'Emperors and Empresses,' he wrote to Doña Manuela, 'are more solidly carpentered than other human beings. They tell me that the voyage through Brittany has not fatigued their Majesties. The reception has been magnificent and I had a letter from there assuring me that the official reports gave rather less than the truth. . . . I hope that these many speeches and fêtes did not have the sort of effect on the Empress they would have had on me. I have discovered long ago that women are far stronger than men, and that sovereigns are a herculean race.'

In this year 1858, which had opened so sombrely with the Orsini outrage, the Second Empire stood at the height of its glory and prestige. The great European questions, the tensions and frontier disputes between Austria, Turkey and Russia, the international repercussions of the national ferment in Serbia, Bosnia, Herzegovina, Montenegro—all the problems which finally exploded into the first world war were then submitted to tribunals and conferences sitting in Paris under the Emperor's effective chairmanship, and found a peaceful solution. The question of Montenegro, for example, whose independence Turkey would not grant despite military defeat, could in the summer of 1858 have led to an armed conflict, since Russia championed Prince Danilo as an independent ruler, and the Prince enjoyed the Emperor's protection in Paris. Turkey and Austria, however, remained hostile to Montenegrin independence. In May a small French naval squadron commanded by Admiral Jurien de La Gravière steamed down the Adriatic coast towards Montenegro, and the Austrian Commander-in-Chief in Dalmatia had orders to offer armed resistance to any French attempt to force a landing in the Gulf of Cattaro. The French admiral was a man of tact and firmness: pointing out that his government had charged him to deliver a written communication to the government of Montenegro, he landed on the Montenegro coast and, accompanied by an aide and the Austrian consul, delivered his note. Then, on the way back to Toulon, he steamed sufficiently close to land for the French flag to be shown in these regions which were longing to shake off Turkish rule. The Emperor sent Admiral Jurien a signal thanking him for his tact. Over thirty years later Jurien remembered the episode and spoke of it in a letter to the Empress: 'Then were we treated as the arbiters of the world. How proud we were! It is easy to be tactful when one serves a strong and glorious government.'

We shall encounter Admiral Jurien again. A Breton like Mlle Bouvet, he became one of the Empress's most devoted and at the same time critical admirers, perhaps her truest friend of all. He had served in the navy since 1828 when he was sixteen and Charles X had another two years to reign. His career had never been perturbed by the turmoil of French politics, and he had served in all parts of the world. Queen Victoria had met him in 1856 and had found him a 'quiet, gentlemanlike man who had always helped to keep matters straight between the two navies [in the Crimean war]'. The successful conclusion of his Adriatic mission in 1858 brought him to the Emperor's notice. After the Mexican expedition, he was attached to the Emperor's service at the Tuileries, and conceived his deep devotion to the Empress that survived the catastrophe of 1870 and made him a convinced partisan of the Prince Imperial as Napoleon IV. His pride and delight in being a servant of Napoleonic France in 1858 which in that year was so typical of many Frenchmen is therefore a good moment for introducing this shrewd and kindly sailor. The cheers and acclamations of Jurien's native Brittany had meanwhile told the Sovereigns how rich a treasure of enthusiasm and good-will they commanded in the country.

'I live in a world,' the Empress had written to Paca as the keeper of her secrets, 'where I must play two parts—my public life, my private life. It always seems to me that my private life would' be profaned if it became involved with the other life, and I would feel I was play-acting if I showed my sorrows, even when I feel them strongly. . . .' Biarritz, so close to Spain and freedom, gave her the solace of a retreat from the world although, even there, the problems and anxieties of both her public and her personal position pursued her. In 1858 Mme Walewska, with her husband and children, formed part of the Court's stay, as Lord Clarendon who had witnessed the *contretemps* at Cherbourg informed the Duchess of Manchester, adding that 'the lady is decidedly in favour still'. From her Atlantic retreat, the Empress organised several excursions into the Basque country where, high up in the mountains, she had a special friend, the monarch of the smuggling routes, whom she called Monsieur Michel. 'Young, active, intelligent and wealthy,' wrote the astonished Dr. Barthez of this fabulous man, 'he wields a great influence in his part of the Basque country . . . a country which adores the Emperor and shouts at the top of its voice: "Long live Napoleon! Long live Papa!"' M. Michel treated his fellow-Monarchs to a Royal feast, having guided them up perilous mountain paths to a huge cave, parts of which were the smugglers' storehouse. There among the stalactites and grottos M. Michel let loose magic fireworks for the entertainment of his visitors. Emerging later into the evening light outside, the visitors were greeted by a group of Spaniards singing and dancing, and to this enticing accompaniment they all sat down to an *al fresco* supper.

'We sat,' wrote Dr. Barthez, 'at table, talking and happy—yes, happy, for we all saw the Empress's delight at the voices and songs of the Spaniards who sang and played with a swing and vivacity, a grace and artistry which were perfect. The emotion of the Empress was so evident, and at the same time so unalloyed—it was so genuine and so generous. Time and the place saved us from the curious, the indifferent and the officious—we were in our own private group—and when, after supper, the Basques began to dance to the sound of the guitar, the Empress could hold back no longer. Flinging aside her hat and cloak, she began to dance a most graceful fandango. She was simple and delightful, and the expression on her face was ravishing. We all felt that the Empress had returned to her native land and for a moment had recovered the freedom of other days. . . .'

The handsome young smuggler-king could be well content with the entertainment he had offered to his Imperial guests.

In 1858 affairs of State intruded even into Biarritz. In pursuit of his Italian scheme the Emperor summoned his cousin Plon-Plon to join him later in September, and initiated him, during early morning walks along the sandy shore, into the secret of Plombières. The radical Prince had returned to public life during the previous June when he had been made Minister for Algerian Affairs, an appointment welcomed only by the opposition. Now the Emperor wished to show his cousin a further mark of favour by sending him on a secret mission to Czar Alexander II, then in residence at Warsaw. The Emperor feared that Prussia might go to the support of Austria in the event of war in Northern Italy, and so hoped to play on Russia's anti-Austrian bias to obtain help against Prussia. This he explained to the Prince as they perambulated on the seashore under the windows of the Villa Eugénie. The Prince accepted the mission, and then the Emperor flattered his cousin further by enjoining him not to breathe a word of this to the Empress or Walewski.

Mérimée was invited to Compiègne later in the year and accompanied the Empress when she paid a visit to several factories at nearby Saint-Gobain and Chauny. 'She was wholly admirable,' he reported to Doña Manuela. 'She talked to the directors and the workers and said to each exactly what was needed to enchant them. When I returned from the visit during which I saw 15,000 workers and peasants drunk with enthusiasm I asked myself whether, when one has the strongest and biggest part of the population on one's side, one need be concerned with what people say and do in the salons of Paris.'

Mérimée had not enjoyed himself particularly at Compiègne in 1858. 'You know,' he wrote to Madrid on December 8th, 'that I have little taste for pedantry, and you won't think me disparaging when I say that in my opinion the Court is not sufficiently literary. When one gets a little bored at times, it seems to me that one should look for slightly more elevated entertainments. The first Napoleon asked for lectures to be given and performances of the classics. At present, there is too much liking for farces and melodramas. . . .' He was present when Mme Walewska was rehearsing for a little vaudeville piece. 'You are playing a peasant girl,' she was told, 'and you have a lover. . . .' Madame blushed and insisted that the offending word should be changed into 'a young man who is in love with you'. 'I protested,' Mérimée went on, 'in the name of the Académie Française but was defeated.' He hated nothing more than hypocrisy, but found that together with prudery it was spreading in French society. The great days of la politesse Française were, he felt, passing away.

To the Empress one of the special pleasures of the country near Compiègne was Pierrefonds, a picturesque ruin of a fortified castle dating back to feudal times, which on the Emperor's instructions Viollet-le-Duc was restoring to its ancient splendour. The Empress never ceased to be fascinated by the gradual transformation and gave the architect a number of ideas.

Viollet-le-Duc, colleague and friend of Mérimée who had brought him to the Emperor's attention, became the first of several architects of note with whom the Empress would hold long conversations about the technical aspects of their craft. He paid the Empress a pleasant compliment by decorating the huge chimney-piece in the Salle d'Armes at Pierrefonds with statues of the nine preuses, the heroines of the medieval chansons de geste and giving the central figure, Semiramis, the features of the Empress. The other statues were allusions in stone to her ladies. The Empress was wholly enchanted when the work of reproduction was at length completed, and always chose the title of Countess of Pierrefonds when travelling, and later when living, incognito. She shared this delight in the Gothic revival with the Queen of England who when visiting Baden or the South of France took her alias from a similar evocation of baronial times and called herself the Countess of Balmoral.

CHAPTER 9

'PEACE?' NAPOLEON said somewhat testily to the Spanish Ambassador in January 1859, 'certainly I want peace, but sometimes one is carried along by circumstances. . . .' Since November, the Italian question, prematurely brought into the open by articles in newspapers closely connected with cousin Plon-Plon, had plunged France and Europe into a new crisis. Rumours of war and invasion, of diplomatic intervention and British efforts of mediation, of new alliances forming, of old ones breaking up, of neutrality and belligerence, of the imminent assembling of a Congress, of a call being made for general disarmament of great and small powers alike, chased each other through the cities of Europe as swiftly and unnervingly as did the rapidly alternating booms and slumps on the Paris Stock Exchange. ' L'Empire, c'est la baisse,' said old James de Rothschild in whose Frankfurt accent the words paix and baisse were never easily distinguished. A howl of rage rose from the capitals of Europe when it was suspected that the French Emperor was planning war against Austria. Only Russia did not join in the chorus: Prince Napoleon's mission to Alexander II in the autumn had led to tentative promises of diplomatic support. In Paris, rumours of war filled the public with dismay and resentment, especially the public interested in the fluctuations of the Bourse which, as James de Rothschild further remarked, meant many more people in 1859 than it had twenty years earlier. 'Nowadays everybody has his railway coupons or his three-per-cents. Bas de baix,' he concluded, ' bas d'Embire.' He was the banker of the Party of Order.

The heroic outlines of France were thus temporarily dissolving into a blurred picture of a jelly shaking in a gale while the rest of Europe recalled that the family name of the French ruler was Bonaparte. The Emperor and Empress preserved an admirable calm and assurance. The Emperor revealed his thoughts and ideas to the public on two separate occasions. On February 4th, the Paris bookshops displayed a pamphlet entitled Napoleon III and Italy of which the Vicomte de La Guéronnière was the nominal, and the Emperor the actual, author. Uncompromisingly hostile to the existing state of affairs in the Italian peninsula, this publication envisaged an Italian Confederation free from all foreign dominance, united under the principle of nationality, protected by the Piedmontese army, and presided over by the Pope: 'If France, who wants peace, were forced to wage war . . . the war . . . would have no other aim than to prevent revolutions by giving legitimate satisfaction to the needs of the people.' The first

123   E*

edition of the pamphlet was sold out in no time, and the Stock Exchange reacted with its swiftest downward plunge yet.

The Emperor's second opportunity for a public statement came three days later when he opened the new legislative session with a speech from the throne. Here he expressed himself with less clarity. He declared that the state of affairs in Italy was abnormal, since order could be maintained only by the presence of foreign troops. 'That gives,' he added, 'no sufficient reason for thinking that there will be war,' but he ended with the imprecise phrase: 'Peace, I hope, will not be troubled.' Such contrasting diarists as Queen Victoria and the Maréchal de Castellane entered in their journals that the Emperor had made no reference of any sort to his respect for the existing treaties, and that the general uncertainty would therefore continue. If one considers that the treaties of 1815 enabled Austria to rule Northern Italy by a system of arbitrary arrests, unlimited terms of imprisonment at Mantua and other prison-fortresses, and wholesale confiscation of the possessions of political opponents, the Emperor's omission of a complimentary reference to the international sanction of such practices was hardly surprising. The Empress fully shared her husband's indignation with Austrian rule in Italy. Hübner, for all his admiration and reverence for her, was often pained to hear her 'imprudently express pro-Italian sympathies', and until well into 1859 he always suspected her of 'making the Court familiar with war-like ideas'. It meant, in fact, that she made no secret of her disappointment at Austria consistently refusing to consider changes and reforms. The possibility that so negative and sterile an attitude made an armed conflict all but inevitable became increasingly familiar to the Empress and she familiarised others with it.

'Tell me what you thought of the Emperor's speech,' the Empress asked Paca in a letter of February 8th. 'Was he not firm and dignified? There are people here who wanted him to say that he would never go to war, that like King Louis Philippe he wanted peace at any price. I am not a partisan of war, quite the contrary, but I cannot approve of this degrading panicking.' When later in the year she was looking back to these months of uncertainty and tension, she told Count Arese, the Emperor's earliest and most loyal Italian friend, that 'the Emperor found it necessary to revive in the French people a feeling of generosity and glory in order to make war acceptable in a country which was still suffering from the terrible experiences of the previous conflict.' She was not a partisan of war, but when a young cavalry lieutenant stationed at Mélun came to her on repeated occasions in March and April to demand active employment in the event of war, she took him under her special protection. His name was Gaston de Galliffet. At twenty-five he had won his cross of the *légion d'honneur* in the trenches before Sebastopol. In bravery he was the equal of Ney and Lannes, but in other respects he anticipated some of the more flagrant heroes of Maupassant, which may explain why, at twenty-nine, he was still, under the Second Empire, a mere lieutenant. With his thirst for battle he reflected the spirit of the younger officers who, as Mérimée wrote to Panizzi, wanted to be 'in the vanguard of the army and be the first to look at the *donne*. . . .' The Empress did what she could to help Galliffet, but in the event she had to be Regent of France before she could get this splendid, if disreputable, *beau sabreur* into battle.

The country certainly needed a change of heart, a better spirit: 'People here,' wrote Mérimée, 'are thinking only of the effect a war could produce on the funds and railway shares. Needless to add that nobody thinks of glory and humanity. . . .' 'It is fear which makes people take leave of their senses,' wrote the Empress. She never presumed to influence the decision between peace and war which was the Emperor's alone, but she shared Mérimée's conviction that the materialistic legacy from Louis Philippe's reign needed an antidote. 'You do not preach the cult of material things for twenty years,' Mérimée had written to Mme de Rochejaquelein,[1] 'without converting the majority of people to that fine doctrine.'

In contrast to the Empress, Prince Napoleon held, in the Italian crisis, the foreground of the stage. As Minister for Algerian Affairs he was a leading member of the government, and since his marriage with Princess Clothilde had been solemnised at Turin Cathedral on January 30th, 1859, he had become closely identified in the public mind with the 'Italian' party. Cousin Plon-Plon led the war-party, a circumstance which caused the Emperor and members of the government to stress the anti-revolutionary character of their policy, their championship of the constitutional and federal solution. The Emperor had made the important distinction between the national and the revolutionary aspirations agitating the Italian mind since 1815. To him, as to the Empress, the revolution meant Pianori, Tibaldi, Orsini and other dagger-happy agents of Mazzini, the ominous prophet of Republicanism. Constitutional Monarchy, as already established at Turin, must be helped to prevail against the disreputable mystique of the secret societies. With Cavour at the helm, this aim appeared to the Emperor and Empress as both honourable and feasible.

The Empress belonged neither to the war nor the peace party. She regarded it as her principal task, as she told Paca, 'to give heart to those who lack it and prudence to those who need it'. Hübner, aware of the country's pacifism—as opposed to the bellicosity of the younger officers of Galliffet's stamp—thought this anti-war mood to represent a crisis of confidence in the Empire, and reported to Vienna that the Empress, having taken fright at the vehemence of the opposition to war, was endeavouring to regain the ground the Emperor had lost. More senior officers, such as the Maréchal de Castellane who commanded at Lyons, were frightened indeed of the internal consequences of war. He told the Emperor that 'the Reds' were rejoicing in the prospect of war, that 'associations'—dreaded word!—were forming among the silk workers who were saying to each other: 'They are going to deliver our brothers in Italy, the time has come to deliver us as well.' The Emperor and Empress were at no time afraid of *le spectre rouge*, the bogy of the Party of Order, and in the Italian

[1] Daughter-in-law of the famous author of the *Memoirs* of the Vendean War.

crisis in particular made it their task to give the people a lead. 'If you could witness the fear and panic here,' the Empress wrote to Paca in February 1859, 'everybody fainting away and telling you how afraid they are, or if you could hear those who predict the end of the world, or those who think that the Emperor had lost his head and cannot be brought back to normal, you would understand that there is much to disgust one here. . . .'

The great question-mark of 1859 was whether Austria would withdraw from Italy after a defeat in the field or be compelled to do so 'by the force of European opinion'. Was there going to be a French expedition across the Alps or a Congress of the European powers? The Empress saw the advantages of a negotiated solution, but Prince Napoleon and his circle insisted that there must be war. When in March the possibility of negotiation seemed promising, the Prince at once resigned from his Ministry. 'Those,' he wrote to the Emperor, 'who have served you in the policy of progress, emancipation and nationality on which you were embarked can now only retire into oblivion and consume their grief in silence.' It was a childish attitude, but the Prince was so identified with a policy of war that he saw in any other solution a personal affront. 'In public affairs,' the Emperor replied to his cousin's letter of resignation, 'one must not put one's *amour-propre* before one's duty, and really I cannot understand what motivates your decision. . . .'

'My plans,' the Empress wrote to Paca on April 15th, 'are at present difficult to make. If we are having peace (*lo que Dios quiera*), I shall go to Fontainebleau in May where, it is useless to add, I should love to see you (I believe I still wish this more than you do), but if there is war, probably I shall have to stay here in Paris where I don't know what they'll tell me to do. . . .' 'I must remain here like a soldier on the breach,' or 'I am as happy as one can be with an excellent husband and a delightful little boy,' were among the phrases that she used in the hurried notes she dashed off to her adored sister in faraway Madrid. 'Sometimes I feel an irresistible desire,' she once confessed, 'to think myself back into the old days at Carabanchel and forget everything, including the existence of Italy and Austria. . . .' Hardly the attitude of the *femme politique*, let alone the clerical fanatic.

In England, the Italian crisis killed what had remained of Queen Victoria's earlier affection for the Emperor. Under Prince Albert's tuition, the nephew merged in her mind with his uncle and predecessor, the first Napoleon. On her journal she lavished expressions of passionate resentment claiming that the French Emperor's and Victor Emmanuel's conduct 'produces universal indignation among all right-thinking people here'. The Queen summed up opinion in the country generally by saying that 'they like the idea of Italian independence, but disapprove of the Emperor of the French attacking another Empire without rhyme or reason'. On April 8th, finally, Lord Cowley put the question of the hour to the Emperor: did he desire peace or war? 'The Emperor replied [reported

Cowley] that he would be very glad if peace could be maintained, but that he was not afraid of war, and he added that his inmost conviction was that war was unavoidable.' The Queen deplored that this reply did not put an end to 'the whole lamentable state of affairs. We have to thank the Emperor Napoleon for all.' It was only in a small voice that she entered in her journal in March: 'The Empress always so grateful and so attached to us. . . .' It was no longer politics.

As in 1914, Austria prevented further negotiations by presenting Sardinia with an ultimatum that was dispatched before other possibilities had been fully explored. On April 23rd, Cavour closed the parliamentary session at Turin with the words: 'The session which ends today was the last session of the Piedmontese Parliament: next year we shall open the first session of the Italian Parliament.' On that day, Queen Victoria wrote that, according to the Foreign Secretary, 'people here are now excited against Austria, though we know that the *whole* is caused by the Emperor Napoleon'. But neither the Court of St. James's which, mainly under Prince Albert's direction, was strongly Austrian in sentiment, nor that at Berlin where Archduke Albert of Habsburg and Prince Windischgraetz were even then appealing for help from the junior partner in the German Confederation, could counteract the effect which the Austrian ultimatum had everywhere caused. Austria was on her own.

'We are about to have war,' wrote the Empress to Paca on Good Friday. 'Austria has *wished* it. The Emperor will depart when the army is ready and I shall stay here as Regent. So, you see, all plans have been changed. My responsibility is great, for you know that the Parisians are not always very easy to manage: but God will, I hope, give me all the knowledge which I lack, for I have nothing but the will to do well and not allow the smallest sign of disorder.' And she went on:

'How bizarre is destiny! Don't you find it so? When we were children, who could have told us what was in store for us? When we listened so closely to M. Beyle as he talked of the campaigns of the Empire, or the scorn they felt for Marie Louise—who could have said to me: you will play an active part in the second scene of that poem, and you will be judged as severely as Marie Louise if you act as she did? Life's events follow one another, often despite ourselves: but I cannot help feeling a sense of pride if, by my presence here, I should reassure the spirit of France.

Adieu, my dear sister. I greatly wish I could embrace you. Give Mama all the news from me.

Your sister,
Eugénie.'

France declared war on Austria on May 3rd. The Emperor issued a proclamation from the Tuileries that he would command the army in person. 'I shall leave the Empress and my son in France. She will show herself equal to her lofty mission.' Giving Austria's ultimatum and her subsequent violation of Piedmontese territory as the causes of war, the Emperor said: 'France has drawn the sword not to conquer, but to liberate. The purpose of this war is to give Italy to herself, not to make her change her master, and we shall have on our frontier a nation of friends who owes us its independence. We do not go to Italy to foment disorder or overthrow the power of the Holy Father whom we have restored to his throne, but to free him of that alien pressure which is weighing on the whole peninsula. We shall, on that classic soil famed for so many victories, find the traces left by our fathers: May God grant that we shall be worthy of them.'

On the same 3rd of May Hübner sadly departed from Paris. No other foreign diplomat had come to know the Empress so well, to understand her better, to love her more: few diplomats of his generation and provenance had come closer to an understanding of Bonapartism. Yet in his inner bias he was, though a moderate, a reactionary. What he called *la bonne politique* which knew neither hatred nor love did not, so he thought, survive after 1848, the year of revolution. Listening one evening to a Verdi opera, he felt that the composer was attempting to 'express impossible emotions', and sighed for the golden days of Bellini and Donizetti. Wistful, backward-looking and opinionated, the departing Ambassador had nevertheless made sincere and persistent efforts to adjust himself to the new Napoleonic Empire and its two principal personages. So far as diplomats have a heart, the Empress filled his with feelings of admiration, respect and affection, and it was certainly a tribute to his honesty that he admitted, at least in his diary, that his first judgment of Mlle de Montijo had been wholly wrong. That the Empress on her side regarded him as a friend cannot be doubted. He must have left her with a vivid feeling that, the Italian controversy once out of the way, the French and Austrian Empires had much to give to each other.

On May 3rd, as the Ambassador was ready to leave, he was surprised to see a man wearing the white tunic of an Austrian Colonel among those waiting to see him depart. This was the Marquis de Pimodan. As an émigré during Louis Philippe's reign M. de Pimodan had served in the Austrian army, and now he was wearing his old uniform as a gesture of legitimist protest. But nobody took much notice and the marquis returned home unhonoured by police action then or later.

The Emperor left Paris for the war on May 10th. 'It is impossible,' wrote an eye-witness, 'to give any idea of the enthusiasm with which he was greeted when, wearing field uniform, tunic and képi, he emerged from the great portal of the Louvre. An overwhelming acclamation of "Long Live the Emperor! Long Live Italy!" arose. The Sovereign's face was radiant with joy. The immense crowd began to sing the Marseillaise. . . .' Another witness, the régime's young enemy Emile Ollivier, tells us that 'in the popular quarters the enthusiasm became delirious—friends as well as enemies were amazed. Even those who since December had looked coldly on the Emperor of the coup d'état, carried in triumph the Emperor of War —not because he was departing for a war of any sort, but because he was departing for a war of liberation.' It was a lonely moment for a member of the opposition. 'The people of Paris,' Ollivier admitted, 'did not share our scruples or imitate our abstention—they rallied behind their Emperor and not behind their deputies although they had elected them to make opposition. It was a lesson which I did not forget and which greatly influenced my later conduct.'

When the Emperor passed through the Faubourg St. Antoine, a quarter of dingy slums and squalor, the enthusiasm reached its height, and a new, less political, note was struck by the people: 'We'll behave ourselves while you're away,' they shouted, and 'We'll look after the Empress for you.' They sang the Marseillaise on May 10th, 1859, and sang it as Bonapartists. There was no official interference, although the great hymn had been suppressed by Napoleon III, as it had been by Napoleon I.

CHAPTER 10

'W E A R E an extraordinary nation,' Mérimée told Panizzi when war was certain. 'A fortnight ago I told you that there was not a single man in France who wanted war, and I believed it to be true. Today, the opposite is true. The Gallic instinct is awake. Now we have an enthusiasm which has its magnificent side, and also its terrifying aspect. . . . The important thing is to be united, honest and moderate, to make cartridges and not constitutions. Bankers and fine gentlemen of that kind continue to deplore the force of events, but the masses are all for war. The Emperor is more popular than ever. A workman said "Old moustachio is stronger than the enemy; he has the plans of his uncle."'

The Empress-Regent did not make cartridges, but in the evenings she gathered her ladies and visitors round her in the garden apartments at Saint-Cloud and made bandages for the wounded. As for Constitutions, she learnt that of the Second Empire by heart and was able to quote, so Mérimée wrote to Doña Manuela, 'decrees and *sénatus-consultes* like the oldest Councillor of State'. Three times a week she presided over the Council of Ministers, which had recently been reshuffled. The Duke of Padua was now at the Interior which the dreaded General Éspinasse had left some time ago to return to an army command. At the Ministry of War, Marshal Randon had succeeded Vaillant whose administration, as the mobilisation had shown, had left much to be desired. Over these men the Empress easily established an authority based on a thorough study of dispatches from abroad and reports from all parts of France. The current session of the Deputies continued until May 28th, but Ollivier and his four irreconcilable colleagues of the opposition spoke and acted circumspectly. On adjournment, the Chamber asked to be allowed to see the Prince Imperial, and the Empress went with her son to the Palais Bourbon. 'I count on your enlightened patriotism,' she told the Deputies who were about to visit their constituences, 'to maintain the faith which we have in the army and, when the time comes, the moderation of the Emperor. However difficult my duty may be, my heart is French and gives me the necessary courage. . . .' She was thanked with an ovation.

It was a businesslike Regency. Before he left, the Emperor had arranged for weekly (instead of quarterly) reports on the morale and activities in all departments of France to be submitted to the government, and these the Empress studied with great care. They proved that there was a national

130

interest in the war that was positive and encouraging. The bookshops could not keep up with the demand for maps and charts; rural communities which had never seen a newspaper were now receiving them in large numbers. 'The people are all in Italy in mind and spirit,' it was reported from Bordeaux. 'They continue to follow the movements of our army with a curiosity which shows no sign of diminishing. Workers take out group subscriptions to local papers, and during the breaks one of them reads them to the others.' 'The public spirit here,' wrote Mérimée to Panizzi, 'continues to be good. Even the salons are behaving themselves. Many rich young men have joined the army, and the Legitimists are saying that, whatever happens, one must stand by the flag. I know nothing about Prussia, except that the fury of the *Franzosenfresser* is strong there. A Russian, M. Turgenev, has arrived from Moscow and says, that the Germans want to swallow France and Russia in one go. From us they want Alsace, and from Russia Courland and Latvia. . . .'

Prussia loomed large among the Empress's preoccupations. Her friend, the Crown Princess Frederick, who was making a slow recovery from her first confinement,[1] had, despite Queen Victoria's fears to the contrary, been able to travel to Windsor to be present at her mother's birthday celebration on May 25th. The Empress took the opportunity to send the Queen her congratulations: 'I have received,' she wrote in the course of this letter, 'good news from the Emperor. Thanks to the attitude taken by friendly powers, he hopes to localise the conflict, for a general conflagration would be an incalculable evil for the whole world. We count on Your Majesty, who always has the peace of the world at heart, to use her personal influence no less than we count on Prince Albert, whose word carries such weight in Germany, in order to arrive at this aim. Your Majesty will be happy to have the Crown Princess Frederick at her side, especially as she has suffered so much. . . .' The Queen replied from Osborne on May 25th:

'You are quite right in thinking that I am animated by the same sentiments for the maintenance of the repose and peace of the world and I can assure you that nobody desires more to spare the world what you so justly call "an incalculable evil" than I do. Alas! my power in this respect is limited, but the Emperor, on the contrary, is all-powerful in this regard. Desirous, as you say, to localise the war, he can achieve that purpose by not carrying the war beyond the territory of Piedmont, after he has succeeded in liberating it from the Austrian invasion. Should he, however, himself invade Austrian possessions, it would be only natural if Germany, alarmed to see one of the most important members of the Confederation attacked and in danger, were to come to Austria's aid, while Europe would be alarmed to see the treaties on which her peace and political existence rest put in question. May God inspire you

[1] The birth of the future Wilhelm II had been as perilous for mother and son as that of the Prince Imperial, but the Kaiser had been less well cared-for by the doctors at birth which was no augury for future peace.

and protect Europe! The Prince is most grateful for your kind remembrance: he suffers as much as I do. . . .'

So far, the war had not led to any major engagements: the French and Piedmontese had won a local victory at Montebello, and Garibaldi's Volunteers were penetrating deep into the area round Lake Como, but no decisive battle had as yet been fought. In her letter to the Empress the Queen went to the very limits of official neutrality to stress that German support of a hard-pressed Austria would find sympathy in England. Prince Albert for his part viewed the conflict entirely as a German and, in reading of movements along the Ticino and Mincio rivers in Lombardy, thought of future movements on either side of the Rhine. He had recently been in correspondence with Thiers, a somewhat doubtful proceeding when one remembers the Prince's position and the French politician's rancorous opposition to the Empire. It may well be that the Empress was aware of this pen-friendship and for that reason added those comments about the Prince Consort's influence in Germany.

In Italy, the first major encounter between the French and Austrian army occurred on June 4th at Magenta in Lombardy. It ended in a resounding French victory, and the moment it was reported, by telegraph, to her the Empress saw to it that the news spread. With Princess Clothilde at her side, she drove down the Rue de Rivoli and along the great boulevards to receive the ovations of the populace. In the absence of more detailed information gossips invented enormous casualty lists and were especially imaginative in ascribing heroic deaths to a large number of generals. 'Neither Canrobert nor Niel have been wounded,' wrote Viel-Castel in his diary on June 10th, after he had read the bulletin, 'nor even General Mellinet whom the gentlemen of the Stock Exchange have in their ardent patriotism ranked among the dead.' The Empress did what she could to counteract such rumours. When she asked Princess Clothilde to share the acclamations with her, she did not yet know that the Piedmontese army had not been engaged. King Victor Emmanuel had had the mortification of appearing on the battlefield too late.

Following their defeat, the Austrians evacuated Lombardy and retired towards the fortresses of the Venetian Quadrilateral. The Emperor entered Milan on June 8th and was received as *liberatore* with unbounded enthusiasm. His critics remarked that the first Napoleon would have remained at the heels of the fleeing enemy, but the nephew was more urgently preoccupied with the political side of events. Napoleon III was the first military leader of modern times to discover that the Italians are not ideal allies, that their political and territorial demands are rarely in proportion to their military performance. In Florence, Modena, Parma and Bologna, for example, the rulers had been expelled by a vociferous, although mostly good-tempered, mob, and in each case a Piedmontese agent had been on the spot with suspicious promptitude to establish a provisional government with dictatorial powers in the name of Victor Emmanuel. Annexation could not be far behind. In Bologna, which belonged to the Papal States, the Austrian garrison had disappeared ten days after Magenta, and a deputation from the city waited on Victor Emmanuel to offer him full powers. The Emperor received the deputation in the place of the King. 'If the people of Bologna,' he told them brusquely, 'had taken up arms against the Austrians, the case would be different. But against whom did you, in fact, rise? Against the Pope. I have not come to Italy to deprive the Pope of his possessions.' The deputation returned to an unannexed Bologna. When Prince Napoleon, arriving in Florence on an official military mission, spoke of raising thirty thousand Tuscans for the war, he encountered irreducible passive resistance and collected scarcely 4,000. The Emperor heard from everywhere that Italians, invited to mobilise their manpower, replied with delightful politeness that they had the utmost confidence in the brave armies of France and Piedmont, and so declined the honour of joining them with their own persons.

Nor did the international scene present an encouraging sight. Prussia mobilised after Magenta, and Queen Victoria's son-in-law Crown Prince Frederick took over the command of the infantry of the Prussian Guard. 'I am getting up all my courage and hope that we shall soon be engaged and pass the Rhine,' wrote the Crown Princess, now back at Potsdam, to Windsor. 'I wish for once I was a man, and baby too, to fight the French. I cannot help being savage when I think that it is their fault that so many poor innocent people are being made wretched, and that so much German blood is being shed, and my happy peaceful life is at an end for who knows how long—perhaps for ever.' This very German outburst mirrored the savage atmosphere East of the Rhine: the Empress daily received reports of troop concentrations at Cologne and Düsseldorf and at once passed them on to Imperial Headquarters.

In Rusisa, where Prince Gorchakov was First Minister, the mood on the whole persisted anti-Austrian and pro-French, but Czar Alexander II watched the disappearance of Legitimacy from widening areas of the peninsula with misgivings. He could hardly pose as the protector of the Pope, but the King of Naples had always been a special protégé of Russian rulers. Ferdinand II, King Bomba, who had imposed the strictest neutrality on his dominions, died late in May and was succeeded by Francis II, young in years, immature in experience—an honourable and timid Prince married to the sister of the young Empress of Austria. The new Queen of Naples had inherited the proud spirit and handsome looks of the Wittelsbachs together with more than a touch of Wittelsbach madness.

In England, the Derby government fell on June 10th and, with the utmost reluctance, the Queen sent once more for Lord Palmerston. The new government included not only the anti-Neapolitan Gladstone, but the pro-Italian Lord John Russell; although no less than three Dukes were given Ministerial appointments, Palmerston had obtained the backing of the radical leaders of the Manchester School. He even asked the Queen to

133

make John Bright a Privy Councillor and offered (also without success) the Board of Trade to Cobden. Nevertheless, he was able to rely on the support of this influential group in the House of Commons, and the Emperor, just before he left Milan, hoped that the new liberal government —despite the three Dukes it could no longer be called Whig—would not yield to the Court's Austrian and Legitimist predilections.

At this point, the Emperor received a letter from the Empress suggesting that she join him for a few days at Milan. This the Emperor declined, for, as he pointed out, would people not lose faith in the Regency if the Regent could absent herself? The Empress acquiesced, but her mind was troubled by the international situation which threatened to turn the war into a more than local one. Queen Victoria's ominous letter had underlined the insecurity of France's Eastern frontier where a nation of *Franzosenfresser* was straining at the leash and General Roon, commanding at Düsseldorf, had been told by the Prussian Prime Minister, Prince Anton of Hohenzollern-Sigmaringen, that Prussia 'was now entering into the historical development of the drama'. By this phrase Prussian statesmen, and especially Generals, always meant revenge for the inadequate territorial awards Prussia had received under the treaties of 1815. While it is not surprising that she at once obeyed the Emperor's order to remain at her post, it is understandable that she should have wished to discuss such matters with him. By now an early peace seemed to her an urgent necessity if a European conflagration was to be avoided.

At the same time she was certain of France, and of the success of her Regency. 'I am of good hope for the future,' she wrote to Paca on June 15th. 'Paris is absolutely quiet and the state of France has never been more reassuring.' She went on to say that the Regency was an excellent arrangement, for even if the 'assassins' should bring off a *coup* it would, with the Emperor away, do no harm to the future of the dynasty. Her dealings with the Press were firm but politic. The first of the three warnings which were needed before a newspaper was closed down had been addressed in the Regent's name to the *Courrier de Dimanche* for meditating editorially on the interesting fact that at Magenta the General preeminently connected with the conception and execution of the Law of the Suspects, Éspinasse, had been killed in action while the Senator-General who had spoken against it, MacMahon,[1] had carried the day. The various uprisings in Papal Romagna after the withdrawal of the Austrian Whitecoats had led to numerous newspaper articles defending or attacking the Pope's temporal power. A left-wing paper, *Le Siècle*, received a stern warning from the Regent, who pointed out that the editor had 'confused the noble cause of Italian independence with that of Revolution. Respect for, and protection of, the Papacy is part of the Programme for the realisation of which the Emperor has gone to Italy'. The Emperor had spoken in identical terms to the deputation from Bologna.

Mérimée dined with the Empress at Saint-Cloud on June 19th and found

[1] After the victory, MacMahon had been made a Marshal and Duke of Magenta.

134

her in excellent health and temper, the Prince Imperial, now three, looking bigger, more handsome and intelligent than ever. He was much struck by the resemblance between the Prince and the Empress as a small girl. The novelist stayed late, chatting and helping to make bandages. That day the Empress had presided over a Council that had lasted for five hours and had afterwards gone on to an exhibition where some new paintings by Delacroix were on view.

Another Empress, Elisabeth of Austria, had also asked her husband to let her come to Headquarters. The Emperor Francis Joseph had, after Magenta, dismissed his Commander-in-Chief Giulay and taken command himself, even as he had dismissed Büol at the outbreak of hostilities and replaced him with the less excitable and more even-tempered Count Rechberg. Austrian Headquarters were at Verona, and there he received not only letters from his beautiful Consort imploring him to let her join him, but reports from his mother, the Archduchess Sophie, and certain courtiers informing him that his Empress, accompanied only by her English riding-master Holmes, spent day after day riding wildly through the country-side, and her nights reading and writing. 'My dear, dear, only Angel,' Francis Joseph wrote from Verona on June 7th, 1859, 'I beg of you, for the sake of the love which you have consecrated to me, pull yourself together, show yourself in Vienna from time to time, pay official visits. You have no idea how much this would help me. It would cheer people up in Vienna and preserve the right spirit which I so urgently need. . . .' Her solitary rides with Holmes were forbidden, and the Emperor told his wife that he could not allow her to come to Verona since he must not set other officers 'a bad example'.

In her boredom the poor distracted woman began to write political letters to Verona: could Naples, where her sister was Queen, not come in on Austria's side? When she heard of unrest in Hungary, she took fright and pleaded with her husband to enter into negotiations with Napoleon. And was it true, she asked in another letter, that Francis Joseph was about to meet the Regent of Prussia?[1] 'She found,' wrote her official biographer, 'no rest or calm, during the night wrote long letters to her husband, her parents and family, feared the future . . . and lost her nerve. . . .' 'The terrible life you are leading,' Francis Joseph wrote from Verona, 'which has now become a habit, makes me feel quite desperate. It is bound to destroy your dear health. I have heard nothing of a meeting with the Prussian Regent which you mention, but, I am afraid, it is not impossible that I shall have to face up to another sort of meeting, namely with the arch-scoundrel Napoleon. I should find this highly disagreeable, but if it would be of profit to our Monarchy, I would have to swallow even that. . . .'

The arch-scoundrel won another victory, that of Solferino on June 24th. The Italian Campaign of 1859 has not yet found the historian it deserves, and this is not the place to make up for the omission. It must therefore suffice to say that the accounts state almost unanimously that the

[1] The future William I. King Frederick William IV was certifiably insane.

Emperor was at the height of his physical and intellectual ability and directed the battle, to use Ollivier's words, *en grand Capitaine*. It was a day of incredible slaughter: as at Magenta, French artillery showed a destructive power that the world had then not experienced. In the evening General Niel, far and away the ablest soldier of the Second Empire, was promoted Marshal of France, though not Duke of Solferino (Napoleon I had never created a Duke of Austerlitz). As is well known, it was his witnessing of the frightful sufferings of the wounded that caused the Swiss philanthropist Dunant to found those voluntary aid societies for the succour of the wounded in war-time which became the parent organisation of the International Red Cross. The Emperor who all his life was haunted by the memory of the screams of that hot summer's day always gave Dunant his unstinting support. Exhausted by his exertions, the Emperor after the battle sat for long in the room at Cavriana which the Austrian Emperor had occupied at dawn. Wearily he sat in silence, supporting his head on his hands, and at length rose. 'The day is ended,' he said, and then dictated a telegram to the Empress: '*Grande bataille, grande victoire*,' was all it said. It caused the Empress on the following day to announce the victory of Cavriana, but three days later she heard that history was to know the day as the battle of Solferino.

In Paris, the Empress ordered a *Te Deum* to be sung at Notre-Dame and the streets and squares illuminated in honour of the victory. She had some difficulty with the Archbishop of Paris, who disliked officiating at a *Te Deum* which in part celebrated the uprisings of the Pope's subjects at Bologna and elsewhere in Romagna, but the Empress in the end prevailed over him. 'The faithful will be flocking to Notre-Dame with a heavy heart,' were the Archbishop's words, but no one knew better than the Empress-Regent how much anguish and dismay the future of the Pope's temporal power was causing in all parts of Catholic France. 'Romagna causes concern,' the Empress had telegraphed to Imperial Headquarters on June 16th, 'please simply tell [us?] whether the King of Piedmont has accepted dictatorship and whether this fact does not violate recognised neutrality.' She was concerned with the legal aspect, the honouring of treaties, and did not speak, as her enemies still allege, as a blind partisan of the Pope. It was her duty to mention Catholic reaction in France to the Emperor, because from among fifty reports from the provinces she read in the second week of June, not one had a good word to say of the Romagnole insurgents.

'I hope,' she wrote to Paca afterwards, 'that peace will now not be too long in coming, for with the means of destruction one possesses nowadays a battle becomes nothing but a butchery. The Emperor had an epaulette smashed by a bullet—you will say that he exposed himself, but I think it was part of his duty to do so because he knows too well how precious his life is to expose it unnecessarily. I have heard all this from M. [name illegible], because he himself has said nothing. . . .'

The victory of Solferino did not increase the Emperor's European popularity. 'May God destroy the wicked French!' wrote the Prince Consort to his Prussian son-in-law, while his reaction to Palmerston's strict observation of neutrality was: 'I am itching to strike a blow at the French.' 'Heaven may grant,' wrote his daughter Vicky in reply, 'that . . . the French be punished for their wickedness and peace be restored to Europe —and,' she added as an after-thought. 'Austria be rather better governed than heretofore.' Queen Victoria, in her dealings with Palmerston and Russell as well as in her feeling towards the French Emperor, behaved very much as the granddaughter of George III, but Palmerston's firmness kept Royal obstinacy well within constitutional bounds.

However, the Prime Minister's insistence on the strictest of neutralities towards the belligerents in Italy was somewhat vitiated by an irrational, but widespread, conviction among England's upper and middle classes that a French invasion, despite the Emperor's heavy commitment in Italy, was imminent. Nobody quite knew whence this odd panic had so suddenly sprung unless it was ultimately inspired by an understandable concern with the unsatisfactory state of the country's defences. The French had the stronger navy. At all events, the Lords held a long debate at the beginning of July during which venerable Peers such as the octogenarian Lord Lyndhurst said in all seriousness that they expected to wake up one morning in the immediate future and find England's inviolate soil trampled underfoot by the French army. Whatever their personal feelings about the French liberating Italy, neither Palmerston nor Russell could afford to treat this vehement anti-French outburst lightly, and both Court and government were united in supporting the famous Volunteer movement that now gripped the country. As has been remarked, Palmerston supplied the rifles for the movement and Tennyson a patriotic poem: *Riflemen, form!* might be said to be the *Ça Ira* of mid-Victorian England. The Emperor, well informed on events in England, realised that Palmerston would hardly be able to come to his aid in any of the many besetting problems facing him as a consequence of his victories in Lombardy.

Seeing no encouraging signs on either the immediate Italian or the farther European horizon, the Emperor, following as always his own counsel, took the initiative and entered into direct armistice negotiations with the Emperor of Austria. The two Emperors met at Villafranca on July 11th and, their minds still filled with the horrors of the recent carnage, agreed on peace terms which gave Lombardy to Piedmont, left Venetia as part of the new Italian Confederation in Austrian hands, insisted on the restoration of the Grand Dukes of Tuscany, Parma and Modena, and offered the Presidency of Italy to the Pope, who was to undertake far-reaching reforms in his territories. These bases accepted, the final treaty of peace was to be signed at Zürich.

The peace of Villafranca represents perhaps the biggest single surprise which Napoleon III sprang on the world. Could he have acted otherwise? Ought he, for the sake of his mission as Liberator and Bonapartist Emperor, to have run the risk of a major European war such as the world entered in 1914? Prussia stood ready on the Rhine and the rest of Germany was in patriotic uproar in which acute observers like Mérimée or Karl Marx's friend Lassalle discerned the symptoms of a budding Socialist upheaval. Where would Russia stand, where England? The Emperor could not tell. How long would his own country stand fast as further revolutions spread through the temporal possessions of the Pope? And were the Italians worth liberating?

Weighing all these factors in his mind, the Emperor, in the fortnight between Solferino and Villafranca, decided against further liberations at French expense—at all events for the present. Receiving the news of the armistice terms, Cavour resigned in fury, but his King was not over-whelmed with grief to see him go—for the present. The revolutionary leaders, Kossuth of Hungary for example, who had hoped to free their countries from the Habsburgs with French support, were bitterly disappointed. Mazzini said that naturally Italy could not expect to obtain her freedom from the French despot. Queen Victoria expressed the same sentiment: 'How clearly can one see the Emperor Napoleon's *real* motives! No wish for *Italy's freedom*!' Yet what would the Queen have written if the Emperor had won a further victory and Venetia had fallen to him? Whatever may have been felt and said in the passion of the moment, under the blinding impact of surprise, Europe in the end did not lose from the Emperor's decision. Nor had he reached it without deep and anguished reflection.

The state of France; Prussian expansionism; the changing faces of English politics; Italian irresponsibility and egoism; the future of the Papal States; and the ghastly character of modern war: all these things the Empress encountered as urgent and real problems for her daily attention while she was Regent of France. In all of them she became something of an expert, and they were all to remain in the foreground of her daily occupation, as the Empire entered upon its further destiny. The future was to show that she had fully grasped the gravity of the problems, especially of those which proved insoluble.

CHAPTER 11

THE EMPEROR returned from Italy exhausted and ill; to some he seemed to have aged by ten years in a few months. Despite his victories, he was bringing back a number of extremely complex and unsolved problems and so prepared himself to find political solutions for the questions that had not been settled by the sword. As he passed through Turin on his way to Paris he rode through streets which were decorated with Orsini's portraits to remind him that his principal war aim of putting the revolutionaries out of business had failed in the eyes of a people who had been promised liberation from the Alps to the Adriatic. Liberation had been halted half way and so had the overthrow of the various petty rulers of the peninsula with the result that the French Emperor, the nephew of a former unifier of Italy, was regarded as the opponent of the aspirations of either side in the Italian theatre of conflict. The Party of Freedom and Unification, led by Cavour and his friends, and that of Order, identified in Italy with the treaties of 1815 and, therefore, Austria, cursed his name with equal fury. The revolutionary movement—and the recent campaign had brought Garibaldi back into Italian politics even though his volunteers had been confined to operations away from the decisive battles—had never trusted him in any case. He hoped to escape from the dilemma by assembling a European Congress that would give the Continent a more up-to-date territorial and political settlement in succession to that of 1815. Was France to be the arbiter of Europe once again? The Emperor's project was defeated by an alliance between Cavour and Garibaldi to which England gave its blessing. The scene would have looked very different if Napoleon had been able to invade Venetian territory after Solferino and offer peace and arbitration from this last Austrian stronghold south of the Alps.

As on some other occasions in the future, the present crisis coincided with a marked deterioration in his health. Many rumours were floating about in Paris and elsewhere about the nature of his ailments, but the Emperor paid no attention either to the gossip or to the nature of his symptoms. The Empress decided to move the Court to Biarritz at the earliest possible moment, as soon as the speech-making and victory celebrations permitted. The Regency was over. She had every reason to be satisfied with its success. She had easily established her authority over the Ministers at her side, had acquainted herself with the administrative machinery and the fluctuations of internal opinion, and had silenced the defeatism of her

139

more doubtful counsellors such as ex-King Jerome, Plon-Plon's father, to whom she had said that unlike the Empress Marie Louise in 1814 she would not be deterred from her duties by the sort of advice the first Napoleon's brothers had offered at crucial moments. In handing back the ship of State in such excellent order, the Empress felt a strong regret and she told her ladies that she feared she might be bored without her recent position at the helm. She had regarded herself as a Prime Minister who stood between the country and the Emperor in the sense that mistakes, errors and hostility (in which she always included the threat of assassination) would be for her to deal with while the Emperor himself could pursue his aims behind that protection.

Even so, the Emperor's health made her leave Paris for Biarritz without regret and the Court arrived at the Villa Eugénie in September; the Prince Imperial, with Dr. Barthez, had already been there for several weeks. King Leopold of the Belgians spent a few informal days at what he called the French Osborne, but the most notable event of the 1859 visit was the appearance, late in September, of Richard and Pauline Metternich who thereafter represented Austria, in more senses than one, at the Court of the Tuileries.

Prince Richard, the son of the famous Chancellor, had served for some years in Paris under his half-brother Hübner, and now entered upon his first important post. Thirty years of age in 1859, he was a grand seigneur of natural charm of manner, an intelligent, if slightly complacent, judge of human nature, fond of women, a patron and friend of 'modern' composers such as Verdi, Johann Strauss and the Wagner of *Tannhäuser*, rich, cultured, spoilt and a little indolent. His wife, who was also his niece, he had married in 1856. Pauline Metternich became one of the great names of the Second Empire: unlike the Empress she seems hardly to have existed before she came to Paris and is lost to view once the Empire had fallen. She was attractively ugly—'I may look like a monkey, but at least I am a fashionable monkey,' she frequently remarked. Strong-willed, capricious, immensely ambitious socially and yet possessing an honest warmth of heart, Princess Pauline must be one of the very few ambassadresses on record whom a member of the Court to which her husband was accredited first encountered singing 'broad—very broad—Parisian songs'—but this was the experience of Dr. Barthez at the Villa Eugénie on the evening of October 2nd, 1859. The excellent doctor hastened to add to his account that when he encountered her again later on, in the setting of her own home, she struck him 'as the most accomplished great lady, serious in her manner, and wrapped up in her home and children'.

Although Prince Richard had not yet presented his credentials, he and his wife were informally invited to call at the Villa Eugénie. Princess Metternich met the Empress first one evening late in September in the big drawing-room where, seated among her ladies at an enormous round table, she was playing patience. This being her first encounter with the most discussed European Court, the Princess was at first somewhat taken aback by the family atmosphere, the absence of etiquette, by the whole tone which she had hitherto associated more with life in a country house ('*de très grands seigneurs*') rather than with a Palace. The Empress rose, went over to the Princess, shook her by the hand, said how delighted she was to make her acquaintance, that she and the Emperor were very fond of the Prince, her husband, and were happy that he had, as requested, brought his wife to Biarritz. Then she went back to her chair, adjusted behind her the big leather cushion which she always used to ease the pains in her back, and invited her guest to sit at her side. 'The charm,' wrote the Princess, 'which the Empress exercised on all who approached her, affected and captivated me for ever—her gracefulness, her kindness, her ravishing beauty. I admired that beautiful sovereign lady without reserve, and she astonished me by the extreme simplicity and the quality of her elegance— she whose appearance and judgment had made her the uncontested Queen of fashion.' They chatted, and presently a door opened at the far end of the room and the Emperor entered.

'Everybody rose,' narrates the Princess, 'including the Empress, whom incidentally I always saw get up when the Emperor appeared, even when one was alone with her in her study or small drawing-room.' The Emperor, with that odd, slightly shuffling gait of his, walked up to the Princess, also shook her hand and said that he hoped she would come to see them often, 'not only at Biarritz, but, later on, in Paris'. She thought him older-looking than she had expected, found that he had great charm of manner, exquisite manners, and above all 'that great simplicity, that absolute absence of all pose which distinguished the *grand seigneur* from the ordinary run of mortals. He was wholly without self-consciousness, and I am convinced that he felt not the slightest concern with the effect he produced. His voice was deep in tone and slightly nasal.'

'From that day onwards,' she wrote in later years, 'the Emperor and Empress did not let a single occasion pass without showing us their kindness, benevolence and affection. To his last breath my husband felt for them the greatest and, if I may say so, most lively attachment; as for me, I shall never forget the great debt of gratitude I owe to the Emperor and Empress. My remembrance of the Emperor is one of profound respect, and my heart is full of tenderly devoted sentiments for the Empress.' This was written on the eve of the First World War.

In October, Eugénie's old friend Mme de Contades was married to Comte de Beaulaincourt. The event gave the Empress the greatest pleasure, for she had the gift, rare at all times, of taking sympathetic pleasure in the happiness of others. She had, moreover, done more than anyone else to make the match possible. Mme de Contades had survived in society only because the Empress, defying the scandalised pose of virtuousness struck by the Faubourg Saint-Germain, had gone out of her way to take Sophie de Contades under her protection, especially by regularly inviting her to Compiègne. Fleury, her lover at the time of Louis Napoleon's Presidency, had introduced her, as we saw, into the Elysée set, but had in the end married somebody else. She seemed irretrievably isolated and compromised, but the Empress drew her into her circle and made her respectable. When therefore M. de Beaulaincourt, a man of good family, intelligence and breeding, fell in love with her and, soon after M. de Contades's death, proposed, Sophie accepted him, and both she and her father, the Maréchal de Castellane, felt an abiding gratitude for the Empress. She was capable of such gestures because she was never influenced by people's sexual misdemeanours, thinking them unimportant and ephemeral. The wedding took place in Paris on October 14th, 1859, just before the Court returned from Biarritz. Stéphanie Tascher represented the Empress. The couple spent their honeymoon in Naples, and on their return Captain de Beaulaincourt was appointed military attaché at the French Embassy in Berlin. Poor Sophie was pursued by an unforgiving fate; he was killed in August 1860 in an accident during manoeuvres in the Prussian capital. She survived until 1903, and we shall meet her again. Not unlike the Empress, she proved to be stronger than her trials, and men like Mérimée, Edmond de Goncourt and Marcel Proust found her an unending source of wit, delight and inspiration. Mérimée had not liked Mme de Contades and her public tantrums during the previous reign, but, greatly impressed by the Empress's steadying protection, he became a devoted friend of Mme de Beaulaincourt.

The Peace Treaties of Zürich—between France and Austria, between France and Piedmont, and between Piedmont and Austria—were signed on November 10th, 1859. They confirmed the preliminaries of Villafranca —an Italian Confederation under the Pope, Austrian Venetia to become a member of that Confederation, the rights of the rulers of Tuscany, Parma and Modena to be reserved, reforms in the constitutional and representative direction to be carried out in all parts of the peninsula. In accordance with Napoleon III's desire, the signatory powers agreed to convene a European Congress in the near future to work out the details of the programme under which the absolutist rulers at Venice, Rome and Naples were to be transformed into Constitutional Monarchs. Victor Emmanuel was to be invited to withdraw his provisional commissioners from the various capitals in which they had so quickly established themselves. So long as the Congress remained a serious possibility, so long did the Emperor remain arbiter of Europe, as he had been at the end of the Crimean War. He was determined to find a solution without war and without revolution but, although it was his greatest hope to make constitutional rule strike roots in Italian soil, he was given no support by England. That country was still in the grip of its artificially engendered invasion scare. While Palmerston[1] and Russell had an Italian policy of their own that soon outstripped French policy in the backing of the 'popular' movements, the Court remained

[1] Palmerston, moreover, had expressed the view that 'unfortunately, man is a fighting and quarrelling animal'. Despite his frequent resort to doubtful expedients, the French Emperor took a less cynical, a more hopeful view of the nature of political man—hence his insistence on a Congress.

strongly pro-Austrian. Mérimée wrote to Panizzi (who was on calling terms with Palmerston) that 'like the Crimean War, the [Italian] enterprise should have been undertaken jointly with England. It might have been possible with the Whigs; it was wholly impossible with the Tories, and difficult at all times with a German Prince and a country which has little sympathy for foreigners and whose patriotism is a little egotistical.' But France and England had moved apart, even before the Congress idea was killed by the rapid movement of events.

At Compiègne that autumn, the Empress entertained the representatives of both the warring factions of Italy. Mgr. Sacconi, the Papal Nuncio, was among the guests and so was Count Arese, her correspondent during the Italian War, who was one of the nobler minds of the Risorgimento and much respected by her. Metternich represented Austria. There had been elections in the various Italian cities occupied provisionally by Piedmont, and the new assemblies had all voted for annexation by Victor Emmanuel who, hitherto, had correctly refused to accept these 'popular' offers, since this would have gone against the peace of Zürich. Yet in what Metternich called the 'battle of Compiègne' the representatives of the traditional powers were in total darkness as to the Emperor's real intentions. Would he hold out against Piedmontese pressure and insist upon the enforcement of the Zürich terms? The Empress, once again, was on the side of honouring pledges and treaties and believed that the Emperor would back, not the popular clamour for a centralising unification, but the project of a Confederacy between equals who would each swear an oath of allegiance to the new Constitution. As Italy, or at least the new democracies at Florence, Modena and Papal Romagna, hovered on the brink of revolution, she conveyed a message to Metternich that 'despite appearances, the Emperor will remain faithful to his obligations'. She added that her 'irrevocable motto was: "*fais que dois, advienne que pourra*".' 'I sent back a message of thanks,' Metternich reported to Vienna, 'and expressed to Her Majesty that the strengthening and beneficent force of her mediation was implicit in that motto.'

Do what you must, come what may: the Empress remained faithful to this motto beyond the battle of Compiègne. The contest entered upon a more acute phase soon after the Court's return to Paris. Already, the question of the Papal States, and more especially that of Romagna, was producing a vehement controversy all over France, the Roman Catholic hierarchy publicly speaking out against any diminution of the Pope's territorial possessions, while liberal opinion of all shades was condemning, equally loudly but more justifiably, the priests' corrupt and inefficient administration in all the Papal States. As the debate was at its height there appeared, on December 22nd, 1859, another pamphlet written jointly by the Emperor and M. de la Guéronnière, entitled *The Pope and The Congress*. It caused a European sensation.

Briefly, the political suggestions made by this publication were based on the principle that the more the Holy Father was relieved from the duties and pressures of a secular Prince, the more would his spiritual power increase. The smaller his territory, the greater his authority! Rome, with its own municipal government and membership in the Italian Confederation, should remain the dominion of the Papacy in addition to a territory which though not defined with precision was assumed to be roughly the equivalent of the patrimony of St. Peter. The imminent European Congress was to define and sanction all necessary territorial redistributions, as the Congress of Vienna had done in 1815. The pamphlet was unequivocal in saying that Romagna must not return to the Papal dominions, but that, within the confines of his Roman patrimony, the Holy Father must remain an independent Sovereign. No doubt was left in the reader's mind that the fact of Papal Sovereignty and independence must remain inviolate while its geographical extension should be a matter for European statesmanship. As a learned writer said approvingly in the *Dublin Review* of July 1936, this solution harmonised with that first advocated by Gibbon, who postulated for the Pope 'an intermediate degree between the humble poverty of an apostolic fisherman and the Royal state of a temporal Prince whose dominions extend from the confines of Naples to the banks of the Po'. It will also be realised that Napoleon III first put forward a solution which was finally accepted by Pius XI in 1929, although by that date his territorial sovereignty was to be confined to Vatican City alone.

How did these bold ideas strike the Empress? The pamphlet's repercussions were on a European scale, and even Paca, never the most assiduous of correspondents, felt sufficiently moved to write to the Empress and ask what it was all about. In her reply the Empress remarked that in her excitement Paca had failed to read the brochure and so after telling her that it had been 'written by M. de la Guéronnière and the Emperor had known it', the Empress explained its contents to her sister. There was no question, she said, of depriving the Holy Father of his temporal possessions. However, 'since he cannot keep Romagna by force would it not be better to indemnify the Pope and take these territories, which he has been holding *only since the treaties of 1815*, away from the rest?' It would only make him stronger elsewhere. 'I rather fear,' she confessed, 'that great complications will be coming from the States of the Church and it breaks my heart. The unfortunate thing in all this is that people want to be more Catholic than the Pope, and that his friends, who always abandon him when it suits them, wish to show him their respect by inducing him to take a road which will be as thorny for the Holy Father as for everybody else. . . .' To make a province return obediently to the fold, she wrote next, required one of two methods: wise concessions granted at the right time—for which it was now too late—or force. And who would employ force under present conditions? What then was to happen? 'God knows, only I hope with all my heart that the responsibility will not be the Emperor's.' She added a special prayer that the whole world might become 'penetrated by the Spirit of the Gospel'.

The Empress could not, then or later, subscribe to the view that a good Catholic must support the temporal power without questioning. She was the kind of Roman Catholic who fervently hoped for a reconciliation between the Holy See and modern times. How horrified the Pope's partisans and close associates such as Cardinal Antonelli would have been to read that the Empress was expecting 'wise concessions' from them! How disappointed the clergy of France, Mgr. Dupanloup, Bishop of Orléans, or Mgr. Pie of Poitiers! The Empress was a Christian, not a clerical, a Roman Catholic, but not an ultramontane, believed in God, but always insisted on the freedom of the individual conscience. On more than one of her Monday receptions in the past, on several memorable occasions in the future, she would declare with vehemence that the greatest mistake in French history had been the revocation of the Edict of Nantes.

Yet when Lord Cowley saw Queen Victoria early in January during a brief visit to London, he told the Queen that 'the Empress was in despair about the pamphlet, but will not believe that the Emperor has written it!' The latter we know to be untrue, while 'despair' must be regarded as something of an exaggeration. Not unnaturally, the Empress felt distress at the dangers and menaces threatening Christendom, but not, as Cowley implied, simply as a devoted partisan of the Pope. Where did Cowley get this impression?

The question brings us back to Mme Walewska. Not long after the Italian campaign her hold over the Emperor began perceptibly to wane while her husband's position as Foreign Minister became seriously threatened. Faced with the loss of power and influence, the Florentine beauty conceived the notion of founding 'the Empress's Party' behind the scenes, with herself as its head and principal inspiration. Was the Emperor not becoming increasingly identified with the cause of Revolution? Did the European Chancelleries not suspect him of having committed himself irretrievably to the ideal of Italian unification under his ally Victor Emmanuel? Did his radical cousin's marriage to Victor Emmanuel's daughter not establish 'Italian' influence in the heart of the Empire? Very well, argued the Emperor's fallen mistress—in that case the Empress, so famous for her devotion to the Roman Catholic religion, so well-known for her predilections for Austrian ambassadors and so widely assumed to exercise a strong influence on the Emperor's decisions, must become known for her partisanship of the other, the conservative, the traditional, the clerical side in the great European conflict. Mérimée, who had detested both Walewskis all along, and was aware of the lady's purposeful intrigues, noticed with despair that the Empress seemed to suspect nothing. Mme Walewska, with her established position in the household, was well able to clothe her allegations in a spurious authenticity. Augustin Filon who, admittedly, joined the Court only in 1867 but was initiated into such matters by his friend Mérimée, went a step further and said[1] that the

[1] In his biography of the Empress, which was published after her, and his, death in 1920.

145

Emperor approved of Mme Walewska's activities for reasons of propagandistic expedience. It enabled him to keep up his policy of the see-saw in which he now seemed to give Prince Plon-Plon his support and now the Empress who must, in order to have a see-saw at all, maintain her position at the opposite end of this political device. He hoped to hold a middle position between the extremes of Radicalism and Traditionalism, and for that he needed an Empress Consort who reassured French, and European, opinion on the Right.

This machiavellian plot which, says Filon, Mme Walewska kept going 'by sheer force of intellect', would, of course, never have had the slightest chance of success had the Empress not unwittingly contributed to it. Its satanic cleverness consisted in its systematic exploitation of the good as well as the imperfect qualities of the Empress's character. She was assiduous in observing the rules and duties of her religion, and so people soon said that with her Spanish superstitiousness she was praying for the Pope, her son's godfather, regarding the Holy Father as a kind of mascot for the dynasty. She said that treaties must be honoured and was at once presented as an unreasoning partisan of the Pope's temporal power, of Austrian despotism in occupied Venetia. She was seen in earnest conversation with Mgr. Sacconi at Compiègne and it was forthwith believed that she allowed no distinction to be made between the Pope's temporal and spiritual power, that to her he could do no wrong in either capacity. From a believing she was turned into a political Catholic, a neo-ultramontane and clerical fanatic.

That image Mme Walewska and her helpers were able to invent and project, because, even after her successful Regency, the Empress's impulsiveness, her temperamental yielding to the mood or inspiration of the moment, still caused her to make rash and angry remarks and so outrun her powers of reflection as well as her sense of discretion. As nothing roused her anger more easily than ambiguity and dishonesty, she found, as the Italian crisis grew into the reign's most besetting difficulty from 1860 onwards, numberless opportunities for voicing her passionate objections to what she would regard as a betrayal of pledged promises, or a desertion of principles and standards of conduct. As the impetus of Italian unification increased in speed and power, she spoke out, on more than one occasion, against the illegality and anarchy of the 'Piedmontese thieves and robbers'. Not alone among European rulers and leaders of opinion, she adjusted herself only gradually to the political realities produced by the principle of nationality: and there is no question that in the midst of the great conflict she committed a number of mistakes. This the future was to show, and we must not anticipate. Yet even before the major complication of the whole Italian problem, the intervention of Garibaldi and his Thousand, occurred, the Empress's position had been discredited by a campaign of deliberate calumny and distortion that, while exaggerating one side of her beliefs and convictions, completely suppressed all that was far more typical of her. Certain passing reactions were interpreted as a rigid and dogmatic attitude, insofar as they were useful to the image of the reactionary and clerical Empress, but her sincere and unceasing search for a political formula that would combine the demands of progress and emancipation with a respect for the authority of tradition and the sanctity of treaties remained largely ignored.

Thus even as the Empress was writing to Paca on the necessity of separating the Romagna from the Papal States, foreign diplomats and wide sections of French opinion believed her to be narrowly opposed to all concessions by the Holy See. Walewski, that harassed mediocrity at the Quai d'Orsay, contributed, half-wittingly as it were, to his wife's campaign, and it was mainly from him that Cowley and others obtained information on such matters. That, in the age of the Catholic revival, the Emperor needed a Consort who could reassure Catholic opinion, is, of course, easily understandable. He had, as Prince-President, relied on political and electoral support from such Catholic leaders as Montalembert and Falloux. Now that the hierarchy, its preachers, political followers and journalists, declared themselves hostile to the notion of diminishing the Pope's territorial possessions for the benefit of his spiritual authority, Napoleon the Liberator was threatened with losing the support on which Napoleon the Defender of the Pope had been able to count. He was aware that the Empress did not belong to 'the Empress's Party', but that the usefulness of the expedient appealed to him is beyond doubt. How far he went in giving it his full support is not easily determined. It may well be that with an adulterer's guilty conscience he found himself forced to let his former mistress have her way beyond his own inclination.

The La Guéronnière pamphlet killed the project of a European Congress. The people of Modena, Parma, Tuscany and the Romagna were now enabled to decide on their own future and voted in overwhelming numbers for inclusion into the domains of the House of Savoy. To Paris wags, Victor Emmanuel became Annexandre I, since his new kingdom now extended from the Alps to the frontiers of Venetia and had become contiguous with the Papal States which still included Umbria and the Marches. England, never enthusiastic about the Congress, viewed these changes without undue anxiety, but the French Emperor did not forgive Austria for having prevented the Congress from taking place. The Austrian government had foolishly insisted on an official disavowal of the La Guéronnière pamphlet, without which she was not prepared to take part in its deliberations.

The speed of events increased, their portents deepened. In Turin, Cavour returned to office in January, a few days before Walewski was removed from the Quai d'Orsay and replaced by Thouvenel. The latter was a career diplomat of great ability and integrity, a conscientious, reliable and efficient figure among the strutting peacocks from which the political stage of the Second Empire was never wholly free.[1] In March 1860 he issued

[1] He had been French Minister at Athens at the time of the famous Don Pacifico incident when he had to some extent succeeded in curbing Palmerston's exuberance. Thouvenel's appointment was not received with unalloyed enthusiasm in Whitehall.

a circular informing the Concert of Europe that as a result of the substantial enlargement of Piedmontese territory on her Eastern flank, France would annex Savoy and Nice, providing that plebiscites would show the inhabitants to be in favour. The people giving their approval in overwhelming majority, France's frontier in the South-East was thus extended to the 'natural' frontier of the Alps where it had been at the times of the Revolution and General Bonaparte. H.M. Government or, rather, Her Majesty and the Palmerston government, were at once united, for the first time since the beginning of the Italian crisis, and roundly condemned this not extravagant expansion of France, an indignation which the Cabinet forthwith expressed in a note worded, as Palmerston told his delighted Queen, 'as strongly as is consistent with international courtesy'. In this, the British government acted in temporary harmony with the Pope, who as emphatically refused to accept the *fait accompli* of the solution in Central Italy and the loss of Romagna. In his capacity as a temporal Prince, Pio Nono took the surprising step of appointing a Minister of War, who sent out rousing calls for the organisation of a Corps of Papal Volunteers. The non-convening of a Congress produced some very odd results. France withdrew the rest of her armies from Lombardy and let it be known that her armies of occupation would soon be withdrawn also from Rome. Napoleon III hoped that his term as Liberator of Italy had come to an end. Having made the constitutional Kingdom of Sardinia stronger and more independent than it had been at any time in its history and having secured France's frontier against any surprises from that new power, he felt, not without justification, that he need do no more.

Another corner of Europe, her own native Spain, briefly claimed the Empress's attention in April 1860. Ortega, Captain-General of the Balearic Islands and a Carlist, made a landing on the Spanish mainland, proclaimed the overthrow of Queen Isabella's government and the succession of her cousin, the Count of Montemolin, as King Carlos VI. It was an amateurish enterprise, put down without difficulty by the army, but even so Palmerston at once accused the French Emperor of using the Carlists in order to obtain the Balearic Islands for France. The Empress had met the absolutist Spanish Pretender some months earlier, when she had exhorted him to refrain from these enterprises 'which might cost the lives of brave people'. His reply had been biblical in style: 'Happy the subject who dies for his Sovereign.' 'Doubtless,' the Empress had drily remarked, 'so long as the Sovereign is equally prepared to die for his subjects.' And now from the safety of his retreat he had sent a handful of misguided young men to their deaths, one or two of whom were the Empress's relatives. For these she interceded successfully with Queen Isabella, pleading that 'clemency and greatness of soul make more partisans of the throne than a thousand bayonets'. Ortega himself had to be executed as the leader. On the eve of his execution he wrote a moving letter to Doña Manuela.

'What misery,' the Empress wrote to Paca during the drama, 'always having to tremble for the life of friends.' She was, by the spring of 1860, deeply anxious about Paca's health. She had no confidence in the various measures the doctors proposed for Paca's mysterious illness, and was, moreover, greatly perturbed by Paca's stubborn disinclination to let medical advice interfere with her enjoyment of life. The Empress insisted in letter after letter that Paca should leave Spain and be properly cared for. The patient was finally brought to Paris in July.

Parisian and international society gathered on April 24th for a grandiose fancy-dress ball given by the Empress in the house of the Duchess of Alba on the Champs Elysées. 'It was sheer magic,' Mérimée told Doña Manuela, 'all the rooms, galleries, stair-cases crowded with women in brilliant costumes and everything bathed in electric light. . . . It seemed to me,' he continued, 'that many things were shown, feet for example and legs, which one has not seen since 1825. . . .'

The Empress was hostess also to a large house-party at Fontainebleau in June when again Mérimée was present. 'There is no Republic,' he wrote to Jenny Dacquin from there, 'where one can be more free, nor a host or hostess who could be kinder to their guests. . . .' 'What with feasts and banquets, walks in the forests and navigating on the lake there is no time here to write to one's friends,' he told Panizzi. With the Emperor, he talked history and archaeology. He found himself closely cross-examined by his Imperial host, who wanted to know things 'which we will never know. I have read in Greek and Latin that Caesar had been the lover of Pompey's wife and Cato's sister, but I was never able to discover what sort of hat or cap he was wearing. . . .' Yet Mérimée's admiration for the Emperor was being nourished from other sources as well: 'Everybody, I think, is mad,' he wrote to Jenny Dacquin à propos of Italy, 'except the Emperor who, like the shepherds of the middle ages, makes the wolves dance to the music of his magic flute.'

Late in the spring of 1860 the Italian problem took an unexpected and sensational turn. On May 11th, Garibaldi landed with his Thousand in Sicily, and sixteen days later Palermo fell to him. 'How can the critics say,' Mérimée wrote to Doña Manuela when the news reached Paris, 'that novels are improbable? If there is anything improbable nowadays, it is history.'

CHAPTER 12

GARIBALDI'S EXPEDITION brought the Revolution back to Italy, this time under the protection of friendly British warships. It made the French evacuation of Rome impossible. As the Emperor had stressed to Cavour from the beginning, he could not afford to permit the Pope to be driven from the Holy City a second time and now that only the Kingdom of Naples stood between the Holy Father and Garibaldi's high-minded Revolutionaries, the disengagement had to be deferred. When the young King of Naples asked for an international guarantee of his fragmentary kingdom on the mainland, the Emperor sounded the other powers for their views, but, while he waited for their reply, gave the Neapolitan emissaries to understand that Sicily would at any rate have to receive its full independence from Bourbon rule.

As it happened, the Dukes of Alba had for long possessed property in Sicily, and Paca's husband therefore wrote asking the Empress what the future might hold for foreign-held possessions in the rebel island. The letter reached her at Eaux Bonnes where she had gone for rest and treatment in preparation for a prolonged tour of Savoy, Nice and, finally, Algeria, which she was to undertake with the Emperor later in the summer. 'Tell James,' the Empress wrote to Paca on August 4th, 'that I can't do anything from here. Anyway, the King of Naples has no authority now in Sicily. It is necessary for claims to wait until a government has been formed.' Garibaldi's expedition roused far less hostility from her than young Ortega's had done and the Bourbons' losing Sicily evinced no criticism from her. Her mind, that summer, was preoccupied with two things: the imminent journey through the newly-acquired provinces, and Paca's health.

Paca and Doña Manuela had arrived in Paris late in July and the Empress from her spa exhorted her sister by letter to 'mend your ways and endeavour to behave yourself', for Paca was never a docile patient. Back in Paris by mid-August, the Empress called every evening on her sister, and sometimes the two of them would drive together to the Bois. 'Elegant, beautiful, stretched out in her *calèche*, immobile, pale, dying,' wrote someone who caught a glimpse of Paca on one of those summer evenings, 'her eyes and lips were half-open as if she inhaled the light and had not enough air to live.' On August 22nd, the Empress called to say goodbye and next morning she and the Emperor left Saint-Cloud on the first stage of the journey.

Dijon, Lyons, Chambéry all received the Imperial visitors with enthusiasm. 'Despite my tiredness,' the Empress wrote to Paca, 'I am delighted with this voyage. Impossible to describe the enthusiasm, which bordered on the delirious.' She telegraphed to her sister daily, she wrote as often as she could snatch a moment, she prayed for Paca's recovery at all the shrines on her way. Yet no one ever noticed her deep anxiety; as always her radiance shone unimpaired through a long series of public engagements and mass functions. At a banquet at Chambéry, she had Farini, Piedmontese Minister of the Interior on her left, the Piedmontese General Cialdini on her right. Both had arrived ostensibly to superintend the illumination and other arrangements for the reception of the Sovereigns in this once Savoyard town, but in fact in order to consult the Emperor on the next step to be taken in the situation created by Garibaldi's progress in Southern Italy.

The Thousand had crossed the Strait of Messina on August 20th and were marching on Naples, after the conquest of which it would be the turn of the Papal States. Was the initiative to be left to the Redshirts? In the midst of the festivities at Chambéry the two Piedmontese leaders asked for the Emperor's approval of Cavour's plan to send armed forces through Papal Umbria and the Marches in order to link up with, and eventually to control, Garibaldi's troops on Neapolitan territory. The Emperor gave his approval on condition that a call for help from the population in the remaining Papal States would justify the march across their territory and stressed that the Pope and the patrimony of St. Peter would remain under the protection of the French garrison until Cavour's statesmanship had found a workable agreement with the Pope at Rome. Of all this the two envoys did not say a word as they sat next to the Empress at dinner.

'Savoy,' the Empress wrote to Paca from Annecy, 'is a lovely country and not at all as poverty-stricken as everybody says. It seems that the Swiss are furious because Savoy wanted to be united to France, and I hear that they will be trying to make all kinds of unamiable demonstrations against us on Lake Geneva tomorrow. But I think like the Emperor—the big dogs should let the little dogs bark as long as they don't start biting them in the leg. Anyway, we have been received in Savoy far too well to be perturbed by these latest expressions of ineffectual rage. When you are better, you must come and visit this part of the world. . . .' The visit to Annecy was one of sheer enchantment. In the evening, the Emperor and Empress were rowed in a Venetian bark across the lake, followed and surrounded by illuminated boats while on the mountain tops fire answered fire and fireworks sparkled to the sound of songs and serenades. All along the shore a thousand torches lit up the warm enthusiastic night, and when next day the Empress drove through the narrow winding streets of Annecy, she fell in love with the tranquillity of the little town over which the mountains stood like ramparts. 'Perhaps for the first time in my life,' she wrote to Paca, 'I understood the attractiveness of calm which we can enjoy so rarely—we especially, condemned as we are to restlessness like the wandering Jew. . . . All my prayers are reduced to one: your dear health. . . .' On to Lake Geneva where Arese came to see the Emperor at Thonon, with more messages from Cavour.

Great surprise at Grenoble: Monsieur Beyle! 'This morning,' she told Paca on September 6th, 'I went to the museum here and the first thing I saw was his portrait which I instantly recognised. Our whole childhood came back to my mind. . . . How far were we from thinking that my son would become the descendant and representative one day of the dynasty of the Napoleons! No doubt you will know that Grenoble is the most Bonapartist town in all France, and so you can imagine what our reception has been like. They have never forgotten that the Emperor chose Grenoble as the base for his triumphant march on Paris, and all the executions of 1815 could not extinguish in their hearts the cult of the Emperor. . . .' Shades of Colonel Portocarrero, shades of La Bédoyère!

Thereafter, Avignon, no longer Papal, Arles, where Mistral celebrated the Empress in a *Provençal* poem, Marseilles, from where, a little overawed, she told Paca that she was facing a ball for 150,000 invited guests. 'Adieu, my dear sister,' the letter from Marseilles of September 9th ended, 'I don't know whether I shall be able to write again before we return from Algiers, but you may be sure that if I don't it will be through lack of time and not from laziness, for you know that I love you tenderly.' And so on to Nice, the second new department of France, which was reached aboard the Imperial yacht *Aigle*.

On September 13th, the Sovereigns embarked for Corsica and Algiers. Two days earlier two Piedmontese army corps had crossed the frontier of the Papal States, even though no cry for help had come from Umbria or the Marches. The *Aigle* reached Algiers on Monday, September 17th, and the Empress found waiting for her grave news of Paca's health. 'I don't know what I am doing or saying,' she wrote at once to Doña Manuela. 'The thought of Paca being worse and I so far away prevents me from living, for I am in mortal fear . . .' and she asked both her mother and the Duke of Alba to telegraph news by return. On September 18th, the Papal army, which Mgr. de Mérode had organised and which was commanded by the French Royalist General Lamoricière, was beaten by the Piedmontese at Castelfidardo. In Algeria on the same day a great ceremony took place in which the Beys and native Chiefs of North Africa paid their homage before the French Sovereigns. 'The festive day,' wrote the historian of the occasion, 'ended in an apotheosis. Admiration for the Empress's beauty was reflected on the bronzed faces of the Algerian chieftains who prostrated themselves before her.' Fleury, who was in the Imperial suite, judged that the artless and spontaneous tributes paid to her by these formidable figures 'pleased the woman in her'. When it was over, she enquired for further news about her sister, and the Emperor indicated that there had been no improvement in the patient. It was decided to return to France next day, cutting the tour short by two days.

Would she reach Paris and Paca in time? The Empress aboard the *Aigle* was filled with unbearable anxiety. They reached Marseilles on the 21st, and, just before disembarking, the Emperor told her quietly that her sister had died on Sunday, September 16th. He had known all along, the fatal telegram had reached him on the day before the solemnities of homage in Algiers. The funeral had taken place at the Madeleine on September 20th; the Emperor had from Algiers telegraphed to the Duke of Alba to wait for the Empress's return before taking the remains to Spain.

No words could describe the bitterness and cruelty of the blow delivered at a moment when she least expected it. She had been the last to hear of Paca's death, of the being she loved and cherished above all else in the world. Her innermost life, the deepest and darkest instincts implanted in her nature had all her life sought out the gentle, strong-willed, gay and undemonstrative sister who alone had known her secrets, who had shared in silence the passions and defeats of the early years—who had been the very anchor of her own unquiet soul, had been her childhood, youth, home. The Emperor had told her of this death only when it suited him. Like a thief he had stepped between her and news that was meant for her alone. He had not trusted her. It seemed to her then, it took her years to overcome it, as though at one blinding blow she had lost her sister and her faith in the Emperor.

The Emperor and Empress arrived at Saint-Cloud from Marseilles in the afternoon of September 22nd.

On September 28th, Ancona, the last stronghold remaining to the Pope outside Roman territory, surrendered to the Piedmontese fleet and army. Umbria and the Marches were ready for annexation. General Cialdini, the Empress's dinner companion at Chambéry, made ready to march on Naples, where Garibaldi had established his dictatorship. The young King of Naples, meanwhile, had withdrawn to Gaëta, the most strongly fortified sea-port of his kingdom.

CHAPTER 13

'I DON'T KNOW whether there will be any invitations to Compiègne this year,' Mérimée wrote to a friend on October 16th. 'They tell me that the Empress, whom I have not seen, is still much distressed. She has sent me a beautiful photograph of the Duchess of Alba, taken more than twenty-four hours after death. She looks serenely asleep. Her death was very gentle. She laughed at the Valencian dialect of her maid five minutes before she died. I have not heard from Mme de Montijo direct since she left. I fear that the poor woman will not be able to bear the loss.'

A week later he was asked to luncheon at Saint-Cloud with the Emperor, Empress and 'Monsieur fils'. He found the Empress looking better than she had done before the voyage—'the rest and solitude,' he told Doña Manuela, 'in which she has been living these six weeks have given her strength and health'. Few other people saw the Empress at this time. Her old friend, Hübner, was passing through Paris late in October and the Emperor had a long and frank discussion with him at Saint-Cloud, but the Empress did not show herself even for him.

Paca's coffin had been transferred to the little church at Rueil near Malmaison which the Emperor had restored as the final resting place of the Empress Josephine and his mother, Queen Hortense. There she went daily to pray, greatly fearing the moment when the coffin would be taken to its final resting place in Spain. She often wrote to Alba, knowing that he would be exposed to the full force of Doña Manuela's grief, and so endeavoured to make the widower understand his mother-in-law's somewhat demonstrative temperament. 'One must remember,' she wrote on October 28th, 'that this final blow has been the worst she has ever experienced. My sister was her idol, the joy and pride of her heart, and now she has lost it all in a few hours. The emptiness around her is immense. I am telling you this so that you may be gentle towards a poor sick heart and not become angry with her for things she is reported to have said and which may not even be exact. . . .'

About herself she wrote: 'To think that I was not there, near her, doubles my grief. Your house in Madrid, sad though it may be at present, at least reminds you of her life, but her house here brings back only the memory of the last days and her death. I feel that a voyage would do me good, for always being reminded of my loss weakens me—but where can I go? I want to flee and I don't know where. Write to me, dear Jimmy. . . .' Paca's son was with her still, the two girls having gone back with Doña Manuela in September, and she had found a tutor for the eleven-year-old boy. 'The tutor, M. Meunlier,' she told Alba, 'is an erudite and conscientious man . . . his character pleasant and easy-going, simple, modest, and he knows that he should amuse his pupil as well as instruct him. . . . Tell me whether you like him, for it has been a big responsibility to arrange all this on my own. Above all, don't be alarmed by his appearance, which is that of a professor and not a man of the world.' And she ended this letter to the man she had once loved so much:

'Adieu, my very dear James: believe in the affection of your sister Eugénie.'

The Duke of Alba was the only person to be told of her desire to flee from Paris. She kept, once again, her own counsel and made her own plans. Shortly before November 10th, she suddenly informed the Emperor that she was going on a visit to Scotland. There was a hastily-arranged farewell on the 14th and a statement was issued to French diplomatic missions abroad that 'Owing to the effect on Her Majesty of the death of her sister, the doctors have recommended a change of air. The Empress will visit Scotland in the strictest *incognito*. The Emperor will go to Compiègne until the end of the month.' So simple an explanation as the desire for a change of scenery after much silent and lonely suffering was widely disbelieved, and the wildest rumours immediately circulated in Paris and elsewhere. 'She wants a divorce;' 'she cannot forgive the Emperor's treatment of the Pope;' 'she cannot overlook the Emperor's latest love affair,' and so on. Only Mérimée believed the simplest explanation to be the true one, and only the Duke of Alba knew for certain.

The Empress arrived in London late on November 14th, and remained until the 17th at Claridge's Hotel. She was accompanied by four members of her household. Queen Victoria, naturally most surprised at this unexpected visit, did not hear of the arrival until November 16th. The Queen confided to her journal that the Foreign Secretary, Lord John Russell, had told her that 'the Empress's nerves had become so shattered and affected by her sister's unexpected death, she having hoped still to find her alive on her return from Algeria, that a journey was thought absolutely necessary. It would not have been possible in Italy, Germany or Spain, so there was nothing left but England and Scotland.' Almost at the same time the Queen received a brief note from the Empress herself which said in the utmost simplicity that she had felt the necessity for a change, was travelling *incognito* and hoped to see the Queen on her way back from Scotland. When Lord Clarendon called on the Queen on November 21st, he offered his opinion that the sudden journey had been due a good deal to fear of an illness like her sister's and the anxiety to see Dr. Simpson at Edinburgh. Clarendon, like Leopold, thought that a subsidiary motive might have been disagreements between her and her husband.

Clarendon's medical theory was correct. Paca had died of a mysterious ailment of the spine which had baffled her doctors, and the Empress had for some years been complaining of pains in her back, so that a thorough medical check seemed advisable. Dr. Simpson found her physically in excellent condition. While at Edinburgh, she paid a visit to Holyrood and the relics of Mary Queen of Scots, but here her incognito broke down. The city fathers could not forgo the opportunity provided by the first visit from a Royal Lady of France since Mary Stuart. The Empress, dressed in mourning, received an address from the Town Council and, to their delight, replied briefly in English. After this, she introduced a more official note into her journey, telling for instance the Provost of Glasgow in reply to another address of welcome that, encouraged by the friendly reception she received everywhere, she 'sincerely hoped that the amity and friendly feeling at present subsisting between Great Britain and France would ever continue'. Local and national newspapers carried reports of such speeches and so did the French press, gratefully noting that these 'manifestations of sympathy on the part of the British nation were drawing closer the ties which bind together the two nations'. Scottish and English friendliness and spontaneity had their therapeutic effect on the Empress.

Her destination in Scotland was Hamilton Palace, the Duchess of Hamilton now being one of her more intimate friends. A fellow-guest at Hamilton, Lord Lamington, arriving shortly after the Empress, was amazed to see that 'a dense crowd lined the road all the way from Motherwell Station to Hamilton Palace. The one anxiety was to obtain a glimpse of the Empress.' At the house, he found the visitor and her suite in deepest mourning, and the luncheon to which the small company presently sat down 'a very funereal one. The whole scene was suited to the Empress's frame of mind. By the time luncheon was over (and it lasted two hours), the crowd of people in the park outside was immense. It seemed as if the whole country had collected to stare, not at any grand procession or military display, but simply at a graceful lady who wore such a thick veil that not a feature was discernible.'

She next visited the Atholls at Blair, unannounced, the Duke meeting her by chance on the road and showing her over the castle, shut up at the time, in the light of tallow candles which he carried from room to room. At Dumfries, the local archivist begged for the favour of presenting her with a genealogical table of her Scottish ancestry, which 'she was graciously pleased to accept'. Other than noting that Scottish papers were printing a good deal of nonsense on the subject, the Empress showed little interest in her Kirkpatrick descent.

Passing through Manchester where she visited several factories and the new Free Library, the Empress received another address of welcome from the Town Council, and an ovation from the people of Lancashire. By then, her sense of duty and opportunity had proved stronger than her desire for privacy. She arrived back at Claridge's on December 2nd, and two days later she went to Windsor. 'How does the Empress wish to

156

be received,' Queen Victoria had enquired from Lord John Russell, 'As Empress? in which case she would have to be received with all possible ceremony—here (at Osborne, of course, the case is different as *there all* ceremony is done away with)—or incognito and privately? 'The Empress expressed a strong preference for the second alternative. Consequently, Prince Albert met her at Windsor Station and brought her to the Castle where the Queen was waiting with a few members of her family.

'She looked thin and pale and unusually melancholy,' noted the Queen, 'but was as kind, sensible and natural as she had always been. . . . She talked a good deal of her journey, with which she was much pleased, but when she spoke of her return from Algeria, her eyes filled with tears and she said it was only since she had come here that she had been able to sleep and eat again. She only mentioned the Emperor once and that was *d'offrir ses compliments.* Politics were not approached, which was much pleasanter. But she gave me a melancholy impression, as if some deep grief and anxiety weighed upon her. Poor thing, one must feel much for her. . . . The Empress left at ¼ p. 3. What a contrast to her visit in 55! Then all a state of excitement, thousands and thousands out and the brightest sunshine. Now, all in private and a dreadful, foggy, wet December day!'

The visit to Britain was fulfilling the Empress's expectations, despite the sneers from King Leopold that few people chose Scotland for health reasons in November, and of *The Times* that now that France had annexed Nice a better choice of health resort should have suggested itself to the Empress of the French. She extended her stay at Claridge's by as many days as possible. Among her private visits the most interesting was to Panizzi at the British Museum. He was a political refugee from the Duchy of Modena and therefore no friend of Austria or of the Pope. Mérimée, his close friend and fellow anti-clerical, had often spoken of him to the Empress. Who among the Empress's detractors would have expected her to call on a man like him? Mérimée replied to Panizzi's account of the visit, saying how delighted he was at Panizzi's being 'on such good terms with Monsieur as well as with Madame. Believe me, she was not at all against seeing you, despite the mediocrity of your Catholicism.'

On December 9th, the Duchess of Sutherland gave a reception for the Empress at Stafford House (as she was to do four years later for Garibaldi). Lord Clarendon received his invitation too late to be present, but evidently he had seen the Empress earlier, for he wrote to the Duchess of Manchester that 'the Eugenian mind' had found luncheon at Windsor a little stiff. 'I am sure,' wrote Clarendon, 'the Q. *intended* to be civil but she doesn't understand scrambles & larks & hack cabs which give her a vague impression of impropriety & curdle the blood in The Consort's veins.' Nevertheless, on December 10th the Queen paid a return visit to the

Empress at her hotel. 'She looked very pretty,' reads the entry in the Royal journal, 'and was in better spirits, telling us all she had seen, but again never mentioning the Emperor or politics. It is evident she likes being here. . . .' With the Queen were Prince Albert, Princess Alice and her fiancée Louis of Hesse-Darmstadt, and 'Affie', the future Duke of Edinburgh.

On December 12th the Empress left London. She was attended to the station by Mr. Claridge, to whom she was heard to express from the carriage window, just before the train started, 'her great satisfaction at the comfortable privacy she had enjoyed while under his roof'. It was a milestone in the progress of that famous hostelry for Kings, and no doubt Mr. Claridge was highly gratified when the Empress's gracious words were subsequently reported in the London papers.

The Emperor went to Boulogne to welcome her. Great changes had occurred during the Empress's absence. On November 23rd it was announced that Achille Fould, Minister of State, was to be replaced by Walewski, who had remained unemployed since leaving the Foreign Ministry in January 1860. Mérimée had been prophesying this turn of events for some weeks previously, his opinion being that Fould, who, in his other capacity as Minister of the Imperial Household, controlled the Court's and Emperor's expenditure, was exercising too tight a hold on the purse-strings for the liking of a good many people, including, it would seem, the Emperor himself. Mérimée, always sharp-eyed in these things, also thought that Mme Walewska had focused her ambitions on Fould's influential office for a long time.

The gossips at once spread the tale that Fould had been dismissed to appease the Empress, who could not forgive him for not delaying Paca's funeral until her return nor for the parsimonious manner in which the solemnities had been held. The Emperor himself denied the story at once, saying that her grief at not being able to be present at the funeral had been 'of short duration' and that she had left for Scotland in 'absolute ignorance' of any Ministerial changes. In the not too distant future, the Empress was to show in a striking manner in what high esteem she held Fould. Other changes announced at the same time included the recall of Persigny from London to become Minister of the Interior, the promotion of Marshal Pélissier, Duke of Malakoff, to be Governor-General of Algeria, and of Charles de Flahaut to succeed Persigny at the London Embassy, an appointment much welcomed by Queen Victoria. Talleyrand's natural son, although deeply implicated in the coup d'état of 1851, had become a universally popular figure in London, where he had established terms of easy friendship with all the leading figures in politics and society.

Even more important changes were announced in Paris on the following day, November 24th. Parisians could hardly believe their eyes when they read in the Moniteur of that day that henceforth the two legislative chambers, the Deputies and the Senate, could deliberate upon an address in reply to the speech from the throne, that debates could be published in full by the press, and that the government would appoint Ministers without ordinary departmental duties to explain the government's policy in the chambers. The Emperor had taken a bold step forward on the road of liberalising the Empire. 'Obviously,' wrote a declared enemy of his, Thiers, to the Duke of Aumale, 'he wanted to prepare the future for his son. . . . To preach liberty, sword in hand, to the whole world, to tell the Pope, the King of Naples, the Dukes of Tuscany and Modena, to tell the Emperor of Austria himself that they were perishing, or would perish, for having refused sufficient liberty to their subjects, and to make us live under the institutions of the first Empire . . . without even the corrective of the Additional Act [i.e. Napoleon I's constitution of 1815]—all this had become an intolerable contradiction. . . .' All the Duke of Aumale, fifth son of Louis Philippe, could say in reply from Twickenham was: 'We shall see how [the new decrees] are carried out in practice,' seeming to question their sincerity. These Orleanist doubts roused Thiers into making the most statesman-like pronouncement to fall from his lips throughout the new decade: 'What matters,' he told Aumale, 'is not the sincerity of the offer, but the sincerity of its acceptance.'

Three days after this momentous announcement, the Emperor and the Prince Imperial went to a sadly quiet and deserted Compiègne. Among the aides attending the Emperor were Fleury, Edgar Ney, the Empress's protégé Galliffet who had, thanks to the Regent's active help, arrived in Lombardy just in time for the battle of Solferino and was now one of the Emperor's Ordnance Officers. The Duke of Montebello, French Ambassador at St. Petersburg, represented diplomacy among the few guests, and Morny, eminently associated with the reforms just announced, the government. The Prince was still under the supervision of the formidable Miss Shaw. The Emperor held a Council of Ministers one afternoon; there were shooting parties and a hunt. After dinner, he worked with Viollet-le-Duc on the plans for Pierrefonds, went pheasant shooting in the morning of November 30th and, after the Prince Imperial's dinner at six, returned to Paris that same evening.

One more change was decreed by the Emperor before the year 1860 came to an end. It was well in keeping with the new liberal thaw and was the happiest measure of all: on December 18th, 1860, he liberated all British subjects from the necessity of carrying passports when travelling to, and in, France. 'His Majesty has decided,' wrote that normally pungent critic of the Emperor, The Times.

'that from and after this day fortnight British subjects coming into France "shall be admitted and allowed to travel about without Passports". Thus speaks the Emperor NAPOLEON, and the victory proclaimed over political superstitions is as memorable as that illustrated by the easy capture of Peking[1]. . . . With great force it was intimated that a swarm

[1] On October 7th, 1860, an Anglo-French punitive expedition sacked and burnt the Summer Palace near Peking and later occupied the Chinese capital.

of officials lived and prospered upon the profits of the [passport] system, and that to destroy these gains would be like destroying a profession. All these arguments have now vanished into air. The thing is decreed, and it will be done—done, we venture to predict, with the utmost facility, and with the best possible results. . . . For the first time we can now go to France and mingle with Frenchmen on terms of perfect freedom, and the removal of the barriers is not only a national compliment, but an expression of amity and a pledge of peace. Six months hence both nations will be wondering how an institution so preposterously mischievous could ever have been maintained.'

Other London papers joined The Times in expressing the view that this measure would have a far more immediate and beneficent effect on Anglo-French relations than the commercial treaty recently concluded between the two countries. Cobden had negotiated it in Paris at the beginning of the year and it had been signed on January 23rd, 1860. It embodied the free trade principles of the Manchester school and the Emperor's own Saint-Simonian concepts of political economy. This, however, had not prevented Englishmen later in the year from rallying to their country's aid against that immediately threatening French invasion which continued to be conjured up before their eyes. Cobden, it is true, had commented on these invasion scares to the effect ' that a delusion more gigantic or a hoax more successful was never practised on the public mind since the days of Titus Oates ', but even after the signing of the Free Trade Treaty his voice carried little weight in mid-Victorian London. All that, however, was politics, the business of the politicians and the ruling classes. As the year drew to its close the acclamations accorded to the Empress had shown the people of these islands in a wholly friendly mood.

'I hope,' the Empress had written to James Alba from London, 'that my return to Paris won't be too sad, for I want to fight against my grief.' She knew that soon after her return Paca's remains would be taken for interment in Spain. The terrible day came on December 19th, and she went to Rueil to watch over the final details and arrange the flowers—'I did everything for the poor corpse which I would have done for her when she was ill. You will understand that I have no courage or strength left to write much, but I have done my duty to the end.' 'A month ago,' she wrote to Alba in her next letter, 'I would have been unable to be present, I was so weak. Now that God has given me back my strength, I wanted to be near her until the last moment. . . .'

'I lived through a terrible moment,' were her final words to Paca's husband, 'when they removed my sister's body. I felt that they were tearing my soul from me.'

CHAPTER 14

T H E Y E A R 1860 marks a water-shed in the history of the Second Empire, in the development of modern Europe and in the life of the Empress Eugénie. She gradually succeeded in mastering her grief at Paca's death, and was able in time also to forgive her husband for the way in which he had informed her of it. The Anglo-Scottish interlude had restored her courage and her determination to distinguish scrupulously between her private and public selves. She returned to a France that had taken the first step towards a greater liberalisation of the interior and this demanded new adjustments from her, and not only from her. The Emperor associated her with the new era from the beginning by making her regularly attend the Ministerial meetings—a not uncalled-for measure in view of the fact that her Regency in 1859 when she herself had presided over such meetings had been an unqualified success. We have a few comments from the Empress on this early phase of the liberal Empire which show that, so far as internal politics were concerned, she was, at first, a learner accepting some of the lessons taught and rejecting others. She was, for example, little enamoured of the new freedom of the Press which anyone who has read French newspapers of the period as carefully as she did will not find surprising. But she was far more in favour of freedom of debate in the two Chambers than her friend Mérimée or her mother in Madrid, whom she lectured once or twice on the desirability of constitutional liberty. Within three years of the beginning of the great experiment she was to show how politic she could be in exploiting the opportunities for reforms which this forward-looking side of the Empire provided.

Foreign affairs, on the other hand, roused her more immediately and, as it were, audibly than the new trend in internal politics. She felt herself, her whole position as Empress and mother of the heir to the throne, to be deeply involved in the Italian question, and this for two reasons. She saw, in the first place, that Victor Emmanuel and Cavour were pushing forward their solution for Italian unity not only wholly unimpeded by any reference to a European forum, but by paying little, if any, attention to the Federalist programme laid down by the Emperor on several occasions, notably in the La Guéronnière pamphlet. Secondly, she saw—and the Emperor confirmed her impression—that France was slipping into a subordinate place in an evolution to which the costly carnage of the Italian campaign had given so powerful an impetus. By March 1861, Victor

Emmanuel called himself King of Italy. Garibaldi, it was true, had retired to the island of Caprera after handing over the kingdom of the Two Sicilies to Victor Emmanuel. Diplomatic relations between France and Piedmont, it was also true, had been broken off when Papal Umbria and the Marches had been invaded by the Piedmontese on their march south. All these territories had been joined to the new Italian kingdom, while the Pope's temporal possessions had been reduced to 'Rome and a garden', as the patrimony of St. Peter came to be called in France. Would the inexorable march of events not soon sweep the Holy Father out of even that fragmentary territory? Cavour had publicly announced that Rome must become the capital of the new Italy. The French army was still in occupation of the Eternal City and so stood between Italian nationalism and the representative of a universal and supra-national idea. If it came to a show-down, would the Emperor fight?

For many years, this complex problem was to give the Empress her greatest political anxieties because, for many years, she regarded the Piedmontese, 'the Prussians of the Alps', as the despoilers of Naples and the Pope. Like the majority of Roman Catholics in France and elsewhere in the world, she could not picture a Pope who had no territorial independence, who would not rule from Rome as the Vicar of Christ and command spiritual submission of the Kings and nations of this earth. This to her had all the force and sanctity of a great historic tradition. She had, as we saw, shed no tears over Victor Emmanuel's annexation of the Romagna and so showed that she did not subscribe to the view, formulated by Pio Nono early on, that *all* temporal possessions of the Church formed 'the indivisible robe of Christ'—a claim that might strike many Christians as blasphemous. Her objection to the rapid swallowing up of Naples, Umbria and the Marches by Annexandre I stemmed from her conviction that the onward rush of the Italian movement was bound to chase the Pope from Rome and make him an exile in Malta or Wuerzburg, the guest of the Queen of Protestant England or the Emperor of Austria. And was it in the French interest to allow the neighbour across the Alps to grow into a major European power? She soon conceived it to be her duty to oppose what was called the 'Italian' line in the Empire's foreign policy, and this she did with her accustomed vehemence, outspokenness and intensity. It was exceedingly useful to the Emperor as the master of the see-saw.

Yet, disdaining to hide the strength of her convictions and being incapable of taking a dispassionate view of any issue that touched so closely on the future of the Empire and its position in Europe, she exposed her reputation and position within the Empire to further sneaking attacks by her hidden enemies. The Emperor, throughout the first six months of 1861, was engaged upon secret negotiations with Cavour which aimed at obtaining sufficient guarantees by Italy of the Pope's continued residence in Rome after which it would at last be possible to withdraw the French garrison from the Eternal City. Only a man of Cavour's forcefulness and authority could achieve a solution that would be acceptable to both his King and the Pope, but Cavour died in the midst of these negotiations: 'an event,' wrote the Belgian ambassador at Paris, 'which is considered a disaster by everybody, even his political enemies.' The Emperor nevertheless decided to resume diplomatic relations with Victor Emmanuel, which entailed the latter's recognition as King of Italy, but to leave the garrison in Rome for the time being. At a Ministerial meeting which the Empress, as usual, attended, he asked Thouvenel to read to the Council a document defining the new measure. Half way through the reading the Empress showed signs of violent agitation, tears came to her eyes and finally she rushed from the room. The Emperor sat silently for a moment, pensive and impassive, and then asked a courtier to see 'whether Her Majesty required any assistance'. The reading was then resumed.

Napoleon III, like his predecessors or his Republican successors immediately after 1870, could not afford openly to break with the Pope. Nor could he afford any act of commission or omission which would enable his Catholic subjects or enemies—the two groups were not, of course, identical—to blame the Pope's loss of independence on him and his government. Of this, the French Ambassador at Rome, the Duke of Gramont, was fully aware: 'France needs,' he wrote to Thouvenel in March 1861, 'not a Pope who is content, but a Pope who is free.' Thouvenel himself, widely known to be 'Italian' rather than Papal, entirely agreed with this formula which to him was good politics. Yet the radical wing of the Italian Party, led, naturally, by Prince Plon-Plon, went much further. In a speech to the Senate during the debate on the speech from the throne, one of the innovations introduced in November 1860, the Emperor's cousin vehemently demanded that Rome be given to Italy, and that the Tiber should form a line of demarcation 'between the Catholic part and the city of the ancient Caesars'. In the same speech he launched a violent attack on the House of Bourbon, since other Senators had praised the resistance offered by the young King and Queen of Naples at Gaeta until lack of European support had forced them to evacuate. The new freedom of debate had shown a France hopelessly divided between the partisans of Naples and the Pope and those of the King of Italy. Public opinion at all levels knew that the Imperial family itself was divided along the same lines, the Empress upholding the Pope's temporal freedom and Prince Napoleon wishing to reduce him to virtual impotence. On whose side was the Emperor?

Napoleon III was on both sides. It was this calculated ambiguity, this cautious and impenetrable manoeuvring and opportunism, the latter not necessarily a disparaging term, that put the Empress's patience and nerves to hard and frequent tests. Her doubts and anxieties were confirmed in public places, in the debates in the chambers and the reports in the newspapers. 'Piedmont could be stopped,' a deputy from Alsace, Keller, had exclaimed during the debate, 'but you must want to do it.' He addressed these questions to the Emperor's government:

163

'Who are you and what do you want to be? Are you revolutionary? Are you conservative? Or are you simply sitting on the fence? You write on the same page of the inviolability of the Pope and the dethronement of the Holy Father. Come out into the open and tell us what you are!'

The see-saw politics were not without their dangers. Yet the Emperor, having begun the tremendous experiment of giving back to France some of the liberties which he had taken from her in the coup d'état, had to tread warily and gingerly across a field that was heavily mined with dangerous and explosive possibilities. In contrast to England, which had cut herself free from Rome three centuries before and now advised him to follow the example of Henry VIII at least in this respect, the Emperor's freedom of action was narrowly circumscribed by dire political necessities. He was himself only a very moderate Catholic, but as an astute politician he realised that the Pope's territorial freedom was a problem that closely affected his own position and future.

For that reason the Empress's loyalty of conscience represented to him, especially in the anxious months after Cavour's death, a considerable political asset—not only her loyalty, but her persistence and staying power, her courage and unconditional honesty. For the other make-weight on the see-saw, his cousin Plon-Plon, not only did not show any of these qualities, but was the Empress's inferior in both self-control and courage. His anti-Bourbon speech in the Senate, when he had singled out the Orleans branch for a specially unmeasured denunciation, led to a reply, in pamphlet form, by the Duc d'Aumale, Louis Philippe's fifth son, who lived in England. Although confiscated by the French police, the pamphlet had been widely read, and the whole of Paris knew that Aumale had made remarks of a nature that would induce any gentleman to issue a challenge. He had called Prince Napoleon a coward. The Emperor advised his cousin to arrange for the duel to be fought on neutral territory such as Belgium, but Plon-Plon replied that he had no intention of taking any notice of the 'agitation' which was entirely due to the Empress's hostility towards him. 'I have given you advice,' the Emperor replied,

'which I thought was in your own interests. You think otherwise, and I have nothing to add. You are quite wrong if you think that the Empress feels any hatred towards you. She is always lively in her impressions, but she has always shown you friendly feelings.'

With her feeling for the necessity of family unity she had certainly always *shown* him friendly feelings, whatever her own judgment of his character and talents. On the present occasion, when once again he had covered the name of Napoleon with shame on a European scale, she cut him at a reception. 'The military,' wrote Mérimée to Panizzi, 'are furious [with Prince Napoleon] and that, in war-time, could be serious.' Soon afterwards,

Plon-Plon gave the Emperor another embarrassing problem to deal with. He allowed himself to be elected Grand Master of a Masonic Lodge, but the Emperor cancelled the election and appointed Marshal Magnan instead. Plon-Plon went on a prolonged cruise on his yacht, visiting the United States shortly after the outbreak of the Civil War. He called on President Lincoln at the White House, but declined to enter into a conversation since the President, not without preoccupations of his own, had kept his visitor waiting for a few minutes.

Prince Napoleon was a man of many gifts, had personality, wit and eloquence. The Emperor, who had known him since his childhood, some of which Plon-Plon had spent in Queen Hortense's house at Arenenberg, never abandoned his turbulent cousin who was fourteen years younger than himself and to whom he had, for long, stood *in loco parentis*. Even so, Plon-Plon's career, if that is the appropriate word, consisted of a series of impulses, followed by hot-tempered resignations at the first sign of resistance from above. The Emperor did always what he could to make his cousin's return to office and position as easy as possible, and so did the Empress, who breathed freely only in a climate of conciliation and accord. Yet what a contrast between the Corsican egoist with his childish *amour-propre* and the Empress who despite so many provocations and opportunities for self-pity and unhappiness remained faithful to her profession! His attitude stemmed from the conviction that, by rights, the Empire belonged to him, hers that she belonged to the Empire. In this, as in other questions, Prince Napoleon, during the Empire and after, remained the same. The Empress developed upwards, learning to accept what once she had rejected. Her friendship with Constantine Nigra is a case in point. He was the first representative at her Court of the new kingdom of Italy, presenting his credentials on August 8th, 1861. At first, she treated him with a distant coldness; a little later, she flung her whole passionate objections to Italian methods and proceedings into his face, not mincing her words, not hiding her conviction that Victor Emmanuel was a bandit, the despoiler of others' possessions. Yet in the years to come, when Roman intransigence and pettiness began to disillusion her, she changed her attitude towards him. He, for his part, gradually wore down her hostility, introducing Italian writers and poets to her, arranging her Italian lessons, affording her glimpses of the abiding beauties and wonders of his native land. Nigra remained at Paris until 1870, and in the hour of her greatest peril proved to be her devoted and courageous friend.

Not that successes of this kind came to her easily, or that the stand she took in the Italian problem was merely an exercise in politics to be conveniently pushed aside in the private sphere. To the Emperor, as to Thouvenel and other politicians, the freedom of the Pope was a matter of politics only. To the Empress, the question was one of conscience and represented a spiritual as well as a practical issue. At Biarritz, in September 1861, Mérimée was distressed to see, as he told Panizzi, that there were 'grave dissensions between host and hostess, especially in spiritual

165

matters'. He added that the Emperor was 'as attached to the Pope as you and me'. Mérimée was, of course, completely anti-Papal and so was Panizzi. It is interesting to note in passing that although Mérimée filled his letters with constant denunciations, now amusing and now vehement, of the Pope, he never once permitted himself a single sarcastic remark on the Empress's attitude to religion. He was revolted by the ostentatious religiosity then much in vogue in the fashionable world, where dowagers and elderly generals shivered in fear of Satan, 'the grim gentleman below', as Mérimée was fond of putting it in English. He himself was entirely in favour of telling the Pope that 'his kingdom is not of this world'.[1] As the declared enemy of all humbug, as one of France's leading Voltairians, Mérimée had neither time nor patience for the pretentiousness of modish Catholicism, while in political Catholicism, the alliance between throne and altar, he saw an acute danger for the future of the Empire. A careful examination of his correspondence shows that he identified the Empress with neither of these manifestations of neo-ultramontanism. He regretted she did not agree with him that such things could be dangerous to the upstart Empire, as he saw through Mme Walewska's game of falsifying the Empress's motives behind her championship of the Pope's territorial independence. To Doña Manuela especially, he issued warning after warning about the lady's treacherous exploitation of her position in the household, but with no success. At the same time, he respected the Empress's personal sincerity and, in exemplary tolerance, they agreed to differ. As for Panizzi, the Empress always treated this Italian anti-clerical and anti-Austrian as a favourite guest.

Biarritz in 1861 was an intimate occasion, Mérimée being one of the very few guests who were not members of the family or Court. He watched the Prince Imperial take his first sea-bathe and was appalled to see that 'they' just threw the child into the element, 'head first, like Achilles into the Styx'. The heir of the Bonapartes emerged from the ordeal in tears. They pointed out the unsuitability of this attitude—had he not shown already that he was unafraid of guns and cannon? 'The difference is,' he gasped, regaining his composure, 'that I can command the guns, but I can't command the sea.' Mérimée was so delighted with this Napoleonic *dictum* that he quoted it in his letters for weeks on end. Otherwise he assisted the Emperor further in his researches for *Julius Caesar*, a project that filled the Empress with little enthusiasm.

Among the house-guests at Biarritz in 1861 was the Dowager Duchess of Alba. In her suite travelled a young Mexican diplomat, José Hidalgo, who was a familiar friend of the Montijos and the Empress. He was a handsome young man with an insinuating and ardent elegance of manner, but was also an intelligent reactionary so far as the chaotic politics of his

[1] In this the Anglophile Mérimée was close to the English attitude. 'So far as the Roman States are concerned,' wrote Odo Russell, British diplomatic agent at Rome, 'I will answer for the most anxious desire of the Pope's subjects to send his Holiness to Jerusalem.' (See *The Roman Question*, Russell ed. Noel Blakiston, Chapman and Hall, 1962.)

country were concerned. In that late summer of 1861 Mexico, where the Republican Juarez had recently become President, was causing a European crisis, and so the Empress enabled Hidalgo to talk to the Emperor about a problem which, as she knew, had interested her husband since 1857 and earlier.

CHAPTER 15

'IN THE Middle Ages,' remarked an English wit of the times, 'Rome was the centre of the world and its motto was "Credo". Nowadays, the City of London is the centre of the world and its watchword is "Credit".' The origins of the Mexican campaign were financial. President Juarez, on taking over the government from his defeated conservative opponents in the civil war then current, had announced that all payments on foreign loans were suspended for the present. England, France and Spain, hardest hit in their exchequers by this arbitrary measure, decided to mount an amphibious debt-collecting expedition to the New World. England agreed to sending several hundred marines under Admiral Dunloup, France assembled some 2,000 *Zouaves* and sailors under the command of Jurien de La Gravière,[1] while the Spanish prepared a force of about 6,000 men under General Prim. Before the operation got under way, the three powers had agreed in a Convention signed at London that interference in the internal affairs of Mexico was to form no part of the three powers' objectives.

However, from the day when they first discussed the expedition with Hidalgo at Biarritz, both French Sovereigns conceived the notion of giving Mexico an Emperor. This was partly due to the insistent propaganda by Mexican émigrés of the conservative type who had, literally for decades, been offering the Mexican crown round the capitals of Europe. They had been unsuccessful even in Vienna, for all its reserves in unemployed Archdukes. During the Biarritz conversations, the name of Archduke Maximilian cropped up, and the Empress had an intuitive feeling that her pleasant-spoken guest of 1856 would accept. Maximilian, now married to Princess Charlotte of Belgium and so the son-in-law of Leopold I, 'the Nestor of Kings', lived in his dreadful fairy-tale castle of Miramar in the bay of Trieste, severely shunned by the Court and government of Vienna, who continued to mistrust him as a dangerous liberal. Like the Crown Prince of Prussia, almost his exact contemporary, he had married an ambitious wife who, just before the Mexican throne was seductively conjured up before their eyes, had written that her husband ought to be given 'a position where he will govern, for he was made for that and blessed by Providence with everything necessary to make a people happy. . . .' Others misjudged his character in the same way, mistaking good intentions for ability. He himself, deeply unhappy at being cold-shouldered by Vienna,

[1] Whom we last saw engaged in successful nautical diplomacy in the Adriatic (see page 120).

168

felt that the House of Habsburg, 'once so fine and powerful', ought to show to the world that its sons still had the stuff of which modern rulers were made. He had visited Brazil in 1860, and told its Braganza Emperor, Pedro II, that he ought to build more railways and emancipate the slaves. Otherwise he would be 'not an Emperor, but only the master of some customs houses in a few sea-ports and lord of the small districts around them'. Perhaps Maximilian was, after all, a man with a 'modern' mentality? For both Napoleon and Eugénie regarded a progressive spirit as the first necessity for the regeneration of a country that had sunk into anarchy, poverty and backwardness tempered by savage civil wars ever since Canning had sponsored its independence at the time of the French expedition to Spain in 1823.

Despite the Convention of London, therefore, the French Sovereigns launched their part of the Mexican enterprise with the intention of causing an upheaval in the internal affairs of Mexico. The Palmerston government, itself protected by the Convention against any unwelcome extension of the expedition's initial purpose, did not show any dismay at the French desire to find a monarchical solution for Mexico. Palmerston said that he thought a Monarchy would suit that country best, and Thouvenel, not a romantic or idealistic Foreign Minister, wrote to the French Ambassador in London, Charles de Flahaut:

'Is government in Mexico possible outside the monarchical form? I do not think it is, and I am assured that all honest and reasonable people in Mexico share this opinion. The only legitimate pretext for an armed demonstration is, it is true, to be found in our [financial] grievances, but I think that it would be in the general interest to make the demonstration in such a way that the Mexican nation itself—if it has any vitality left—could profit from it, and emerge with Europe's help from the abyss into which it has fallen.'

The Mexican enterprise carried within itself the germs of another possibility, which, for the first eighteen months or so, was not without its attractions to the British government. That aspect, not connected with the Mexican émigrés and their propaganda, was the anti-American bias of the operation. Throughout the early part of the American Civil War, it seemed possible on more than one occasion that Britain and France might jointly give modified support to the Southern States in the conflict and it was thought that, in the event of victory by the secessionist States, a recognition of a new Mexican Empire under a European Prince would present no difficulty.

The anti-American, anti-Washington, potentialities of the 'demonstration' provided the only aspect of the whole Mexican enterprise that ever made it popular in any sense, even in France. Throughout the earlier decades of the nineteenth century, the United States, exploiting the civil wars and anarchy of Mexico, had grabbed large slices of Mexican territory and incorporated them in the Union which, many Europeans thought, was now about to break up. An economic motive for help to the South was provided by the dilemma, illustrated in a famous *Punch* cartoon, between the rival claims of cotton and slavery. Other matters reinforced the anti-American emotion of those months, the hope, for example, that the defeat of the North would see the end of the Monroe doctrine,[1] that a barrier would be erected against the further spread of Anglo-Saxon materialism in the Southern hemisphere, and that Europe, including England, would gain greater independence from the industrial leadership by the United States. The latter point was very close to Mérimée's heart. In this he was not alone. 'Will America become Europe's protector and master,' Parisians read in a book published in 1862, 'even as a hundred years ago Europe was America's? Our pride revolts in the face of these formidable problems while in America the insolent audacity of an ambitious race makes ready to solve them to its own advantage before the end of the twentieth century.'

The difference, the fateful difference between the British and French approach to the Mexican enterprise was that whereas Palmerston and his colleagues could examine its various possibilities in a non-committal and open-minded way and drop it without compunction should it turn out to be unviable, the French Empire, once it had committed its resources and prestige, could not afford to draw back without incurring grave political risks at home. This is, in fact, what happened. When the allied expeditionary force landed at Vera Cruz and began its march into the interior, they encountered no trace of the ecstatic welcome as liberators which the Mexican émigrés had promised. They merely found a country in the grip of terror which Juarez, the ablest leader Mexico had produced for generations, was organising with ruthless efficiency. The 'honest and reasonable' Monarchists of Mexico, of whom Thouvenel had written, either did not exist or were too frightened to come forward, while the émigrés in Europe were neither honest nor reasonable. Britain withdrew, the Minister, Sir Charles Wyke, telling Jurien that the Mexicans had best be left to work out their own salvation.[2] Prim, meanwhile, was engaged upon obscure negotiations of his own, probably with a view to giving the vacant throne to one of the Spanish Bourbons. Jurien himself began hopefully to enter into negotiations with Juarez about the financial question and found the dictator's attitude entirely promising. Before he could proceed, however, he was recalled to Paris, where negotiations with Juarez of any sort were

---

[1] In 1853, Clarendon had told the American Minister in London that 'the Monroe doctrine can only be viewed as the dictum of the distinguished person who delivered it. . . . Her Majesty's government cannot admit that doctrine as an international axiom which ought to regulate the conduct of European states.'

[2] In June 1862, Wyke concluded a bilateral settlement with Juarez of British financial claims. 'What sympathies,' wrote Thouvenel in exasperation, 'can England have for the men at present in power in Mexico? She has complained about them as much as we have.'

roundly condemned. The Emperor sent military reinforcements across the Atlantic and from then onwards France was pursuing the Bonapartist dream of Mexican regeneration on her own.

We need not concern ourselves with either the ups and downs of the Mexican campaign in which General Bazaine made his name nor with the prolonged campaign of persuasion by which the French Sovereigns and various Mexican émigrés induced Maximilian and Charlotte to accept the proffered crown. The Empress was, since first she had brought Hidalgo to the Emperor's study at Biarritz, irretrievably committed to the whole enterprise, burning her boats almost at the very beginning. Even so, her motives for flinging herself so unreservedly into the enterprise were once again so completely misunderstood and distorted that it is as well to stress that the initiative for the operation came, in the first place, solely from the Emperor and his government. The Emperor had long dreamt of building up a French sphere of influence in Central and South America, and it was by his decision alone that the debt-collecting expedition was extended into an Empire-founding campaign. It should also be added that Morny, the reign's most able and astute second man, furthered the scheme with all the authority he commanded at home and abroad. It is an absurd over-simplification to allege that he did so merely for shady financial motives. Being Talleyrand's grandson, he was never averse from adding to his already considerable wealth, but he interested himself in the Mexican project as a statesman and not as a speculator. He and the Empress became close allies in the enterprise.

However, although it was the brisk breezes of her husband's interest and instigation which carried the Empress along into the Mexican enter-prise, she soon assumed a leading part in, and a great personal responsibility for, its whole course. No other venture of the reign revealed so clearly the defects of her qualities, even as no other Imperial enterprise taught her so much about responsibility and about herself. As the dangers of the whole scheme hardened into a major diplomatic, military and financial liability, she closed her eyes to its utopian and chimeric side, allowing only the necessity of success to influence her actions. This was particularly the case in the question of prevailing over Archduke Maximilian to overcome his recurrent hesitation about accepting the Mexican throne. For the Arch-duke, despite his initial enthusiasm and his wife's ambitions, did not throw himself into the enterprise in the spirit in which the young Bona-parte had marched into Italy or Napoleon III gained power in his coup d'état. Maximilian was attracted to the idea, but he wanted full guarantees from the European powers, with an international military force to occupy the country until its pacification was complete. In fact he wanted security before he was prepared to risk his person and his future. Such individual encouragement as he received, notably from his father-in-law King Leopold, did not always drown those other more pessimistic voices which kept tell-ing him the regeneration of Mexico was beyond the strength of any European ruler.

171

The Empress admitted no such doubts. Sharing the Emperor's view that Maximilian's presence in Mexico would be 'worth an army of 100,000 men', she devoted her correspondence with the exiles of Miramar as well as her personal powers of persuasion during a visit from them in 1863 to urging them to accept. In this respect she went farther than the Emperor himself who late in 1863 said to Metternich that 'I would not be angry with Maximilian if he deferred his departure for Mexico until the country's affairs have progressed a little further. In his place I would do the same.' Almost on the same day the Empress wrote to Charlotte saying that only their speedy departure could redeem Mexico from her many evils. 'We hope,' had been her words,

'that news we shall soon receive will be of such a kind as to hasten the departure of your Highnesses, for none but a strong and vigorous hand can carry the work of regenerating the country to a successful conclusion.'

When early in 1864 Maximilian suddenly announced his withdrawal from the Mexican candidature because it would entail the renunciation of all his Austrian possessions, titles and prospects for himself and his descendants, the Empress's fury knew no bounds. She summoned Metternich to a nocturnal interview at the Tuileries and, largely as a result of her insistence, Francis Joseph inserted a clause into his family pact with his younger brother guaranteeing Maximilian's personal inheritance as a Habsburg.

This proved decisive. Maximilian accepted the crown from a delegation of Mexican monarchists in a ceremony at Miramar and set out for Mexico City. The new Emperor and Empress made their solemn state entry into the capital on Sunday, June 12th, 1864. The French army and authorities had them welcomed with 'popular' acclamations. On his way across the Atlantic, Maximilian had drawn up a volume of some 500 pages laying down the ceremonial and etiquette to be observed at the Court of the Second Mexican Empire. He was a Habsburg still.

No one who hesitated could be the man required. This the Empress would not admit. Ignoring her protégé's limitations and giving no thought to the possibility of failure, she acted throughout these years on the assumption that Maximilian was Mexico's man of destiny. The Emperor, more cautious as usual, still hoped to avoid premature commitments and often muttered his favourite motto: Il faut rien brusquer, the famous 'wait and see' of the Second Empire. The Empress, however, allowed no practical considerations to weaken her conviction that a liberal-minded Habsburg prince ruling the country on the principles of an exported Bonapartism—'throwing in his lot with that of the people'—was bound, as if by magic, to succeed. Maximilian and Charlotte, the latter more willingly than her husband, became the victims of this unhappy application of her Bonapartist convictions.

Her surprisingly inflexible, blinkered attitude was particularly unjustifiable because, as the Mexican negotiations dragged on from 1861 to well into 1864, the whole aspect of events in Europe and America was changing beyond recall. It had become obvious that the North was not the losing side in the Civil War, that all hopes of a break-up of the Union and an abandonment of the Monroe doctrine would never be fulfilled. Palmerston now expressed the view that the people of Mexico was 'destined to be devoured by the Anglo-Saxon race, before which it will disappear sooner or later, as the redskins did before the white man'. The Empress shut her eyes to this possibility because she hoped that the non-racist civilisation of the Latin nations would preserve the Mexicans from, as Mérimée put it, 'the Yankees, lynch-law and Anglo-Saxon colonisation'.[1] Wholly ignoring the powerful forces arraigned against this mission, the Empress insisted that Latin standards of civilisation were capable of erecting a barrier against the Anglo-Saxons.

Her persistence must be the more deplored since she seemed deliberately to be closing her eyes to the all too obvious dishonesty and the reactionary political tendencies of the Mexican émigrés and of such senior Roman Catholic clergy as became involved in the enterprise. Although fully aware of the canker, she forced herself to believe that Maximilian the Progressive could provide the remedy. When the Emperor asked her opinion of one of the exiled Mexican leaders, Gutierrez, she said: 'If that man goes to Mexico, people will believe the Inquisition has returned. He talked to me as if Philip II had come to life again. Lord Palmerston will never approve of such a man.' When, some months later, Gutierrez spoke to her again of his ideas for Mexico she told him: 'One should not live in a world that does not really exist.' He replied:

'We ought to have a dictatorship in Mexico on the pattern of that established in France.'

'Yes,' she interrupted him, 'but a dictatorship which will bring liberty. We need a man able to maintain both side by side.'

'Liberty!' muttered the old man, 'we have had only too much of that, without ever finding a dictator of the required ability.'

When she found that the Papal government intended to cancel all Juarez's laws of expropriation and restore the clergy unconditionally to all its former monopolies and possessions, the Empress's anger blazed forth. She told the Papal Nuncio at Paris, Mgr. Chigi, that as Mexico had to choose between becoming a Catholic Empire or 'annexation and Pro-

---

[1] The Empress built a shrine near Biarritz to Our Lady of Guadalupe whose cult Arnold Toynbee has described as 'the key to post-Cortesian Mexican history'. This image of the Virgin had 'the likeness of a pre-Columbian Mexican goddess' and had appeared to a native Mexican in the first generation after the Conquest. 'Hispanic Roman Catholicism,' Prof. Toynbee wrote, 'has the same unifying power as Islam . . . it creates a sense of cultural and social solidarity that is strong enough to overcome racial and political barriers. . . . In Mexico . . . there has been a racial as well as a cultural and social fusion between the descendants of the oppressors and the oppressed.'

testantisation by the United States', the clergy's demand for a wholesale restitution of their former vast possessions could only harm true Catholic interests. She even said that the Pope was endangering 'the grand moral idea of regenerating a whole country for the sake of the temporal possessions of a regrettably dissolute clergy'. When she saw that both the émigrés and the Monsignore persisted in what she called 'this seventeenth-century attitude', she summoned Hidalgo and freely expressed her anger. A friend of Hidalgo's who had watched the scene said afterwards: 'I admired you just now, you didn't turn a hair.' 'No,' replied Hidalgo with a shudder, 'but I have all hell within me.'

Nevertheless the Empress continued to support the enterprise and this fateful attitude was strengthened by factors outside her control: the French army had been defeated in battle in 1862 and so the Emperor could not enter into negotiations with Juarez without the certainty of political humiliation. 'There is not one man in France,' wrote even Mérimée, who was not chauvinistic, 'who would dare maintain that we should negotiate with Juarez rather than treat him with cannon shots, expensive though this may be.' That the Emperor, for this reason, went on sending military reinforcements to Mexico cannot be blamed on the Empress; it was the official policy of the Imperial government.

The Emperor had said: 'France goes to war for ideas.' This conviction made him pursue the Mexican dream with an idealism that had much in common with that of the Empress, who, however, overtook him at several important junctures with her compulsive determination to speed the operation on its way. Altogether, the Emperor's sights were trained at more limited objectives. 'I hope,' he had written to Maximilian, 'that the Party of Order will now raise its head in Mexico and our projects be realised.' It was a dangerous abandonment of the origins of his own power, which, as has been stated, had been won in defiance of the Party of Order at home. What could the Emperor expect from that group of unenlightened landowners and corrupt politicians who had hitherto managed Mexico under the auspices of the Conservatives and the clergy? The clergy in particular had been responsible for the people's extreme ignorance as well as for the glaring contrast between poverty and wealth that had been so typical of Mexico since independence.

In May 1862, not long after the French defeat in the first battle of Puebla, the Maréchal de Castellane received a letter from a friend who fought in the campaign as a Captain in the *chasseurs*. 'The Emperor,' said this man,

'has been scandalously deceived about the situation in the country. We sustain a cause without partisans, and we have among our followers men like Almonte who are viewed with horror in the country and make us detested, even by our own countrymen. We are too weak . . . I dare not say what we are all thinking, but we cannot go on like this. We need another General, a different diplomatic representative, and we need more men. Once we have 50,000 we can go where we like and take Mexico: but we shall not have a single partisan.'

At about the same time the Empress was writing to Miramar:

'Mexico now feels safe enough to express its wishes, and all men are rallying round Almonte who, an émigré yesterday, is today the dictator of the provinces through which we have advanced. . . . Unfortunately, many mistakes were made at first, but I have never had any doubt of the success of the enterprise.'

She had been misled not merely by the émigré sources on which she and the Emperor had uncritically placed too much reliance; she had been deceived by her own high-mindedness. It only remains to add that, when the consequences of her attitude were brought home to her, she made no attempt to deny her responsibility or make excuses.

During these years when the government's difficulties called for the strongest leadership, the Emperor's health was showing grave signs of deterioration. Never fully trusting any of the many doctors at his Court—Conneau, Corvisart, Larrey—the Emperor always refused to undergo a regular examination, preferring to deal with the symptoms rather than the causes of his disease. He had frequent attacks of acute pain and in consequence was often in a state of drugged torpor. The Empress had witnessed the violence of these attacks and had heard him calling out for her in agony, but he would not let her arrange for proper medical attention. Their contrasting attitudes towards bodily afflictions typified the difference in character between Emperor and Empress. His was a policy of evasion, of improvising quick treatment of the symptoms, and of continuously postponing expert diagnosis. The Empress, for her part, fought a life-long battle against her body, always consulted the best European authorities and then followed their advice. Her principle was to subjugate her physical side to a strict régime, to keep herself informed of what must be done and do it, to be stronger than her body and independent of it. There were thus after 1860 many critical moments when she urgently felt that she must, so to speak, do the work of two, since her husband could not always rally himself to face up to the daily problems. All this she could have brought forward, had she ever chosen to defend herself in relation to Mexico. As it was, it was always others—Mérimée, Filon, one or two of her ladies such as Mlle Bouvet or Sophie Tascher de la Pagerie—who wrote of the burden she had to carry as the sick Emperor's consort.

That the circle around Mme Walewska entirely misrepresented her Mexican policy need not be specially stressed. Their task was easy. It was immediately plausible to say that the Empress was committed to Mexican Imperialism as a Spaniard who wanted to resurrect the former Spanish Empire across the seas, that as a clerical politician she wished to restore the hierarchy to its former exclusive and repressive power. The Eugenian legend had even graver consequences, both for her and the Empire, when in October 1862 the régime underwent one of its major Cabinet crises in the course of which the Emperor replaced Thouvenel with Drouyn de Lhuys at the Quai d'Orsay.

The Italian Revolution had returned to the mainland in July 1862, when Garibaldi landed in Southern Italy and began another march on Rome. Victor Emmanuel's army defeated the popular hero and his volunteers at Aspromonte and Garibaldi, who had been wounded in the battle, withdrew once more to Caprera. Yet the Italian government associated itself officially with the objective of Garibaldi's expedition, the conquest of Rome, calling it 'the expression of an imperious need', and addressing a note to the European powers, which demanded the immediate cession of Rome. In reply, the Emperor dismissed Thouvenel, under whose auspices the kingdom of Italy had been recognised. With Drouyn a politician returned to the Foreign Ministry who was more Austrian than Italian, more conservative than liberal, and less prepared to bury the Pope's temporal independence than Thouvenel, rightly or wrongly, had been assumed to be.

The Italian demand that the Emperor should abandon the Pope led to a number of new appointments abroad as well as to a major Ministerial reshuffle at home. They were announced to the world on October 16th, 1862, and were, perfectly correctly, interpreted as a gesture of encouragement addressed to the Pope in the face of the latest provocation from Italian nationalism. The Empress was widely credited with being the moving influence behind the reshuffle. In a private letter to Clarendon, Lord Cowley wrote of 'this disreputable intrigue in which the Empress has been so successful, but only because she had to do with opponents equally disreputable and who lacked at the same time her courage and energy. She has now got complete influence over the Emperor, who does what she likes, and with a woman of her passions such influence is very dangerous.' Dangerous, it might be asked, to whom? England's policy was to support the Italian claim to Rome unconditionally, an attitude that had been christened by Lord John Russell 'our policy of non-intervention'. But in the case of Venetia, still an Austrian province, though reduced to a starving and depopulated shadow of its former self, England took the Austrian line, opposing Italian claims to annex it. On the assumption, therefore, that the Empress was a fanatic partisan of temporal power (which she was not), and on the second assumption that her influence over the ailing Emperor was total and complete (which it was not), she would have been dangerous indeed to the major British interest of giving Italy national unity to the detriment of the Pope and of France.

A less prejudiced examination of the facts behind the reshuffle shows that the Empress, far from 'doing what she likes', was called in by the Emperor to help him in carrying through the changes in the way he judged would bring the greatest political benefits. Not unnaturally, both the tone and the contents of the Italian note summoning him to pursue a certain course had infuriated and disappointed him, and his first reaction

176

had been to give the Quai d'Orsay to Walewski whose Papal tendencies were a European byword. However, the other Ministers expressed unanimous opposition to that incompetent and hag-ridden Minister's return, offered their collective resignation and so forced the Emperor to think again. The most serious case was that of Fould, the determined advocate of orthodox finance and an undoubted master in his field. At her husband's bidding, the Empress asked Fould to call at Saint-Cloud on October 15th and invited him to name his conditions for withdrawing his resignation. He insisted that Walewski be dropped, but Persigny, probably the most rabid enemy of the Pope among the Ministers, retained. The Emperor, joining the conversation a little later, accepted these terms, and Fould remained in charge of the Empire's financial policy for many years to come. A clerical Empress, sweeping all before her, would certainly have removed Persigny rather than Thouvenel. Yet when at the first session of the new Cabinet Persigny said that his intimate knowledge of opinion in the country had convinced him that the Pope must go, the Emperor replied: 'I also, gentlemen, know the sentiments of France and I shall not abandon the Pope.'

In ordering the reshuffle of October 1862, the Emperor had acted in anticipation of the general election, which was to take place in 1863. Since their annexations of Naples and the Papal States, the Italians had lost a great deal of sympathy among the French, less because the annexations themselves were condemned than because the methods had angered and provoked French susceptibilities and pride. It has been estimated by an expert that out of 229 groups of voters in France in the early 1860s, 92 groups were sympathetic to the Italian cause (especially since the ceding of Savoy and Nice), 68 groups took the side of the Pope, while 69 were indifferent to either party. In the coming elections, the first since the liberalising decrees of 1860, the Emperor could scarcely afford to ignore the considerable pro-Papal minority groups.

Mérimée, so anxious to finish once and for all with 'the antiquated idol at the Vatican', was, at the time of Thouvenel's dismissal, convinced that in view of Italian behaviour the French nation would never allow the Pope to be overthrown. He had many conversations with the Empress at Biarritz that autumn. They discussed the Italian desire to take Rome. 'Why,' she asked him very reasonably, 'do the Italians not take Venice instead? Suffering there is much greater than among the Romans.' 'It is a very popular argument,' admitted Mérimée, and to Panizzi he wrote:

'How illogical the British are! They think it a good thing that the Romans want to get rid of the Pope, but a bad thing that the Ionian Islands want to get rid of the British. It is in their interest that Italy should be free and united, but they do not want to give up the Ionian Islands, and they even say that the Turkish government is excellent. . . .'

And he put his finger on the problem at the base of all other problems:

177

'On the Continent unfortunately, and especially in France, national interest is not a principle of government.'

As the Empress, though *papalina*, was not a clericalist, the allegation that she had removed Thouvenel from office for that reason falls to the ground. Those who were able to discuss such things with her were able to form a truer picture. To Hübner, for example, who visited Paris privately in April 1862, she deplored that 'the Pope takes up so absolute an attitude of refusal. He could very easily agree to some sacrifices.' 'Do not,' Hübner warned her, 'count on concessions from the Holy See. Rome never yields and it is always wrong to pick a quarrel with priests—and with women. The former always pose as martyrs and the latter as victims.'[1]

'Perfectly true,' replied the Empress, laughing. 'There is nothing stronger in politics than weakness.'

Not long after the reshuffle, Lord Malmesbury had a long talk with her on the Roman question. 'The Empress,' he wrote in astonishment, 'did not, as I expected, treat the subject as a *dévote*, though she said that no scandal could be greater than an exiled Pope with no foot of earth belonging independently to himself.'

But the legend had already turned her into a *dévote* and a Hispanic fanatic, which explains Lord Malmesbury's astonishment at meeting the real Eugénie.

While her active interest and involvement in the questions of the day grew constantly, she still found time for more intimate and gentler pursuits—her care for Paca's children, for example, the education of the two girls, of the heir to the title, now a boy of thirteen and known as the Duke of Huescar. For him the Empress had found a tutor in Paris, a university man and not a priest. 'My wish for you is,' she wrote to her nephew on New Year's Day, 1862,

'that one day you may become the man your mother wanted you to be—useful to your country, worthy of your name. I hope also that your childhood may be happy. . . . Au revoir, my dear Carlos, do your work well and enjoy yourself. . . .'

She kept the peace between Doña Manuela and the widowed Duke of Alba, pleading with him not to remove Paca's coffin from the tomb her mother had built near Carabanchel. 'My poor mother's only joy in life,' she told Alba, 'lies in that brief pilgrimage which allows her to look after her beloved child. Do not, I beg of you, separate her from that coffin: all personal considerations must fall silent before so much suffering.'

Doña Manuela briefly saw her daughter at Madrid in the autumn of

---

[1] It is interesting to note that when in 1867 Hübner was appointed Austrian Minister at Rome, the Papal authorities soon insisted on his recall, because he had been advocating modifications to the 1855 Concordat which the Empress had once described to him as 'medieval'.

PROSPER MÉRIMÉE

A SOIRÉE AT THE TUILERIES, GIVEN IN HONOUR OF THE VISIT OF
THE CZAR OF RUSSIA AND THE KING OF PRUSSIA TO THE PARIS
EXHIBITION OF 1867

EUGÉNIE

1863. The Empress had sprung something of a surprise on the Court at Biarritz by announcing that before returning to Paris she was going on a voyage aboard the Imperial yacht *L'Aigle*, calling at Lisbon, Cadiz, Malaga and Valencia and returning home via Marseilles. At Valencia a pressing invitation from Queen Isabella reached her, and so reluctantly the Empress attended an official banquet at the Royal Palace in Madrid. Her drive through the streets turned into a triumphal progress. 'Her dress!' wrote the American Ambassador who saw her at the banquet for the first time. 'The ladies contemplated it in silent awe, and even grave diplomatists were in raptures.' It may have been on this occasion that some Spaniard remarked, in the hearing of the French ambassador, on the peculiar way women dressed in Paris. 'What about Spain?' asked the Frenchman haughtily, 'how do you dress your ladies in Spain?' The Spaniard neatly delivered his *coup de grâce*: 'Oh, in Spain, we usually dress them as Empresses of the French.'

The American Ambassador watched Doña Manuela, as she sat facing her daughter across the table, sunk in silent wonderment, crumbling a roll of bread in her fingers, scarcely noticing what she was eating or drinking. The Papal Nuncio, Mgr. Barili, heard the Empress say that there could never be any question of returning the Romagna to the Pope, that further-more the Holy See must initiate governmental reforms within its remaining possessions—sentiments that were deeply shocking not only to the Nuncio, but to most of the guests gathered round the table of the Queen of Spain.

The Empress returned home late in October. The six weeks at Compiègne that year were an occasion of great splendour. On November 15th, Saint Eugenia's day, the Cuirassiers beat the retreat by torch-light. 'The band,' wrote Mérimée in English to Fanny Lagden, his very superior housekeeper, 'was accompanied by torches, paper lanthorns and flags carried by men with glittering breast-plates or in long red cloaks: it was the most beautiful sight in the world.' Among the guests that year figured Lord Dufferin, 'the great-grandson,' Fanny Lagden was informed, 'of Sheridan, with his wife, a pleasant sort of Irish woman, much afraid of everything, and especially of sitting near to H.M.' In the words of Lady Dufferin's nephew, Harold Nicolson, Dufferin and the French representative at Beyrout had worked out a solution for a régime in the Lebanon and Syria which, 'strange to relate, worked admirably until the outbreak of the [first] European War'. Whether strangely or otherwise, Syria certainly vindi-cated the sounder potentialities of Anglo-Bonaparte co-operation, nor was it always the fault of the Emperor and Empress that such examples of old jealousies being intelligently overcome were comparatively rare. In 1863, at any rate, the Dufferins were the guests of honour at Compiègne. Their nephew, many years later, asked Lady Dufferin about the visit. 'She remembered [writes Sir Harold Nicolson] the long passages lit by china globes, and the way the chamberlains would summon them to meals, and the dresses worn by the Empress Eugénie, and the drives in the forest. "But, Aunt Lal," I asked, "weren't you shy? It must have been a terrible ordeal." She smiled silently to herself, searching back along the corridors of memory to these four days, seventy-three years ago, when she had stayed as a young bride at Compiègne. "Shy?" she repeated, "but I was always shy. And your Uncle Dufferin, I remember, was much interested by his conversations with the Emperor."'

That year, the Mephistopheles of the Second Empire, cousin Plon-Plon, went beyond the limits that even he had hitherto observed in his behaviour towards the Empress. On November 15th he was sitting on her right. At the end of dinner, the Emperor invited him to drink the health of the Empress and make a little speech. The Prince remained seated and silent: the other guests had risen already. 'No speech from you, please,' said the Empress lightly and laughingly, 'you are very eloquent and sometimes your speeches make me feel afraid.' The Prince pulled a face, and still remained seated and mute. 'You won't give the toast, then?' said the Emperor at length. 'I am no good at public speaking,' said the Prince. 'You won't,' said the Emperor incredulously, 'drink the health of the Empress?' 'If Your Majesty will excuse me, I shall dispense with it.' Joachim Murat now grasped his glass and, with a voice vibrant with anger, proposed the Empress's health on her name-day. 'Their Majesties,' Mérimée told Panizzi, 'kept their accustomed *sang-froid*.' Presently they rose from table and taking Prince Plon-Plon's arm, the Empress led the company to the drawing-room.

Later in the evening, the Prince sought out Mérimée and began abusing everything and everybody. Mérimée rose and like the others left the Prince alone, but not before saying to him in his gentle and precise voice: 'Do you think, sir, that these days the Bonapartes can afford to be divided?'

CHAPTER 16

IT WAS about this time in the early sixties, that the Empress Eugénie took on that magnificent, somewhat theatrically majestic, and intriguing appearance by which she is best remembered: the elaborate coiffure showing her broad forehead to advantage and admirably suited to her severe Spanish cast of feature; the severity of her looks again contradicted by the elaborate bodice and crinoline, as we see them in the portraits by Winterhalter and others.

Her appearance, like her reputation for neo-ultramontane Catholicism, is deceptive. The immense artificial magnificence with which she surrounded herself gives a very false idea of her character. She dressed as she did for a purpose. She used to refer to her 'political' costumes, meaning those sumptuous and heavy creations from Lyons silks and other materials which she wore on the great days with a slight sigh of despair. Her own preference was for light and quiet garments, for an informal and even austere simplicity. But these robes of state were political in the sense that the distinction with which she wore them sang the praises, as it were, of the Lyons silk industries and the art of the great Parisian dressmakers led by Mr. Worth, late of Swan and Edgar. Other dresses, such as one presented by the town of Nancy, served a different purpose, since in wearing it the Empress paid a splendid compliment to the ancient capital of the Kings of Lorraine. She used several costumes of this 'political' variety in order to stress the importance of various provincial cities. When in 1864 the dye works at Hoechst near Frankfurt produced the hitherto unknown 'aldehyde green', which they exhibited at Lyons, an enterprising local manufacturer, M. Renard, bought the entire production of one year and presented the Empress with an evening dress dyed in this new shade. She wore it for the first time at the opera and earned an ovation for her own gracefulness, the Lyons industries, the enterprise of M. Renard and the Emperor's commercial policy of Free Trade agreements with the German States. That appearance at the opera 'resulted', as the gratified manufacturers testify, 'in a demand for the Hoechst green that assumed proportions never known before'. Like her graver political activities, this dutiful encouragement of French dressmaking and textile industry was artfully misrepresented by her enemies.

We may, while on this subject, briefly draw attention to a minor revolution for which the Empress, being a feminist, was responsible; the introduction of shorter skirts. She judged the fashion for long and full dresses

181

laden with long trains to be cumbersome and overdone and gave a lead in preferring functional to merely ostentatious dresses. Nor was she ever in sympathy with the resultant flirtatious jokes about glimpses of feminine ankles and legs. So at Compiègne as a beginning, but gradually elsewhere as well, the Empress set a new fashion of dressing sensibly. Her reasons were practical as well as emancipatory. On all but the most sumptuous 'political' occasions, she gave an example of simplicity and comfort intended to lead women away from the luxurious exaggerations which had become the vogue since the 1850s. 'These happy changes in fashions,' writes Mlle Bouvet, 'we owe entirely to the Empress, yet they were not adopted without difficulties. Certain dowagers deplored the unseemliness of abandoning long and imposing trains, and shorter skirts at one moment assumed the importance of a political question. But young people took to them and won. . . . The Empress endeavoured to modify the frantic emulation of elegance which had seized people received at Court. During the day, Her Majesty at Compiègne preferred plain dresses, cloth garments which were more comfortable for walks in the forest or for excursions. Instantly, velvets and satins were given up, since everybody wanted to imitate the example given from on high. Some critical spirits saw in all this nothing but a caprice of our elegant sovereign lady, but in truth it was a protest. . . .'

Compiègne was an excellent place from which to launch this little feminist revolution. It had become her unique domain. The Emperor left the composition of the guest-lists almost entirely in her hands, only occasionally adding names whose inclusion he desired for reasons of his own. The Empress's reputation as an affable and tactful hostess was by now becoming world-wide, and not even the Mexican imbroglio prevented Americans from eagerly seeking invitations. Not the least reason for the success of these autumnal gatherings was that the Empress always had the infectious gift of genuinely enjoying herself. There was the week when, at her special invitation, the kilted Duke of Atholl and his sons danced a reel or two after dinner, having brought their own pipers along. Mérimée was a little dismayed by 'those eight naked knees in the drawing-room', by the 'devilish' music, by 'the turning and jumping and the very alarming tossing of the kilts'. Or there was the other occasion when he and Morny had written a little duologue to be performed by themselves in which various idiosyncrasies of the Sovereigns and some of the guests were gently lampooned. Lord Hertford, for example, one of the world's richest men, who lived a life of lonely eccentricity among his priceless collections at the château of La Bagatelle in the Bois, was apostrophised by Morny for 'having a vast fortune and never spending it, beautiful houses in England and never seeing them, fine pictures and never showing them: he is content with a bagatelle'. The Emperor's mania for archaeology came in for comment, as did the Empress's taste, in Mérimée's words, 'for furnishing rooms so richly that there is no space left in them for people'. Hertford, a shy and misanthropic man, did not relish hearing his name bandied about, even by such distinguished performers, but the Emperor and Empress laughed loudly at the jokes against themselves. It was, again, at Compiègne that Nigra was able to present Count Alberti, from whom the Empress took Italian lessons. When on another Saint Eugenia's day, Nigra offered her an enormous bouquet wrapped in the Italian national colours, the Empress accepted it with a friendly smile. Her powers of self-control were growing.

Another, more secret, aim which she pursued at Compiègne was to keep the Emperor amused and happy. Not unlike King Edward VII, Napoleon III overcame moods of despondency and irritability in the society of attractive women; the Empress saw to it that feminine beauty was generously represented at Compiègne. She intended to ease his moods of depression and exhaustion, to lighten his mind and to rescue him from the importunities of a foreign ambassador, from the boredom of conversing with some visiting official personage, by presenting at the right moment some accomplished lady. She did not provide him with mistresses —that was the task of Bacciochi, who remained the Imperial *maître de plaisir* until his death from a cruel and degrading disease. The Empress endeavoured, on the contrary, to give the Emperor more harmless and intelligent pleasures than those he found in the many casual affairs which were arranged for him at the Tuileries and elsewhere. The Empress, aware of that evil, if inevitable, aspect of her husband's life, saw to it that at Compiègne at any rate he was more worthily surrounded. He responded to the treatment with some gratitude.

Mme Walewska's reign as acknowledged mistress had ended during 1860, which, as has been said, only caused the lady to promote her invention of ' the Empress's party' with redoubled vigour. At that time also there had been an explanation between Emperor and Empress during which he had spoken with great frankness about his love affairs, confessing that they began to tire and exasperate him. Only Mérimée had heard of this and hinted in one or two letters how pleased he was by the new understanding between husband and wife on this torturing side of their conjugal life. Yet in the course of 1863 the Empress was once more confronted with a testing ordeal. The Emperor had found an attractive new mistress in Marguerite Bellanger, tall, strong, blonde, plebeian, and aged twenty-five. With a little more breeding, she would have been a *demi-mondaine*. She was installed in a house at Passy, and embarrassingly haunted the park of Saint-Cloud; Mérimée, still assisting the Emperor in his work on *Julius Caesar*, began to make sly remarks about Caesar and Cleopatra. The Empress realised her husband's newest passion seemed far from casual or temporary. When she heard he was taking her off to one of the notorious chalets at Vichy in the summer, she decided to spend a few weeks at Schwalbach, a pleasant watering place in Hesse-Nassau. This latest crisis, showing how totally the Emperor could on occasion surrender to feminine aggression, had reacted so acutely on the Empress's health that in the end she could neither eat nor sleep. It was on her doctor's advice that

183

she went to Schwalbach, leaving the Villa Eugénie by the Atlantic shuttered and deserted throughout 1864.

The Empress had consented to take the cure on the strict understanding that her incognito as Countess of Pierrefonds would be respected. She was not to be granted that simple wish. Within the first few days of arrival, Queen Sophie of Holland bustled noisily and importantly into the quiet little villa where the Empress had installed herself. She had heard of the marital difficulties, had impulsively taken the first available train and now stood before the Empress imploring her to return to Paris forthwith. Nothing could have been more tactless or unnecessary, but then Queen Sophie, although a woman of intellect, was an opinionated busybody who had already enraged Queen Victoria with her high-minded meddling. A cousin of Prince Plon-Plon's, her own marriage to the King of the Netherlands was a total failure. While she was capable of writing well-informed letters on European questions, she was singularly unqualified to act as marriage counsellor to the Empress. This was soon made clear to her; Queen Sophie left Schwalbach piqued and dissatisfied, and the Empress continued her cure.

Once left in peace, the Empress began to recover. With her were the two beautiful sisters, Mme de La Bédoyère and Mme de La Poëze, also Mlle Bouvet, M. de Cossé-Brissac and Admiral Jurien de La Gravière. Mlle Bouvet has left an engaging account of the *villegiatura*, saying that the Empress was undergoing ' the most sorrowful crisis of her personal life '. She saw with admiration that in the present idyllic setting the Empress's resilient vitality came quickly to the fore, and nothing could be more appealing than Mlle Bouvet's account of the Empress's conversation in the intimacy of their little vacation. ' She had,' wrote Mlle Bouvet, ' a prodigious memory, remembered everything, and by a vivid and natural turn of phrase made the smallest things interesting. Then, suddenly in the middle of some trivial conversation, as at the beat of a wing, Her Majesty revealed a width of vision, a natural eloquence united to an enormous fund of observation, of reflection, of knowledge of life. . . .' Jurien, one of the Emperor's equerries since his demotion from the Mexican command, had been added to the little group at the Emperor's special wish.

Soon, there was another intruder. The King of Prussia was visiting his son-in-law, the Grand Duke of Baden, at nearby Karlsruhe, and called on the Empress unexpectedly one morning with an enormous bouquet of red roses. She had first met William I in 1861 when his visit to Compiègne in the year of his coronation had proved a triumph for the Emperor's foreign policy and therefore caused much heart-searching in London and Windsor. Later in the same year, Lord Clarendon had been sent to Berlin to warn the King against involving himself too closely with French intrigues, and when Clarendon wanted to return home via Paris, Queen Victoria indignantly forbade the detour. For her part, the Empress had liked the King, then a courteous, merry and youthful man of sixty-four, regarding him, quite correctly, as an obstacle to the ' popular ' movement to unite the whole of Germany under an Imperial crown. The King, like many Prussians of his generation, was opposed to letting Prussia lose her historic identity by merging her with the differently constituted lands of Southern Germany, while the Empress viewed the possibility of a united Reich rising beyond the Vosges and the Rhine with alarm. She feared that Prussia, which she was in the habit of calling 'a kind of German Piedmont', would simply annex the German States south of the river Main. King William's 'honesty', she felt, would never allow this, but she was suspicious of the 'democratic' ambitions cherished by the King's English daughter-in-law, Victoria.

Yet by the time King William I was calling at Schwalbach, the first of Prussia's three wars of German unification had been fought and won. Denmark had gone down before the combined Prussian and Austrian armies and was being forced to conclude a peace of doubtful justice. France and England had, for a time, come close to agreeing on armed intervention but, as in the various crises between 1933 and 1939, a working agreement had eluded them and each country was blaming the other for its lack of resolution.

Delicate political issues were therefore at least hinted at when the King of Prussia called with his red roses and asked to see the Countess of Pierrefonds. Prussia after the Danish war was temporarily isolated—even though Bismarck's[1] pro-Russian policy during the Polish rising of 1863 had strengthened the traditional friendship between those two countries—so that a friendly visit by the King to the Empress would, however unofficial, serve a useful purpose. The Empress could scarcely turn her august caller away, and the King spent a happy day at the little villa. 'His gallantry with women,' wrote Mlle Bouvet, 'is well-known. He manages to give it that touch of respectful admiration which is highly flattering.' The King, exploiting his initial advantage, further prevailed on the Empress, after a good deal of resistance, to break her journey home at Karlsruhe. The Grand Duke of Baden gave a reception for her at which she made the acquaintance of Queen Augusta of Prussia, subsequently first German Empress; King William was most attentive, never leaving the Empress's side, and finally accompanied her to the railway station to see her off.

The Empress was back in Paris early in October. She found the exacting Bellanger as greatly in favour as ever, and in her despair opened her heart to Mérimée. 'I had,' wrote the latter to Panizzi, 'a little chat with her lasting four hours. It is all very sad, more so even than you think, but do not say a word about it to anyone.' Not long after this, the Emperor was brought back from Passy in a state of complete collapse. The Empress forthwith decided to confront his mistress and tell her that she was 'killing the Emperor and must give him up'. She ordered Mocquard, the brother of the Emperor's secretary, to accompany her and the poor man,

---

[1] Bismarck, after serving for a short time as Prussian Ambassador in Paris, had been William I's *Ministerpräsident* since 1862. The appointment had been sponsored by army circles because Bismarck undertook to eliminate parliamentary opposition to the new army programme, which was very close to King William's heart.

aghast at the scandal which, reasonably enough, he anticipated, had no choice but to go along. Arrived at the love nest, the Empress came straight to the point and accused the startled Marguerite of every crime under the sun. But the lady, not a Parisienne for nothing, answered back volubly: 'What do you want here?' the unhappy Mocquard heard her say. 'I owe you no explanation. If you don't want the Emperor to come here, you must keep him at home by your charm, your kindness, your gentleness, your good temper. If he comes here, it is because you bore him and annoy him. . . .'

Mocquard could bear no more and fled to another room. There he awaited anxiously. After a while, hearing nothing, he tip-toed back and cautiously peeped round the door. To his amazement, he found the two combatants sitting peacefully on the sofa, chatting away and laughing together like the best of friends. Presently the Empress rose to leave and cordially embraced the now silent Marguerite in her most courtly manner. By the beginning of 1865 Mérimée was able to tell Panizzi that 'Caesar thinks no more of Cleopatra'. A quarter of an hour with Caesar's wife had been enough.

We know in truth little enough of the Emperor's love affairs, especially as he usually managed to retrieve and destroy any letters he may have written to those who had captured his roving fancy for a time. We know that he was a man of strong amorous needs and desires, that an uncontrolled sexuality was as much part of his nature and character as his visionary intelligence, subtlety of mind and goodness of heart. The voluptuary and the idealist, the incontinent amorist and liberalising Bonapartist, the libertine and the statesman were one and the same man. In the case of Marguerite Bellanger, his last mistress in the accepted sense, an impression persists that the ageing Napoleon was the victim of genuine passion, that, emotionally speaking, the affair with this young woman went deeper than the amusements which the deplorable Bacciochi arranged for him behind the scenes. It is perhaps significant that, one after another, his best-known mistresses ultimately exchanged their short season of splendour for bitter years of loneliness and oblivion. The vanished sun of Imperial favour was followed only by a chilling darkness. Miss Howard, dropped on the eve of the Emperor's marriage, lived on until 1865 in the vast château of Beauregard near Paris, where a suite of rooms was kept ready for an Emperor who never called. Mme de Castiglione returned to Paris, became involved with dubious bankers and murky manipulators, ending her days behind permanently closed shutters in a sordid apartment near the Place Vendôme from which she ventured forth only after dark. Mme Walewska, after the death of her husband in 1868, declined into a bourgeois marriage, and Marguerite Bellanger later led a penitent life of the greatest respectability and charity.[1] For all these, normal life ended

[1] Mme de Mercy-Argenteau's claim to have been 'the Emperor's last love' can be taken no more seriously than the other extravagant claims she makes in that work of fiction which she calls her Memoirs.

with their fall from the dangerous heights to which the Emperor had briefly raised them. He was always generous, making their material existence easy, but he forgot them, and so did the world.

Invariably he returned to the Empress. Too many writers have alleged that for this she exacted her price, that for tolerating, virtually conniving at, his infidelities, she obtained compensation in large drafts of power. Unimaginative Victorians like Lord Cowley, or frivolous Regency survivals like Lord Clarendon, with the conventional English clubman's attitude towards women, gleefully accepted this interpretation which, though adopted by many historians, does the Emperor and Empress the gravest injustice. In his own way the Emperor was determined to associate the Empress with all the great issues and conflicts of the reign. He held back in certain matters—the Italian question in the past, the problem of Army reform after 1866—because he did not invariably feel certain of her discretion and powers of dissembling, just as in other respects, pre-eminently the complex Roman question, he pushed her forward into a distorting limelight. It has correctly and often been said that the Emperor never wholly lost the mental habits and outlook of the conspirator, that even the liberalising Emperor or the re-arming Emperor conspired rather than initiated, albeit for creative and not subversive purposes. The more complex certain developments tended to become—in the later 1860s relations with Prussia or the question of an alliance with Austria—the more exclusive grew his preference for working matters out alone. The Second Empire was never poor in intelligent, capable, and even loyal public men, but he trusted none of them completely, although his half-brother Morny came perhaps closest to achieving the position of a fully established Prime Minister. But it is clear beyond doubt that in his mind the Empress stood high above all those who, for one motive or another, were dedicating themselves to making the Bonapartist Empire strike root in the soil of France. Similarly, his life-long admiration, respect and affection for her was never impaired by his amorous experiences, for in this field the Empress, having made a conscious act of renunciation, never competed. The essence of the situation was summed up by Filon, who knew them both much better than most of their other friends. 'The only party,' he wrote, 'to which the Empress ever belonged, was the Emperor's Party.'

Yet why in that case had she gone to seek out Marguerite Bellanger at Passy? What had she said to Mérimée during those long four hours at Saint-Cloud? To her, with her instinctive awareness of the daily and hourly dangers to which the future of the dynasty was exposed since the end of the Italian war, the Emperor's absorption in that strenuous love affair was tantamount to abdication. So, on a different level, was his absorption—ridiculous as it appeared to her and some others—in his work on *Julius Caesar*. The former preoccupation alarmed her also for the Emperor's health, that central mystery of the reign, where once again the Emperor gave his full trust to nobody, always ordering such doctors as hinted at the seriousness of the disease to keep the information from the Empress. It was therefore, so to say, as Regent that the Empress braved the tigress in her suburban den, not as the wronged wife who afterwards extracted her quid pro quo from a blushing husband. Moreover, the whole position caused her prolonged and acute additional distress because she knew that the Emperor's infidelities were common knowledge and much gloated over by her enemies, especially by those gifted intellectuals who foregathered at the Magny dinners or at Princess Mathilde's soirées in the Rue de Courcelles.

CHAPTER 17

THE FRENCH general election of 1863 had nearly doubled the votes cast for the opposition and the new Chamber contained thirty-three, instead of five, opposition deputies. The creating of a working and, dynastically speaking, loyal opposition on the English model was of course one of the Emperor's most cherished hopes, but he had few illusions concerning the difficulties which that programme was bound to produce in a country like France where the borderline between opposition and revolution was never regarded as insurmountable. His aim was to create a parliamentary machinery which under the firm leadership of the Imperial majority would become capable of working out the country's laws, liberties and reforms until France would learn, in the words of one of his leading collaborators, Baroche, 'how to govern herself'. It was that aspect of the Liberal Empire that always interested the Empress most. 'Rulers,' she had told Hübner in 1862, 'must anticipate the demands of the age and grant concessions before they are forced from them by circumstances.' Morny interpreted the election results of 1863 in the same sense when he said that now was the time 'to concede, if not complete liberty immediately, then at least civil liberty, and to study social questions'. The elections had also shown that clerical influence had been weakened proportionately as general Catholic hostility towards the Empire had decreased in consequence of Thouvenel's dismissal. 'Help me to declericalise myself,' had been the prayer of one defeated candidate, and Mgr. Dupanloup, Bishop of Orleans, said that the elections had gone against the Church. In the years to come, the Empress was to make important contributions to the Empire's educational and social progress, but until her second Regency in 1865 her mind was dominated by the burning questions of foreign policy. The man to whom she communicated her ideas and apprehensions in that field more openly than to anyone else was Richard Metternich, Austrian Ambassador at the Court of the Tuileries.

The numerous and persistent conversations which the Empress held with him between February 1863 and August 1870 form one of the most bizarre and fascinating chapters of European diplomatic history. They certainly fascinated Metternich who reported them verbatim to Count Rechberg, Büol's more temperate successor at the Ballhausplatz. The truth was that the Empress's impassioned pleading for a full Franco-Austrian alliance frequently took the Ambassador's breath away. Although a devoted admirer and friend of the Empress he was on occasion reduced to protesting against the intensity, against what the Empress herself called her *furia Francese*, with which she pressed forward with this plan that to her represented the Empire's sole chance of survival as the arbiter of Continental Europe. 'I cannot in all honesty say,' Metternich once told her in the excitement of battle, 'that you possess diplomatic subtlety, a feeling for the finer shades and a sense of the right opportunity which to me are the first necessity in politics and an essential pre-requisite of success. . . .' Four months after this protest, the Prussians beat the Austrians at Sadowa and the Viennese, for the first time since 1805, could watch the enemy's camp fires from the hills of the Vienna Woods. Francis Joseph and his Ministers looked in vain in the direction of the Rhine in 1866: no French army crossed into the lands of Southern Germany, then Austria's allies, or took the undefended road towards Berlin. Such was the harvest reaped by diplomatic subtlety and an aversion from pursuing an active policy.

Her very first attempt, made under the impact of the Polish rising of 1863 with its ghastly excesses of Russian brutality and oppression, had led to bitter disappointment. Like the whole of France,[1] the Empress felt the greatest sympathy for the cause of Polish independence, and once again England and France hovered on the fringes of acting together, only to fall apart through lack of mutual confidence. The failure was Prussia's advantage. Bismarck made an agreement with the Czar which included sending back Polish rebels who had sought refuge on Prussian soil. In her talks with Metternich, the Empress, having been briefed by the Emperor, developed a plan that not only stipulated the restoration of Polish independence, but envisaged a whole series of territorial and dynastic readjustments among which, from the Austrian point of view, the gravest change suggested was the ceding of Venetia to the kingdom of Italy. As the Polish restoration would also entail Austria's ceding the province of Galicia, the problems facing Vienna were not inconsiderable, but they were linked to the offer of a full offensive and defensive alliance with France which had as its objective the strengthening of Austrian influence both in the Balkans and in Germany south of the river Main. When Metternich communicated the plan to Rechberg he implored him to study it carefully and Rechberg replied that the Emperor Francis Joseph was greatly interested in the project of an alliance with France. Metternich travelled to Vienna in March 1863 to follow up his memoranda by personal advocacy; the ten days he spent there have often been described as one of the most pregnant moments in the history of the nineteenth century. He returned to Paris with nothing in his pocket but a few polite letters, from Rechberg to Drouyn de Lhuys, from Francis Joseph to Napoleon III. He

[1] 'The *Siècle*,' wrote Pierre de La Gorce, 'spoke the same language as *Le Monde*, the clergy and the University agreed, as did the Académie Français and the Faubourg Saint Antoine. Strangest and most unbelievable of all, on the Polish question the Empress and Prince Napoleon saw eye to eye.' An interesting letter in the Alba archives shows that the Empress successfully intervened with the Russian Governor of Poland for the lives of captured freedom fighters.

also carried secret instructions telling him that although 'closer relations with France' should be further explored, 'an active policy' was not in accordance with Austrian interests: 'Austria has need of peace, she cannot engage in an active policy, and circumstances alone can compel a change in her attitude.' 'The mountain has given birth to a mouse,' were the Empress's words when Metternich reported to her on his talks at Vienna.

The Polish question was settled by the Concert of Europe in a compromise that delivered the Poles gagged and chained into the hands of their Russian oppressors while leaving the Czar full of resentment against those who had expressed their sympathy with that heroic nation. Henceforth the Empress pursued her Austrian policy on a more limited scale, keeping it separate from the larger vision of a new European distribution, but persevered to advocate the voluntary cession of Venetia to Italy as an unavoidable necessity if Austria was to acquire the strength to deal with the dangers facing her north of the Alps. 'Rightly or wrongly,' she told Metternich in 1864, 'the Emperor entered Italy to turn you out. We shall be against you if you want to undo the results of that unfortunate war . . . but we shall be your loyal allies if you would only give up Venetia. . . . You do not like Italian unity, but Germany unity under Prussia repels you even more.' On another occasion she spoke to Metternich of how her husband had been told by one of the leaders of the German national movement that there was 'complete agreement between ourselves and our comrades in Hungary. We count on Austrian weakness to obtain our aim of German unity, and shall force the King of Prussia to abdicate in favour of his son, that weak young man who is eager to be dipped in the waters of German unity'. Metternich informed Vienna that 'Her Majesty's impatience to see us effect a reconciliation with Hungary is extreme and here we have one of her principal preoccupations'. In the Empress's talks with Metternich, the problem of Hungary figured indeed as largely and urgently as that of Venetia, for the Austrian alliance could obviously not be expected to work if Vienna had its hands tied by the hostility of these two centres of disaffected nationalism. In both problems the Empress never let up in her advocacy of boldly anticipating the inevitable by voluntary action, but found that in the event Austria acted only when circumstances, i.e. defeat in battle, forced her to do so. Venetia went to Italy as a result of the war of 1866, while the recognition of Hungarian national and political rights within the Empire was symbolised by Francis Joseph's coronation at Budapest on June 8th, 1867, the birthday of the 'Dual' Monarchy of the Habsburgs, nearly a year after the day on which Prussian troops had crossed the Austrian frontier.[1] The tardy recognition of Hungarian equality was therefore understood as being due at least as much to Bismarck's policy and Prussian military might as to Austrian statesman-

[1] June 16th, 1866. The battle of Sadowa was fought on July 3rd following, and the Peace of Prague concluded on August 23rd.

ship and good-will—a lesson that was remembered in the great crisis of 1870.[1].

The year 1864 witnessed a number of European events which closely affected the destinies of France. On the Danish war, in which Prussia and Austria shared the spoils of the campaign in a treaty that struck few statesmen as very durable, the Empress merely remarked that the Prussian annexations along the Danish border were preferable to the founding of yet another independent pocket principality. The Emperor's suggestion of holding plebiscites in the affected areas was not carried out until 1918. The Danish *Blitzkrieg* had the result of leading to an improvement in Anglo-French relations, as the Palmerston government found it now no longer quite so expedient to build up the French Emperor as a potential enemy and aggressor. Cowley lamented throughout the Danish crisis that 'the Queen has inherited the unreasonableness of the poor Prince Consort on the subject'. Prince Albert, who had died in 1861, had indeed raised Prussian goodness and Napoleonic evilness to the status of primary political dogmas, and for many years after his death his distracted widow conceived it as her mission to follow him with undeviating obedience in this as in other respects. Yet now that her eldest son, the Prince of Wales, was married to Princess Alexandra of Denmark, the tensions of Continental politics made themselves felt in the Queen's closest family circle, especially as her eldest daughter Victoria was as eager as ever to be 'dipped in the waters of German unity'. The Prince of Wales further distressed his mother by paying frequent and enthusiastic visits to Paris, Fontainebleau and Compiègne. On one occasion he was told by the Queen that 'the style of going on there is quite unfit for a young and respectable Prince and Princess like yourselves'. The Queen was prepared to permit him a day's shooting at Compiègne every now and again, and even dinner with the Emperor and Empress, 'but', she underlined, 'nothing more'. He took no more notice than did his younger brother, the Duke of Ediburgh. The British government showed no concern at the slight political implications of these visits. Lord Clarendon, Chancellor of the Duchy of Lancaster in Palmerston's last government, himself visited Paris in 1864, where he was universally greeted as 'the saviour of the Anglo-French alliance'. When in August 1865 the British and French navies held joint exercises and French warships visited Portsmouth, they received so tumultuous a welcome from the people of England that the aged Palmerston became positively

---

[1] It should be added that Hungarian liberty provided the Austrian Empress Elisabeth with the opportunity of playing an active part. With much courage and application she held talks with a number of Hungarian liberals, urged her husband to receive leaders of the moderate Hungarian 'Left' and at one time wrote to him 'in the name of our son Rudolf do not miss these opportunities'. Once crowned at Budapest, however, she relapsed into her accustomed absenteeism. It is interesting that the two Empresses, although not in communication with each other, pursued an almost identical course in this question. The French Empress drew attention to the urgency of the problem three years before the Prussian invasion, while Elisabeth's energies were roused mainly after the outbreak of war.

alarmed. A few weeks later, the great British statesman died, and Clarendon returned to the Foreign Office.

A further *détente* in Anglo-French relations was achieved when in September 1864 France and Italy concluded a Convention intended to provide the definitive solution of the Papal question. The Italian government undertook to respect the territorial integrity of Papal Rome and to defend it against all attacks, including those still to be expected from Garibaldi. In return France promised to disengage her troops from Rome over a period of two years. Victor Emmanuel, in order to prove the sincerity of his renunciation of Rome, declared Florence to be the capital of Italy. The Pope, for his part, replied to the new arrangement by issuing, at the end of 1864, his famous *Syllabus of Errors*.

This document, which condemned all the major aspirations of the nineteenth century as fundamental errors, is of interest in the present context because, as became clear in 1865, the Empress acted resolutely against all its major definitions. Of the eighty propositions listed in it, No. 80 has the greatest relevance. It laid down that the Sovereign Pontiff must not be expected to reconcile and align himself with 'progress, liberalism and modern civilisation'. Religious tolerance, secular, or university, education, equality between the confessions, equal rights for State and Church and the diminishing of the Pope's 'civil princedom' were all castigated as grave sins. With the consternation which this pronouncement caused in all parts of the world we are not here concerned. In France Mgr. Dupanloup, Bishop of Orleans, published a pamphlet which simultaneously attacked the September Convention with Italy and attempted to reduce the stipulations of the Syllabus to more intelligible terms. Dupanloup, who as a young abbé had received the dying Talleyrand back into the Church, was even able to explain the eightieth proposition by saying that the 'Pope does not have to reconcile himself to what is good in modern civilisation as he has never ceased to encourage it while naturally he must continue to condemn what is bad'. Dupanloup was well versed in making the most of unpromising material. Cardinal Darboy, Archbishop of Paris and Grand Almoner of the Empire, came closer to expressing what the Empress felt in her own mind when he addressed this appeal to the Holy Father:

'You have pointed out and condemned the principal errors of our time. Now turn your eyes towards what is good and honourable in it, and give your support to its generous efforts. It is you who must reconcile reason with faith, liberty with authority.'

Within a few months of the Syllabus having disturbed the souls of good Catholics everywhere in the world, the Empress decided to launch a project that, so she hoped, would remind Christians of all denominations of the origins of Christianity above the political wrangles of the day. She suggested rebuilding the decaying Church of the Holy Sepulchre at Jerusalem by international co-operation, the new building to consist of two lateral churches, one for Roman Catholic, the other for Greek Orthodox worship, while the central nave was to be given over to worshippers of all Christian denominations. She approached other Courts with this revolutionarily ecumenical idea. Queen Victoria replied that she 'admired and respected' the suggestion, but Clarendon soon saw that she could not, as Queen of England, take official action, adding that he for his part would have welcomed the Queen's co-operation for 'political reasons'. The scheme was quickly and finally scotched by Rome. Count von der Goltz, Prussian Ambassador in Paris, who was on amicable terms with the Empress, sounded the Nuncio, Mgr. Chigi, on her behalf and reported on March 8th, 1865:

> 'The Pope refuses in the most absolute manner to approve the plan of rebuilding the Holy Sepulchre by all Christian communions. His Holiness bases himself on the absolute rights of the Latins in this matter and also on the antiquity of the present building, but will be glad to leave the dome of the present building to be restored by the Empress.
>
> If this is His Holiness's last word he will have rendered Russia a great service by making it unnecessary to her to say No.'

In our own times, any endeavour to give convincing expression to the unity of the Christian communions is receiving greater encouragement at Rome. Since the days of Pio Nono the Papacy has undergone a powerful inner transformation. Few will deny that the Second Empire's policy of making the Holy Father great by rendering the temporal ruler humble provided the basis for this historic process. The Empress's conscience never permitted her to abandon the Pope altogether or to envisage the possibility of exiling him to Malta or Jerusalem. The Emperor, surrounded by politicians who were either basically indifferent to the question or, like his cousin Plon-Plon and his earliest follower Persigny, actively hostile to every form of Papal rule, was at times tempted to abandon the Pope—a prospect which English pressure and Roman silliness frequently made very tempting indeed. As has been stated, he resisted such temptations for reasons of internal politics. Yet among the leaders of the Empire it was only the Empress who was pervaded by the conviction that in this world the Papacy represented a spiritual principle and a hope. To this conviction she remained faithful even after her disappointment with Papal intransigence towards her suggestion for the Holy Sepulchre. Future experiences with the Court of Rome taught her that although the institution of the Papacy was great and eternal, Pio Nono and those who served him were, as temporary incumbents, small and fallible. The Pope himself was not always unaware of the more doubtful aspects of his 'civil' government and once said to the French Ambassador Gramont: '*Buffoni, buffoni, tutti buffoni, buffoni di qua, buffoni di la, noi sono tutti buffoni.*'

The Empress's opportunity for identifying herself with internal reforms and progressive policies came with her second Regency, which began in April 1865. The Emperor, having at last published his *Julius Caesar*, decided to go on a prolonged tour in the interior of Algeria. By his special wish, Prince Napoleon, vice-president of the Council since February, was prominently associated with the Regency. His conduct was of particular importance at this time, as Morny, the most successful politician among the Imperial family, had died in March at the early age of fifty-four. It was an irreparable loss. As President of the Chamber of Deputies he had come close to creating a working opposition in the Palais Bourbon, teaching men like Emile Ollivier that constitutional liberty must be achieved by gradual evolution from within the régime, not by a sudden revolution from without. Combining the velvet manner with a will of iron, Morny had succeeded in considerably narrowing the gulf between Empire and Republic on the one hand, between Bonapartism and Bourbonism on the other. His astonishing skill in transforming an enemy into a sensible opponent had won respect on all sides, and although he had become one of the Second Empire's most picturesque public figures with his love of the opera and his libretti for Offenbach and his lavish parties at his official residence, the political world took him very seriously indeed. 'He would have been a great man,' was Cowley's epitaph, 'had he been an honest one.' Morny had certainly inherited Talleyrand's lack of conscience in financial matters, but also his finesse and strong-willed statesmanship. One would only wish that he had also inherited his grandfather's longevity. At all events, Prince Plon-Plon was now under an added obligation to give the Empire all the support that was in his power, and it seemed to Mérimée early in 1865 that the Prince intended to do so. 'He is wiser,' Mérimée told a correspondent, 'more moderate and on a much better footing with the Empress than ever before. *Tant mieux* provided that it lasts.'

The Empress-Regent continued the missionary work which Morny had started in the political field. She invited a number of opposition deputies to the Tuileries, not only for her regular dinner parties but, as in the case of Ollivier, for prolonged and concentrated discussions of the problems which they themselves had proposed for debates in the Chamber. In 1865, Ollivier was interesting himself particularly in penal reform and juvenile delinquency. After several conversations with him, the Empress paid a surprise visit to the children's prison of La Roquette, where she was appalled to find some 500 children and adolescents kept in solitary confinement. At the next Ministerial Council she made a strong plea for ending this barbaric system. When a red-tape-ridden official reminded her of the departmental complications her proposal would involve, she replied: 'It is not a matter of administration, Monsieur, but of humanity and policy.' La Roquette was shut down, its inmates distributed among less gruesome penitentiaries in the country where, instead of being kept in solitary confinement, they were often employed as agricultural labourers. Nor did the Empress confine her efforts to impersonal reform. During one of her visits to the prison, she talked to a boy who told her that after his release he would kill his father for having denounced him to the police. She had several talks with the boy, sent for the father, and eventually induced him to withdraw the charge. The boy became a normal member of society. All this made a lasting impression on the Republican Ollivier, who now wrote of the 'Emperor's Montijo':

'More than by her beauty . . . I was impressed by her ability to understand and discuss everything, by her resilient intelligence, her vivid talk animated by original flashes of wit and, occasionally, heated eloquence. I formed the conviction that a nature like hers could err only at the high level of a character in Corneille.'

The Empress's most effective collaboration with a Minister was with Victor Duruy, who, in his six years in office, changed the face of French education as radically as Haussmann changed and modernised the face of Paris. The basis for this work was laid during the Empress's Regency of 1865 when, undeterred by the postulations of the Papal syllabus, she boldly associated the future of the dynasty with the education of the generations of the future. As a university man, classical scholar and free thinker, Duruy was a declared enemy of the clerical monopoly and nobody had been more surprised than himself when, in 1863, the Emperor sent for him to preside over the Ministry of Education. Two years later, at the time of the second Regency, two of his bills for primary education were to be debated in the Chamber and, as they were first to be discussed in the Council, the Empress invited him and his experts to brief her on the details. When both bills were passed, first by the Ministers, then by the deputies, Duruy wrote to the Empress on May 11th, 1865, saying it had been her 'clear and firm language at the last Council which brought this happy result about'.

The Minister had in his gift a number of apartments and studios in Paris where needy scholars and artists could be accommodated. In his gratitude for the Empress's support, he suggested three names for vacancies, and asked the Empress to communicate the good news to the recipients, for, he wrote,

'grace must be seen to come from the throne while refusals, when they become necessary, must come from the Minister.'

The Empress's practical interest in educational reform did not end with her Regency. Until Duruy left the Ministry in 1869, he could always count on her active support. He reported to her regularly and in detail about legislation he intended to introduce, particularly his highly controversial programme of secondary education for girls under the auspices of the University. This was a cause particularly close to the Empress's heart, but both middle-class and clerical opinion in France was scandalised by the thought of young ladies between sixteen and eighteen receiving instruction in the sciences, and from male professors at that. 'Violent protests are pouring in,' Duruy wrote to the Empress early in

196

1867, 'as if something highly dangerous was being attempted.' Yet what was his aim? 'French girls,' he told her, 'are to be enabled to exercise and strengthen their minds by the same education as their brothers are getting in the lycées and to which they are equally entitled and fit to receive. . . .' The Empress gave a lead by sending her two Alba nieces to the courses at the Sorbonne, and Duruy wrote in another letter that her efforts in support of women's equality had 'defeated unjust attacks by the sole authority of her example'.

The attacks came from Rome. In an open letter to Mgr. Dupanloup, Pio Nono accused the Minister of Education of promoting 'impious designs by new and unheard-of measures, lending his hand to the work of ruining the social order'. In reply Duruy wrote that the 'old pastors of the Church' wished to retain the new generations 'in the darkness of the Cathedrals', but would be unable to prevent them from 'emerging into the sunlight of knowledge and study'. In a personal letter to the Empress, he summed up his wider aims, expressing the hope that 'the future historian of Napoleon III will be able to say: "When he took over the government of France half the population lived in spiritual darkness, but when he was gone, all could read, write and count." This will mean unusual glory, for I know of no Prince who ever acquired it.' Duruy's co-operation with the Empress extended to her family, for it was he who recommended his former pupil, Augustin Filon, as tutor for the Prince Imperial, while in Mlle Redel he provided an *institutrice* for the two Alba girls. For her part, the Empress was at pains to associate the Prince Imperial with the new educational reforms, allowing him to distribute annual awards and prizes at the Lycée du Prince Imperial and elsewhere, while Duruy was always anxious to establish a close link between the dynasty and his own Herculean work. In his letters he often told her that a 'contented teacher will vote correctly', that a conscript who could read and write would be a better soldier, that her support of his reforms would 'heighten the dignity of wives, increase the authority of mothers and expand the influence of women in society'.

The Empress showed greater zeal in this field than the Emperor. The historian Ernest Lavisse, who was Duruy's right-hand man at the Ministry of Education and later became the Prince Imperial's history tutor,[1] wrote:

'The Emperor hovered over the Empire instead of governing it. . . . The most striking public testimony of Imperial confidence which Duruy received was given by the Empress who, despite what has been alleged, always gave him unstinting support. In connection with clerical outbursts, the Emperor merely said to Duruy "Why don't you defend yourself?". . . .'

The Empress's relationship with Duruy was, from the beginning, as friendly as it was unceremonious. She particularly relied on him to submit

[1] Also that of the present Comte de Paris.

names of guests to be invited to her informal dinners. When, in May, 1865, Duruy had to go on a tour of inspection in the provinces, he applied for leave from the Regent and ended his letter with these words: 'I have just read the speech by Prince Napoleon and am deeply distressed.'

Plon-Plon had upset matters once again. Speaking at the unveiling of a monument to Napoleon I at Ajaccio, the princely vice-president of the Council had launched an attack on the Pope that was extreme in vehemence even for him. Describing Rome as 'the last fortress of the Middle Ages', he exclaimed that Rome in the hands of the Pope was 'a centre of reaction against France, Italy and our society'. The orator's tactlessness and violence were equalled only by his abominable sense of timing, for the September Convention had led to a considerable lessening of tensions within France and the first steps of the French withdrawal from Rome were even then in progress. The speech provided the Empress with the most vexing and thorny problem of her Regency, but she showed a politic moderation in dealing with her enemy's latest transgression. At the next session of the Ministerial Council, she suggested that the speech should be ignored officially, but that in the Emperor's absence no reprimand ought to be publicly addressed to Prince Napoleon. A number of Ministers were in favour of publishing an official censure of the speech and the speaker in the *Moniteur*, but the Empress, who felt that a policy of silence would be best, prevailed with her opinion, and the *Moniteur* merely printed a brief item that a monument to Napoleon I had been unveiled in Corsica.

The Emperor surprised everyone by a swift and angry reaction from Algiers. He wrote a letter to his cousin disavowing him completely and accusing him of giving aid and comfort to the Empire's enemies:

'In leaving you during my absence by the side of the Empress and my son, I wanted to give you a proof of my friendship and confidence, and I hoped that your presence, your conduct and your speeches would bear witness to the solidarity existing in our family. . . .'

The Emperor ordered that this letter be published in the *Moniteur*, before which he had sent his special ordnance officer, Col. de Galliffet, to the Palais Royal to deliver the document in person. The Prince at once resigned from the vice-presidency, also from the presidency of the Committee preparing the Great Exhibition of 1867, and retired, a discredited Achilles or a frustrated Brutus,[1] to his villa at Prangins, near Geneva.

---

[1] It may be noted in passing that the Emperor, in his foreword to *Julius Caesar*, had written: 'Brutus, by slaying Caesar, plunged Rome into the horrors of civil war; he did not prevent the reign of Augustus, but he rendered possible those of Nero and Caligula. The ostracism of Napoleon I by allied Europe has been no more successful in preventing the Empire from being resuscitated. . . .' The Emperor may well have felt that his cousin was, like the friends of Brutus, 'disguising himself under the *mask of liberty*'.

Shortly before the Emperor's return in June 1865, the Regent caused something of a sensation by conferring the Cross of the *légion d'honneur* upon Rosa Bonheur, then at the height of her success as a painter. She was also an ostentatiously unconventional woman, wearing her hair short and dressing not fashionably, but sensibly. The Empress had unexpectedy called one morning in the spring of 1864 at the cottage in the forest of Fontaine-bleau, where the artist lived and worked, had admired her pictures and engaged her in a long conversation on feminist subjects. Mérimée, who had been present, had greatly admired the Empress's ease and affability with the artist, about whose outward appearance, however, he had felt a little unhappy: it seemed difficult to tell whether you were talking to a man or a woman. Mlle Bonheur became the first woman to be honoured with the decoration, and the effect on the country was profound. *L'Opinion Nationale*, a newspaper generally mildly in opposition, commented:

'We applaud with both hands. Decidedly, our civilisation begins to recognise that women have a soul. And the signature underneath the degree proves that women have also intelligence, even when they are on the throne.'

On the eve of the Emperor's return, the Empress cancelled all warnings[1] which had been addressed to peccant newspapers. The amnesty was greeted with delighted applause in which slightly ironic undertones were audible. A liberal newspaper wrote that the Regent evidently wished 'to restring the Imperial lyre with the democratic cord which has been missing since the speech at Ajaccio.'

The Emperor returned on June 8th. 'I had the honour,' wrote Metter-nich to Vienna on June 10th, 1865,

'to be received by the Empress yesterday to whom I addressed my con-gratulations on the happy results of her interregnum. Her Majesty admitted that she had done this work with the greatest interest and that she was proud to have "managed the ship" so well. "The Ministers never quarrelled among themselves and I have kept them so well under control that I almost regret surrendering the reins. I shall tell the Emperor that I am handing him a firm and united government, and I shall ask him to be careful not to relax the bridle too much." The Emperor's health is excellent. . . .'

The Emperor came back in excellent form indeed. Mérimée heard him describe his North African journey later in June. 'Don't you find it extra-ordinary,' he wrote to Panizzi, 'that after having had four or five hundred thousand men killed by the Christians, after having many of their women

[1] It will be recalled that after three warnings a newspaper could be heavily fined and closed down.

raped, after having lost their autonomy and I don't know what else, the Arabs have received so wonderfully the Chief of the people who have done all this to them? The Emperor went into the desert with, at the most, twenty Frenchmen and spent forty-eight hours among fifteen or twenty thousand Saharians who deafened his ears with rifle shots (their way of salutation) and cleaned his boots with their beards. They gave him whole oxen roasted, they made him eat ostriches and I don't know what other impossible animals besides, and received him everywhere as a beloved Sovereign. He has come back very proud and very happy. . . . '

The Empress, wishing to take the present happy time at the flood, persuaded the Emperor to spend some days that summer at Arenenberg, Queen Hortense's château on the Swiss shore of Lake Constance. The Emperor consented with gratitude. While imprisoned at Ham, he had been forced to sell the property, but in 1855 the Empress had bought it back from the purchasers, had it repaired and restored in the style of Queen Hortense and the First Empire and presented it to her husband on his forty-seventh birthday. The Imperial party spent four days in August 1865, at Arenenberg. On the first evening, a local male choir serenaded the Emperor, who appeared on the terrace and made a little speech in German. Was anyone there, he asked, who remembered his departure from Arenenberg— and Switzerland—twenty-seven years ago? A vigorous 'Ja' rose from almost all the serenaders confirming that they well recalled the humiliating moment when Louis Philippe's government had insisted on the Bonapartist claimant's being expelled from their hospitality. Two days later, the Emperor invited the entire neighbourhood to a magnificent display of fireworks. He entertained the Cantonal authorities to luncheon, contributed to local charities, presented the famous Benedictine Abbey of Einsiedeln with two magnificent candelabra, called on the Queen of Württemberg in nearby Gottlieben, took the whole party on a steamer round the Lake— he spent, in fact, four days of the most perfect happiness.

Departure had to be timed for August 24th, since an important visitor was expected to visit Biarritz in October: Bismarck. The Imperial party travelled by train to Neuchâtel, to continue the journey to the frontier by road. The carriages, the first with the Emperor and Empress, the second with the Empress's four ladies, were waiting outside Neuchâtel station, ready to start, when the driver of a stationary locomotive sounded his steam whistle with such prolonged force that the horses of the second carriage panicked and tore away into the huge crowd that had assembled to witness the departure. Anna Murat, Mme de Montebello and Mlle Bouvet were thrown and badly injured. The Emperor at once dismounted and helped to get the ladies away to hospital, and the Empress 'like a sister of charity', says Mlle Bouvet, spent the night at their bedsides tending them. Incredibly, the engine driver was a French republican who later explained that he had wished to revenge Orsini's failure in 1858. The pilgrimage to Arenenberg ended on a bitter note, and the Sovereigns returned to Paris separately, the Empress taking care of the injured ladies until September 3rd.

Mérimée had dined with the Regent in May and saw her again soon after her return from Neuchâtel. 'It seemed to me,' he wrote after the first occasion, 'that the whole tone in the house is changed. One is less gay, but one is calmer, with greater steadiness of poise. I think that in the course of a year the Empress has learnt much about things and people.' In September, shortly before she departed for Biarritz, he saw her again at luncheon, and afterwards wrote to Panizzi: 'Eugénie is no more, there is only an Empress. I mourn, and I admire.'

CHAPTER 18

BISMARCK STRODE into the drawing-room of the Villa Eugénie at
Biarritz in the morning of October 4th, 1865. He found only Mérimée
present to receive him, as the Court had gone to Mass. 'He pleased me
much,' Mérimée wrote in English to Fanny Lagden, 'but I doubt whether
he was pleased with his conversation with the Emperor.' Bismarck was
now a Count, having been promoted by a grateful King for successfully
checking all parliamentary interference with Prussian army reform. In his
capacity as Prussian Foreign Minister, he brought to Biarritz the fresh
laurels of the Convention of Gastein, by which Prussia and Austria re-
affirmed their alliance. In the days to follow, the Empress saw her husband
and her guest walk along the sandy beach below the villa deep in conversation, retiring later to the Emperor's study for further talks. Bismarck,
who was then evolving his plan for a united 'little' Germany aimed at
the elimination of Austrian influence in Southern Germany, had come to
Biarritz to sound the French Emperor on his attitude in the event of an
open conflict between Austria and Prussia. He found the French Emperor
inclined towards a policy of neutrality, heard him even advocate a Prussian
alliance with Italy in order to speed up the cession of Venetia. In return
for his toleration of the shift in the balance of power within the Germanic
system, Bismarck suggested compensations for France in the direction of
Belgium and Luxembourg, and the Emperor later told Lord Cowley that
the Prussian statesman had been profuse in offering him territory that was
not his to give away. Bismarck's overriding impression was that, whatever
the future held, the Emperor of the French was determined not to go to
war for any of the problems then facing the concert of Europe. Back in
Berlin, he told his friends that in France he had seen 'two remarkable
women and nothing else'. This alluded, apart from the Empress, to the
beautiful Mme de La Bédoyère, with whom he had enjoyed flirting at
Biarritz. He was not impressed by an Emperor who preferred peace. Nor
was it difficult for a man of Bismarck's experience to see through
Napoleon's intention of remaining outside any armed conflict between the
two leading Germanic powers and then, as *tertium gaudens*, claiming to be
the arbiter in the peace talks between the exhausted combatants.

This was the exact antithesis to the Austrian policy pursued by the
Empress in her talks with Metternich. The Emperor encouraged her to
continue with these, but to him the possibility of an Austrian alliance was
merely another card that might be played one day, a potential sword of

Damocles with which he might threaten either Prussia or Italy in the case of complications. To the Empress, the alliance represented the Empire's most vital duty. As the tension between Austria and Prussia grew and the European sky darkened, she once more urged Metternich to settle the Venetian problem by a gesture of voluntary renunciation, as this would 'make the whole of Italy march at your side'. French opinion, she correctly told him, was already instinctively anti-Prussian, and it would only require that one act of statesmanship to make France also swing over to the Austrian side. This remained the theme of her talks with the ambassador, the most important of which took place on March 22nd, 1866, on April 14th, May 1st, 16th and 21st. On the latter occasion she went further than ever before: 'Don't you see,' she told Metternich, 'that the Emperor is committed to a policy of neutrality only until the first shot has been fired? If I tell you to go ahead, it is not to lure you into a trap . . . *en avance, en avance* . . .' She broke off abruptly.

After many months of international crisis and unrest, Austria took a first active step by renouncing her alliance with Prussia on June 1st, 1866. This made war a certainty, and so on June 10th Austria at long last made a secret agreement with France, undertaking to cede Venetia to France, who was to act as a broker between Austria and Italy whatever the outcome of the conflict. The countries of Southern Germany as well as the kingdom of Hanover ranged themselves on the side of Austria, the Prussian army crossed into Bohemia, and on June 24th the Austrian army defeated the Italians under Victor Emmanuel in the battle of Custozza. Late on July 3rd, Metternich received the following telegram from his Foreign Minister:

'Endeavour to make Emperor Napoleon give up his passive neutrality in Germany which is the cause of our disasters. Only French armed intervention can now prevent Prussia from achieving exclusive domination of Germany. Obtain positive reply quickest. . . .'

On that day the battle of Sadowa had been fought and the Austrians completely routed. They lost 24,000 men killed and wounded and some 13,000 prisoners. The day was a triumph of Prussian resolution, speed and efficiency, an impressive vindication of their new needle-gun and army organisation. By one mighty stroke, Bismarck with his impeccable timing established the superiority of his diplomacy over that of the Emperor Napoleon, who now found himself reduced to isolation and impotence in Europe. Although Austria had ceded Venetia to France, the defeated Victor Emmanuel marched into the province without waiting for French permission. Nor did Bismarck, or indeed the King of Prussia, take much notice of French offers of mediation between Austria and Prussia. King William, having smelt powder, wanted to enter Vienna at the head of his victorious army and, like Napoleon I, dictate the peace terms there, but in a famous and dramatic scene Bismarck prevailed on his Sovereign to agree to a moderate and conciliatory peace. The peace of Prague, concluded in August without any reference to France, established Prussian hegemony over Germany north and south of the river Main, and removed the last vestiges of Austrian influence from Southern Germany, tying that territory to Prussia by a number of military agreements that were to run for the next five years. Otherwise, Bismarck had the statesmanship not to interfere with the outward independence of these countries, leaving their little Kings and Dukes unpunished after the defeat of their Austrian ally and erstwhile protector. Only the blind King of Hanover was driven from his kingdom and had his considerable private fortune confiscated by Bismarck, who re-christened it the 'Guelph Fund'.

Before that fateful shift in the European power system had been consummated, however, the Empress, in two Council meetings at Saint-Cloud on July 5th and 10th, made a final bid to compel the Emperor to side openly with Austria. At the former meeting, her urgent suggestion to make a military demonstration on the Rhine had the backing of Drouyn de Lhuys and the Protestant Marshal Randon, but was opposed by Lavalette, Baroche and Eugène Rouher, respectively Ministers of the Interior, Justice and State. The Empress, remembering the fatal effect which Prussian mobilisation had exercised on the Italian campaign of 1859, was convinced that Prussia could be turned back from Bohemia by French mobilisation. This Bismarck confirmed in a speech in 1874 when he said that 15,000 French soldiers and the armies of Southern Germany would have been able 'to force us to cover Berlin and abandon all our successes in Bohemia'. Towards the end of the meeting on July 5th, the Emperor seemed persuaded that France should mobilise, but changed his mind again during the night and went back on his promise to summon Parliament and announce that 80,000 troops were to be sent to the Eastern frontier. The Ministers of the Interior and Justice had shown him reports from all parts of the country that public opinion was overwhelmingly opposed to war. At the meeting of July 10th, the Empress and her supporters returned to the charge, but the Emperor and the appeasing Ministers remained firm and said that the country was not ready for 'a policy of adventure'. 'My voice,' wrote the Empress to Metternich after the meeting.

'no longer carries any weight, and I am almost alone in my views. They are exaggerating today's dangers in order to make us forget tomorrow's. The one thing I can answer for is that the Emperor will do everything in his power to obtain the best possible peace terms for you. I am deeply grieved and cannot go on writing.'

And she added a postscript that expressed her simple war-aims in one sentence:

'If only you could give them a good hiding!'

After the two Council meetings of July, 1866, the Eugenian Legend was played with a new variation. The clerical Empress now became the war-mongering Empress, the woman bent on war in order to assure the future of the dynasty. It was a new distortion of the truth. She was convinced that the Empire could not afford to watch the growth of Prussia in idleness, but was it possible to draw a distinction here between régime and country, between the Empire and France? She understood that the Prussian system, where political life was subordinated to the needs and requirements of the armed forces, represented a deadly challenge to the life and future of France and Europe. The Empress was convinced that Prussia, bent on uniting Germany by Italian methods, and France could not live together in peace, unless the Empire was able to inspire its Eastern neighbour with a healthy respect for its striking power. Most French parliamentarians, several Ministers and a large number of influential intellectuals thought that this was a typically reactionary attitude, dangerous to the programme of internal liberalisation. Yet two public men in France, both determined and active progressives, fully shared the Empress's apprehension of the Prussian danger to the future development of France: Victor Duruy and, in the Franco-Prussian crisis of 1870, Léon Gambetta. Duruy was in favour of armed intervention and wrote to the Emperor in the week after Sadowa:

'We are faced today with a young and ambitious neighbouring country that wishes to become a great Continental and maritime power. That power will not be able to hold what it has and take what it wants until after it has humiliated France, as it has humiliated Austria already. . . .'

We shall study Gambetta's conception of the Prussian system in due course. Duruy's attitude in 1866 shows that the wish to threaten the victorious Prussians militarily was not a party matter or a question of dynastic selfishness, but a logical attitude inspired by the concern for the future of French power and independence. With her sharp and instinctive understanding of the dangers of the future, the Empress realised that Sadowa had been a defeat not only of Austria, but of France.

The preliminaries and aftermath of the Seven weeks' war of 1866 taught the Empress another and even graver lesson: the Emperor was no longer physically capable of dealing with the complexities of his reign. His chairmanship at the two Council sessions during July had been feeble, confused and ineffectual; he patently vaccillated between the various courses open to him without being able to reach positive decisions or insist on their implementation. His health, throughout 1866, was further deteriorating. 'The Emperor,' wrote Dr. Barthez, 'has not the will-power to deprive himself of the things he likes which do him harm.' 'I assure you,' the Empress told Metternich on July 26th, 'we are moving towards our fall, and the best thing would be if the Emperor suddenly disappeared, at least for a time. He can't sleep or walk, and he can hardly eat. For two years he has been living in utter prostration, has not occupied himself with the government, but written *Julius Caesar* instead. . . .' The idea of the

Emperor's modified abdication, with herself succeeding him as Regent on her son's behalf, occurred to the Empress under the impact of these appalling conditions. It seems possible—the surviving evidence is weak—that she tentatively discussed this notion with her husband, who may have seen its force, but put off a decision to some future date. Metternich at all events wrote to Vienna that

> 'never since I have known the Imperial couple have I seen the Emperor to be so completely nothing and the Empress take our interests to heart with such fury and zeal.'

They were not only Austrian interests.

Despite the crisis—or was it because of it?—the Empress's public standing in the country, her personal popularity were higher than ever. On July 4th, the day after Sadowa, she visited Amiens, which had been hit by a cholera epidemic, inspected the hospitals, arranged for energetic measures to be taken and distributed large sums of money both to hospitals and individual cases. The speech which the head of the local Council addressed to the Empress must have reminded her of the France that was now slipping from the Emperor's grasp:

> 'The Emperor has given France peace and prosperity. He has made her great and the arbiter of the world. At this moment, the whole Empire vibrates with pride because His Majesty, whose genius and lofty wisdom inspire universal confidence, has been called upon to act as mediator between the three belligerent powers.
>
> Near the throne live sublime and moving virtues which make us love and bless our sovereigns. Your Majesty has condescended to visit us in the midst of misfortune, consoling us and giving us an example of heroic courage. . . .'

Two weeks later, the Empress and the Prince Imperial went to Nancy to represent the Emperor at the centenary celebrations of the union of Lorraine with France. 'The Empress's journey,' wrote Mérimée to Mme de Montijo on July 18th, 1866,

> 'is an uninterrupted triumph. It seems that the papers only report half the enthusiasm which she rouses wherever she goes. I am delighted that she appears alone with her son and am sure that she is not only as graceful and charming as ever, but that she is as skilful and politic as the most accomplished diplomat.'

In August, she and her husband were faced with the ordeal of receiving the Empress Charlotte of Mexico, who had come to Europe to ask for further credits and armed support for Maximilian's crumbling Empire. The United States government was now openly supporting Juarez from their side of the border, but apart from that Maximilian had shown himself an incompetent and soft-willed ruler who had antagonised conservatives and liberals alike and even lacked the acumen to remain on sensible terms with the French army under Bazaine. It must be admitted that the attitude of the Roman Catholic hierarchy backed by Rome rendered his task almost impossible from the start, but even so his lack of fibre came as an unpleasant surprise to the Empress. 'He is too sporadic,' she told Metternich, 'too inclined to demand the impossible, such as a guarantee from all the great European powers.' He had certainly shown himself a man of pleasure rather than of action, more expert at dealing with ceremony and etiquette than politics and government, and his marriage with the impatient and wild-eyed Charlotte had become one in name only.

When the Empress of Mexico appeared uninvited in Paris in that tragic summer of 1866, the Emperor had to drag himself back from Vichy to receive her at Saint-Cloud. He had to refuse all further military and financial support and broke this to her in his gentle and apologetic way. Fould and other Ministers whom Charlotte saw on the following days expressed the same facts more brutally. She rushed on to Rome, where Pio Nono and Cardinal Antonelli also gave her to understand that they were disinclined to raise a finger for her husband's throne, adding acid comments on Maximilian's flirtations with liberal opinion. It was while she was the guest of the embarrassed Pio Nono in the Vatican that Charlotte showed the first alarming symptoms of the madness that was to envelop her from then until the end of her long life in 1927.

The summer of 1866 not only saw the Empire's most acute political crisis before that of 1870, it also witnessed the nadir in the relationship between Emperor and Empress. She left Paris for Biarritz in mid-August in a mood of despair; the Prince Imperial, Dr. Barthez and Mérimée accompanied her. Five weeks later, on September 21st, the Emperor arrived at Biarritz. During the month which they spent by the Atlantic shore, the relationship between Emperor and Empress was restored to its former intimacy and mutual confidence. How did this miracle come about?

In the first week, he suffered attacks of fever. But these soon ceased and there was a marked improvement in his health. Thereupon, to the Empress's profound relief, he began to work with something of his former energy and resolution on the urgent problems of the day. Fould, still the leading financial expert in the government, was summoned for a discussion of the big rearmament programme on which the Emperor was now determined, and Lavalette for talks on how best to persuade French public opinion of the necessity for army reform.

'It seems to me,' Mérimée wrote to his friend Victor Cousin, the historian and philosopher, 'that Roman history has been abandoned and that the Emperor occupies himself exclusively with his own.' Mérimée had brought one of the new *chassepot* guns to Biarritz and the Empress watched him practise with it on the beach. They were widely believed to be better than the Prussian needle-gun that had won them the day at Sadowa. The Empress had heard of the new weapon just before she left for Biarritz and during a luncheon at Saint-Cloud closely questioned Marshal Canrobert on its range and performance. 'The disaster experienced by Austria,' she told the Marshal on that occasion, 'has injured the moral and material power of France. If our country is not to lose its standing in Europe, it is essential to strengthen the national forces.' She was thankful to see the Emperor taking the first steps to form the 'Commission for Army Reform', which was to submit new and comprehensive army bills to the Chamber in the course of 1867.

Other factors contributed to the miracle of Biarritz and restored the Empress's confidence. There was the exuberance and intelligence of her son, now a child of ten. The Emperor doted on him, as did Mérimée and Panizzi and, with the important exception of the Empress and Miss Shaw, everyone was inclined to spoil him. The sculptor Carpeaux had discovered that the Prince had an unusual gift for drawing and sculpture and was giving him regular lessons. His other studies were, until Filon took over in 1867, in the hands of a M. Monnier, a professional teacher and philosopher. From the soldiers' sons with whom he associated in Paris and Saint-Cloud the Prince had picked up a good deal of Parisian slang. When at Biarritz one day the Empress reproved him for using a particularly earthy expression, he replied: 'Mama, you speak French very well, but you are a foreigner and don't know the finer points of the language.' The Empress was speechless.

Mérimée, too, knowing so much about the Empress's dilemma, did much to ease and relax her mind. He taught her the virtue of patience—'we have to swallow insults from Prussia until we have our own needle-gun'. But he also lightened her anxieties by supervising her reading, telling her respectfully that she was 'not literary enough'. In the evenings he read to her and her ladies his latest short story, a faintly risqué and wholly delightful tale called La Chambre Bleu, after which he read stories by his friend Turgenev. He prevailed on Victor Cousin to present a copy of his work on French Society in the seventeenth century, for which the author was rewarded by a letter from the Empress in which she expressed her appreciation at seeing 'a society of the past' brought back to life in an 'admirable style which is one of the glories of our literature'. Mérimée also unsuccessfully endeavoured to establish a link between the Empress and another literary friend of his, Adolphe Thiers, who was then bringing out his monumental work on the First Empire. But Thiers, in 1866, was still hovering between opposition and collaboration, and his vanity proved so overwhelming that Mérimée was powerless to introduce him at Court.

The Empress always enjoyed Mérimée's racy and acute conversation and was grateful for his efforts to amend her cultural imperfections. It was therefore with special delight that she informed him at Biarritz of his promotion to Grand officier of the Legion of Honour. 'They could,' wrote the recipient to Mme Prezdjecka, the witty and agreeable *présidente* of the Empress's famous Courts of Love,[1] of which he was secretary, 'have made a better, a more politic use of the decoration. I cannot love them more or serve them more devotedly because of it.'

Although the stay at Biarritz in 1866 clearly marks an important point in the personal relationship between Napoleon and Eugénie, there is, in the final analysis, a mysterious element in the situation, since their ability to return to each other is a phenomenon rarely found in relationships at their level. For they did return to each other in sincere and mutual affection—they did not keep up a mere façade for the benefit of the Court and the official world. Many of the details, the gradual steps and mutual efforts by which they worked out their difficulties, are hidden from us, since little correspondence between them survives. The exception, as will be seen, are the letters they exchanged when the Emperor was a prisoner of war at Wilhelmshöhe and the Empress an exile at Chislehurst. Augustin Filon wrote that the Emperor 'came to regard the Empress as his second conscience, and his second conscience was often better and more reliable than his first'. He needed her because in the battle between his will-power and his recurrent illnesses she remained steadfast, reassuring and as firm as a rock. Beyond the disagreements, despite his many betrayals, and above the difference in age, temper and outlook, she had proved that he could rely on her. Although their physical and emotional limitations had imposed abnormal burdens on their marriage they were united by their faith in the future of the Prince Imperial. They were both convinced that in the age and the world in which they lived their mission was to lead France towards a future of unity and strength—so long as they remained united themselves. As Filon rightly hints, the Emperor's 'first conscience' stood in great need of being encouraged and refreshed by another conscience that was less tainted and worn down by the subtle sophistication of politics and diplomacy. That he ultimately never absconded from his other conscience reveals a certain goodness of character in Napoleon III who as Emperor and man is only now beginning to come into his own.

---

[1] The 'Courts of Love', about which much misleading gossip has survived, consisted of regular meetings attended by the wittier conversationalists of the Court, mostly held at Fontainebleau. Its members were under the sworn obligation to speak nothing but the truth on the themes proposed for debate at these verbal tournaments. As the name indicates, the subjects discussed were usually concerned with the relationship between the sexes. Mérimée's secretaryship, and incidentally Mme Prezdjecka's wit, kept these occasions at a not unworthy level.

CHAPTER 19

IN THE autumn of 1866, the Emperor summoned a number of military experts to Compiègne, among whom Marshals Niel and Canrobert and General Trochu were the best-known, to work out the details of the projected army reforms. The *Moniteur* of December 12th, 1866, published a commentary on the plan which stressed the necessity of creating an army of 800,000 men by a system of universal conscription and of simultaneously establishing an 'auxiliary force for the defence of the frontiers'. The project was immediately attacked by the opposition on the Right and Left while in the country itself the Prefects reported widespread aversion from all forms of military service illogically going hand in hand with acute uneasiness and hostility caused by Prussia's stunning successes. War, according to the Prefect of Caen, was coming to be regarded as inevitable in view of 'Prussian arrogance and the susceptibility of our national dignity', but any increase of the military forces in peace-time 'encountered almost general opposition'. Reports from other parts of the country confirmed this contradictory attitude. 'The formerly Gallic nation,' wrote Mérimée, 'shows an invincible aversion from dealing out blows or doing anything that might prejudice financial speculations. We have changed indeed since the days of Brennus or even Napoleon I.' The Emperor and his military advisers had therefore to proceed with great caution before their project could be submitted to the Chambers with any hope of success. It was not until December 1867 that a much modified and vitiated army bill was discussed by the deputies. The government meanwhile made every effort to rally an Imperialist majority against the cynical alliance between Right and Left in the Chambers and the country.

The Empress was not one of the government's military advisers, but nevertheless she contributed towards making the country aware of its mortal danger. In the face of the pacifism of the opposition and the lethargy of the middle classes, she conceived an idea which later governments in France and elsewhere were to follow up, but which was scarcely popular in the France of 1867. She addressed this letter to the Ministers of War and the Interior:

'They say enthusiasm is dying out. We must revive it. There must be a democracy of rewards, and we must do for the village what is already being done in towns. I should like to see the name of a simple soldier who was killed on the field of honour in an act of heroism remembered

THE PRINCE IMPERIAL DRIVES OUT FROM THE BAGATELLE

THE EMPRESS ELISABETH OF AUSTRIA IN THE HUNTING FIELD

SAINT CLOUD IN THE FIFTIES

THE VILLA EUGÉNIE, BIARRITZ

ARENENBERG

FARNBOROUGH HILL

in his village. A street or a square might be named after him while a plaque on the school building tells future generations what gave him the right to have his monument.

The best way to bring about good is to make it known. Even as a criminal sees his name, his crime and his punishment announced for universal reprobation so should devotion and patriotism have their publicity.'

The Empress continued to devote her energies to social work, and to her official and personal charities. The former are too numerous to list here; the record of her private charities does not exist. A very few letters from those who benefited have survived, such as two from Georges Sand ('I join to the wishes of the poor shipwrecked man whom Your Majesty has saved from misery, the wishes of my soul for the happiness which Your Majesty deserves so well, having given it to so many others . . .'), but otherwise the Empress drew a veil across her innumerable acts of personal charity.

Yet by the middle sixties she felt, as she put it to Henri Chevreau, Prefect at Lyons, that 'private charity is always insufficient'. Lyons had been hard hit by the cotton famine and when Chevreau came to Paris to discuss how to relieve the silk workers' suffering, the Empress had several discussions with him, following them up by correspondence. She suggested establishing a government fund to guarantee losses incurred by manufacturers who employed surplus labour during the depression. Chevreau discussed this idea with a group of Lyons employers, but had to report to the Empress their unanimous opposition to all forms of State intervention, which might set a dangerous precedent and give rise to 'unrealisable hopes'. Workers might even accuse the management of 'speculating with their misery', and certainly no management would wish the State to examine its account books. The Prefect saw no alternative but for the State to continue relying on private charity, however inadequate. Their correspondence ended with the Empress donating a large sum of money with which the *hospices* of Lyons purchased a château as a convalescent home for sick workers.

With the Prefect of Marseilles, a city in which the alliance between reactionaries and revolutionaries was specially active, she also corresponded about progressive social legislation, exploring the question of what she called 'retirement pensions for workers', but it was not until the spring of 1870 that the Prefect of that 'red' city produced a detailed pioneer scheme to be applied in the first instance to Marseilles alone. The Third Republic was to continue, in this as in other respects, what Bonapartism had begun. We may note in passing that the bishop of Marseilles, unlike Mgr. Dupanloup a real Catholic liberal and therefore a staunch supporter of the dynasty, was one of the few clerics with whom the Empress discussed political questions. Like herself, the bishop was appalled by the unceasing political agitation in his diocese where Gambetta and M. de La Rochejaquelein propagated the same venomous ideas. When the Vatican Council held its historic assembly late in 1869, the bishop, who belonged to the 'inopportunist', or anti-infallibility, minority, became her informant on the struggles behind the scenes.

The Roman question cast its unsettling shadow across the French political scene in the critical twelve months after Sadowa. The evacuation of Rome by the French garrison was scheduled to be completed by November 1866. It was generally supposed that if the Pope could last one week after the French withdrawal, his possession of Rome would be assured. The Empress conceived the notion of spending a month in Rome during the final days of the evacuation. Her presence, she considered, would reduce the likelihood of an attack from outside or of revolutionary events within, besides giving her an opportunity to insist on the Roman government carrying out constitutional and judiciary reforms. From Florence, where General Fleury was obtaining the necessary assurances from Victor Emmanuel, it was made clear that the Italian government would welcome the Empress's visit. Mérimée, though horrified by the idea, thought it might do the Empress good 'to see with her own eyes the disorder, ignorance and obtuseness of the Roman Court and so disabuse her of her chivalrous enthusiasm'. Others such as Magne, who was Minister of Finance whenever Fould was not, told her frankly during dinner at Compiègne early in December 1866 that he thought the plan disastrous. 'But surely,' she replied, 'when a house is on fire it must be extinguished at once. At all costs the Pope must be prevented from leaving Rome. No one but myself can persuade him to remain and secure certain concessions.' Magne agreed that for the Pope to leave Rome would be a defeat of the policy the Emperor's government had pursued for the last fifteen years and must be prevented, but insisted that her journey 'would be both useless and dangerous'. She listened carefully and thanked him for his frankness.

A traveller returning from Rome reported that when His Holiness was asked whether he expected a visit from the Empress of the French, he had replied: 'I have already received an Empress who was mad. That was quite enough.' We do not know whether this ungracious statement was repeated to the Empress, but she most certainly was informed of the Pope's speech when General de Montebello and his comrades went to the Vatican for a farewell audience. 'Depart,' said the Pope on this highly official occasion, 'with our benediction and paternal good wishes. If you see the Emperor of the French, your Emperor, you will tell him that I am praying for him. They say his health is poor, and so I am praying for his health. They say his soul is unquiet, and so I am praying for his soul. The French are a Christian nation, its Chief ought to be Christian as well. . . .' French papers were told not to print this tactless allocution, and the Empress lost all desire to make the Pope's personal acquaintance. Her visit to Rome, which had already been announced in the papers, was abandoned. On December 10th, 1866, the Tricolour flag of France was lowered for the last time on the Castello Sant'Angelo, and the yellow and white standard of the Pope was raised instead.

Within nine months, Garibaldi returned to the Italian mainland and launched his third march on Rome. In pointedly reluctant obedience to the September Convention of 1864, Victor Emmanuel mobilised against the new aggression, but the Pope sent an appeal for help to the Emperor, as a result of which the French army returned to Roman territory. Garibaldi, now far more closely identified with revolutionary and anarchist movements than hitherto, was defeated at Mentana. General Failly, in command of the French expedition, reported to Paris that 'the chassepots have done wonders', a phrase which, against the Emperor's express wishes, was leaked to the Press by Marshal Niel to impress the Prussians. This in turn caused Victor Emmanuel to retort that the chassepots had killed all hope of a Franco-Italian alliance. Public opinion in France was disappointed to see that even after Garibaldi's defeat a French garrison was back in Papal territory, at Città Vecchia this time and not in Rome itself. In the Chamber of Deputies, Rouher, now the Empire's First Minister, exclaimed that France would 'never allow Italy to have Rome—never, never, never!' for which the Emperor afterwards reproved him, saying that 'never' was a term that must never be used in politics. What would happen to that fine phrase if Victor Emmanuel and the Pope came to an agreement between themselves? As in the days of Cavour, Napoleon still hoped that this bilateral solution would be eventually achieved.

The Empress had been present at the Council which decided for intervention against Garibaldi and, like Marshal Niel, had supported the measure. The images of the war-mongering and clerical Empress were now fused into one. 'All is over,' said a leading journalist after Mentana, 'from now on, the Spanish woman triumphs and the reign of Philip II has begun.' Another said: 'The liberal Empire is finished, the clerical Empire has begun.' Yet military intervention against Garibaldi had been the unanimous decision of the whole government. French reactions to Mentana revealed once more that the country was reluctant to allow the government to create an efficient striking force, as it was feared in many circles that conscription and militarisation were incompatible with the liberal reforms which the Emperor's government were pursuing at the same time. The speakers of the left-wing opposition, with Gambetta and Jules Favre at their head, voiced these suspicions in many public meetings and were rewarded with much popular acclaim from the streets. A sinister element was added to the situation when General Trochu, a member of most of the military commissions set up by the Emperor and Marshal Niel, published confidential material about the proposed measures in a pamphlet and thus made a clear bid for popularity with the opposition and the *communards* of Paris.

Simultaneously with army reform, the Emperor decided to revise his foreign policy. But, whereas on military questions the Emperor now showed unwavering determination to create a more up-to-date instrument for attack and defence, and himself contributed a number of valuable ideas and suggestions, his foreign policy was less single-minded.

Although he now examined the possibilities of an Austrian alliance more actively than he had before, his old dislike and suspicions of Austria never wholly left him. Despite Mentana, he still hoped that Italy could be induced to accede to any agreement he might be able to make with Francis Joseph, and certainly it became noticeable after 1867 that personal relations between the Austrian Emperor and the King of Italy were growing friendlier. Negotiations for a tripartite alliance had to be carried out secretly as the opposition was just as suspicious of a diplomacy aimed at strengthening France politically as of a policy of making her more effective militarily. Yet in Beust, a Saxon by birth whom Francis Joseph had appointed Chancellor after his defeats in 1866, Austria now had a statesman who was firmly opposed to any further expansion of Prussian influence in Germany. Mostly behind the back of his own diplomats such as Gramont, French Ambassador in Vienna, the Emperor opened confidential talks with the Austrian chancellery, while Nigra made many trips to Florence to pave the way for an alliance between the two countries. In Florence he found an influential party advocating closer relations with France in gratitude for her assistance in 1859; others, however, remembered no farther back than 1866 and Prussian help over Venetia. Memories of 1866 also influenced the leaders of Hungary, now governing at Budapest on terms of equality with Vienna, who had little wish to see the Austrian Monarchy defeat Prussia in the field, thus reaffirming the hegemony of German Austria over the rest of the multi-racial Habsburg dominions.

Apart from encouraging both Metternich and Nigra to promote *pourparlers*, the Empress took little share in these complex and often half-hearted negotiations. The principal ideological difference between her and the Emperor was that whereas the Emperor still felt a lingering doctrinaire preference for the principle of nationality and was thus inspired from time to time with a measure of sympathy towards German unitarian ideas, the Empress was wholly free of any such intellectual preoccupation. 'Her Majesty,' a French Minister had written in 1866, 'does not hide her aversion from the theory of nationality. She thinks that Italian unity is for us a source of danger rather than of strength, and that German unity will be a patent and immediate danger.' Two events in foreign policy showed in the course of 1867 how strong the latter danger was. The first was Bismarck's announcement of an offensive and defensive alliance between the North German Confederation and the German States south of the Main which, in addition to the military provisions agreed to between North and South after the latter's defeat in 1866, turned Germany, even before official unification, into a 'nation-wide training school for war'. The second event, more immediately fatal to the prestige and authority of the Imperial government, was the crisis over the status of Luxembourg, 'the Gibraltar of the North', which then belonged to the King of Holland but had been garrisoned, since the Congress of Vienna, by the Prussian army. Soon after seeing his hopes for compensations on the Rhine dashed by Bismarck's refusals, Napoleon had entered into negotiations with the King of Holland to purchase the fortress of Luxembourg for a sum of money and so remove an irksome threat to the security of France. Bismarck raised no objections and was even opposed to making Luxembourg a member of the German *Bund*. Very few people doubted that in the event of a plebiscite the Luxembourgers would vote overwhelmingly for France since they had already forced their Dutch governor to copy a number of reforms from the liberal Empire next door. The German liberal nationalists, however, were less ready than Bismarck to leave their Luxembourg cousins to France, and the King of Holland, impressed by the alliance between North and South in Germany, abandoned the negotiations for fear of offending the North German *Bund*, his immediate neighbour. The impasse led to a major European crisis which was eventually settled in a conference held in London at the invitation of the Tory government. Luxembourg became an independent Grand Duchy, though dynastically still united to the Dutch crown; the fortress was dismantled and the Prussian garrison withdrawn. Both France and Prussia had hoped that Luxembourg's neutrality and independence would be the subject of an international guarantee by the great powers, but in this they were disappointed. 'The treaty,' Lord Derby told the House of Lords, 'becomes invalid if one of the contracting parties violates Luxembourg's neutrality.' Since the crisis had made war between Prussia and France seem imminent, this formula was hardly calculated to relax the tense atmosphere on either side of the Rhine. When the Emperor opened the parliamentary session of 1867, he was unable to announce any territorial gains for France, but instead indicated a new series of liberal reforms. These included the right of the legislature to interpellate, the duty of the various Ministers to answer questions concerning their departments, and a new press law. The Emperor's hands trembled as he read his speech quickly and badly, and its reception was extremely cool. From now on Mérimée, whenever he made plans to travel or spend the winter in Cannes, added the phrase 'M. de Bismarck permitting'.

This discouraging background must be kept in mind when we contemplate the dazzling and, on the whole, successful enterprise which the Second Empire achieved in that same year of 1867: the Universal Exhibition. It was opened in April and at once attracted a vast concourse of visitors from all over the world. The Czar of Russia, attended by Prince Gorchakov, arrived on June 1st and the King of Prussia, attended by a genial and debonair Bismarck, on June 5th. The Prince of Wales and his brother the Duke of Edinburgh had been enjoying Paris *en fête* since May, and the Exhibition gave Napoleon III's unaggressive claim to be the Emperor of Europe an impressive confirmation.

Nothing could demonstrate to the world the strangely dual character of the Second Napoleonic Empire, its creative and its Offenbach side, so clearly as the events of the following six months. The Exhibition itself stood for everything that was bold, progressive, idealistic and enlightened in the Empire. It was a statement of faith in the arts of peace, in Free Trade, in the blessing of Science. It was a whole-hearted affirmation of the nineteenth century. 'If Paris is hated, our duty is to love it,' visitors read in the introduction to the guide of the Exhibition, which went on to say:

'Why do people hate Paris? Because she is home, life, work, breeding-ground, change, melting-pot, rebirth. Because she is the opposite to all the things in force today—superstition, stagnation, scepticism, obscurantism, reaction, hypocrisy, lies. In an epoch when the *syllabus* decrees immobility, it is necessary to render mankind a service, to show movement. Paris shows it. How? By being Paris. To be Paris, is to advance.'

Who wrote the introduction? Victor Hugo, *hélas*.

'Let Europe be welcome! [he concluded.] In Paris, Europe will find herself at home. Let Europe take possession of Paris, for Paris belongs to Europe as Europe does to Paris. May Europe take her ease here and fill her lungs in that city which has the privilege of fostering European action.'

It was odd that the great poet who still refused to give up his pose as the irreconcilable exile should have found words to celebrate the Empire's keenest aims and hopes. It was one more proof that the French are capable of all forms of greatness except unity.

Parisians of all shades of opinions were proud to see, laid out in the heart of their city, the fruits of the inventive genius of mankind, achieved by the toil of every race, creed, and social order and offered to the critical appreciation of the whole world. They were proud to be hosts to the globe. Their pride was being kindled daily by their knowledge that at the centre of the festive hospitality extended to the world there moved a woman of unrivalled beauty and grace, over whose hand Emperors and Kings and Sultans and Pashas bowed in respectful reverence. When on the great days that summer the Empress drove from Saint-Cloud to the Tuileries, the outriders in green and gold preceding her open *calèche* with its postilions in powder and tricorn hats, with her handsome equerries and ladies at her side and the giants of the *Cent-Gardes* cantering in the rear, Parisians all along the route raised their hats and waved to this cavalcade of elegance and colour and said to each other in possessive pride: 'Qu'elle est jolie!'

All this mirrored the constructive, the hopeful, the confident side of the Second Empire. The Offenbach aspect was equally strongly in evidence. In the literal sense, the witty Maestro from Cologne attracted vast audiences with two of his shows, *The Grand Duchess of Gerolstein* with Hortense Schneider in the title role, and *La Belle Hélène*, featuring Cora Pearl as Cupid. Bismarck visited the first of these repeatedly and was heard to guffaw approval at this parody of a small German Princedom and its trenchant satire of militarism. In a wider sense, the rule of Offenbach was expressed when night after night the ball-rooms of the Embassies, of the great houses in the Faubourg and of the Tuileries itself saw brilliant and cosmopolitan assemblies dance through the night to the tunes which he and his disciples had been pouring forth for nearly ten years.

The Empress had met Offenbach once, after a *première* at the *Bouffes Parisiennes*, and, never feeling wholly at ease with men of music whose work she did not understand, had forced herself to utter a few gracious remarks.

'You are, I believe, a Rhinelander, M. Offenbach? '

'Indeed yes, Madame.'

The Empress struggled bravely on : 'You were born in—Bonn, were you not? '

'Ah no, Madame, I was born in Cologne. The composer who was born in Bonn was called—let me see . . .' there was a pause while the maestro searched his brains for this lesser name . . . 'ah yes—he was called Beethoven.'

She and the Emperor honoured most of the great Offenbach first nights with their presence, but they both understood so little of music and opera that the profoundly subversive character of the performances remained mercifully hidden from them. The artful and artistically successful combination of luxury and frivolity, the seductive danceability of the tunes and the delightful lyrics, which mocked every aspect of the Empire, became a hallmark of the Parisian social scene of the 1860s.

Perhaps inevitably, in the minds of the visitors to the Great World Fair the ostentatious and determined gaieties of the minority called Parisian society became identified with France itself. Many of the foreign guests, crowned and otherwise, regarded Paris as a kind of gas-lit Venusberg in which distinction between classes and even between sexes became increasingly blurred while the pursuit of pleasure offered stimulating vistas of temptations without limit.

'Who are all these ladies? ' enquired a Russian Grand Duke of a friend at Longchamps. 'They are all *gay* ladies,' replied the friend meaningfully. 'And where are the respectable ones? ' 'There are none left.'

'You look like a Duchess tonight,' an admirer breathed into the ear of a famous courtesan. 'How do you know I am not one? ' she replied coldly.

'I saw you with the Princess last night,' one gay lady said to another. 'Yes, I know,' came the reply, 'I am going to cut her in future, she really is too compromising.'

If the frontier between the *haut* and the *demi-monde* was thus being obliterated, a new vogue of transvestism, the wide popularity of male and female impersonation, a half-hidden spreading of homosexual self-absorption and similar cults seemed to herald the vanishing of other hitherto accepted lines of demarcation. Two commodities were necessary to gain admittance to and prestige in this world : money and wit—more especially the latter since money was, as in Regency London, often a matter of luck and courage at the gaming tables. As in Edwardian England, the nobility married either money, as when the Prince de Polignac married Mlle Mirès, or ladies of the stage, as in the case of the Marquis de Caux who married Adelina Patti, the great operatic soprano. But conversational versatility and a certain verbal prodigality were as highly treasured in this world as was the capacity to spend money lavishly, recklessly and grandly.

Second Empire Society in Paris may have set the world new examples in dissoluteness and moral neutralism, but it did so not without style and spirit. The work of Jacques Offenbach gave it at once a mirror and a stimulus, and we may remember that it provided the ancestral material for the novels of Alphonse Daudet, Emile Zola and Marcel Proust.

The Empress, so strict and conscientious in her own conduct, never viewed the social scene around her with an apprehensive or censorious eye. What some of her guests in 1867, such as the Crown Princess of Prussia, liked to call the 'depravity' of Paris was as much a figment of political silliness as was the allegation of decadence made against English society before 1939. The Prussian Crown Princess expressed to her mother at Windsor concern at the 'mischief' which the French Court 'and that very attractive Paris' seemed to be doing to her two eldest brothers—an apprehension which they themselves certainly did not share, even though the Prince of Wales was already conscious of the dignity and obligations of his position. The Empress had great faith in stylish entertainments as a kind of political tonic, and perhaps the Court's most notable contribution to the gaieties of 1867 was a repeat performance at the Théâtre des Variétés of *The Commentaries of Caesar*, a revue written and produced by Philippe de Massa at Compiègne in 1865 and performed by a group of distinguished amateurs, among whom Princess Metternich was the uncontested star. She was *commère*, she sang a little ditty as a *vivandière* of the Zouaves, another as a Paris cabby and finally appeared, wearing a gorgeous dress of white satin trimmed with musical notes in black, as the embodiment of the *Chanson* of which the chorus went:

> *Dérider tous les fronts,*
> *C'était mon privilège*
> *Et les bouchons de Liége*
> *Sautaient jusqu'aux plafonds.*

According to Mlle Bouvet, the Austrian Ambassadress sang her couplet 'with more dash and spirit than one has ever heard in any theatre'. She had taken lessons from Theresa, the Marie Lloyd of the Second Empire, and on both occasions she stopped the show. In another scene Mme de Galliffet, unloved wife of the Empress's military protégé, appeared as Britannia with Mme de Pourtalès, an Alsatian lady married to a Prussian diplomat, as France. They exchanged vows of eternal friendship and loyalty:

France: Free Trade!
Britannia: Yes, and no more passports! Let us have a bridge over the Channel!

France: Very well—we will prolong the Boulevard Haussmann to Piccadilly.

Others participating in the entertainment included Mr. Ashton Blount from London, a son-in-law of the Duke of Bassano, who was dressed up as the great Theresa herself and gave a successful imitation of her singing her greatest hit: *Rien n'est sacré pour un sapeur*. Grand Opera also came in for a witty parody, and Count Solms of the Prussian Embassy had much success with his impersonations of a Parisian pick-pocket, a cocoa vendor, and, finally, Robin Hood.

The revue was a brilliant mixture of *café-concert* and light-hearted propaganda for certain policies close to the Emperor's heart. Mme de Galliffet appeared also as 'Industry', and two ladies represented Deauville and Trouville having an extremely feminine quarrel about their rival attractions as bathing resorts. Here the Marquis de Caux acted as the harassed umpire. In the final scene, General Mellinet came on as a veteran of the First Empire, while Galliffet, very appropriately, embodied the spirit of the present army, after which Princess Metternich went down to the footlights and announced that she was calling on the future to appear. This was the cue for the Prince Imperial, now eleven years old and the official President of the Exhibition. He made his entrance in the uniform of the Guards and sang an effective little couplet ending in:

> Voilà, voilà, voilà, voilà le grenadier français.

After this, the little Prince presented the veteran of the First Empire with a wreath of laurels and sang:

> Mais en voyant le noble visage
> Du vieux soldat et son front sillonné
> J'aime à penser aussi qu'à mon courage
> Pareil honneur, un jour, sera donné.

Mlle Bouvet tells us that the 'grace and feeling' which the Prince put into this final scene were so touching that he was rewarded with instant and thunderous applause. 'The Empress's face was radiant with happiness. The Emperor's eyes filled with tears, as he sat gazing at his son, that child who was already so intelligent and on whom reposed so many hopes.'

Politics erupted into the Imperial feast with dramatic inevitability. The Czar, who took his sons to all the Offenbach shows with almost offensive regularity, was greeted with a shout of 'Vive la Pologne, Monsieur' when he was conducted through the Palais de Justice on June 5th. Next day, the Czar was returning in the Emperor's carriage from a military review, when a Polish exile fired on him from close range. It was only thanks to Raimbaut, in charge of the mounted escort, throwing himself promptly between the assassin and the Imperial carriage, that the lives of the French and Russian Emperors were saved. The Empress, following not far behind with the King of Prussia in her carriage, called on the Czar at the Elysée immediately to express her horror at the attempt. At the Russian Embassy ball that evening, she appeared at the Czar's side, still white as marble. Some thought it due to her exertions, which went pointedly beyond the normal requirements of etiquette, that the Czar did not leave Paris there and then.

Before the attempt on his life, the Russian ruler had been coldly received in public, but afterwards, feeling swung round in his favour and Parisians made it clear that they condemned the crime. The elderly King of Prussia, as benign and pink-faced as ever, was acclaimed joyously whenever he showed himself, while Bismarck, always wearing the white uniform and spiked helmet of a Prussian cuirassier, was the object of open-mouthed curiosity. He showed himself frequently in public, taking a glass of beer in the Café de Bade, or walking about in the corridors of the Variétées in the intervals during *The Grand Duchess*. 'Tiens, c'est Bismarck,' they whispered to each other. 'He doesn't look wicked,' and 'he doesn't look like an ogre,' they said. The story that he ate Danish or Hanoverian babies for breakfast was clearly untrue. 'Parisians are liking you,' Marshal Vaillant told him one evening, 'you have conquered them, and when you returned from the review the other day, they shouted, "vive Bismarck".' 'I heard them,' he replied, smiling, 'they weren't shouting "vive Bismarck" they shouted "v'là Bismarck". Not quite the same thing, but still, I felt flattered.' He was assiduous in paying calls, and was always full of praise of the Emperor Napoleon's excellent political principles. He told Marshal Canrobert that the principle of nationality in particular was one of the great ideas of the age. 'There lives south of the mouth of the Rhine a people whose way of thinking and whose language are French—the Belgians. Why don't you make a move in that direction?' It was the *leitmotif* of all his visits and talks.

To Mme de Pourtalès, on the other hand, who everybody knew belonged to the Empress's intimate circle, he developed another idea. A woman of her beauty and wit, he told her, ought to live in Berlin, where a brilliant position was hers for the asking. And were the Counts of Pourtalès not faithful servants of the King of Prussia? She pointed out that she herself was Alsatian. 'True,' he replied, 'but Alsace is part of the greater German fatherland.' 'Alsace,' she said, 'is one of the finest flowers of France.' He seemed scarcely to hear her protestations.

CHAPTER 20

THE WORST eruption of politics into the World Fair occurred on July 1st. In the middle of a great prize-giving ceremony on the Champ-de-Mars, the Emperor received a telegram with the news that Maximilian of Mexico had been executed at Queretaro on June 19th. Faced with total failure after the withdrawal of French support, Maximilian had been unable to cut his losses and abdicate. His own incapacity and the intransigence of the Roman Catholic hierarchy had made the collapse of the Mexican enterprise inevitable. Its purpose was beyond his strength and it was perhaps symbolic of the reign that on the day when he fell before Juarez's firing-squad at Queretaro, 2,000 nightingales were being embarked at Trieste, destined for his private pleasure garden at Cuernavaca. The Queen of Holland, writing to Lady Salisbury, provided a fitting epitaph:

'Maximilian thought he filled a mission of civilisation, but he was little shaped for that. He ought to have brought the qualities of a squatter, hard-working, energetic, self-denying. Instead of which he was a spend-thrift, a man of pleasure, full of that sort of foolish Liberalism which never stands the test of sacrifice. Poor man and poor mother! He was her pride.'

The Imperial Court went into mourning for a month. The disaster of Queretaro inevitably caused the Austrian Emperor and Empress to put off their promised visit to Paris, much to Napoleon's and Eugénie's regret who, under the political conditions of 1867, had both been looking forward to receiving Francis Joseph and his consort with special fervour. Before the news from Mexico had reached Europe, Queen Victoria had invited the Empress to attend a naval review at Spithead, but since this could not be done during Court mourning, the invitation was changed to a private visit to Osborne in July. So for the first time since their meeting in 1860, when the Prince Consort had been still at her side, Queen Victoria welcomed her old friend, finding her 'looking very lovely in a simple black short walking dress and a small hat. She was very kind, saying under what altered circumstances she saw me. She is but little altered.' There were few opportunities for lengthy conversations, especially as the Queen did not feel equal to much talk—'my head being very bad', she noted in her Journal. 'The Empress alluded to poor Max's murder, Charlotte's state of health, etc. . . . She is extremely discreet and, luncheon over, would not remain.' The Queen was grateful for this understanding attitude. 'Nothing could have been kinder,' she noted after her guest's departure on July 24th, 'or more amiable than the Empress was. I took the opportunity of urging peace (mutually, on the side of France and Prussia) and no arming, laying all the blame on Prussia. Greatly relieved the visit was over, as I am feeling far from well, and everything tires me so.'

In order to make up for the cancellation of Francis Joseph's visit to Paris, the Emperor and Empress travelled to Salzburg in August to convey their condolences to Maximilian's family. Metternich had greatly encouraged this encounter and overcame the misgivings which both Emperor and Empress felt. 'For me,' the Empress had told him, 'it will be the most painful thing in the world to face a brother and a mother to whose grief I contributed by pushing the Mexican expedition. If I had met the Austrian Emperor, the Empress and the Archduchess Sophie before, I would have rushed to see them to express my feelings to them. As I don't know them, I fear they will think me either too cold or too tragic.' Against these scruples, Metternich argued that, on the contrary, the shared grief would bring the two Sovereign families closer together. Beust whole-heartedly agreed.

The French Sovereigns travelled via Karlsruhe, Stuttgart, Ulm and Munich. Their reception demonstrated what high hopes were placed in these South German States on the conclusion of an anti-Prussian alliance. There were extremely friendly demonstrations as they passed through Baden, Württemberg and Bavaria; the King of Württemberg greeted them at Ulm —a name with pleasant associations for a Napoleon—and the King of Bavaria travelled with them from Munich to the Austrian frontier.

The encounter at Salzburg lasted from August 18th to the 23rd. Maximilian's mother, the Archduchess Sophie, did not accompany her other son, the Austrian Emperor, but instead addressed a letter to the Empress, which Francis Joseph presented. 'May you, Madame', she wrote, 'keep only happy memories from your stay at Salzburg and on your return find your dear child in perfect health. Assuring you, Madame, once more of my great gratitude for your affectionate interest, I am Your Majesty's most grateful, Sophie.' It was a letter of unusual warmth, implying and hinting more than it said.

Beust, who attended the Austrian Emperor during the Salzburg conversations, tells us that throughout the five days the Empress Eugénie 'endeavoured to efface herself', when in the company of the Empress Elisabeth. The latter had only with some difficulty been persuaded to be present, but it seemed to all observers that the two ladies got on together surprisingly well. Elisabeth's reproachful attitude towards the Mexican enterprise was confined to the criticism that her brother-in-law had voluntarily consented to accept a crown, to her the hated symbol of inhuman bondage in any circumstances. Neither Empress appears to have contributed very much to the political discussions which were attended, in addition to the two Emperors and Beust, by Count Taafe and Richard Metternich on the Austrian side, and by Gramont on that of the French.

These ranged over questions like the future of Germany, relations between Austria and Russia on the one hand, and between France and Prussia on the other. The whole nature of the meeting precluded the conclusion of a formal agreement, but the fact that the French and Austrian Emperors had met in this intimate setting was widely taken as an important first step.[1]

The Austrian Sovereigns' return visit was scheduled to take place in October, but early in that month the Empress received a letter from Elisabeth announcing that 'heaven is once again blessing my marriage and the gentle hope which is thus offered me imposes the greatest prudence'. So Francis Joseph travelled to Paris alone, but the reception which the French Sovereigns and the people of Paris gave him, eclipsed everything that the earlier visitors to the Great Exhibition had experienced.

After all these travels and exertions in 1867, the Emperor's health underwent a new crisis. His periods of languor and depression returned, and spasms of acute pain became more frequent. He often had to retire to bed and on these occasions the entourage, including Mérimée, were told that he had rheumatic pains aggravated by haemorrhoids. He still evaded proper consultations with his doctors, and the Empress remained unaware of the true nature of his ailment. During a solitary drive through the park of Saint-Cloud late in 1867 the Queen of Holland asked her point-blank whether there was any danger. 'No,' replied the Empress, 'but he is so changed, he has become so *inamusable*.' After a while she added: 'He can never take a decision.' She herself recovered only slowly from the disasters of Queretaro and Sadowa, as one observer who saw the Court in its daily intimate life noticed. This was Admiral Jurien de La Gravière, the Emperor's naval equerry, who since Schwalbach had often been seconded to attend on the Empress. Grieved by the Empress's despondency, he sat down in November 1867 and wrote her a most singular letter.

His principal purpose in writing was, he explained, to present the Empress with two large collections of documents and correspondence concerning the origins of the Mexican expedition of which he had then been in supreme command. 'Your Majesty will find therein all the reasons for the illusions and confidence which were entertained in Paris at the time. Today these seem astonishing, but, in view of the almost unanimous information on which they were based, they may be explained quite naturally.' He continued:

'I wanted to give the Empress further proof of my devotion and at the same time to inspire Her with greater confidence in Herself. I have been granted the great privilege of knowing all the nobility and virile pride that live in Her soul. God has selected Her to contribute to the splendour and prosperity of the reign. She has no right to efface herself when She

[1] Bismarck at once caused a circular to Prussian diplomatic missions abroad to be published which said in offensive terms that questions of German unity were no concern of Austria or France.

can be so useful. She is one of our social forces. We are in peril, and it would be a sign of weakness to abandon us. All the political experience which She has acquired at the price of twelve years' training She must now use to our profit. If She does not do that, if She should abdicate, even temporarily, I fear that posterity will call Her to account for defaulting.

I know only too well that the memory of the Mexican expedition underlies Your Majesty's misgivings. But if the course of events which nobody could control turned this expedition into a misfortune or a blunder, has it not also made it a lesson? Why be afraid of associating oneself with the government of the Empire, that school attended by the Empress? Where are the statesmen who since 1852 have been able to learn so much about the business of the world? Despite the unjust responsibility which has been put at Your Majesty's door, nobody denies Her liveliness of mind, or wisdom, or firmness of views and resolution. People merely deny Her a sense of continuity (*l'esprit de suite*). Consequently, to have been in the midst of political affairs and then to withdraw for a while in order to return later is not without its danger. To work merely intermittently will give many people the appearance of capriciousness.'

This letter gives us a rare insight into the real state of her mind and soul after the collapse of her Mexican and Austrian hopes. The despondency, born from self-reproach, the thought of withdrawing from all political activity, the awareness that the world blamed her more than she deserved: all these things seem to have driven the Empress to the very limit of her staying power: if it had been otherwise, would the Admiral have felt compelled to remind her of the great qualities of her character, of the value of her unique experience? Yet the most remarkable fact about this letter, as about the future correspondence with Jurien, is that it has survived. In the last year of her life, the Empress burnt a great many documents and letters, but she kept Jurien's, despite their allusions to her weaknesses. Her immediate reaction to the letter in 1867 is not known, but the later correspondence suggests that she reproved him for wishing to raise her on a pedestal beyond her merits.

She always showed wonderful tact towards those who loved her in a way to which she could not respond. The most poignant case was that of M. Levesques-Desvarannes, a lieutenant in the navy, and since May 1866 ordnance officer to the Emperor. He had become incapable of hiding what his friends called his 'romantic love for the Empress'. In the end, the smitten man was sent off on a mission to Indo-China and Japan to help him overcome his fatal passion. Before setting out, he had, in the autumn of 1867, a farewell audience of the Empress at Saint-Cloud. Filon was in the antechamber when he emerged from it. 'Who is this man?' he asked, being greatly struck by the expression of 'some tragic suffering' on the sailor's face. 'Madly in love with the Empress,' he was told, 'and being sent away to die at the other end of the world.' Mérimée, less callous towards someone who loved the Empress, urged the unhappy young man to write down his impressions of the exotic countries he was about to visit. 'Write,' he told him, 'as if you were writing only for yourself, without bothering about style and beauty, and then send it to someone who could communicate it to the reading public. I would offer to be your correspondent, but at my age and with my asthma, the postman would probably not find me at home and would write on the envelope: "Try the cemetery of Père Lachaise."' But it was the young lover who died first. When the news of his death at the other end of the world reached Paris, the Empress travelled to the little town on the Loire, where his old mother lived, to offer her condolences.

She began to find more time for private pursuits. Filon had called in Ernest Lavisse to teach the Prince Imperial history, and with him the Empress not only discussed the affairs and concerns of the Ministry of Education, but the general problems of the hour. 'A coup d'état,' she said when they were discussing the liberal reforms of 1868-9, 'is like a convict's ball and chain, you drag it along and eventually it paralyses your leg.'

History had become the principal interest of the Empress's leisure hours, and she asked Duruy to recommend a teacher who could help her with these studies. He sent her Fustel de Coulanges, one of the great academic teachers of his day, who told his audience: 'Do not applaud me—it is not I who talk to you, but History, using me as her mouth.' The young historian went regularly to the Tuileries and addressed a small group consisting of the Empress, her Spanish nieces and one or two personal friends. 'Those who knew Fustel's integrity as an historian,' wrote one who did, 'felt sure that the special character of his audiences did not lessen the seriousness or the authority of his lectures.' On some days—when he felt well enough to do so—the Emperor dropped in to listen.

The major debate on army reform began in December 1866 with Jules Favre expounding the strange dogma that 'the strongest nation will be the one which disarms the most', while the confusion of the French mind was expressed in the equally odd attitude that peace was assured because France did not want war. 'Do you want to turn France into a gigantic barracks?' asked Favre of Marshal Niel when he explained his plans for creating auxiliary forces in the *Garde Mobile*. 'Take care,' replied the Minister of War, 'that you do not turn it into a gigantic cemetery.' With certain cuts and modification, the army bill became law in February 1868, but even then the whole programme was hampered by parliamentary unwillingness to grant the necessary funds and by the fear, on the part of certain vested interests, that it was dangerous to arm French workers with weapons that could be turned against their employers. Only somebody of Morny's stature could have succeeded in getting the bill accepted in full, but he was dead and Bismarck's mastery in silencing democratic opposition found no equivalent in France.

The Emperor was gravely ill in August 1868, and in his delirium was once heard to call for Marshal St. Arnaud, who had died in 1854. Marshal Niel, suffering like the Emperor from the stone, died in August 1869 and his loss was a serious set-back for the Empire. He was succeeded at the War Ministry by Marshal Leboeuf, whom the latest and best historian of the Franco-Prussian conflict[1] describes as 'active and competent . . . if he lacked Niel's political adroitness, [he] was quite as energetic and possibly more popular with the Legislature'. In the general election of 1869, the Republicans achieved further gains, mainly in urban and industrial constituencies, while the Legitimists and Orleanists were decisively defeated all over the country. The political issue henceforth lay clearly between Empire and Republic, and in the streets of Paris and other large cities the masses were staging almost permanent riots, shouting for revolution. The Court did not move to Fontainebleau, Biarritz or Compiègne in 1869, and the Emperor, yet again recovering almost miraculously from his illness, showed much energy in putting the finishing touches to the great transformation in which the liberal Empire was finally to liquidate the remnants of the authoritarian rule of the past. 'The old régime,' wrote Theodore Zeldin, 'was finished and the only possible solution was to create a new majority around a new régime.'[2]

The moment of transition was full of hidden danger. 'We have a police, but no government,' wrote l'Opinion Nationale. 'Order reigns in the streets, thieves are arrested, the gas is lighted and the queues form quietly for Frou-Frou, but all the higher qualities of government are for the moment in abeyance.' The final step from Caesarism to representative government was long and arduous, but neither the Emperor nor Empress wavered.

In the autumn of 1869, the Empress travelled to Cairo in order to represent France at the opening of the Suez Canal, which her cousin Ferdinand de Lesseps had that year completed for the Khedive of Egypt. Host to the Monarchs and Princes of Europe, the Khedive distinguished the Empress of the French before all his other guests and on the day of the official opening her yacht L'Aigle led the line of ships sailing down the Canal. This was in acknowledgement of the unceasing and courageous support which the Empire had all along afforded to this visionary scheme. She delighted in her reception and won universal praise for her poise and unostentatious demeanour. What made her particularly happy was to see that Francis Joseph never left her side. Yet she had left Paris oppressed by misgivings, for she had heard that the police were expecting a major mass demonstration on October 26th, sponsored by the opposition because opening of Parliament was being delayed. The Empress wrote to her husband on October 27th:

---

[1] Michael Howard, author of The Franco-Prussian War (Hart-Davis, London, 1961).
[2] See Theodore Zeldin, The Political System of Napoleon III (London, 1958).

'My very dear Louis,

I was extraordinarily uneasy yesterday, knowing you to be in Paris without me, but now I see from your telegram that all has gone well. When one sees other peoples in their countries, one appreciates the injustice of ours so much better. Despite everything, I think that we must not be discouraged, but persist on the path which you have inaugurated. The only way is to persist with the concessions which have been granted. The more need one has for strength later on, the more necessary it is to prove to the country now that one is following ideas and not expedients. I am far away and out of touch, but it is my inner-most conviction that our real strength lies in ideas and their realisation. I do not believe in violent action, and I am convinced that one cannot have a coup d'état twice in a reign.

Here I am, preaching to one converted, who knows more about such things than I do. I wanted to speak to you if only to prove what you know already—that my heart is with both of you. My life is over, but I live again in my son, and I find that the real joys are those which have passed through his heart and then come to mine. . . .'

She was, not without effort, coming to terms with the liberal Empire. She had received Emile Ollivier before leaving for Cairo and assured him that she was withdrawing from all forms of public activity, apart from her social and charitable work. Ollivier, the Emperor's principal assistant in the final stages of the great experiment, had already succeeded in getting her excluded from all Ministerial and Council meetings.[1] Renunciation did not come easily to someone of her temperament and experience, but she loyally, if sometimes a little bitterly, complied with this new obligation to efface herself. When early in 1870 she was asked to assist in someone's career, she replied:

'Formerly I would have promised my help. Now all I can promise is to pass your request on to the Emperor. But let me give your protégé one piece of useful advice—may he never let it be known at the Ministry of the Interior that I am interested in his career.' When her friend Jurien was asked by a politician what the Empress really thought of certain Ministers, the Admiral said:

'The Empress abstains from all participation in affairs. Towards people, she feels neither antipathy nor predilections. All she is interested in is the good of the country and the consolidation of the Empire. She will raise no objections to any man capable of serving those two great interests.'

In her heart of hearts she continued to be more alarmed by Prussian designs and attitudes than the Emperor and Ollivier were. Her friend, Mme

---

[1] The public were told of this step by the official papers which said that the Empress would cease attending Ministerial meetings 'in order that opinions may not be attributed to her which she does not entertain and that she may not be suspected of an influence which she does not desire to exercise.'

de Pourtalès, returned from a visit to Berlin quoting sinister reports from high Prussian sources concerning the imminent cession of her native Alsace to Germany; others cited more than one Prussian general inviting his friends to a parade to be held by the German army on the Champ-de-Mars 'sometime in 1870'. 'There is no greater calamity for a King, President or Dictator,' the Empress wrote, 'than to hand on his territory smaller than it was when he received it.' Deeply concerned for her son's future, she was constantly aware of the menace that Prussian action would one day complete the work begun at Sadowa and force the Empire into helpless subservience before Prussian and German might.

Amid these besetting anxieties, she found as always solace in the company of Prosper Mérimée. The novelist's health had been failing for some years, and by 1869 he was an ailing and ageing man. The Empress put him in charge of the Alba archives, and Mérimée spent many fascinated hours in deciphering the correspondence between Philip of Spain, the Pope and the sixteenth-century Duke of Alba. In the same year, he had completed a new story, a Lithuanian tale entitled *Lokis*, which he dedicated to the Empress. She made him read it to her one summer evening at Saint-Cloud, seated at her side under the marble bust of Napoleon II in the large drawing-room on the first floor, with her ladies of honour, Paca's daughters and Mlle Redel, Filon and the gentlemen of her household distributed about the room. 'The windows remained closed out of consideration for Mérimée,' writes Filon. 'The doors of the adjoining rooms, which were lit, but deserted, stood open, and soon there was only his voice echoing through the stillness and seclusion of the great sleeping Palace. A heavy lamp lit up the white pages of the note-book in which *Lokis* had been written with a strong and firm hand, fans were gently beating the air. . . . Mérimée was reading in a cold and monotonous voice, interrupted only by smiles or slight murmurs of approbation for which the Empress gave the sign.

The friendship between the Empress and the leading Voltairian writer of the times had stood the test of the years. Since her earliest youth he had been something of a tutor to her, exercising a beneficent influence on her intellectual development; he was responsible for the growing seriousness and selectiveness of her reading, for her ability to discriminate and appreciate. Few men were so profoundly aware of what the transformation of Eugénie into Empress had cost her in terms of sacrifice. He remained at her side to the end of his life. In May 1870, he wrote to Doña Manuela, during the last season the Court was to spend at Fontainebleau:

'There is only one person who resists the herculean fatigues of life we lead here, and that is the Empress. They seem to glide off her like water from a rock of granite.'

It was not his last word about her.

CHAPTER 21

THE LIBERAL Empire was officially proclaimed in January 1870. The Emperor was justified in thinking that ten years of reforms and concessions had produced auspicious and encouraging results, and that his early ideal of 'crowning the edifice with liberty' had at long last provided the country with representative government and far-reaching constitutional freedoms such as France had not known at any period since 1789. It would appear—again the evidence is not conclusive—that he now regarded the possibility of his own retirement and the succession of his son as Napoleon IV as the best possible dynastic and personal solution; in all probability he thought that the opportunity for this would occur in 1874 when the Prince Imperial would officially come of age. Once the new government, led in fact, though not in appearance, by Emile Ollivier, had been installed in office, the Emperor decided to consult the country in a new plebiscite. Did Frenchmen of all classes, parties and creeds affirm or refute the new political institutions—extended franchise, secret ballot, Ministerial responsibility, freedom of the press, of speech and association? Eighty-two per cent of the electorate, an unusually high proportion, gave their vote, sixty-eight per cent answering with Yes and fourteen per cent with No. It meant that seven million Frenchmen welcomed the transformation of the Napoleonic into the liberal Empire, thereby giving the dynasty a vote of confidence while simultaneously expressing distrust of the Republican form of government such as had been recently foreshadowed by Gambetta in his famous Belleville programme. The lesson was not lost on the great tribune, who described the results of the referendum as *un écrasement*.

In the afternoon of May 7th, the Emperor and Empress went to the room where the Prince Imperial was at his studies. The Emperor handed him a piece of paper with the final results of the plebiscite. The Prince read it eagerly; father and son looked at each other with radiant eyes and it seemed to Filon that the parents were saying to their son: 'It is your throne that is rising on seven million votes. France is with us.'

The Prince Imperial, fourteen in March, 1870, had grown into a strong, tall and passably good-looking boy. In the oval of his face, the blue eyes flashing below a fine forehead, he resembled his mother. Filon thought that 'his greatest joy was to court danger deliberately and in cold blood', but the tutor was less impressed by his pupil's academic progress. During the classes, which were attended by the Prince's two Spanish girl-cousins

229

as well as by his greatest friend, Louis Conneau, son of the Emperor's old companion in Italy and Ham, Filon found that the Prince's 'blue eyes became vague and lustreless and assumed that look of unhappiness which comes from lack of understanding'. His proficiency in sculpture and drawing had made admirable progress, but intellectually he developed late.

As future Emperor of the French, the Prince had undergone his baptism of fire on the afternoon of August 10th, 1868. Under the Duruy system of identifying the dynasty with educational reforms, the Prince and Filon had travelled that day from Fontainebleau to the Sorbonne to award the prizes in the *Concours général*. Among the pupils was the son of General Cavaignac, the Emperor's rival in the Presidential election of 1848 and subsequent enemy of the regime until his death in exile in 1857. The name was called, the Prince made ready to embrace the recipient when Mme Cavaignac angrily motioned her son to sit down again and not receive awards from the hands of a Bonaparte. She was applauded by others in the hall, by pupils, according to Duruy, of the lycée Bonaparte, 'that involuntary nest of Orleanism'. The Prince remained completely impassive as if he had not understood the meaning of the demonstration, but Mérimée, who was a guest at Fontainebleau that summer, saw him return from the ordeal and throw himself crying into his mother's arms. 'He showed,' Mérimée told a friend, 'the most admirable sang-froid to the point of making his tutor think he had misunderstood the audience's intentions. The lesson was a little hard, but, I think, useful. One must learn distrust at an early age.' Sainte-Beuve wrote to Princess Mathilde : 'In such situations one needs tact, intelligence and character. It is impossible to become practised in these things too early. The whole incident is a most happy augury.'

If the plebiscite of 1870 had strengthened the political bases of the Empire within the country the Emperor's other two tasks, army reform and a new system of alliances, were by that date less close to realisation. Parliamentary interference with rearmament and universal conscription no less than the illogical pacificism of the propertied classes, acutely described by Pierre de La Gorce as a disguised form of chauvinism, had made it unlikely that the army envisaged by the Emperor and his advisers would be fully ready much before 1874. Yet the experts were not dissatisfied with the progress made, and shortly before his death in 1869 Marshal Niel said to the Empress : 'We are ready, you are not,' meaning that the Austrian alliance should now be concluded in order to give the new army its political complement. In 1869, France had suffered another defeat in her foreign policy when a French project to buy and extend certain railway lines in Belgium had at the last moment been vetoed by the Belgian government. As in the case of the Luxembourg crisis, it was widely assumed that Bismarck had been responsible for the new 'slap in the face'. The Emperor had said at the time :

'A government, like a man, must accept a challenge when it is provoked, and, when the occasion presents itself, must take it up in order to prove its virility. French public opinion is convinced that Prussia was behind Belgium's refusal. It will be necessary to act as if war will arise.'

Even so, the Emperor found that the triangular talks between Paris, Vienna and Florence were little more than academic conversations, especially as he was not prepared to buy Italian co-operation by abandoning the Pope to Victor Emmanuel without first obtaining precise safeguards. Relations with England, on the other hand, were now better than they had been since the Italian war. In 1867 Lord Lyons, one of the ablest British diplomats of the century, had succeeded Cowley as ambassador. After he had discussed the Roman problem with the Empress he reported that she 'spoke with much grace of manner and expression and I think with very great ability'. The Russian Ambassador in Paris told a friend at this time that the Empress had become far more 'lukewarm' on the Roman Question than formerly; Mérimée wrote in the same year that she was Empress first and Roman Catholic second. A scrutiny of diplomatic and other correspondence between 1867 and 1870 shows no trace of the Empress interfering with her husband's and Nigra's endeavours to seal a treaty of alliance.

It was Lord Lyons' general opinion that 'Europe, and England in particular, are more interested in maintaining the Emperor than in anything else'. Lord Clarendon, recalled by Gladstone to the Foreign Office in December 1869—'kicking and screaming against it', he wrote—agreed with this view. Like Lord Castlereagh in 1813, the British Foreign Secretary travelled to the Continent, this time to obtain from France and Prussia certain measures of mutual disarmament, in which he was successful in Paris, but failed utterly in Berlin. 'People everywhere,' he told Bismarck, 'must obtain a larger share in the administration of their own affairs and, in proportion as they do so, the chances of causeless wars will diminish. The people well understand the horrors of war. . . .' Bismarck countered this sane attitude with various arguments. How would Her Majesty's government react to a Prussian invitation to reduce its naval armament? was one of these. In answer to Clarendon's notion of the inter-relationship between rearmament and parliamentary control, he told the British ambassador:

'If the present Constitutional Government of France had been three years instead of three months in existence, then there would be some chance for its duration and the maintenance of peace. At the present moment, however, there is a party anxious to restore the former state of things, a personal government. Amongst that party is the Empress Eugénie, and they would not be sorry to divert public attention from home affairs by raising some question of Foreign Policy.'

Clarendon, without taking much notice of Bismarck's accusation of the Empress, understood only too well what the North German Chancellor

231

meant when he voiced Prussia's feelings of insecurity or described the disarmament proposals 'as being put forward in favour of France and French policy, and without regard to the safety of Prussia'. 'I know well the suspicious character of the King of Prussia,' the Foreign Secretary wrote to Lyons on March 23rd, 1870, 'and if he thought we had cast in our lot completely with that of France, he would straightaway set about a more intimate alliance with Russia, which would not be in the interest either of England or France.'

Bismarck's insinuation that the Empress favoured war for dynastic and internal reasons shows that her reputation as a war-monger was well-established by the spring of 1870. According to Germain Bapst, Imperial jeweller before 1870 and biographer of Marshal Canrobert thereafter, a Captain Pierron, once military secretary to Maximilian of Mexico, alleged that as the Empress was watching the results of the plebiscite come in and saw that most of the wards of Paris had voted No, she remarked that only a war could save the dynasty from revolution. 'Several aides-de-camp,' wrote Bapst, 'took up the idea and henceforth the notion of consolidating the dynasty by a popular war was under way.' Although in his biography Bapst advanced and developed this accusation as an alibi for Canrobert, whose attitude during August 1870 certainly needed a good deal of explaining, the notion of Eugénie as the war-criminal became widespread before and after Sedan. We shall examine it presently.

An English journalist caught a glimpse of the French sovereigns at Longchamps where the *Grand Prix de Paris* was run on Sunday, June 12th: 'The reception they met with was respectful, but by no means cordial. The Empress looked smiling and pleasant, as she invariably does, as though she felt an interest in what was going on, but the Emperor soon relapsed into a careworn expression, so different from his habit a few years ago. From the moment he entered the tribune until he quitted it he continued to be seated, instead of advancing to the very front, and leaning jauntily on his cane, or promenading down below among the spectators, as was formerly his custom. The Empress's toilette was the simplest that the eye could detect in a survey from one end of the tribunes to the other.'

The constant problem of the Emperor's health was by now exercising not only the Empress but the generals, who, as war with Prussia became increasingly probable, were uneasy about his fitness to command. When, in January 1870, the Empress's close friend Mme de Montebello fell ill, General de Montebello was surprised to see that the Empress's visits to her sickroom always coincided with those of her physician. This was Dr. Nelaton, who for the past four years and particularly since the crisis of 1868 had been principal medical attendant to the Emperor. Observing how the Empress would take Dr. Nelaton aside for whispered consultations, the General suddenly understood the reason: 'Good God,' he exclaimed. 'she was questioning him about the Emperor's health.' It was her only means of getting information but even this was ineffective since Nelaton's lips had been sealed by the Emperor's orders. On July 3rd, 1870, Nelaton and others at last persuaded their patient to undergo a proper examination by a group of medical experts. One of those, a young surgeon named Germain Sée, had been called in for the first time. He urged an immediate operation. When the others demurred, Sée put his diagnosis in writing and handed it in an envelope to Dr. Conneau. This the Empress found, unopened, among the Emperor's papers in 1874.

By the time this consultation took place, it had been known in Paris for twenty-four hours that Prince Leopold of Hohenzollern had accepted the Spanish throne. This was a tragic nemesis of the Emperor's life-long policy of evasion. The news reached Paris not from Berlin, but from Madrid, where Marshal Prim, currently the strong man since the overthrow of the Spanish Monarchy in 1868, had casually informed the French Ambassador of the *fait accompli*. French reactions were immediate and strong. 'We are thirty-eight million prisoners,' wrote a newspaper, 'if this news is not false. It has to be false; it will be if we want it to be. But is the French government still able to will it?' The crisis quickly intensified when the French Ambassador in Berlin, Benedetti, reported that the Prussian government was blandly denying all interest in the question, claiming that Prince Leopold's acceptance was purely a family concern of the Hohenzollerns whose head, by coincidence also King of Prussia, had decided the question in exclusive consultation with Prince Leopold and the latter's father, Prince Anton. Prussia was clearly getting ready to administer another 'slap in the face'. Yet on January 30th, 1870, Ollivier had already spoken to Lord Lyons of 'the importance of not exposing France to the appearance of being slighted; in fact he would not conceal from me [wrote Lyons] that a public rebuff from Prussia would be fatal. "*Un echec*," he said, "*c'est la guerre*."' It was therefore not surprising that Gramont, whom Ollivier had called from Vienna to the Quai d'Orsay in May 1870, should make a bellicose speech in the Chamber on July 6th, openly threatening war if the candidature, 'placing in peril the interests and the honour of France', were not withdrawn.

The events of the following days, culminating in France declaring war on the North German *Bund* on July 19th, have been too often described to need repetition here. The two countries now facing each other for the supreme contest had for the previous ten years been ruled on diametrically different principles, Bismarck utilising the Prussian military and caste system at the expense of parliamentary evolution and Napoleon endeavouring to channel the pressures of the mass age into representative institutions to the disadvantage of military efficiency. Yet, in both countries, the Generals claimed that the summer of 1870 offered the most favourable opportunity for war. Moltke said that with every year France would become stronger; he also realised that the countries of Southern Germany were showing signs of wishing to throw off Prussian military tutelage when the agreements of 1866 came up for revision in 1871. In France, Leboeuf argued that the army ought to strike before Prussia had time to copy various French weapons and 'before the opposition has destroyed the

233

army altogether'. Each government made efforts to influence the other's 'opposition', Bismarck by 'waving the red flag before the Gallic bull', while Napoleon hoped to use for his own ends the anti-Prussian bias that existed in Southern Germany. Bismarck calculated that the more the temper of France was provoked by diplomatic and journalistic means, the greater would be the country's final humiliation. Although in this respect he roused forces which eventually proved uncontrollable even by him, he certainly foresaw immediate French reactions to his political warfare with amazing accuracy.

The governments of Southern Germany, on the other hand, conveyed to the French Emperor that they would be his allies after one successful battle. The same answer was, with variations, returned by Austria, Italy and even Denmark. France was therefore under the necessity of opening the conflict with a bold aggressive move that would take the enemy by surprise. This was beyond the capacity of a country which had so recently undergone a profound political transformation. The transition inevitably produced a passing crisis in leadership, with executive officials such as Prefects in the provinces living in constant confusion about the extent and legitimacy of their own powers. This had a disastrous effect on the country's preparedness and mobilisation; the liberal Empire had had no chance to extend its system effectively from Paris to the rest of the country. Here also the German military system proved its initial superiority over the political system of France: after four years of Prussian hegemony the all-German mobilisation proceeded relatively swiftly. Events were to show only one man in the whole of France to be capable of leading the roused masses of France to victory. That was Léon Gambetta. The Empire's sole chance of survival lay in co-operation between him and the Imperial authorities, a possibility towards which the government, from Emperor and Empress downwards, were unforgivably blind. Morny, had he lived, would have grasped the opportunity with both hands, while Gambetta himself, deeply impressed by the results of the recent plebiscite, was during the whole crisis in a far more 'governmental' frame of mind than any of his Republican colleagues from whom he pointedly separated himself at various crucial moments.

Even so, the emotion of unity and unanimity that swept across France as a result of Prussian provocations was so overwhelming that no government, least of all a constitutional one, could afford to ignore it. 'Constitutional government,' Lord Lyons reported to London, 'has so far established itself in France that a Ministry in a minority in the *Corps Legislatif* is as much bound to go out as a Ministry in the House of Commons.' The majority in the two Chambers fully shared the country's indignation and fervour, a mood with which the Empress actively allied herself. Metternich on July 8th found that the possibility of 'a political triumph or war has made her look ten years younger'. Faced with Prussia's pretended lack of responsibility in the question of Prince Leopold's acceptance, she thought, as she told Metternich, that Prim 'whom I know well will publish Bismarck's correspondence . . . M. de Bismarck must give in or confess'. It was, of course, well known in Paris that Bismarck had sponsored the Hohenzollern candidature for some considerable time, and only some ten months earlier Napoleon had presented a formal protest against it in Berlin. Yet Gramont, who had been at the Quai d'Orsay for only a few weeks, did not possess the diplomatic skill required to force Bismarck's hand. The result was that Leopold's withdrawal from the candidature, once more presented to the world as a matter concerning only the Hohenzollern family, appeared as a diplomatic defeat for France so long as it did not have official Prussian backing. Even the Emperor, perhaps the least bellicose man then alive in France, thought that the withdrawal merely meant 'peace for the time being'. When Ollivier reported Leopold's renunciation to a group of deputies, they replied with such expressions as 'Prussia is making a fool of you'; 'Prussia has sought us out, we must have it out with her'; 'this means your downfall'. The newspapers described the renunciation as 'insufficient and derisory', as a 'Sadowa of the salons' and its acceptance by the government as 'cowardly', but it seemed to the Emperor and Ollivier that, for the time being, peace was assured. This was the moment when Bismarck gave his drastically cut version of the famous Ems telegram to the world in which an encounter between the King of Prussia and Benedetti was, falsely, presented to the world as having been insulting to the Ambassador and the country he represented. The old King had in reality told Benedetti with his accustomed courtesy that Leopold's withdrawal had his entire and unreserved approval. Bismarck saw to it that his version of the telegram received the widest publicity in Germany and abroad. Although the French Emperor at the last moment produced his favourite idea of submitting the conflict to European arbitration, peace could not be preserved after the publication of the Ems telegram.

Nevertheless, the Second Empire has been widely blamed for going to war over a diplomatic formality after the substance of the crisis, a Hohenzollern on the throne of Spain, had been settled in a sense favourable to France. The Empress, in particular, has often been judged guilty of overriding the Emperor's and his government's efforts to avoid war in 1870. 'Her hand,' wrote Michael Howard for example, 'was to guide Napoleon's pen [during the crisis]'. This is certainly overstated so far as direct political action, as implied in Mr. Howard's image, is concerned. 'May God grant that there be no war,' the Empress exclaimed to Princess Metternich during the early stages of the crisis, adding, 'But peace bought at the price of dishonour would be as great a misfortune, and France would never put up with it.' When she heard of the Emperor's hopes for a European Congress, she said: 'I doubt that this does justice to the feelings in the Chamber and the country.' It was the country's fervour and temper and not the Empress's belligerence that was guiding the government's hand. 'In spite of Leopold's renunciation,' Gramont frantically telegraphed to Benedetti on July 12th, 'the animation of opinion is such that we do not know whether we can control it.' On the same day, he told

Lord Lyons that the government could not hope to survive 'if it went to the Chamber tomorrow and announced that it regarded the affair as finished without having obtained more definite satisfaction from Prussia'. When he saw the Ems telegram as edited by Bismarck he rushed to Ollivier with the words: 'Behold a man who has just been slapped in the face.' Also on July 14th, Ollivier said to the Emperor about the notion of calling a Congress: 'I think the same as you, Sire. If we took the proposal to the Chamber, they would throw mud at our carriages and hiss us.' The most decisive of the various calumnies spread after the débâcle about the Empress's war-guilt came from Gramont who said that at the Council meeting of July 14th she made a 'strong and most excited speech' which tipped the scales in favour of war, but Ollivier, not a warm partisan of the Empress in this respect, says that she was not even present at the meeting. The country's new-found mood of unity and boldness roused by four years of Prussian provocations and Bismarck's well-calculated war of nerves in 1870, found in her a ready and whole-hearted response, but she had done nothing to create that mood and had no opportunity for influencing the Emperor and his harassed Ministers in any vital issue. Morally and emotionally she preferred war to the prospect of a new humiliation, but politically events took their course under the impact of the impersonal forces which had been unleashed in that historic year. Napoleon III and his government were no more in a position to stem and tame the French people's impulse to settle accounts with Prussia once and for all than Bismarck was able to control the dynamic impetus of the Prussian military machine or to curb Moltke's and Roon's determination to go to war against France in 1870. Ultimately, the leaders of Prussia and France were at the mercy of the forces they had hitherto manipulated to impose their contrasting political system on their countries, even though the difference in degree between them was considerable. Napoleon and Bismarck both showed an odd mixture of reluctance and determination throughout the crisis and in neither case could it be said that war resulted from a definite decision of theirs. All that can be safely recorded of the Empress's share in the declaration of war is that her personal determination not to appease Prussia at the expense of the future integrity and self-respect of France was greater and stronger than the Emperor's, who alone knew that war in 1870 might well prove premature for France. This he never admitted either to her or others. 'Like almost all the world,' wrote Ernest Lavisse, 'the Empress believed that victory was certain and would be swift.'

CHAPTER 22

THE CHAMBER OF DEPUTIES voted the necessary military credits on July 15th. Thiers used the opportunity for making a speech which in view of his repeated advocacy of a strong policy against Prussia was surprisingly anti-war, and Gambetta criticised the government less for deciding on war than for not putting its cards on the table before Parliament. The liberal Empire, he implied, was not liberal enough:

> 'You are asking France to give you men and money, you precipitate her in a war which may mean the end of the Nineteenth Century, which may decide whether the Germanic or the French race is to predominate in Europe, and yet you refuse to make the origins of this gigantic enterprise absolutely clear. . . .'

He attacked the government for not taking the country and Europe sufficiently into its confidence, and so showed himself a responsible member of the opposition rather than an all-out enemy of the regime: a statesman and patriot rather than a party-man. In that respect he differed from his more doctrinaire colleagues, Jules Favrie, Ferry, Arago etc., seven men in all who voted against granting the credits whereas he voted for them. Since the plebiscite, he had mostly lived hidden in the country, out of touch with his party, 'isolated and grazing happily', repairing his health, preparing his strategy for the elections of 1871. After the debates in the Chamber in July, he vanished again, bidding his friends farewell with the words: 'We shall thrash the enemy.' He reappeared in Paris on August 7th.

Despite the reluctance of the opposition to let the government have the day to itself, the debates of July 15th did not detract materially from the country's impulse of unanimity. The Empress was at Saint-Cloud throughout the day and heard late in the evening of the government's overwhelming majority in the Chamber. From the terrace in the garden she could see the lights of Paris, and they told her the people were milling about in the streets, singing the Marseillaise. The Emperor, like his uncle in 1814, had specially withdrawn the ban which had made the revolutionary anthem a forbidden song, and perhaps snatches of it were audible as the Empress walked to and fro under the old trees in the park of Saint-Cloud, gravely absorbed in her thoughts. A courtier allowed himself to remark upon her mood. 'How can I feel anything but concern on the eve of great events?' she replied. 'Here is a great country like France, peaceable, prosperous, and now engaged in a conflict from which, even if all goes well, so much destruction, so much sorrow will come. The honour of France is engaged: but what disaster if fortune should go against her! We have only one card to play. If we are not victorious, France will not only be diminished and robbed, but swallowed up by the most frightful revolution ever seen.'

Nor did the Emperor show any signs of light-heartedness. When the Senators and Deputies came to the Tuileries on July 18th to deliver a loyal address, he replied with a sombre and unboastful speech: 'We are entering upon a long and arduous war,' he said several times. The Prince Imperial was in transports of delight because he knew that he would soon be leaving for the front at the side of his father. Filon was a little disconcerted when he caught his pupil teaching the Marseillaise to Louis Conneau and his Spanish cousins. Where had he learnt it? The Empress was appointed Regent on July 26th, and two days later the Emperor, the little Prince and a numerous suite, consisting of all the great military names of the Crimean, Italian and Mexican campaigns, left for the war from the little private railway station below the Palace of Saint-Cloud. 'The Empress,' writes Mlle Bouvet, 'although agitated to the bottom of her soul showed the self-control of a Sovereign.' She marked the sign of the cross on her son's forehead and embraced him: 'Louis, do your duty.' The Emperor extended both hands to Ollivier: 'I count on you,' he murmured. Presently he waved to them from the wide window of his saloon, the eager face of the Prince bobbing up at his side. 'Dumanoir,' he called out in his strong deep voice to one of the courtiers standing below, 'I did not say goodbye to you.' Dumanoir bowed low, and an odd silence spread along the platform at these kindly words, the last most of them were to hear the Emperor speak. Then the train steamed out, away to the war and the Prussians. The little railway station emptied, and Filon saw the Empress drive by, returning to the Palace with Princess Clothilde, no longer able to hold back her tears. Next to Filon stood Parieu, President of the Council of State, and they walked back together, 'Everyone is saying, of course,' Parieu remarked to Filon, 'that the Empress has been exerting her influence for war. Well, I know that this is quite untrue. When I was leaving the Council the other day, she said to me: "What do you think of the situation, M. de Parieu?" I replied: "Madame, I think that if England were to offer her mediation, we should be very wrong not to accept." And she answered: "I think so, too."' It is indeed conceivable that even after the Ems dispatch Lord Clarendon might have travelled to Paris or Berlin in order to stop the war. But Clarendon had died on June 30th, and events had moved too swiftly for his successor, Lord Granville.

Among the Empress's first acts in her new Regency was a visit, late in July, to the Fleet at Cherbourg. A French squadron was ready to sail to the Baltic, where Denmark was preparing herself to join in against the Prussians after the first French victory. The Empress received an enthusiastic welcome in the beflagged streets and wharves of the harbour town.

Aboard Admiral Beuet-Willaumez's flagship the naval officers in charge of the expedition were presented. 'We are accustomed,' said the Admiral in his speech of welcome, 'to see our Empress come forward whenever there is danger to be faced.' She was always happy among sailors and made an inspiring and warm-hearted little speech in reply, ending by reading out the Emperor's proclamation to the army. Then she returned to the prosaic work of her new Regency.

The Empress remained at Saint-Cloud from July 28th to August 7th, and at the Tuileries until September 4th. In many ways, she was less well prepared for the new Regency than she had been in 1865. She had, as we saw, bowed to the insistence of the men to exclude her from the daily business of government. Ollivier, a formalist to the point of pedantry, now made a great show of the constitutional independence of the Ministers. So at first she was reduced to the merest representative duties such as bestowing the *légion d'honneur* on deserving recipients like Dr. Adrien Proust, the novelist's father, who had done heroic work in combating cholera under one of those officially sponsored research projects that were so characteristic of the Second Empire. Or—and this cause had always been very close to her heart—she visited, early in August, the Jewish *maison de refuge* at Paris and handed its secretary a sum of money.

When she was able to, she took a mild degree of initiative. Early in August, for example, she heard that two papers, *La Presse* and *Le Rappel*, faced closing down because of their inability to pay a fine that had been outstanding for some time. She sent Filon to Ollivier's secretary Adelon with a plea not to make enemies of journalists at a time when national unity was the first duty of all. Adelon was greatly surprised that 'the Empress was more liberal in her ideas than he was himself', and the two papers survived. The Regent also addressed an appeal to her friend Paul de Cassagnac (who, journalistically speaking, was something of a Second Empire Loyalist and as such often guilty of grossly inflated language), to show moderation in his writings, to think less of making enemies and more to making friends. Cassagnac, an intelligent and gallant man despite his occasional exaggerations, replied, and complied, most handsomely. Filon acted as the Regent's secretary, because Conti was away ill, and his deputy Franceschini Pietri, a distant Corsican relative of the Chief of Police, was at the Emperor's side. Also with her at Saint-Cloud were her two Spanish nieces, the widowed Duchess of Malakoff (the Marshal had died in 1864), Jurien de La Gravière (at the Emperor's special insistence), M. de Piennes, M. de Cossé-Brissac (who, so to speak, had been at his Sovereign's side in good days and bad since the days of Louis XIV), Mme de Rayneval, Princess d'Essling, Mme Clary, Marie de Larminat, and the ladies on duty. In these first days of the Regency, the Empress received a letter from Octave Feuillet, the writer and her ardent admirer, which put into words what many felt:

'You are at this moment, Madame, the living image of the motherland.

On your noble forehead we can read all the sentiments which animate you, all that you suffer, all that you hope, all your anguish, all your pride, your enthusiasm, your faith. The soul of France is with you.'

Filon, familiarising himself with his secretarial duties, was amazed at the paucity of information reaching the Regent from the Ministers, who barely communicated decisions even after they had been taken. Neither he nor the Ministers knew that within two days of the Emperor's arrival at Metz she had received a letter from him in which he described the whole mobilisation as disastrous, spoke of confusion and chaos, of the lack of co-ordination and supplies, of disorder and quarrelling. On the very day that he had proclaimed that 'on our success hangs the fate of liberty and civilisation', the Emperor had to recognise that the first necessity of his strategy—launching an attack into German territory—was out of the question. No wonder Abbé Puyol, one of the Chaplains of the Tuileries now on duty at Saint-Cloud, found the Regent in tears on the day when she received this letter. At luncheon, the Duchess of Malakoff attempted to console the Empress. 'Don't,' the Empress replied, 'I must not weaken,' and unaffectedly dried her tears with her napkin.

Better news came on August 2nd when in a telegram the Emperor announced a slight advance near Saarbrücken. In a private wire to the Regent, he added that the Prince Imperial had undergone his baptism of fire, showing as complete coolness in the midst of a skirmish 'as if he were strolling in the Bois'; a bullet that fell close to him he kept as a souvenir. That evening the Ministers came to dine, and the Empress showed her private telegram to Ollivier who deplorably enough decided to publish it. 'The bullet of Saarbrücken' was to haunt the Prince to the end of his short life. Metternich, wearing the red ribbon of the Legion of Honour, was also at dinner, and heard the Empress exclaim: 'I am sure he has a charmed life. August is the month of the Bonapartes.' Metternich, with his eyes on the Empress's, raised his glass to his lips and silently drank a toast. 'For sure,' wrote Abbé Puyol, 'he did not give a toast to the victory of the French army—no, Bismarck will never be able to prove that the Austrian Ambassador violated the laws of neutrality. Nevertheless, M. de Metternich that night gave a toast.'

The turn for the worse came on August 6th. On that day the armies of MacMahon and Frossard were beaten at Forbach and Froeschwiller, but by a ghastly and inexplicable mischance Paris at midday was filled with news of a splendid victory. An excited crowd invaded Ollivier's Ministry in the Place Vendôme and asked for confirmation. He dismissed them saying that he had no news of any sort, but sent a telegram to the Empress asking her to come to Paris because 'the revolution' was raising its head. Before this, she had heard Abbé Puyol's eye-witness report of the strange doings in Paris, and now she sent an equerry, General Lepic, to Ollivier, whom he found presiding over a meeting of discordant Ministers. That same after-noon, the Regent received a telegram from the Emperor which said that

Frossard was engaged, there was no news from MacMahon and that 'success was uncertain'. Lepic returned to report that the Ministers had issued a proclamation asking Parisians to be calm. They had not consulted the Regent. 'What is the point of being Regent?' she said and added: 'I shall say nothing. No personal question must raise so much as the shadow of a difficulty.' Lepic told her that at the Police Prefecture he had also seen Pietri, who had said the news-mongers were clearly up to something sinister. 'Quite,' said the Empress, 'a kind of conspiracy à la Malet.'[1] Baraquay d'Hilliers, Commandant of Paris, had told Lepic that he would act as soon as he received his orders, and when Lepic called once more at the Place Vendôme he heard that the Ministers had decided to send someone to the Emperor's Headquarters to let him know what was happening in Paris. 'But why add to the Emperor's worries?' the Empress exclaimed at once. 'Can't they let him direct the war without bothering him with our problems?' Finally Lepic submitted for her signature a decree drawn up by Ollivier putting Paris under martial law, together with a letter from him repeating his demand that she should return to the Tuileries 'at the head of the troops at your disposal'. She looked aghast at Lepic: how many troops, she asked, did she have at her disposal? '160 voltigeurs, Madame,' came the reply. The Empress signed the decree, said that she would return to Paris next day, and retired to her rooms.

Filon, Cossé-Brissac, M. de Piennes and a few others remained in the drawing-room, chatting. Soon after ten a new telegram from the Emperor's headquarters was brought in. Filon began deciphering it, but the first sentence made its meaning only too clear:

'Our troops are in full retreat. Nothing must be thought of now beyond the defence of the capital. . . .'

It was the news of the twin defeat sustained on the day which Paris had begun with victory celebrations. Piennes looked at the others: 'Who is going to tell the Empress?' There was no answer. 'Very well,' said Piennes, 'I will go myself.' He returned a few minutes later, looking pale. 'Do you know what her first words were?' The others looked at him in silence. 'She said the dynasty is lost—we must think only of France.' Fifteen minutes later the Empress came downstairs, dressed for the drive to Paris. Mme d'Essling rushed over to her: 'Ah, Madame,' she began. 'No sentiment, please,' said the Empress, 'I shall need all my courage.' She called a meeting of Ministers for that very night at the Tuileries, and so Ollivier and she faced each other in the Council Chamber at three in the morning of Sunday, August 7th, 1870.

She conducted the meeting admirably. Ollivier, knowing his Ministry to be threatened in the Chambers, spoke in favour of a new coup d'état— to prorogue Parliament, suspend the right of assembly, muzzle the Press

[1] It will be recalled that in 1812 General Malet, a convinced Republican, had attempted to rouse Parisians against the Empire while Napoleon I was in Russia.

and arrest the irreconcilables, were among his main suggestions. The Regent, in vivid contrast to the principal pilot of the liberal Empire, insisted on the strictest and fullest constitutional collaboration between Crown, government and the Chambers. The majority of the Ministers were on her side. When Ollivier demanded the Emperor's immediate return to the capital, she opposed it with the argument that he must not come back to Paris 'under the shadow of defeat'. Ollivier further proposed making General Trochu Minister of War, and she agreed, asking Jurien de La Gravière to go off and sound him. Trochu, an eloquent critic of the government's army policy since 1867, was by now the idol of the opposition and Ollivier hoped that his appointment might save the life of his Ministry. But during the following two days the Regent was told by several senators and deputies, including the Presidents of the two Chambers, that, whatever Trochu's reply to the overture, the Ollivier government had lost the country's confidence and should be dismissed. To this she replied that she had no powers of dismissal, but that if the Chambers voted the government out of power, it would be her duty to appoint a new one.

Much to Ollivier's irritation, she recalled Parliament for August 9th and when, as expected, the government fell, she sent for General Cousin de Montauban, Count of Palikao since his successful leadership of the Chinese expedition in 1860, to form a new Ministry. Palikao at once submitted a drastic programme to put Paris in a state of preparedness and obtained an overwhelming majority from the Chamber. The response to this swift and energetic change in Paris and the country was excellent, and the Regent gave this mood of grim determination appropriate expression in a proclamation: 'I am here in the midst of you. Faithful to my mission and my duty, you will see me first in the place of danger to defend the flag of France.'

'The French people and Government,' says Michael Howard of the events in Paris of August 7th-9th, 'faced the invaders with a spirit of self-sacrifice and resolution not inferior to that of their grandfathers, in 1792, and their children in 1914.'

She had negotiated this perilous passage without reference to the Emperor, but merely sent him a reassuring telegram when it was over. 'You are acting in a revolutionary manner,' Filon told her. 'I must,' she replied. She wanted the Emperor to be able to direct the war without being deflected by the politics of the capital, and felt that his presence in Paris would only serve as a rallying point for the revolutionary party, especially if he separated himself from the army in days of adversity. Trochu, whom she would have been quite willing to accept as Minister of War on this occasion, spoilt his chances by assuming a deliberately unreasonable attitude, probably because she was already committed to a different political course. When she heard that he made his acceptance of office conditional on being allowed publicly to expose all the faults which in his opinion had been committed towards the army since 1867, she felt that this was not the time for inquests, and so Palikao took on the War Ministry as well.

He quickly organised two further Army Corps, the 12th and the 13th, and removed Trochu from Paris by putting him in command of the former at Châlons.

Like the Empress, Gambetta had returned to Paris on August 7th. Like the Empress's, his energies, the full vigour of his character and feeling, were dedicated not to politics, but to the prosecution of the war. Again he stood in some contrast to his party friends by insisting, not that the Empire must be replaced by a Republic, but that the liberal Empire, if it was to save France, must extend its war policy and arm the people. 'We must show,' he thundered, 'that a régime based on parliamentary institutions can be a régime of action.' 'We are fighting,' he exclaimed, 'to re-establish, against the retrograde invasion that threatens us, the civilising principles of Europe.' All his interventions, his vitalising and amazing flood of exhortations and admonitions, came from a deep awareness of national danger which he expressed in these words:

'We are faced by the whole of the Prussian nation in arms. That nation has trained its children for war. Against it, you have sent out an army whose heroism no one admires more than I do, but remember: In the presence of a nation in arms we also must raise a nation in arms.'

With this phrase Gambetta highlighted the difference in attitude between the Government and himself. Palikao and his Ministers shrank from the policy of arming 'the people', fearing the workers more than the Prussians, and Gambetta had to wait for his opportunity until after Sedan when he put that timidity to shame. Only one Minister, Jerome David, enjoined the Chamber in 1870 to 'learn from M. Gambetta's patriotic enthusiasm', but no one else had the statesmanship to grasp the hand which Gambetta was, in fact, stretching out. His reputation as a fanatic demagogue obscured the fact that he had moved beyond the distinction between régime and country, that the recent referendum had marked a turning point in his political thinking, and the Empress and her harrassed Ministers did not detect the muffled note of willingness to serve struck in his speeches. By saying 'we must raise a nation in arms', he was, too indirectly, announcing his wish to head the Government's Committee of Defence. It all flowed from the nemesis of a premature war. A year or two later Gambetta would in all probability have taken the step from opposition to government—especially under Napoleon IV. It may be sterile to speculate on what might have been, but we need not doubt that the Empress would have made the transition as easy and honourable for him as she did for Duruy, Ollivier and others—even as, twenty years later, she turned Gambetta's disciple and secretary, Joseph Reinach, into a declared partisan and, very nearly, a biographer.[1]

From August 7th, the Empress presided twice a day over Ministerial meetings. 'She had,' wrote someone who was present at all of them, 'so exaggerated an idea of the rights of responsible Ministers that she never

[1] See page 339.

interrupted them, but when opportunity offered, always brought the wayward discussion back to the point under debate and kept it there to the best of her ability until a solution was found. Misfortune had purged her spirit, had freed her of all feminine weaknesses and futilities and of her preoccupation with the future of the dynasty which she considered lost. She thought exclusively of the country, directing her speeches, her whole effort only towards saving France, to obtain for the Empire an end worthy of the name of Napoleon. The Emperor's death at the head of his troops seemed to her desirable. . . .' Lord Lyons wrote to London that she showed 'pluck, but not hope', and Mérimée told Panizzi that he had no doubt 'the Emperor will let himself be killed, for he can only return as a victor, and victory has become impossible'.

During the days which followed, the Empress could hardly eat, could not sleep without taking chloral, and yet there was not a single man or woman who approached the Empress-Regent during that August and did not come away with courage braced and confidence strengthened. Mérimée, who had suffered a stroke on the day of the first defeats, dragged himself almost daily to her side until August 25th and wrote: 'She is as firm as a rock.' As the three German armies were closing in on Paris he heard her say: 'We shall hold out in Paris if we are besieged, or if we are out of Paris we shall still hold out to the end. There can be no question of peace.' The sentiment is familiar, and so is, almost, the language. 'She told me,' Mérimée wrote again, 'that she did not feel the fatigue. If everybody had her courage, the country would be saved. Unfortunately, M. de Bismarck has a fourth army, and that is in Paris itself.'

Prince Napoleon, unemployed since the previous Regency, was present at Imperial Headquarters during August. It was largely due to him that on August 17th the Empress had for a second time to combat the suggestion that the Emperor should return to Paris and resume the reins of government. The Emperor had, at Metz on August 12th, already handed over supreme Command of the Army to Bazaine and now, on August 17th, at Châlons, his cousin told him:

'You have abdicated from the government at Paris; at Metz you have abdicated from the supreme Command. Short of going to Belgium, you must resume the one or the other. The High Command is out of the question. The Government will be difficult and perilous, for you must go back to Paris, but, what the devil! if we must fall, let us at least fall like men.'

With this suggestion Prince Napoleon coupled the demand that Trochu should be made military Governor of Paris. Also largely under Prince Napoleon's impulsion, it was further decided to send the new Army of Châlons, which thanks to Palikao's excellent measures was a respectable force of some 130,000 men, to Paris under command of Marshal Mac Mahon, Duke of Magenta.

The Empress and Palikao first heard of the new plan when Trochu appeared in the capital, with the Emperor's decree in his pocket, towards midnight on August 17th. He at once submitted a proclamation addressed to the people of Paris to the Minister of the Interior, the Empress's old correspondent Henri Chevreau, in which his appointment and the Emperor's imminent arrival were to be simultaneously announced. Chevreau refused to act without the Regent or the Prime Minister, and so later in the day there was a consultation between the Regent, Palikao and Trochu. The Empress, who had not been edified by Trochu's behaviour when she had offered him the War Ministry, nevertheless accepted him reluctantly as Governor, since Canrobert had declined. But on the question of the Emperor's return, she and the Ministers remained absolutely firm. 'Do you know, General,' she said to him,

'that fifty armed men could walk straight into this room and murder me without any difficulty? But they do not attack me. Why? Simply because I do not defend myself, and because they know that if I disappeared the Empire could still remain. But imagine the Emperor in this Palace, which is a trap for Sovereigns. What would happen to him? Imagine the onslaught of all the bitter enemies who are now combined against him. There would be two alternatives: either the Army would side with him, and then there would be civil war between the Army and the people of Paris; or else the troops would desert him, and revolution and massacre would follow. In either case who would profit? The Prussians.'

Palikao and the government fully supported her stand, and Palikao added that the plan to withdraw the army of Châlons towards Paris would be most ill-advised, since it delivered the army of the Rhine, commanded by Bazaine and based on Metz, to a Prussian onslaught without support. Like Trochu, Bazaine, the ranker who had become a Marshal, was popular with the Left and in the streets. To leave him to fend for himself while the army of Châlons was drawn back to the defence of the capital and the dynasty would have been impossible under the conditions prevailing in Paris. Besides, Palikao's entire system of supply and reinforcements would have to be readjusted—not the kind of practical detail likely to bother a strategist like Prince Napoleon.

Trochu's appointment as Governor of Paris was Plon-Plon's last contribution to his cousin's Empire, as the Châlons Conference was the last time that he prevailed over the Emperor's judgment. The Emperor had not welcomed Trochu's appointment, but had not found the strength to resist. As was to be expected, Prince Napoleon was furious that the Regency had prevailed against his advice about the Emperor's return and on August 19th he accepted a mission to his father-in-law, the King of Italy, to see whether the Italian army could not be persuaded to create a diversion in Bavaria. In his rage and fury, Plon-Plon spread the rumour that the Empress, thirsting for personal power, wished the Emperor out of the way.

The immediate effect of Bazaine's and Trochu's appointments was to make the atmosphere in Paris calmer, and the Empress was able to pursue her exacting duties. showing remarkable attention to all manner of detail. She it was who arranged to have the art treasures in the Museums and national collections removed to Brest. She had the Crown jewels put into a place of safety and had the foresight to obtain an official receipt. Her private jewellery she entrusted to Princess Metternich. She paid daily visits to the two hospitals she had installed in the Tuileries, one in hutments along the Terrace, the other in the large hall between the Chapel and the Pavillon Marson, the scene of the sessions of the Convention after 1792. It was the Regent who gave the Ministers the idea of providing the fortifications of Paris with naval guns, of destroying the locks, blowing up bridges and blocking the tunnels. She also instructed Grandperret, Keeper of the Seals in the Palikao Ministry, to organise a second government that could carry on at Tours, should Paris become paralysed as the governmental nerve-centre. Filon, her secretary on duty, watched the Regent in open-mouthed astonishment. 'The Salic Law is quite wrong,' he told her one day, 'because the men will do far more for Your Majesty than they would for the Emperor.'

She even continued her diplomatic efforts. No less aware than Gambetta of the long-term issues behind the struggle against Prussia, she told the Austrian military attaché that 'Austria will be lost, if she does not enter quickly into an alliance with France.' As usual, the Austrians understood too late. 'What a nightmare!' wrote Metternich to Beust on August 16th, 'and what a future for us, this omnipotence of Bismarck!'

Trochu continued to be the disturbing question mark. His offices in the Louvre were becoming a meeting place for the hostile and the discontented of the Left. As soon as there were more than about six people assembled in his antechambers, the Military Governor would emerge and make a speech. He also flooded every Ministerial meeting with his eloquence and one day treated them to a repetition of the speech he had just delivered to the National Guards about—dying: 'In supreme agony you must maintain the attitude of pride and tragedy which alike becomes men, citizens, and soldiers. . . .' The Regent interrupted: 'Good God, General, one dies as one can.' Was he a buffoon or a tribune, Filon wondered, a hero or a traitor? Duvernois, Minister of Agriculture, who had provisioned Paris with an enormous amount of livestock against the siege, asked the Governor point-blank: 'General, if the Regent were attacked, what would you do?' 'I should lay down my life on the steps of the throne,' he replied without a moment's hesitation. At the same time, he felt that his intimacy with the oppositional Ultras, headed by Jules Favre, could not have escaped detection, and so he struck a pose of manful honesty towards the Empress: 'Madame, if your police are really efficient they will have told you that I have seen the Deputies of the Left. . . . I feel it my duty to keep in touch with public opinion.' The Empress said nothing.

'We are doing what we *must* do,' she wrote to her mother, who offered refuge in Madrid. 'Thank you for your offers but I cannot accept.' Her private language, and sentiments, were no different from her public ones: 'I think,' she wrote to Paca's children late in August, 'that the Prussians will be before Paris within a few days and that the siege will begin. Courage, then! I view the situation calmly. Maybe this is because of tiredness and uncertainty, but I regard this development as good and I have hope. . . .' To her mother she allowed herself to show the weight of her burden: 'All things in this world may cause envy—except a crown. One gives up everything—repose, happiness, affection, to find oneself surrounded by nothing but weakness or worse. At the same time, I must say that I have found true friends in places where I did not think they existed, and devotion in moments of trial.' 'Believe me,' she wrote again, 'I am not defending the throne, but *honour*, and if after the war, when not a single Prussian will be left on French soil, the country does not want us, I shall be only too glad to forget, far away from the noise of the world. . . .'

As long as she thought that the issue of the war would be decided beneath the walls of Paris, she did not lose confidence, but her heart sank when late in August she heard that the Prussians had slowed down their march on the capital and that the decisive battle might be fought elsewhere, where German superiority in numbers and striking power could prove overwhelming. 'In a few days from now there will probably be a great battle,' she wrote to her Alba nieces. 'How terrible war is!'

The decision to send Marshal MacMahon and the army of Châlons northwards to effect a junction with Bazaine's army of the Rhine at Metz had been taken by Palikao, as Minister of War, and the other Ministers alone: 'The Regent,' says Filon, 'whatever may have been her personal opinion, made no comment.' The government felt that any action which left 'our glorious Bazaine' unsupported at Metz, would lead to instant revolution in the capital and the other cities. The fate of France was in the hands of MacMahon as he marched northwards, and in those of Bazaine, who was waiting at Metz for the right moment to break out and effect the junction of the two armies of which Parisian and foreign newspapers were speaking quite openly from August 26th onwards. Neither Marshal measured up to such opportunities as, even in the circumstances of August, 1870, they were granted. Communications between them across enemy lines were almost non-existent and, when established, subject to disastrous delays. Although there cannot be any question of treason, Bazaine's determination to break out was very slow in forming and half-hearted when made, even as MacMahon's tactics were cautious to the point of uselessness. What was needed was a Commander-in-Chief with absolute authority over both these inhibited and fumbling Marshals, but the Emperor, rendered useless by the acutest physical agony, was now in a state of drugged torpor. He took special care not to let the Empress know the truth about his health, sending Nelaton to Paris with soothing bulletins. As MacMahon was groping towards Metz, the Emperor, a passenger in this movement, decided on August 27th to separate himself from the Prince Imperial 'for a few days'. Attended by Count Clary and three equerries, among whom Charles Duperré, of the Navy, was also a great personal friend, the Prince moved uneasily from place to place in order to avoid being captured by the enemy. The Regent was not in favour of these wanderings from town to town. 'I am in terrible anxiety,' she wrote to Duperré on August 30th, 'but I wish above all things that each of you should do his duty. Always remember one thing: I can weep for my son dead or wounded, but to think of him running away! I could never forgive you if you allowed such a thing. I appeal to your honour as soldiers. Do everything for the best, but act like soldiers. I will take all responsibility.' The Prince himself was restrained only with difficulty from rushing away towards the sound of the guns: had he been twenty and not fourteen he might have become a rallying point.

On August 31st, MacMahon's army had blundered into what Moltke called 'the mouse-trap of Sedan', and the decisive battle began at 4 a.m. on September 1st with a Bavarian thrust across the Meuse. MacMahon was wounded early on, and General Wimpffen, who had arrived at the front only two days earlier, took over from him. The battle was fought in brilliant autumnal sunshine. The King of Prussia, surrounded by all those German Princes who a few weeks earlier had vainly looked for an escape from the Prussian grip, watched from a vantage-point which provided 'a view of the battle such as no commander of an army in Western Europe was ever to see again'. The Emperor, on the other hand, spent the morning riding to and fro on the battlefield, five hours of agony heroically borne. Like Ney at Waterloo, when night and the Prussians came, he hoped for death from a bullet which never found him. Like the Empress, he thought that death in battle would be the greatest service he could render his son. The battle went against the French from the first, and their fiercest bravery bought no improvement during the livelong day. Among the last actions were the French cavalry charges led by Galliffet against the victorious German infantry. The first charge overran the German lines, but was helpless against the firing power of the supporting formations and so was beaten back with huge losses. Galliffet was asked whether they could return to the attack. 'As often as you like, General—as long as there is one of us left.' From his vantage-point, the King of Prussia saw the splendid horsemen plunge down the hill to their destruction: 'Brave people!' he exclaimed, and the words are still carved on the memorial erected by the Third Republic to the Imperial Cavalry on the field of Sedan. The day ended when at five p.m. German artillery, with a massive precision not hitherto experienced on a battlefield, decimated and demoralised the fugitive remnants of the army of Châlons. Simultaneously, the Emperor issued his first independent order since his 'abdication': an immediate cease-fire. The white flag was hoisted above the walls of Sedan, and the Emperor sent General Reille to the King of Prussia with this letter:

'Sire, my brother,

Having been unable to die among my troops, there remains nothing for me to do but surrender my sword to Your Majesty. I am Your Majesty's good brother

Napoleon.'

This was followed, later in the evening, by Generals Wimpffen and Castelnau meeting Bismarck and Moltke to obtain terms from the victors. The Chancellor and the Chief of Staff had little difficulty in thwarting French attempts to offer merely 'an honourable capitulation' with a promise by the whole army to lay down their arms and not take the field again. Instead, it was made clear to them that the day's defeat must be taken to mean the end of French predominance or, as Bismarck put it to Wimpffen, of her 'excessive pride'. 'You seem to think,' said the Iron Chancellor, 'that victory is a property reserved for you alone, that the glory of arms is your monopoly. Now this must end. We must have land, fortresses and frontiers which will protect us for good from enemy attack.' France had been Germany's enemy for two hundred years and now, in the words of General von Blumenthal, the Prussian Crown Prince's Chief of Staff, the French must be crushed 'so that they will not be able to breathe for a hundred years'. Faced with this way of thinking, the Emperor indicated, on September 3rd, that he surrendered merely his own personal sword and not that of France, that he and his army were the prisoners of the Prussians, and that his surrender affected neither the Regency in Paris, nor the army of the Rhine at Metz. This was accepted, and the Emperor was taken to the château of Wilhelmshöhe near Cassel from where his uncle, Plon-Plon's father Jerome Bonaparte, had ruled over the kingdom of Westphalia at the beginning of the century.

The news became known in Paris in the afternoon of September 3rd. When Filon went to the Palais Bourbon towards three o'clock, someone who had learnt it by heart recited the Emperor's telegram announcing his and the army's captivity. He went back to the Empress's study at the Tuileries, where he found Conti, the Emperor's secretary, who despite his illness had gone to the Palace to offer his help. The poor man sat shivering in the hot September sun, and Filon began to light a fire in the grate. Suddenly the Empress appeared at the head of the little winding stair-case which connected her apartments with those of the Emperor below. One glance at her face told Filon that she knew. 'Do you know what they are saying?' she began. 'That the Emperor has surrendered, that he has capitulated! Surely, you do not believe that abomination?' They dared not speak. She became very angry and demanded vehemently: 'You do not believe it?' Conti tried to find words: 'There are circumstances, Madame, where even the bravest . . .' She understood.

'Without waiting to hear more,' wrote Filon of the scene which haunted him to the end of his life, 'the Empress cut short his words, and, her soul stirred to its innermost depths, poured forth its agony in a torrent of incoherent and mad words. What she said then Conti never repeated to anyone, and I shall die, like him, without repeating it. I was so overcome at the time that my memory was as if paralysed. It lasted five long, terrible minutes. The Empress then left the room and went down the little staircase. We remained speechless and stunned, like men who have come through an earthquake.'

CHAPTER 23

SHE REGAINED her calm, and later in the evening sent for Henri Chevreau and General Trochu. The Governor of Paris sent his excuses. She summoned him again next morning and he said he would send his Chief of Staff who, however, failed to appear. Plon-Plon's nominee was living up to her expectations. In the morning of Sunday, September 4th, a day of autumnal radiance, two deputies counselled her to hand over her powers to the Legislative Body to avoid being forced to abdicate. She objected that she could only follow whatever course the Legislature might prescribe: if they believed the dynasty was an obstacle, then they must pronounce its overthrow. 'I am convinced,' she went on in what both deputies later called 'her firm and calm manner', 'that the only sensible and patriotic course would be for the country's representatives to rally round me, round my government, leaving aside all internal questions, so that we could unite our efforts exclusively against the invasion.' She spoke of her prepared plan of evacuating the government from Paris: 'I am ready to face all dangers and follow the *Corps Legislatif* wherever resistance can be organised. If resistance becomes impossible, I should still be able to obtain less unfavourable peace conditions.' She told them that the day before 'the representative of a great power' had offered mediation by the neutrals on the basis of territorial integrity and the maintenance of the dynasty: 'I replied that I was inclined to accept mediation on the first point, but energetically turned down the second. The maintenance of the dynasty concerns the country alone, and I will not allow foreign powers to meddle in our internal affairs.' The deputies remained unmoved: abdication in some form was the only answer. 'Such is not my feeling, gentlemen,' she replied, 'but I am leaving all personal things out of this. My sole intention is to act in a regular manner. If my Ministers agree with you, no obstacle will come from me. Go and see Count de Palikao.'

Soon afterwards, Chevreau rushed into the room: 'All is lost, Madame!' he cried. 'Has poor General Trochu been killed, then?' she replied coolly. Chevreau told her that the mob had flooded across the Pont de la Concorde and was inside the Palais Bourbon. All the approaches to the Tuileries were filled with an armed crowd shouting for abdication, and there was no sign of any measures against them being taken by Trochu. Among that crowd was an Englishman, Lord Ronald Gower: 'It seemed as if 1792 had come back [he wrote]. Had the Empress been found there and then, her life would not have been worth a moment's purchase.'

I*

Inside the Palace, General Mellinet, who was in charge of the guard, offered to open fire on the crowds, but the Empress forbade him. She did not know that at that moment Gambetta in the Palais Bourbon was vainly trying to keep the invading mob under control. Like the Empress, he fought vehemently for legality and wanted the authentic voice of the deputies to be heard above the din of the masses: 'Remember,' he shouted 'that the enemy is on our soil! . . . I implore you to await the return of your representatives.' For a moment the mob seemed prepared to allow the session to resume its deliberations, but when Palikao returned, there were cries of 'down with the majority'. 'Do you want us to make orderly decisions?' cried Gambetta for the last time. 'No phrases! No treason!' came the reply. Gambetta gave up, and they marched off to the Hôtel de Ville to proclaim their Republic.

So it became finally clear that the Military Governor of Paris was on the side of the insurgents. The mob, not Parliament, decided the issue, and the founders of the Republic acted on the principle of 'I am their leader, I must follow them.' Gambetta in the Palais Bourbon and the Empress in the Tuileries were the only people of stature who were able and willing to provide a different leadership, but, instead, the public images created by the free press prevailed—Gambetta, the revolutionary demagogue and the fanatic Empress determined to risk the army in defence of the dynasty. For not the last time in modern history, propaganda proved stronger than the truth.

At the Tuileries, the Regent yielded at length to the pleas of Metternich and Nigra who, remaining at her side in the most unneutral manner, urged that if she fled now, she would carry the authority of the Regency with her, wherever she went. To stay would only endanger the lives of those who had so faithfully stood by her during those nightmare weeks. Reluctantly, the Empress gave in. From her ladies, she asked only Mme Le Breton to accompany her. Since the shouting crowds made it impossible to leave by the Place de Carrousel, they left by a disused gallery of the Louvre. Here came the final farewell from her suite and household, and presently the two ambassadors guided the Empress and Mme Le Breton through the deserted Museum towards the exit in the Place Saint-Germain l'Auxerrois. Outside, the mob was shouting: 'A mort! A mort!' Metternich stopped a passing cab, a street urchin recognised one of the ladies and shouted: 'Look—the Empress!' Nigra dealt with him, and the Empress drove off with Mme Le Breton. The sole manifestation of the Franco-Italian-Austrian alliance they had all hoped to achieve was at an end.

After one or two knocks on closed doors, the Empress decided to seek the help of her American dentist, Dr. Evans, and she and Mme Le Breton spent the afternoon sitting in his library waiting for him. When at last Dr. Evans returned, the Empress told him she wanted to go to England. At once this splendid American volunteered to make the necessary arrangements.

If it was a little prosaic that the Count Fersen of the new flight to

Varennes should be a middle-aged dentist, the Empress had made a wise choice. Rich, level-headed and devoted, Evans was entirely responsible for the fact that, after two days on the roads, the Empress reached Deauville in safety. Aided by an equally dependable fellow-countryman, Dr. Crane, Evans procured horses, squared inn-keepers, got his passenger through barriers and toll-gates and generally shielded the Empress's incognito. Not that she was a difficult traveller. Despite the superhuman strain and anxieties of recent days, she was calm and composed; it was poor Mme Le Breton who throughout looked woebegone and tragic. As they passed by the defensive installations she had ordered, the Regent's regret at not being allowed to share the ordeals of Paris found a measured expression: 'It has sometimes seemed to me that the French set up their heroes, so to speak, on pillars of salt, so that when the first storm strikes them they tumble down to lie for ever in the mud. In no country in the world is the step from the sublime to the ridiculous so often made.' She was wholly without self-pity: 'Only a few days ago I said that I would never leave the Tuileries in a cab, like Louis Philippe—well, that is exactly what I have done.' And she laughed. Or she cried with equal freedom, such as when she opened the little *médallion* with a miniature of the Prince Imperial inside it. Where was the boy? Nobody knew.

They spent the night at La Rivière. Evans tells us that when the Empress emerged from her room in the morning she triumphantly showed them some handkerchiefs she had washed and ironed 'in some ingenious way'. 'When there is no necessity to move us,' she said, 'we little suspect our own cleverness or ability to do things.' Her father's austere upbringing had accustomed her to face up to poverty from an early age and, at this moment of total uncertainty, she was ready to face up to it once more. Luxury and power had not corrupted her.

Evans's wife was on holiday at the Hôtel de Casino at Deauville and while she looked after the two fugitives the dentist and Crane looked round the harbour for a vessel to take them to England. A sailor drew their attention to a yacht, *Gazelle*, alongside the quay, which belonged to an Englishman, Sir John Burgoyne. Evans sent his card aboard and Sir John expressed his willingness to show the two Americans over his ship. Presently Evans took him aside, told him about the Empress's plight and asked him to assist her escape to England. Burgoyne replied at once that it could not be done. The conversation threatened to deteriorate into an Anglo-American wrangle, Evans saying that in his country 'every man will run any risk for any woman', and Crane adding that such an opportunity came only once in a lifetime. The unhappy yachtsman finally referred them to the highest authority he knew: 'If Lady Burgoyne is willing to have the Empress come on board, she can come.' 'Well, why not?' Lady Burgoyne instantly replied when the two Americans had explained their mission. 'Let her come to us tonight, or as soon as she can safely do so.' At midnight, Evans escorted the Empress to the yacht.

As Burgoyne had prophesied, *Gazelle* ran into very rough weather soon after raising anchor, violent squalls and high seas making it almost impossible to keep on course for England. The Empress, however, would not hear of altering course for the French coast, and 'Sir John', Dr. Evans tells us, 'observing Her Majesty's fearlessness, made no further reference to turning back'. Rain came down in torrents, and there were vivid flashes of lightning and sharp thunder; *Gazelle* was tossed about helplessly like a plaything of all the fury of the elements. The Empress lay awake in her cabin. 'I was sure we were lost,' she told Evans in the morning, 'but singular as it may seem, I did not feel alarmed in the least. I have always loved the sea, and it had for me no terrors. Were I to disappear, I said to myself, death could not come more opportunely nor give me a more welcome grave.' Presently the storm abated, and at four in the morning of September 8th, *Gazelle* dropped anchor at Ryde. There they learnt that the Prince Imperial had arrived at Hastings, and that H.M.S. *Captain*, commanded by Sir Hugh Burgoyne, their own skipper's cousin, had gone down in the night's storm with all hands. When Evans came with these two items of news to the Empress in her hotel room, he found her with an open Bible in her hands, agreeably surprised that English hotels provided such reading. She showed him the passage at which she had opened the book:

> 'The Lord is my Shepherd: I shall not want.
> He maketh me to lie down in green pastures;
> He leadeth me beside the still waters . . .'

Mother and son were reunited the same evening at Hastings. The Emperor had ordered his son to leave French soil and go, via Belgium, to England. The Prince and his three equerries had reached Dover on September 6th and the same day moved on to the Marine Hotel, Hastings. Here they were joined by Filon on September 9th.

The first letter from the Emperor did not reach Hastings until September 20th. Even before leaving the Tuileries, the Empress had heard an account of her husband's conduct under fire at Sedan, of his five hours on horseback in search of death. She had written him at once a tender letter of compassion and now from Hastings she wrote twice again. All three letters reached him at Wilhelmshöhe on September 17th, and he replied:

'. . . The affectionate expressions in your letters have done me a world of good, for I was much grieved by your silence. Certainly, the misfortune which has struck us is very great, but what aggravates it is the state France will find herself in, a prey to invasion and anarchy.

You are quite right to tell me to be economical. I have on me 260,000 francs, which is all I have with me in cash. Like you, I am proud to have fallen from the throne without having placed money abroad.'

This crossed with a further letter from the Empress to which he replied on September 19th:

'Your letters are a wonderful consolation, and I thank you for them. To what can I attach myself if it is not your affection and that of our son? You say nothing of your own ordeals and the dangers to which you have been exposed. All that I had to find out from the newspapers. Everybody praised your courage and your firmness in difficult moments. It did not surprise me.'

She had written about their future arrangements. Where should they live? There was the villa near Trieste which had been left to the Prince Imperial by one of his Murat relations. The Emperor did not like the idea of taking up residence there:

'I know, from the experience of my younger days, that, in our position, we can be happy only in free countries like England or Switzerland. Anywhere else, governmental and ordinary people feel nervous about compromising themselves even when merely showing common politeness. When I am free, I want to come and live with you and Louis in a little cottage with *bow-windows* and creepers. . . .'

The Prince of Wales had at once offered Chiswick House to the Empress, but Lord Granville, as indeed Queen Victoria herself, doubted the political wisdom of this, since the Empress was still Regent of France. The Queen had, as soon as she had heard of the Empress's arrival, told the Foreign Secretary that she wished the Empress to know 'that she is not insensible to the heavy blow which has fallen upon her or forgetful of former days'.

The situation was not easy for the Queen. In the first weeks after Sedan, her eldest daughter, the Crown Princess of Prussia, shared her adoptive compatriots' disappointment that, as the war dragged on into the siege of Paris, opinion in England was swinging round to the other side. While Bismarck was sending circulars to German missions abroad insisting that peace-loving Germany must aim at an expansionist peace that would guarantee her against future French aggression, German spokesmen of another kind, from Prussian Generals to popular journalists, expressed their impatience at the delay in dismembering the enemy country, the destruction of what Roon called 'the inheritance of France'. It was not only the Prince of Wales who became alarmed by these war-aims.[1] The Queen was filled with compassionate tenderness towards the Empress, but had still not forgiven the Emperor for what she continued to call his deception over the war in Italy. 'Papa,' she reminded her daughter, 'had

[1] Lord Salisbury wrote as follows in the *Quarterly Review* of October 1870: 'At the head of 600,000 men, under the walls of beleaguered Paris, Count Bismarck has the courage to pretend that peaceful, idyllic Germany needs to be protected against her formidable and turbulent neighbour. "Pacific Germany" is a mere diplomatic common place. . . . The first object of a treaty of peace should be to make future war impossible. [Europe's] best interests would be served by absolutely prohibiting any change of frontiers. . . . Is there no neutral that will make one effort to rescue Europe from a future of chronic war? *Will England make no sign?*'

the worst opinion of him, which was never removed.' Would Prince Albert not have revised his opinions, had he lived to see the Prussia he and Dr. Stockmar had known changed out of all recognition after Bismarck had became its *Minister-Präsident*? The Prince Consort was essentially a man of peace. The Queen, sharing his devotion, made a not very hopeful attempt to influence the King of Prussia: 'In the name of our friendship and in the interests of humanity,' she wrote to him on September 30th, 'I express the hope that it may be in your power to offer terms which your defeated enemy can accept.'

The Empress was also writing letters in order to obtain a generous peace for France, while taking care to do nothing to embarrass the Government of National Defence that had assumed power in Paris on September 4th. From Hastings, she addressed appeals to Czar Alexander II and the Emperor of Austria. Their replies were disappointing, especially Francis Joseph's. His ambassador Richard Metternich, however, struck a very different note: 'The sovereign ruler here is chaos—I cry with rage,' he wrote in a hasty little letter which he managed to smuggle to the Empress from Paris. To Beust he expressed himself freely in remorseful sincerity:

'Europe's abdication before Prussian might is certainly one of the saddest events of the century. The impotence of Europe, of my own country above all, towards that vital power, growing every day, is the most heart-breaking spectacle I have ever witnessed. I shall say nothing. I have no longer the right to say anything, although I still can make sad and bitter reflections. The opportunity is gone, it was not possible to seize it—*requiescat in pace!* That is all one can say.'

Towards the end of September the Empress found a house which seemed suitable as a more permanent residence—Camden Place, Chislehurst. There, she soon became involved in the negotiations for peace. As early as September 11th, Bismarck had let it be known that 'the German Government' (not, it may be noted, that of the North German Confederation) could not treat with the Government of National Defence since it represented merely 'a part of the Left Wing of the former Legislative Assembly'. They could, however, negotiate with the Emperor Napoleon, or with the Regency he had appointed, or with Marshal Bazaine 'who has his command from the Emperor'. Bazaine had, since Sedan, been sitting inactive and isolated in besieged Metz with over 150,000 men of the army of the Rhine, an Imperial island surrounded on all sides by Prussians and the Republic. Paris itself was similarly cut off from all outside contact after September 20th, but part of the provisional government had withdrawn to Tours where they were joined on October 7th by Gambetta after his famous balloon flight. The Prussian Headquarters was first at Ferrières and later at Versailles. While Gambetta organised new armies to fight the enemy, Bismarck's desire to conclude a quick Prussian peace grew in urgency.

Jules Favre had seen him at Ferrières on September 18th, but came away defeated, empty-handed and in tears.

Pursuing his efforts to play the Empire against the Republic, the Iron Chancellor received, on September 20th, a melodramatic personage by the name of Edouard Regnier, whose sole credentials consisted of a picture-postcard of Hastings which the Prince Imperial had been persuaded to address to the Emperor at Wilhelmshöhe. This was good enough for Bismarck, who sent him, not to Wilhelmshöhe, but to besieged Metz where he was to find someone who could be sent to Chislehurst as a liaison between the Regent and the French Army. General Bourbaki, Mme Le Breton's brother, was chosen for the mission, but when he presented himself at Chislehurst, he found the Empress not only in total ignorance of Regnier's mission (she had at this point not even set eyes on the man and had upbraided Filon for allowing himself to be hoodwinked), but wholly unwilling to be drawn into any action that might prejudice the freedom of action of the Government of National Defence. Bismarck's next move was to use Boyer, another General shut in at Metz, to reopen negotiations. General Boyer saw him at Versailles on October 14th, and the Regent at Chislehurst on October 22nd.

The Empress understood at once that Boyer's mission represented a final chance to save the Empire's last army from the humiliation of surrender and provide a basis for a peace parley. What terms, she therefore asked, did M. de Bismarck offer? Boyer was unable to tell her. After an exchange of telegrams, she gathered that Bismarck wanted Bazaine to issue a *pronunciamento* from Metz in favour of the Imperial Dynasty, while she herself was expected to come to France and sign whatever peace terms the German government were to dictate. The Empress was entirely untempted by the suggestions of launching a coup d'état on the Spanish model and, suspecting that German terms would include demands for cession of territory, she decided to address a personal appeal against making such demands to the King of Prussia. The King replied on October 25th with a letter destined to have a decisive influence on an important Allied issue during the First World War.

'I love my country,' the King wrote from Versailles, 'as you, Madame, love yours. I understand the bitterness which fills Your Majesty's heart, and I sympathise with it sincerely. But, after having made such immense sacrifices for her defence, Germany will have to be assured that the next war will find her well prepared to repulse the attack which we may expect, as soon as France shall have recovered her strength or gained Allies.

'It is this sad consideration alone, and not the desire for the aggrandisement of my country, the territory of which is large enough, which forces me to insist on cessions of territory, which have no object other than to push back the point of departure of the French armies which, in the future, will come to attack us.'

257

And the King ended up by expressing regret that hitherto the Regent had not agreed to enter into negotiations, for by doing so, the King somewhat naïvely told her, she would have preserved France from 'the anarchy which threatens a nation whose prosperity the Emperor has successfully promoted for twenty years'.

Even before she received the King's letter, there arrived at Chislehurst on October 26th a top-secret letter from Richard Metternich, who was writing on behalf of the Government of National Defence. He explained that when the Boyer mission became known in Tours, they had asked him (Metternich did not specify who precisely 'they' were) what the Empress was likely to do. Would she and Bazaine treat with Prussia? He had replied that he was sure she would do nothing that would impede the defence of the country, that she would think of nothing but the welfare of France, and that she would not enter into any negotiations that would entail cession of territory. These replies, singularly accurate, having caused universal satisfaction at Tours, 'they' went one step further. They thought the Empress might be able to prevent the capitulation of Metz until an armistice, sponsored late in October by England and other neutrals, had been concluded. This would strengthen the hand of the Tours authorities very considerably.

'The news from Paris,' Metternich concluded his highly unneutral letter, 'is really good, and the army of the Loire is no longer a myth. Apart from the fear of seeing Metz capitulate, the situation improves daily. Who knows?'

'The capitulation of Metz,' the Empress telegraphed by return on October 26th, 'is a matter only of hours. They have no food. Hurry on the armistice.' And she assured them that it was her ardent hope to save the Empire's last army even at the cost of all hope for the dynasty. Metz, in fact, capitulated on the following day, the chance of an armistice was lost, and the army of the Rhine, like that of Châlons, went off to Germany and captivity. The Empress was informed of this final blow in a letter from General Boyer, who was still in London, on October 27th. The last chance of the Empress and Gambetta working together to save France was lost.

The Emperor, more tactfully treated at Wilhelmshöhe than his uncle had been in St. Helena, had not been actively associated with the various peace feelers. He was delighted to find that the Empress had been acting entirely in accordance with his own ideas. 'It really is extraordinary,' he wrote, 'to see how despite the great distance between us our reflections lead us to the same results.' After the surrender of Metz he told her:

'I am entirely of your opinion, and the letters which I wrote and which crossed with your last one will prove that we understand each other in our hearts and our thoughts: A thousand times better to live forgotten

258

and miserable than to owe our elevation to the abandoning of our dignity or of the interests of the country.'

Soon after the Emperor wrote this letter, the Empress arrived at Wilhelmshöhe in person. She had announced her visit to no one, not even the Emperor; she was accompanied only by Count Clary and Mme Le Breton. Husband and wife first saw each other in one of the castle's big reception rooms, the prisoner receiving her surrounded by his fellow-captives, who came forward one by one to kiss her hand. Suddenly she began to sob, and the Emperor led her gently away to his study. There they both broke down in unrestrained weeping.

III. EXILE
1871-1880

CHAPTER 1

FROM THIS moment onwards the relationship between husband and wife, between Emperor and Empress, entered upon its final phase of reconciliation. She herself confessed, in a letter she wrote to Wilhelmshöhe on their wedding anniversary on January 30th, 1871, that in 'times of happiness' she had thought the ties between them had broken. 'It needed a day of storm to show me how strong they are,' she added. He on his side stressed in a good many letters from his comfortable prison that as long as he felt sure of her and of the Prince Imperial's affection he could face whatever the future might hold. After due allowance has been made for the circumstances, this correspondence gives us much insight into the true nature of a relationship which, both in their lifetime and afterwards, has been grossly distorted. The most widely accepted version is that she often prevailed over him by making scenes until he feebly gave in. A glance at a difference of opinion between the Emperor and Empress while he was a captive throws a light on the manner in which they were accustomed to examine any given question together.

In December 1870, when the war in France was still raging, the Empress communicated to him a plan for achieving peace and the return of the dynasty. Could not she as Regent establish herself in some town in the unoccupied part of the country, summon the old *Corps Legislatif* to her side, enter into peace negotiations, and then submit the peace treaty to the country in a plebiscite? The Prussians would be certain to offer more favourable peace terms to the Empire than to the revolutionary Republic; the terrible suffering of Paris and the country would be brought to an end; was it not her duty to intervene constructively at this moment of agony? The Emperor, writing back on December 21st, 1870, had little difficulty in demolishing this dream.

'I regret to say,' he began, 'that I completely disapprove of the ideas in your letter.' With ruthless briskness he showed her the impracticability of her plan: four French policemen would be enough to arrest her and send her back to England. The Senators and Deputies would not, or could not, respond to her summons: and anyway, were they the best people for the present crisis? 'For new circumstances,' he pointed out, 'you need new men, yet elections at the present moment are unthinkable.' And if the King of Prussia would really offer better terms to the Empire than to the Republic, then let him show this by disclosing his terms to the Government of National Defence. 'The peace cannot be advantageous to France and is bound to be more or less disastrous,' he stressed. 'One part of France is in the hands of the Prussians and the other in those of energetic demagogues'; the latter would prevent the country from responding to the Regent's appeal. 'Our duty is to remain in obscurity and allow events to take their course. . . . After the role which we have played in Europe, all our actions must bear the stamp of dignity and grandeur in accordance with the position we have held. . . .' And in a postscript he finally dealt with her idea of a plebiscite on the peace terms:

> 'To submit the treaty of peace to the direct vote of the country, to its Yes or No, would amount to hiding behind the inevitable response of the country, which would accept with its eyes closed a question submitted to it in an abstract form: peace or war.'

The consequences of their fall from power were immediately felt in various parts of the Continent. Victor Emmanuel took advantage of the French defeat and occupied Rome on September 20th. The Pope, deprived of the protection of French troops, became the prisoner in the Vatican seventeen days after the Emperor of the French had became the prisoner of Wilhelmshöhe. Russia immediately denounced the Black Sea clauses of the Treaty of Paris, and the Emperor wrote wistfully to Chislehurst that Gorchakov's note to this effect 'has brought *The Times* over to our side'.

The most important European consequence, however, of the disappearance of the Second Bonapartist Empire was that it made possible the foundation of the Second German *Reich*. The King of Prussia, reluctantly accepting the Imperial Crown from the other German Sovereigns, was proclaimed German Emperor in the Hall of Mirrors at Versailles on January 18th, 1871. Europe, in the words of an English diplomat, exchanged a mistress for a master. The moment, as indeed the setting, was ill-chosen, for Paris was still under siege. Although the Germans by that date had defeated the various armies which Gambetta and his friends at Tours had organised with such astonishing energy, peace still seemed far from certain. Thus the Germany which dominated Europe until 1945 came into existence to the accompaniment of Prussian guns spitting death and destruction into the city which until then had been the capital of Europe. 'Not one single voice,' wrote the Austrian Ambassador in London, Apponyi, to Lady Salisbury, 'will be lifted to protest against these unspeakable proceedings. . . . We are back in the time of the *Faustrecht*—the boldest and strongest is always right. As for the neutrals, they are cowards, ourselves most of all. Nobody will say a word; the world will bow its head before Bismarck Pasha and his Sultan.'

Apprehensions that Prussian victory and German unity would lead Europe into what Florence Nightingale described as 'the abyss called Military Despotism', were not confined to French patriots like the Empress and Gambetta, or to officially neutral Europeans. On the German side, one man, though acutely interested in a victorious outcome of the struggle for his fatherland, viewed the continuance of the war after Sedan with the gravest misgivings. This was Crown Prince Frederick of Prussia. ' The longer the war lasts,' he wrote at Versailles on the last day of 1870,

' the better it will be for the French and the worse for us. . . . We are no longer regarded as the innocents who have been attacked, but rather as the arrogant victors. We are considered capable of every evil, distrust of us increases more and more. That is not the result of this war alone— it is the theory of blood and iron, invented and acted upon by Bismarck, which has brought us to this pitch. He has made us great and powerful, but he has robbed us of our friends, of the sympathies of the world, and of our conscience. . . . How hard will it be to combat the worship of brute force and outward success ! '

As a Corps Commander, the Crown Prince had, both in 1866 and 1870, made important contributions to the success of German arms in the field, but as the war continued he underwent a crisis of conscience similar to that suffered by later German military Commanders under a different political régime. It was greatly to the credit of this Hohenzollern Prince that he should let these secret doubts take root in his mind at a moment of great military success, that he should have understood the tragedy of victory even before it had become final.

So, in Rome, in Russia, and in the heart of Europe, the fall of the Bonapartist Empire wrought immediate changes for the worse, as with Napoleon and Eugénie two rulers who were also good Europeans disappeared from the centre of power. Peace, when it finally came in February, confirmed the Empress's belief that the dynasty would not be able to accept Bismarck's terms and remain on the throne. The Germans insisted on the cession of Alsace and Northern Lorraine, including Metz, an indemnity of five thousand million francs, occupation of parts of France until it was paid in full, and, mainly because the old Kaiser wanted to repeat the triumphs of 1814, a victor's entry into Paris. It had fallen to Thiers to accept these terms from Bismarck, because on January 28th, 1871 (the day on which the Palace of Saint-Cloud was burnt down just before the end of the bombardment), an armistice had at last been agreed to by the two belligerents. France was enabled to elect a new National Assembly. The elections secured an overwhelming victory for the Orleanist and Legitimist factions, and Thiers himself was elected in no less than twenty-six constituencies. This made him the obvious choice as head of the new government, causing Gambetta and the minority party of war to the last to resign, and finally produced the man who could grant Bismarck his concessions. ' After signing a peace like that,' said Napoleon at Wilhelmshöhe to Count Monts, his chivalrous jailer, ' I would not have remained in power for a week.'

The treaty of peace between France and Germany, known as the Peace of Frankfurt, was finally signed on May 10th. Before that date, Europe witnessed another effect of the void left by the disappearance of the Bona-partist Empire. The people of Paris, emerging from the then novel ex-perience of indiscriminate bombardment, rose against the Republican authorities at Versailles, and the short reign of terror by the Paris *Com-mune* began. The Hôtel de Ville and the Tuileries were set on fire as the government troops, led by General de Galliffet, moved in on the *com-munards* from Versailles, and only blackened ruins remained of these two monuments of the revolutionary and Royal history of France. Galliffet showed the utmost ferocity and ruthlessness in suppressing the Commune. He was acting on orders issued by Thiers, who, unlike the Empress-Regent on September 4th, had no hesitation in using the army against the revolutionary mob.

At Chislehurst, the Empress was endeavouring to accustom herself to the novel experience of being unemployed. Since the fall of Metz she had remained outside all negotiations, but a number of friends managed to reach Camden Place with news, and others succeeded in getting letters through to her. As the winter went on, Mlle de Larminat, the Empress's youngest reader, joined Mme Le Breton as lady-in-waiting; the Duke of Bassano took charge of the tiny household, the Aguados moved into a house across Chislehurst Common, her beloved friend, Anna Murat, Duchess of Mouchy, stayed at Camden Place itself while the Duke had gone back to France to fight. The Prince and Princess of Wales, the Tecks, and Prince Arthur of Connaught paid subdued but well-intentioned visits to Chislehurst. 'What particularly struck me,' Prince Arthur wrote to Queen Victoria afterwards:

'was the Empress's utter absence of bitterness against those who had so shamefully cast her out. . . .'

Finally, at the end of November, the Queen herself called informally at Chislehurst, and, on December 5th, the Empress went to Windsor to return the call. Writing to Queen Augusta of Prussia on December 7th, 1870, in another attempt to improve feeling in the victor-country, Queen Victoria commented:

'The Empress bears her sad fate with the greatest dignity. Not one word of complaint or bitterness is ever heard from her, and she accuses no one. . . . She is looking miserable and infinitely sad, but is still very beautiful and her whole attitude so simple and moving. . . .'

Although memories of 1855 kept breaking through the December gloom of 1870, these reunions were more than merely sentimental occasions. Victoria and Eugénie had suffered and lost much since those days of promise and splendour, but each found in the other much to like and admire—strength of character, a certain ingrained toughness and power of endurance.

Though the Empress thus was living, even before the Emperor's return from captivity, in an atmosphere of friendship and respect, we cannot doubt that in the first six months or so of her stay in England her inner mood was one of black melancholy. What was to become of her son? Filon was there to resume his lessons, and the Prince's old class-mate, Louis Conneau, had arrived from France, as had Tristan Lambert, his boisterous playfellow from Saint-Cloud. 'I reorganised the Prince's studies as best I could,' wrote Filon, 'his French, the dead languages, history . . . but how could he take an interest in the lessons or in the distractions London offered, while Paris was burning?' His recent experiences in the war had left their trace, and some of the visitors to Camden Place were slightly shocked when he spoke with a queer sense of pride of the French army. 'His presence with the army has rather spoilt him,' wrote Lt. Col. Elphinstone, Prince Arthur's equerry, to Queen Victoria, 'and made him very conceited.' It is not difficult to understand that he felt the need for a defensive armour in the presence of British officers. Elphinstone found him 'curiously inquisitive' and Lord Sydney, as Lord Lieutenant of Kent a frequent caller at Camden Place, 'common-looking, but very intelligent'. The Empress confided to Sydney that, until the Emperor returned, she did not want the Prince to go about too much, but that 'it would soon be very dull for him here'. Would a boy of his high spirits ever be happy in England? The Empress looked out through the windows of the old house into the damp, cold, raw winter outside. The rain-soaked park looked forbidding and dead. 'Don't you think we are like fishes in an aquarium?' she asked.

The Emperor returned from captivity with the spring. He landed at Dover in the early afternoon of March 20th, 1871, and as he painfully made his way down the gangway, looking wan and ill, a tremendous cheer broke from the crowds on the quay, waving their hats and sticks in the air and bombarding him with flowers. A public British voice, however, struck a note of primness. 'What,' asked *The Times* next day,

'are we to think and what will the German people think and what will the French people think, of all this effusive and unqualified admiration? What, indeed, will Louis Napoleon think of it, when the quietude of Chislehurst enables him to review the events of the day?'

For anyone present at Dover that day it was not difficult to fathom what the Emperor thought. When the first cheers went up he stopped half-way down the gangway and glanced at the multitudes in momentary amazement. Then he waved to them, tears running down his cheeks. On the quay, a man approached him, hat in hand, and said he had been Mayor of Dover in 1855. The Emperor stammered that he remembered; the former Mayor conveyed that he was on the Borough Council still, and that he welcomed the Emperor also in the name of his colleagues. The Emperor summoned his professional manner; what, he asked courteously, was Mr.

Worsfold's position on the Council now? 'I am the Borough Coroner, Sire,' came the reply.

Policemen cleared a path for him, and presently the Emperor stood before the Empress and his son. The party was quickly hustled into the Lord Warden Hotel, and soon afterwards they walked along the narrow covered passage to the railway station. A further ordeal awaited them, for down the passage strode members of the Orleans family about to embark for France where the recent elections had gone so strongly in their favour. Who should give way? Gracefully, the Empress stepped aside and made a curtsy; the Emperor and the young Prince, drawing to her side, lifted their hats and bowed. The junior branch of the Bourbons nodded, bowed, smiled and were on their way, while the more recent victims of the French revolutionary tradition went to catch their train to Chislehurst.

CHAPTER 2

THE EMPEROR'S final exile in England lasted less than two years. With uncomplaining dignity, he fitted himself into life at Camden Place, a house of modest proportions, but hardly the creeper-covered, bow-windowed cottage of his imagination. His presence bestowed an odd, but welcome distinction on the rural neighbourhood. The Empress organised as various a life of social and intellectual intercourse as circumstances permitted. Men of science and literature predominated among the regular guests, the press was represented by Algernon Borthwick of the *Morning Post*, and politics by a sprinkling of M.P.s from both sides of the House. There was a group of friends from the old pre-Imperial days—Lord Malmesbury, who had known the Emperor as a young man in Rome and noted that he, once one of Europe's most athletic and accomplished horsemen, was now hardly able to drive out in a carriage. And there were many other visitors whose friendship for the man had remained untouched by the poison of politics and the events of the intervening decades. Political attacks on the Empire, the slandering and vilification of their persons and their circle, were now in full flood in France, but the Emperor insisted from the beginning that no replies, no counter-accusations or any other recrimination should ever come from them. He resumed his work, spending most of his days in his study, smoking innumerable cigarettes, studying reports, reading, sifting, analysing. At his side was Eugène Rouher, his most powerful Minister in the years between Sadowa and the advent of the liberal Empire.

The Empress's principal source of information in France was Jurien de La Gravière, with whom she maintained a regular correspondence. The Admiral, now a man of sixty, told her as early as May 1871 that opinion in the military and naval circles in which he mainly moved had wheeled round to a complete vindication of the Emperor's personal conduct during hostilities. There remained, however, what Jurien called the 'responsibility for a badly prepared and badly conducted war'.

In pooling the information that reached them from France, the Emperor and Empress became aware of a gradual reaction in their favour. The impression was confirmed elsewhere. 'If the Napoleonic party succeeded in calling a plebiscite,' wrote the mysterious C. de B., the Paris correspondent of the London Rothschilds, to his employers on September 9th, 1871, 'it would obtain between 5,000,000 and 6,000,000 votes. This is only 1,500,000 fewer than the Emperor received in his tremendously successful plebiscite of May 1870 when, just before the war with Germany, he wanted to make contact with his people and test their feelings towards him.' The Rothschild correspondent had throughout the Empire been an Orleanist, which gives additional interest to his reports after 1870. 'In the Paris salons,' he wrote, 'you can well imagine that the question of a Bonapartist restoration is the one subject of conversation'. Jurien asked the Empress whether she had the perseverance to give herself entirely to the 'great task' of her son's education. He continued:

'That you should succeed in forming the Prince for whom France is waiting and whose hand could sustain our crumbling century is the wish of the man who loves you most and appreciates you best.'

What was the Prince's education? Not long after his arrival, the Emperor decided to widen the range of his son's and young Conneau's studies by sending them up to King's College in London. But Filon, who had not been consulted, thought that all the Prince reaped from these daily expeditions was the novel experience of being about, unrecognised, in the streets of London—'to stare without being stared at, to make his way into a café and order an ice, to be a spectator and not a spectacle'. Academically, he learnt little at King's College.

He was growing up. *The Times*, not invariably the most friendly commentator on the Imperial family, wrote that this formerly 'slight and somewhat effeminate lad' had become 'a strong, healthy, well-conditioned youth, an excellent horseman, and in all respects as ruddy and hardy as the majority of English boys of his age'. Mr. Gladstone, who encountered him at Chislehurst railway station late in 1871—the Prime Minister had only just paid his first visit to Camden Place—was captivated by his charm. He had begun the conversation on a distant and slightly pompous note, but as the Prince replied in his gay and ingenuous way, Gladstone, says Filon, 'gradually relaxed and softened, and on parting looked down on the Imperial boy with a sort of fatherly interest mingled with pity'. Filon felt, rightly or wrongly, that the Prime Minister at Camden 'was perhaps not quite at ease with regard to the causes of the misfortunes of France and the disasters to the Napoleonic dynasty', but another cause for his stiffness while in the house may well have been due to his overhearing Prince Louis Lucien Bonaparte say in an aside to the Empress: 'I never knew that an English Liberal could be a gentleman.'

The Empress certainly did not believe that the Prince's education would be furthered by nagging and meddling. 'If my son,' she once said, 'could learn how to be bored he will have achieved something of which almost all Frenchmen are incapable. It should be extremely useful to him.' 'Let his life be free and honourable,' she said on another occasion. 'If he has to undergo the rigours of exile, let him be spared all financial embarrassment, so painful for one who bears his name.'

The Empress, unlike her mother and her husband, understood the value of money. Despite her professional obligation as a leader of fashion and her widespread charitable work, she had always been a model of thrift: unlike the Emperor, who gave money to the first needy person appealing to him, she had mastered what might be called the economics of generosity. In exile, the financial management of the household was in her capable hands. She was fond of stressing that she had been taught the importance of poverty by her father in early childhood. Her attitude to money was revealingly demonstrated in 1872 when Prince Pierre Bonaparte, the head of the Lucien branch and something of a liability to the Empire before 1870, demanded from the Emperor a continuance of his allowance from the civil list. Gently the Emperor replied that this was no longer possible, whereupon Prince Pierre threatened that he and his wife would open a shop in Bond Street. Surely this would shame Chislehurst into paying up? Not at all, replied the Empress: 'If one has no money, honest work is much more commendable than expedients.' And presently London society was able to buy its handkerchiefs from Princess Pierre, the wronged woman serving behind the counter in person. The business, not surprisingly, flourished, but some people whispered: 'How mean of them—how heartless of the Empress!' Undeterred, she planned their budget narrowly and conscientiously for her husband's comfort, for her son's unembarrassed future. She began quietly to sell some of her personal jewellery which Princess Metternich had had deposited, through a minor Austrian diplomat, at the Bank of England. The Emperor, through his old friend Arese, sold his Italian estates and received a capital sum which the Empress invested.

The Emperor gave much of his time to initiating the Prince into the complexities of French party politics, often having him in the room when he was working with Rouher and others on the problems of the day. At dinner one evening, a little incident occurred that shows that the Prince was learning something of the paradox of exclusive political allegiances. A visitor from Paris, Mme de Sancy de Parabère, was holding forth on how the great political changes had caused great changes in manners. She had found in Paris the most violent language, the most vitriolic discussions and debates going on in houses once famous for their well-conducted and civilised conversation. 'Nowadays,' someone concurred, 'when ten people are assembled together, you have at least five different opinions.' The Emperor glanced languidly round the table: 'Exactly,' he remarked, 'look at us here.' This provoked scandalised cries of protest, but he merely smiled his smile of benevolent malice and turned to the Empress: 'You, for example, have always been a Legitimist,' he said, 'a fanatical partisan of the Count de Chambord—you admire his character and even his proclamations.' The Empress, smilingly, denied nothing. 'And look at Mme Le Breton,' continued the great student of political opinion, 'entirely Orleanist! And you, Conneau,' he went on, turning to the companion of his Italian adventures and the prison of Ham, 'I know you: you are a Communist. You always have the most subversive ideas, you are an enemy

271

of society. I have seen you at work among the secret societies in Florence. You are a Carbonaro!'

And here he went into a slight digression about the legend of his own membership in the gruesome fraternity that had sent Orsini to assassinate him. Amusedly he told them how people had invented the melodramatic boulevard story of his visit to Orsini's cell on the eve of the execution to help the condemned man to escape, and that he had desisted only because of the man's arrogance. 'I was always opposed to the death penalty,' he added, 'but that man had to die for simple reasons of common law.' He had always known, he went on, of the other myth spread about him—that because of the early peace after Solferino and his refusal to give Rome to the Italians he, as the former Carbonaro, had lived under constant threats of new assassinations. Had he ever been a Carbonaro? Stuff and nonsense! It had been not he, but his elder brother, then known as Prince Louis Napoleon, who up to his early death in 1831 had been an initiate of that secret society. After his brother's death, he himself had come to be called Louis Napoleon; confusion was complete, and the two brothers' personalities were fused into one. 'So much for the fable of my membership of the Carbonari,' concluded the Emperor.

His son had listened to it all in complete absorption. 'But, Papa,' he burst out at the end, 'if Mama is a Legitimist, Mme Le Breton Orleanist, and Dr. Conneau a Republican, where are the Imperialists among us here?'

Through heavy eyelids the Emperor gazed at his son in silence. Then he put a hand on the boy's blond head and said:

'The Imperialists—that's you.'

This was the aspect of things which the Empress stressed least in her conversations with the boy, for she felt that he had far to go before becoming, in Jurien's words, the Prince for whom France was waiting. The time was not yet ripe, and neither was he. News from France showed a widening of the conflict between Thiers and the Monarchist majority in the Assembly. The country's new leader intended, whatever happened, to cling to power: 'Politics,' he said to the Duc d'Aumale, 'mean only one thing, the art of jockeying oneself into power, and then remaining in the saddle.' On this principle he gradually abandoned the Monarchists who had raised him to Presidential power and allied himself more and more with the Republicans who in the many by-elections of July 1871 had won a striking victory. Chambord, meanwhile, despite the disastrous effect of his manifestos, felt no doubts at all about his mission. To a visitor from France, who spoke to him of the country's grave sickness, of its inclination to entrust its cure to the first available quack, he replied: 'You are seeking a solution for the present crisis? But what solution, my dear sir? I am the solution.' Between Thiers' Republic and Chambord's return to the ancien régime many minds perceived an opportunity for Napoleon IV. But for the present the country wanted tranquillity and peace, at least until the war indemnity was paid and the last German soldier had left the soil of France.

The Empress continued to give help where help was needed, even if it meant braving the Prussian lion in his den. Friends reported that Count de Bizemont, once a frequent guest at Compiègne and a very gallant officer afterwards, had been sentenced by a German Court at Melun to fifteen years in a fortress. Through Princess Marie of Baden, the Empress appealed to Kaiser William I. 'I am delighted to tell you,' the old gentleman wrote to Princess Marie on March 3rd, 1872, 'that M. de Bizemont has been released. That he was given fifteen years shows that his offence was a grave one, and I could never have obtained his pardon had he been one of my own subjects. I hope this explanation will find favour in the Empress's eyes, for whom I was only too happy to do this, for I remain under her charm before, during and afterwards!' And the old Kaiser underlined his gay *avant, pendant et après*. 'Although I realise,' he went on, 'that she does not like Prussia—with my exception, I am vain enough to hope —I hope that this little act will please her.' The Empress conveyed a last word to him through Princess Marie:

'He is ill-informed about my feelings towards his country. I have never felt either prejudice or antipathy towards any country then or now. My feelings were always subordinate to the interests of France. I trust that this manner of feeling will assure me respect, if not happiness.'

It was during the summer of 1872 that his parents decided on a great change in the Prince Imperial's life. The Emperor had discussed the boy's military education with an old English friend, Col. Manby of the Gunners, who recommended sending him to the Royal Military Academy, Woolwich. In consequence, General Sir Lintorn Simmons, Governor of Woolwich, presented himself at Camden Place. After a lengthy talk with the Emperor and Empress it was decided that the Prince should prepare himself for the entrance examination and thereafter train for the artillery, the traditional service of the Bonapartes. Louis Conneau was to do the same. The two boys worked extremely hard that summer, and a master from Harrow was called in to coach them in mathematics. They passed their examination in November, and one afternoon later in the month the Prince had the strange experience of putting on the uniform of an officer cadet in the British Army. He, Conneau and Filon went to live in a small house near 'the Shop'.

The Prince Imperial quickly sensed the difference between his position and that of his new class-fellows. 'They have all had three years' mathematics, and I have hardly had one,' he complained to Filon after a few days. Urged on by him, Filon went to see Sir Lintorn, who replied there had been at Woolwich plenty of precedents of Princes passing through without taking too much trouble. They had been taking classes and so on —as Princes. Filon objected that in this the Prince Imperial would never find satisfaction: he wanted to take his work, his career, more literally, more seriously. Sir Lintorn understood, and henceforth looked on the new cadet with new respect. The Governor soon became a regular visitor at

Camden Place, and the Empress as well as the Prince found no stauncher or sturdier friend in the British Army than this distinguished officer whose military career, as we saw, began in the trenches outside Sebastopol when England and France had been allies.[1]

Sending him to Woolwich was the last service the Emperor was able to render his son. His old bladder complaint, still unattended except for some rather casual attempts to soften the symptoms by hot sea-water baths, became worse in November 1872. Yet, by this date, he was feeling with greater confidence that an early return to France, with himself leading his followers on horse-back, promised success. So after a holiday at Cowes he took a mild amount of exercises on a wooden horse which the Empress had commissioned a French sculptor to make from fruit-tree wood. Onto this delicately carved model he painfully climbed each day. Prince Napoleon visited Chislehurst that autumn and persuaded the Emperor to drive over to Woolwich in a carriage. It was his first outing for a long time, and on the following day he developed a high temperature with violent pains. Knowing that his entourage were preparing for his restoration in the following March, he told them: 'My health will never stand in the way. I will do what it is my duty to do.' At last he promised to bow to medical advice.

The doctors examined him in December. They were the Queen's physician Sir William Gull and Sir Henry Thompson, the leading specialist in diseases of the bladder. Both advised an immediate operation; the Emperor consented. Did he really believe in the possibility of success, that his return to France was near? His consent is some indication that he was hopeful. He submitted to a series of operations with the utmost fortitude. After the first, Sir Henry wrote a not unoptimistic account to the Prince of Wales on January 2nd, but two days later he confessed himself to be 'very anxious'. Queen Victoria became acutely alarmed. She had seen the Emperor three times since his arrival from Wilhelmshöhe, and, re-awakened by personal contact, her old tenderness for him had proved stronger than Albert's faded strictures. Like the Prince of Wales, she sent daily telegrams enquiring after the Emperor's health. 'I am so anxious to hear,' wired the Prince of Wales to the Empress, 'how His Majesty is today. My thoughts and sympathy are with you, dear Madame.' Similar enquiries came from members of the British Royal Family and the Sovereigns of Europe.

The Empress was at first able to telegraph back that there was hope, finally that he had, during the night of January 8th, slept well. Another operation was planned to take place at midday on the 9th. The Empress saw him briefly in the morning and was told it was safe for her to drive over to Woolwich and see her son, as planned. The Emperor, his mind dimmed by chloral, dozed in his bed; Dr. Conneau sat at his side. Suddenly he murmured a few words. 'We weren't cowards at Sedan, were we, Conneau?' was what his old friend heard. Thompson looked in, and

[1] See page 87.

274

realised that a crisis was developing; the Empress, about to drive off, was recalled. She took off her hat and hastened to his bedside; as she entered she heard Thompson send for Father Goddard, of the Roman Catholic parish church. The priest, escorting the Empress gently away, remained alone with the dying man, and at a quarter to eleven on Thursday morning, January 9th, 1873, Napoleon III, last Emperor of the French, was released from his sufferings and from his hopes. The Empress, in tears, knelt at his bedside and prayed, and presently there could be heard in the room the strong, young voice of the Prince Imperial reciting the *Pater Noster*. He had rushed over from Woolwich, but had not reached the sickroom in time.

'I will never forget,' wrote Queen Victoria to the Empress, from Osborne,

> 'the constant kindness of the Emperor when I had the pleasure of seeing him; and the days we passed together in England and France will never fade from my heart. Your Majesty has the whole country's sympathy, for the dear Emperor was much loved here. I wish I were near London to be able to go myself to offer you the expression of my most earnest sympathy. . . . Accept once again all my loving sympathy and believe me, *Madame et chère Soeur*, ever Your Imperial Majesty's affectionate Sister,
> Victoria R.'

And in her Journal the Queen wrote:

> 'Had a great regard for the Emperor, who was so amiable and kind, and had borne his terrible misfortunes with such meekness, dignity and patience. He had been such a faithful ally of England . . . too tragic and sad.'

Not a word of condemnation now! The Queen's vocabulary contained few terms of higher praise than 'faithful ally'. Had the Emperor known of this proud epitaph, he would have smiled a little ironically, but he would have smiled. Before his death he had been granted the consolation of knowing that since the German victory people in England understood much better what his reign had signified. Not long before the end there had been the day when the Empress and he heard a great commotion going on outside Camden, shouts, bands, a great and boisterous noise, and they had walked down to the gates to investigate. They found the employees of the Greenwich Board of Works having their annual outing. As the Imperial family appeared, someone stepped forth from the crowds and made a speech—saying that they hoped the clouds at present hanging over France would soon disperse, that there would be an Imperial Restoration soon, and that Anglo-French relations would get back to those bonds of friendship on which the Emperor had always insisted. The Emperor was deeply touched and was just able to say that he had always been a good

friend of England. This simple truth produced a most astonishing reaction:
'We know you have!' They all shouted for minutes on end, 'You have,
you have, you have!' They all came up and shook the Emperor, Empress
and Prince Imperial by the hand, and the cheering rang in their ears as
they walked back slowly to the house.

In his last months the Emperor had worked further on a scheme that
had occupied his thoughts since 1863: the Council of Europe, an international body that would meet regularly and create a code of public
law to regulate relations between the great powers. A few weeks before
his death, he met again the man, Thornton Hunt, with whom he had
first discussed this vision at the Tuileries and Compiègne during the
previous decade. 'The day will come,' wrote Mr. Hunt after his wintry
talks at Camden Place, 'when the world will rejoice at the inauguration of
that institution in which civilisation is still wanting . . . the International Council; and when that time arrives, if memory still exists among
men, mankind will recognise that Napoleon III, the exile of Chislehurst,
was the founder of this court of legislation and of judicial appeal for
nations.'

So among the lengthening shadows of Chislehurst he must have felt that
the two pilot lights of his policy as a European, friendship with England
and the creation of a supra-national body for the defining and safeguarding of public law, would still shine after he was gone, that he had
not striven after these ideals wholly in vain. In the second decade of his
reign he had been defeated by two statesmen who were his superiors in
single-mindedness and ruthlessness, Cavour and Bismarck, as he was also
defeated by his own inner weakness and illness which, in the field of
foreign policy especially, prevented him from giving his country the leadership it so urgently required in the age of nascent Italian and German
nationalism. There, he fell below the level of the Empress's unhesitating
clear-sightedness and resolution, and acquired, not without justification, the
reputation of an ambiguous intriguer. But in the field of internal policy, in
his great and bold experiment of transforming an autocratic into a representative and responsible government, he never wavered and his Empire came
closer to success than any other régime between the Restoration and the
advent of General de Gaulle.

Following so soon upon the terror of the Commune and the experience
of the occupation, the Emperor's death did much to soften and assuage
anger that was strongly felt by Frenchmen at the inexplicable swiftness
of the Empire's collapse. Jurien, who shortly before it occurred had written
to Chislehurst that 'the Bonapartist formula was France's last life-belt',
wrote to the Empress before the Emperor's funeral:

'May God sustain your forces, may He protect and keep you, may He
give you the courage to live for your son, for France. France will realise
what she has lost. The day of justice has arrived: it always arrives after
death.'

The Emperor's funeral at Chislehurst was attended by members of Europe's reigning families, by the vanished Empire's military and political leaders, and by a large deputation of Parisian workmen holding aloft the tricolour banner. Crowds from all over Britain made the pilgrimage to Chislehurst and lined the route to the little church of St. Mary where the Emperor was laid to rest. He was buried in the uniform of a French General and among the decorations he wore was a personal Order bestowed by the Kings of Sweden upon those who had won distinction on the field of valour.

CHAPTER 3

'WHEN LIFE produces grief and trouble,' the Empress wrote to Doña Manuela early in February 1873, 'then we must drink all the more deeply from the springs of duty to find the courage to carry on. Sorrow might have beaten me down, but perplexing irritations soon roused me from momentary sleep. . . .' Prince Plon-Plon had provided the irritations immediately after the funeral. She had offered him reconciliation and co-operation for the sake of the future of Bonapartism. The Republican Prince made his acceptance dependent on two conditions—his recognition as the sole leader of the Imperialist Party and the handing over of the Prince Imperial 'to his sole care and surveillance'. She gasped with horror at the second demand, and the peace negotiations were at an end.

Even if Prince Napoleon had not represented a political tendency which she distrusted, revolutionary Radicalism, she would never have consented to her son being forced to undergo an exclusively political education before his character had been completely formed. Not that there was any love lost between Prince Napoleon and the Prince Imperial, for the older man had never overcome his jealous hatred of the Imperial heir, while the boy had not forgotten his uncle's rough and evil conduct in the old days. Thwarted once again in his desire to become the first representative of Bonapartism, Prince Napoleon invented new lies about the Empress for consumption in France. He now alleged that the Empress, with the help of Rouher and Franceschini Pietri, had suppressed the Emperor's latest will in favour of that of April 1865, which appointed her Regent until the Prince Imperial's majority. Stories of mysterious second wills are always welcome to what the Emperor called the boulevard imagination, and journalists and other gossips made use of the latest slander with much glee. The Empress took no notice, but the affair showed that the breach between the two branches of the Bonapartes remained unhealed.

Although one or two people in her entourage tried to dissuade her, the Empress decided to let her son continue at Woolwich. There, for the next two years, the Prince worked hard, did well in examinations and was moderately happy. He, Conneau and Filon continued to live in their little house on Woolwich Common, and the Prince was allowed his own servants. He also continued his private tutorials with Filon in history and literature at the expense, Filon tells us slightly guiltily, of outdoor games such as cricket and football ('not that the Prince despised them, but, not having taken to them early enough, he had no liking for showing himself,

278

when it could be avoided, inferior to his colleagues'). The tutor was astonished at the boy's growing knowledge, keen judgment, his irrepressible interest in the questions of the day. He read all the newspapers, French and English, friendly and hostile, and then bombarded his tutor with questions. 'Memorable evenings,' writes Filon, 'when I watched this intellectual expansion for which I had waited so long, and that I had vainly tried to hasten with all my wishes and all my efforts! People sometimes say to me: "You formed the Prince." That praise I can in no way accept. I did not form the Prince. No one formed him. The Prince formed himself.'

The difficulty was that Bonapartism became, after the Emperor's death, a party issue, one among many, and this involved the Imperialists, still led by Rouher, in various political manoeuvres which often filled both the Empress and the Prince with grave misgivings. While Thiers was Chief of the Executive and moved, as we saw, towards the Republican Left, the Prince's interest in the parliamentary game was small. Rouher, who usually shepherded his band of Imperialist deputies into voting with the two Legitimist parties of the Assembly—in other words the conservative majority—was, since the Emperor's death, able to act on his own. His frequent visits to Chislehurst were made to report rather than to discuss. In May 1873, the majority overthrew Thiers and elected, as his successor, Marshal MacMahon, who formed his first government with Duke Albert de Broglie, grandson of Mme de Staël and erstwhile admirer of the Empress in Madrid, as Prime Minister. This was generally understood as a prelude to a Restoration of the Bourbons, especially after the Comte de Paris had paid a much publicised visit to Frohsdorf, Chambord's official residence near Vienna, and made the official submission of his branch of the family to Henry V. In return the childless Chambord was expected to adopt the descendant of Louis Philippe (and Philippe Égalité) as his dauphin. The gesture remained ineffective, turning out to have sealed not a marriage of convenience, but a suicide pact, the Mayerling of French Royalism. The real issue lay between Empire and Republic, between Napoleon IV and Gambetta. When the armistice with Prussia was signed and his hopes of war to the last were disappointed, Gambetta left France, but he had now returned to become the most considerable figure among the Republican minority at Versailles.

Rouher urged that the Prince's official coming of age, his eighteenth birthday, on March 16th, 1874, should be celebrated in a great public ceremony of Bonapartist solidarity. Although neither the Empress nor the Prince himself were particularly anxious to interrupt his education for this purpose, they yielded in the end to Rouher's insistence and invitations were sent out. Not the most devoted Imperialist could have foreseen how reverberatingly successful the celebration would be. Adherents from all parts of France travelled to England in what was probably the biggest flotilla of small ships to sail across the Channel before 1940. 'Majority of the Prince Imperial,' announced giant red, white and blue posters everywhere. The day seemed to be practically a national event and even the music-halls added special turns with the playing of *Partant pour la Syrie* as their climax. Chislehurst itself that week-end (March 16th was a Monday) reminded people of a Paris suburb on holiday, and the customary restraint of an English Sunday was cast aside by the local people, who greeted this extraordinary invasion with the warmest hospitality.

On the day itself, there was a brief morning service at the little Catholic church where the Emperor's sarcophagus stood and to which only a small number of the guests could be admitted. Father Goddard gave an impassioned oration in French which, horribly enough, was loudly applauded. Then the Prince led his mother over to Camden Place, where a huge marquee, packed with delegates from the departments and districts of France, had been erected in the park. On the platform sat former Ministers and officials of the Empire, only serving soldiers having been forbidden to attend. Looking slightly pale, slightly nervous, the Prince escorted the Empress to her seat, and presently he stood before his audience, crumpling a few sheets of notes in his hands. On behalf of the delegates the old Duke of Padua offered him their congratulations, and then the Prince, looking tall, young and erect beside the bent figure of the Duke, began his speech. His voice rang out strong and clear, and he did not once look at his notes:

'Your presence around me proves to what extent France is uneasy about her future destiny. Order is safe under the sword of the Duke of Magenta, that old comrade of my father's glories and misfortunes. . . . But order in material things is not security. The future remains unknown. . . .

Will France, if she is openly consulted, look towards the son of Napoleon III? The thought gives me, not pride, but distrust of my strength. The Emperor taught me how heavy is the burden of sovereign authority, and how essential are faith in oneself and the sense of duty to carry out so lofty a mission. Here, faith will make up for what youth lacks. United to my mother by the most tender and grateful affection, I shall labour without pause to outstrip the march of years. If, when the time comes, another system of government attracts the votes of the greatest number, I shall bow with respect before the decision of the country. If, for the eighth time, the name of Napoleon should come out of the people's ballot boxes, I am ready to accept the responsibility that the nation's suffrage would lay upon me. . . .'

Something about the Prince Imperial's first bow to history since his father's death still arrests the attention. Filon says that the fire and sincerity in the Prince's voice when he spoke of his father and mother were unmistakable; when he spoke of the plebiscite his tone and voice 'assumed the vigour of an oath'. Nobody present doubted his sincerity, his longing to restore France's greatness, his deep love of the country, heightened and not dimmed by exile. It all came as a great surprise to those present who since the end of the Empire had been reading and hearing stories about 'Napoleon 3½', about his feebleness, his alleged cowardice, about his being kept at Woolwich by influence and fraud. 'Would anyone have thought it possible?' they whispered to each other when he had finished, and *The Times* wrote next day:

'Napoleon IV is holding in his hands the Second Empire, and only awaiting an opportunity to turn it into a Third. The Empire [went on the adaptable Thunderer] was overthrown by the Prussians and Republicans, but its organisation remains intact. In Paris, they talk more than ever of the Empire and the Prince Imperial. They return unceasingly to the same topic, as if there were no other political prospect—as if, beyond that, there are only darkness and chaos.'

The Empress's private correspondence from France confirmed the accuracy of *The Times* both as regards political opinion and the feeling for the Prince. Jurien had been to Chislehurst in January 1874 and returned in July. 'The Prince,' he wrote after his first visit,

'has impressed me very much. I think he is born to inspire real affection and sincere devotion. I loved him already because of you, but now I begin to love him for himself.'

In the same letter, he spoke of the feeling in the country:

'I have been to Toulon, that Red city, and found that your memory continues to be honoured there. Public opinion has changed, the uncertainty has turned many minds back to a régime from which the present government are daily compelled to borrow the formula.'

The Rothschilds' man in Paris, C. de B., encountered Bonapartism in unexpected places:

'Yesterday [he wrote to New Court on June 27th, 1874], I was driven to the Bois de Boulogne by a talkative cabby. He was complaining about the lack of a real government and the instability of things in general, and added that the best thing would be to return to the Empire.'

And C. de B. added the information that the man and his colleagues were all Bonapartists and Socialists at one and the same time. 'Order', as the Prince had said in his speech, was not enough.

The swing in public opinion was also reflected in the letters from a very differently placed observer—Richard Metternich—who wrote to the Empress during his first visit to Paris since the war on April 17th, 1874:

'Now that Legitimacy looks as if it had abdicated and we none of us

281

have any confidence in the ability or good-will of the legitimate pretender, we all think that the future belongs to you know whom, and we
are telling each other quite openly that this would be the most natural
and also most welcome solution. We detest the Commune and the
umbrella [i.e. the Orleanists] equally. . . .'

And on May 5th he wrote to Chislehurst:

'Will the Marshal call for a plebiscite? Is it not much too early to ask
the country for a decision? What if they decide for the Republic? This
would give the Gambettists a basis which at present they lack. Is it not
much better to let the assembly talk and gesticulate in the void? Much
progress must still be made in the cause which I love. Instead of precipitate action, I prefer an organic ripening—slow, but fruitful and sure,
like child-birth.'

In the summer of 1874, the Empress followed the celebration of her
son's majority by assembling a house-party at Arenenberg. There the
Prince could meet a number of Imperialist friends under the relaxed and
informal conditions which Queen Hortense's delightful house above Lake
Constance could provide more easily than Camden Place. The Empress
vaguely regarded Arenenberg as the Compiègne of their exile, and for the
next few years she took her son and her entourage there every summer
to recuperate among her Parisian friends from the severities of the English
social and physical climate.

The sojourn of 1874 was the longest—July to October—as well as the
gayest and most diversified of the four summer visits she was able to
arrange for her son. Richard Metternich was there, as was old Count Arese,
who had done so much to show her the nobler aspirations of the *Risorgimento*. Joachim Murat and his son, who was the Prince Imperial's exact
contemporary, were present, and so was Edgar Ney, Prince de La Moscowa
and his Princess, once Mme de La Bédoyère, and as brilliant and beautiful
as ever. M. and Mme de Pourtalès, the Clarys, a Talleyrand-Périgord, the
Dukes of Cambacérès and Treviso, M. and Mme de Piennes (whose son
was married to MacMahon's daughter), the Duchess of Hamilton, now
among the Empress's most intimate friends; Ernest Lavisse, the Prince
Imperial's favourite historian, and Octave Feuillet. The names in the guest-
book reached back into the First Empire and pointed forward into the
unknown future which the young Murats and La Bédoyères grouped
round the Prince seemed so engagingly to represent.

Or let us take a glimpse at Arenenberg a year later, the summer of
1875, when the house attracted a concourse of European Royalty—the
Queen of Holland and her two sons, the Prince of the Asturias, the King
and Queen of Württemberg, the Grand Duke of Baden all paid homage
of a kind to Napoleon IV, while the Duke and Duchess of Mouchy, the
Bassanos, the Darus, the old Duke of Padua, the young Tristan Lambert

stayed on through the summer months and made it difficult for the spies from Paris to decide just what social or political groups and personages should be denounced to the government as 'Bonapartist sympathisers'.

The Prince made excellent progress in his career between these two summers at Arenenberg; in February 1875, he passed the final examinations at Woolwich seventh, coming out first in the preparatory examination at artillery. The Shop celebrated the success of its most romantic cadet by adding a special fervour to the breaking-up ceremonies. The Examination Review was attended by the Duke of Cambridge, who rode up to the Empress's carriage to congratulate her on her son's prowess, and in the evening the Prince was chaired by the other cadets. His joy at all this was much modified soon afterwards when Louis Conneau left Chislehurst for France and Saint-Cyr, interrupting a friendship which had begun with their birth. 'I begin to fear,' wrote the Empress to Paca's daughter Louise,

'the loneliness of Chislehurst for him, now that he does not have to work so hard. It was heartless of Conneau to leave him when more than ever he needs a friend of his own age. . . .'

In this spring of discouragement the Prince at last found a true English friend. Arthur Bigge, one of the twelve children of the Rev. J. F. Bigge, vicar of Stamfordham in Northumberland, was seven years older than the Prince, having been born on the thirty-fourth anniversary of the battle of Waterloo and named after its victor. They first met at Aldershot where, thanks to the Queen's and the Duke of Cambridge's intervention, the Prince had been allowed to join a battery. There he was immediately in his element. The new life with its discipline, its discomforts and hardships, its opportunities for self-reliance, its nights under canvas, all found an enthusiastic response from him, and Lt. Bigge soon realised that the Prince's passion for soldiering was serious and professional. With Lieutenants Slade and Wodehouse, he and the Prince formed a quartet of inseparable comrades. On free week-ends, the Prince took his new friends to Camden Place, where the Empress, always delighting in the company of young people, encouraged them to come back as often as they liked. In the summer, the three young English officers stayed at Arenenberg, where the Prince presented them with some pride to the other guests: they were, so to speak, an achievement all his own, a new justification for his life in England. He singled out the quiet and solid Bigge for his special friend, wrote him long letters when they were separated and opened out his heart and mind to him as so far he had done only to Conneau. Bigge, for his part, formed a deep, silent and enduring affection for the Prince. The Empress was delighted with the friendship, and Bigge—Lieutenant Bigge, Captain Bigge, Sir Arthur Bigge, Lord Stamfordham—remained a close friend and correspondent to the end of her life.

The Prince filled his day with academic studies and political work, and did so under his own discipline, as Filon was ill in France with a dangerous eye ailment. He read the vast correspondence of Napoleon I, as published during his father's reign, and made copious notes from this work, which in a letter to Louis Conneau he described as essential reading for officers. He studied his father's writings of which the Empress was making a careful collection. He read Hippolyte Taine's *Origins of Modern France* and wrote to the author afterwards:

'All those who want to understand the situation of our country and find the causes of our social instability owe a great debt of gratitude to your work. I want to discharge that debt by writing you this letter. Your book has not only answered a need of my mind, but has given my heart real satisfaction. Exiled from my country, I have lived there in spirit and thanks to you I have been able to spend long hours in France.
Believe me,
Napoleon.'

In his political contacts, the Empress allowed him full freedom, although she kept a sharp eye on the danger of the Prince's eagerness being exploited by unscrupulous party politicians. 'He is not ambitious,' she wrote to Doña Manuela in March 1876, 'but he has a strong sense of duty and is audacious. By appealing to these sentiments, they might succeed in making him commit some imprudence or folly. . . . Fortunately, while I am about, they won't succeed so easily.'

The danger that the precarious balance between the parties in France might tempt some of his supporters to strike prematurely was considerable. On January 30th, 1875, France had officially become a Republic, for on that day the Assembly at Versailles had voted for this form of government with a majority of—one. The Constitution of 1875 was an excellent instrument for avoiding leadership: it prevented Napoleon IV as well as Gambetta from reaching their political goal. As Jurien expressed it to the Empress, 'France wants a Governor, but does not know how to keep him.' In the Prince Imperial's lifetime the Constitution allowed the various party groups to combine effectively against anyone putting himself forward as the candidate of a national solution, as opposed to a party one. Political power was in the hands of the shifting and changing factions in the Chamber of Deputies, who could make and unmake governments and control the President without reference to any form of special allegiance or loyalty.

At the same time, administrative power, the actual running of the country, was vested in the hands of certain institutions such as the *Conseil d'État*, the departmental and municipal councils, the Prefects and their organisations, all of which were able to fulfil their functions far more continuously and efficiently than the changes on the open stage of politics seemed to indicate. The Constitution of 1875 was, after all, drawn up under the hostile vigilance of Bismarck. The Republic, for all its practice of anonymous responsibility, its vagueness and apparent shapelessness, hardly offered a point for attack. The system was not without practical wisdom, however equivocal its political character.

The greatest difficulty, therefore, facing men of vision and mission like the Prince Imperial and Gambetta was that the new system worked. The indemnity had been paid to Germany in full, the last German soldier had departed from French territory ahead of scheduled time. The Stock Exchange was steadier and far less neurotic between 1875 and 1880 than it had been during the corresponding years of the previous decade. Bonapartism's greatest difficulty was expressed in the phrase that appeared increasingly in public print and on people's lips: Paris is herself again. 'What people love Paris for,' wrote Henry James after a tour of the Boulevards at Christmas time in 1876, became almost absurdly obvious: charm, beguilement, diversion was stamped upon everything. Beaten and humiliated on a scale without precedent, despoiled, dishonoured, bled to death financially—all this but yesterday—Paris is today in outward aspect as radiant, as prosperous, as instinct with her own peculiar genius as if her sky had never known a cloud. The friendly stranger cannot refuse an admiring glance to this mystery of wealth and thrift and energy and good spirit.'

For these reasons, the most vexing problem facing the exiles of Chislehurst was not the hostility, but the indifference of France, not the continuing slander in the papers, but what Henry James in the same letter called 'the amazing elasticity of France'. The Third Republic's political shoddiness was offset by its administrative efficiency, and so it seemed increasingly probable that Frenchmen preferred their present easy-going materialism to remain undisturbed by those who, like Gambetta and Napoleon IV, offered them the politics of dedication to bolder and more stirring ideals. The Empress had no faith in MacMahon's ability to prevail against the new system, even though she knew the Marshal to be no Republican. When the elections of 1876 had returned a Republican majority she wrote that

'the first effort of the present majority will be directed towards dislocating all means for action. Quietly and legally, they will disarm all resistance, the Marshal will follow that road and when he wants to act he will find himself isolated vis-à-vis the others who will be better armed.'

This was an accurate and prophetic analysis of the shape of things to be expected from the venerable Marshal's timid leadership. Who could blame either Gambetta or the Prince Imperial for refusing to leave the destinies of France in the hands of a man whose political intelligence and initiative were as incisive as those of a stubborn sheep? Just because the Marshal was neither King nor Republican, the Prince felt that he and his cause had a right to the future.

The Empress was not so confident. 'The age of men of destiny is over,' she wrote to Doña Manuela early in 1876. 'In a sceptical society, redeemers become the victims.' Her comments on the political situation were always acute:

'M. Gambetta,' she wrote to Doña Manuela on April 6th, 1876, 'is the President of the Budget Commission, the most important body of all, which proves that the majority belongs to him. . . . The Marshal will continue to accept this order of things, but he will always believe that he rules through the Conservatives. I have no doubt at all that Gambetta, once he is in power, will ask nothing better than to put liberty into his pocket and create order, for liberty to him is a means and not an end. . . .'

She understood, better than most Bonapartist politicians, that Gambetta was not an enemy, but a rival, and that he was much better placed to rally the masses for his Republic than the Prince could hope to do for the Empire.

'The world as you see it,' the Empress wrote to her mother from Arenenberg in September 1876, 'belongs to the Middle Ages. . . . We must reckon with new forces.'

Her mind moved with the times. 'The Marshal,' she told her old mother,

'has no force behind him because he has not a single principle to rest on and is therefore followed by nobody. Gambetta is really more logical and more independent than he is, and is therefore more respected by the people. He has always been a Republican, whereas the Marshal owes his position, rank and titles and honours to the Emperor whom he allows daily to be insulted. . . .'

Her interest in the political scene, moreover, was not confined to the problems of France. When the government of Spain, in drawing up the first Constitution since the recent Bourbon Restoration, seemed to move in the direction of religious intolerance, the Empress wrote:

'You cannot use two different weights and measures in these things. To demand, in the name of the Catholic faith, religious freedom in Ireland, China, Japan, Sweden and to refuse it in Spain is both illogical and impolitic. You know very well that I am not saying this in opposition to the Church; on the contrary, it seems to me that *justice* should come from those who believe in the truth of their *credo* and that one should fight, not against the diversity of religions, but against unbelief. . . .
The Revocation of the Edict of Nantes was a grave political error. Must it be repeated in the middle of the nineteenth century? I hope not—*because* I am a Catholic to the bottom of my soul.'

Or, when she read that during a railway strike in the United States soldiers had been called in against the strikers, she wrote:

'A grave incident, but it did not surprise me. The whole thing was a perfectly logical development and will no doubt find its European imitators. Do not let us have illusions: the problems of today are social much more than political. It would be stupid to ignore this and to think that if one is strong enough one can charm these problems away. Bayonets have never prevented an idea from taking root, but only strong governments are able to distinguish between what is equitable and what is not and say: I safeguard the freedom of all.'

She had not lost her faith in the Bonapartist formula of freedom and order. She had merely begun to feel that France was no longer in a mood to accept it from the Napoleonic dynasty. At the same time, she was careful not to discourage her son, but continued to avoid anything that smacked of tutelage or interference. He must form his own judgment.

The Empress and her son regarded their active and unceasing study of contemporary France as a school in which to learn new vital lessons. On occasion, they both felt distrust with certain politicians or with the game of party politics, but they never felt, or spoke, ill of France. Here, the Empress was able to set her son an example in restraint and self-control, nowhere more impressively so than in the incident of the Le Sourd letter. Le Sourd, First Secretary at the French Embassy in Berlin in 1870, had delivered France's declaration of war. In an interview with this diplomat, published several years after the event, a Parisian newspaper wrote that when Le Sourd saw the Empress at Saint-Cloud late in July 1870, she had said to him: 'This war belongs to me! It is *my* war!' On seeing the newspaper in question, Le Sourd wrote at once to Benedetti, his former Chief at Berlin, that

'The Empress has never used in my presence the language, or the particular expression, which this article alleges. It would be, it seems to me, useless, or even difficult, to publish a denial in the papers, but I wish there might be an opportunity to let the Empress know that I entirely disavow the piece of fiction which it has pleased these people to attribute to me.
Georges Le Sourd.'

The original of the letter was sent to the Empress at Chislehurst, and her friends urged her to have it published. She knew, however, that this would mean the end of Le Sourd's career and so the letter remained hidden in her archives for fifty years until the late Duke of Alba published it in the early 1930s. As we have seen, her bellicosity in 1870 and before was one of the principal accusations raised against her. Remaining uncontradicted, the newspaper article seemed to confirm it.

Shortly before this incident, the Empress was being greatly plagued by the Duc de Gramont rushing into print with untruthful versions of the origins of the war. The former Foreign Minister, unemployable since his speeches of July 1870, was staying in London with relatives and was also spreading his lies by word of mouth. He slandered the Empress, and used letters from Beust and Metternich to establish his own innocence. Again, the Empress took no steps to vindicate herself, not from inability to do so, but as a matter of principle.[1] No explanations, no arguments in justification, were ever addressed by her to European public opinion. The past was a matter between her conscience and herself, not to be aired in public. It took some time before her contemporaries and the generations whom she survived understood the power and significance of her silence. It took even longer for the world to grasp what it must have meant to someone of her temperament to forgo the easy victories that in the case of her war guilt and other calumnies would have been hers to win. The Prince Imperial followed her example, again at a price. As was to be revealed later, he always carried with him in his wallet a particularly odious article on the 'bullet of Saarbrücken'[2] and the cowardice of the Bonapartes which had been written by a French journalist.

If one glances at the upbringing of Crown Princes of the Prince Imperial's generation elsewhere, for instance that of Kaiser Wilhelm II or of the Archduke Rudolph of Austria, one is agreeably struck by the sane realism and freedom in which the Crown Prince of Bonapartism was allowed to reach manhood. The Empress was delighted that the Prince took his studies so seriously and she particularly approved when during 1877 she found him tackling economics and reading Proudhon and Karl Marx. But she was equally delighted when in the autumn of the same year he went on a round of country house visits for the shooting and hunting.

In town, the Prince enjoyed the special patronage of the Prince of Wales, who took him to the Marlborough Club and summoned him to soirées at Marlborough House. At one of these, he danced with the famous Lady Waldegrave, most splendid of London's hostesses, who, although married four times in the last twenty years, had been, politically speaking, singularly faithful to the Orleans Princes. One always ran into at least one of them at her dinners in town, her lavish house-parties in the country. The Prince of Wales was much amused to see the young Prince Imperial make a hit with Lady Waldegrave, and when he saw them dance together exclaimed laughingly that he would send a telegram denouncing her to the Duc d'Aumale. Like many other people, Lady Waldegrave suddenly became aware of some aspects of the Second Empire which she had overlooked at the time of its existence. The Prince having attended her first ball of the 1878 season, she was heard to remark that he had inherited his father's feeling for England. 'One of the fine things in the late Emperor's

[1] Richard Metternich, however, effectively silenced Gramont.
[2] See page 240 for the origin of this lie.

character,' she wrote to a friend, 'was his courage in owning his good feelings towards this country and his contempt for the French prejudice against it. The Orleans Princes have never had the pluck to take the same line.' The Prince had often, in all innocence, the strange effect of causing people to behave uncharacteristically: for Lady Waldegrave to speak well of the Emperor was as unexpected as for Mr. Gladstone to unbend after exchanging a few words with the engaging and serious-minded youth.

Queen Victoria was no exception. It was the opinion of Sir Henry Ponsonby, her private secretary, that the Prince Imperial and John Brown were the only two people who were totally unafraid of the Queen. 'Didn't the Queen terrify you, sir?' a courtier asked the Prince after he had sat next to her during luncheon at Osborne. 'Good heavens, no!' came the reply. 'Why should she? We like each other.' Unlike the Queen's sons and daughters, who in public usually addressed her in nervous whispers, the Prince always spoke to the Queen in the most natural manner in the world. The Queen was conquered by more than boyish charm, for not long after the Emperor's death she wrote:

'For the peace of Europe, the Queen thinks it would be best if the Prince Imperial was ultimately to succeed.'

She accepted him as a member of her family.

This was the time when bright people, wishing to be regarded as being in the know, spread the interesting story of a warm friendship linking the Prince to the Queen's youngest daughter, Princess Beatrice. Being the Queen's constant companion, the Princess was always at her side during visits to Camden Place, or when the Empress and her son were at Osborne or Windsor. The Prince, not unnaturally, paid much attention to the Princess on these occasions, while she, never wholly at ease in the company of young men who were not her brothers, was sometimes seen to blush and stammer and generally display signs of confusion when he engaged her in polite conversation. There is no evidence to suggest that the Prince had any thought of proposing to the Princess.[1] What the two august mothers hoped or planned is a matter of speculation.

The Empress further widened her son's knowledge of the world by travel. In the winter of 1876-77 she took him to Italy for several months. She herself settled at the Villa Oppenheim near Florence while the Prince, in the company of Joachim Murat, Pietri and Espinasse, travelled about the country, visiting Venice and the battlefields of Magenta and Solferino. King Victor Emmanuel was in residence at the Palazzo Pitti, and so the Empress went to pay him a courtesy visit. He received her in his study upstairs. Speechless with amazement, the Empress found that the man whom her husband had made King of Italy had portraits and

[1] Princess Beatrice's eldest son, the late Marquess of Carisbrooke, told the author that the often quoted story of his mother hinting to him she had been in love with the Prince Imperial before she married Prince Henry of Battenberg, was not true.

photographs of the entire Hohenzollern family on his writing desk and the walls, but no single memorial of the Emperor. The King noticed her amazement: 'You are astonished at what you see?' he asked uneasily. She replied: 'I am astonished at what I don't see.' Old Count Arese came to see her often at her villa, and when the Prince arrived from his travels, Arese took him to the studio of an artist whom the Prince immediately asked as a special favour to give him lessons in drawing and sculpture. These lasted for several weeks, until the Empress took him to Rome, where he paid his respects to his godfather, the prisoner in the Vatican, old Pope Pio Nono. 'I did not go,' wrote the Prince to Tristan Lambert from Rome,

'with any political aim; I did not go to ask for the support of the Catholics in France. I went to lay my homage at the feet of a saintly old man, the dethroned sovereign, still the powerful head of Christendom. I went to assure the Holy Father that the Third Empire, like the First and Second, would be the protector of all liberties . . . but I gave him to understand that I considered the Church should keep outside the arena of politics and that, on pain of losing her influence and prestige, she ought not to identify herself with any party.'

This implied considerable censure of the officially encouraged religious fervour, bordering on hysteria, that went on in France during MacMahon's interregnum. At no time during the Empire had clericalism been so triumphant as during the Marshalate, when the cult of the Sacred Heart spread through the country and the pilgrims to its countless shrines sang 'the Marseillaise of Ultramontanism':

> Sauvez Rome et la France
> Au nom du Sacré-Coeur!

The Assembly on whose behalf nearly 22,000 Communards had been summarily executed, ordered, by way of expiation, the erection of the Basilica of the Sacred Heart on Montmartre as 'the Church of the National Vow'. In other fields the clergy were able, for a while, to re-establish a far greater hold over the country's mind than had been possible in the time of Victor Duruy and the Empress. In later years, Charles Péguy castigated the 1870's new wave of religiosity as 'a kind of superior religion for the superior classes of society, a miserable kind of genteel religion for allegedly genteel people'. The Empress was profoundly apprehensive of the consequences of this amalgam of religion, politics and doubtful architecture and so was her son, whose conversation with the Pope signified that the Third Empire would endeavour to lead the country back to a less exalted and intolerant state.

Movingly enough, the old Pope was entirely of the Prince's opinion. The fanatics among his collaborators, Cardinal Antonelli, Mgr. Talbot and Mgr. Mérode, had been removed from the battlefield, and Pio Nono, glowing with the kindliness and warmth of feeling that Antonelli had so often found so irritating, had nothing but words of encouragement for the son of Napoleon III. 'I hope,' His Holiness said at the end of the interview,

> 'that a speedy return will restore you to France; I wish it for the sake of the Church, I wish it for the sake of your country, I wish it for the sake of Europe. For when France is quiet within, calm reigns throughout the world; but when she is agitated by revolutionary passions, the security of the world is threatened.'

The Pope had experienced the consequences of Sedan not only in the final 'spoliation of Rome' by Victor Emmanuel, but in the persecutions and brutalities of Bismarck's *Kulturkampf*, which must have made him look back to his little differences with the Emperor of the French with nostalgia and, possibly, remorse. In those years he, or at least the Cardinals speaking in his name, had mobilised the Legitimists and clergy of France against Napoleon III as the champion of Italy. Now he told the Prince Imperial that when recently a partisan of the Count de Chambord had asked him to back the Bourbon Pretender in his fight for the white Standard, he had replied that he recognised 'no other banner than the Cross of Calvary'.

The Empress did not see the Pope. Under her well-known incognito as Comtesse de Pierrefonds she stayed quietly in what was still 'the dim, unmodernised, unexcavated Rome of papal days'. She freely saw her friends, her various Bonaparte cousins and their Italian clans, but she did not go to see the Pope.

From Rome the Prince travelled back to England with Pietri, while the Empress went to Spain to see her aged mother once again. It was their last meeting. Doña Manuela, undefeated and octogenarian, was now nearly blind, but, not wishing to become an object of pity, would endeavour to hide her affliction, angrily pushing away all helping hands and continually colliding with furniture and knocking things over. Old Miss Flowers, Eugénie's and Paca's governess and confidante, was still with her. Doña Manuela was as lively and imperious as ever, was still the great Countess of Montijo, fascinated by the ways of the world, eagerly discussing the topics of the day with callers at the Plazuela del Angel, her guests at Carabanchel. The Empress called at the Palacio de Liria where her former suitor, Paca's widower, the Duke of Alba lived out his lonely life. Paca's son was engaged to be married that year. One of her daughters, Maria, had been Duchess de Tamamès since 1873; the other, Louise, had married the Duke de Medinaceli in 1875 and died in the following year from a miscarriage: she had been the Empress's favourite niece.

The Empress was still in Madrid when on May 16th, 1877, Marshal MacMahon and his advisers attempted in the notorious coup of the *seize mai* to finish off the Republic and embark on some not clearly announced Conservative programme of their own. The Marshal dismissed the moderate Cabinet, presided over by the mild Jules Simon, and once more summoned

Duke Albert de Broglie to his side. The Chamber was dissolved, new elections were called for October and all other arrangements made to avoid the one opportunity for the country to speak its mind—a plebiscite. Instead, Broglie and his friends resorted to the old election technique of official candidates, which the Empire had dropped after 1863, and generally hoped to obtain a Conservative victory by such means as were in their power, and by some which were not. Much to the Empress's and the Prince Imperial's disappointment, Rouher allied the hundred or so Bonapartists of the Chamber to these proceedings, the outcome of which could hardly be favourable to the Empire. The elections returned the Republicans, although with a reduced majority. Although the Republican vote increased by 212,000 over that of 1876, and the Conservative vote by 437,000, the Republicans had a majority in the Chamber of 90, compared with 216 in 1876. The only immediately obvious result of the election was that the Marshal had lost it. He had asked the country to decide between himself as unfettered head of the Executive and what Gambetta called 'the omnipotence of the Chamber'; the country had decided for the Chamber, the Constitution of 1875.

The Republican victory of 1877 taught the Prince an important lesson in his political apprenticeship. Everyone had prophesied that a Republican victory would be synonymous with the victory of the revolution, leading to new outbursts of anarchy and violence reminiscent of the worst moments of Parisian history in 1793, 1848 and 1871. Instead of which he noticed with baffled surprise that the country showed complete indifference. Everything went on much as it had before—on the surface. 'Another ten years of such a regime,' he wrote to Raoul Duval after the elections, 'and France will be governed, like the United States, by a clique of politicians, discredited in other careers, whose game is to exploit their popularity.'

The Empress, for her part, looked elsewhere for the reason why the country had shied away from a bolder course: 'You turn your nose up at Germany,' she wrote to Doña Manuela in November 1877, 'but her weight lies on everything, and she bars the way to everybody.' In a later letter she said more emphatically that Germany was deliberately encouraging a weak and divided Republic:

'Germany does not see that a moderate Republic will become a powerful argument against Monarchy, while violent Republicanism will be a menace to the peoples.'

In the summer of 1878 the Prince Imperial, accompanied by Joachim Murat and the faithful Pietri, went on a tour of the Scandinavian Courts, while the Empress travelled to Ems to take the waters. The Bonapartes had always been popular in Copenhagen and Stockholm, and the King of Sweden did everything to turn the visit into a public triumph.[1] Under the

[1] King Oscar II was, of course, the Empress's visitor and friend of 1856, when he had been Crown Prince of Sweden.

Bernadotte dynasty, Sweden was ruled under a close approximation to the Bonapartist formula, which may explain why King Oscar treated his cousin with all the honours due to reigning Royalty. 'Need I tell you,' the King wrote to the Empress at Ems,

'how greatly I rejoice in your son's visit here? You have known for long my feelings towards you and yours, but what I should like to say now is that I am absolutely enchanted with him, and that this sentiment is shared by all who come near him. I have rarely, or never, met a young man who was so mature at twenty-three.[2] He is interested in everything, enquires about everything, and his questions always show wide knowledge and excellent education. Already, he is extremely popular here and has been acclaimed all along his route with a warmth which is rare among us inhabitants of the North.'

And to an acquaintance the King said during the visit: 'You would certainly have to bring your knowledge up to date if you were going to be with the Prince Imperial for long. He asked me yesterday how long it took a ship to get up steam. I had no idea, but said "ten minutes". Though he evidently did not know the answer either, I could see he wasn't satisfied. However, he has forced me to learn something. I have now discovered that it takes an hour and a quarter at least.'

Mother and son were re-united at Arenenberg later in the summer, where, from among his English friends, the Prince found Captain Wodehouse waiting for him. To his great joy, Ernest Lavisse was also there. Mme Octave Feuillet, who had not seen him for some years, wrote that she

'hardly recognised him, so tall has he grown, so noble and animated has his face become. He is a fine fellow of two and twenty, with the grace of the perfect gentleman. Everybody speaks feelingly of his charm, his heart, the sincerity of his sentiments. At dinner I sat beside him. He talked with the utmost liveliness of everything that concerns France.'

Back at Camden Place in October, the Empress received a letter from Lavisse:

'I have been staying with my family in a part of the country which seems deeply divided, full of hatred and unrest, and suffering from a general sickness. This is, I think, an accurate description of the whole of France.'

As the year 1878 drew to a close it appeared to the Prince that he and his friends among the Imperialists remained the only group of people who could cure the country of the *malaise générale* of which Lavisse had written. He did not feel this in any spirit of rashness or arrogance. Only

[2] The Prince was, in fact, twenty-two.

recently a delegation of Bonapartists had invited him to use the current excitement of the 1878 Exhibition (here again the Republic was borrowing from the Empire) as a kind of diversion to launch his long-awaited coup d'état. He heard them out with his accustomed courtesy and then said:

'What would happen if I did as you wish? I go to an hotel: a demonstration is made under my windows. Some poor wretches are taken to the police station for crying "Vive L'Empereur". Next day, very early a police official and two plain clothes men come to fetch me and take me to the frontier. . . .

You tell me that I must make myself known to France: is this the way? No, gentlemen, I will go to France, you may be sure: but I will choose the hour.'

And the delegates went back to Paris full of enthusiasm: 'We have a real sovereign,' they told everyone. President MacMahon at length resigned in January, 1879, to be succeeded by Jules Grévy, a moderate Republican, who, though in opposition at the time, had behaved extremely well in the crisis of September 1870. The Prince directed his party to vote for him in the Presidential election, thereby at last achieving his object of separating his man from Broglie's orthodox and now largely discredited Conservatives. In common with a great many Frenchmen all over the country, the Prince took it for granted that the Republic, once it was fully in power, could not possibly last for long: 'It is not our efforts that will overthrow the Republic,' he told Rouher in a letter of February 3rd, 1879,

'but it is up to us to take advantage of its fall. If the adherents of the Empire show themselves inaccessible to the depression as well as to the exaltation of party spirit, if they remain united and always ready to defend our institutions which were born with the century and are so suited to its genius, if they steep themselves in the Imperial teachings and never lean either towards the Royalists or the Jacobins, then the country, disillusioned by the Republic, will not hesitate for long and ten million voices will exclaim pointing to us: Those are the men who must govern us.'

The Empress wrote of the same events:

'Our premonitions were not fulfilled: the transmission of power went quietly, and difficulties cannot arise for some time—or perhaps for some days? . . . The country, at present, regards its saviours merely as spoilsports. . . .'

And of the Prince she wrote:

'My son goes hunting in the country from time to time and is enjoying it all round: they dance in the evenings and hunt in the mornings. . . .'

He also travelled to London on various occasions, official ones such as when Monckton Milnes, now Lord Houghton, asked him to speak at the Press dinner, or for his social activities and visits to the Marlborough Club. Or he just went up to dine with Bigge and be with his military friends. After dinner at the Café Royal one evening, he and Bigge had to rush to the railway station to catch the last train to Chislehurst. Somewhat to Bigge's surprise, he found that they were being cheered on with shouts like 'Vite, vite, mon Prince' or 'How he looks like his mother!' by what the Prince laughingly described as '*les petites dames de Leicester Square*'. He had certainly established himself with all classes of the population.

CHAPTER 4

IT WAS due to the Empress that the Prince Imperial was allowed to go out to South Africa and fight in the Zulu War. He had, it is true, made up his mind to seek permission without telling anyone, but she easily guessed his purpose. At first, after he had admitted that he had written to the Duke of Cambridge at the War Office, she endeavoured to dissuade him, principally by appealing to his sense of duty as the head of his party: 'If anything should happen to you,' she warned him, 'your adherents will not weep for you, they will bear a grudge against you.' He was not to be moved. He told her that he found his present mode of life futile: 'I am not a man of pleasure,' he exclaimed with the utmost conviction, 'I care nothing for going out into society, refusing endless invitations. There is nothing I can do for my own country.' Another argument was that now all his friends had gone to South Africa he could not show his face at Aldershot. Then, on February 21st, 1879, the Duke of Cambridge's letter of refusal arrived, and he was thrown into the blackest despair:

'. . . I looked upon this war [he told the Duke in his reply] as an opportunity for showing my gratitude towards the Queen and the nation in a way that would have been after my own heart. I hoped that it would be in the ranks of our allies that I should first take up arms. Losing this hope, I lose one of the consolations of my exile. I remain none the less deeply devoted to the Queen. . . .'

The Empress soon realised that he was wholly incapable of accepting the refusal as final. It seemed to make him ill, his face had gone ashen when he said: 'On m'a refusé'. 'Tears came rushing from his eyes,' the Empress later told Queen Victoria, 'he, who never cried.' Realising the strength of his resolution, the Empress conquered her repugnance towards the project and went in person to see the Duke of Cambridge at the War Office. Her intervention proved the turning point. The refusal had been decided upon at Cabinet level, but the Duke now hit on the solution of letting the Prince go to South Africa as an ordinary traveller. On arrival, he could be attached to the staff of the commanding General, Lord Chelmsford, in some innocuous capacity. The Duke put this idea to the Queen, and showed her the letters the Prince had written about his urgent desire to go. Queen Victoria yielded. 'I am greatly touched,' she wrote,

296

'at the kind and gratifying expressions he makes use of, and cannot but admire his desire to go out on service with my brave troops. But I am glad I am not his mother at the moment. He *must* be careful not to expose himself unnecessarily, for we know he is very venturesome. I should like to see him before he goes.'

The government, thus circumvented by the Court, looked with no great favour on the new arrangement, but felt unable to stop 'two obstinate old women', as Disraeli said, from having their way. And so, on February 27th, the Prince Imperial sailed away to the wars. 'Bébé s'en va t'en guerre,' wrote a Republican French journalist as a caption to a caricature.

What were the Prince's real motives? 'Entirely political,' he himself wrote from South Africa in a revealing letter. He felt that with Mac-Mahon's dismissal from the Presidency and the succession of a moderate Republican, any expectation that the Empire would be restored through the party alone had been killed. 'All hopes,' he wrote,

'are centred in my person; if that becomes great, the strength of the Imperial party becomes tenfold. I have had proof that no one will be followed but a man of conspicuous energy, and my principal concern has been to find a way of making myself known.'

And he expressed the same thought in a different way:

'If one belongs to a race of soldiers, one finds recognition only sword in hand, and he who wants to learn by travel, must travel far.'

He repeated the argument he had used to his mother, namely that a merely social life with its inevitable conclusion in an arranged marriage could never satisfy him:

'I have not cared to let my wings be clipped by marriage and my dignity refused to stoop to the part of a princely commercial traveller . . . to view all the princesses and boast of my political elixir that will heal all social evils. . . .'

To Rouher, who had rushed to Chislehurst in the vain hope of inducing him to change his mind, the Prince wrote a letter intended for publication and therefore defining his motives slightly differently:

'. . . For eight years I have been the guest of England. I completed my education at one of her military schools, and on several occasions I have strengthened the ties which unite me to the English army by taking part in manoeuvres. The war which England has been carrying on for more than a year at the Cape of Good Hope has assumed a gravity which it had not presented before.

In France, where, thank God, party mentality has not yet killed the soldierly spirit, they will understand that I could not be satisfied to remain aloof from the fatigues and perils of that army in which I have so many comrades. . . .'

Elsewhere he said more simply: 'The disaster of Isandhlwana gave me the opportunity I wanted.' His old battery at Aldershot, commanded by Major Ward Ashton, had gone out soon after that stunning defeat, and Bigge and Slade had departed with it.

On the night before sailing, the Prince made his will. The final bequest in it read:

To my Mother, the last uniform I shall have worn.

He departed for South Africa on February 27th, 1879, aboard *S.S. Danube*. The Empress and Laurent de La Bédoyère went to Southampton to see him off. On the quayside the Empress was handed a telegram from Queen Victoria of whom the Prince had taken his farewell at Windsor on the previous day. The telegram was in French and read:

'I ask you, dear Sister, to accept the expression of all my good wishes for your beloved son, who is departing accompanied by good wishes of the entire nation. May God bless and keep him.'

On the next day the Empress wrote to her mother from Chislehurst:

'I returned from Southampton last night worn out with tiredness and grief. You will understand what emotions I passed through. I have sent you some English newspapers so that you can see what they have said about my son. His departure was being loudly acclaimed, and it was consoling to see that they cheered him and blessed him wherever he showed himself. He himself, although sad at saying good-bye to us, was very happy about going. He gave me the enclosed letter for you. You must understand that I cannot write more today.'

The Empress spent the next three months in solitude 'at the mercy of the telegraphic wire', waiting for news as she had waited in the summer of 1870. Far away in Madrid, she knew, old Doña Manuela was waiting in the same anxious suspense. When news from South Africa reached Chislehurst, which took three weeks, she passed it on to Madrid at once. This dutiful correspondence apart, the Empress hid herself from the world, could hardly eat, read or sleep. Marie de Larminat, on holiday in France, was discouraged from returning; Franceschini Pietri, now her secretary, was sent to Corsica on leave. It was some consolation to the Empress to know that as he came nearer to the battle area, the Prince would meet Aldershot friends again, Bigge, Slade and Wodehouse.

'They are devoted to him,' she wrote to Doña Manuela on April 28th.

'They are excellent officers and, better still, slightly older than he, more experienced in knowing what they have to do to avoid risking their lives without necessity or reason.'

Bigge had, in fact, promised to keep in touch with her and be a restraining influence on him. The Prince wrote to him soon after arrival at Maritzburg:

'The General has most kindly taken me on his staff as an A.D.C., but an attack of fever[1] has retained me here, or rather the Doctors would not allow me to go on.

I have seen Wodehouse yesterday, he is following the same route as I am and he will soon go to the front. I told him how pleased you would be to see him and he was much touched by your message.

Goodbye, my dear Bigge, I hope to be soon with you, we will fight side by side!
Yours most affectionately,
Napoleon.'

It was not the letter of a non-combatant spectator. When the two met a few days later, Bigge felt it necessary to sound a word of caution. He wrote afterwards to his battery commander, Major Ward Ashton:

'Knowing his temperament, I implored him not to do anything rash and to avoid running unnecessary risks. I reminded him of the Empress at home and his party in France. He said: "Oh, of course, yes, you are quite right, I shall take care." '

Soon after this meeting Bigge went down with a bad attack of the same local fever from which the Prince had just recovered and so was separated from him. Those who were now responsible for the Prince were concerned with two conflicting duties: to see that he came to no harm and yet to satisfy his urgent longing for active service. The Prince had arrived with dangerously vague letters of introduction from the Duke of Cambridge, Sir Lintorn Simmons and other military friends: being infinitely more agile mentally than Lord Chelmsford or other superior officers, he soon succeeded in getting himself sent on missions which brought him face to face with danger. With every show of respect, he made rings round the military figures in whose charge he officially was. These officers, Chelmsford, Redvers Buller, Evelyn Wood, William Butler, Colonel Harrison, Major Grenfell, were all immersed in the task of preparing the expedition into Zululand that would avenge the defeat of Isandhlwana. Of these, Colonel Harrison was in charge of reconnaissance. The Prince, using his charm to camouflage his determination, now appealing to Harrison's feelings

[1] French newspapers, hearing of the malady, spoke of the Prince suffering from 'the hereditary disease of the Bonapartes', namely cowardice.

now asking Evelyn Wood to intercede with the Commanding General, managed to get permission to join several of these patrols which took them into the *kraals* of the Zulus, leaving the security of the camp for days and nights on end. Major Grenfell (who died in 1925 as Field-Marshal Lord Grenfell) described in a letter home one such operation:

> Head Quarters Camp
> Zululand.
> May 24th, 1879.

'The Prince Imperial is with us, and was in great danger last Tuesday. He and Col. Harrison joined a reconnaissance of Buller's, missed their escort and went on with only five men. The Zulus caught them on the top of a hill, where they came under fire. The Prince drew his sword and charged up the hill, shouting. His ferocious yells (and, I conclude, his likeness to his great-uncle) alarmed the Zulus, who fled, but they had to pistol a Zulu before they got out, which they did all right, but slept two nights in the open, very cold and miserable.

He is a plucky little chap and will, I think, get himself shot before the campaign is over. We shall, I expect, have a good fight in the rough ground near Ulundi and that, I hope, will end the campaign.'

Another time, he was allowed to go on a prolonged patrol under the command of Major Bettington, an officer legendary for his knowledge and cunning in local warfare. There was no ruse or trick in which he could not forestall the native Zulus, and the Prince felt the greatest respect for this tough and experienced officer. Bettington on his part admired and liked the Prince, and, so long as they were together, gave him his opportunities to prove himself a soldier. When on their first patrol together they occupied a Zulu *kraal* after charging at a group of Zulus around their plumed Chief, Bettington suggested that the place should be marked as *kraal Napoleon* on their maps. Their return to Head Quarters Camp produced further adventures, as the Zulus harassed them day and night, and they had to abandon their camping sites several times during one night. 'Even to strike a match,' wrote Bettington in his diary about one of their nocturnal halts,

'or to say a word, except in a whisper, was strictly forbidden. In front, in the rear, on the right and left, Basutos were stationed as sentinels with orders to walk towards each other. Then the men could take some rest; the Prince was stretched upon the ground beside the others, sharing his scanty covering with Lomas, his orderly. . . . So the night passed, troubled only by false alarms given by Lieutenant Carey.'

Carey, a young officer of much promise, who had volunteered for service in South Africa after having done well at the Staff College, had commended himself to his superiors, especially Harrison, through his zeal in gathering and collating information and was frequently sent out on these forward map-making expeditions. He was, of course, inexperienced in the field of native warfare, seemed a little emotional and voluble, but for all that was very keen. He spoke French fluently, and the Prince took a liking to him. Carey had been greatly impressed by the Prince in action at the *kraal Napoleon*, and he may have overheard the Prince say to Bettington when the latter condemned swords as 'useless in this kind of work':

'I always wear one, not for attack, but defence. If I could die fighting, I should not mind death at all.'

Sword or no sword—this was the life which the Prince had come out to Africa to experience. The privations, the dangers, cold nights under a blanket in the open—it all appealed to what the Empress called his Spartan side. He took good care that she did not hear too much of his activities. He wrote frequent affectionate letters, he kept in touch with Rouher and other political friends, but on his return from the patrol of which Major Grenfell had been so critical, all he wrote home was:

'I have just come back from a reconnaissance: we were away for six days. Some shots were fired on both sides, but nothing very serious happened. We were in the saddle for twenty-four hours out of twenty-four. . . .'

Later on, Filon was allowed to see Bettington's diary, after he had already studied the letters the Prince had written to Camden Place. 'Bettington,' he noted with some surprise,

'had never spoken to the Prince before May 14th, but six days later was absolutely devoted to him. These curious pages show the manifold and continually recurring dangers of these rides by day and by night through an unknown country, in the presence of an untiring foe who was following the foreign invaders step by step and laying new traps for them wherever they could.'

However, at the time of these events, Filon was not at the Empress's side, but still in Paris, his eye ailment having taken a turn for the worse. The Empress had the Duke of Bassano and his son and Mme Le Breton with her at Camden Place. She lived for the next arrival of the mail, for the cables from Madeira, at this time the farthest point of the cable to Africa, but her vital energies threatened to become exhausted during the three weeks' interval of waiting: 'My nerves,' she wrote to Doña Manuela, who demanded from her news she did not have, 'cannot bear this tension of the spirit. I cannot reply to your letters when I have received no news myself.' Visitors were kept to the unavoidable minimum, but she always made an exception for Sir Lintorn and Lady Simmons, with whom she felt at ease to speak about her soldier son. Late in May, she read in the *Daily News*:

'Prince L. Napoleon has distinguished himself with a reconnaissance party,' and *The Times* of 21st May told her:

'The Prince Imperial, while riding out from the camp with several officers, was surrounded by the enemy. Three of our Zulus [*sic*] were killed. The Prince put his horse at a *krantz* (i.e. rocky descent) and had a narrow escape. All are well.'

Finally she saw it mentioned in a French paper that the Prince 'had taken a *kraal* by assault, which in his honour had been called *kraal Napoleon*.' Passing this piece of news on to Madrid, the Empress added that:

'In good things and bad I mistrust the imagination of the Latin races and keep to the *Daily News*, which says more simply that he had distinguished himself, without saying where or how.'

But all this while she was waiting for news from her son direct. 'All the old sensations,' she told her mother, 'come to life again under the influence of fear.'

'Not assegaied yet, sir?' Evelyn Wood cheerily asked the Prince when he returned to Head Quarters Camp from the patrol with Bettington. 'Not yet,' replied the Prince laughingly and then grew serious:

'If I had to be hit,' he said, 'I think I would prefer an assegai to a bullet. It would show that I had been close to the enemy.'

Also at Head Quarters Camp to greet him was another recent acquaintance, a journalist called Deléage who had been sent to South Africa by the *Figaro*. Reporting about the Prince was part of his assignment. He had gone out expecting to find the spoilt, insipid and anglicised figure of Republican propaganda. Instead he found,

'not just a young Prince, but a striking and superior personality of overwhelming charm, a Frenchman with all the qualities of his race, a true Parisian speaking with the accent of the *boulevards*.'

'I enjoy these little outings, M. Deléage,' the Prince, fresh from his exploit at *kraal Napoleon*, called out to him. 'Still—

'I should hate to be killed in some obscure skirmish. A big battle—yes: that would be Providence. But just a skirmish—no.'

And later that day Deléage was stopped by an officer who insisted that as a reporter he must know the full story of the Prince's conduct on that

302

patrol—his courage, intelligence, amiability had been prodigious. The gratified journalist took it all down and then asked for his informant's name. It was Lieutenant Carey.

Others were less enthusiastic about the little outings. Colonel Redvers Buller complained to Chelmsford, and forthwith the Prince was given staff duties. He became Deputy Assistant Quarter-Master General to Colonel Harrison—'I comprise,' he wrote to his mother on May 26th,

> 'Colonel Harrison's whole staff which is and will remain a very slender one, though I am getting fat. . . .'

In this new capacity he drew up plans for fortified points along the lines of communications of the army for their imminent march on Ulundi, and began writing a treatise entitled *South African compared with European Warfare*. While he was thus desk-bound in a tent, everything around him was seething with the preparations for the march on Ulundi. Was he to be left behind, out of it all? Deléage, at their next meeting, found him looking ill and dejected, unable to bear the thought of not being allowed to fight in the coming battle. The journalist, both a friend and an Imperialist convert by this time, had had a political conversation with the Prince a week or too earlier, which had been sparked off by his mentioning reports of certain speeches which the Prince's supporters had made on March 16th, his twenty-third birthday. The Prince had asked:

'Did they strike you as exaggerated?'

'They might have had that effect,' had been Deléage's reply, 'on people who don't know Your Highness. I read them with great pleasure, and I liked particularly the brilliant paradoxes of M. Robert Mitchell.'

'Oh? And what were they?'

'That on the most democratic and republican grounds, your return was both necessary and imminent.'

'Indeed,' the Prince had replied and galloped off.

Now, at their meeting at the end of May, Deléage was able to tell the Prince that a Bonapartist deputy had been elected in one of the Paris wards. The Prince expressed delight to hear this excellent news from a fellow-countryman, but presently vented his bitter resentment of his present position. Far from being allowed to express any words of admonition, the journalist had to listen to a lecture from the Prince on rashness, for that day Deléage, having lost touch with his escort, had returned from a patrol alone. 'Really,' said the Prince, 'you'll get yourself killed before I do.'

It became known on May 31st that the big advance on Ulundi was to begin on June 1st. Colonel Harrison, remembering the unhappiness of his chafing assistant, thought it safe to send him out on a patrol to select suitable camping ground for the second day of the advance. This would not take him far from the camp, and besides he would give him Bettington as escort. The Prince, moderately happy at this chance of a new outing, however unadventurous, accepted the gesture: and from this moment things went fatally wrong. Harrison forgot to warn Bettington that night, and when he sent for him the following morning, June 1st, found that the Major had gone out on another duty. Carey at once volunteered to take Bettington's place. Harrison agreed, giving Carey a warrant for an escort of six white and six Basuto scouts. The white soldiers were assembled by nine o'clock, of the Basutos there was no sign. The Prince, mounted on his horse, became impatient, and Carey yielded to his suggestion to make a start and let the Basutos catch up with them. So the small party moved on towards the Ityotyozi Valley, where the camp was to be. They had with them a Kaffir guide to whom the Prince had lent one of his horses. He himself was on the high-spirited horse he had purchased at Durban a month earlier and which he had taken with him on his earlier adventures. Its name, not bestowed by the Prince, was *Fate*.

On the way, they overtook Colonel Harrison and Major Grenfell. Where, Harrison wanted to know, were the Basutos? They were following on behind. Why not wait for them? 'There are quite enough of us,' replied the Prince with a laugh. Harrison forbore to interfere, while Grenfell thought that the Basutos were probably covering the party from afar. The Major had finished his morning's work and so he told the Prince he would ride along with him and have a look at the site in the Ityotyozi Valley. He and the Prince led on, and Carey was riding behind.

They were riding along the long ridge which finally descends into the valley, a landscape 'bare of trees or cover', says Grenfell, 'and therefore, as the Zulus had no horses, even with the smallest escort perfectly safe'. Before they descended into the valley, Grenfell thought he heard his own team approaching, and so turned his horse and said goodbye. 'Take care of yourself, Prince, and don't get shot!' 'Oh no!' came the gay reply, 'Lieutenant Carey will take good care that nothing happens to me.'

He was killed soon after four o'clock. Carey had taken his patrol down into the valley, choosing a deserted-looking *kraal*, to which he had been before, for their rest. He had allowed them to unsaddle, had posted no sentinels except the Kaffir guide, and after a little sketching and map-making, had relaxed with his party over some coffee. The *kraal* was in an opening by the tall grass of the region, and under this cover a party of forty Zulus had crept up.

At four the Kaffir reported having seen a Zulu, and Carey gave orders to saddle. A volley of shots rang out as they did so, and thereafter all was panic. 'Some were mounting,' one of the escort, Sam Hully, said later, 'while their horses were starting, some half in and some just in, their saddles. Trooper Rogers was killed and another, Abel, fell shot, or missed his stirrup, and shared the fate of the Prince.'[1] The Prince was waiting for

[1] Sam Hully gave his account to a friend who published it in a letter to *The Times* on November 21st, 1928, adding that it 'generally corroborates that given by Augustin Filon'.

the others to mount, Carey was already mounted: and now Carey's horse plunged away. The Prince ran over to *Fate*, which had begun to gallop off with the others, but as he tried to mount, the girth gave way and he was thrown to the ground. He turned to face the enemy, he walked towards them contesting every inch of ground, firing from his revolver; his foot caught in a hole, and he fell. With their assegais they rushed up to him, yelling, and a minute later all was over.

Major Grenfell was with the party which, next morning, rode out to find his body. 'It was a sad sight,' he wrote:

'as we, his English brother-officers, stood round the dead body of the hope of the Imperialists of France, the Prince's two servants weeping bitterly, and we all felt the great disaster and the deep disgrace which had fallen on the British Army.

He was assegaied in seventeen places, his arms were crossed over his chest, and his face, which was beautiful in death, was disfigured by the destruction of the right eye from an assegai wound.'

And Captain Molyneux reported to Lord Chelmsford:

'The body was stripped naked except for a gold chain with medallions, which was about his neck. His sabre, his revolver, his helmet, and his other clothes had disappeared, but we found in the grass his spurs with their straps, and a sock marked N.

The body had seventeen wounds, all in front, and the marks on the ground as on the spurs indicated a desperate resistance. At ten o'clock a bier was made of lances and blankets and the body was brought out of the donga by officers: Major-General Marshall, Captain Stewart, Colonel Drury Lowe and three officers of the 17th Lancers, Surgeon-Major Scott, Lieutenant Bartle Frere and myself. Mr. Deléage, the correspondent of the *Figaro*, claimed the honour of joining us which was immediately granted.'

Before the coffin was carried aboard H.M.S. *Orontes*, bound for England, an Order of the Day was issued at Natal:

'In following the coffin which contains the body of the Prince Imperial of France, and in rendering to his ashes the last tribute of respect and honour, the troops in garrison will remember:

(1) That he was the inheritor of a powerful name, and one of great military renown.
(2) That he was the son of England's strongest Ally in times of danger.
(3) That he was the only child of a widowed Empress, who now remains without a throne, an exile and childless, on the shores of England.

To enhance the sorrow and respect which they owe to his memory, the troops will bear in mind that the Prince Imperial of France fell in fighting under the English flag.'

Paul Deléage spoke with the voice of the Prince Imperial's France:

'I alone in that sad procession had the civilian's privilege of walking along bareheaded. Seeing the flag of England droop slowly to the ground giving a royal salute to this body wrapped in the tricolour, I thought how deep shall be the repentance of those whose insults drove the unhappy Prince to prove his manhood even at the cost of his life, when history shall relate how, in this faraway land, the last of the Napoleons brought by his death honour to the banner of France.'

England and France knew nothing of these events until June 20th, and even Lieutenant Carey's Court Martial had been held before the Empress knew of the disaster. On the night of June 1st, Carey had written a letter of crushing self-indictment and replete with self-pity to his wife. But, by the time he stood before his judges he was cool and self-possessed. Not he, but the Prince, was in command of the patrol, was the burden of his defence: the moral responsibility for the disaster was not his. 'I can only,' he conceded, 'be blamed for the selection of the camping place.' This was, in itself, a damaging admission, but when he said, 'I did everything to save the Prince,' he received the well-deserved answer: 'You did absolutely nothing.' This reproach followed him to the end of his days. Major-General Marshall presided over the Court, and its verdict was that, subject to the approval of the Commander-in-Chief of the British Army, Carey was to be cashiered. To this, the Court added a recommendation to mercy. Carey had been a promising officer with a good service record, and they all knew what it meant to have the Prince Imperial under orders. In the latter respect there was a certain amount of instinctive solidarity among the English officers, as the following letter from Carey to Major Grenfell implies:

'My dear Major,
I return you the residue of the foolscap with very many thanks. Kindly let me know what I am indebted to you for my share of messing. I cannot close without thanking you from the bottom of my heart for all your sympathy in my trial. My military career is now closed but I can never forget your sympathy, even on the night of the 1st June. Five superior officers have found me guilty, but to the end of my life, though I bow to their decision, I cannot think that I could have done anything else.
Kindly say goodbye to Colonel Buller and Colonel Harrison for me and tender them my sincere apologies for having so bothered them at my

THE PRINCE IMPERIAL

Photo: Spearman, Windsor

THE PRINCE IMPERIAL, 1878

Photo: Francis, Camberley

A DRAWING BY THE PRINCE IMPERIAL SAID TO REPRESENT THE
ANGEL OF DEATH RECEIVING THE SOUL OF A YOUNG WARRIOR

trial—I could do nothing else and wanted Colonel Harrison's evidence to clear myself.

    Forgive my bothering you and believe me,
               Yrs. very sincerely,
               J. Brenton Carey.'

19th June, 1879.

He was sent back to England to await the Duke of Cambridge's final decision. The question of responsibility, as opposed to that of legal guilt, affected the whole hierarchy of command. To have a person of the Prince Imperial's character and situation in one's charge required an understanding and authority that though not provided for in the Queen's Regulations need not have gone, as Arthur Bigge showed, beyond the imagination of those whose professed calling was the leadership of men. Who, during his short service at their side, thought of calling him a 'brother-officer' as Major Grenfell did standing before the corpse? Lord Chelmsford had written when the Prince first reported to him that 'his desire to serve under my command is a set-off of those who consider that I am quite unfit for my present command', but after the disaster he said less proudly:

'I have always felt that it was somewhat unfair to saddle me with the responsibility attached to such a charge, but I had to accept it with all the rest.'

So he passed the Prince on to Colonel Harrison, whose responsibility, both in putting Carey in charge and in not stopping the patrol when he met them without their Basutos a few hours before the end, was at least as grave as that incurred by Carey.

CHAPTER 5

HITHERTO, ALL accounts of how the Empress received the news of her son's death derive from that given by Filon in his book on the Prince Imperial. However, in June 1879 Filon was lying desperately ill in a darkened room in Paris and heard the story two years later from the old Duke of Bassano who was present at Camden Place on that 20th of June. It is now possible to correct the traditional narrative in certain details from the unpublished diary of someone who, unlike Filon, was at Camden Place on the day itself and who wrote down what happened in a diary immediately afterwards. This was Lady Simmons, wife of the Governor of Woolwich, who himself had done so much to enable his erstwhile disciple to go to the wars. Both Sir Lintorn and Lady Simmons had become, as we saw, intimate friends of the Empress, and so it was natural that Lady Simmons, having seen the terrible news in the papers, should hasten to Chislehurst to see whether she could be of help. Sir Lintorn was in Somerset, but she took a friend, Lady van Straubenzee, with her.

The two ladies reached Camden Place in the early afternoon of June 20th, and were received by the Duke of Bassano and Baron Corvisart, the Emperor's doctor and friend. 'They both told me,' wrote Lady Simmons,

'that Earl Sydney had sent them the intelligence at 7 a.m., begging them to keep all the newspapers from the Empress, till he should arrive at 9.30 to break the news to her.[1]

The Empress was reading her letters and accidentally opened one for her secretary, M. Pietri, who was in Corsica. The writer alluded to having just received "*les affreuses nouvelles*". The Empress gave a loud cry, and Baron Corvisart ran into her room. He found her dreadfully excited and agitated, demanding what it was. He told her the Prince was wounded and (by degrees) dangerously so, and then that Lord Sydney was coming to bring the details. She said, "Alors, il faut que je m'habille", and he advised her to do so. Thus the time, Baron Corvisart told me, passed on with alternations of terrible anxiety and agitation

---

[1] Queen Victoria, who had received the news late in the evening of June 19th, had asked Lord Sydney—as Lord Lieutenant of Kent well known at Camden—to tell the Empress before she saw the papers. Princess Beatrice was with the Queen when John Brown came in and said: 'The young French Prince is killed.' 'My accession day forty-two years ago,' the Queen finished her entry in the Journal for that day, 'but no thought of it in the presence of this frightful event.'

on her part, till Lord Sydney arrived. He entered the room with the Duc de Bassano and Baron Corvisart, and when the Empress saw them come in together (for she always received visitors singly) she seemed at once to guess the truth. When the sad tidings were broken to her at last, she sat as white and motionless as a statue for some hours, to their great alarm. It was long before tears happily came to her relief.'

By this time, the park and the surroundings of the house were swarming with reporters, pestering Bassano and others for news and details. The Duke told Lady Simmons that he would give them no information of any sort. The two ladies, unwilling to intrude on the Empress, or perhaps even afraid of doing so, then walked away to the station, but a policeman came after them and said that the Empress wanted to see Lady Simmons. So they turned back and, leaving her friend downstairs, Lady Simmons went up to the Empress's room.

The room was in darkness; the Empress was sitting alone, with her back to the windows. When she saw her friend enter,

'she threw herself [continues the narrative] on my shoulder, clasped me tightly with both arms round my waist, and lay there sobbing convulsively. I put out my arms, and clasped her; I could only exclaim "Oh! Madame", very heartily. As her cheek lay on my shoulder, I could not help kissing her fervently, and tried to murmur faint expressions of what I—and we all felt. After a while she made me sit down.

She asked me if I remembered her saying at our last visit, how sure she felt that this mail would bring her decisive news: I well recollected this.

She told me of her opening the letter to M. Pietri, after reading one which Major Ward Ashton had forwarded her from Mr. Bigge, giving such excellent news of the Prince's health, and saying that she might make her mind quite easy, for they would all see that no harm happened to him.

She said that only two days previously she had heard from the Prince, who told her that he had got his friends, Lieutenants Bigge and Slade and Wodehouse with him—that he was so happy, and only wanted to hear more frequently from her to be perfectly so. She told me of the gentlemen coming in to break the news to her, and added: 'I don't know which it was of them who told me.'

She . . .'

Here, the diary abruptly breaks off.

Filon did not see the Empress and her circle again until 1881. He himself could be told nothing in June 1879, for his doctor warned Mme Filon that if in the present state of his eyes he wept, his sight, and perhaps his life, would be lost. For nearly three months the heroic Mme Filon and the nurses kept the news from the Prince Imperial's tutor and friend: and when, on September 9th, the doctors at last thought it safe to let him know, they could not tell him that it had happened so long ago or go into any detail. These singular circumstances give Lady Simmons' diary added importance. It has been hitherto believed that, on being told the news, the Empress fainted and remained unconscious for long periods. We now see that she was not granted this escape and had to bear the blow with all her feelings and awareness fully awake. Nature was never merciful to the Empress Eugénie. Or so she felt herself, for the first sign of life she was able to give to her mother sounded almost like a cry of protest against living:

> 'Today I have the courage to tell you that I still live, for grief does not kill. Your devoted daughter,
>> Eugénie.'
> June 25th.

Friends endeavoured to do for her what they could. Major Ward Ashton, the battery commander, was in England and saw her the day after the news had come, and soon afterwards her beloved friend Anna Murat, Duchess of Mouchy, came to Chislehurst with her husband. Letters of condolence were numberless and sincere. Queen Victoria, who had lost her daughter, Princess Alice, a few months earlier, found words of genuine sympathy:

> '. . . You have one great consolation in knowing how very good he was, loved and respected by all. My daughter and I have shed bitter tears for the dear young Prince who was so promising and the loss of whom is a misfortune for the future and who died doing his duty in my service. This will always form a link between us.'

The Queen went to Camden Place on June 23rd, and two days later wrote to Disraeli:

> 'The accounts from the Cape fill one now with redoubled anxiety, for if *so precious* a life was not more cared for, how much less will others be!
> The dear Empress Eugénie's conduct is *beyond* all praise. Her resignation, her unmurmuring patient submission to God's will, her conviction that it could not be otherwise, and the total absence of all blame of others are admirable.
> But her heart is broken and her poor health seems sadly shaken. She can eat nothing and hardly sleeps. But *how* could it be otherwise?'

Resignation and submission, which the Queen so praised in the Empress, did not come easily or soon. On June 28th the Duchess of Mouchy gently prepared her for the imminent arrival of H.M.S. *Orontes* with the coffin aboard. 'This,' the Duchess told the Duke of Connaught, who reported it in a letter to the Queen:

> 'upset her dreadfully and brought on a nervous attack which was *most* violent and distressing. The Duchess described it as being the most fearful thing she ever witnessed and that her cries were heard even downstairs. . . .'

And to her mother the Empress wrote:

> 'You tell me that Carlotta says I am resigned. No, alas, I am not, I am crushed, I no longer live, I wait for death, for it alone can reunite me with those who are waiting for me. I hope that calm and solitude will return. I badly need to be left alone with my thoughts, my memories, and nothing must come between them and me from outside.'

And later on:

> 'I am without purpose and courage. The weather is cold, I have a fire, but nothing can warm me and my heart is turned to ice.'

We may be brief with the outside events. The coffin was brought to Camden Place on July 11th, and the funeral at St. Mary's, Chislehurst, where the body of the Emperor rested, took place on the following day. Her Majesty's Government, anxious not to offend the French Republic, had no wish to be represented, but yielded to the Queen's furious protest and in the end sent two Ministers, not of the first rank, to Chislehurst. The Court, however, was fully represented.[1] The Queen, accompanied by the Princess of Wales and Princess Beatrice, reached Chislehurst in the morning at eleven o'clock. The Prince of Wales, the Duke of Connaught, the Duke of Cambridge, and the Crown Prince of Sweden together with the Duke of Bassano and Rouher acted as pall bearers. The chief mourner of the Bonaparte family was Prince Napoleon, who with his two young sons walked behind the coffin. The Second Empire was represented by its surviving representatives, but the Republican Minister of War had not given permission to its Marshals, MacMahon, Canrobert, Leboeuf, to attend. Nor was Jurien de La Gravière permitted to represent the navy. The cadets of Woolwich formed a square, as the cortège set off; the Prince's French friends, Conneau, Espinasse, Laurent de La Bédoyère, and

---

[1] Lord Salisbury, now in office as Foreign Secretary, wrote to Lord Lyons in Paris 'for M. Waddington's confidential information', that H.M. Government had seen 'the ceremonial growing to its present importance with great disquietude', but that the presence of the Royal Family did not give the funeral an 'official' status. He added: 'The strong feeling which exists is due in some degree to the general esteem in which the late Prince was held—much more, I think, to a sentiment of something like national self-reproach.' (Lord Salisbury to Lord Lyons, London, July 10th, 1879, Private. Salisbury Papers.)

after them his two servants Uhlmann and Lomas followed the coffin walking behind Prince Napoleon and his two sons. The cadets broke the square and marched in the procession with sabres reversed. Guns boomed over the common, and the band of the Royal Artillery marched to the sound of muffled drums. It was a soldier's funeral, but the end of the procession was brought up by ordinary French and English people mingling together in their thousands as a gesture of spontaneous comradeship. Late in the afternoon the exhausted Empress was engulfed again by the solitude of the deserted house, alone with her voices and her thoughts, shivering in the new climate of loneliness.

External matters continued to intrude, however. When Pietri returned from Corsica, the Prince's will was opened and was found to contain the following codicil:

'I being dead the task of continuing the work of Napoleon I and Napoleon III devolves upon the eldest son of Prince Napoleon, and I hope that my beloved mother in aiding him to her utmost power will give to us who are no more this last and supreme proof of affection.'[1]

He had expelled Prince Plon-Plon from the Imperial succession. It had been entirely his own decision; the Empress, for all her disagreements with the Imperial cousin's eccentric policy, disliked this arbitrary setting aside of the laws of succession. However, the Bonapartist party in France heaved a sigh of relief when they learnt that the unpredictable Prince had been excluded from its leadership. Prince Victor, his eldest son, was then seventeen. Lord Lyons wrote of him:

'He is said to be a remarkably clever, attractive youth and a thorough Bonaparte in appearance. No hereditary responsibility for Sedan can be cast upon him; he is undoubtedly of the Bonaparte race, and he has been brought up in France. For the present, however, the Prince Imperial's melancholy death is a decided accession to Republican strength.'

The Empress was distressed that any reconciliation between herself and the only other considerable survivor of the Empire was now less feasible than ever, but when, despite her invitation to see her, Prince Plon-Plon drove off immediately after the funeral without a word of explanation she felt that she must leave him to the 'perversity of his instincts'.

The second major intrusion from outside was caused by Carey. The finding of the Court Martial had yet to be confirmed and when, on July 17th, Queen Victoria and Princess Beatrice called once more at Camden Place, the Empress suddenly spoke of Carey:

[1] The Prince left a considerable sum of money and several valuable possessions. The will proved conclusively that the allegation of the Empress keeping him short of money was entirely unfounded.

'Tell me, they will not do anything to that poor man? Oh no! He may have a mother!'

Queen Victoria hardly knew what to reply. Reminding the Empress that matters were not entirely in her hands, she promised to try and see what could be done. The Queen added that she knew Carey to be extremely unhappy, but also alluded to the 'grief and shame we all felt'. The Empress immediately interrupted, saying that she wished to know nothing about that. 'All I know is that he has been killed, and that is all.' She thanked the Queen for her promise to speak for mercy, and she herself issued a statement in the form of instructions to Pietri:

'The only earthly consolation I have is the knowledge that my beloved child fell as a soldier, obeying orders, on a duty that was commanded, and that those who gave them did so because they thought him competent and useful.

Enough of recriminations. Let the memory of his death unite in common sorrow all those who loved him, and let no one suffer, either in his reputation or his interests. I, who can desire nothing more on earth, ask this as a last prayer.

Eugénie.'

She was sincere to her innermost heart in wishing that the circumstances of her son's death should not poison relations between the two countries. For in France, the country's rich fuel of Anglophobia was feeding a huge flame of resentment such as the French had not enjoyed since the Orsini affair. Rumours floated about like ashes after a conflagration: the Prince's death had been decided by a conspiracy between the Prince of Wales and Gambetta; Carey had had orders to slash the girth; he had been assassinated by the freemasons, Bismarck's agents, the Communist International. The country was genuinely angry, and the sense of loss was widespread and vivid. Some blamed him for going, but all blamed England, her government, army and, especially, her Queen for allowing him to go.

In England, public emotion became greatly agitated from the moment Carey landed at Plymouth. It was felt, not wholly unjustly, that he was being made a scapegoat to camouflage the negligence of higher-ranking officers. Carey, with a neurotic lack of method, continued publicly to lay the blame, not on his superiors, but on the Prince. He might have achieved a measure of vindication had he remained silent. Instead, his hysterical flight into publicity, which involved him in resorting to lies and very obvious evasions, lost him such sympathy as he might have found from his fellow officers. In his frenzy, he even began sending letters to Camden Place, but received no satisfaction. It would have been quite easy for the Empress to show up his lies, for, incredibly enough, someone had sent her, on behalf of Mrs. Carey, the original of the letter he had written to his wife a few hours after the catastrophe. No more self-incriminating document could be imagined. But she kept the letter among her papers until

313

after the Duke of Cambridge had pronounced on the Court Martial's findings. Only then did she forward it to Queen Victoria, saying in her covering note:

'While Lieutenant Carey's fate was undecided, I did not wish to put before Your Majesty the enclosed letter, written on the *day itself*. Mrs. Carey had it sent to me, no doubt hoping that I would make it known. To me it seemed, on the contrary, to be of a kind that would influence in an unfavourable sense the decision to be made about him, and so I thought I ought not to show it.'

The Queen had herself been conducting a private enquiry into the events of June 1st, personally interviewing anyone who had been near the scene of the tragedy at the time.

'This evidence is terrible,' she wrote in her Journal. 'Indeed, every word seems to me *most* unfavourable in every way towards *all* those who deserted the poor young Prince. All seem to have been indifferent to his fate.'

The Duke of Cambridge nevertheless was told about the Empress's desire for leniency: the verdict of the Court Martial was reversed, and Carey restored to his rank. We are not concerned here with the indignation which the army, speaking through Sir Lintorn Simmons, Evelyn Wood and others, expressed at this 'justification of the *sauve qui peut* principle on reconnaissance', of thus condoning, as Simmons put it, the betrayal of 'the law of comradeship'. The controversy raged on in both countries, but the Empress wrote to Queen Victoria:

'Neither my son nor I would wish that Your Majesty should be exposed to annoyances for our sakes. Truth, however slowly, will see the light of day in the end. This is a consolation which God gives to those whom He tests.'

Arthur Bigge recovered from his attack of the fever after his friend's death. In a letter to his future mother-in-law, Mrs. Neville, he summed up the event with conspicuous fairness to all involved:

Natal Club,
Durban.
August 17th, 1879.

'. . . Whenever I think of the last moments of his life, when I think of the desperate struggle he must have endured while the helping power was disappearing further and further in the distance, I sorrow for his cruel death and think how different it all *might* have been, indeed *ought* to have been. Everyone has sympathised with Lord Chelmsford, especially

314

those like myself who knew how difficult it was to restrain the Prince. The Empress was well aware of his rashness and in all her letters entreated him while doing his duty thoroughly not to incur unnecessary risks. I cannot tell you how I have felt for her, and Major Ward Ashton's account of her utter prostration and grief is most distressing. Dean Stanley's sermon preached the following Sunday most truthfully described the dear fellow's character[1]—His enemies in France will now at all events learn what a formidable foe he might have been had he lived— We still talk of him and you may be sure I shall never forget him.'

The last word on the tragedy may be given to Major Bettington of the *kraal Napoleon*, who wrote to the Duke of Bassano:

'I trust that Her Majesty knows that had it been fated that I should have been in Carey's place I should have taken the same care of His Highness as I did on former occasions, and that if I could not have saved him I would have remained with him.'

Only to her mother did the Empress permit herself to reveal the full agony of the sorrow:

'. . . My thoughts cannot leave that donga in Zululand where the drama was enacted. I want to interrogate everybody to know what he did and what he said. But with indifferent people I have an absolute horror of talking about my child, if they have nothing to tell me. Misfortune has its shame as much as wrong-doing, and I hide myself away as far as possible. My grief is savage, unquiet, irascible, I am in no way resigned and I don't want to hear about resignation any more than about consolation: I don't want to be consoled, I want to be left in peace.

I want to be sufficiently alive to be able to go to where he has been killed, see the places, all that happened: but let no one talk to me of the consolations which come from God and which I cannot accept at present.'

Her greatness was, not that she bore and suffered so much, but that she was so pitilessly determined to bear her cross alone and involve no one outside her, not even God.

Doña Manuela survived the death of her grandson by only a few months. When the Empress heard of the gravity of her mother's malady she asked the French government for permission to travel to Madrid overland. This was granted, but, just as when Don Cipriano lay dying forty years earlier, she reached Madrid too late. Now there was only Miss Flowers left at the Plazuela del Angel, still calling her Miss Eugenia, still speaking in her unbeautiful mixture of Spanish and English: and inconsolable

[1] On the same Sunday, Cardinal Manning praised the Prince in a sermon at St. Mary's, Chislehurst.

at the death of her mistress, who had unceasingly bullied her for half a century. The Empress left no word concerning her feelings at the final separation from the mother who did not love her, whom she never loved. Among the effects left by the last Countess of Montijo in her vast town house she found the letters Mérimée had written to his *chère Comtesse* through forty years of European history. Attracted by the perfume of politics and love affairs of a vanished age, of the ghosts of Narvaez and Lord Clarendon briefly rising from the dust, she browsed through the letters and read the passages where in his sharp irony Mérimée wrote of the young officers in blue and gold eagerly crowding round Doña Eugenia in the now deserted rooms where Paca had been dancing too late into the night, before the Duke of Alba silently took her away to his Palacio de Liria. She brought the letters back with her to England.

In March, 1880, a few weeks before her fifty-fourth birthday, she set out on her voyage to South Africa. With her went Sir Evelyn and Lady Wood, Napoleon de Bassano (the Duke's son), Bigge, Slade, Surgeon-Major Scott, and Mrs. Ronald Campbell. They arrived at Cape Town on April 16th, where they were received by the Governor, Sir Henry Bartle Frere, as the Prince had been eleven months earlier. 'I need not tell you,' the Empress wrote from there to Queen Victoria on April 18th,

'what cruel emotions I felt when I saw the places from where my poor child started full of hope and believing that he had found the opportunity for showing that he was worthy of his name—that heritage which is so hard to bear.'

Her deepest lament and despair came out in this letter to the Queen of England:

'What misfortune that the Emperor should have married a Spaniard and I a Napoleon! Our son naturally had to be the victim. Through my race I gave him the gift of Quixotism, the readiness always to sacrifice all to the ideal: the Emperor gave him the obligations of his name. And all in the middle of the nineteenth century when materialism closes in on us like weeds from all sides. . . .'

Thereafter, the Empress and her party spent fifty days under canvas. They reached their sad destination on May 25th; the Empress's tent was pitched in front of the *kraal* that had seen his last moments. The Queen had ordered a simple stone cross to be erected on the spot where he fell, and nearby were the graves of the two troopers who had been killed with him. It was meant to surprise the Empress, and it did. 'The place,' wrote Filon, possibly echoing her disappointment, 'presented the peaceful and orderly appearance of an English cemetery, instead of a wild ravine which had witnessed death and carnage.' A layer of cement, surrounded by an iron railing, was hiding the ground, but this was removed by Slade on the day

after their arrival: they none of them liked the alien War Memorial effect
in this primitive landscape. Otherwise the scene was exactly as he had
seen it, the tall grass, the maize, the deserted huts and pens of the *kraal*,
the seasonal heat of day and cool of night facing the Empress as they had
faced him. 'Yesterday morning,' the younger Bassano wrote to Pietri, on
June 1st,

> 'the Empress insisted on going alone to the spot selected by the Prince
> for the camp, where he made his last sketch. She had to walk for
> over three hours. I accompanied her in the afternoon, and we went
> over the same ground together. She ate nothing all day, her wonderful
> energy alone sustained her, and she walked with a sort of feverish
> strength.'

At the Empress's wish, Evelyn Wood interrogated some of the Zulus who
had taken part in the skirmish—'they all agree,' wrote Bassano, who
attended the interrogations,

> 'that the Prince turned and fought like a lion, and fired three revolver
> shots, and that they left the medals on his corpse, as their custom is not
> to take ornaments from the necks of brave men who died fighting. They
> all confirm the flight of Lieutenant Carey. . . . One of the Zulus even
> told me that if the fugitives had but turned round, they would have
> stopped the pursuit. . . .'

The Empress spent the night of June 1st alone by the cross down in the
donga, and from time to time she thought she could see silent Zulus
against the sky on the top of the banks, moving and watching above the
tall grass. Candles had been placed at the foot of the cross and shone
through the quiet night. There was no breath of air, but towards morning
they suddenly began to flicker as if blown by a wind that was not there.
'Is it you beside me?' the overwrought woman called out. 'Do you want
me to go away?'

By June 17th, they were on their way back. 'In two days,' the Empress
wrote to Pietri,

> 'we shall once more have a roof over our heads, and I am counting the
> hours, for the interest that has sustained me to this point is now over.
> At Camden Place, I wish to find only its usual occupants, and these
> only if they wish it. My one longing is for rest; any visit would be
> unwelcome.
> The farther I travel down the sorrowful road of life the greater is my
> need for rest and solitude. Nobody can fill the immense void which has
> opened in my existence. . . .'

Shortly before she went on the voyage, she had heard that a daughter had been born to the Alba family. They proposed calling her Eugénie, but the Empress wrote:

'I hope you will call the little one Doña Sol, for my name does not bring luck.'

The little one was baptised Eugenia nevertheless, although, to appease the Empress, they addressed her in the family as Doña Sol. She grew into one of the great ladies of her generation, became the Duchess of Santona, famous for the brilliance of her social life, celebrated for her horsemanship:[1] a Spaniard, a European. She died in Madrid at the beginning of 1962. She was to encounter the Empress frequently, but nothing ever caused her to complain of her baptismal name or of the godmother from whom it had come.

[1] And shocking some by taking part in bull-fights.

IV.   THE FINAL YEARS
1880-1920

CHAPTER 1

'I CAN live with the irremediable,'[1] the Empress had written on a former occasion. The forty years between her return from South Africa and her death in 1920 formed a period of submission, acceptance and self-fulfilment that gave those of her contemporaries who knew her a new understanding of such words as humility and greatness. 'The merit of her self-restraint,' wrote a friend, 'shines the brighter, when it is compared with the conduct of fallen greatness in some of the most famous of rulers and statesmen. Napoleon spent much time and labour in re-arranging history during his captivity at St. Helena; Bismarck, the man of "blood and iron", disgraced himself by impotent scolding and vituperation when he was forced to resign his power. She chose, as more consonant with her dignity as Empress, and still more with her dignity as a woman, to keep unbroken silence.'

Her innate qualities of sincerity, honesty and loyalty, her passion for ideas, her belief in the traditions and values of history, her faith in Europe, did not fade away under the impact of her many defeats, but grew stronger and deeper now that her sole obligation in life was to be, or become, herself. She did not really change, even in minor ways: to the last a pretty face, the manifestation of beauty in the human form, whether male or female, continued to delight her. Her temper did not become placid nor did her restlessness lessen with old age. Her life was not a requiem or a museum-piece, but one of activity, of movement, of growing upwards.

At first, her life was centred on the memory of her son. She could not bear to be separated from her two tombs for long. But St. Mary's Church, Chislehurst, was too small to house the two Imperial dead in permanence. Also, she wanted to leave Camden Place. In 1880, Sir Lintorn Simmons found Farnborough Hill for her, the Hampshire property of Mr. Longman, the London publisher. This she purchased together with considerable land on both sides of the Portsmouth Road. The house was a pleasant shooting lodge, standing on a hill-top above the pines and rhododendrons. Another hill rose across the railway line, and this she purchased as the site of the mausoleum for her dead and her own final resting place. A small house would be built for the monks, who would sing masses for their souls, while Mr. Longman's house would be enlarged.

When it came to choosing an architect she called in not her old friend Viollet-le-Duc, who had become a violent Republican, denying his Imperial

[1] As the term she used was irrémédiable, a literal rendering may be excusable.

321

past with shameful persistence, but M. Destailleur who had done excellent restoration work on various châteaux of the Loire. Destailleur was at this very moment busy erecting a Loire château in Buckinghamshire, Waddesdon Manor near Aylesbury, for Ferdinand de Rothschild. The Empress had met him in 1873 when he had designed the side-chapel of St. Mary's, where the Emperor's coffin rested. Work was begun in 1881. The Empress was being advised on the legal and financial side of these ambitious enterprises by her solicitors, Messrs. Markby Stewart, and by Messrs. Baring, who had been the Emperor's bankers from the beginning. Both firms remember their long connection with the Empress to this day.

Her son's friends were another element that drew her back into life. Conneau, who had been left 100,000 francs by the Prince, was a Lieutenant in the French cavalry now, and Bigge and Slade were Gunner Captains. Bigge she had presented to the Queen at Balmoral in 1880 when the Queen invited her to spend the summer months at Abergeldie. The Empress had recommended him to the Queen in the warmest terms, and soon she was able to write to him:

'Dear Captain Bigge,
    I am so glad that the Queen as [sic] appointed you to the position of Assistant Private Secretary. I know that you will always be devoted to your duties and they will always come before everything for that reason. I am not only glad for you, but also for the Queen as I know that you may be relied upon and that no better choice could have been made for that position. I always thought it would be so, you deserve all the happiness that God granted you. I am sure you will be thankful to Him for all. My dear child would have been so pleased! And as to me, although my heart bleeds, I am thankful to see those my son liked happy.
    I am not very well, I feel very fatigued. I hope to see you soon. *Croyez à mes sentiments affectueuses*.
                                                            Eugénie.
I hope you will be able to read me in English——'

Her English was not as good as Mérimée's, who in writing did not drop his aspirates, but she was making progress. Arthur Bigge was launched on his eventful career.

Among her son's older friends, Evelyn Wood, even before the journey to South Africa, had won her heart by the way he spoke of him. Wood proved the value of his friendship, when trouble arose over the project of a public monument to the Prince Imperial. It had started when the Dean of Westminster, on his own initiative, called for subscriptions for the erection of a monument to the Prince in Westminster Abbey. The French government at once protested, but Lord Salisbury replied through Lord Lyons that the Dean being 'absolutely supreme' as regards the Abbey—

'he might put up a statue to Nana Sahib, if he chose', were the Foreign Secretary's words—H.M. Government could do nothing to stop him. This was followed by an unpleasant debate in the House of Commons, where Joseph Chamberlain and Sir Charles Dilke spoke of the effect the project would have on the working classes in France. The Queen thereupon decided that the monument should instead be erected in St. George's Chapel, Windsor. The Empress was so deeply hurt by what had been said in the House that she thought of asking those in charge to drop the project altogether: it was, however, Evelyn Wood who, writing to her at Queen Victoria's command, found the kind of language that tipped the scales. Telling her respectfully, but firmly, that the debate had been an attack on the Dean of Westminster rather than on the Queen ('the English mind is not systematic,' he pointed out), he urged her to accept the Queen's offer of St. George's Chapel. He concluded:

'I imagine all of us would sooner see the monument in St. George's than in any other place except the Abbey, and I fear your refusal must pain your English friends more than it can please your countrymen. I entreat Your Majesty to pardon my frankness. No one can live for several months in your society without feeling a deep interest in all that concerns you, and although I am conscious that my life of continuous action is not favourable to the framing of arguments for sovereigns yet I believe no one feels more warmly for you than
Your devoted servant,
Evelyn Wood.'

The Empress withdrew her objections and was able to write to Bigge after a visit to St. George's Chapel later in the year:

'I have been glad to see the beautiful monument and the place where it stands. The Queen, who feels with those that suffer and, what is rare, has the courage to show her feelings, has completed the work of those that by affection for my dearest child wished a durable monument for him.'

Conneau, the Prince Imperial's companion from the earliest years, was the youngest Captain in command of a French cavalry unit and patently marked out for a brilliant career. By then also, he had spent his legacy from the Prince, and shown a natural talent for living beyond his means, including the allowance he received from the Empress. It was not, as the Empress was well aware, the first time, but now he was writing from Bezière on February 2nd, 1886:

'. . . With a broken heart, I turn once more to Your Majesty. Thanks to you, I have received an education which has enabled me to achieve a position in the army which is almost unique. Thanks to you also, my past

323

sins are unknown here, or have been forgotten. Soon I hope to get married and give up this bachelor's life which is so bad for me. What I need is a capital sum of 25,000 francs. . . .'

The Empress dealt with the young man's difficulties effectively and anonymously. Through her Paris solicitors she paid his debts, which amounted to 36,800 francs, instructed the solicitors to tell his creditors to allow him no further credit and to cut his allowance of 5,000 francs by half 'until further orders'. The treatment, the strictness within the generosity, do not seem to have been wasted. Conneau remained in the service and, after 1914, did his country much honour.

In the Prince he had lost his closest friend, and the letters which he sent to the Empress twice a year, on March 16th, the birthday, and on June 1st, the anniversary, always glowed with an engaging sincerity. Those of 1887, the year following the financial rescue, were no exception, and the Empress replied from Farnborough, where she was supervising the final completion of the mausoleum:

'My dear Conneau,

I feel like you that the steady march of the years cannot diminish the memory of him who felt for you so strong and constant an affection. It seems incredible that eight years have passed. The void which he has left has not been filled for any of us. Here, I find that work has made little progress, because the winter has been grim, but I hope that the year will not end without my having the two coffins brought to me here.

Do your work well for the sake of his memory, and believe in my affection:

Eugénie.'

Among the Empress's first guests when she moved into Farnborough Hill at the beginning of 1833 were the Lintorn Simmonses and their daughter. Lady Simmons' diary gives vivid glimpses of the Empress entertaining her guests, including the Portuguese Ambassador and, for one afternoon, the Duke and Duchess of Connaught, 'with the greatest ease and kindness': the house, though still half-finished, might have been Compiègne. She quickly put everyone at their ease, amusing them with a flow of anecdotes. She told them of the stranger who was constantly writing letters offering her an invention for the new house, beginning his letters with 'Darling Eugénie', and with 'My own loved one'. Or she spoke of poor Miss Flower, still all alone in the town house of the Montijos in Madrid and refusing to come to England because she did not trust the new-fangled inventions of steamships and railways. She also recounted how she had abruptly terminated an interview recently granted to a lady journalist when her questioner remarked:

'What a pity you were not beheaded like Marie Antoinette—then you would have lived in history,'

and how the lady quoted this in the published account, adding:

'The Empress did not seem to like the suggestion, but rose and dismissed me.'

She astonished them by her powers of mimicry and imitation, of caricaturing the way in which Spaniards said goodbye to each other at railway stations. 'The Empress acted,' wrote Lady Simmons,

'in the most entertaining manner how they embraced, and wept, and violently waved their handkerchiefs. One husband and wife, who were parting for only a few days, howled terribly, especially the man, and his friends patted him on the back saying, "but it's only for eight days!"'

But on other occasions, especially when she found herself alone with the Simmons family, she would suddenly grow serious and comment on the torturing contrast between the truth, as she had experienced it, and the fictions that were being spread and believed. 'People always say I am fanatical,' she once said to them. 'We have often remarked,' said Sir Lintorn, 'that there is not the slightest foundation for this mis-statement.' 'Ah,' replied the Empress, 'a few of my personal friends know this, but they cannot outweigh popular feeling.'

One evening, pacing up and down for hours on end, she spoke to Lady Simmons of all her closest memories—of the night at Biarritz when the Emperor suddenly cried out 'Ugénie, Ugénie' revealing the agony of his disease to her for the first time, and how always when he was ten minutes late returning from some visit or parade, she expected to hear he had been killed: and how she knew they were doomed when in August 1870 a messenger fresh from the Emperor had woken her in the middle of the night and told her Trochu had been appointed Governor of Paris: and how deeply her son had felt the insults in the French papers, the insinuations about the Bonapartes' *maladie de famille* and the bullet of Saarbrücken, and how his servant who was with him in Zululand had said: it was these things that killed him. And after that she told Lady Simmons of the first time the Prince had been drunk, and it had been mentioned in a London paper, and he swore never to exceed again. It was an astonishing, an irrepressible torrent of trivial detail and history that came tumbling out helter-skelter before the ears of the enthralled Lady Simmons. Was the life of a Sovereign to be envied? The Empress told her friend that from all the splendour and glories of her former position, from all the glittering life in the great palaces of France, she missed only one thing: and that was her yacht. Otherwise—'she spoke of her life of constant anxiety with *émeute* and mentioned with horror the cries of the people against them which she could hear from the Palace, and of the agony of mind she endured.'

On the walls of a long corridor up and down which she liked to walk there hung what Lady Simmons describes as 'a very large portrait of the Empress in red velvet, holding the Prince as a baby on her lap, but it does not do her justice'. Several times in their perambulations, the Empress stopped in front of it. During one of these sudden silences Lady Simmons remarked shyly that there had been nothing in the Prince 'to regret or wish otherwise'; the Empress, in a different voice, exclaimed, 'but he was so young', began to sob convulsively and ran from her friend to her private sitting-room. Lady Simmons's entry for this day concludes:

'When the Empress rejoined us later in the salon, she entered into conversation with Lintorn, and was as kind and pleasant to all as ever.'

At the beginning of 1883, the Empress exercised her powers of conciliation in one of the least congenial political acts of her life. Prince Napoleon had been sent to prison by the Republican authorities in January, because, hoping to take advantage of Gambetta's sudden death in the last five minutes of 1882, he had issued a proclamation calling for a plebiscite as a preliminary to the overthrow of the present system. It had been the first of the feeble coups d'état which the Third Republic was so easily to master; Prince Plon-Plon's attempt had been no more effectual than those of Boulanger and Déroulède were to be later on. Yet it had been a coup d'état of sorts, and the Empress certainly incurred a grave risk of antagonising both the British and French governments by going to Paris so soon after the event. Her principal concern, however, was to preserve unity among Bonapartists of all shades, and as the party wanted to save its own skin by disavowing the Bonaparte Prince, she travelled in order to make a personal appeal against this. Although her old enemy had been excluded from the succession to the throne, she did not want him excluded from the party as well. Like the Emperor in the old days, she realised the value to the party of so strong and bold a personage. 'I detested him,' she said after his death in 1891, 'but I never despised him, he was always frank.' So to Paris she went, forgetting all the injuries he had done her, and assembled the party leaders around her in her rooms at the Hôtel du Rhin in the Place Vendôme. 'I have forgiven him, why can't you?' she asked and implored them not to drop him from the party at a time when Gambetta's death offered new opportunities. But the party-men refused to have him back and Prince Napoleon, liberated soon after the Empress's visit to Paris, went into exile in Switzerland and Italy. In gratitude for the Empress's endeavours on his behalf, he travelled to Chislehurst a few months later and appeared, wearing the *Grand Cordon* of the *légion d'honneur*, at the memorial Mass for the Prince Imperial on June 1st, 1883. But at no time was the stubborn Corsican capable of a gesture of lasting reconciliation. When he lay dying in a Roman hotel in 1891, he forbade his son, Prince Victor, to come to his deathbed: the claimant of the Imperial throne was on too friendly terms with the Empress. In his will he disposed:

' I leave nothing to Victor. He is a traitor and a rebel. I do not wish him to be present at my funeral.'

It meant that the Empress became responsible, financially and otherwise, for the Pretender's future. To her, he was the Emperor to the end of her life.

The Empress had regarded Gambetta as a dangerous demagogue and expected that his advent to power would lead to civil strife and anarchy. But in his last years he had grown into a statesman of stature, determined to transform the Republican Constitution into an instrument, his instrument, of responsibility. Even some of the Imperialists felt that after the death of the Prince Imperial, only Gambetta could give them the government of which they dreamed. He dominated the parties, the Ministries, the Chamber, the Elysée itself. In the evenings the former left-bank bohemian dined—white tie, black coat, scented, fresh from his barber— with Prince de la Trémoille, Prince d'Arenberg, Marquis de Lau, General de Galliffet and Alphonse de Rothschild, with Henri de Breteuil and the Prince of Wales. At one of these banquets he gave a toast:
' To France saved ! '
Alphonse de Rothschild rose and turned towards Gambetta:
' To him who will save her ! '
Had the mantle of Empire fallen on his shoulders? ' Gambetta is decidedly our master ! ' and ' He is the Grand Elector of France,' were sayings of this period. It was the classical moment with which the Third Republic was so supremely qualified to cope. They conspired, they allowed him to become Prime Minister, they gave him the appearance of power and prevented him from exercising it. Three months after taking office, he fell. The Chamber had remained the master of France. When next Gambetta rose to speak, attacking the Chamber's latest nominee, Freycinet, he was shouted down, and the government of the day was given a huge majority. ' Such are the people who govern us,' wrote Ludovic Halévy[1] in his diary. His entry for January 1st, 1883, brings us back to the Empress:

' Gambetta dead. The year has begun with a thunderbolt. He died last night at five minutes to midnight. He really was ill, despite the denials of his friends. Why this mystery? Gambetta was lovable, witty and kind. As a person, he must be regretted. Politically—one does not know what to say. He had ceased to be anything, was neither a conservative nor a revolutionary: he was a Gambettist.'

[1] Halévy had been a friend of Morny and had, in 1860, pointed out Gambetta to Morny. The latter studied the then uncouth figure through his lorgnon from a distance and that, alas, was all.

And this was the moment when the Empress appeared in the Hôtel du Rhin and wished to forge a new unity out of the Bonapartist remnants. Was there not a great lesson to be learnt from the manner in which Gambetta had failed? 'We shall never bargain over our principles,' she told Fleury, 'but it is always necessary to efface those little susceptibilities which do our cause so much harm.' To her, the survival of the party and its identity was a matter of conscience and duty, and she had gone to Paris for that reason.

When she returned, Bigge was waiting for her with a letter from the Queen which said:

'I should like to tell you how greatly I admired your courage and self-denial on the present occasion. The motives which caused you to sacrifice your personal feelings are admirably expressed in an article in today's *Morning Post*.

You know how great are the affection and friendship which I feel for you, and you will, I hope, understand that for a few hours I have been feeling anxious for you. . . .'

The Queen had always shared the Empress's detestation of Prince Napoleon, but realised that the French authorities might have sent the Empress to the Conciergerie as well. In her reply the Empress showed concern not with that danger but with the possibility of political repercussions from Mr. Gladstone's government. She wrote:

'. . . Your affectionate letter has touched me deeply, for your friendship is a necessity for my heart. My life has not only been full of sorrows, but it seems that circumstances demand more sacrifices from me than from other people. Self-denial is a duty for me.

Had it become necessary to modify our relationship, my grief would have been great, even though I would have kept my confidence in your sentiments, because you understand that in certain circumstances momentary sacrifices are unavoidable. . . .'

Among the outward influences which guided the Empress from her grief and her tombs back into life, Queen Victoria's practical and tactful concern for the Empress, her hospitality at Abergeldie and Osborne and her awareness that the Empress could not be pitied or consoled, exercised a great healing power. It was not a one-sided friendship, for with the years the Queen came to cherish the lively and always slightly exotic presence of the Empress among her family and Court. In the first years of exile the Empress, with characteristic diffidence, had always addressed the Queen formally with *Madam* and *Your Majesty* and in the third person. Soon the Queen insisted that she must call her *Ma Soeur* as in the days before 1870. It put the seal of sincerity on a relationship that meant much to both: harmony between two intransigent solitudes.

Work on the Memorial Church and the Empress's house at Farnborough was completed in early 1888. On January 9th, the fifteenth anniversary of the Emperor's death, his and the Prince Imperial's remains were transferred to the massive Norman crypt of the church. The two sarcophagi were placed in the transepts to the right and left of the altar above which an empty space was hewn into the thickness of the wall: there the Empress's own coffin was eventually to stand. From the roof of the church a small dome reaches skywards, and this subdued architectural allusion to the Invalides met the Empress's gaze on her hill across on the other side where the turreted roofs, timbered gables and clock-towers of the now considerably extended houses added something wholly unfamiliar to the Hampshire skyline. Below the church M. Destailleur had built a small, château-like house in warm red brick for the four Premonstratensian Canons who had declared their willingness to sing the services for the dead and take charge of the welfare of their souls. The Prior, Fr. Ambrose Garreau, had been a secular priest in the Orléannais and been carried off as a hostage by the Prussians in the 1870 war. The Order itself had been expelled from France in 1882, in which year they founded their new house at Storrington in Sussex. They remained at Farnborough until 1895.

At the Empress's wish, monastery and church were dedicated to Saint Michael, the patron saint of France. Queen Victoria and Princess Beatrice, Princess Henry of Battenberg since 1885, paid the first of many visits to the Priory on March 3rd, 1888. King Oscar of Sweden and Norway re-affirmed the devotion of the Bernadottes to the Bonapartes and his own affection for the Empress and her son by a visit in June, and in the following month the Prince of Naples, later King Victor Emmanuel III, paid his homage at the tomb of the man to whom the House of Savoy owed its elevation to the throne of Italy. The Empress Frederick of Germany came to Farnborough in December. To her, the year 1888 was everything that 1870 had been to the Empress Eugénie: her husband, having at last succeeded his father as second German Emperor in March, had died in June, and her son Wilhelm II was the new Kaiser. Even in the old Emperor's lifetime, Frederick and his English wife had been barred from all participation in the shaping of the new Germany by Bismarck and the circle hopefully gathering round their son, and now the Dowager Empress could almost be described as an exile from her son's *Reich*. On her visit to Saint Michael's she gave the coronation robes she had not been destined to wear to the monks who worked them into some of the beautiful vestments used at the Abbey to this day. In later years the Empress Frederick sought solace in the liveliness of her conversation at Farnborough Hill as often as she could. She never modified the admiration for the Empress as Sovereign which she had first felt as a young girl. 'The perfection of a hostess,' she wrote to her daughter Sophie, as Crown Princess of Greece a novice in the profession of Royalty, 'was the Empress Eugénie—no one ever came up to that.' During her final illness, the Empress offered her stricken friend the hospitality of her house in the South of France as a

329

refuge in the sun. 'Her kindness,' wrote the Empress Frederick to her daughter,

'touches me so much, it is just like her. She does not stop to ask whether it will do her good or harm in the eyes of her party in France, but follows the dictates of her kind heart.'

Although no French government before 1920 could afford to recognise the Empress's existence officially, unofficial relations behind the scenes, carefully hidden from the public, became friendlier and even produced, in the case of Hanoteaux, Delcassé, Poincaré and finally Clemenceau, muted expressions of respect and gratitude. The Republican authorities never raised any difficulties when the Empress wished to retrieve her personal possessions from France. She had always most scrupulously observed the difference between her private property and the possessions of the Crown. Immediately after the Emperor's death, she had sold the Villa Eugénie at Biarritz and other possessions to pay the debts of the civil list. In return, the authorities restored to her such items of furniture or works of art as could be identified as hers. Others, however, which had mysteriously reached public collections, became the subject of litigation. So she was able to hang on the walls of Farnborough Hill her various Winterhalters, his paintings of the Emperor and of herself in robes of state, his portraits of Paca and of the Duchess of Mouchy, his leafy study of herself and her ladies. From Biarritz came the beautiful set of seven Gobelin panels depicting the history of Don Quixote, from Compiègne the Louis XVI chairs, cabinets and fire-screens, the Beauvais tapestry chairs, the circular tables, Sèvres vases and other period pieces which she had been collecting during the reign. In the big drawing-room downstairs she hung Cabanel's not unimpressive full-length portrait of Napoleon III, on another wall de Dreux's excellent picture of the Emperor on horseback. In one of the smaller reception rooms was the Golden Rose which the Pope had sent her for the baptism of the Prince Imperial. This particular treasure had been brought to her soon after the Tuileries fire of 1871 by a gentleman who insisted on anonymity.

The Empress's personality was revealingly expressed in the library which she gradually built up at Farnborough Hill. It ranged from La Rochefoucauld, Pascal and Montesquieu to Kipling's *Jungle Book* (in French) and works on the Russian Revolution of 1917. History figured with special prominence, that of France and of the two Napoleonic Empires holding pride of place. But her reading was not confined to the works of partisans: Maxime Du Camp's mordantly Republican commentaries on the Second Empire shared the shelves with orthodox Bonapartists like Giraudeou, the two Cassagnacs, Henri Houssaye. The books of Darimon, the irreconcilable Republican of 1857, were read and kept as was Paul Deléage's moving account of the Prince Imperial in Zululand.

Reading was to her one of the ways to keep up-to-date. She eagerly took up new books dealing with scientific inventions and the problems of medicine. As she sat alone among her books browsing, comparing, remembering, the Empress saw the course of her life transformed into history. Pierre de La Gorce and Emile Ollivier completed their voluminous histories of the Second Empire in her lifetime, men like Baron Haussmann, Persigny and Philippe de Massa published their memoirs before the end of the nineteenth century. Hübner's confidential diary of his ambassadorial years in the 1850s was published by his son in 1905. The Franco-Prussian War was raging on in unending paper-battles fought with ink and venom, but when in 1910 a British journalist called Norman Angell published a book which described the concept of victorious wars as a *Great Illusion*, the Empress was among his earliest readers.

Two safes let into the walls of her private study housed her other, her secret library. It was composed of the documents and correspondence she had permitted to survive. She preserved all the letters the Emperor had ever written to her; the documents dealing with various episodes of her Regencies, her correspondence with the Ministers, the personal notes from foreign diplomats such as von der Goltz, Nigra and Metternich. Letters from the Sovereigns of Europe, appeals for help from friends and begging letters from strangers; the whole correspondence between the Emperor and Mme Cornu; the most authoritative collection of documents dealing with the peace feelers of 1870 and the fall of Metz; small curiosities of history—a letter from Rossini accompanying a *Stabat Mater* dedicated to her, a dignified letter of condolence from the King of Siam, a call to accept Fate from Abd-el-Kader—all these were kept in meticulous order and constantly reviewed in the light of her determination to let facts speak louder than the din of controversy, to make the authentic voice of the Napoleonic Empires heard without explanation and justification. No brief summary can do justice to the rich and varied interest of the documents which survived her periodic *auto-da-fés*; she regarded them as the substitute for the memoirs she at length decided not to write.

Jurien de La Gravière had come very close to persuading her to put down her memories and experiences on paper, but in the end she judged that the time was not yet ripe. The octogenarian Admiral had become a serious naval historian and a member of the Académie Française. Their correspondence continued as lively as ever. As a father and grandfather, Jurien formed his own judgment of the problems facing the growing generations. 'Education,' he wrote to the Empress, 'has become so universal that it no longer confers distinction.' He added:

'A new society is being born, a society of the largest numbers. We are being tossed about between Germanism and Americanism, although our own standards are neither Germanic nor American. In our hearts we remain French, but I fear that we will not for long remain the easygoing and good-tempered Frenchmen we once were. . . .'

His last letter to the Empress was written after he had fallen ill. It was dated January 28th, 1892:

'The savage beast has paid me the honour of a visit. I have not left my room and bed since January 1st. But I reckon to emerge victorious from the struggle and to be about when the time comes to avail myself of your kind invitation. You know how great my pleasure always is to exchange ideas with you. Then time seems too short however long our conversation! Nor do we lack subjects for discussion: and what heights of philosophy do we seem to reach.

I beg Your Majesty to accept the respectful homage of my deep affection.

E. Jurien de La Gravière.'

He died on March 5th, 1892.

From the 1890s, the Empress spent her life constantly moving between the three focal points of her existence: Farnborough, the South of France and her yacht *Thistle*. So far as she thought, and felt, in terms of 'home', she thought of Farnborough, of her spacious house set in its pleasant parkland, where the stables housed the horses Arthur Bigge had brought for her, and the Prince Imperial's two servants, Uhlmann and Lomas, who had been with him in Zululand, kept an eye on the visitors from the two lodges at the gates. But she needed her escape from the English winter, to breathe the air of France, and, however transitorily, the air of Paris. Mérimée had always encouraged her to build a house somewhere along the Mediterranean coast of France. At Cap Martin, between Monte Carlo and Mentone, she found a strip of land running out into the sea, where she built herself a villa and called it Cyrnos, the Greek name for Corsica. 'The sea,' she told a visitor, 'is my element—it is the cure *par excellence* for every physical and moral sickness. I should like to live on the sea all the time. . . .' She bought *Thistle* from the Hamilton estate in 1888. Until 1914 the sturdy little ship carried her to Venice and Naples and Palermo, Athens, Constantinople and Corfu, Cairo, Tangier, Gibraltar. Cruising on *Thistle*, even in the Empress's company, was not always viewed as an unmixed joy by her guests, for the yacht pitched and shook and rolled in the slightest of swells. The Empress was wholly immune from sea-sickness, and in times of storm would climb up to the bridge.

Her household was small. The most indispensable of the regular members was Franceschini Pietri, who fulfilled the function of Chamberlain as well as Secretary. Mme Le Breton and Mlle de Larminat, her principal ladies in the first decades of exile, were gone: the former died in 1899, the latter had left not long after the Prince Imperial's death. The Empress had liked Marie de Larminat: she was a handsome, sharp-tongued and witty person, somewhat Anglophobe in bias and apt to vent her spleen in public. 'We gave them,' she had said when the Prince Imperial's coffin was brought to Camden Place, 'a young man at the height of his charm and beauty, and they return us a corpse.' When an English visitor propounded somewhat original religious views one afternoon, she said equally audibly: 'My dear, what do you expect? She believes in the Gospel according to Saint Anne

332

Boleyn.' 'In England,' she moaned, 'they treat the sun with the affection due to a friend who is always absent.' She left the Empress's circle early in the 1890s, and as poor Mme Le Breton was more an invalid than an attendant, the Empress, reversing their roles, was mostly in attendance on her.

Others, coming as friends volunteering to be at the Empress's side, took their place. There was, in the first place, Christine de Arcos, née Vaughan, and there was Antonia d'Attainville, née Nava del Tajo and, as such, a relation. Between them, the English woman with her Spanish husband (the Arcos family were old friends of the Montijos) and the Spanish lady with her French husband became inseparable from the Empress and shared her life with devotion, intelligence and helpfulness. Isabel Vesey, daughter of neighbours in Farnborough, became the last and the most understanding of the friendly guardians watching over the Empress in her final years.

The Empress's mail always included a large number of begging letters, the most painful one perhaps being that written by Marshal Canrobert's son Napoleon who, although her godson, had sent no word since 1870, until in 1899 his debts made him turn to her. The most astounding series of appeals for help came from a retired tax official in Brittany who told the Empress that he found himself in acute financial trouble owing to his unrepublican mentality: this was Trochu, one of the sons of the General who was not killed on the steps to the throne in September 1870.

CHAPTER 2

THE EMPRESS kept open house at Farnborough and Cap Martin, and in both places during those last two decades before the 1914 War gathered round her a circle of people remarkable for their conversation, their character, their erudition, their manners, their public positions, their youth, their looks. She barred bores and never liked old people, especially after her eightieth birthday, in 1906. 'Is old Lady X still alive?' she would say in wonderment when some matron of sixty or so was mentioned. With her wide sympathies and insatiably inquisitive mind she valued all visitors who excelled in their chosen profession. There was Maurice d'Ocange whom she made explain to her the curative and other properties of radium; the young and unknown Marconi who spoke to her of wireless telegraphy and to whom she lent *Thistle* to experiment with his invention between Nice and Corsica. When in 1901 wireless communications were formally inaugurated between Canada and England, the first message to be flashed went to King Edward VII, the second to the Empress Eugénie. Aviation held a never-ending fascination for her, and she studied its development in technical publications.

But her favourite field remained that of foreign affairs. Sir Donald Mackenzie Wallace, who was in charge of the foreign department of *The Times* from 1891 to 1899, was a frequent guest at Farnborough Hill. Ambassadors from many countries came to her dinner-parties and weekends. The Marqués de Villalobar, who represented the King of Spain in Lisbon, Paris, London, and, during the First World War, Brussels, valued her friendship so highly that he built himself a house at Camberley to be her neighbour. Nephew of her father's friend and fellow-Bonapartist, the Duke de Rivas, Villalobar had been born legless, yet had achieved mastery of his artificial limbs with astonishing courage and determination. The Empress had known him all his life and had insisted that he be fitted with prostheses and taught to walk, despite the resistance of his parents, who with fatalistic indifference had simply regarded him as the monster of the family. She had recognised his exceptional promise and had helped with his education. In her guest at Farnborough and Cap Martin she admired his steely will-power, devotion to duty and wit. They had both much to teach each other in the matter of disciplining misfortune by unyielding self-control.[1]

[1] Villalobar's son, the present Marqués, told the author that Alexander Woolcott's account of his father in *While Rome Burns* errs greatly on the side of sensationalism. A serving Spanish Ambassador wrote to the author recently: 'I began my diplomatic career under Villalobar and it was from him that I learnt most about my profession.'

Anyone who ever discussed the international scene with her, or listened as her mind ranged over the problems and tensions of Europe, came away with the conviction that, as an eminent man who was no friend of hers expressed it, 'the Empress is one of the great politicians of our time.' 'She was,' wrote Abbot Cabrol of Farnborough, 'like a man in her appreciation of facts and her brave ability to face truths.' These qualities were tested and proved to a remarkable degree during the Spanish-American War of 1898 in which she felt herself involved both as a Spaniard and a politician. Her interest was roused immediately when the Cuban insurgents showed their fighting strength. 'May God give,' she wrote to her niece, Rosario, sixteenth Duchess of Alba, on October 22nd, 1897

'that they [Spain and the rebels] will reach an understanding and that Cuba, in the event of becoming independent, will take over a large part of the Spanish national debt. Italy did this when she took Venetia, and we in the case of Nice and Savoy. As soon as one makes concessions, one is in a position to stipulate conditions, and in this way the Spanish finances would be improved, one evil out of the way. Yet to a Latin country honour counts for much, we do not have the cold and balanced reasoning of the Anglo-Saxons, and the country is not ready for the amputation. . . .'

When in the spring of 1898 war with the U.S.A. was imminent, she wrote:

'. . . I cannot get used to the idea of war, the parties are too unequal: my poor, dear, adored country has the courage, the energy, the senti-ment of honour pushed to the limit of temerity, but America has the nerve for war, the possibility of replacing fleet after fleet. . . . May God inspire the Government to avoid war. I do not doubt that the Spaniards will perform splendid feats of arms, but afterwards. . . !'

And her *mais après* went through her letters to Madrid as a constant warn-ing.

Lord Salisbury, now Prime Minister, said in a speech in April 1898 that, although England would remain neutral, nations of the world could be divided into 'the living and the dying', that the 'efficacy of destruc-tion, the concentration and increasing power' advanced continuously on the side of the strong, and implied that England's sympathies could hardly be on the side of moribund nations which were 'drawing nearer and nearer to their fate'. The speech, which *The Times* called 'a justification of aggression', had a devastating effect in Spain, and not only in Spain. The British Ambassador at Madrid, Sir H. Drummond Wolff, was told by the Duchess of Alba that it had undermined the position of the Queen Regent's government vis-à-vis the Carlist and left opposition, but Salisbury, replying to Wolff's representations, maintained that by moribund States he had alluded, not to Spain, but to the Central and South American Republics. He had been misinterpreted 'by one of those lying telegraphic agencies'. Yet when urged to make public amends, he curtly refused, saying that 'explanations are always impossible'. Henceforth, many people in Spain thought that, in Wolff's words, 'England is going to join the United States in the present war.'

The Empress also was shocked by the Prime Minister's speech. She wrote to the Duchess of Alba:

'Outside their immediate interests on which the British base their policy we cannot expect anything from them. I have not spoken to a single Englishman who did not admire the courage of the Spanish, but who at the same time did not approve of Lord Salisbury's attitude which amounts to this: If you are weak we admire you and if you are strong we help you.'

Haunted by the fear that the recently restored Spanish Monarchy would not survive military defeat and the onslaught by its internal enemies, the Empress broke the rule of a lifetime and made a direct appeal to Queen Victoria. She hoped that a gesture of monarchical and European solidarity from the Queen of England would strengthen the Spanish government and throne. 'I spoke to the Queen,' she wrote to the Duchess of Alba,

'of the Queen-Regent, of the little King, of Spain. She listened to me. her eyes were full of sympathy, but she did not utter one word. She had become the constitutional sovereign once more, with her Ministers being the sole organ of policy: it was infuriating!'

The Empress underrated the old Queen's strength of feeling, however. When the United States declared war, the Queen had written privately to Salisbury urging a united protest by the great powers 'against such unheard-of conduct'. If Cuba was to be independent why not Ireland as well? she asked. After the Prime Minister's speech she wrote again imploring him 'to get the powers to help the Queen-Regent of Spain. Unfortunately, Lord Salisbury's speech seems not understood', she added. She could not, of course, inform the Empress of these intercessions with her Prime Minister, but her sympathy with Eugénie's outlook was far from mute.

On June 3rd, 1898, a letter, signed 'Neutral', was published in The Times which so closely reflected the Empress's own ideas that it deserves a brief quotation. 'Neutral' wrote that Cuba, for long merely a drain on the Spanish economy, should be given up, especially as the United States was pledged to secure its evacuation by Spain. However, he continued—

'there remains the point of honour as to which the countrymen of Cervantes are naturally and rightly sensitive. No one can have read the

336

account of the devoted gallantry of the Spanish seamen at Manila without feelings of the warmest admiration. If we are proud of the action of the little *Revenge*, Spain has an equal right to glory in the devotion of her sailors. . . .'

'Neutral' followed this up by putting these terms to the two belligerents: the U.S. to raise the Cuban blockade, Spain to evacuate in nine months, the Cubans to choose their future allegiance and government.[1] The Philippines to be held by U.S. only until the Cuban evacuation was completed, but Porto Rico to go to the U.S. Drummond Wolff immediately telegraphed to London that these proposals—'they must have been written behind the scenes'—might prove successful. The Empress grew impatient. 'Time passes,' she wrote to Rosario Alba on June 17th, 1898:

'the chances of a favourable peace diminish, and the illusions grow. To what purpose? I cannot understand it—are they trying to pretend that the Philippines can be defended, when everybody knows that they can't? I should like to believe that those who live in their comfortable houses in Madrid will not cast stones at our poor soldiers who were not given any support from the motherland. I wish that those who shout for war to the last ditch would share the perils and fatigues of the fighting men.'

Finally, an American force was landed in Cuba on June 24th, and although in the face of fierce Spanish resistance it looked at first as if the enemy might be thrown back into the sea, General Linares surrendered Santiago de Cuba on July 16th. Spain had to accept the loss of Cuba, Porto Rico and the Philippines. The Empress, back at Farnborough Hill, wrote to Madrid on August 14th, 1898:

'This is a terrible year for Spain, and will inevitably leave its mark on the younger generation. . . .

One thing has struck and, I must admit, humiliated me in this sad episode of Spanish history: to see that all the great names of Spain were absent from it all. Their heroism remained confined to being warriors in the Chamber and clamouring against those who were doing the fighting.'

Her close involvement in Spain's tragedy had made her physically ill and she had conducted most of her battle for sanity and compromise from her bedroom at the Hôtel Continental opposite the Tuileries Gardens, where a suite of rooms was always kept ready for her.

Paris was her half-way house between Farnborough and Cap Martin and the Empress went there annually in the last decade of the old century and

[1] 'Cuba should be independent and not American,' Queen Victoria wrote to Lord Salisbury.

in the first fourteen years of the new. Many people found it incomprehensible that she should choose to face from the Continental the gardens where her son had played, where a vacant space now yawned between the two wings of the Louvre once linked by the Tuileries. Did it not show that she was heartless? The Empress knew that this was being said, but did not feel compelled to change her hotel. She received her friends in the drawing-room of her suite with its huge chimney-piece of marble, its rich gilt, its looking-glasses and brocades.

In the Dreyfus affair, the Empress was staunchly *Dreyfusiste*, convinced of the innocence of the prisoner on Devil's Island, of the guilt by blind prejudice and a diseased *esprit de corps* animating the General Staff who sent him there. She hated injustice and hoped that there would be a new trial leading to a reversion of the original verdict, but it was known only to a few that the Empress, despite the legends, was on the side of Zola, Clemenceau and the revisionists and not on that of the royalists, political Catholics and professional aristocrats. Gustave Schlumberger, the Byzantine scholar whose rather specialised erudition she admired and who was a frequent guest at Farnborough and Cap Martin, was a convinced anti-Dreyfusist. He was quite unable to face the fact that the sacred cows of the General Staff could be fallible, let alone guilty, and so was in the habit of cutting short any one who argued Dreyfus's innocence, asking him sharply not to pursue this theme in his presence. When he called on the Empress at the Continental at the height of the *Affaire*, some remark of his prompted the Empress to an impassioned exposition of the Dreyfusist view, which he neither interrupted nor contradicted.[1] In the following year Schlumberger and his friend the Duc de Rivoli called at Cap Martin for tea. With the Empress that day was the Prince of Monaco, who before the second Dreyfus trial at Rennes had written to Mme Dreyfus to say that should the verdict once more go against her husband he and his family must be his guests at Monte Carlo. As Schlumberger entered, the Prince walked up to him with an outstreched hand. Schlumberger ignored it, the Prince, embarrassed, made his excuses and left. 'I had no idea,' the Empress later told Rivoli, 'that your friend is so strongly against Dreyfus.'

'Has Your Majesty forgotten the recent letter which the Prince wrote to Mme Dreyfus?' replied Rivoli.

'Last year,' said the Empress, 'I explained to Schlumberger my ideas, which were entirely favourable to the prisoner on Devil's Island. He made not a single objection.'

'That was because it was Your Majesty who spoke.'

Intolerant of all forms of intolerance, impatient of fanaticism in all

[1] It is interesting to find that in the same year Princess Mathilde, still, at seventy-seven, leading an active social life, was assuring her friends that ' the War Office has letters to Dreyfus in the Kaiser's own handwriting'.

THE EMPRESS IN OLD AGE

ARTHUR BIGGE (later LORD STAMFORDHAM)
1881

THE EMPRESS AT FARNBOROUGH HILL. FROM LEFT TO RIGHT:
MISS VESEY, MISS COCHRANE, GENERAL BOURNE, THE EMPRESS,
DR. HUGENSCHMIDT AND DR. ATTENBOROUGH

THE FUNERAL OF THE EMPRESS
(Heading the procession: Prince Victor Napoleon and Princess Clementine of Belgium)

guises and wholly free of both the shabbiness of anti-Semitism[1] and the narrowness of chauvinistic nationalism, the Empress had watched the convulsions of the Third Republic from Boulanger to Dreyfus's final vindication without taking any delight in the Republic's tribulations or without losing her faith in France. The Dreyfus affair had caused many Frenchmen to remember the Prince Imperial. 'If only the Prince Imperial had lived,' wrote Giraudeou to her, 'is the cry to be heard on all sides today.'

Bismarck's public revelations of his reasons for starting the Franco-Prussian War blunted an important weapon in the propagandistic armoury of the Republic, namely that the dynasty had provoked the war to ensure its own survival. The Empress saw that in the last decade of the century the whole image of the Empire was brightening and improving. There was, in 1892, a long article in the *Moniteur* praising the Empire's attempt to save Mexico from political and economic domination by the United States. 'History,' she read, 'will, in its impartiality, judge the Mexican venture differently from contemporary judgment.' She had, moreover, the extraordinary experience of winning over, almost despite herself, the most unlikely enemies of former times. Jules Claretie, most influential of journalists and notoriously hostile to the Empire, emerged from a conversation of several hours at the Continental and announced that she was entirely unlike the woman he had hitherto assumed, and written, that she was. Then there was Joseph Reinach, once Gambetta's secretary, former owner of the Gambettist *République Française*, determined enemy of Boulanger, and convinced Dreyfusist. He conceived so strong and deep an admiration for the Empress that he decided forthwith to write her biography. It is to be regretted that in the end he had to desist because the Empress, faithful to her iron resolve never to encourage any public vindication or explanation of her record, would not give him her support. She would not consent to so much as a statement to the Press, a quotation or *démenti*. 'I died in 1870,' she would say in accents that ranged from the playful to the angry.

At the same time, she acquired great skill in keeping her movements and visits secret. In 1894, she heard that Victor Duruy lay ill in his apartment in Paris, and so one afternoon slipped into the house of the anti-clerical educational reformer and historian. It is only from a letter of Filon's that we know of this event. He wrote:

[1] Edouard Drumont, author of the notorious *La France Juive* and founder of French right-wing anti-semitism, had attempted to draw the Empress into his sordid controversies by alleging that as a strong Roman Catholic she was anti-semitic. The Empress at once wrote a letter of protest which Filon, who had known Drumont in their student days, delivered. 'Drumont,' Filon wrote to the Empress, 'is the mouthpiece of others and dangerous only to his friends. . . . Your Majesty's letter has said all that is necessary to say. . . .' Although Drumont was largely responsible for the downfall of Lesseps over the Panama affair and the imprisonment of the canal-builder's son, he was, after the Empress's discreet but outspoken protest, unable to use her name for his odious purposes. During the Panama scandal, the Empress gave the Lesseps family every moral and financial support and was officially represented by Prince Murat at the funeral of Ferdinand de Lesseps in December 1894.

'I was greatly touched to hear of the visit Your Majesty has deigned to pay to my poor old teacher. The thought was charming and worthy of Your Majesty—but those stairs! ! I always have the greatest difficulty in forcing myself to make the ascent. But when next I succeed in getting there, and if my strength does not fail me on the third floor, I shall recall with him the memory of Your Majesty's visit.'

Her contacts were wide, varied, and limited by no prejudice. A note written to Pietri by Gaston Calmette, the famous editor of *Figaro*, and unfortunately undated, tells its own story:

'I send you [wrote Calmette] a copy of *Figaro* in which the Empress will recognise some of the ideas which came from her marvellous brain and also from her no less exquisite heart. It is an interview with Delcassé. . . .'

Her numerous 'progresses' through Paris brought her other experiences and delights. Many are the anecdotes told of her picking a flower in the Tuileries Gardens and being warned off by a keeper who recognised her too late, or of the old lady in black moving silently through the deserted rooms of Compiègne and being told not to touch the furniture. . . . Isabel Vesey who, like Pietri, was often at her side in Paris remembers different incidents: the Empress, driving about Paris in her electric brougham, pointing out 'each familiar spot and relating the incidents she remembered as clearly as though they had happened the week before'. Or the visits to Versailles, the Trianons and Fontainebleau, the visits to Malmaison to which the Empress added new treasures from her Napoleonic collections year after year. Or the drives through the countryside to visit the Murats at Rocquencourt, Mme de Beaulaincourt and her son at the Château d'Acosta, or old Raimbaut at Saint-Cloud—the same Raimbaut who in 1867 had pushed his horse between the carriage bearing the Emperor and the Czar and the gun of their Polish would-be assassin. Then there was the occasion when they passed a large car which had broken down by the wayside with a grey-bearded gentleman standing next to it who looked up as they passed: it was M. Loubet. Recognising him at the last moment, she ordered her chauffeur to drive on, since it would scarcely have been etiquette for her to take the President of the Republic in tow. Miss Vesey remembers, too, the callers assembling in the big drawing-room at the Continental, well-established friends like young Walewski, the now aged Mme de Pourtalès, Gustave Schlumberger, the three Bassano girls mingling with a group of mere sightseers, waiting for the Empress to make her entry, and the Empress saying afterwards: 'They come to see me like a Fifth Act.' Or the starlit autumn night when, standing by the open window, suddenly the Empress stood transfixed and exclaimed:
'Listen!'
She had heard, above the noises from the street, the sounds of a distant

hunting horn, and it brought back memories of Fontainebleau and Compiègne. She to whom music meant so little burst into a flood of explanations of what the various musical calls on the big French horns meant, and seemed to relive the excitement of the hunt, the wild gallops through the forest, the killing of the stag to the final unison of the *Hallali*. 'The sound of those two or three solitary notes,' wrote Miss Vesey, 'borne to us on the evening breeze touched a chord in her memory and carried her back to other days and other scenes.' Had not the Emperor first shown that he loved her when these sounds had echoed through the autumnal air at Fontainebleau?

Among those who called on her at her Paris hotel was Jean Cocteau. 'I saw the Empress again,' he wrote, 'at the Hôtel Continental, where stupid people reproached her for staying opposite the Tuileries. What could remain from the past to affect a woman who had died several times, but habit? The habit of living in a certain district, which is stronger than any other. When I took my leave, she invited me to return soon. I saw a flash of youth illuminate her whole face and her whole frail mourning-clad figure, like the lightning flash of the salamander which gives life to ruins.'

Cocteau had been presented to the Empress by his friend Lucien Daudet who had become, soon after his famous father's death in 1897, very much a permanent member of her intimate circle.

'The Empress came out of a winding alley,' Cocteau wrote of his first meeting with the Empress at Cap Martin. 'The face was the same. It had kept its delicate oval shape. The eyes had kept their heavenly blue, but the gaze had been diluted. An expanse of blue water inspected you. The blue, and the black eye-shadow which underlines it, recalled the tattooed eyes of young sailors who are released from prison when they are old. In these old men you find to your surprise the indelible signs of angry beauty.

'The Empress stopped: the blue water looked me up and down. Lucien introduced me. "I can no longer decorate poets," she said, "here you are, I can give you this"—and with a rapid movement she tore off a white bunch of daphne, offered it to me, watched me put it in my button-hole and went on with her walk. I walked beside her. She questioned me about dancing—Isadora Duncan and the *Ballet Russe*. She stopped and sometimes she burst out laughing. That voice and that laughter—where had I heard it before? It is a memory of the bull ring, the laughter and chatter of the young Eugénie de Montijo which were to frighten and fascinate the shy Napoleon III. . . .

'"Preceded by her suite." This little joke would hardly have any meaning at Cyrnos. The Empress exhausted her attendants, trotted along, was surprised that people complained of tiredness, and suggested accompanying me part of the way back. . . .'

Lucien Daudet, Cocteau's sponsor in this meeting, had been drawn by the Empress into the small regular circle of those whom she trusted as friends. Born in 1878, he was the second son of Alphonse Daudet and the lame duck of a brilliant family. Moving in the circle dominated by Marcel Proust, Lucien had acquired a reputation for conversational brilliance which was deserved, but it was also noted, equally justly, that he lacked the will-power to put his talents as artist or writer to some constructive use. Slim, slight and handsome, highly-strung and deeply discouraged, he had a natural gift for making himself unhappy, especially as with the years he became increasingly enslaved to homosexuality which inevitably inflicted a great deal of misery on his whole adult life. The Empress, recognising from the first the goodness of his heart and the sincerity of his devotion, rescued him from total futility and gave his life a purpose.

He walked, one spring day in 1899, into her study at the Villa Cyrnos, bowed at the door, kissed her hand, and stood speechless. She asked him to sit down, and told him that she remembered his mother reciting his father's verses at Saint-Cloud in 1857. Fighting down the tears which he felt welling up, he said that he had always worshipped her, the Emperor, the Prince Imperial. He told her that he had brought his bicycle to Cap Martin, that sometimes he went on trips of as much as 100 kilometres a day: he hardly knew what to say in the presence of this mythological figure. The Empress asked him to stay to tea, and invited him to come to Farnborough in the autumn.

She had taken an instant liking to him. Whether she was more moved by his cult for the Bonapartes or the devotion to his bicycle, more touched by the homage from a Daudet or the reverential sincerity of his manner, more taken with his good looks or amused by his nervous elegance and precocious sophistication, it would be difficult to say. At all events she accepted him, and thereafter showed him an affection that was as warm-hearted as it was astringent. 'You must work, work, work,' she would tell him when she caught him idling away the hours or found him in his room surrounded by water-colours that were unfinished and pages of manuscripts that had been abandoned. One day he told her that he had been exempted from military service. 'I hope,' she replied, 'that you will start working in earnest now. You have, I believe, a studio somewhere?'

'Yes, Madame. in the Place Dauphine.'

'What an extraordinary idea!' she said, not liking the slummy location of this alleged temple of art.

'I love the neighbourhood,' he assured her, 'and it is not very far from our part of Paris, as Your Majesty knows. It is a little studio on the mezzanine floor, in a very old house.'

The Empress burst out laughing: 'A studio on the *entresol*!' she exclaimed. 'Really, only you could invent situations like that.' And he felt an urgent desire to hide himself away from this terrible laugh.

'Despite the sun at Cap Martin,' Lucien wrote in 1910, 'despite her cruises on the *Thistle*, the Empress's true life is lived among the low skies and green fields of England, the only country in Europe where sovereigns without a throne may live in dignity.' She soon distinguished him with the rare accolade of addressing him by his Christian name. She called him Lucien and Luciano and *mon cher enfant* and, simply, *cher*.

The Empress was entirely out of sympathy with the then fashionable cult of sickness, and the gospel spread by, among others, the Goncourts, that all great writing needed 'the stimulant of neurosis to the point of illness', found no echoing response from her. She could understand and tolerate eccentricity, as she proved in thirty years of friendship with Ethel Smyth: even though Miss Smyth's lack of respect for convention exasperated her, once or twice practically to the point of physical violence. But she respected in her friend the creativeness of the musician and was in sympathy with her aims, if not methods, as a suffragette. She always believed that to preserve one's moral and physical health was among the first duties in life, and, although she at once dealt rigorously with any symptom of illness, she found being an invalid an almost degrading state, regarding those who cherished their ailments with no sympathy. Lucien Daudet may have splintered off from the sick-room world of Marcel Proust to be in attendance on her, but after his many years under the Empress's influence, he at last demonstrated that he was, despite everything, a writer.

This he proved by writing a book on the Empress. An enterprising publisher had suggested the idea to him in 1910 and he showed the letter to the Empress one afternoon when they were alone. Would she authorise him, he asked, to write a book on her, a little work without indiscretions or anecdotes, but describing her character, her mind, her tastes—'a kind of written portrait'?

'Impossible!' she replied. 'How could you write about me without giving new historical information? As you know, I always refuse permission for that. Surely you could not write without making me speak? And you know what I think of those who make me say "I" despite myself?'

'I ask,' he pleaded, 'because I am aware of this, Madame. I am thinking of a book which would provide, as it were, the psychological and moral references, would be a key for those who will later on read books about Your Majesty and who will form ideas, sometimes correctly, sometimes not. . . .'

'That,' she told him, 'I could not prevent you from doing. But you must be just and say what you think of me—not only the things which would be agreeable for me to read. . . . I know how devoted you are to me,' she went on. 'You are one of those who are more attached to people than to ideas, and you would be capable for my sake to show bravery, or even courage, if necessary. Still, this is no reason for speaking too well of me— nor too ill either, of course. . . .'

Lucien wrote his book in the summer of 1911. In the autumn of that year *La Revue* published certain extracts from it and the author wondered uneasily about reactions at Farnborough Hill. 'Her Majesty,' wrote Joachim Clary from there in October, 'is amazed that all this could have been written without containing one word of injury. For the first time she has read a book about herself in which not one phrase displeased her.'

At the end of October the happy author appeared at Farnborough Hill with the final proofs. In two long sessions Lucien read his book, facing her across the room in her private study where the two tall windows framed the view across to the other hill with the dome of the Abbey Church sailing against the clouds above the pine trees. She did not interrupt, except when once or twice she corrected little errors of fact. When the reading was completed late in the afternoon, Lucien, feeling like a prisoner in the dock, hardly dared raise his eyes towards her. What would she feel about the references to her great age, the narrative of her son's death? At last he glanced towards her. He saw her eyes full of tears, her face pale and agitated with emotion: and although she seemed to force herself to smile, all she was capable of was a quick gesture with her hands signifying: 'no words'. Silently he moved over to her and in a gesture of expiation knelt before her. Silently, she embraced him.

The book, called *L'inconnue*, was published in Paris early in 1912 and remains one of the more important works so far published about the Empress. Lucien had learnt from the principles which she had taught him.

'Do not dramatise life,' she had written to him on June 30th, 1909. 'I am always telling young people this. Life is difficult, sad and even sorrowful enough without burdening it further with anxieties, which we induce ourselves. . . .' And on another occasion she wrote this down for him:

'If among the great events of life you are searching for truth and justice you must, above all, disengage your own personality. This you can do only after living through revolts, disillusionment and suffering. Then you will reach a great calm, a peace of the soul.'

It was not the least merit in Lucien's book that he showed that a personality of her vitality could not be identified with any particular period of the past, not even with that of the Second Empire. 'Nothing about the Empress dates,' he wrote, 'and she belongs to no out-of-date epoch of history.' 'She is,' he wrote again, 'the least "Second Empire" lady imaginable.' 'She is the only woman I know whose whole aspect, from her clothes to her attitudes, does not bear the imprint of the times of her greatest glory.' The book was the first to say that the myth of the Empress's clericalism was not based on the truth, and it stressed her moderation, her aversion from all forms of proselytising, the absence in her entourage 'of all black or purple *soutanes*'.

Lucien had a special copy of his book printed and bound for the Empress, which he sent to Cap Martin early in 1912. He received the following letter in reply:

344

'My dear Daudet,

I feel inclined to reprove you. Why have a special copy made for me? Was it not enough to have been the first to dispel the legends which are so cruelly forming round the vanquished when their destiny has raised them to a role above the common run?

You have judged me indulgently. Your heart guided you, and your talent did the rest.

I cannot conclude this letter without thanking you for yours and for the book with which I was charmed.

Affectionate sentiments,
Eugénie.'

Although Lucien was still closely connected with Marcel Proust and although the Empress frequently called on her old friend Sophie de Beaulaincourt on whom Proust modelled his Mme de Villeparisis, there was no direct contact between the Empress and the novelist. Proust had grown up in the tradition that writers and intellectuals properly belonged to the salon of Princess Mathilde, a tradition which had survived the collapse of the Empire, even though the Princess and the Empress had long since composed their differences and lived on terms of friendly co-existence. Proust wrote somewhat disdainfully of the Bonapartist aristocracy—'those people who are named after a bridge', says for example Baron Charlus of the fictitious Jéna family—even though his own adored Comtesse Greffuhle, the very embodiment of the Faubourg St. Germain, was a frequent visitor at Farnborough and Cap Martin. As those two leading Proustians, Jean Cocteau and Lucien Daudet, realised, the Empress's personality did not lend itself easily to the Proustian treatment, but needed the authentic light of history and reality as its true element. Proust wisely left well alone, and no place worthy of her has ever been given to the Empress in a work of fiction.

CHAPTER 3

T HE E MPRESS was able to participate in the problems of Europe because of the unique position she held in England, especially with the Royal Family, most of all during the reign of Edward VII.

This position she owed to Queen Victoria. The trust in her honesty and sincerity which the Queen had placed in her since their first meeting at Windsor in 1855 had stood the test of the long years, and so had the Queen's delight in the Empress's company. In a number of special situations, moreover, they found themselves in agreement. The Queen, like the Empress, had been pro-Dreyfus, and when in 1899 the Empress took the Duke and Duchess of Alba to Balmoral and the Duke was able to give the Queen a first-hand account of Paris at the height of the battle, the old conviction that the Prince Imperial would have reigned reappeared before their eyes like a tragic ghost. The Queen was grateful for the Empress's presence because there was no one else now outside her family to whom she could unburden her anxieties and find so sympathetic and tactful a listener. The tensions invariably aroused by the visits of Kaiser Wilhelm II; the despair of the Queen's eldest daughter, the Empress Frederick of Germany; the loneliness of her youngest child Beatrice, whose husband Henry of Battenberg had died after a few years of marriage in 1896 and whose friendship with the Prince Imperial remained unforgotten; the thorny question of relations with the Prince and Princess of Wales; these and other problems the Queen was able to discuss with the Empress, who took no sides in any of them but was, on the contrary, on terms of reasonable friendship with the Prince of Wales and his beautiful Danish Princess, with the Kaiser, the Empress Frederick and others. Queen Victoria's confidence was handed on to her children. When the Queen died in January 1901, the new King wrote :

' I knew how deeply Your Majesty would sympathise with us all in our profound grief. Our dear mother was deeply attached to you.

Edward R.I.'

King Edward's admiration and affection for the Empress lasted to the end of his life, while Queen Alexandra continued her habit of unpredictably dropping in at Farnborough Hill, thereby often disconcerting the Empress, who liked having sufficient warning to produce at least a red carpet.

The Empress's friendship with Edward VII was, however, more than a mere continuance of the pleasant relationship begun at the Tuileries and Compiègne. They understood each other on the subject of France. This created problems of its own. As long before as 1875, Bismarck had blamed a deterioration in Anglo-German relations partly on the Empress's influence on Queen Victoria; it was desirable to avoid any repetitions from Bismarck's successors. Edward VII's French sympathies had for long caused thought and comment in the capitals of Europe. Both as Prince of Wales and King, he had become acquainted with a number of people who, like Mme de Pourtalès, Mme de Galliffet, Charles Haas and the famous Mrs. Standish, had belonged to the Empress's world before 1870 and been to her houses of exile. Not unnaturally in this spy-ridden period when new alliances between the Great Powers were slowly taking shape, the King's activities in Paris were kept as much under suspicious observation by other powers as were the Empress's travels and cruises in the *Thistle*. For had not that yacht been fitted with wireless installations by Marconi himself? The German Admiralty harboured the darkest suspicions.

This is not the place to investigate to what extent King Edward's personal contacts in Paris were connected with laying the groundwork of the *entente cordiale*, nor to determine whether the Empress's fervent desire to see France strong and respected, under whatever government, played a part in King Edward's own preferences in this respect. That the King was interested in the Empress's intermittent contacts with some of the leading French politicians and publicists seems highly likely. Sir Frederick Ponsonby, the King's private secretary, tells a curious story of a meeting between the King and the Empress in Paris in 1905 when the Empress received him, not at the Continental but at the Grand Hotel and spent an hour with him in private conversation while Sir Frederick talked to Mme de Arcos downstairs. In England, matters were easier. There the Empress was received by the King at Windsor as she had been during his mother's reign.

The Empress accepted the continuity of friendship with the Monarch with her accustomed diffidence. 'I was delighted,' she wrote in August 1902 to Bigge, now Sir Arthur and a full colonel,

'to find the King so well. Like the Queen, his mother, he has, thank God, a marvellous constitution. I was greatly touched by the affectionate manner in which he received me at Cowes. He has, I think, some friendship for me and this gives me great pleasure.

I have been to visit Osborne which I found very empty and silent. If it is to be a Royal residence no longer, I would prefer to see it turned into a place for convalescent officers. This would be less sad than to abandon it altogether, for it is always a painful thing to find places one has known deserted. One feels that death has passed that way. . . .'

Possessing as she did the confidence of the Kaiser's mother, the Empress was well aware of the unhappy relationship between mother and son which began with that ghastly moment at birth when the new-born baby had been ignored for two whole hours while the doctors were fighting to save the mother's life. She knew that as a result his left arm had withered and was stunted for life, but she had not met him in person until 1894 when he called on her together with the Duke of Connaught during manoeuvres at Aldershot. After the visit Bigge, who had made the arrangements, wrote to the Queen:

'The Duke of Connaught told Colonel Bigge that the visit to the Empress was most satisfactory. There was no stiffness and soon the Emperor and Her Majesty were joking with each other. He was struck with Her and altogether interested in seeing Her.'

The Empress Frederick died at Schloss Friedrichshof near Frankfurt on August 5th, 1901, having survived Queen Victoria by barely seven months. Not long afterwards, the Empress received this letter from the Kaiser:

Neues Palais, Potsdam,
2 January 1902.
Madame my cousin,
   The Empress Frederick, my beloved mother, had throughout her life preserved for Your Majesty a sincere friendship and deep sympathy. This, together with the memory of the gracious reception which Your Majesty accorded me when I had the honour of visiting Aldershot, now encourages me to address myself to Your Majesty's benevolence. I have arranged to have a miniature made of a portrait of my dear mother in the form of a bracelet and I solicit the honour of having it accepted by Your Majesty as a memento of a faithful friend whom the heavens have tested with a terrible martyrdom.
   In the hope that I have not taken too much advantage of Your Majesty's patience, I sign myself as Your Majesty's obedient servant and cousin,
      Guillaume.'

He had, of course, written in French. There is no reason to suspect that the tone of almost exaggerated reverence in which the letter was couched was not completely sincere and genuine. He had written in much the same accents to his adored grandmother Queen Victoria.
She heard from the Kaiser again when one day in 1905 old Count Solms, lately German Ambassador at Rome, came to the Villa Cyrnos with a personal message. Solms, now a man of eighty-five, had been an attaché in Paris before 1870 and taken part in one or two of the *revues* at Compiègne. 'Madame,' said the old man, 'the Emperor, my august master, has sent me to offer his respects and express the admiration which he feels for Your Majesty. He has charged me to tell you that to him you are always the Empress, that times are bad and all sovereigns should remain close to

348

each other.' It was a charming gesture, charmingly delivered with the formality and expertise of former times. 'What part did you play in M. de Massa's *revues*?' the Empress presently asked him, 'the postman, I believe?'

'No, Madame,' he replied sadly, 'I was Robin Hood.'

The second and last meeting between the Kaiser and the Empress took place in 1907 aboard the *Thistle* in a Norwegian fjord. The Empress had been cruising that summer in Northern waters and when *Thistle* steamed into the port at Bergen on July 25th, Miss Vesey wrote:

'We found it full of German cruisers. We were told that they were awaiting the arrival of the *Hohenzollern* with the Kaiser aboard. Pietri suggested to the Empress that we should leave before the Emperor came in, but as we had already missed him twice while cruising in the fjords, she said: "No, if we leave now, he will know that I am trying to avoid him, so we must remain." We steamed in and anchored between the line of cruisers, the *Thistle* looking like a miserable little prisoner of war in their midst. The French members of the party did not care much about meeting the Kaiser while on the Empress's yacht. . . .'

The *Hohenzollern*, followed by a cruiser and a gun-boat, arrived at Bergen at 11.30 the same night, and although it was after sundown the guns of the German warships boomed out their salutations. A little later an A.D.C. from the *Hohenzollern* climbed aboard the *Thistle* to enquire whether it would be convenient for the Emperor to pay his respects to the Empress the following morning—and what should His Majesty wear? The Empress, who had retired for the night, conveyed that she would be charmed to receive His Imperial Majesty at eleven o'clock and that she thought civilian dress was most appropriate in the circumstances.

It was pouring with rain next morning, but they had the awnings up so that the Empress could receive her august visitor on deck at the head of her little party all of whom, with the exception of Miss Vesey, assumed expressions of near-hostility as they stood waiting for the Kaiser to appear. Walewski *fils*, Miss Vesey wrote home, looked as if he had swallowed a dose of medicine, while Mlle de Castelbajac kept her eyes on Miss Vesey to make sure that she would not 'look too agreeable'. At the appointed hour the Kaiser 'skipped up the ladder, and he and the Empress went through the formality of embracing'. The Empress then presented her party, with all of whom the Kaiser amiably shook hands, and then she escorted him downstairs to her state-rooms while the angry Bonapartists of the party had to exert themselves to entertain the Kaiser's suite on deck. It was heavy going. The rain was beating mercilessly against the awning, the A.D.C.'s French was wearing out and the two sovereigns remained closeted together for an eternity. At one o'clock the Kaiser at last emerged, again shook hands with the assembled party and disappeared down the ladder. Miss Vesey wrote home the same day that he had struck her as an odd mixture of effusiveness and awkwardness—'not at all imposing, but very determined-looking, wore too many rings, a bracelet and bright yellow shoes. He spoke French with a very German accent, and his manners were certainly pleasant, no stiffness about him.'

What had he discussed with the Empress during what Miss Vesey called 'two mortal hours'? The Empress did not tell Miss Vesey much, except that he had declared himself anxious to pay an official visit to Paris where, the Empress added, 'they won't have him at present'. A tense moment was reached when his eyes fell on a photograph of Queen Victoria and he burst out that '*They*' would not let him have the smallest souvenir of her after her death. Finally he had asked to be shown over the *Thistle* about which he said some complimentary things to Miss Vesey, although he added that the whole ship could easily be fitted into one of the cabins of the *Hohenzollern*. And he guffawed. He had inherited his mother's tactlessness but, Miss Vesey wrote home, 'as a matter of fact, the Empress rather likes him and says he is always most agreeable and charming to her, and he always makes a great point of being very friendly with her, I believe'. Miss Vesey's final impressions of the Northern encounter are interesting:

'The *Hohenzollern* departed on Saturday. I don't think the Kaiser meant to be offensive, but you can see he can't help drawing attention to himself. He left orders that the fleet of cruisers were all to hoist the French flag and the crews to parade on deck as they passed us, but as they left at seven o'clock and we were all in bed, only our Captain and crew had the benefit. They, of course, are very anti-German—even our first Officer, Mr. Neal, a very nice youth, put on a bored expression while waiting to hoist the German Imperial standard during the Emperor's visit. . . .'

The Kaiser had certainly gone to some length to show that to him she still remained the Empress, and although she, for her part, had consented to the meeting mainly from a sense of duty she did what she could to turn the chance meeting into a conciliatory occasion.

Miss Vesey's letter, written immediately after the episode, deserves close study, for in 1928 the late M. Maurice Paléologue published, in his *Conversations with the Empress Eugénie*, a version of the meeting which, he would have us believe, was based on what the Empress had told him herself. There, the Empress is made to speak with violent loathing both of the Kaiser and of his country. M. Paléologue claims to have held intimate conversations with the Empress, both at the Continental and Cap Martin, on numerous occasions between 1901 and 1919. He says that she not only opened her heart to him on all the problems of the Second Empire, including the events of 1870, but that she also passed on to him what Edward VII, the Dowager Empress of Russia and others had told her in confidence. He represents himself as a secret liaison man between the Empress and Delcassé when the latter was French Foreign Minister and makes the further claim that in 1905 the Empress authorised him to publish the record of these conversations so that they might take the place of the Memoirs she had decided never to write. Casting himself in the kind of part the Empress permitted only Filon and Lucien Daudet to play, Paléologue let eight years pass after her death before publishing his *Conversations.* The book turned out to be an eloquent and carefully written tribute to the Empress's 'hieratic' impressiveness and his own crushing superiority. While appearing to be reverential, Paléologue is, in fact, often preposterously patronising. While he holds the strings in his practised hands, the Empress, speaking an academic French of the rarest distinction, turns before our eyes into a kind of secret agent *de luxe* used by Paléologue and his Chief Delcassé as a pawn in their far-sighted European diplomacy which ended in war and Armageddon.

M. Paléologue was not only a French diplomat of considerable standing, but a literary craftsman of much skill. The portrait he has left us of the Empress is a forgery, a Van Meegeren and not a Vermeer. He did not scruple to use published material, disguising it as personal confidences addressed by the Empress *to him.* He claims, for example, that it was to him at the Continental that the Empress made that somewhat sardonic comparison between the manner in which Louis Philippe in 1848 and she herself in 1870 had fled from the Tuileries in an unheroic cab,[1] whereas the story had been published as long before as 1894, in Dr. Evans's Memoirs. As for the record of the encounter with the Kaiser, M. Paléologue, like Miss Vesey in her letter, makes the Empress say that her visitor had spoken of his desire to visit Paris and of his resentment at his treatment by Queen Victoria's heirs. Miss Vesey had published her account in *The Times* of October 11th, 1920. The Empress's narrative in Paléologue's book is identical, word for word, with Miss Vesey's article, but superimposed on it are the anti-Kaiser outbursts of which there is no trace in Miss Vesey's letters written at the time, nor in her article of 1920, nor in Miss Vesey's excellent memory today. The human undertones of a modified sympathy and liking, on the other hand, are omitted.

The tenor and contents of these conversations are in glaring contradiction to some of the Empress's most cherished principles. She had the strongest aversion to justifying herself, to fishing for pity, compassion or even partisanship. Yet confronted with that superior personality, she does all these things, *with him.* There are several major mistakes in her accounts, as given by Paléologue, of her Regency during the Italian War, the Ministerial sessions at Saint-Cloud in 1870, the negotiations with Bismarck after Sedan, but such things are expertly mixed together with phrases and sentences which ring true and carry conviction. All that can be said with certainty is that M. Paléologue did see the Empress on the days which he specifies, that they talked, and that after an interval of eight years he came out with a book which as historical evidence is worthless; it is one of the poisoned wells. Since some serious historians have used these un-

[1] See page 253 for the real story.

corroborated conversations as a source concerning, among other things, the outbreak of war in 1870, it is necessary to say this with some emphasis here and not relegate the matter to a footnote or an appendix.

The Empress's third and last contact with the Kaiser occurred in the summer of 1912. On August 1st, 1911, Lt. Bertrand Stewart of the West Kent Yeomanry, eldest son of the Empress's lawyer, was arrested at Bremen, charged with espionage, put on trial at Leipzig early in 1912 and, after a hearing *in camera*, sentenced to three and a half years' imprisonment in the fortress of Glatz. The whole case, the manner of arrest and trial and the ensuing campaign in the Press highlighted the tense and overwrought atmosphere prevailing between the two countries. On May 20th, 1912, the Empress wrote a letter to the Kaiser interceding for the convicted man's release.

The Kaiser replied on July 16th, 1912. 'Madame, my Cousin,' he began,

'Your Majesty has been good enough to write to me about the English Lieutenant Bertand Stewart, at present detained in my fortress of Glatz. Since setting him free will raise important questions of principle, the question will have to be examined in detail. I have therefore asked the competent authorities to submit a report to me. Your Majesty may rest assured that, before taking a final decision, I shall not fail to take into account the benevolent interest which Your Majesty has so kindly shown for the officer in question.

I am delighted to have this opportunity to repeat the assurance of the high esteem with which I am,

Madam, my Cousin,
Your Majesty's good Cousin,
Guillaume.'

When in the spring of the following year, King George V and Queen Mary paid their State Visit to Berlin, the Kaiser was able to tell them that the prisoner had been released. Bertrand Stewart arrived on May 22nd, 1913, at Victoria Station, where a large crowd greeted him as a hero and martyr.

Lucien Daudet once described the Empress as the *doyenne* among the sovereigns of Europe, and most of them regarded and respected her as such. Even the unhappy Empress Elisabeth of Austria, always abnormally reluctant to talk to anyone of the official world, sought her out and unburdened her soul to the Empress during long drives and walks in the hills and mountains surrounding Cap Martin. 'It was like driving with a ghost,' the Empress told Miss Vesey, 'for her spirit seemed to be living in another world. She seldom saw what went on around her, or noticed the salutes of those who recognised her. If she did, she merely acknowledged them with a curious tilt of her head, instead of the usual bow.' The Austrian Empress had abdicated all but formally soon after the Franco-Prussian War. The sensational suicide of her son Rudolph in 1889 finally drove her into the total escape of aimless travels and panicky wanderings across the length and breadth of Europe. 'I should like to die,' she once told the Empress at Cap Martin, 'from a tiny wound in my heart through which my soul could escape.' She died of just such a sound, inflicted by the anarchist Lucheni, at Geneva in 1898. The Emperor Francis Joseph, grateful to the Empress for the long hours she had spent with his consort at Cap Martin, sent to Farnborough the sad objects she had carried with her on the day of her death—her sun shade, her fan, her prayer-books. These the Empress, with her horror of such reliquary, kept out of sight in an inaccessible attic.

She never lost her fondness for the old Austrian Emperor and in 1906 spent three days with him at Ischl, an occasion which with the most delightful tact he turned into an event of State, wearing the *légion d'honneur* as his sole decoration in her presence. 'With what mission, if any,' wrote an Austrian courtier, Baron von Margutti, about the visit, 'she may have been entrusted by King Edward, I have not been able to ascertain for certain, but in any case she was a clever choice, for the Emperor would find it more difficult to resist this highly gifted lady, who was associated in his mind with brilliant memories.' 'The Empress,' wrote Miss Vesey to her mother from Ischl, 'looked beautiful at dinner last night. Her black silk dress with its long sweeping train, her white hair crowned with a jet diadem, her lovely neck and shoulders. . . .' The Empress was Francis Joseph's superior by far in intelligence and feeling for the climate of the times, but even so she revered in him the legitimate sovereign of a great Empire, the anointed embodiment of a great idea and ideal. 'I feel,' she said on this occasion, 'that I am enveloped in a dream.' Once Austria had been a reality. Whether she sounded Francis Joseph about the possibility of a meeting with Edward VII is not known: the King certainly paid a state visit to Austria in the following year. Of her affection for the sad old Emperor, gratitude for his stately courtesy and expressions of friendship there is no question. The contrast in awareness between the two old sovereigns is mirrored in two conversations which they each of them held in their most familiar circle. 'When war comes,' Francis Joseph once told his daughter, 'I suppose that Austria will be allied with Germany, Italy, and, perhaps, with England. Russia will be allied to France, but even without France Russia's preponderance will be overwhelming.'

'But what will the war be about?' asked the Archduchess. 'What cause will they be fighting for?'

'That nobody can say,' replied the Emperor, 'for, really, there will not be any cause.'

At the Villa Cyrnos in 1912, the Empress was discussing the shipwreck of the *Titanic*. For days she seemed haunted by the ghastly catastrophe, and when someone remarked that it had been a bad year for ships—the *Delhi*, the *Oceanic* and now the *Titanic*, the biggest and newest of them all, she said, 'What a bad name to give a ship! At long last the Titans have been roused.' Lucien Daudet was struck by the remark. 'The Empress,' he wrote to his mother,

> 'talks almost exclusively politics these days. Every incident reminds her of something analogous in the past, and her incomparable memory, her unique experience reminds one of that splendid ruined city in the *Jungle Book*, from where a persistent voice rises: "I am the guardian of the treasure in the city of Kings." Really, she is the last to guard the treasure of tradition, experience, foreign policy. . . .'

And Lucien attempted to say something on those lines to her. 'Bah!' she exclaimed, 'I am like an old bird that makes a noise without meaning and nobody listens to.'

'Yes, Madame,' one of them replied, 'the prophet bird.'

Lucien once said: 'How is it possible that so restless a soul can be so close to you, so accessible, so capable of inspiring confidence in the present, in reality? That is the constant miracle—that, and also that she never deceives you, not even for an instant. . . .' 'The woman,' wrote Gabriel Hanoteaux, who often came to Cap Martin, 'who had listened to Stendhal and understood Mérimée, did not deceive herself about the human heart.'

When Prince Victor Napoleon came to visit her, she always treated him as the Emperor, giving him precedence, curtsying to him when he departed —for had her son not appointed him to the succession? She performed these duties with more grace than conviction, for the Empress was unable to feel that here was the First Consul for whom France was waiting. She knew far too much about the inner workings and increasing efficiency of the Third Republic to expect great things from Prince Victor. When Aristide Briand formed his first government in 1909, the Empress said that he was 'the first statesman France has produced in the last thirty years'. Prince Victor lived mostly in Brussels, where he had married Princess Clementine, youngest daughter of King Leopold II of the Belgians, and soon became known as 'the Pretender without pretensions'. He was devoted to his family and was content, under the circumstances, to leave it at that.

The Empress was not so complacent. While she was alive, Farnborough Hill remained the living centre of Bonapartism. When Prince Victor appeared, he must be reminded of its significance. The domed mausoleum on the hill; the museum in the grounds, with its carriages of state, the uniforms and robes of the first Napoleon, the saddle with the broken girth, the portraits and other mementos of the reign, the souvenirs from the Palaces of France: all these she wanted to be understood as the tokens and symbols of an idea that could not die. And when after an evening's conversation in the large drawing-room the Empress rose to dismiss her guests for the night, she went first across to Angeli's portrait of the Prince Imperial and extinguished the light above it, then turned towards the guests and gave the exquisite *révérence de l'impératrice* that had been famous throughout Europe during the Empire and in her oldest age still reminded all who witnessed it of a flower bent and released by the wind. Of all this, Prince Victor was an essential part, however rare his visits, however discouraging his personal limitations.

Another visitor reminded the Empress of the Emperor in another way. This was Dr. Hugenschmidt. He had taken over Dr. Evans's prosperous practice in Paris and numbered the political and fashionable world among his patients. When he was first brought to Farnborough Hill at her request, she exclaimed in amazement: 'How you resemble him!'—for the doctor was her husband's illegitimate son. Hugenschmidt himself did nothing to contradict the rumour that his mother had been Mme de Castiglione. He had been born soon after the Prince Imperial's birth, had been in Pietri's care and afterwards apprenticed to Dr. Evans. The Empress had not wished to see him in her son's lifetime, but after their first meeting the doctor spent a regular week or two each year at Farnborough Hill. Someone who knew him remembers him as a 'delightful, intelligent, cosmopolitan man who looked amazingly like the Emperor, although in build he was taller'. With him the Empress frequently discussed medical science. As he had men like Doumergue, Poincaré and Clemenceau among his clients, she was also able to talk politics with him. The doctor was no Imperialist, but the Republican offspring of the Emperor was destined to play a brief, but historic part at a critical moment in the first world war.

One great change had meanwhile taken place at Farnborough and the Empress had not welcomed it. The monastery below the Church now housed a larger community than at the time of the Premonstratensians, the Benedictines of Solèmes having taken over from them when religious persecutions in France had forced them to give up their famous mother-house. They had added two wings to M. Destailleur's original building, copied from the romanesque architecture of Solèmes. The new superior was Fr. Cabrol, a scholar of strong personality, a man who understood and admired the Empress.

As a result of the Empress's personal intercession at Rome shortly before Pope Leo XIII's death in 1903, the status of her foundation was raised from Priory to that of Abbey and Dom Cabrol had been elected its first mitred Abbot. She had been present at the ceremony of consecration by the Bishop of Portsmouth on 29th May, 1903, the feast day of St. Michael, but otherwise, according to Abbot Cabrol's successor at Farnborough, 'relations between the Empress and the authorities of St. Michael's Abbey were not friendly . . contacts were reduced to the minimum'. Priests from the Abbey went over to Farnborough Hill to celebrate Mass in the Empress's private oratory upstairs; she herself came to the Abbey Church on certain feast-days, but otherwise she did not get on with the monks. She kept her feelings in the matter almost entirely to herself, yet one remark escaped her that tells us something of her attitude. When she presented the Abbey with the Golden Rose which Pio Nono had given her after the Prince Imperial's birth she cast a last glance at the treasure and sighed: 'It has never brought me any happiness.' The Empress had much to forgive to many people and it may well be that she found it hardest of all to forgive political Catholicism for its attitude towards Mexico, towards the political and social ideals of the Second Empire, towards herself. Compared to the policy of Pio Nono in Mexico hers had been almost statesmanlike. But she, unlike the Vatican, recognised and admitted her responsibility for that catastrophe of good intentions.

CHAPTER 4

DOM PETER CONWAY, one of the Benedictines of St. Michael's Abbey, wrote in his diary on August 21st, 1914:

> 'The Germans have entered Brussels. Dom Prior sang High Mass, a votive Mass *tempore belli*. The Empress turned up unexpectedly during the little hours before the Mass.'

When she heard of the Austrian ultimatum to Serbia in July 1914, the Empress prepared herself for a long war with the minimum of fuss, with the maximum of resolution. The *Thistle* was handed over to the Admiralty; servants of military age were encouraged to volunteer; a wing of Farnborough Hill was turned into a hospital for officers. Lady Haig—she and Sir Douglas had often been over from Government House, Aldershot, after the General had taken up the Command there—was invited to be the Commandant of the hospital, while Dr. Wilfrid Attenborough, in practice at Frimley and a friend of the house since 1910, was asked to act as medical officer and surgeon. Shortly before Brussels fell, Prince Victor's family—first his baby son[1] and daughter with their nurse, then the Prince and Princess Clementine—arrived at Folkestone, were fetched by the Empress in her motor, and remained at Farnborough Hill for the duration of the war.

'My dear Daudet,' she wrote on August 13th, at the time of the German advance,

> 'I wonder whether this little letter will reach you? You will know how much I take part in what is happening and how the memory of the past makes the present moment so bitter. To be far away and not be able to do anything in this supreme struggle is inexpressibly hard to bear.
>
> The Belgians have behaved admirably, and the spirit of France is above all praise, and gives one confidence. But how much disaster on the road to glory!'

From the beginning, the Empress had exceptionally good sources of information about the war. Sir Douglas Haig was in the habit of sending his

---

[1] Now Prince Napoleon.

357

wife leaves from a diary he kept, and these Lady Haig would copy on her typewriter and show the Empress and some of the patients. 'Tell the Empress,' Sir Douglas wrote from France in October 1914,

> 'that there is no cause for anxiety. The French are now in superior number to the Germans in France, but I gather that the Commander-in-Chief, General Joffre, is a very prudent man and won't run any risk of a check through attacking the enemy's entrenchments unless he is certain of success. But do get a nice comfortable house! We shall have lots of money after the war, so please don't stint yourself on my account.'

At first there were red-tape difficulties about the allocation of patients to the hospital; beds stood empty and Lady Haig wrote despondently to France. Her husband promised to put in a word at the War Office. He added in a note of November 6th,

> 'when all the new troops are put into the field I doubt that there will be enough hospital accommodation for all the wounded.'

Lady Haig remained Commandant-Matron at Farnborough Hill until August 1915. It was not a happy period for her, for those working under her, or for the Empress. When finally Dr. Attenborough objected to the distribution of the General's diaries on security grounds, the smouldering conflict came out into the open and Lady Haig forced the Empress to choose between her and the young doctor. With her accustomed tact, the Empress smoothed things over by saying that the hospital would be closed for some time during the summer of 1915, which gave Lady Haig her chance to depart. After that, the Empress made Miss Vesey Commandant, while Dr. Attenborough remained in his previous position until he went to fight in France in 1917.

The hospital was a small establishment, but the Empress kept it going for five years entirely from her own resources, spending something like £30 a month per patient as well as buying all the latest equipment which Dr. Attenborough needed for his operations. 'She took,' writes Miss Vesey,

> 'the deepest interest in each case, showing a knowledge of nursing and medicine well above the average. She sent to Paris and London for all the latest surgical appliances, and might occasionally have been seen trying a new wheeled chair in the long corridor, or propelling herself up and down on the latest invention in crutches. It happened once or twice that some small hurt or injury to herself was treated at the Hospital, and it amused her immensely to identify herself with her patients and feel that she was one of them.'

One of these 'hurts or injuries' the Empress suffered at the age of ninety in 1916 when she lost her balance at the top of the broad staircase in the main building, fell backwards and rolled down to the bottom. Antonia d'Attainville, rushing towards the noise, was shocked to find her lying on the ground, her face bruised and covered in blood from a deep cut on her forehead. However, she was perfectly collected and insisted on walking upstairs to her bedroom, although this time with the help of two nurses from the hospital. One of them said timidly she hoped that going up did not hurt Her Majesty? 'My dear,' she replied, 'it hurt me a great deal more going down.'

The Empress who had wanted to be a nurse during the Franco-Prussian War went to endless trouble to make her patients comfortable. 'We were spoilt,' wrote Mr. H. E. L. Mellersh, a young Lieutenant in 1917,

'an ancient and venerable Renault car was at our service to go shopping in Aldershot or tour round the countryside on most afternoons: there was a small lake to row on: those who were well enough could use the tennis court.'

Another former patient, Mr. Phillip Bateman, late of the Royal Flying Corps, writes:

'The atmosphere was delightful and patients were at once made to feel that they were honoured guests at a country-house party. It was my first break from army life for two years and at first I found it hard to accustom myself to the change. I had lost the habit of being treated as an intelligent human being. Even the doctor at Farnborough was a civilian and the nurses, selected by the Empress herself, were darlings. Visitors such as Princess Clementine, sister-in-law of Crown Prince Rudolph and thus a link with the tragedy of Mayerling, and the Empress's jolly lady-in-waiting, Mme d'Attainville, helped to entertain the patients, and I was taken to see the Imperial Museum, with its relics of three Napoleons and its memories of Austerlitz and Moscow, of the Crimea and Sedan and of Zululand.'

Among the later patients was Captain Vaughan. The Empress was interested in the name, for the Vaughan family, of whom Mme de Arcos had been one, were her oldest pre-Empire English friends. But the young Captain was no relation to them; indeed, as he sadly told her, he was quite alone in the world, did not know where to go or what to do after the war and had nothing to look forward to except living on a meagre pension. The Empress was immediately moved by his story, for Captain Vaughan was a very handsome man. So she summoned a member of Messrs. Markby Stewart to her side and added a codicil to her will that Captain Vaughan was to be paid the sum of £250 per annum free of tax for life, payment to start forthwith. Once again, she had fallen for a good-looking face.

When the news from the war was bad, the Empress did not show herself in the hospital. 'It is not good for them to see me anxious and gloomy,' she told Miss Vesey. 'Invalids must be cheered and not depressed.' 'The person of my acquaintance I most intensely longed to see at all critical moments in the last five nightmare years was the Empress,' wrote Ethel Smyth in 1920, 'so sane and unshakeable was her faith in ultimate victory. She was blessedly free from that belief in their own strategical powers which temporarily clouded the intellects of many of one's most revered friends.' When Haig, a Field Marshal since 1916, yielded to Foch in the matter of unified supreme command, her admiration for him was powerfully revived. 'This triumph of commonsense over vanity,' she said, 'could only happen on this side of the Channel.' And she added enviously: 'You are an easy race to govern.' 'England and France,' she told Colonel Willoughby Verner, who since the war began had been making notes of the Empress's conversations,

'England and France are meant by nature to work together, for each of them possesses high qualities which the other lacks. Combined they are invincible. In England you find wonderful endurance, great steadfastness and a determination that nothing can alter. In France you have the dash, the sanguine temperament, but, above all, you have *foresight*. That is what England lacks and has always lacked, and today your statesmen seem to have very little or none, for they act on the spur of the moment and do not stop to see where the action they take today must certainly lead them in the future.'

She viewed the political prospect, Allied war aims, the future of Britain and Europe, with apprehension. Wilson's Fourteen Points she regarded as a disastrous document:

'It is absurd [she told Col. Verner] for English people to discuss such things as "Freedom of the Seas". England must always be the strongest Power at sea. You *must* be. I foresee trouble for England with America, trouble about Ireland, for example. Unless you are careful, Ireland will become a second Bohemia. . . .'

She saw with the greatest mistrust that the pronouncements of the President of the United States increasingly influenced the Allied conduct of the war, for she remained unimpressed by Wilson's high-mindedness. His postulate, expressed frequently during the spring and summer of 1917, that the coming peace must be 'scientific', must not reproduce 'the enormity committed by the Germans when they took Alsace-Lorraine from France', stirred her, and not only her, profoundly: was it to be understood that Alsace-Lorraine would remain in German hands? No clear-cut announcement on this question had been made at any time during the war; by the end of 1917 the recovery of those two border provinces was not an Allied war aim. On June 5th, 1917, the French Deputies debated a peace resolution which demanded the return of Alsace-Lorraine together with the liberation of invaded territories and 'just reparations for war damage', but the Socialists insisted on a plebiscite being held in Alsace-Lorraine after the war. At the same period, the revolutionary authorities in Russia were propagating a peace 'without annexations or indemnities'. Britain equivocated. When Mr. Lloyd George addressed a large meeting at Glasgow on June 29th, 1917, no mention of the return of the provinces was made. In the House of Commons, Mr. Arthur Balfour expressed it as his 'personal opinion' that Britain should support France over this problem, but in the Reichstag Herr von Kühlmann implied that Britain would be ready to sign a peace which, though entailing the evacuation of Belgium, would preserve the *status quo* in Alsace-Lorraine. On October 11th, Lloyd George made another speech. 'However long the war may last,' he said,

'this country intends to stand by her gallant ally France until she redeems her oppressed children from the degradation of a foreign yoke.'

But were the inhabitants of the disputed provinces the children of France? Alsace was German-speaking. Surely what under the Second *Reich* was called the *Reichsland* had always been German by race and blood? Had the provinces not gone to Germany in 1871 on the basis of the principle of nationality?

The Empress remembered the letter King William of Prussia had written to her on October 25th, 1871, when she had appealed to him to grant France a peace without annexations.[1] It will be recalled that in it the King had argued, not the principle of nationality, but what he called 'the sad consideration' of strategic necessity. Alsace-Lorraine had to become German so that Germany could feel more secure in the next war with France. Dr. Hugenschmidt, who throughout the war was paying his annual visits to Farnborough Hill, mentioned this letter to a patient, Georges Clemenceau, who immediately expressed an urgent desire to have this document. Hugenschmidt quietly stressed the difficulty the Prime Minister might have in communicating with the hated Spanish woman, but Clemenceau bluntly ordered him to go to Farnborough Hill and ask for the letter. Somewhat doubtfully, Napoleon III's son consented.

The Empress raised no difficulty whatever. When Hugenschmidt explained the purpose of his unexpected appearance and quoted what Clemenceau had said, she immediately took him upstairs and from the safe produced the letters which the sovereigns of Europe had written in reply to her appeals to preserve the integrity of France. He read the letters in silent amazement. 'How much there is here,' he said, 'to justify the conduct of Your Majesty.'

'Justify it?' she exclaimed; the remark nearly ruined the mission. 'I want no justification.' And she took from him the letter from Francis Joseph, the letter from Alexander II, but in the end left him with that

[1] See page 257.

from the King of Prussia. She gave it to him unconditionally. Ethel Smyth's story that she said 'I give it, not to the Government, but to France', is a piece of biased fiction, as Hugenschmidt wrote to Miss Vesey when he saw Miss Smythe's article in a periodical. The Empress, who had already described Clemenceau to Verner as 'a most useful man for the present time',[1] allowed him to make whatever use of it he wished, without fuss, without ostentation. Clemenceau had the document read out during a solemn session at the Sorbonne, in the presence of the Allied, including the American, representatives. The recovery of Alsace-Lorraine was henceforth a major Allied objective. 'Good work,' said Clemenceau to Hugenschmidt, but to the Empress he wrote a letter of appreciation which the French Ambassador, M. Cambon, handed to Abbot Cabrol for delivery.

Her morale remained unimpaired as the war progressed. 'The *Zeppelins* have been to Sandringham,' she wrote to Jimmy Alba at the beginning of 1915,

'but the King and Queen had left a few hours earlier. No panic; people are reconciled to the fact that these visits will be repeated, and the effect they are having is no greater than that of a railway accident. It is a mistake to think that the morale of this country can be subdued. While this lasts, people are merely laying bets for and against *Zeppelins*.'

Later in that year she wrote to Alba:

'England has become a camp. Soldiers everywhere, not merely conscripts. This peace-loving country has become military in no time at all, and they show in this, as in everything else, their "*erectness*".'

She had her own experiences of Zeppelin raids. When Aldershot was attacked during the night, she would wake poor Mme d'Attainville excitedly: 'Quick, Antonia, quick! They are here!' and, rain or no, dash out into the night. Miss Vesey and Antonia remonstrated with her. 'Bah!' she replied, 'at my age you don't start learning fear!'

The Titans were astir indeed. When, in the critical summer of 1918, there was an anxious lull and the expected German attack did not come, the prophet bird spoke again:

'What are the reasons for the delay in the German attack? There must be *some* reason. People suggest that many are down with influenza. Depend on it, there must be some *very strong reason* to cause them to waste all this, the best time of the year.'

She said this, Verner remarks, 'long before any rumours of the serious state of affairs in Germany were whispered abroad'.

[1] 'He should be First Consul,' she said to Wickham Steed in 1919.

It was after the German offensive of 1918 had failed that the Empress and Allied policy parted company. 'It is a great mistake,' she told Verner,

'to let your politicians go about as they do declaring that you are going to "crush" the Germans. You cannot crush 60 million people in the very centre of Europe.'

As rumours of an impending armistice were ripe, she told him:

'The Kaiser will certainly abdicate; the other Crowned Heads will also go—in time they will all go. King George will be the only one left and he will remain, for the nation likes him and he is also the ruler of the great Overseas Colonies of Great Britain. But he will be very lonely, like a lighthouse in a stormy sea.'

She was horrified when the dismemberment of the Austro-Hungarian Empire was raised to the dignity of a political principle:

'All these talks and speeches and theories of Wilson's are most dangerous and more dangerous to England than to anybody else and are also dangerous to France. This "League of Nations"; what folly! This "self-determination of the nations"; what madness! You, you, you English' (and she pointed at Colonel Verner with tremendous energy) —what are you about? Why should you run risks by creating nations such as Czechoslovakia and I know not what?

And then this idea of putting the Americans into Constantinople, Americans of all people?[1] What will the Indian Princes think of this? You did one very clever thing in recognising the King of the Hedjaz. But beware! You and France combined will provide materials for a Holy War if you go on as at present.'

While the peace-makers met at Versailles and redistributed the countries of the world in a manner compared to which her own geopolitical flights before the bewildered eyes of Richard Metternich were realism itself, the Empress's despair grew until it hurt her: 'I have always,' she told Verner on his next visit,

'all my life had great faith in England, but now I feel I am losing it. You want a *Government*—not people who make promises to everybody to do anything—for example to abandon Russia and so drive her into the arms of Germany. It is the old want of foresight. Think of the thousands upon thousands of well-trained German officers, most of whom will have no employment when their own army is abolished, and think of the millions of Russians who would supply them with men and so create a terrible force which some day could crush Europe.'

[1] Soon after the end of the war President Wilson asserted that the United States might accept a mandate at Constantinople.

Nobody had been more deeply moved than the Empress when the armistice was signed in November 1918. 'Thank God the killing is over,' she said. When Verner called, she walked towards him with both hands outstretched and simply said 'Enfin'. Yet when Dr. Attenborough came to her study on the day when the details of the Treaty of Versailles were published, he found her bending over *The Times*, holding the now indispensable magnifying glass to her good eye. She flung the paper angrily to the ground: 'What have you done?' she exclaimed in horror. 'This is no peace—these are the seeds of future war.' And to Verner she said:

'I see in every single Article of this peace a little egg, a *nucleus* of more wars. . . . You know what I always say about enforcing all possible terms. But the Allies are enforcing impossible terms. Not content with this, the Allies are going to crush German shipping, trade, everything! How can Germany ever earn the money to pay her just obligations? Madness! Folly!'

No jubilation over the downfall of the Hohenzollerns was mingled with her gratitude for the Allied victory. Ought the Kaiser to be tried and hanged? asked Verner. 'No!' she replied at once.

'That is not the way to treat a man in his position. What is the use of killing him? His punishment is to live. Think of what his fall means to him. He was above everybody and everything or rather believed he was—except, of course, his God, and sometimes he was perhaps even above Him!'

She carried on. The hospital was not shut until the last patient could be discharged in September 1919, for she would not consent to having 'her' cases transferred to other hospitals. In her private life she had had her own share of sorrows. Her faithful Franceschini Pietri died at Farnborough Hill in November 1916 after half a century of devotion. Few of her regular friends could come to see her in those years. The Duke of Alba who was a liaison officer on the Western Front came to stay when he could, and so did the Marqués de Villalobar, who, early in 1915, brought her his account of how he had vainly endeavoured to save Nurse Cavell from execution as a spy. King George and Queen Mary came, both as her guests and officially to inspect the hospital, for her traditional friendship with the British Monarch lasted uninterrupted in the new reign. Of other members of the Royal Family, Princess Beatrice was the most frequent caller. Widowed, motherless, one son killed in Flanders, her daughter Queen of Spain, the Princess was now engaged in copying out Queen Victoria's Journal—not without exercising some obscure principles of censorship of her own. Once she had finished with a volume of the original, she consigned it to the flames.

Towards the end of the war, the Empress made one of those gestures of conciliation in which her life had always been so rich. Lady Haig, as we
364

have seen, had left Farnborough Hill in a whirling cloud of discord. In March 1918 she gave birth to a son, and the Empress became his god-mother. All strife was buried and forgotten and the present Earl Haig, artist, landowner and most delightful of hosts, to this day exhibits among the historic treasures of Bemersyde the christening cup with which the old Empress had greeted his birth.

The Empress's personal life in the war had been secure in the devoted friendship with which her small entourage safeguarded her need for independence and continuity. Miss Vesey, efficient, humorous and observant; Antonia d'Attainville, warm-hearted, boisterous and frequently flirting with the officers (the therapeutic value of which the Empress did not underrate); Dr. Attenborough, excellent surgeon, vigilant and dedicated to the Empress and his duties (when he left for France in 1917, the Empress, remembering another parting, made the sign of the cross on his forehead); the Duke of Alba and other nephews, great-nephews, from Spain; Pietri, until he suddenly declined into mental confusion and death; from among the domestic staff Bristol, the major-domo, who had joined the Imperial family as a kitchen boy at Chislehurst, Aline Pelletier, who had been in attendance on the Empress since the last two years at the Tuileries, and Bizou, the chef, who knew how to prepare the Empress's beloved Spanish *jambons*: all these enabled her to lead the life she preferred

In March 1919, the Prince of Wales, later King Edward VIII, and his brother, the future King George VI, called at Farnborough Hill to invest, on behalf of their father, the Empress with the insignia of a Dame Grand Cross of the British Empire. The Prince of Wales knew the place well. He had paid his first visit in August 1909 when the Empress showed him (as the Prince wrote to his father) 'all the things that had belonged to the Prince Imperial', including the sad relic of the saddle with the broken girth, which she rarely took out from its hiding place. The Prince had returned during the war to inspect the hospital. On the visit in 1919 he astonished Dr. Attenborough by remembering the names and medical details of patients he had seen and by his compassionate concern for them. The Empress was greatly touched by the presentation of the decoration and she wrote to the King:

'Sire,
I thank Your Majesty for the G.B.E. which the Prince of Wales gave me in Your Majesty's name. I owe this much more to the kindness of Your Majesty than to any merit of my own, and I appreciate this token of friendship very much. The charming young Prince who presented it has doubled this pleasure for me.
Please believe in the sentiments of sincere affection with which I am,
Your Majesty's most devoted,
Eugénie.'

Incipient blindness forced her to dictate this letter. What she resented so bitterly about her failing eyesight was that it increased her dependence on others, but such specialists as she had consulted since the end of the war had not been hopeful about restoring the affected eye by surgery. Moreover, for the first time people began to notice that she was ageing rapidly.

As October slipped into November and the leaves began to fall in the woods, the Empress conceived the idea of travelling southwards, to the sun at Cyrnos, to the sea she loved so much. She had not moved from Hampshire for five years, a fact which did nothing to increase the confidence of her entourage in this alarming project. Yet Dr. Attenborough, who gave her a thorough examination, saw no physical reason for advising against the journey and soon it became known that the Empress was leaving for France and Spain early in December 1919. Arthur Bigge, now Lord Stamfordham, went to Farnborough Hill with an offer of the loan of the Royal Yacht from the King which the Empress declined. She suddenly interrupted their conversation and went across to where von Angeli's portrait of the Prince Imperial was hanging. For long it had presided silently over the gatherings in this huge drawing-room. With her strong arms she took the picture down and gave it to the surprised Royal Secretary and Counsellor.

Before leaving England for the sun, she had one more duty to fulfil. Among her most treasured possessions was a relic of the True Cross, a present from the Caliph Harun al Rashid to Charlemagne. The Canons of Aachen had presented it to the Empress Josephine in 1804, and through her daughter Queen Hortense it had come to Napoleon III, and so to the Empress. She had often wondered what her duty was with the 'Talisman of Charlemagne', as the relic was known in the world of learning, and had thought of returning it to Aachen Cathedral by asking the Kaiser to hand it to the Archbishop of Cologne. The war, and more especially the bombardment of Rheims, decided her otherwise. Eventually she entrusted it to Fr. Cabrol to hand over to the Cardinal Archbishop of Rheims and so, as the learned Abbot wrote, ' a marvellous jewel of medieval art was returned to France. By an inspiration as lofty as it was touching, she wished the relic to return to the land of her adoption that she might pay in part the ransom of what that land had undergone under the assault of the Saxon '.

She had made her final will in 1916. Her considerable fortune was divided between three principal legatees, Prince Victor, for the sake of the Napoleonic succession, the Duchess of Tamamès, because she was Paca's daughter, and the Duke of Alba, because in him Paca's family continued in the male line. Numerous bequests and legacies showed the breadth of her sympathies and charity, and the whole document proved again and finally what a conscientious and able administrator she had always been, a thrifty expert in the economics of generosity.

On the way to Cap Martin, she stopped once more at the Continental in Paris. Many old friends rushed to see her, but when Lucien Daudet called one afternoon she was, for the moment, alone. He saw her sitting in the big drawing-room, against the marble chimney-piece, her profile set off against the flames in the fireplace. She turned her unseeing face towards the door when she heard that someone stood there. 'It's Lucien Daudet, Madame,' he said.

'Ah, Lucien, the little Lucien,' she called out, and five years of separation fell away. They had written to each other in the war, and she had sent him a large sum for one of the mobile canteens for front-line soldiers which had been his form of war service. Now she said to him:

'If I know anything about you, I am sure you never said *Les Boches*?'

'Never, Madame.'

And, he says, she gave a little smile, as if to say: 'That one has been to my school.'

She abruptly changed the subject and said: 'You know I wanted to make this present journey in an aeroplane, but people would only have said that I was an old mad woman.' She soon reverted to the war, and to the peace, and told him: 'It became clear to me in the war that I would have sacrificed the only things that meant anything to me, conscience and honour, if that would have saved the country.' It was her spirit of 1870. And then she spoke in her spirit of 1919, of the League of Nations, the principles of which she admired without feeling a great faith in its workability. 'All that,' she concluded, 'is terrible, but we must think ourselves fortunate to be living in times like these. Our epoch is a new beginning, everything must be built on new foundations: do men know this?'

Lucien went daily to the Continental and soon found that she had not given up her old ways. 'Now tell me, have you been dancing again last night? What—up until four o'clock in the morning? Really! You'll need Cap Martin this spring, God knows! Now what was the name of that book I mentioned the other day? Do you remember, Antonia? or you, Luciano? No? That none of us three can remember it—a nice state of affairs. . . .' And there was a knock at the door: Aline Pelletier, 'like the phantom of the Tuileries', said firmly: 'Does Your Majesty realise it is half-past eight and dinner is served?' And the Empress left them with a *bon soir* that at once struck a formal note of ceremony.

Cap Martin, Gibraltar, Algeciras, Colonel Verner's house at Jerez: as she drew nearer and nearer to her origins, the anxieties of Europe fell from her shoulders and with every breath she seemed to find new inspiration. From Jerez, the Duke of Alba motored her to his house in Seville, and there the King and Queen of Spain called on her in the morning. She motored on to Madrid and on the way they passed a house that had once been hers. It stood empty, decaying and neglected. As from the car the Empress gazed at this picture of desolation, an old peasant came past and said: 'Here there once lived a beautiful Countess who went away to marry a King.'

At Madrid she stayed at the Palacio de Liria, and they all flocked to the house to pay their homage to the greatest Spaniard of their times. 'Ah, the Miraflorés girl,' the Empress would exclaim when some dowager of advanced age was presented. Or young Carlos de Arcos came up, the son of her old friend Santiago de Arcos, and nephew of her unforgotten Mme de Arcos who had died in 1912. She could hardly see him: 'Bring a cushion,' she told him, 'and sit here, close to me.' And she bent down towards him and when still she could not see she took his young face between her hands and said: 'How like your father you are!'

The end came swiftly. Dr. Barraquer of Barcelona, unlike all the English and French doctors she had consulted, declared himself ready to perform the operation for cataract. It was a complete success. To her, to see was to live, and within a week of the operation she felt all her old energies and love of activity returning. She went out and paid calls in Madrid and the country, she went to a bull-fight: Spain had given her back her delight in life. 'I have returned home—*je suis revenue chez moi*,' she said, and it expressed her strongest joy.

She planned to return to Farnborough by the middle of July: Jimmy Alba was engaged to be married and she sent him ahead on July 9th to make the arrangements for the wedding to take place from Farnborough Hill. She would stop in Paris for only a day or two, but with her usual foresight ordered a car to be at her disposal there after July 12th.

On July 10th, during her breakfast, she felt suddeny ill, shivering in the hot day, unable to swallow her food. A few hours later she allowed herself to be put to bed, for the first time in her many illnesses. Soon her face showed a strange lassitude and tiredness. The priest came during the night. She confessed. In the room next door her relatives were on their knees while the priest administered extreme unction. At eight o'clock on the morning of Sunday, July 11th, 1920, the Empress died in Paca's room, in Paca's bed, at the Palacio de Liria. Spain that had given her life and restored her to life, had also given her the release of death: but her final resting place stood waiting for her in England ready to receive her in the setting she had created with her courage and single-mindedness in defiance of the laws of probability.

The coffin travelled, with all the pomp and state that only the King of Spain could order, from Madrid through France to England. Yet before it had left the Palacio de Liria, Princess Beatrice was writing to someone who was familiar with the Empress's personal arrangements:

Kensington Palace
(Clock Court)
W.
July 13th, 1920.

'Knowing all your friendship for and connection with the dear late Empress's affairs I think you ought to know that all her correspondence with Mme de Arcos was left by the latter to her niece. It seems to me that anyone who has the carrying out of the Empress's last wishes ought, if possible, to make sure that they are destroyed. The dear Empress was so particular about none of her correspondence, which

368

must have been of a very intimate character, being kept that I think I
ought to write to you on the subject.

I am sure you will have felt the dear Empress's death as we all do,
but one cannot help feeling that for her it will have been a happiness to
end her days in the land of her birth. She was so attached to it.

> Believe me,
> Yrs. sincerely,
> Beatrice.'

What secrets of the past alarmed her? That there might have been an
engagement with the Prince Imperial? Or that there was never any hope
of one? The incendiary Princess certainly showed great haste.

The coffin reached Farnborough on Sunday, July 18th. 'Just before
twelve noon,' writes Father Conway,

> ' we went in procession from the Church down to the station. Troops,
> mounted and on foot, were already in position and holding the dense
> crowds back. Lord Rawlinson, G.O.C. Aldershot, and his staff were on
> the platform. As we approached the cavalry drew and presented arms.
> The train arrived punctually. There was a guard of Irish soldiers accom-
> panying the coffin and many mourners with Prince Victor at their head.
> The coffin was mounted on a gun carriage and covered with the Union
> Jack. At the moment the coffin was taken off the gun carriage, the band
> played the Marseillaise. . . .'

The funeral ceremony was held at Farnborough on July 20th. King
George and Queen Mary, King Alfonso and Queen Ena, the King and
Queen of Portugal, attended in the sanctuary; other Monarchs, dethroned
or otherwise, were represented. The French Republic confined its interest
in the ceremony to making official protests against the honours to be
shown to the last Empress of the French. In consequence the War Office
gave orders that the salutes due to a Sovereign were not to be fired from
the guns, which were already in position behind the Abbey buildings. The
Cardinal Archbishop of Westminster officiated and Abbot Cabrol gave a
sermon that was masterly in its proud and delicate simplicity.

So far everything had gone as it should have done: the ceremony of
farewell had been worthy of her life. The slight touch of farce that followed
would not have been lost on her: the sarcophagus of granite which had
stood waiting to receive the coffin all these years could not be found, not
at the Abbey, not at Farnborough Hill. How it had been possible to
mislay so unwieldy an object is a mystery that will remain unsolved; it
was never found. A replica was made and this, with the simple inscription
EUGÉNIE, stands today ensconced above the altar of the crypt and the
tombs of the Emperor and the Prince Imperial.

The immediate consequence of the loss was that for the time being the
simple Spanish coffin remained on the floor of the crypt where from the

day after the funeral onwards unending crowds of people came to see it. The coffin was buried beneath a mountain of flowers, although at the funeral itself, in obedience to the Empress's wish, none had been allowed. On July 28th, Abbot Cabrol opened the coffin and through the inner glass saw her lying robed in white, 'the habit of some Order, third order of St. James, I was told,' wrote Father Conway. The precise naming of the Order is of small importance—according to a pleasant saying, not even God can know how many Women Orders there are in the Roman Catholic Church. Yet it was not inappropriate that on the threshold of eternity the Empress should wear the habit of a nun, for she had overcome the world and founded her own discipline.

Of all human beings of whom we have detailed record, none seems to have suffered so cruelly from interested detraction. In her lifetime, she helped the process by her refusal to combat libel, by her proud Spanish faith in the ultimate justice of history. The libels persisted. Even so perceptive a man as Ronald Knox could use the words 'a spiritual sedan' of the crypt in St. Michael's Abbey. If ever there was a monument to the triumph of the spirit over temporal defeat it is here. She lived on into our own times when 'efficacy of destruction' became the accepted criterion of national greatness, even in France. Her own sense of greatness, learned in the very frontline of history, was higher and rarer. 'Everything must be built on new foundations', she said in 1919, 'do men know this?'

REFERENCES

ABBREVIATIONS:
R.A.: Royal Archives, Windsor
A.A.: Alba Archives, Madrid
C.G.: Mérimée, *Correspondance Générale*, ed. Maurice Parturier
L.F.: *Lettres familières de l'impératrice Eugénie*, publ. by the Duke of Alba

CHAPTER I

Page
3   Col. Verner: *Nineteenth Century and After* (August 1920).
4   Lord Stamfordham: communicated by his daughter, the Hon. Mrs. Adeane; gardener's bill at Cap Martin: papers of Messrs. Markby, Stewart & Wadesons. Other remarks at Cap Martin: MS by the Duke of Alba, A.A., and Miss Vesey's MS.
5   Kirkpatrick genealogy: information supplied by the late Count de Albiz and Sir Ivone Kirkpatrick. William Kirkpatrick's correspondence as American Consul survives in the National Archives at Washington.
6   Ticknor: see *Life, Letters and Journals of George Ticknor*; Mme de Lage is quoted in Gabriel Hanotaux's introduction to *Correspondance inédite de Mme de Montijo et Prosper Mérimée* from the lady's *Mémoirs*: 'Tyrant of genius' and other details on the Teba ménage: Fleury's *Memoirs of the Empress Eugénie*, a work, though misnamed, usefully based on memories of relatives and personal friends; Primoli, *L'Enfance d'une Souveraine* (*Revue des Deux Mondes*, 15 Oct. 1923), though written by an intimate friend of her later years, is often wildly inaccurate.
7   Teba's career from Spanish and French military archives: Villeneuve's mission in Comte de Rilly's MS; see also Comte de Rilly, *La reine Hortense à Cauterets* (*Revue des Deux Mondes*, 1 Sept. 1959).
8   Teba in 1814: Filon, *Mérimée et ses amis:* for Montijo's career before and after 1814: A.A.; Teba's légion d'honneur: ibid.
9   Montijo-Teba correspondence: A.A. In 1823 Montijo offered his services to the Duke of Angoulême, just as Teba had done to Joseph Bonaparte in 1809.
10 Pena: L.F., vol. I note to letter X. A few letters from Louis de Viel Castel survive in A. A. Earthquake: see acknowledgements. Eugénie's certificate of baptism at Granada: confirmed by Father Antonio Due, S.J.

CHAPTER II

12 The changeling: see L.F. vol. II, letter CCLXI and note; Torriglia, *Mintijo*; Primoli, op. cit; Filon, *Souvenirs de l'impératrice Eugénie*. Other details on childhood from Fleury, op. cit; L.F. vol. I, letters I-VIII; Mérimée, C.G. passim.
14 Stendhal: Filon, *Mérimée et ses amis, Souvenirs;* see also André Billy, *Stendhal et Mérimée. Revue de Paris.* Oct. 1956.
15 Massacre of the Friars: Duke of Alba, *The Empress Eugénie* (address to the Ark Society, Oxford 1943); Abelino: L.F., vol. I., letter III.

16 Clarendon: Maxwell, *Life and Letters of the Fourth Earl of Clarendon*; Eugénie's and Paca's letters are in L.F., vol. I, passim.
17 Clifton: Ethel Smyth, *Streaks of Life*.
18 Col. Amoros: A.A. Stendhal: sources as before; Doña Manuela's letters to Mérimée were lost when his house in the rue de Lille was burnt down in 1871. His letters to her were published separately in two magnificently illustrated volumes in Paris in 1935, but all quotations here come from C.G. which is the definite edition.

CHAPTER III

20 Eugénie's letter to Stendhal: Filon, *Souvenirs*; 'own dishonour': Eugénie's letter of 16 May 1843 in L.F., vol. I, letter IX, original in A.A.
23 The first meeting between Eugénie and Prince Plon-Plon has often been wrongly placed in 1849, when he was, briefly and unsuccessfully, French Minister at Madrid (e.g. Thompson, *Louis Napoleon*), but the right dates may be gathered from Mérimée, C.G. vol. 3, No. 773, and Fleury, *Memoirs*.
24 Doña Manuela's, Eugénie's and Mme Gordon's letters to Ferdinand Huddleston are all in the possession of Captain Huddleston at Sawston Hall. There are a few references to Ferdinand Huddleston in Rumbold, *Recollections* and Lord Newton. *Retrospection*. According to a Sawston tradition, Huddleston in September 1870 wanted to rescue the Empress from France in his yacht, but was prevented by a private mutiny of his crew. Mérimée met Huddleston several times in Paris. For other details on Mme Gordon see F. A. Simpson, *The Rise of Louis Napoleon*, and Filon, *Souvenirs*.
25 Miraflorés: Mérimée, C.G. vol. 5, No. 1328. Another admirer of Eugénie's at this time was Prince Albert de Broglie, Prime Minister after 1873: for Monckton Milnes: James Pope-Hennessy, *The Flight of Youth*.
27 The only available reference to the Alcañisez affair is in Ethel Smyth, *Streaks of Life*, but there is one letter from Doña Manuela to Paca written soon after their arrival in Paris which makes it clear that Eugénie suffered deeply from his treachery. Several references to Pepe Alcañisez occur in both volumes of L.F. which show that in later years he became a friend who had been forgiven.

CHAPTER IV

28 The President: G.G. vol. 5, No. 1443. Miss Howard: C. André-Maurois, *Miss Howard and the Emperor*; Mme Gordon's death in Fleury, op. cit.
29 Doña Manuela's letter to Paca: A.A. The Montijo ladies rarely dated their letters, but it was possible to give the exact date of the first meeting from Doña Manuela's references to other events, including the première of Meyerbeer's *The Prophet*. Eugénie's remark about Mme Gordon and the dinner party at Saint-Cloud: Filon, *Souvenirs*, based on the Empress's recollections. Bills to extend the Prince-President's term of office were sponsored by enlightened Orleanists such as Duke Victor de Broglie, by de Tocqueville and Comte Falloux. Tocqueville's *Recollections* contain an interesting account of various negotiations behind the scenes, including his own, mainly negative, impressions of the Prince, and of Falloux's opportunism.
30 The Prince's speech: Simpson, *Louis Napoleon and the Recovery of France*; Eugénie's offer in Filon, *Souvenirs*; Lady Clifford-Constable's letter: A.A. The Clifford-Constables were Roman Catholics, and their eldest son, then aged 23, wanted to marry Eugénie—or so a family tradition still alive at Burton Constable in Yorkshire has it. The quotation on the coup d'état: P. Labracherie, *Le Second Empire*, vol. I; 'saviour of society'; Guedalla, *Second Empire*.
31 'The hour had been reached'; d'Antioch, *Le Général Changarnier*. The best

books on Donoso Cortés are: A. Maier, *Donoso Cortés*; d'Antioche, *Deux Diplomates (Racynski et Donoso Cortés)*.

32 The essay, first published in 1851 and widely translated, was entitled: *An Essay on Catholocism, Liberalism, Socialism*.
The Adeanes of Babraham: private information.

33 Doña Manuela's letter: A.A.; Eugénie's letters: L.F. vol. I, IX-XIX.

CHAPTER V

35 Hübner: *Neuf ans de souvenirs d'un ambassadeur*. Bordeaux speech: Simpson, *Recovery*.

36 Rumbold, *Recollections*: for Hübner's background, see Engel-Janosi, *Der Freiherr von Hübner*.

39 Hübner's report is quoted in full in Wellesley & Sencourt, *Conversations with Napoleon III* (original in Vienna State Archives).

40 Details of house-party communiated from Compiègne Archives by M. Max Terrier; clover leaf in Maupas, *Mémoirs*; other details in General le Comte de Fleury, *Souvenirs* and, for Cowley's reactions, Wellesley, *The Paris Embassy*, also Maréchal de Castellane, *Journal* vol. III.

41 Eugénie on her métier, L.F., letter XXVI. Donoso Cortés's dispatch: Maier, *Donoso Cortés* (Paris, 25 Jan. 1853, Confidential).

43 Doña Manuela's famous remark, first noted by Lady Clarendon in her private diary, is from Villiers, *Vanished Victorian*. Eugénie's letters: L.F., vol. I, letters XXIII-XXVI.

CHAPTER VI

45 The Hohenlohe proposal: Queen Victoria, Journal, December 1852/January 1853, passim (R.A.), Queen Victoria, *Letters* (first series), Earl of Malmesbury, *Memoirs*, Wellesley, *Paris Embassy*.

46 Napoleon-Eugénie conversation: Queen Victoria, *Letters*, Greville, *Memoirs*. Lord Westmeath: Clarendon Papers.

47 Letters of credence: Simpson, *Recovery*, Hübner, *Neuf ans*.

48 The incident at the ball, frequently misreported, is in Hübner, *Neuf ans*—he was present.

49 The original of the Emperor's letter: A.A.

49-51 The fullest version of the Emperor's speech is in Simpson, *Recovery*. Comte de Rilly's MS gives René de Villeneuve's unfavourable reaction to both speech and marriage, typical of the older generation of militant Bonapartists; Eugénie's letter, L.F., letters XXIV; Donoso Cortés in Maier, *Donoso Cortés*.

52 Queen Victoria, Journal (R.A.); O'Reilly: Clarendon Papers.

PART 2

CHAPTER I

55 Pope's reply: Simpson, *Recovery*; Eugénie's letter, L.F., vol. I, letter XXVII.

56-59 Wedding: Best account in Ferdinand Bac, *Le mariage de l'impératrice Eugénie*; Lady A. Bruce's letter was copied by Queen Victoria in full and inserted into her Journal; Hübner, *Neuf ans*; O'Reilly, *Clarendon Papers*; 'C. de B.': R. Henrey, *Letters from Paris*; René de Villeneuve: Comte de Rilly's MS.

CHAPTER II

Page
60 Assassination: Mérimée, C.G., vol. 7, No. 225. Drouyn de Lhuys: d'Harcourt, *Les Ministères de Drouyn*; immediately after the reconciliation the Minister wrote an enthusiastic letter about the new Empress to Doña Manuela (A.A.) Queen Victoria to Uncle Leopold: *Letters*, 1st series.
61 Republic: d'Antioch, *Changarnier*; Ollivier: *Journal 1846-1869*, vol. I.
62 A very good description of the Empress's household with further information on its individual members is in *The Court of the Tuileries* by 'le petit homme rouge' (Henry Vizetelly).
66 Eugénie's letter: L.F. vol. I, letter XXXIV; Montpensier story: Mérimée, C.G., vol. 7, No. 2081.

CHAPTER III

68 Hübner, *Neuf ans*; Hübner was present at Donoso Cortés's death-bed and funeral and has left a moving description of both events.
69 Empress on sex: Mme Carette (Mlle Bouvet); *Souvenirs intimes*, vol. I; 'men are worth nothing': Duchess of Sermoneta, *Things Past*; Queen Victoria's letter: Sencourt. *The Empress Eugénie*; Clarendon to Cowley: *Paris Embassy*, to Doña Manuela: A.A.
70 Assassination attempt: Hübner, *Neuf ans*, *Paris Embassy*, Clarendon Papers. The 'mirror' incident: Comte de Rilly's MS.
71 Hübner, *Neuf ans*.
72 Queen Victoria, Journal (Buckingham Palace, 28 February 1854) R.A. to Paca: L.F. vol. 1, letter XLII.
73 Lieutenant's remark: Mérimée, C.G., vol 7, No. 2098; Queen Victoria, *Journal* R.A., 28 February 1854; 'changed climate': Pope-Hennessey, *The Years of Promise*, who also quotes Hawthorn's comment; Mérimée, C.G.; Hübner, *Neuf ans*.
74 Habsburg wedding: Hübner, *Neuf ans*; E.C. C. Corti, *Elisabeth, die seltsame Frau*.
75 Spanish participation: Empress to Duke of Alba, L.F. vol. I, letters XLVIII and XLIV.
76 The Concert: Queen Victoria, Journal (Windsor, Oct. 29th/30th, 1854) R.A. Prince Albert's visit to St. Omer, ibid, and Martin, *Prince Consort*, vol. III.
77 The Emperor's Crimean journey: Queen Victoria, Journal (January-March 1855, passim); Mérimée, C.G., vol. 7, No. 2225 and 2231.
78 Baron d'Ambès, *Mémoires inédites*. The theory propounded by J. M. Thompson and others that the Empress regarded the Crimean War with the fervour of a Roman Catholic crusader has no foundation. That had been the mentality of Montalambert and his circle which provided Napoleon III with one of his reasons for breaking with the tutelage of that group. The Emperor, in the Empress's presence, strongly criticised that outlook to Stratford Canning when the latter passed through Paris en route to Constantinople and was singled out by the Empress for special attention, much to Hübner's annoyance. To Paca; L.F., vol. I, letter LI. Queen Victoria to Clarendon: Journal, 23 March 1854, R.A.: Cowley: *Paris Embassy*.
79 Mr. Worsfold: Ivor Guest, *Napoleon III in England*. The book on the State visits mentioned in the foot-note on page 80 is, of course, based on the edition published by Queen Victoria in 1880 which omitted several details contained in the Journal. Mr. Guest, like the present author, was permitted to consult the Journal itself.

374

CHAPTER IV

CHAPTER V

CHAPTER VI

Page

supplied by M. Max Terrier; Hübner, *Neuf ans*; Decaux, op. cit.; Castellane, Journal; Queen Victoria, Journal 9 July 1857 R.A.; Ilchester, *Chronicles of Holland House*. For Tibaldi see Vizetelly, op. cit.

CHAPTER VII

105-112   To Paca: L.F., vol. I, letter LXIX; Pack *The Bombs of Orsini*; Queen Victoria, Journal 15 January 1858, R.A. Mérimée, C.G., vol. 8, No. 2541; de Cassagnac in Fleury *Memoirs*; letters from Emperor and Empress to Queen Victoria: R.A. m 57/76 and m 57/77. Blanche of Castile: Hübner, *Neuf ans*. Laws of Public Safety: Ollivier, *Empire Libéral*, vol. IV, and *Journal*, vol. I, Pierre de La Gorce, *Histoire du Second Empire*, vol. II; Zeldin, *Political System of Napoleon III*. Clemenceau, cf. John Roberts, *Clemenceau. History Today*, Sept 1956: Empress's letter to Cowley: *Paris Embassy*.

113   Lady Combermere's letter: A.A. Queen Victoria, Journal, 21 April 1858, R.A. Princess Royal's Wedding: Queen Victoria, *Letters*, vol. III.

CHAPTER VIII

114   Pélissier's appointment: Queen Victoria, Journal, 22 March 1858, R.A. Mérimée, C.G., vol. 8, No. 2598. Rumania: Hübner, *Neuf ans*.

115   Venice etc. Corti, *Elisabeth*; Maximilian in Milan, Corti and Montgomery Hyde, op. cit. For Cavour, and Plombières, see P. Matter, *Cavour et l'unité Italienne*, also Hübner, *Neuf ans* and Wellesley, *Paris Embassy*.

116   Mme Walewska: Hübner, *Neuf ans*; Wellesley, op. cit., and Clarendon Papers, Bodleian. Mérimée, in very many of his letters, and Filon, in his book on the Empress, have drawn the best portrait of the lady and her ambitions. Unpublished documentation, if it exists, has not yet been made available by the Walewski family.

117   Cherbourg: Queen Victoria, Journal, 31 July 1858 and August 4-6, 1858, R.A.

118   Brittany: Hübner, *Neuf ans*; Mme Carette (née Bouvet): *Souvenirs intimes*, vol. I; Mérimée, C.G., vol. 8, No. 2635.

119   For Napoleon III's foreign policy at this date see especially A. J. P. Taylor, *Struggle for Mastery*, Corley, *Democratic Despot*, R. W. Seton-Watson, *Britain in Europe 1789-1914*. The Montenegrin problem figures frequently in Hübner's *Neuf ans*.

120   Jurien's letter: A.A.; Queen Victoria on Jurien: Journal, 23 April 1856, R.A. Clarendon on Mme Walewska in Kennedy, '*My dear Duchess*'. Biarritz: Barthez, op. cit.

121/122   Plon-Plon: d'Hauterive, *Napoleon III et le Prince Napoléon*; Compiègne, Mérimée, C.G., vol. 8, No. 2669; Pierrefonds: Mme Carette, op. cit.

CHAPTER IX

123/124   Hübner, *Neuf ans* is very informative on the Empress's attitude towards Italy; her letters to Paca: L.F., vol. I passim. For feeling in the country, especially towards the La Guéronnière pamphlet, see Case, *War and Diplomacy*. For Galliffet: Thomas, *Le Général Galliffet*.

125/128   Mérimée, C.G., vol. 9, No. 2717. Castellane, *Journal*, vol. IV; for Plon-Plon, d'Hauterive, op. cit.; Queen Victoria, Journal, January to April 1859, passim (R.A.).

Cowley's interview with the Emperor: Wellesley & Sencourt, *Conversations with Napoleon III*: For preliminaries of Italian War: Malmesbury, *Memoirs of an Ex-Minister*, Hallberg, *Franz Joseph and Napoleon III*, Case, *War and*

376

Diplomacy, L.F., vol. I., letter LXXXI. M. de Pimodan later joined the Papal Volunteers and was killed at Castelfidardo. Ollivier, *Journal*, vol. I and *Empire Libéral*, vol. IV.

CHAPTER X

130-133 Mérimée, C.G., vol. 9, No. 2736. The Regency is amply documented in A.A. where many of the special reports on morale etc. survive. For other reports see Case, *War and Diplomacy*. Prince Consort and Italy, Th.Martin, vol. IV; also Jagow, *Letters of the Prince Consort*. Correspondence between Empress and Queen, R.A. 319/81, 319/119; Napoleon III in Italy: Ollivier, *Empire Libéral*, vol. IV; de La Gorce, vol. III. Crown Princess of Prussia: R.A., CHY 28/6. The Italian War in relation to English internal politics is masterfully described in Beales, *England and Italy 1859-1860*. For Palmerston see Connell, *Regina v. Palmerston*, for Russell, Gooch. *The Later Correspondence of Lord John Russell*.
134-135 To Paca: L.F., vol. I, letter LXXXII; Empress of Austria: Corti, *Elisabeth*.
136-138 Ollivier, *Empire Libéral*, vol. IV. Empress's telegram: A.A., *Prince Consort*: Martin, vol. IV; Prussian Crown Princess: R.A. Invasion scare: Woodward, *Age of Reform*, Beales, *England and Italy* (where the Tennyson anthem is given in full); Kossuth, *Memories of My Exile*. Queen Victoria, Journal, 12 July 1859, R.A. The Prince Consort echoed the Queen's anger at Villafranca, see Corti, *The English Empress*.

CHAPTER XI

139-141 Turin: Pack, *Bombs of Orsini*. End of Regency: Tascher de La Pagerie, *Mon séjour aux Tuileries*. Barthez, op. cit. Princess Metternich, *Souvenirs, 1859-1871*; for Mme de Contades (later de Beaulaincourt), see Mérimée, C.G., vols. 9-15, passim; also G. Painter, *Marcel Proust*, and Tascher de La Pagerie, op. cit. (where she figures as Madame de —).
142 Footnote: from Guedalla, *Palmerston*.
143 Compiègne: Salomon, *L'ambassade de Richard Metternich*, Hallberg, *Franz Joseph and Napoleon III*.
144-146 For La Guéronnière pamphlet, see Case, op. cit; *A new view of Pio Nono*, by Rev. H. Johnson (*Dublin Review*, July 1936. To Paca: L.F., vol. I, letter LXXXIV; Cowley and Queen Victoria: Journal, 5 January 1860, R.A. Mme. Walewska: same sources as before.
147 Franco-Austrian relations: Salomon, op. cit., Hallberg, op. cit.
148 Thouvenel: The best published source is by his son, entitled *Le Secret de l'Empereur*. The Ortega episode: L.F. vol. I, letters LXXXV and VI, and other material in A.A. and Torriglia, *Condesa de Montijo*.
149 Mérimée, C.G., vol. 9, No. 2930.

CHAPTER XII

150-153 Garibaldi: Trevelyan, *Garibaldi and the Thousand*; Mack Smith, *Cavour and Garibaldi 1860*; letters to Paca: L.F. vol. I passim (including note on Paca in bois). The Emperor's Italian negotiations: Case, *War and Diplomacy*. Algiers; General de Fleury, *Souvenirs*, de La Gorce, op. cit.

CHAPTER XIII

154 Mérimée, C.G. vol. 10, No. 2995. L.F. vol. I, letter CI.

155-158 Scottish journey: Queen Victoria, Journal Windsor, 16 Nov. 1860 R.A.: Queen Victoria, *Letters*, first series, vol. III; *The London Illustrated News*, Nov./ Dec. 1860. Queen Victoria, Journal Windsor, 4 Dec. 1860. R.A. Panizzi: Mérimée, C.G. vol. 10, No. 3035. Lord Clarendon to Duchess of Manchester: Kennedy, *My Dear Duchess*. Mr. Claridge: communicated by the Savoy Group of Hotels from their archives. There is no evidence that the Empress did not find Paca's funeral sufficiently grandiose, although she wrote many letters at this time to Paca's widower, the Duke of Alba L.F. vol. 1, letter IC-CIX.

159/160 Liberalising decrees see especially Zeldin, *Political System of Napoleon III*, Corley, *Democratic Despot* and Gooch, *Second Empire*. Compiègne 1860; communicated by M. Max Terrier. Cobden's remark quoted in Corley, op. cit. To Alba: L.F. vol. I, letter CVI.

CHAPTER XIV

163-165 Council Meeting: Thouvenel, op. cit.; Gramont: ibid. Plon-Plon's and Keller's speeches quoted in Mérimée, C.G. vol 10. Two unofficial letters of appeal from the Queen of Naples to the Empress are in A.A. Plon-Plon and the Duke of Aumale: d'Hauterive, op. cit. Plon-Plon's cruise and American visit: *Prince Napoleon in America, 1861*.

CHAPTER XV

168 'Credit': From '. . . and *Mr. Fortescue*', by O. W. Hewett. The principal sources for the Mexican expedition are: C. Scheffer, *La grande pensée de Napoléon III*, Corti, *Maximilian and Charlotte of Mexico*, H. Montgomery Hyde, *Mexican Empire*.

169 Thouvenel, op. cit.

170 On future power of USA: *Prince Napoleon in America, 1861*, first published as *Lettres sur les Etat-Unis d'Amérique* (Paris, 1862).

171 Morny: Christophe, *Le Duc de Morny*.

172 To Empress Charlotte: Salomon, op. cit.

173 Palmerston's remark in Maxwell, *Life of Clarendon* which also quotes the remark by Clarendon's brother-in-law, Sir George Lewis, that absorption by USA was Mexico's 'manifest destiny'. Conversation with Guitierrez: Montgomery Hyde, op. cit.

174 Nuncio: Corti, *Maximilian and Charlotte*; Mérimée, C.G., vol. 11, No. 3319. Emperor's letter: Corti, Montgomery Hyde, Salomon op. cit.; Castellane, Journal, vol. IV.

175 To Charlotte: Salomon, Corti, op. cit.; Emperor's health: see Dr. Macdonald Critchley's interesting account in *Second Empire Medley* (1952), also Feraud, *Le Baron Hippolyte Larrey*, one of the doctors whom the Emperor forbade to inform the Empress of the gravity of his disease.

176 Garibaldi: Trevelyan, *Garibaldi and The Making of Italy*. Cabinet crisis: Taylor, *Struggle for Mastery*, excellent, but too ecstatic about Thouvenel. Cowley's letter: Clarendon Papers. Fould and Persigny: Persigny, *Mémoires*,/ Zeldin, *Political System*, Corley, op. cit., Case, op. cit.

177 Conversation with Mérimée: C.G., vol. 11, No. 3319.

178 Hübner to Rechberg: Vienna State Archives. Malmesbury, *Memoirs*. To Huescar: L.F., vol. I, letter CXIV.

179 Spanish cruise: see Mérimée, C.G., vol. 11, No. 3474 and No. 3483 for his initial objections and subsequent approval. American ambassador and sartorial anecdote communicated to author by Conde de Bailén. Nuncio Barili: Pirri, *Pio IX e Vittorio Emanuele II dal corteggio privato* (Rome, 1944-51) (I am

greatly obliged to Mr. E. E. Y. Hales for this reference). Mérimée: C.G., vol. 11, No 3498. Harold Nicolson, *Helen's Tower.*

180 Plon-Plon: Mérimée, C.G., vol. 11, No. 3495, cf. d'Hauterive, op. cit.

CHAPTER XVI

181-184 Aldehyde Green: details from archives of manufacturers, Hoechst, W. Germany. 'Political dresses'; Mme Carette, Tascher de La Pagerie, op. cit. Compiègne: information from M. Max Terrier; Mérimée, C.G. Falk, *Old Q's Daughter* (for Lord Hertford). A large number of letters from Nigra survive in A.A. The Empress's initial hostility from Metternich's dispatches in Salomon, op. cit., and Sencourt, *Empress Eugénie*; Empress's health in 1863: Mme Carette, op. cit., which also gives a detailed and most attractive account of Schwalbach. See also L.F., vol. I, letter CXV, where the Empress writes of her 'blue devils' and '*idées noires*'.

185-186 William I and German unity: The Empress discussed this with Hübner in 1862: Hübner to Rechberg, Paris, April 1862, Vienna State Archives. She distrusted the 'popular' ideas of Crown Prince Frederick and the ambitions of his English wife. The Bellanger scene: M. Chevalier, *Journal* (*Revue des Deux Mondes*, 1 Nov. 1932). Mérimée, C.G., vol. 11, No. 3718.

187-188 Filon's remark is in his *Souvenirs*. For Magny Dinners see Baldick, *Pages from the Goncourt Journal*.

CHAPTER XVII

189-192 Elections of 1863: Zeldin, *Political System*, Case, *War and Diplomacy*, Hübner to Rechberg, loc. cit. Conversations with Metternich: Hallberg, op. cit., Salomon, op. cit., supplemented by five unpublished dispatches from Metternich to Rechberg, kindly communicated by Dr. Blaas of Vienna State Archives. Drouyn de Lhuys's parallel efforts for closer Franco-Austrian understanding in d'Harcourt, *Les Ministères*. Danish War: A. J. P. Taylor, op. cit. and E. W. Mosse, *The European Powers and the German Question*. The same author has written a lucid account of Queen Victoria's attitude to the Danish War in *English Historical Review*, April 1963. Palmerston and French Navy: Woodward, *Age of Reform*.

193-194 *Syllabus of Errors*: Fliche et Martin, *Le Pontificat de Pie IX*, Case, *War and Diplomacy*. Holy Sepulchre: to Queen Victoria, R.A. from Queen Victoria, A.A.; von der Goltz's letter: A.A.; '*Buffoni*'; Gramont to Thouvenel, in Thouvenel, op. cit.

195-197 Cowley on Morny: *Paris Embassy*. The Empress's social work: Ollivier, *Empire Libéral*, vol. VII, Filon. *Souvenirs*, Mme Carette, op. cit. Duruy's letters to the Empress, hitherto overlooked, are all in A.A. See also: Duruy, *Notes et souvenirs*, Lavisse, *Victor Duruy*, Gooch, *Second Empire*.

198 Plon-Plon in Corsica: d'Hauterive, op. cit. (which also gives the Emperor's letter from Algiers). The quotation from *Julius Caesar* comes from the English translation (Cassells, 1865).

199 Rosa Bonheur: the original citation for her legion d'honneur is in A.A., as are the two newspapers comments. Mérimée, C.G., vol. 12, No. 3608, gives an amusing account of the Empress's first meeting with the artist. Metternich in Vienna State Archives.

200-201 Arenenberg: Hugentobler, *Die Familie Bonaparte auf Arenenberg*. For Neuchâtel incident: Mme Carette, d'Hauterive, op. cit. (Plon-Plon sent the Empress his expression of sympathy). Mérimée, C.G., vol. 12, No. 3753 and No. 3798.

CHAPTER XVIII

Page
202   Mérimée, C.G., vol. 12, No. 3818, Bismarck, *Gedanken und Erinnerungen*. Mr. A. J. P. Taylor's assertion that the Emperor and Bismarck became close friends is untenable. The Emperor very rarely kept political discussions on the coldest official level as markedly as he did with Bismarck.
203-209   Metternich: the conversations listed here are all in his dispatches, some of which were published by Salomon and Sencourt. Telegram of 3 July: Salomon, op. cit. General background: Mosse, *European Powers*; A. J. P. Taylor, *Struggle for Mastery* and, less impressively, *Bismarck*. Two Council meetings: Case, *War and Diplomacy*, d'Harcourt, *Les Quatres Ministères*, Randon, *Mémoires*. Duruy's letter: A.A. Barthez, op. cit. Metternich: Salomon, op. cit. Visit to Amiens: see *Souvenir Napoléonien* for July 1958, quoting the eye-witness report of a South American diplomat. Nancy: Mérimée, C.G., vol. 13, No. 3951; Empress Charlotte: Corti, Montgomery Hyde: Biarritz 1866: Mérimée, C.G., vol. 13, No. 3991 and No. 3987; Empress and Canrobert: see Bapst, *Le Maréchal Canrobert*, vol. IV. Empress to Victor Cousin: A.A. Second conscience: Filon, *Souvenirs*.

CHAPTER XIX

210-220   Army Reform: Bapst, *Canrobert*, vol. IV; Michael Howard, *The Franco-Prussian War*; Case, *War and Diplomacy*. Copies of the Empress's letter on War Memorials: A.A. Letters from Georges Sand, Chevreau, the Prefect and Bishop of Marseilles: ibid. Conversation with Magne quoted in Gooch, *Second Empire*. Pope's allocution quoted in notes to vol. 14 of Mérimée, C.G. Rouher's 'Never': Schnerb, *Rouher*. Mentana reactions: Case, *War and Diplomacy*, Trochu: a very good account in Michael Howard, op. cit. For Luxembourg, see Case, op. cit., for the French influence within Luxembourg see *Internationales Jahrbuch für Geschichtsunterricht* (International Institute for Text Books, Braunschweig 1957/58); Liberal reforms: Zeldin, Gooch, Cornly, Ollivier op. cit. For Offenbach: S. Krackauer, *Offenbach and Paris*. Society and morals: see F. Lollié, *Les courtisans*. Fleury et Sonolet, *La société du Second Empire*, *Commentaries of Caesar*: Mme Carette, op. cit. Attempt on Czar, Ollivier, vol. IX, de La Gorce, vol. V; Bismarck: Bapst, *Canrobert*, vol. IV, Mme de Pour-talès: ibid.

CHAPTER XX

221-228   Queretaro: Corti, Montgomery Hyde, op. cit. Queen of Holland: Lady Burghclere, *A Great Lady's Friendships*. Osborne: Queen Victora, Journal 22-24 July 1867, R.A. Salzburg: Beust, *Memoirs*, Salomon, op. cit., Corti, *Elisabeth*. Bismarck's circular was in all major British and Continental papers. Francis Joseph in Paris: Corti, *Elisabeth*. Queen of Holland: Lady Burghclere, op. cit. Jurien's letter: A.A. Desvarannes: Filon, *Souvenirs*, Mérimée, C.G., vol. 13, No. 4107; Fustel de Coulanges: Acton, *Lectures on Modern History*. Lavisse, Duruy. Diary of Cécile de Nardaillac (née Delessert) who accompanied her old friend, the Empress see Mérimée, C.G. notes to vol. 14. The Empress's letter : published by revolutionary Government, 1871. Jurien: A.A. Mme de Pourtalès: Mme Carette, op. cit. Mérimée reading: Filon, *Mérimée et ses amis*. 'Rock of granite': Mérimée, C.G., vol. 14, No. 4388.

CHAPTER XXI

Page
229-236 Gambetta: D. W. Brogan, *The Development of Modern France, The French Nation;* Tank, *Frankreich Zwischen Freiheit und Diktatur.* Ghensi: *Gambetta.* Prize giving: Duruy to Empress, A.A. Mérimée, C.G. vol. 15 which quotes Sainte-Beuve's remark. Franco-Italian-Austrian talks in Beust, *Memoirs,* Salomon, op. cit., A. J. P. Taylor, *Struggle for Mastery,* Engel-Janosi, *Oesterreich und der Vatikan.* Newton, *Lord Lyons.* Clarendon: Kennedy, *My Dear Duchess,* Maxwell, op. cit. Bismarck in 1870: Michael Howard, op. cit., Bonnin, *Hohenzollern Candidature,* Newton, *Lord Lyons;* Empress's War Party: Bapst, *Canrobert,* vol. IV. Emperor's health: ibid. Sée's diagnosis: Filon, *Souvenirs.* Scene at Longchamps: *Illustrated London News,* whose Paris correspondent was H. Vizetelly. Gramont: de Grunwald, op. cit. Empress and War: Princess Metternich, *Souvenirs,* Ollivier, *Empire Libéral,* vol. XIV; Filon, *Souvenirs,* Lavisse, *Duruy.*

CHAPTER XXII

237-250 Gambetta: same sources. Empress at Saint-Cloud: Mme Carette, op. cit. Filon, *The Prince Imperial.* Farewells: Mme Carette, Filon, *Souvenirs.* Painter, Marcel Proust. Maison de Refuge: Rabbi's letter of thanks in A.A. L.F., vol. I, letters CXXI-CXXIV. Feuillet's letter A.A. Filon, *Souvenirs.* Abbé Pujol's account of last days at Saint-Cloud: *Revue des Deux Mondes,* 15 July, 1929. 'The dynasty is lost': Filon, *Souvenirs,* Ollivier, *Empire Libéral,* vol. XIV. Empress presides: Bapst, *Canrobert.* Newton, *Lord Lyons.* Bismarck's Fourth Column: Mérimée, C.G., vol. 15, No. 4796. Trochu: Filon, *Souvenirs,* Bapst, *Canrobert.* Metternich to Beust: Salomon, op. cit. Empress to Duperré: Filon, *Prince Imperial.* Galliffet: Thomas, op. cit. Surrender after Sedan: Michael Howard, op. cit. September 3rd in Tuileries: Filon, *Souvenirs.*

CHAPTER XXIII

251-259 Filon, *Souvenirs,* R. Gower, *My Reminiscences;*   Dr. Evans, *Memoirs.* The Wilhelmshöhe correspondence: *Revue des Deux Mondes,* 1 Sept. 1930. Chiswick House: see Tisdall, *Unpredictable Queen.* Salisbury's article: Salisbury Papers. Queen Victoria's letter: Letters from Alexander II and Francis Joseph: A.A. Metternich to Empress, ibid., same to Beust, Salomon, op. cit. Peace negotiations: Michael Howard, op. cit., Filon, *Souvenirs;* for Regnier, see Guedalla's engaging account in his *Second Empire.* William I to Empress: A.A.

PART 3

CHAPTER I

263-268 Wilhelmshöhe as before. The best account of the Emperor's captivity is by Graf Monts. Apponyi's letter: Burghclere, *Great Lady's Friendships.* Crown Prince Frederick: *The War Diary of the Emperor Frederick III,* Woodham-Smith, *Florence Nightingale.* Duke of Connaught: R.A. 383/153; Queen Victoria

Page

to Queen of Prussia, ibid. I65/149 Elphinstone and Sydney to Queen: ibid. Add A15/1666. Emperor's return: Ivor Guest, op. cit.

CHAPTER II

269-277 Chislehurst: Guest, op. cit., Filon, *Souvenirs* and *Prince Imperial*, L.F., vol. II, letter CXXXI, Malmesbury, *Memoirs*. Schnerb, *Rouher*. Jurien's letters all in A.A. 'C de B': R. Henrey, op. cit. Filon, *Prince Imperial*. Empress on value of boredom: L.F., vol. II, letter CLXXVI: 'free and honourable': Filon, *Prince Imperial*. Prince Pierre: Information from his great-granddaughter, Princess Eugénie of Greece; see also Lucien Daudet, *L'Ombre de l'Impératrice Eugénie*. The anecdote on page 221, frequently misquoted, is from Mme Carette, op. cit. For Chambord (Henry V) see Monti, *Chambord*. Letters about de Bizemont: A.A. Woolwich: Filon, *Prince Imperial*. The Emperor's wooden horse: Information supplied by Royal Military Academy, Sandhurst. Little concrete evidence on the Emperor's desire to return to France has come to light and any indications of it are purely circumstantial. 'C de B' in *Letters from Paris* (e.g. letter of 5 Dec. 1871) and Maxime du Camp in his *Souvenirs* took the possibility seriously, as did Jurien in his letters to Chislehurst (A.A.). In her letters to Doña Manuela late in 1872, the Empress sometimes wrote that she did not 'dare' to trust the post, especially concerning the Emperor's health. The Emperor's operations, Ivor Guest, op. cit. Prince of Wales's and many other telegrams: A.A. 'Faithful Ally': Queen Victoria, Journal, 9 January 1873. Greenwich Gas works and Mr. Hunt: Guest, op. cit.

CHAPTER III

278-295 L.F., vol. II, letter CXXXIX: Filon, *Souvenirs* and *Prince Imperial*. Schnerb, *Rouher*. *The Times*, 17 March 1874. Jurien and C de B as before; Metternich: A.A.; Arenenberg: Hugentobler, op. cit. Empress to her niece Louise, Duchess of Montoro: L.F., vol. II, letter CLIV: Arthur Bigge: both John Gore and Sir Harold Nicolson say in their books on George V that his appointment as secretary showed the Queen's judgement of character, but in fact he was appointed on the strength of the Empress's recommendation and because of his friendship with the Prince Imperial. Liaison between the Empress and the Queen was among his principal initial duties. All Bigge's letters are in the possession of his daughter, the Hon. Mrs. Adeane. Prince Imperial to Taine: A.A. (Taine had been Mgr. Dupanloup's *bête noire* during the Empire). Henry James: *Parisian Sketches*, 1875-1867. Elections of 1876: L.F., vol. II, letter CLXII. Men of destiny: L.F., vol. II, CLXII; Gambetta: ibid., letter CLXVII; from Arenenberg: ibid. letter CLXVIII (also about MacMahon); Intolerance: ibid., CLXV; Strike: ibid., CLXXI. The original of the Le Sourd letter is on permanent display in the library of the Palacio de Liria, Madrid. Gramont: Metternich's letter in A.A. Lady Waldegrave: O. W. Hewett, *Strawberry Fair*; Ponsonby, *Recollections of Three Reigns*: Queen on Prince Imperial, Queen Victoria, *Letters*. Prince Imperial in Florence and Rome: Filon, *Prince Imperial*. French Neo-Ultranism: Fliche and Martin, op. cit. Doña Manuela in old age: Hanoteaux, loc. cit. Miss Flowers: Lady Lintorn Simmons's unpublished diary. *Seize Mai*: see Brogan, *The French Nation*. Empress on Germany and France: L.F., vol. II, letter CLXXV and CLXXXI. For Prince Imperial in Sweden: Filon, *Prince Imperial* and E. E. P. Tisdall's book; King Oscar II's many letters: A.A. Lavisse, ibid. Prince Imperial in 1878/79: Filon, op. cit. ' *les petites dames*': communicated by Hon. Mrs. Adeane who heard the story from her father.

382

CHAPTER IV

Page

296-307 Prince Imperial going to South Africa: Filon, op. cit. Queen Victoria's letter: R.A. R5/12 Filon quotes the Prince's letters here given. Queen telegram: R.A. R5/(L) Empress to Doña Manuela: L.F., vol. II, letters CLXXXIII, CLXXXIX. Prince to Bigge: original in possession of Hon. Mrs. Adeane. Bigge to Ward Ashton, ibid. Grenfell's letter in Lord Grenfell, *Memoirs* Bettington quoted by Filon. Empress at Chislehurst: L.F., vol. II, letters CXC-CXCVIII; Filon, *Souvenirs*. Deléage, *Avec le Prince Impérial en Zululand*. Grenfell on 1st of June and finding the body: Grenfell, op. cit. Order of the Day: K. John, *The Prince Imperial*. Carey's letter is in the possession of Lord Grenfell's descendants and was communicated by John Grenfell, Esq. Chelmsford: E. G. French, *Lord Chelmsford and the Zulu War* (1939). Carey's Court Martial and subsequent conduct in the three books on the Prince Imperial listed in the bibliography.

CHAPTER V

308-318 Mme Filon wrote several very moving letters to Chislehurst which are preserved in A.A.; Lady Simmons's diary was left by her to her daughter who bequeathed it to Mrs. Wroughton. 'Cry of protest': L.F., vol. II, letter CXCIX. Queen's letter: A.A.; same to Disraeli: H25/62, R.A. Duke of Connaught to Queen: R.A. Add 1A/15/3219 R.A. To Doña Manuela: L.F., vol. II, letters CC-CCV; Funeral: Filon, op. cit., The Prince's Will is in the possession of Messrs. Markby, Stewart & Wadesons. Prince Victor: Lord Newton, op. cit. Empress to Queen on Carey: R.A. R8/65. Bigge's letter: Hon. Mrs. Adeane. Bettington to Bassano: A.A. Empress's letter of 18 April: original in A.A., copy (in Princess Beatrice's handwriting) R.A. 1Z169/14 R.A. Empress in South Africa: Filon, and the other two books on the Prince Imperial. Doña Sol: Empress to Duke of Huescar, L.F., vol. II, letter CCXIX ('*Espero que llamareis a la chica Doñ Sol: mon nom ne porte pas bonheur*'), and private information.

PART 4

CHAPTER 1

321-333 Self restraint: *The Times*, 20 July 1920 (Wickham Steed). To Bigge: Hon. Mrs. Adeane. Arthur Bigge was the grandfather of H.M. The Queen's private secretary, Sir Michael Adeane. Salisbury in Newton, *Lord Lyons*; other correspondence between Salisbury and Lyons: Salisbury Papers. Wood's letter: original A.A., copy R.A. (Dilke had been in Paris during the mob attacks on Tuileries on 3 Sept. 1870). Young Conneau's letters all preserved in A.A.; The Empress's letter to him in possession of St. Michael's Abbey, Farnborough. Lady Simmons's diary as before. Plon-Plon's coup: outlines in Filon, *Souvenirs*. A fascinating account of Gambetta's last years in Halévy, *Trois Diners avec Gambetta*, (*Revue des Deux Mondes*, July 1929). Empress to General Fleury. An excellent article on the early years of the Monastery, by Dom Placid Higham, O.S.B., appeared in *Pax*, Summer 1959.

A diary in the possession of the Premonstretensians at Storrington, Sussex gives many interesting details on those early years, including the Empress's journeys and visitors. Empress Frederick: see Gould Lee, *The Empress Frederick writes to Sophie*. The Empress's Republican friends: Hanoteaux loc. cit., for Delcassé, see page 340. Briand and Poincaré, see Lucien Daudet, *L'Ombre*, Clemenceau, see page 362. Furniture and pictures at Farnborough Hill: Catalogue of the Farnborough Hill Sale, 1926, in the files of Messrs. Markby, Stewart, which also have a list of the Library. Secret Library: In 1920 Messrs. Markby Stewart asked Captain Lascelles, now Sir A. Lascelles, G.C.V.O., C.M.G., to compile an inventory of all papers found at Farnborough Hill. That list, meticulously draw up by Sir Alan, represents the index to the Empress's unwritten Memoirs and exists in the Alba Archives, those of Prince Napoleon at Prangins, and in the files of Messrs. Marky, Stewart and Wadesons. When Captain Lascelles first went to Farnborough in 1920, Bristol, the Empress's old major-domo, warned him that he was unlikely to find much—the Empress had spent three days in 1919 burning papers! It makes the surviving papers, and Sir Alan's inventory, all the more valuable. Captain Lascelles' correspondence with Messrs. Markby Stewart is in the latter's files. Sir Alan very kindly communicated his recollections of Farnborough Hill to the author in 1960. Jurien's, Canrobert's and Trochu's letters: A.A.

CHAPTER II

334-345 The original Marconi telegram in A.A. Villalobar: private information from sources in Madrid and London. 'Great Politician': Abbot Cabrol, *Dublin Review*, Oct.-Dec. 1920. Correspondence with Rosario, Duchess of Alba: L.F., vol. II, letters CCXXX-CCLIII, Salisbury's speech in *The Times*, 5 May 1898. Drummond Wolff's letters: Salisbury Papers; Queen Victoria to Salisbury, ibid.; 'Neutral' as indicated (*The Times* archives contain no indication of the identity of this well-informed man). Schlumberger, *Mes Souvenirs*. Filon was in Paris at the time of the Boulanger crisis and reported on it to Chislehurst. Like the Empress he deplored the pseudo-Bonapartism of this hollow affair. These letters, and those on Drumont, are in A.A. Jules Claretie, Joseph Reincach: Lucien Daudet, *L'Ombre*. Filon on Duruy, Calmette to Pietri: A.A. Empress in Paris: Miss Vesey MS. The principal sources for Lucien Daudet are his introduction to the third edition of *L'Inconnue* and the letters he wrote to his mother from Farnborough and Cap Martin which he published in *L'Ombre de l'Impératrice Eugénie*. Mme de Beaulaincourt: Painter, *Marcel Proust*.

CHAPTER III

346-356 Albas at Balmoral: Queen Victoria, Journal. King Edward's telegram: A.A. Sir F. Ponsonby, *Three Reigns*. Empress to Bigge: Hon. Mrs. Adeane; Bigge to Queen: R.A. I6o/86 Kaiser to Empress: A.A.; Solms at Cap Martin: Daudet, *L'Ombre*. The Bergen encounter: Miss Vesey MS; Kaiser's letter in 1912: A.A. the Bertrand Stewart case: Public Record Office for correspondence between F.O. and Berlin Embassy. Empress of Austria: Corti, *Elisabeth*, Miss Vesey MS. Ischl; Marguttix, *Kaiser Franz Joseph* and Miss Vesey; Francis Joseph on next war: Corti, *Elisabeth*; 'Titans': Daudet, *L'Ombre*. Dr. Hugenschmidt: briefly mentioned in Decaux, *La Castiglione* and Painter, *Marcel Proust*; both Miss Vesey and Dr. Attenborough remember him very well (he died in 1929) and Miss Vesey has some interesting letters from him in her possession. Abbot Cabrol's papers are at Quarr Abbey, I.O.W. Golden Rose: Dom Placid Higham's article in *Pax*, Spring 1959.

CHAPTER IV

BIBLIOGRAPHY

UNPUBLISHED SOURCES

The Royal Archives, Windsor Castle.
The Alba Archives, Madrid.
Lord Stamfordham's letters, in possession of Hon. Mrs. Adeane.
The Salisbury Papers, Christ Church, Oxford.
The Clarendon Papers, Bodleian Library, Oxford.
The Haig Papers, in possession of Earl Haig.
Miss Vesey's MS and letters.
The Rilly Archives, at the Château de Rilly, France.
The Huddleston Papers, Sawston Hall, Cambridge.
The Rev. Dom P. Conway's Diary, St. Michael's Abbey, Farnborough.
Lady Simmons's Diary, in possession of Mrs. Wroughton.
The Papers of Messrs. Markby, Stewart & Wadesons.

PUBLISHED WORKS

(This list makes no claim to completeness but represents the published works on which the author has relied).

Alba, Duke of (Editor): *Lettres Familières de l'Impératrice Eugénie.* 2 vols. Paris 1935.
Allain-Targé: *La République sous l'Empire.* Paris 1939.
d'Ambès, Baron: *Mémoires inédites.* 2 vols. Paris 1909.
André-Maurois, Mme. S.: *Miss Howard and the Emperor.* London 1957.
Anonymous (probably Frédéric Masson): *L'Impératrice, notes et documents.* Paris 1877.
d'Antioche, Cte. A.: *Deux Diplomates, Le comte Raczynski et Donoso Cortés.* Paris 1880.

Bac, F.: *Le Mariage de l'Impératrice Eugénie.* Paris 1928.
Bapst, G.: *Le Maréchal Canrobert.* Vol. IV. Paris 1909.
Barthez, Dr. E.: *The Empress Eugénie and her Circle.* London 1912.
Beales, D.: *England and Italy 1859-60.* London 1961.
Berkeley, G. F-H.: *The Irish Battalion in the Papal Army of 1860.* Dublin 1936.
Beust, Ct. F. F. von.: *Memoirs.* 2 vols. London 1887.
Bonnin, G. (ed.) *Bismarck and the Hohenzollern Candidature.* London 1957.
Boulenger, M.: *Le Duc de Morny.* Paris 1925.

Burghclere, Lady.: *A Great Lady's Friendships.* Letters to Mary, Marchioness of Salisbury, Countess of Derby, 1862-1890. London 1933.

Cambridge History of British Foreign Policy. Vol. 2. Cambridge 1923.
Camp, Maxime du.: *Souvenirs d'un Demi-Siècle.* Paris 1949.
Carette, Mme (Mlle Bouvet): *Souvenirs Intimes de la Cour des Tuileries.* 3 vols. Paris 1888-1891.
Case, L. M.: *French Opinion on War and Diplomacy during the Second Empire.* University of Pennsylvania 1954.
Case, L. M.: *Franco-Italian Relations 1860-65.* Philadelphia 1932.
Cassagnac, A. Granier de: *Souvenirs du Second Empire.* 3 vols. Paris 1881-84.
Castellane, Maréchal de: *Journal.* 6 vols. Paris 1895-1903.
Chesnelong, Ch.: *Les Derniers Jours de l'Empire.* Paris 1930.
Chevalier, M.: *Journal. Revue des Deux Mondes.* 1 November, 1932.
Christophe, R.: *Le Duc de Morny.* Paris 1951.
Connell, B.: *Regina v Palmerston 1837-65.* London 1962.
Corley, T. A. B.: *Democratic Despot. A Life of Napoleon III.* London 1961.
Cortés, Donoso: *Obras Completas de Donoso Cortés.* Madrid 1946.
Corti, E. C. Ct.: *Maximilian and Charlotte of Mexico.* London 1928.
    Elisabeth, die seltsame Frau. Salzburg-Leipzig 1934.
    The English Empress. London n.d.

Dâudet, Lucien: *L'Inconnue. L'Impératrice Eugénie.* (New revised edition with a preface, an epilogue and numerous notes). Paris 1922.
    Dans L'Ombre de l'Impératrice Eugénie. Lettres intimes addressées à Mme Alphonse Daudet. Paris 1935.
Darimon, A.: *Les Cinq sous l'Empire, 1857-60.* Paris 1885.
    Histoire d'un Parti. Paris 1888.
    Histoire de 12 ans. 1857-69. Paris 1883.
Decaux, A.: *La Castiglione, le Coeur de l'Europe.* Paris 1953.
Deléage, P., *Trois mois chez les Zoulus et les derniers jours du Prince Impérial.* Paris 1879.

Elliott, Hon. G.: *Sir James Hudson and Earl Russell.* London 1886.
Engel-Janosi F.: *Der Freiherr von Hübner.* Innsbruck 1933.
    Oesterreich und der Vatikan. Vienna 1958.
Esslinger, E.: *Der politische Einfluss der Kaiserin Eugénie auf die Regierung Napoleons III.* Tübingen 1932.

Evans, Dr. T. W.: *Memoirs.* 2 vols. London 1894.
Falk, B.: *Old Q's Daughter.* London 1937.
Filon, A.: *Souvenirs sur l'Impératrice Eugénie.* Introduction by E. Lavisse. Paris 1920.
    The Prince Imperial. London 1913.

Fitzmaurice, Lord. E.: *The Life of the 2nd Earl Granville*. 2 vols. London 1905.

Fleury, General Comte F.: *Souvenirs*. Paris n.d.

Fleury, Comte M.: *The Memoirs of the Empress Eugénie*. 2 vols. London 1920.

Fleury et Sonolet: *La Société du Second Empire*. 3 vols. Paris 1911-13.

Fliche A. and Martin, V., (ed.): *Histoire de l'Eglise*. vol XXI. Paris 1952.

Frederick III, Emperor: *The War Diary of the Emperor Frederick III*. London 1927.

French, E. G.: *Lord Chelmsford and the Zulu War*. London 1939.

Fuye, L. de: *Louis Napoléon Bonaparte avant l'Empire*. Paris 1951.

Garets, Comtesse de: *L'Impératrice Eugénie en Exile*. Paris n.d.

Gheusi, P.-B.: *Gambetta par Gambetta*. Paris 1909.

Gooch, G. P.: *The Second Empire*. London 1959.

    (ed.) *The Later Correspondence of Lord John Russell*. 2 vols. London 1925.

Gorce, Pierre de La: *Histoire du Second Empire*. Paris 1908.

Gower, Lord R.: *My Reminiscences*. 2 vols. London 1883.

Gramont, Duke of: *La France et la Prusse avant la Guerre*. London 1872.

Grenfell: *The Memoirs of Field-Marshal Lord Grenfell*. London 1925.

Grunwald, C. de: *Le Duc de Gramont*. Paris 1951.

Guedalla, Ph.: *The Second Empire* (new edition) London 1957.

Guest, Ivor: *Napoleon III in England*. London 1952.

Hales, E. E. Y.: *Pio Nono*. London 1954.

    Mazzini and the Secret Societies. London 1956.

Halévy, L.: *Trois Diners avec Gambetta*. REVUE DES DEUX MONDES July 1929.

Hallberg, C. W.: *Franz Joseph and Napoleon III*. New York 1955.

d'Harcourt, Comte: *Les Quatres Ministères de Drouyn de Lhuys*. Paris n.d.

d'Hauterive, E.: *Napoleon III et le Prince Napoleon*. Paris 1925.

Henrey, R. (ed.): *Letters from Paris 1870-75*. London 1942.

Hewett, O. W.: *Strawberry Fair*. London 1956.

    . . . . *And Mr. Fortescue* London 1958.

Holden, E. W. (ed.): *Second Empire Medley*. London 1952.

Howard, Michael: *The Franco-Prussian War*. London 1961.

Hübner, Count: *Neuf ans de Souvenirs d'un Ambassadeur d'Autrichex*. 2 vols. Paris 1904.

Hyde, H. Montgomery: *Mexican Empire*. London 1946.

Ilchester, Earl of: *Chronicles of Holland House 1820-1900*. London 1937.

Jagow, K. (ed.): *Letters of the Prince Consort*. London 1938.

James, Henry: *Parisian Sketches (1875-76)*. New York 1957.

John, Katherine: *The Prince Imperial*. London 1939.

Kennedy, A. L.: 'My Dear Duchess'. Social and Political Letters to the Duchess of Manchester (1858-69). London 1956.
Kerry, Earl of: The Secret of the Coup d'Etat. London 1924.
Kossuth, L.: Memoirs of My Exile. London 1880.
Krackauer, S.: Offenbach and the Paris of his Time. London 1937.

Lavisse, E.: Victor Duruy. Paris n.d.
   Correspondence avec le Prince Impérial. Revue des Deux Mondes, March 15, 1929.
Labracherie, F.: Le Second Empire. Paris 1962.
Lenotre, G.: The Tuileries. London 1934.
Lee, Arthur Gould: The Empress Frederick writes to Sophie. London 1953.
Lucas, R.: Lord Glenesk and the Morning Post. London 1910.

Mack Smith, D.: Garibaldi. London 1957.
   Cavour and Garibaldi 1860. Cambridge 1954.
Maier, A. H. (ed.): Donoso Cortés, Briefe, Reden und Diplomatische Berichte. Cologne 1950.
Malmesbury, Earl of: Memoirs of an Ex-Minister. London 1885.
Margutti, A. von: Kaiser Franz Joseph. Vienna 1921.
Martin, Sir Th.: The Life of H.R.H. Prince Consort. 5 vols. London 1873-80.
Matter, P.: Cavour et l'Unité Italienne. Paris 1927.
Maupas, C. E. de: Mémoires sur le Second Empire. Paris 1884.
Maurain, J.: La Politique Ecclésiastique du Second Empire. Paris 1930.
Maxwell, Sir H.: Life and Letters of the Fourth Earl of Clarendon. London 1913.
Mérimée, Prosper: Correspondance Générale, établie et annotée par Maurice Parturier. 16 vols. Toulouse 1946-1961.
Metternich, Princess Pauline: Souvenirs 1859-71. Paris 1922.
Monti de Rezé, Cte. R. de: Souvenirs sur le Comte de Chambord. Paris 1930.
Monts, Graf: Napoleon III auf Wilhelmshöhe. Berlin 1909.
Morley, John: The Life of Richard Cobden. London 1881.
Mosse, W. E.: The European Powers and the German Question 1848-71. Cambridge 1958.

Napoleon III: Oeuvres. Paris 1856.
   Julius Caesar. 2 vols. London 1865.
Newton, Lord: Retrospection. London 1941.
   Life of Lord Lyons. 2 vols. London 1913.
Nicolson, Hon. Sir H.: Helen's Tower. London 1935.

Ollivier, E.: L'Empire Libéral. 18 vols. Paris 1895-1918.
Ornano, Cte: Le Comte Walewski. Paris 1958.

Pack, Michael St. 3. The Bombs of Orisini. London 1958.

Painter, G.: *Marcel Proust*. London 1959.

Papiers et Correspondance de La Famille Impériale.

Papiers sauvés des Tuileries. Paris 1870-1872.

Pares, R. and Taylor, A. J. P. (ed.): *Essays Presented to Sir Lewis Namier*. London 1956.

Pemberton, W. B.: *Battles of the Crimean War*. London 1962.

Persigny, V. F. Duke of: *Mémoires*. Paris 1896.

Pisani, C. F.: *Prince Napoleon in America, 1861*. London 1960.

Pirri, P.: *Pio IX e Vittorio Emanuele II dal loro corteggio privato*. Rome 1944-51.

Ponsonby, Sir F.: *Recollections of three Reigns*.

Poirson, P.: *Walewski*. Paris 1943.

Pope-Hennessy, James: *Monckton Milnes*.
>> vol. I, *The Years of Promise*. London 1949.
>> vol. II, *The Flight of Youth*. London 1951.

Puyol, Abbé: *Les derniers jours du château de Saint-Cloud*. *Revue des Deux Mondes* 15 July, 1929.

Rilly, Comte de: *La Reine Hortense à Cauterets*. *Revue des Deux Mondes* 1 Sept., 1959.

Rumbold, Sir H.: *Recollections of a Diplomatist*. 2 vols. London 1902.

Salomon, H.: *L'Ambassade de Richard de Metternich*. Paris 1931.

Schlumberger, Gustave: *Mes Souvenirs*. Paris 1934.

Schnerb, R.: *Rouher et le Second Empire*. Paris 1949.

Seignobos C.: *Historie de la France contemporaine*. vols 6–8. Paris 1921.

Sencourt, R.: *The Life of the Empress Eugénie*. London 1931.

Sermonetta, Duchess of: *Things Past*. London n.d.

Simpson, Rev. F. A.: *Louis Napoleon and the Recovery of France*. new ed. London 1951.

Smyth, Dame Ethel: *Streaks of Life*. London 1920.

Tank, K. L.: *Frankreich zwischen Freiheit und Diktatur. Gambettas Kampf gegen Napoleon III*. Hamburg 1958.

Tascher de La Pagerie, S.: *Mon séjour aux Tuileries*. 3 vols. Paris 1894.

Taylor, A. J. P.: *The Struggle for Mastery in Europe 1848-1918*. Oxford 1954.
>> *Bismarck*. London 1956.

Temperley, H. W. V.: *England and the Near East; The Crimea*. London 1936.

Thayer, W. R.: *The Life and Times of Cavour*. 2 vols. Boston 1911.

Thomas, L.: *Le Général de Galliffett*. Paris 1911.

Thompson, J. M.: *Louis Napoleon and the Second Empire*. Oxford 1954.

Thouvenel, A. (ed.): *Le Secret de l'Empereur*. 2 vols. Paris 1889.

Tisdall, E. E. P.: *Unpredictable Queen* (Alexandra). London 1954.
>> *The Prince Imperial*. London 1959.

Tocqueville, A. de: *Recollections*. ed. J. P. Mayer, London 1948.
Torriglia, Llanos y: *Maria Manuela Kirkpatrick, Condesa de Montijo*. Madrid 1935.
Trevelyan, G. M.: *Garibaldi and the Thousand*. London 1909.
    Garibaldi and the Making of Italy. London 1912.

Victoria, Queen: *Letters*. 9 vols. London 1907-1932.
Viel Castel, Cte. Horace de: *Mémoires sur le Règne de Napoleon III*. 6 vols. Paris 1884.
Villiers, Hon. N. C.: *A Vanished Victorian. The Life of the Fourth Earl of Clarendon*. London 1938.
Vizetelly, H. *The Court of the Tuileries 1852-70*. London 1912.
Vitzthum, Graf: *London, Gastein und Sadowa*. Stuttgart 1889.

Wellesley, F. A.: *The Paris Embassy during the Second Empire*. London 1928.
Wellesley, V. and Sencourt R.: *Conversations with Napoleon III*. London 1934.
Woodward, Sir L.: *The Age of Reform*. Second Ed. Oxford 1962.

Zeldin, Th.: *The Political System of Napoleon III*. London 1958.
    (ed.) Emile Ollivier, *Journal*, vol. I (Paris 1961).

Special acknowledgements are due to the following authors and publishers for permission to quote:

Mrs. Robert Henrey and Messrs J. M. Dent for quotations from *Letters from Paris 1870-1875*;
The Hon. Sir Harold Nicolson and Messrs. Constable for quotations from *Helen's Tower*;
Mr. Michael Howard and Messrs. Rupert Hart-Davis for quotations from *The Franco-Prussian War*.

INDEX

Emperor), 43-4, 55-6; opposition to marriage, 45-7, 48, 51-2; insulted at Court Ball, 48-9; Emperor's proposal, 49-51; wedding, 56-8

Supports Emperor in conciliation policy, 60-1, 62; household, 62-3; Winterhalter's paintings of, 63; Court life, 63-5, 140-1; adds Biarritz to royal residences, 65-6; persuades mother to return to Spain, 67-8; influenced by Donoso Cortés, 68; miscarriage, 68-9; frigidity and attitude to sexual love, 69, 95, 142; Emperor's disciple in foreign affairs, 70-1, 75; views on Austria, 72, 86-7, 88-9, 114-15, 124, 126, 127; dissuades him from Sebastopol project, 78; State Visit to England, 78-80; beginning of friendship with Royal Family, 79-80, 84-5; and Pianori's attempt on Emperor, 81-2; pregnancy and depression, 83, 84, 86; entertains Royal Family, 84-5; heavy social round, 86; difficult birth of Prince Imperial, 90-1, 92-3, 94; slow recovery, 94, 95, 97; and Emperor's mistresses, 94-5, 100, 102, 116-117, 183, 185-8; pleasure in good looks, 97, 321, 359; son's baptism, 98-9; visits Osborne, 103; and Orsini attack, 105-7, 111-12, 113; and Bernard verdict, 112-13, 114; nominated Regent, 107-8; not told of Emperor's Italian project, 115-16; Mme. Walewska's scheming against, 116-17, 145-6, 166, 175, 183; tour of Brittany, 117, 118-19, 120; in Basque country, 120-1; factory visits, 121-2; uses Countess of Pierrefonds incognito, 122; and Italian question, 124, 125-6, 127, 143, 146-7, 161; as Regent during Italian campaign, 130-1, 134-5, 138, 139-40, 161-6; fear of Prussia, 131, 134, 185, 204-5, 227-8; anxious for early peace, 134; upholds Pope's temporal freedom, 136, 162, 163, 165, 176; and Papal States, 143-5, 146, 147, 162; anxiety over Paca's health, 149, 150-1, 152; tours Savoy, Nice and Algeria, 151-3; grief over Paca's death, 153, 154-5, 160, 161

Visits Scotland, 155-6; at Windsor, 156-7; in London, 157-8; adjustment to liberal reforms, 161, 227; opposes 'Italian' line in foreign policy, 162-3; Plon-Plon's hostility to, 164-5, 180; and Mexican enterprise, 168-9, 171-5, 206-7, 221, 222-4; attitude to bodily affliction, 175, 343; accused of forcing Ministerial reshuffle, 176-8; care for Paca's children,

178; visits mother in Madrid, 178-9; leads fashion reform, 181-2; reputation as hostess, 182; new understanding with Emperor, 183, 187; takes cure at Schwalbach, 183-5; keen interest in foreign policy, 189-94; desires full Franco-Austrian alliance, 189-90, 191, 202-3, 204-5, 246; and Polish question, 190-1; acts against Pope's Syllabus of Errors, 193-4; suggests rebuilding of Holy Sepulchre church, 193-4; second Regency, 194-9; interest in internal reform, 194-8, 211; urges penal reform, 195; educational reforms, 196-7; at Arenenberg, 200-1; urges Emperor to mobilize against Prussia, 204; warmongering charge against, 205, 213, 231, 232; and Seven-week war, 205-6; considers Emperor's modified abdication because of ill-health, 206; personal popularity, 206; stay at Biarritz and improved relationship with Emperor, 207-9; faith in future of Prince Imperial, 208, 209; tries to revive military enthusiasm, 210-11; social work and charities, 211-12; and Roman Question, 212-13, 231; private visit to Osborne, 221-2; at Salzburg, 222-3; despondency over Austrian and Mexican failures, 223-4; studies history, 225; at opening of Suez Canal, 226; withdraws from public activity, 227, 239; concern over Emperor's health, 232; her share in declaration of war against Prussia, 234-6, 237-8; legend of war-guilt, 236, 238, 287-8; appointed Regent, 238; visits Fleet, 238-9; during Franco-Prussian war, 238-50; limited powers as Regent, 239, 240, 241; distressed by Emperor's news, 240; and twin defeats of Forbach and Froeschwiller, 241-2; opposes Emperor's return to Paris, 242, 244-5; determination to defend Paris, 242, 244-5, 246-7; accepts Trochu as Governor of Paris, 245; and Emperor's surrender after Sedan, 249-50; persuaded to leave Paris, 252; escape to England, 252-4; reunited with son, 254; hears from imprisoned Emperor, 254-5, 258-9; settles at Chislehurst, 256, 266; seeks generous peace for France, 256-8, 361; visits Emperor at Wilhelmshöhe, 259

Final phase of reconciliation, 263; anxiety over son's future, 267; and Emperor's arrival in England, 267-8; organizes social life, 269; and Prince

visits scene of death, 316-17; mausoleum at Farnborough, 321-2, 329, 354, 369; monument in St. George's Chapel, 322-3; Angeli's portrait of, 354, 366
Prophet, The (Meyerbeer), 57
Proust, Dr. Adrien, 239
Proust, Marcel, 142, 342, 343, 345
Public Security, Law of, 107, 108-10
Puebla, 174
Puyol, Abbé, 240

Quarterly Review, 255n
Queen Victoria: Leaves from a Journal (1961), 80n
Queretaro, 221

Radetzki, Field Marshal J. W., 115
Raglan, 1st Lord, 73, 74, 83
Raimbaut (mounted escort), 219, 340
Rama V of Siam, 331
Randon, Marshal, 91, 130, 204
Rappel, Le, 239
Rawlinson, Sir Henry Seymour, 1st Lord, 369
Rayneval, Mme de, 239
Rechberg, Count J. B. von, 135, 189, 190
Redel, Mlle, 197, 228
Redondo, José (El Chiclanero), 33
Regnier, Edouard, 257
Reille, General, 248
Reinach, Joseph, 243, 339
Renard, M., 181
Revue, La, 343
Rheims, 61, 366
Riflemen, form! (Tennyson), 137
Rivoli, Duc de, 338
Rocquencourt, 340
Rogers, Trooper, 304
Roman Question, The (Blakiston), 166n
Rome, 162, 163, 176, 177, 178, 187, 193-4, 198, 207, 212-13, 231, 290-1
Roon, A. T. E., Count de, 134, 236, 255
Rossini, G. A., 331
Rothschild family, 269-70, 281
Rothschild, Alphonse de, 327
Rothschild, Ferdinand de, 322
Rothschild, Baron James de, 48, 101, 123
Rouher, Eugène, 204, 213, 269, 271, 278, 279, 292, 294, 297, 301, 311
Royal Corps of Spanish Artillery, 7
Royal Military Academy, Woolwich, 273, 274, 278, 281, 283
Rudio (assassin), 110, 111
Rudolph of Austria, Archduke, 288, 352

Rueil, 154, 160
Rumbold, Sir Horace, 36, 38
Russell, Lord John, 82, 133, 137, 142, 155, 157, 176
Russell, Odo, 166n
Ryde, 254

Saarbrücken, 240, 325
Sacconi, Mgr., 143, 146
Sadowa, 190, 191n, 203, 205, 208, 228
St. Arnaud, Marshal A. J. Leroy de, 30, 46, 226
Saint-Aulaire, Mme de, 64
Saint-Cloud, 29, 30, 36, 37, 43, 58, 65, 66, 84, 86, 96-7, 99, 103, 130, 134, 150, 153, 154, 177, 183, 187, 204, 207, 208, 223, 224, 228, 237-8, 239-41, 265, 287, 340, 342, 351
Saint-Gobain, 121
St. Helena, 6
St. Malo, 119
St. Michael's Abbey, Farnborough, 355-6, 357, 369-70
St. Omer, 76
Sainte-Beuve, C. A., 230
Salisbury, 3rd Marquis of, 255n, 311n, 322, 335-6, 337n
Salisbury, Lady, 221, 264
Salzburg, 222
Sancy de Parabère, Mme de, 271
Sand, Georges, 211
Santa Cruz, Marquesa of, 46
Santiago de Compostella, 10
Santiago de Cuba, 337
Santona, Eugenia, Duchess of, 318
Sawston Hall, 23, 32
Schlumberger, Gustave, 338, 340
Schneider, Hortense, 216
Schwalbach, 183-5
Scott, Surgeon-Major, 305, 316
Sebastopol, 75, 77, 83, 84, 87, 124, 274
Sedan, 243, 248-9, 254
Sée, Germain, 233
Segovia, 7
Ségur, Philippe de, 76
Seville, 7, 33, 75, 367
Shaw, Miss (Prince Imperial's nurse), 101, 159, 208
Siècle, Le, 134
Simmons, General Sir Lintorn, 87, 273-4, 299, 302, 308, 314, 321, 324, 325, 326
Simmons, Lady, 302, 308-9, 324-6
Simon, Jules, 291
Simpson, General Sir James, 87
Simpson, Sir James Young, 155-6

405